AutoCAD®: The Complete Reference

Nelson Johnson

Osborne **McGraw-Hill**

Berkeley New York St. Louis San Francisco
Auckland Bogotá Hamburg London Madrid
Mexico City Milan Montreal New Delhi Panama City
Paris São Paulo Singapore Sydney
Tokyo Toronto

Osborne **McGraw-Hill**
2600 Tenth Street
Berkeley, California 94710
U.S.A.

For information on translations and book distributors outside of the U.S.A., please write to Osborne **McGraw-Hill** at the above address.

A complete list of trademarks appears on page 819.
Screens produced with InSet, from InSet Systems, Inc.

AutoCAD®: The Complete Reference

234567890 DOC 89

ISBN 0-07-881463-4

To mom and dad, with all my love

CONTENTS

ACKNOWLEDGMENTS

Writing is only a small part of producing a book—there is so much more to be done. The first month or so is the hardest. Until the style and tone are set, nothing seems to fall together. Finally, after weeks of writing, rewriting, editing, and polishing, everything begins to make sense. Without talented editors the process would go on forever. Special thanks to Liz Fisher for her valuable support and vision. Thanks also to Leslie Tilley, Ilene Shapera, Sandra Horwich, Margaret Flynn, and Fran Haselsteiner, for their excellent contributions to this book.

When the idea for this project materialized, it was difficult to imagine how a complex program like AutoCAD could be treated thoroughly in less than 900 pages. Many thanks go to Lloyd Martin for his help in creating the AutoLISP code, preparing illustrations, and writing some of the text for Chapters 11 through 15. My thanks to Robert Callori, who reviewed the book from the user's standpoint, and to Bill Kramer, who reviewed the AutoLISP text and code.

As you read these pages, you should be aware that a lot of love and attention has gone into the creation of AutoCAD. As you use the software, this fact will surely become apparent. The staff at Autodesk are to be congratulated for their superb efforts.

—Nelson Johnson

INTRODUCTION

With the elegance of its command language and the sensitive, open-ended way in which its commands interact, AutoCAD is one of those software packages that will far exceed your expectations. When you start to use AutoCAD, you will be impressed by the simple way it all goes together. You can work with the software at the most superficial level and be quite productive, but if you need to do more complicated things the power is there to do them, too. It's quite easy, for example, to interrupt a command to turn grids on or off. With Release 10 you have true three-dimensional capabilities built right in.

As software grows in size and sophistication, the greatest danger is in its tendency to become "brittle"; that is, very complex, highly evolved software tends to become rigid, unforgiving, and failure prone. Not so with AutoCAD. Even though AutoCAD offers a world of capabilities, it is also flexible and forgiving. You will find many ways to reverse undesired consequences of commands entered unintentionally or inappropriately. Although the first-time user may be a little overwhelmed by any CAD system, AutoCAD goes as far as possible to guide the user to a successful completion of every command.

In AutoCAD you will find all the interaction tools that today's software user has come to expect, including pop-up menus, pull-down menus, a sidebar menu, a command line, and tablet menus. All the user-interaction systems are thoroughly programmable. You can use a host of input and output devices, perhaps more than with any other software package of any kind on the market today. You will find the installation process easy to follow and the features of each device well integrated.

How This Book Is Organized

AutoCAD: The Complete Reference is designed to get you started quickly and to teach you how to use more advanced features, enhance your drawings, and write programs and menu files. The book is divided into four parts that present AutoCAD from the simple to the complex. Part One, "Drawing and Editing," describes the fundamental ways in which you use commands to draw and edit. Part Two, "Enhancing AutoCAD Drawings," shows you how to use special commands to organize, crosshatch, dimension, and plot. Part Three, "Advanced Techniques," discusses the many ways you can use AutoLISP and other programming methods to expand AutoCAD's capabilities. Part Four, "Function and Command References," describes all the Release 10 AutoLISP functions and AutoCAD commands.

Part One, "Drawing and Editing"

You may have just purchased AutoCAD and don't know how to begin drawing. Chapter One gets you into AutoCAD and starts you drawing as quickly as possible.

Chapter Two, "Drawing," shows you how to use most of the commands that draw lines, arcs, circles, and other entities. The chapter gives examples of commands and includes each line of the command sequence. Illustrations include the use of four screen shots on facing pages to show the progression of the command sequence in the same way you will see it on your screen.

In Chapter Three, "Editing," you will find out what to do after you have drawn entities. You can erase them, copy them, move them, and perform many other functions once you have drawn them. No more erasing holes in paper drawings!

Part Two, "Enhancing AutoCAD Drawings"

Blocks are such an important part of AutoCAD that an entire chapter is devoted to them. Chapter Four, "Using Blocks," describes this powerful feature of AutoCAD. Any drawing can be used within any other drawing by being included as a block. You can have drawings that contain drawings that in turn contain drawings.

You will learn how to add dimensions to your drawings in Chapter Five, "Dimensioning." Dimensions in AutoCAD are associative; that is, they can be made to change when the objects they describe change. You will learn how to create many kinds of dimension entities, how to change arrowhead types and sizes, and how to create text callouts.

In Chapter Six, "Crosshatching Techniques," you will read about techniques that you can use to fill or crosshatch areas in your drawings. You will also see how to create your own crosshatching patterns.

Chapter Seven, "Text and Fonts," shows you how to add text to your drawings. Text entities can be in various fonts and styles. You will learn how to use the commands that create and format AutoCAD text.

After you have drawn and edited your drawings, you may wish to plot them. Chapter Eight, "Working with Plotters," gives you a complete description of AutoCAD's plotting options for pen and printer plotters.

The management of attributes is becoming a new frontier for CAD. Chapter Nine, "Attribute Management," is an introduction to this exciting new aspect of CAD. Attributes are text information that can be attached to graphic entities. With attributes you can make your drawings more than a graphical database; each object in a drawing can contain information about itself. You will see how to assign this information to objects and extract the information in the form of reports. You will also see many suggestions for the use of attributes in your work.

Chapter Ten, "Working with Menus," shows you how to write your own menus for use with AutoCAD. Even if you are not a computer programmer, you can make routine tasks less tedious if you standardize them and perform them through menus.

Part Three, "Advanced Techniques"

In Chapter Eleven, "Introduction to AutoLISP," you will learn about this powerful programming language, some of the language's history, and its structure.

Chapter Twelve, "Programs in AutoLISP," contains many useful programs that you can copy and use in your work. By using the techniques shown here you can automate your design process and save a great deal of effort.

Chapter Thirteen, "Putting It All Together in 3D," presents a detailed application, the automated assembly of kitchen cabinets from standardized components. If you follow the principles in this chapter, you will be able to create automated systems for other assembly processes.

In Chapter Fourteen, "AutoCAD's Other Programming Languages," you will read about the "hidden" command languages in AutoCAD and how to use them. You will find out about shape files. You will even see how to write a program in C language that converts files for use with AutoCAD.

Part Four, "Function and Command References"

Chapter Fifteen is a complete guide to AutoLISP's many functions, organized by category for easy reference by programmers. As you use functions you often find yourself working with functions of a certain type; for example, the input and output functions include those that open, read, write, and close files. You will find out about the details of each function and see many examples.

You will find a complete alphabetical list of all the AutoCAD commands in Chapter Sixteen. Each command name is shown in large type so you can quickly thumb through the pages and find the command. Commands are organized alphabetically because you will be using them interactively from the keyboard rather than as functions in a programming language.

Appendixes

Appendix A, "Command Summary," is a complete list of AutoCAD commands in an abbreviated form for quick reference.

Appendix B contains information on AutoCAD's Drawing Exchange Format. You can use this information (including a program in C language) to extract drawing information from DXF files.

Companion Disk

Source code shown in this book is available on a companion disk, including an ASCII text editor that you may find useful for creating and editing menus and AutoLISP code, as well as for other purposes. You will also find an executable version of extraction software. To order your copy, fill out the coupon that follows, and send it together with your check in the amount of $29.95, U.S. shipping included, to

Imagimedia Technologies, Inc.
P.O. Box 210308
San Francisco, California 94121-0308

For international orders shipped airmail, send $32.95 U.S. For shipment to any California address, please add $1.95 sales tax.

Money orders will receive immediate shipment. Purchase orders should be accompanied by payment in full. Purchases from outside the U.S.A. must be drawn on banks with U.S. correspondents. Sorry, we do not accept credit card orders. Please allow 2-3 weeks for delivery.

∫iTi Imagimedia Technologies, Inc.
P.O. Box 210308
San Francisco, California 94121-0308

Name ____________________

Address ____________________

City ____________________ State _____ ZIP __________

Telephone ____________________

Amount enclosed __________ U.S. dollars

Drawing and Editing

PART ONE

Quick Start

ONE

Starting AutoCAD
Starting to Work with AutoCAD
Starting to Draw with AutoCAD

A client has just asked you to work on a big project with a short deadline. You know it would be best to use AutoCAD, but you have never used it before. You purchase the program and install it, and now you must learn to use it as quickly as possible.

This chapter contains all you need to know to begin drawing with a minimum of effort. AutoCAD is a very complex program, but it is also a very powerful and helpful tool. In fact, AutoCAD can be in itself all the tools you will ever need for drawing. Like a carpenter with a hammer or a plumber with a wrench you too can become a master of your craft with AutoCAD.

In this chapter you will find a condensed presentation that covers some of the more fundamental operations you can perform with AutoCAD. If you have already installed and started to use AutoCAD, you may not need to read this presentation but can go on to the more detailed chapters.

Starting AutoCAD

Let's get right into it. This discussion assumes that you have installed AutoCAD in accordance with the AutoCAD installation instructions. It also assumes that you have learned the rudiments of your computer's operating system. This book was written using AutoCAD under MS-DOS, the primary operating system used on IBM personal computers. Because most of your AutoCAD work will be done with little operating system interaction, it is enough for now to only know how to begin the AutoCAD session.

Using MS-DOS, you can change directories with the CD command (also known as CHDIR). For example, if you were in any other directory, the following command would take you to the \ACAD directory:

```
C>cd \acad
```

It is recommended that you make a subdirectory for your own drawing files to keep them from being confused with AutoCAD's program files. Read about the creation of subdirectories in your DOS manual.

Note that more than one drive is used in this book's examples. If you have multiple drives, you may see AutoCAD on the D, E, or any other DOS drive. The drive used in these examples is drive C. For a description of drive designations, consult your DOS manual.

Changing The DOS Command Prompt

You may want to change the DOS command prompt so it will contain the name of the current directory. This is a simple procedure that will prevent you from being in the wrong directory without knowing it. Though you do not need to make this change to run AutoCAD, doing so will make it less likely that you will become confused or make mistakes while running the program.

To make this change, all you need to do is enter "prompt pg" at the command line, like this:

```
C>prompt $p$g
```

When you have done this, DOS will respond

C:\ACAD>

This command prompt will appear only if you are in the ACAD directory. If by some chance you are *not* in the ACAD directory, it will be immediately obvious because a different directory name will appear.

Put "prompt pg" in your AUTOEXEC.BAT file if you want the current directory name to automatically appear as part of the DOS command prompt each time you boot up your system.

Running AutoCAD

You must run the ACAD.EXE file to invoke AutoCAD. You do this as with any other executable file under DOS. Prepare a command line that looks like this:

C:>**acad**

After you have typed the ACAD command (in upper- or lowercase), just press ENTER. Press ENTER again and you will see a screen that looks like Figure 1-1. Now you are ready to run AutoCAD for the first time.

Starting to Work with AutoCAD

The easiest way to get started is to begin a new drawing. To do this choose option 1, "Begin a NEW drawing." Simply press the numeric key 1 and press ENTER. When you do this, you will see an additional line on the display that looks like the following:

Enter NAME of drawing:

```
                A U T O C A D
Copyright (C) 1982,83,84,85,86,87,88,89 Autodesk, Inc.
Release 3.34 (1/16/89) IBM PC
Advanced Drafting Extensions 3
Serial Number: 12-345678

Main Menu

   0. Exit AutoCAD
   1. Begin a NEW drawing
   2. Edit an EXISTING drawing
   3. Plot a drawing
   4. Printer Plot a drawing

   5. Configure AutoCAD
   6. File Utilities
   7. Compile shape/font description file
   8. Convert old drawing file

Enter selection:
```

Figure 1-1. AutoCAD's main menu

At this prompt you can enter any name you want, as long as the length of the name is eight characters or less. Why not use the name "new" for your first drawing? It is as good as any other name.

If you have done everything right until now, you will see a display that looks like Figure 1-2. If you do not see anything that looks like Figure 1-2, repeat the installation and the steps taken until now. If you *still* don't see anything like Figure 1-2, you may need technical support from your AutoCAD dealer.

By the way, don't add the ".dwg" file name extension to the drawing name even though drawing file names are stored this way. If you do you will see the message

"": Improper name for drawing file

If you were to enter "new.dwg" instead of "new" in the above example, you would see the "Improper name" message.

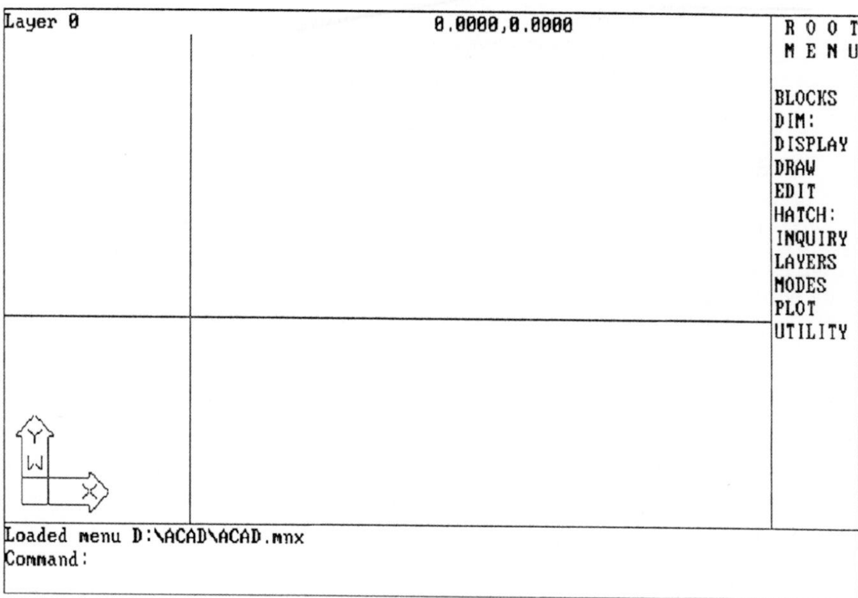

Figure 1-2. Initial AutoCAD display

Getting Familiar with the Display

In order to work with AutoCAD, you must understand the various parts of the AutoCAD display shown in Figure 1-2. Your work with AutoCAD will be done through a complex interaction with this display. The display is divided into a drawing area, a command area, and a menu area.

The Drawing Area

The largest area on the display is the AutoCAD drawing area. It starts at the upper left corner. It is bounded on the right by the menu area and on the bottom by the command area.

The AutoCAD drawing area has several unique features. In the upper left corner you will see the "Layer" indicator. A *layer* in AutoCAD refers to a separate "sheet" on which you can draw. Of course, your drawings are not stored on sheets of paper in AutoCAD. The layer is just a convenient way to simulate the effect of overlaying sheets of paper. You can display layers in various combinations.

To the right of the Layer indicator is a series of numbers, in this case 0.0000,0.0000. These numbers indicate the current *coordinates* of the *crosshairs.* AutoCAD's coordinate system is based on the concept of three directions, denoted X, Y, and Z. The coordinate system is the same one you are familiar with from analytic geometry. The numbers you see on the display refer to the X and Y coordinates of the crosshairs. The crosshairs themselves are two lines, one horizontal and one vertical, that cross at a point on the display. You use the crosshairs to locate the places at which you wish to draw using AutoCAD.

In the lower left corner of the drawing area is the *Coordinate System Icon.* This icon looks like two arrows, one pointing north and one pointing east, connected at their tails. This icon will change as you use AutoCAD. It is intended to show you the orientations of the coordinate axes as you change the coordinate system.

The Menu Area

At the far right of the display you will see the screen menu area. You can use this area to select menu items. The menu you see when you run AutoCAD for the first time contains a selection of AutoCAD commands that are organized to help you use AutoCAD effectively. The menu items are sometimes commands and sometimes words that lead to other menus. You select menu items by moving your pointing device until the crosshairs move into the menu area. When you are in the menu area you will know it, because you will see the letters that make up a menu item selected by the cursor in "reverse video." This means that if your menu area has white characters on a black background, the part you are pointing to will have black characters on a white background.

The Command Area

The bottom of the AutoCAD display contains three lines of text that show the command line and the last two lines that you or AutoCAD have entered. The command area in Figure 1-2 shows that the standard AutoCAD menu (acad.mnx) has been loaded. It also shows the command line itself.

AutoCAD keeps a list of the commands you enter. You can see a full screen of commands if you press the F1 function key. This key toggles back and forth between the command list (of which the command area is just the last three lines) and the drawing display.

Pointing and Picking

In order to use AutoCAD you must first understand how to *point* to objects and how to *pick* them. Pointing involves the use of a pointing device such as a *mouse*, a *digitizer*, or the arrow keys on the numeric keypad. You have probably already chosen your pointing device and installed it by using AutoCAD's installation instructions. Consult the AutoCAD Reference Manual for current information on the requirements of your specific pointing device. There are many variations.

A mouse, shown in the following illustration, is a small plastic device that can fit in the palm of your hand and is operated on a flat surface. It is connected to the computer by a cable. It usually has at least one button. You move the mouse in the direction you want the crosshairs to move.

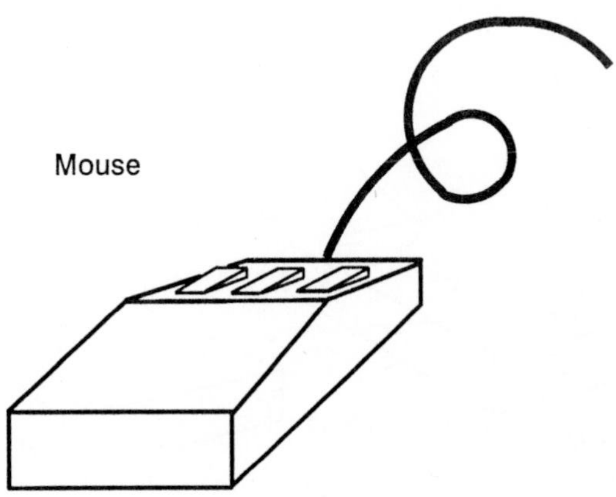

The following illustration shows a digitizer with two different positioning devices. A digitizer has a specially designed surface that uses electromagnetic or electrostatic methods to interact with the positioning device. You place a mouse-like device called a "puck" on the digitizer's surface, and the crosshairs immediately move to that position on the display. Digitizers also sometimes use a pencil-like device called a "stylus" instead of a puck.

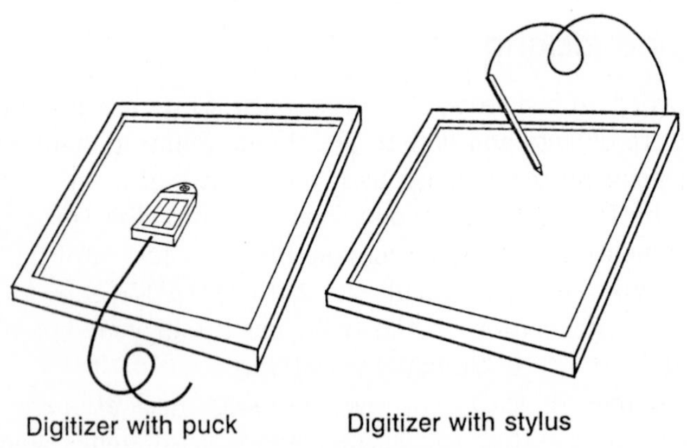

Digitizer with puck   Digitizer with stylus

In addition to the mouse and digitizer, you could use a *trackball* or a *joystick* as your pointing device (shown in the following drawing). A trackball is a plastic ball, usually palm size, that can be rotated to move the crosshairs. A joystick is a rod that you use to move the crosshairs.

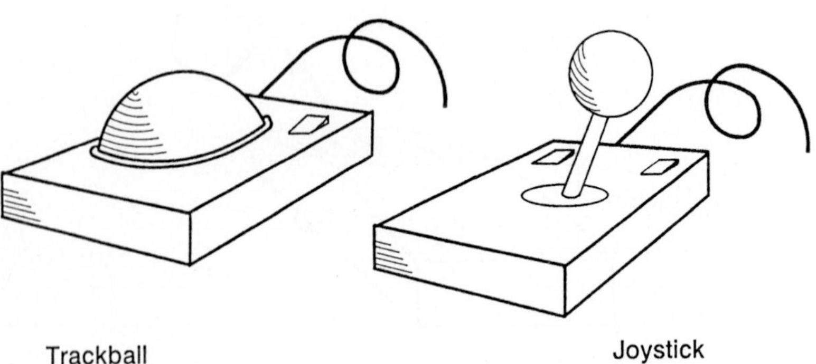

Trackball   Joystick

There is a fundamental difference between the ways a mouse and a digitizer send coordinates to the CAD system. A typical mouse uses relative movement to position the crosshairs. That is, it moves the crosshairs only when it is in contact with a flat surface. When lifted from the surface and moved to another position the mouse does not "remember" the position from which it was lifted. It assumes that the new position is the start of further movement. Digitizers always report the exact position of the puck or stylus on the surface.

Your pointing device enables you to point to any part of the AutoCAD display except the command area. A button on your pointing device enables you to pick the locations, objects, or menu items to which you are pointing. There are many variations among pointing devices: some have only one button, some have many. The "pick" button on a typical three-button mouse, for example, is the left button.

Other Button Functions

In addition to the pick button, you will usually have access to at least two other buttons. Using the common example of the three-button mouse, the middle button performs the same function as the ENTER key. The right button cancels the current command and redraws the drawing. You may or may not have access to all three buttons on a given pointing device.

A typical sequence of button presses might start with the picking of a menu item by pressing the pick button. This results in the beginning of a command sequence. You might enter the default for the first prompt in the command sequence by using the "enter" button (or the ENTER key). After entering the default you might decide you wanted a different command, in which case you might press the "cancel" (or redraw) button.

Starting to Draw with AutoCAD

Now that you know how to start running the program and are familiar with the display area and the functions of your pointing device, you are ready to begin to draw. First, you will learn how to draw a point.

Drawing a Point

The most simple thing you can draw with AutoCAD is a single dot, or point. There is a command to do this, and you will now see how to draw a single point using AutoCAD's command line.

To draw a point using the command line, you must first type the POINT command at the prompt. After you enter this command, you will see yet another prompt, "Point:", appear at the bottom of the display, as shown in Figure 1-3. This prompt is asking for the coordinates of the point. There are two ways to set coordinates. You could type in a pair of numbers here,

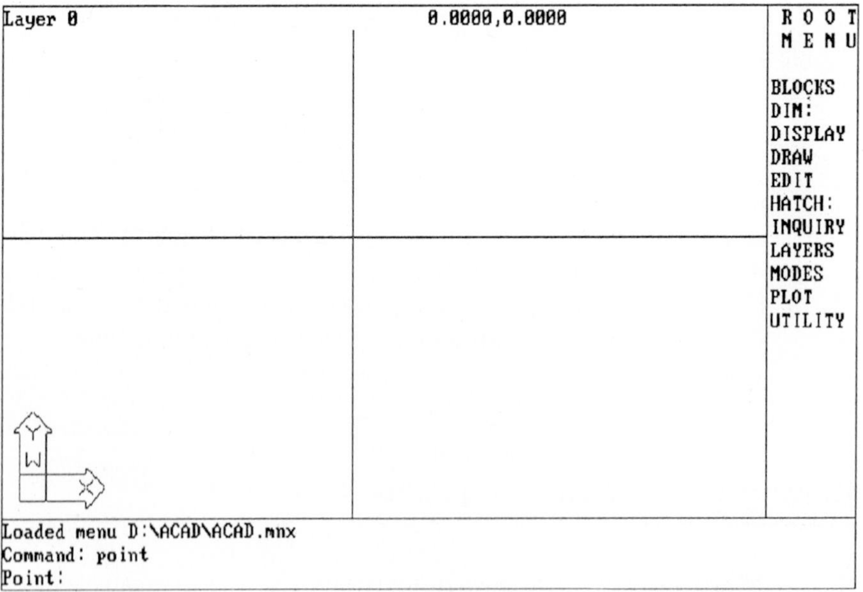

Figure 1-3. Beginning to draw a point

separated by a comma. Or, as you will do now, you can move the crosshairs so that they intersect (cross) where you want to draw the point.

Moving The Crosshairs

If you have installed a pointing device such as a mouse or digitizer, you can use it to move the crosshairs. At any time while drawing you can also use the arrow keys on the numeric keypad to move the crosshairs, even though a pointing device is installed. If you do this, however, you may be frustrated when you try to use the mouse or digitizer again. If you use the arrow keys, you must press another key on the keyboard to resume using the mouse or digitizer. The spacebar or ENTER key is good for this because neither leaves a character on the command line.

If you use the numeric keypad as your pointing device, you can press the "page up" (PGUP) key to increase the speed of crosshair movement. Pressing the "page down" (PGDN) key will decrease the speed of crosshair movement. Pressing the END key removes the crosshairs from the screen. Pressing the HOME key makes the crosshairs appear again.

Using your pointing device, place the crosshairs at the location of the point and press the pick button. You will see a little cross at the crosshairs' location. After you have drawn your first point, the display should look roughly like Figure 1-4.

Recreating The Display

AutoCAD always places little crosses as markers when objects are created. These markers are temporary. You can rebuild the display to see your work with the crosses removed.

There are two commands used to re-create a drawing, the REDRAW and REGEN commands. The fastest way is to use the REDRAW command to re-create the display. This method uses AutoCAD's "display list" to draw very fast. The display list only contains information about what is on the screen. Because the list is usually smaller than the entire drawing workfile, it

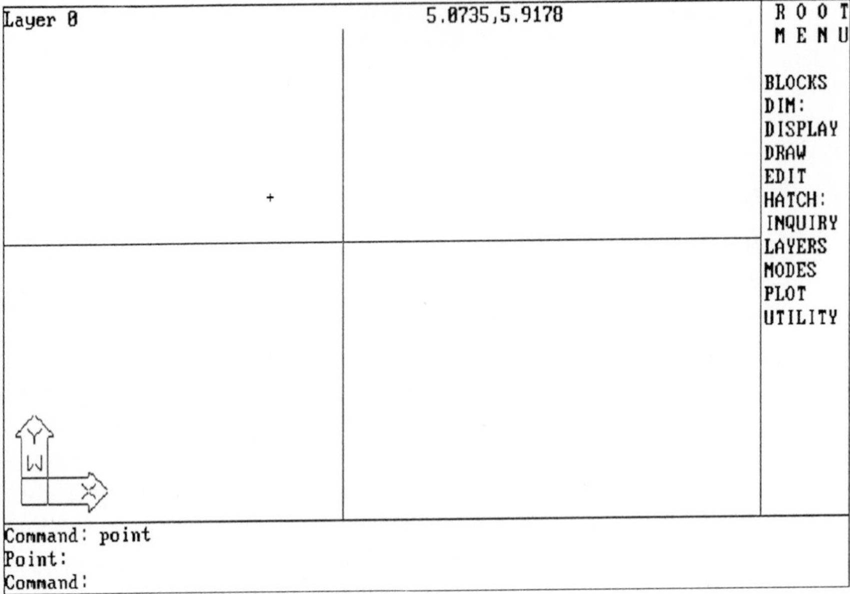

Figure 1-4. The display after drawing a point

takes less time to display it. For most purposes, the REDRAW command will quickly accomplish what you want to do.

A slower but more accurate way to re-create the display is to use the REGEN command. This method actually repeats the steps you used to create the drawing. If you regenerate the drawing completely, you will faithfully reconstruct your work. Under certain circumstances, for example, when you change certain system parameters, AutoCAD will automatically regenerate the entire drawing. It will tell you when and why it is doing this. For this simple demonstration, you will use the REDRAW command.

To get a feel for how to use the REDRAW command, move the crosshairs to the right until you see one of the menu items on the AutoCAD sidebar menu change, probably to reverse video. Position the menu selection bar (the reverse video text line) until the DISPLAY menu item goes to reverse video as in Figure 1-5.

Now "pick" the DISPLAY menu item by pressing the pick button on your pointing device. Notice what happens. The entire

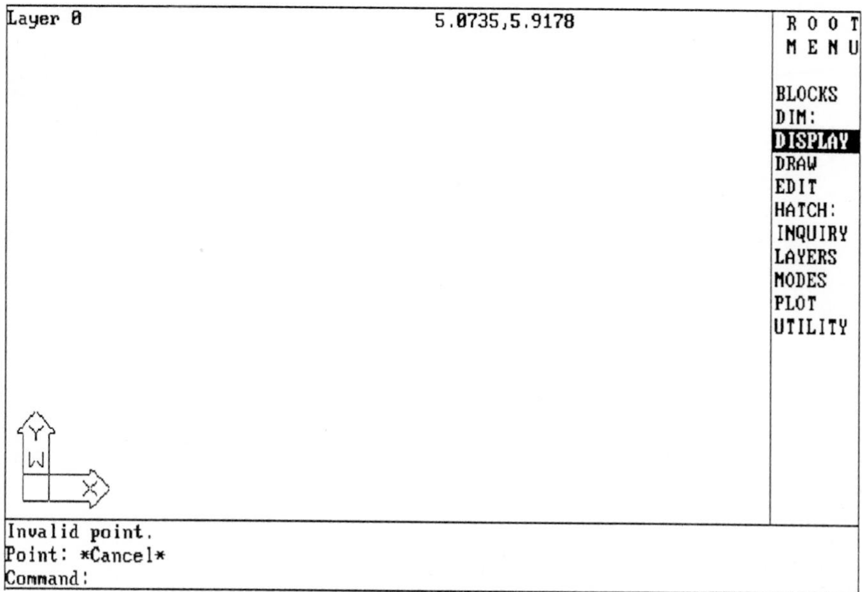

Figure 1-5. Selecting an option from the sidebar menu

sidebar menu changes to look like Figure 1-6.

Now pick the REDRAW command in the same way you selected the DISPLAY menu item. The display is quickly redrawn and the cross disappears.

Note that the REDRAW command has automatically been entered for you at the command line. Note also that the DISPLAY menu item in Figure 1-5 has no colon (:) after it. This means it is a menu item that leads to other menu items. The REDRAW: command does, however, have a colon after it, which means it is to be treated by AutoCAD as if you are entering it at the command line. It is at the "bottom" of the menu hierarchy and does not lead to menus. More about menu hierarchies can be found in Chapter 10, "Working with Menus."

Drawing a Line

When using AutoCAD, you have a choice of two basic methods for drawing lines. The first of these, represented by the LINE

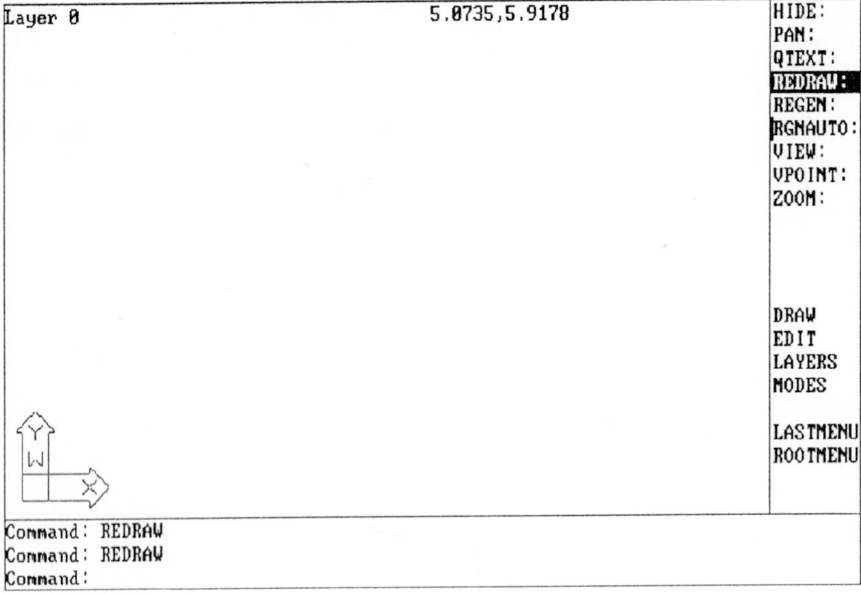

Figure 1-6. Sidebar menu after selection

command, draws simple lines. The second, represented by the PLINE command, draws a variety of lines of different widths and types.

The LINE command is present in all versions of AutoCAD. The PLINE command is present only in the ADE-3 package. PLINE stands for *polyline.* A polyline is a line that can have its own thickness that varies along its length. AutoCAD has a wide variety of possible polyline expressions.

Entering the LINE Command

You will now draw a simple line. Enter the command LINE at the "Command:" prompt. After you press ENTER, you will see a prompt "From point:". In response to this prompt you could enter a coordinate pair, but instead you should locate the crosshairs with your pointing device and pick the beginning point of the line. You will see a small cross appear on the display, and a new prompt, "To point:", will appear. Locate the crosshairs at the desired endpoint of the line and pick the endpoint.

After you have drawn your first line, however, the "rubber-band" line continues to follow the crosshairs. How do you stop it from doing so and keep the line you have drawn? In order to stop the line-drawing process, you must press ENTER or the spacebar in response to the "To point:" prompt. In AutoCAD the spacebar is an alternate way to produce the same effect as the ENTER key, except when you are creating a text string. The ENTER key will terminate the current prompt or select a default and move on to a new command line. The spacebar will terminate the current prompt but the next command option will appear on the same line. An animated illustration of rubber banding is shown in Figure 1-7. Notice how the line follows the crosshairs as they are moved.

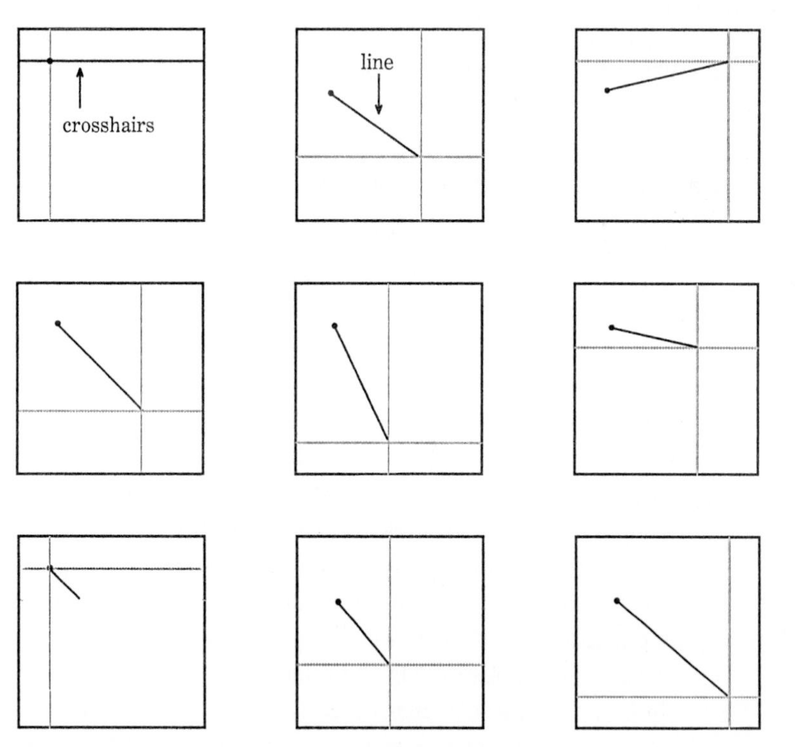

Figure 1-7. Rubber banding in action

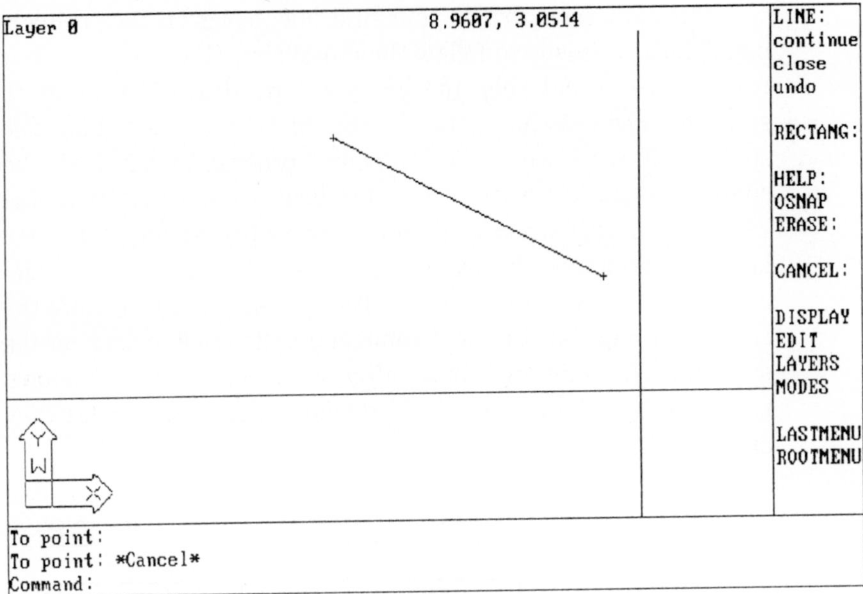

Figure 1-8. Your first AutoCAD line

Canceling Commands

If you wish to turn off the LINE command, you can press the CTRL-C key combination. To do this you hold the CTRL key down and press the C key so both keys are down at once. If you have been using an IBM PC for a while, you will find this action familiar. If not, welcome to the club.

When you execute the CTRL-C combination you will see the "*Cancel*" system message. It will come in handy from time to time as you use AutoCAD. It allows you to escape from command sequences. Sometimes you decide halfway through a command not to continue. After you have drawn your line the display should look something like Figure 1-8.

Congratulations! You have now mastered the single most important part of AutoCAD—you can draw a line.

This is where the art of drawing using manual methods departs from the art of computer-aided design. If you were to draw a line using a straightedge and pen, you would need to build your drawing as a composite of many lines. Using AutoCAD, however, you can use extremely powerful tools to draw lines, arcs, polylines, and much more. No set of mechanical drafting tools can compare to the set of tools you have at your fingertips with AutoCAD.

Drawing

TWO

In the days before AutoCAD you had no choice but to use manual drafting methods, unless you had hundreds of thousands of dollars to spend on a custom CAD system. When you draw manually, you decide which tools to use based on the tasks to be performed. Therefore, the things you normally would do with your compass, straightedge, and templates are described in this chapter in terms of AutoCAD.

Most of the features of AutoCAD have rough equivalents in the drafter's toolbox. For example, the CIRCLE and ARC commands can be thought of as roughly equivalent to circle templates and drafting compasses. The LINE command can be roughly compared to the plastic adjustable triangle or the drafting machine straightedge.

This chapter covers basic concepts that will help you use the tools available with AutoCAD. You will learn about systems of units that express distance and angular measure and how to enter drawing information. In order to draw, you need to understand how to use the many AutoCAD viewing options, which are presented in detail in this chapter. Finally, the actual drawing of AutoCAD entities will be introduced.

Basic Concepts

Now that you have drawn your first line, you have already overcome some of your possible first-time user's reservations. Using a CAD system should seem more natural to you now. As you continue to work with AutoCAD, keep some of the following information in mind. These concepts and techniques lie at the heart of AutoCAD and may help you avoid delays as you learn.

Interaction Techniques

AutoCAD provides you with not just one, but many options for interaction between you and its commands. There are three fundamental ways you can interact. You can enter commands by typing them directly on the command line. You can pick commands from pop-up or sidebar menus. You can also pick commands from tablet menus. These ways used in combination create a rich set of options.

Entering Commands Directly

When you enter commands on the command line, one hand types commands (usually single letters) and the other hand does the pointing and entering. One advantage of this method is that the crosshairs stay in the drawing area while you pick commands. This enables you to keep the crosshairs at a desired location in a drawing while you go on to work with other commands. Of course, this method requires that you know the commands and enjoy typing. You do not have lists of commands on the screen to help you.

Picking Commands from Menus

If you have a three-button mouse, the left button is usually programmed for picking, the middle button for entering, and the right button for redrawing and canceling. You can get a lot done by moving the crosshairs to menu items on the screen and using these buttons. The advantage is that you have menus and submenus of commands and options to help you remember the commands you need. The disadvantage is that you must move the crosshairs from the drawing area to pick commands. Even if you use the pointing device to pick menu items and commands, you will still need to enter some values by typing.

Picking Commands from Tablet Menus

A standard tablet menu is provided by AutoCAD to use with a digitizer. To select from a tablet menu, you must send the exact location of the pointing device to AutoCAD. The advantage of tablet menus is that the entire set of commands you wish to use is shown all at once. With on-screen menus you must descend down a menu hierarchy, so all of your options are known only *after* you get to the bottom of the menu hierarchy.

The disadvantage of a tablet menu is that you must move the crosshairs from your work in the drawing area in order to select the tablet menu item. You cannot use a mouse with tablet menus because the mouse does not point to an absolute location. All the mouse can do is transmit directions and amounts of movement to AutoCAD.

Abbreviating Command Options

If a command in AutoCAD has options, you can usually enter just the first character to select an option. AutoCAD sets up prompts in both upper- and lowercase letters to remind you of this. For example, the following command presents you with series of options:

Command: **ARC**
Center/<Start point>:**c**

On the above command line, you could enter the word **Center** or just an upper- or lowercase letter **C** to specify that the arc is to be drawn centered on a point.

You can use either of two methods to enter commands. You can press ENTER, in which case any command options will appear on the next line. The example of the preceding ARC command shows what happens when you press ENTER to enter a command. Or you can press the spacebar instead of ENTER to enter the ARC command, in which case you will see the following:

Command: ARC Center/<Start point>: **c**

You may respond to prompts with upper- or lowercase letters. The convention in this book is to show user responses in lowercase to remind you of this fact.

Some command options have more than the first letter capitalized. The UCS command, for example, will prompt you as follows:

Origin/ZAxis/3point/Entity/View/X/Y/Z/Prev/Restore/
Save/Del/?/<World>:

In this case, you can enter **ZA** to select the "ZAxis" option. If you just use **Z**, AutoCAD will assume you wish to use the "Z" option. Where AutoCAD requires more than one letter to specify an option, it will capitalize the required letters.

You will find that most AutoCAD commands begin with a command for you to enter manually or from a menu. You then follow a series of prompts and indicate that you are finished by pressing the spacebar or ENTER. You can abort a command by using the CTRL-C key combination to cancel the command.

Using the Keypad

If you use the arrow keys on the numeric keypad to move the crosshairs, they will seem to stop moving when you switch back to the pointing device. To start the crosshairs moving again, press any key. The spacebar and the ENTER key work very well for this because they do not add any text on the command line.

Beware of the NUM LOCK key on the IBM numeric keypad. If this key is toggled on, and you expect to move the crosshairs with the arrow keys, you will see numbers instead. If you see numbers on the command line when you use the arrow keys on the numeric keypad, press the NUM LOCK key once. You should then be able to move the crosshairs with the arrow keys.

You can remove the crosshairs from the display by pressing the DEL key, and you can restore the crosshairs to the display by pressing the HOME key. The PGUP key increases the speed of the crosshairs' movement with each press, and the PGDN key decreases the speed.

Picking Objects

In order to pick an object, use the pointing device to place the crosshairs over the object to be picked. Most commands that request you to pick an object will display a box at the crosshairs' intersection. The part of the object that will be picked must be within that box. When you have properly located the object, press the pick button on the pointing device to complete your selection.

Picking Distances

Some AutoCAD prompts will require the expression of a distance value. Before Release 10, you had to express this distance numerically. In Release 10 of AutoCAD, you can use the crosshairs to locate a point that expresses the distance from another point. You will see a rubber-band line whenever AutoCAD asks for a distance value. Just stretch the line to whatever point you want for the distance and pick the point.

Rubber Banding

When you drew your first line, did you notice that after the first prompt a line was "rubber banded" to the crosshairs location? The line endpoint "leads" the rest of the line to its new position. This is called rubber banding because the line appears to stretch and shrink like a rubber band as you move the crosshairs. Picking the line endpoint places the new line in its position. (See Chapter 1, "Quick Start," for an illustration of rubber banding.)

Expressing Coordinates

In AutoCAD coordinates are expressed with a method attributed to the philosopher Descartes. This method dates from the middle of the seventeenth century. You may be familiar with coordinate systems from your high school or college geometry courses. AutoCAD is designed to augment, rather than interfere with, knowledge you have already gained.

The etymology of the word "coordinate" is as follows. The vertical axis in a coordinate system can also be referred to as the "ordinate" scales of the system, and the horizontal axis is referred to as the "abscissa." The prefix "co" means "together." Coordinate values are thus ordinates (or values on axes) taken together. Since the values are measured on each axis from the origin (where X, Y, and Z are 0), coordinates must be groups of numbers that refer to the same origin. To be coordinate (have the same origin), values must be grouped together. A single numeric value (a scalar) is not a coordinate. To express a coordinate in a two-dimensional system, you need a pair of numbers. To express a coordinate in a three-dimensional system, you need three numbers (a triplet). AutoCAD is a true three-dimensional system.

Each number in a three-dimensional system represents a distance along one of three coordinate *axes.* An axis can be visualized as a uniform line (or scale) of numbers extending outward from an origin at 0. Since numbers can be positive or negative, you can have positive or negative scalars along an axis.

In standard Cartesian geometry, the axes are named X, Y, and Z. If you are familiar with analytic geometry, you may be used to seeing these axes expressed in italics as x, y, and z. Because AutoCAD expresses the axes in uppercase and without italics, this book also refers to them in that way.

The X, Y, and Z axes in AutoCAD are *always* at right angles to each other. When you start an AutoCAD drawing, the positive direction along the X axis extends to the right. The positive direction along the Y axis extends perpendicular to the X axis upward on the screen. The positive direction of the Z axis extends directly toward you, away from the screen. The origin of the default coordinate system (0,0,0) is at the lower left corner of the drawing area.

AutoCAD gives you a great deal of control over the expression of coordinate values. Depending on how the coordinates are expressed in response to a prompt, you can enter *absolute, relative, polar,* or *world* coordinates.

Absolute Coordinates

You can respond to AutoCAD prompts that ask for coordinate values by typing them. When you enter coordinate values in this way, you must separate the coordinates with commas. For example, a two-dimensional point can take the form 2.36,8.965. The X value comes first, followed by a comma and the Y value. If you intend to enter the coordinates of a three-dimensional point, use a second comma, like this: 1.1135,3.39,9.775.

When you enter coordinates in this way, you are expressing the exact location of a point in the coordinate system. The location of such a point is absolute because it is based on measurements taken from point 0,0,0 in the coordinate system. This, the origin, is the place where the values of X, Y, and Z are all zero.

Relative Coordinates

While absolute coordinates refer to the coordinate system itself, relative coordinates refer to the coordinates of the last point specified. For example, if the absolute coordinates of a point are 10,20 and you specify a second point at 5,10 relative to the first point, the absolute location of the second point will be 15,30. You must prefix an @ character to any coordinates that want you to be relative to the last coordinates entered, as follows: @5,10.

As with absolute coordinates, you must use X, Y, and Z values, separated by commas and prefixed by an @ character if you choose to express a three-dimensional set of relative coordinates. The following is an example of three-dimensional coordinates expressed as relative to the last point entered: @1.10,3.14159,−12.34.

Polar Coordinates

If you wish to express the coordinates of a point by the distance and angle from the last point entered you must use polar coordinate notation. Enter the @ character first, followed by the distance, followed by a < character, followed by an angle. The angle specifies the deflection of the new line from the X axis. The following are the coordinates of a point expressed in polar notation: @3.14159<1.618. If you enter the @ character without anything else, you will specify the same point as the last point entered. This is a convenient way to refer to the last coordinates entered instead of specifying @0,0 or @0<0.

World Coordinates

The World Coordinate System (WCS) is absolute. Unlike User Coordinate Systems (UCS, discussed later in this chapter in "User Coordinate Systems"), the WCS cannot be changed. If you wish to refer to the WCS rather than the UCS to plot a point, you must prefix the coordinates with a * character. A typical reference to the WCS is *3.14159,1.618.

You can refer to the WCS from relative coordinates by combining the * and @ characters as follows:

```
@*2.23579,39.75
@*5<6
```

Understanding Units

AutoCAD provides you with a broad range of numerical types to express distances and angles. The UNITS command can be used to change units for a given drawing or session. When entering numbers, you can use the numbers from 0 to 9 (0123456789), the plus (+), the minus (−), the E key, the double quote ("), single quote ('), and the period (.).

Linear Units

Linear units are used to express distances along straight lines. AutoCAD can be set up to use one of five different linear unit modes for expressing distances or coordinates. You can change the units mode at any time in an AutoCAD session. Numbers entered subsequent to a change will be expressed using the then current units mode.

Scientific Units Scientific notation is accepted, in which case an "E" indicates the exponent. For example, the following is a number in scientific notation: 1.2345E+6. This number could be shown otherwise as 1234500. Scientific notation is used where the magnitude of numbers tends to be very large, such as in astronomy or physics. Using the exponent to indicate the number of decimal places reduces the need to enter numerous zeros to express large numbers.

Decimal Units If you do not use the UNITS command, the units you will use (the default units) will be decimal. Decimal units are numbers with a decimal point. You are probably most familiar with such numbers from your daily life. Dollars and cents, for example, are most often expressed in decimal units. You have a choice of from 0 to 8 decimal places after the decimal point.

You might want to use decimal units for English or metric applications. Decimal units are used in many branches of engineering, including machine tool, piping, mechanical, and electrical engineering.

A typical number expressed in decimal units is 123.45.

Engineering Units Engineers often express numbers in a combination of feet and inches, but do not wish to use fractions. If you choose AutoCAD's Engineering Units option, you will express numbers as follows: 12′ –3.45″. You can omit the double quote (″) sign if you wish to save some time entering the numbers. The following expression will work just as well: 12′ –3.45.

Engineering units enable the engineer to express large distances using feet, but control high tolerances using decimal parts of inches rather than fractions. Civil engineers and surveyors will often use AutoCAD's Engineering Units option.

Architectural Units Architects and builders use much lower tolerances than engineers. Standard tolerances in building specifications, for example, call for one-quarter inch per ten feet of length for construction that is to be true and plumb. It is just too difficult, unnecessary, and expensive to require builders to hold to higher tolerances. Traditionally, builders in the United States, Canada, and the United Kingdom use fractional expressions of inches. So AutoCAD provides architectural dimensions that appear with fractions of inches. For example: 12′ –3 3/4″.

Note that the preceding example is how the number will appear on a drawing or when AutoCAD shows it to you on the display. When you enter the number in response to a prompt, it is quite a different matter. To express the preceding number in response to a prompt, you must type it as 12′3 –3/4. As an alternative, you can express the same number with the double quote (″). Usually, however, you will want to omit the double quote to be more efficient. AutoCAD will know what you mean with or without the quotation marks. The following is the same number response entered with the double quote: 12′3 –3/4″.

Remember, in AutoCAD, pressing the spacebar is the same as pressing ENTER. It tells AutoCAD that you are finished typing the command or response. Hence, what you must type is different from what AutoCAD displays.

Fractional Units You can express numbers as fractions without using the feet and inches notations required by engineering and architectural units. For example: 12 3/4. Note that as with architectural numbers, the preceding expression is the way AutoCAD will show the number to you, not the way you must type it in response to a prompt. To respond to a prompt, you must type the following if you want AutoCAD to display the preceding number: 12 –3/4.

Angular Units

In addition to linear units, AutoCAD supports five types of angular units. Different branches of the sciences, engineering, and architecture employ different standards for the expression of angles.

Decimal Degrees Angles are measured in decimal degrees with 0 decimal places by default. Like linear decimal units, the number of decimal places can be varied from 0 to 8. A typical expression of an angle measured in decimal degrees is 12.3456.

Degrees/minutes/seconds When you set AutoCAD to the "Degrees/minutes/seconds" mode, you will use a method that is often found in engineering work according to the English notation system. This method of expressing angles depends on three symbols to divide the non-decimal numbers into three parts. First, degrees are expressed from 0 through 360, followed by the letter "d," standing for "degrees." The next number is the number of minutes of arc from 0 to 60, followed by a single quote. Finally, the number of seconds of arc is expressed followed by a double quote character. A typical expression of an angle in "Degrees/minutes/seconds" mode follows: 12d34′56″. When AutoCAD produces angles in this mode in drawings, the degree symbol will appear in place of the letter "d." Since there is no degree symbol on the keyboard, however, you must use the lowercase letter "d" when you type angles in this mode.

Grads The "Grads" mode expresses angles according to the convention that 360 degrees is equal to 400 grads. This convention is used in scientific and engineering applications. It was adopted in an attempt to make angular measurements more adaptable to decimal expression. For example, a right angle is expressed as 90 degrees and as 100 grads. If you wish to divide a 90-degree angle into four parts, you must use a decimal. The actual number would be 22.5 degrees. Using grads, however, no decimal portion is required, so the angle is 25 grads. The grad system makes angular measurement more like linear measurement and is more consistent with the decimal system as a whole. Because there are 400 grads in a circle as opposed to 360 degrees the grad system is a little more accurate as well. The following is an expression of an angle in grads according to AutoCAD's notation: 12.3456g.

Radians Radian measurement of angles is based on the idea that a circle with a radius of one unit (a unit circle) is 6.283185 units in circumference. The number pi, with which you may be familiar from your high school studies, is derived by dividing the circumference of the unit circle by two. In radian measurement, 360 degrees is two times pi radians. Radians are used by scientists and engineers because the radian unit of measurement is easily incorporated mathematically. A typical expression of radian measure in AutoCAD is 1.2345r.

Surveyors' Units Surveyors use a special method to express angles. The surveyor's compass rose is like a ship's compass. It is divided into four parts. The top of the compass is North and the bottom South. To the right is East and to the left is West. Angles are expressed in no more than 90-degree parts, or quadrants. The quadrant between North and East, for example, starts at 0 degrees due East and goes to 90 degrees due North. The expression of 10 decimal degrees using AutoCAD's default origin for angles would appear as follows in surveyors' units: N10d0′0″ E.

Remember, you cannot use space characters if you type angles in this mode. The example above shows how AutoCAD will present surveyors' units to you, not how you must type them. The following is the same expression as the preceding, but as you must type it from the keyboard: N10d0′0″E.

Angular Measurement Origin Angles are measured assuming a beginning angle or origin where the angle is assumed to be 0. You have a choice of four possible origins for angles with AutoCAD. Angles can start with 0 at due East, due North, due West, or due South. You have the option of setting the assumed 0 angle location whenever you use the UNITS command.

You might wish to change the default (due East) 0 angle direction to conform with standard requirements for a drawing. If, for example, a drawing is oriented so that "up" is to the left for whatever reason, you might want to have the 0 angular direction pointing North.

Clockwise or Counterclockwise Angles The sense of rotation of an angle is very important because all angles in your drawings will be affected by it. Your angles can be expressed either clockwise or counterclockwise (the default) from the 0 direction. Like the origin for angular measurement, the rotational sense of angles can be specified as part of your response to the UNITS command.

Viewing Drawings

Imagine having to produce a complete drawing on a sheet of paper the size of a computer screen. Aside from the eyestrain, it would be impossible to work accurately. Because of this, AutoCAD offers a wide range of different tools for looking at your drawings. This section covers methods for viewing various degrees of detail (called "zooming"), moving across your drawings ("panning"), and choosing what part or parts of a drawing you wish to see (using "viewports"). Also covered are the different types and uses of grid displays.

Zooming for Detail

Think of your drawing as being only the *information* required to draw lines, not as a sheet of paper with lines on it. The CAD system is only a means of presenting and editing that information. Zooming is one way of controlling how the information is presented.

The word "zoom" refers to an action similar to that of a zoom lens on a camera, except that zooming on the computer is not smooth. You zoom in steps, redrawing at the new zoom scale. With some combinations of hardware, you can see the zoom happen almost instantaneously. You will find zooming to be essential to your mastery of AutoCAD. Zooming enables you to see and work with the details in a drawing. Drawing would be almost impossible without the ZOOM command.

The ZOOM command governs an entire series of options. Depending on which option you select for a given invocation of the ZOOM command, you will be able to zoom all or only a selected part of a drawing. The following are the options you will see when you enter the ZOOM command:

All/Center/Dynamic/Extents/Left/Previous/Window/
<Scale (X)>:

Remember, you can select just the first letter of each word to select the desired option. Each option will cause a different zoom effect.

Zooming to See All

If you choose the "All" option, the entire drawing will be zoomed so that all of the drawing area will appear on the screen at once. The entire drawing limits, as set by the LIMITS command, will be visible on the screen.

Zooming Around the Center

If you choose the "Center" option, you will be asked to choose a center point and a magnification or height. The center point you choose will become the center of the display. The magnification you select will be relative to the displayed default value. Thus, if the selection is larger than the default value, the drawing will be enlarged. If the selection is smaller than the default value, the drawing will be reduced in size.

If you follow the height value with a capital letter "X," the meaning of the value will be changed. Instead of being interpreted as a height, the number will be interpreted as a magnification factor. For example, responding with the number 5X will multiply the size of the objects by 5. Zooming using the Center option will be shown in action at the end of this section.

Dynamic Zooming

If you wish to test different sizes and positions of the new, zoomed view, you can use the "Dynamic" method of specifying the zoom. When you use Dynamic zooming, AutoCAD helps you visualize the appearance of the drawing when zoomed. It does this by giving you visual tools to use.

On the display, shown in Figure 2-1, you will see the drawing extents as a solid outline. (The drawing extents border is equivalent to the edges of a sheet of paper on which you are

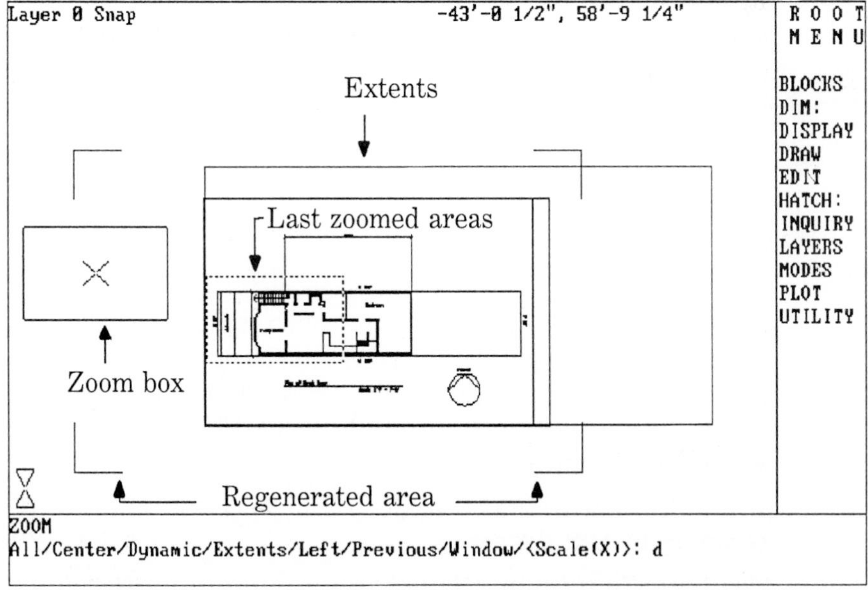

Figure 2-1. The ZOOM dynamic command

drawing.) A zoom box may be moved around on the drawing extents. The zoom box is shown with an "X" in its center. In addition to the drawing extents and the zoom box, the area of the display that has already been regenerated (and thus may be quickly redrawn) is shown by its corners only. The part of the drawing that represents the last zoomed area is shown with a dotted line.

Note that in the lower left corner of the drawing area in Figure 2-1 you see a small hourglass-like icon. This icon appears whenever the zoom box is moved outside the regenerated area. It is intended to remind you that regeneration, rather than redrawing, will be required and that this takes more time.

The key to understanding how dynamic zooming works is in the use of the zoom box. You can move the zoom box anywhere in the drawing area. You first position the zoom box over the part of the drawing you wish to zoom in on. Then you pick that position. When you do so, you will see an arrow appear in the zoom box. This indicates that you can now change the size of the zoom box dynamically by moving the pointing device. When you have changed the size to enclose the area of interest, you can pick again and revert to a panning motion for the zoom box, or you can press ENTER to record the location of the zoom box. When you record the zoom box at the location and size you have selected, the zoomed drawing will be computed and displayed. The contents of the zoom box then take up the entire area of the viewport.

Zooming to Extents

If you use the "All" option described above, you will see the entire limits of your drawing information, up to the sheet size you have defined using the LIMITS command. If you choose the "Extents" option, you will see only up to the farthest extent of any lines or other objects in the drawing. The drawing's lines will be forced to fit just within the viewport.

Zooming by Left Corner

If you wish to zoom by reference to the lower left corner of the drawing, you can use the "Left" option of the ZOOM command.

This option works just like the "Center" option, but it instead asks you for the lower left corner.

Going Back to Previous Zoom

As the option name suggests, you can get back to the zoom specified previously with the "Previous" option.

Zooming by Window

If you choose the "Window" option, you will be able to specify the part of the drawing to zoom by picking a *window*. A window is an area you pick by rubber banding rectangular boundaries in the drawing area. You will be asked for the coordinates of the "First corner:" and the "Second corner:" of the window. The contents of the window will fill the entire viewport when you pick both corners of the window rectangle.

Zooming by Scale

If you zoom with the "Scale" option, the entire drawing will be zoomed around the center of the *viewport*. (Think of the viewport as a rectangular cardboard frame on top of the drawing.) To invoke the Scale option you enter a decimal number. This number is used as a multiplier to compute the zoom.

Zooming in Action

Figures 2-2*a* through 2-2*d* are examples of different zoom options. Figure 2-2*a* shows a drawing in progress of a floor plan in which the viewport corresponds with the drawing limits. Here, a simple architectural plan drawing is shown with its border. The "All" command option was used to show the entire drawing limits. The limits, in this case, go well beyond the drawing border.

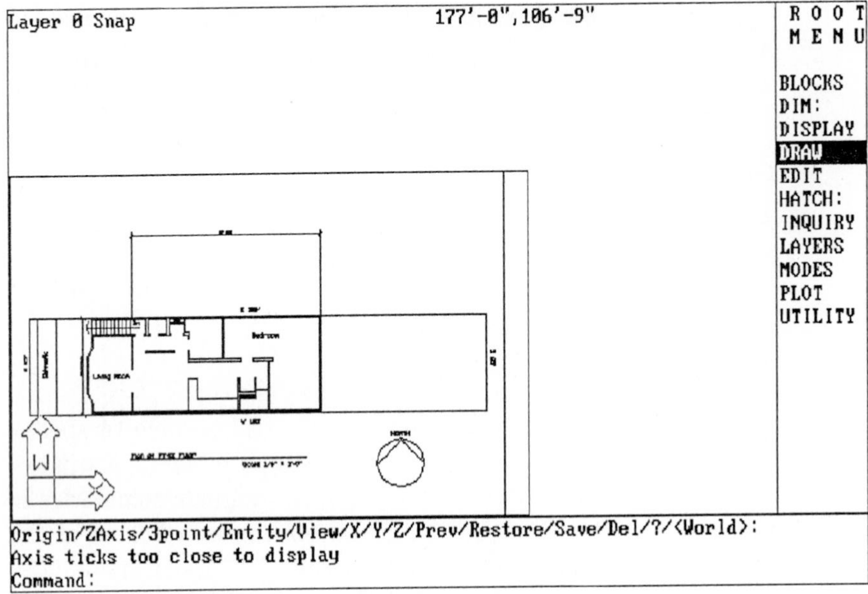

Figure 2-2*a*. A drawing zoomed to show all drawing limits

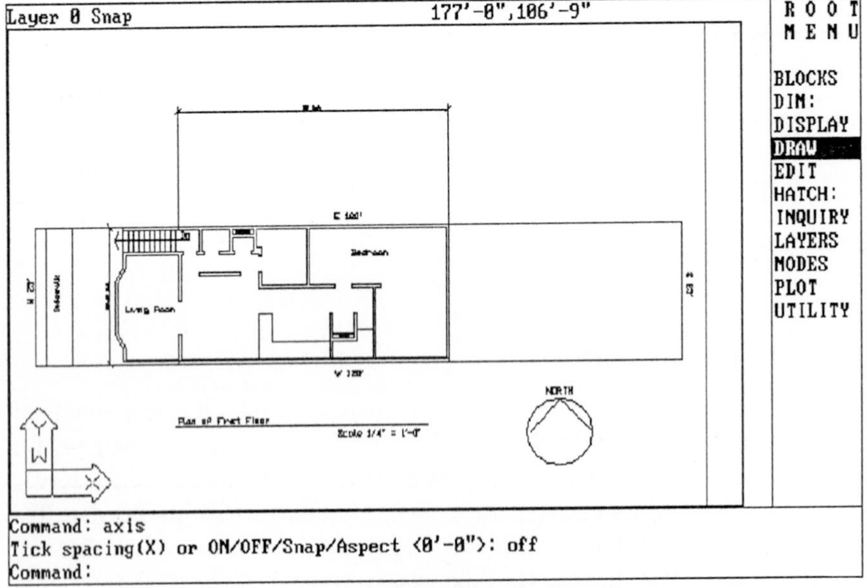

Figure 2-2*b*. A drawing zoomed to show extents

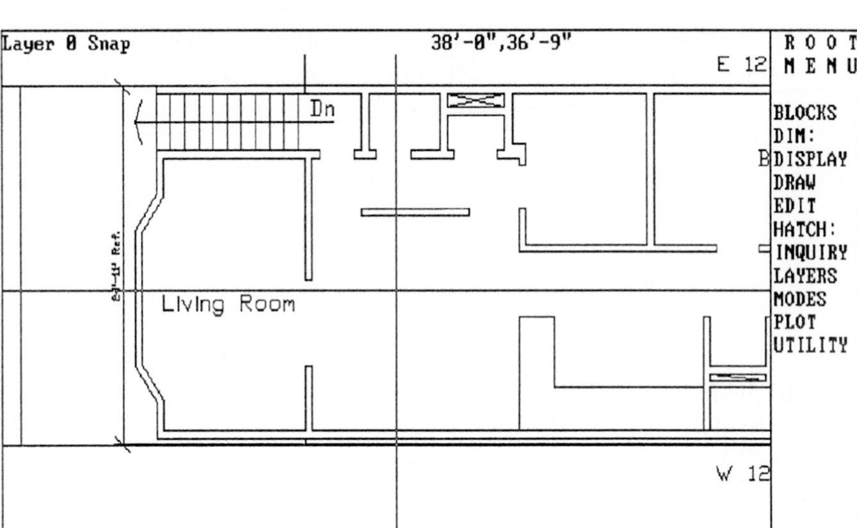

Figure 2-2*c*. A drawing zoomed around a center point

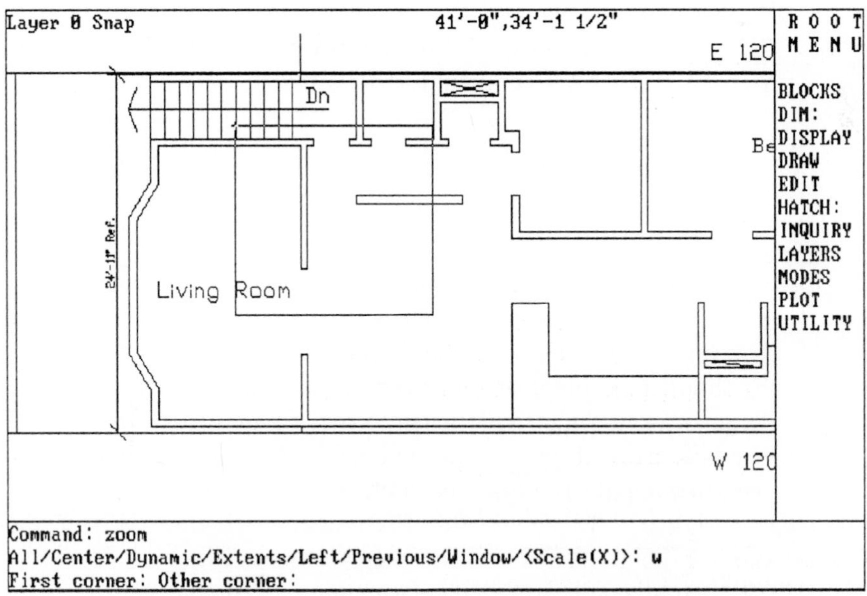

Figure 2-2*d*. Specifying a zoom using the Window option

Figure 2-2*b* shows the same drawing zoomed with the "Extents" option of the ZOOM command. Note that the entire drawing within the border is forced to fit into the entire display area.

The ZOOM "Center" command option is shown entered in Figure 2-2*c*. Note that the center of the image has been selected. When complete, the new image will have this point as the center of the drawing area.

Finally, Figure 2-2*d* shows zooming with the "Window" option. The window for the zoom has been selected. When the command sequence is finished, the contents of the window will occupy the entire viewport.

Panning

If you wish to move the viewport across the surface of your drawing without changing the scale of anything on the drawing, you can use the PAN command. You would typically use panning to work on a part of the drawing that was outside the viewport. While zooming changes the apparent size of all or part of a drawing, panning moves all of the drawing across the viewport. You enter the PAN command as follows:

Command: **pan**
Displacement: Second point:

The PAN command will prompt you for a displacement and a second point. The displacement is the distance and direction the drawing is to be moved. The distance and direction you supply for the displacement are interpreted as relative to the viewport if you enter nothing in response to the "Second point" prompt. If you pick a point for the second point, the coordinates will be used to compute the displacement.

Figure 2-3*a* shows the PAN command entered and the starting point picked for the displacement. Figure 2-3*b* shows the second point of the displacement picked and the drawing panned to its new location.

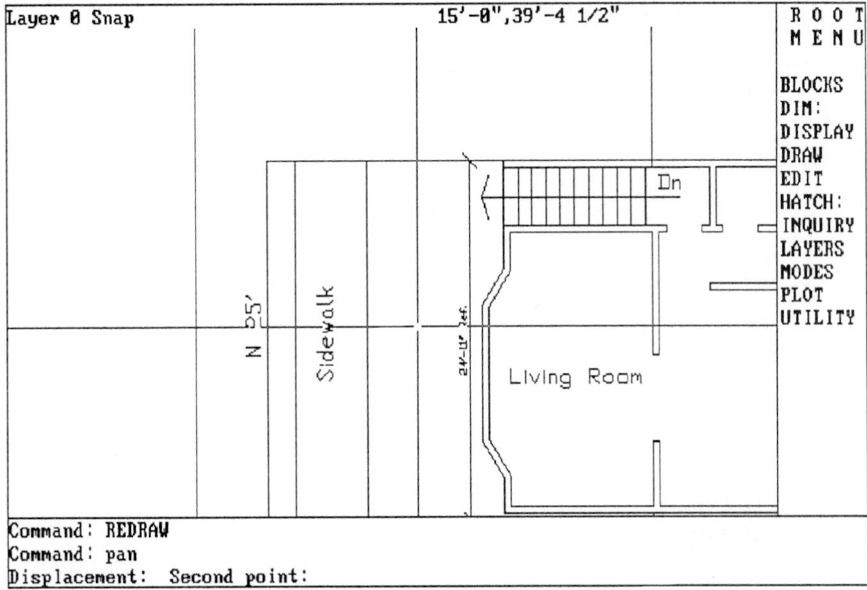

Figure 2-3*a*. Entering the PAN command

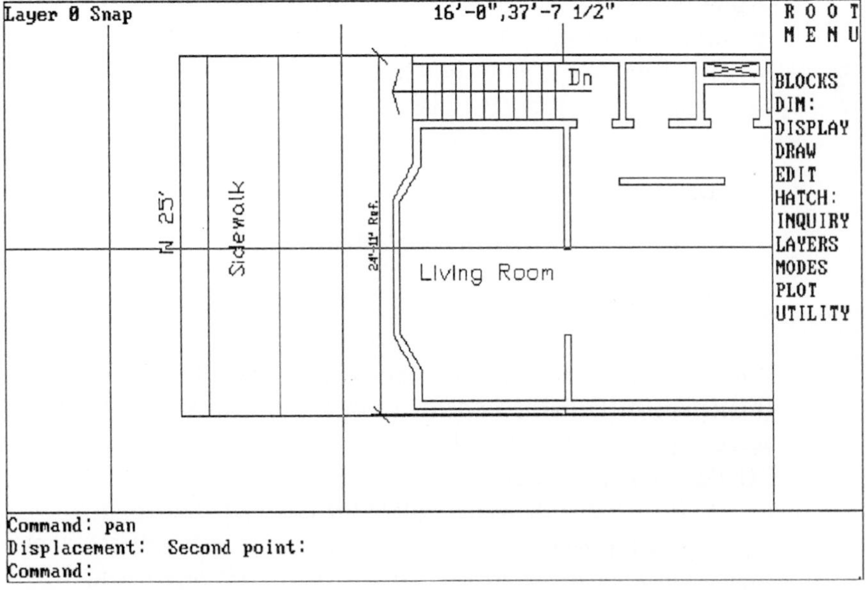

Figure 2-3*b*. The completed pan

Working with Viewports

A *viewport* is, as the word suggests, a "port" through which you "view" your drawing. The port is a rectangle that outlines a specified part of the drawing. You have already used a viewport. When you started working with AutoCAD, the default viewport was the entire drawing area. AutoCAD allows you to specify more than one viewport at a time, so you can work on several different parts of a drawing at once. Viewports help you to relate one part of a drawing to another part at a large enough scale to work on each.

You can create viewports or control the current viewport configuration with the VIEWPORTS (or VPORTS) command. In order to show why and how this command is helpful, a simple drawing will be worked on using viewports. The drawing that will illustrate this command appears in Figure 2-4.

This drawing (symbolic of a flatbed lathe) is long and has detailed components at each end. Your problem is that it would be very convenient if information about one end of the lathe bed could be seen on the screen while you work on the other end. At the scale of the drawing in its single viewport, however, the details are too small to see.

In order to put both ends of the lathe on the screen at the same time, enter the VPORTS command as follows:

Command: **vports**
Save/Restore/Delete/Join/SIngle/?/2/<3>/4: 2
Horizontal/<Vertical>:

When you select the "2" option as above you will see two identical copies of the lathe appear. In order to see both ends on the screen at once, you must zoom in on each end by using the ZOOM command. You can pick each viewport with the pick button. The active viewport will show the crosshairs.

If you zoom in on each end of the lathe you will see something that appears as in Figure 2-5. After setting up your viewports as in Figure 2-5, it will be easy to switch between them

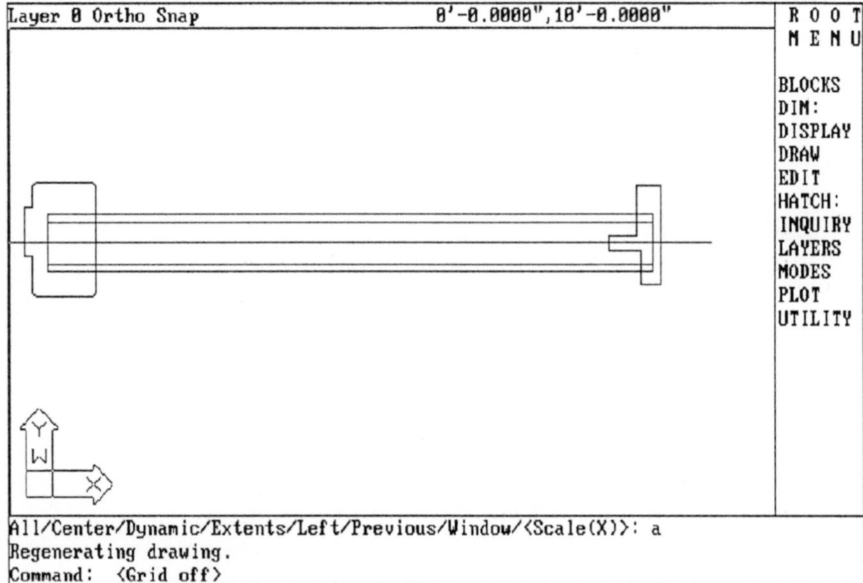

Figure 2-4. A drawing in the default viewport

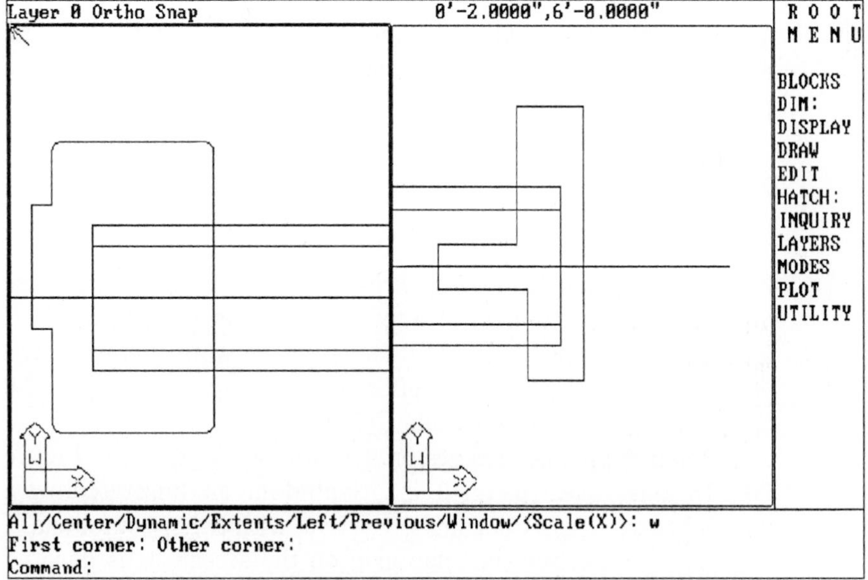

Figure 2-5. Each end of the lathe in its own viewport

and work on both ends of the lathe. You have many other options with the VPORTS command. You can have as many viewports active at once as the display will accommodate.

Snapping to a Snap Grid

AutoCAD has two grid systems. One is the snap grid and the other is the displayed grid. The settings for each grid can be different. In this way, you could have a displayed grid of one unit by one unit and a snap grid of half a unit by half a unit.

Snapping means the crosshairs will move from one grid point to another rather than move smoothly in the drawing area. If the SNAP command has been used to set the snap grid to non-zero values and Snap is on, the crosshairs will jump from point to point on the snap grid. You can toggle Snap on and off by using the F9 function key at almost any time.

Turning the Grid On

You can turn the grid on at any time by entering the GRID command and responding by typing **on** in response to the prompt

Grid spacing(X) or ON/OFF/Snap/Aspect <0.0000>:

You can also turn Grid on by pressing the F7 key, in which case you will not see the grid prompt. Or, you can execute a CTRL-G keystroke sequence (hold the CTRL key down while you press the G key) and achieve the same effect by pressing F7. In Figure 2-6 Snap has been turned on while Grid is also on.

When Snap and Grid are on, you will see a grid as in Figure 2-6. In this case, the grid is oriented in an unrotated way, parallel to the User Coordinate System, with X horizontal and Y vertical. You can see the snap grid on the screen. It is denoted by a field of points. These points are the locations to which the

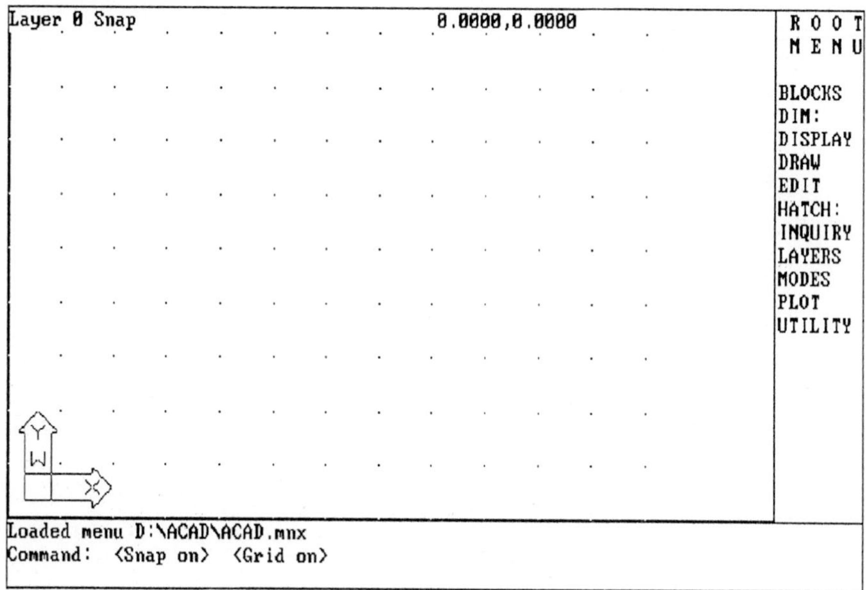

Figure 2-6. Snap and Grid are both on

crosshairs will snap. In Snap mode, no motion is possible *between* the grid points. The crosshairs jump from grid point to grid point. To work between grid points, you must turn Snap off.

Drawing with Ortho On

You can enter the ORTHO command to make lines that are constrained horizontally and vertically with respect to the grid. This means that you will only be able to draw lines that are absolutely horizontal or vertical. The command is useful for situations in which you wish to be sure that your lines are only horizontal or vertical, as for drawing lines that show walls in a typical building plan. You can do this by entering the ORTHO command on the command line, by executing a CTRL-O sequence (hold the CTRL key down and press the O key), or by pressing the F8 key. You draw one line horizontally, snapping to the grid. You then draw a second line vertically. The two lines, because they have been snapped to the grid with Ortho on, are perpendicular to each other. Figure 2-7 shows two lines that have been drawn perpendicular to each other in this way.

Rotating Grids

But what if you wish to draw two lines perpendicular to each other that are not horizontal and vertical? What if you were an architect or building designer and wanted to draw part of your floor plan with walls at an angle to all of the other walls? In order to do this, you must use the "Rotate" option of the SNAP command. This option allows you to rotate the entire grid to any angle you wish. As long as you stay in Snap mode under that grid orientation, you will be able to draw lines that are perpendicular to each other with ease. Figure 2-8 shows the SNAP command line for a rotated grid. Note that the grid now appears at a desired angle to the horizontal.

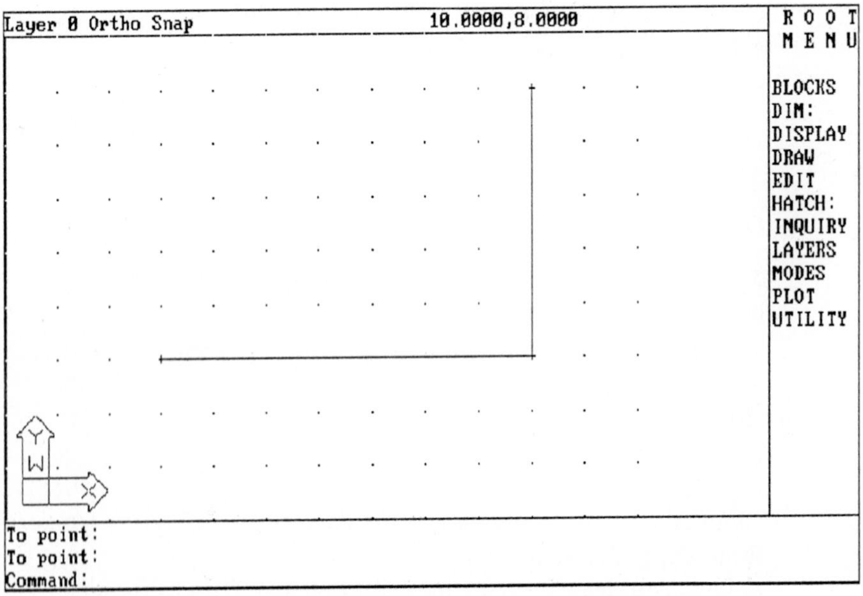

Figure 2-7. Perpendicular lines drawn with Ortho on

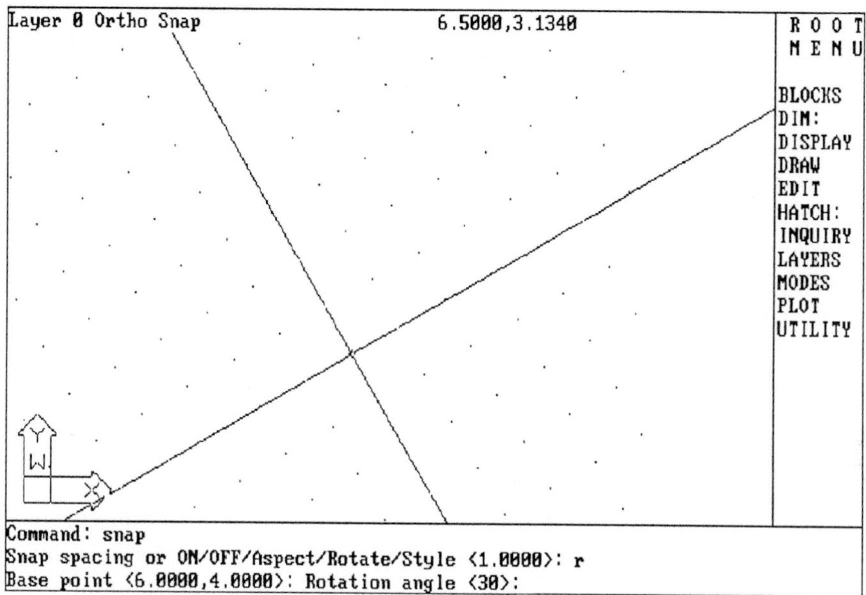

Figure 2-8. A rotated snap grid

If you now draw lines, assuming Ortho mode is still on, you can create perpendiculars just as before. Figure 2-9 shows perpendicular lines drawn snapped to a rotated grid in Ortho mode.

Note that you can use any rotation angle for the grid. This gives you total control over the placement of perpendicular lines.

Cautions Using Snap

It is common practice to set snap to the highest precision used in your drawing. An example would be an architect, contractor, or building designer setting snap to a 1/4-inch interval. This is usually the highest precision for building framing. By leaving Snap on while the walls of a building are being drawn, with Ortho mode and offsets, the designer can work to an acceptable module. If, however, the *origin* of the coordinate system is changed at any time, it might be difficult to re-establish the grid used for the design project. The origin is the place in AutoCAD space where the X, Y, and Z axes meet. The coordinates at that

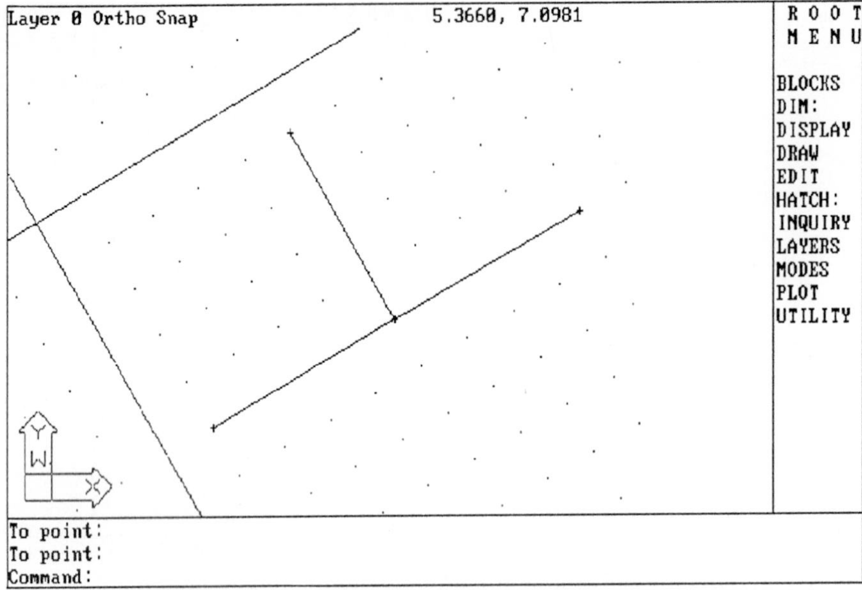

Figure 2-9. Perpendicular lines on a rotated grid

point are 0,0,0. You can use the UCS command to set your own coordinate system to be different from the world coordinate system.

Remember, if you use Snap and you change the origin to be off the grid module, you may find yourself working off the module for some time before you realize what you have done. You can always re-establish the grid by snapping to a line endpoint within the portion of the drawing you want to be on the grid. Your origin can be reset by using that point. Subsequent work will then once again be in register with the grid.

Aspect Ratio

The SNAP command permits you to set the *aspect* of the grid. The aspect is the ratio of the horizontal grid interval to the vertical grid interval. With the "Aspect" option, you can create grids that do not have square cells. Figure 2-10 shows the

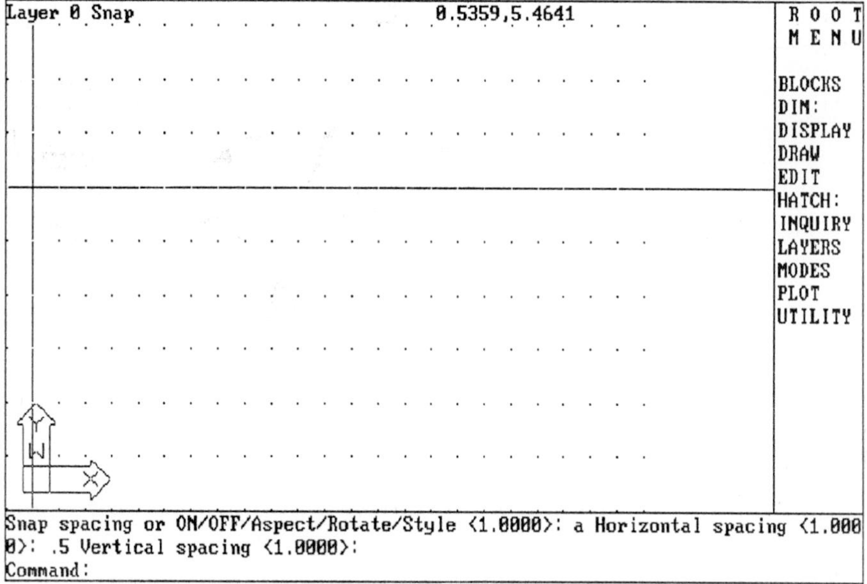

Figure 2-10. Snap used with an aspect ratio

command line and the resulting grid when the "Aspect" option of the SNAP command has been selected.

Snap Style

The "Style" option of the SNAP command allows you to select "Standard" or "Isometric" grids. Figure 2-11 shows an isometric grid. With this form of grid, it is possible to work to angles with intervals of 60 degrees, starting at a 30-degree rotation from the horizontal. This mode is intended to facilitate the construction of 30-degree isometric drawings only.

Drawing Lines

Drafting is the art of drawing lines. There are an infinite number of line combinations, styles, widths, and patterns. What is usually sought in drafting is a clean, neat appearance. Lines

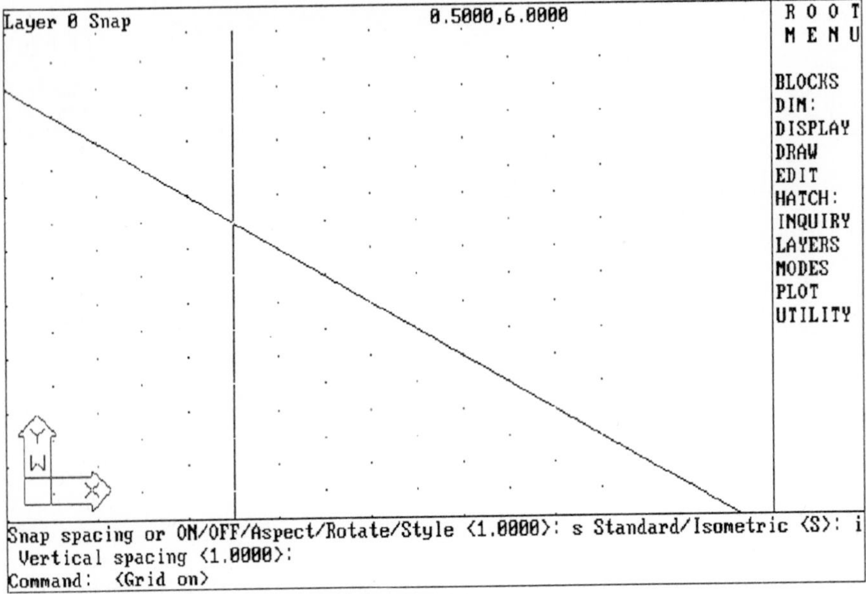

Figure 2-11. An isometric grid

should be crisp, sharp, and of consistent width. Drawings are used to communicate ideas. If you are to get your meaning across, you must avoid anything that will be ambiguous or confusing. There is nothing worse than trying to read a poorly prepared set of working drawings.

AutoCAD can be used to draw lines in many ways. You can even invent your own techniques and implement them with AutoLISP, AutoCAD's programming language. This ability will be discussed in Chapter 12, "Programs in AutoLISP."

Parallel Lines

One way to draw parallel lines with AutoCAD is to use the OFFSET command. As usual, you enter the command at the "Command:" prompt. See Figure 2-12 for a pre-drawn set of lines and the entry of the OFFSET command. Note that you are prompted for

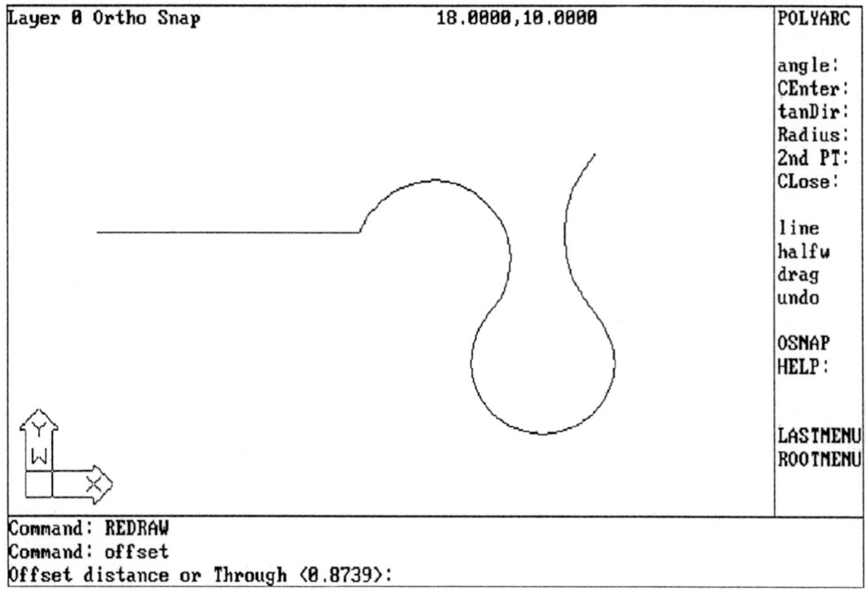

Figure 2-12. The entry of the OFFSET command

Offset distance or Through <last>:

You can respond in one of two ways to this prompt. The first way is to specify a numerical distance. Just enter a number. The second way is to specify a point through which you wish the parallel lines to be drawn. You do this by entering the word **Through**, but the letter **T** will suffice.

After you enter either a number or the letter "T," AutoCAD will ask you to

Select object to offset:

You then pick the object using the crosshairs. The "Window," "Crossing," and "Last" options must not be used to select the object.

After you have successfully selected the object to offset, you will be asked to specify either the "Side to offset:" or "Through point:", depending on whether you chose the "Distance" or "Through" options respectively. Here you indicate to AutoCAD where the offset line is to be drawn relative to the original object.

Distance, Through

If you selected the "Distance" method, AutoCAD already knows the offset distance and the point you select will only show which side of the object to offset. If you selected the "Through" option, the side of the object, as well as the distance from the object to the offset, will be determined by the point you select. Figure 2-13 shows the results of using the OFFSET command.

Perpendicular Lines

AutoCAD has no T-square, triangles, or protractor drafting head which you may have worked with in your manual drafting

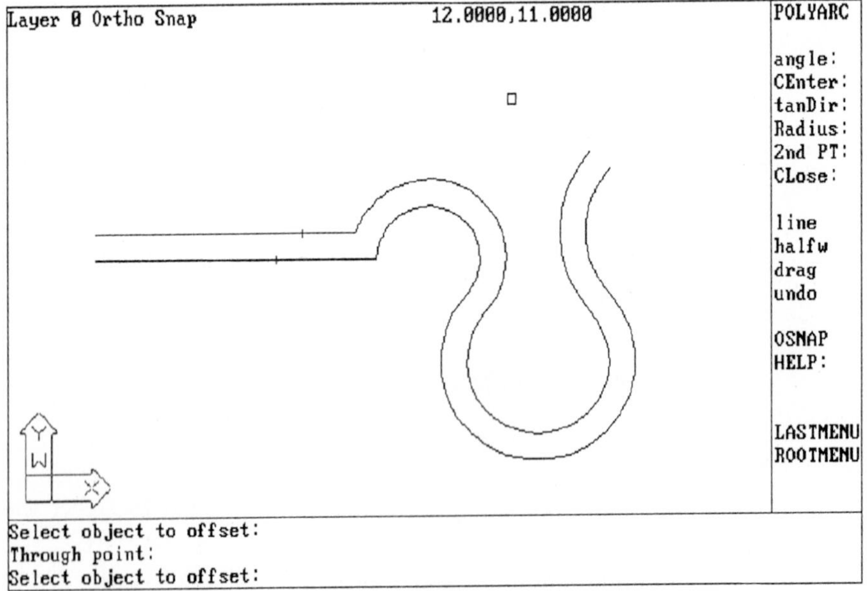

Figure 2-13. The finished offset of a polyline

work. Using real drafting tools and working directly on vellum, the task of drawing a perpendicular to a line is intuitive. When you first try to use a CAD system to do geometric constructions, you may find that your intuition leaves you high and dry. Yet, after a little practice, you will be able to draw from the AutoCAD toolbox just as easily as you drew from that box of drafting equipment you kept by your drafting table. In addition, you will be able to extend the reach of your intuition with the interactive use of perpendicular constructions and other object-drawing techniques.

With manual methods, the simplest case of perpendicular lines, horizontal and vertical, were child's play. When you wanted to draw anything out of the ordinary, however, you needed an adjustable triangle or a drafting machine. With AutoCAD, you can construct perpendiculars with a variety of methods that interact with other AutoCAD features. There is almost always a combination of techniques that will enable you to solve the problem at hand.

Drawing Polylines

Often you will find that drawing a single width of line is not adequate. What if you want to draw a dashed line of a certain width? What if you want your line to start out thin and grow wider, like the stroke of a quill pen?

A polyline is a line that consists of a combination of segments of lines and arcs. Polylines can be drawn in 2D or 3D.

In order to draw polylines, use the PLINE command. As is usual with AutoCAD, you will be given a series of options to help you draw the polyline. The following is a typical command sequence to draw a polyline of a specified width:

Command: **pline**
From point:
Current line-width is 0.0000
Arc/Close/Halfwidth/Length/Undo/Width/
<Endpoint of line>: **w**
Starting width <0.0000>: **.5**
Ending width <0.5000>:

Arc/Close/Halfwidth/Length/Undo/Width/
<Endpoint of line>:

You first pick the starting point of the line. When you do, you will see AutoCAD's usual rubberband line extend from the starting point to follow the crosshairs. You will also see the "Current line-width" message that informs you of the width of the line that will be drawn. If you use the width of 0.0000, the polyline will be a simple line, as though you used the LINE command. If you choose the "Width" option, however, you will be able to specify a line width in drawing units. Figures 2-14*a* and 2-14*b* show the invocation of the PLINE command, the specification of a line width, and the completion of the polyline.

Polylines can vary in width along their lengths. Polylines can even be curved and vary in width from the beginning of the curve to the end. Figure 2-15 shows a polyline that starts at 0 width and changes along its length, including a curved portion.

Drawing Traces

The most basic form of line in AutoCAD literally has no width. The pen that draws the line on a plotter has its own width, but the instructions that move the pen convey no width to the line. If you need to draw solid lines with a constant width, as in printed circuit board work, you can use the TRACE command. The use of the word "trace" to stand for a line with width comes directly from one of the first industries to use AutoCAD—printed circuit board manufacturing.

Just type **trace** on the command line. You will be prompted

Trace width <current>:

See Figure 2-16 for the command line and menu options used in drawing a trace. After you specify the width, you can draw a series of trace segments as shown in the figure. The trace can be continued just as with the LINE command. You can go on constructing new line segments until you press ENTER in response to one of the "next" prompts. You can press ENTER either from the keyboard or from the middle button on a mouse.

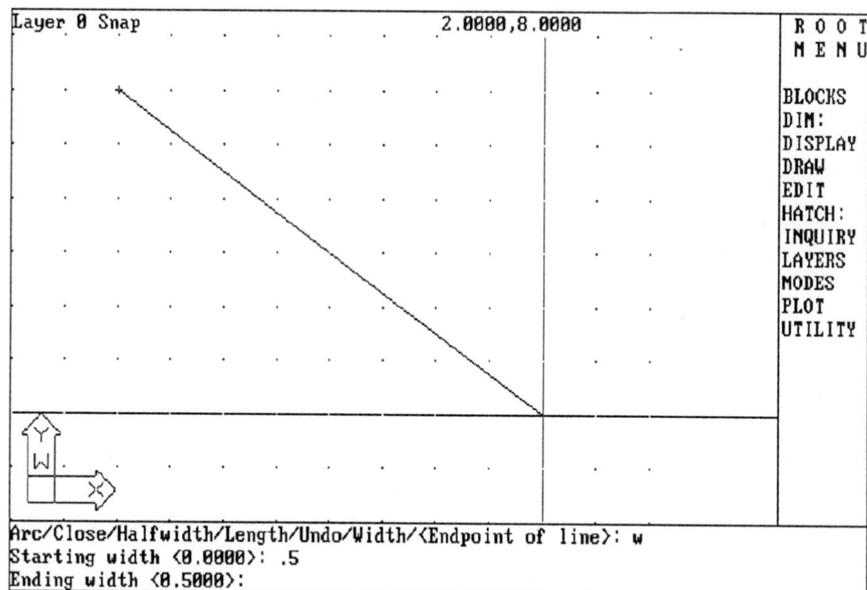

Figure 2-14*a*. The invocation of the PLINE command

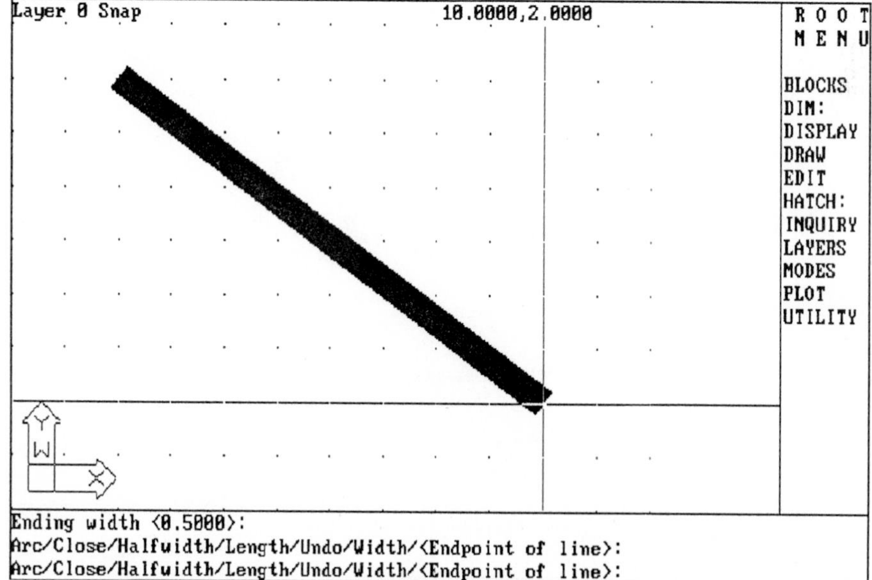

Figure 2-14*b*. The finished polyline

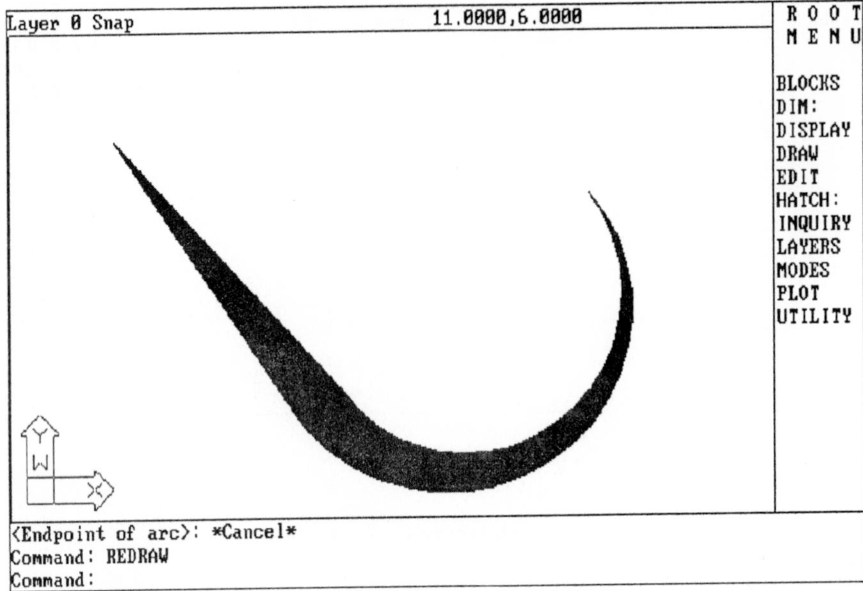

Figure 2-15. A polyline that changes width

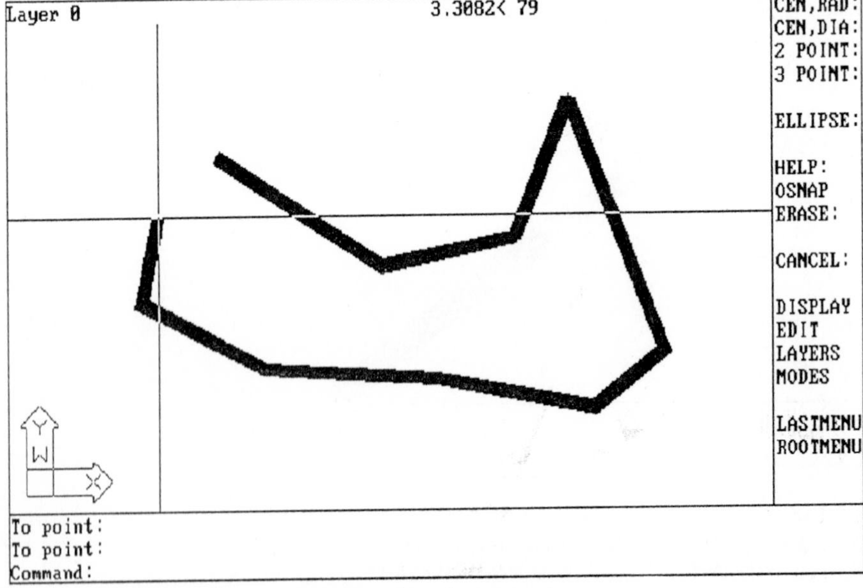

Figure 2-16. A series of trace segments

Dividing Lines Into Parts

With manual methods, you would divide a straight line into parts by using a compass to swing arcs equidistant from the line endpoints. Perhaps you own a proportional divider that you have used to do this task quickly. Proportional dividers are mechanical devices that, by using the principle of the pantograph, make quick work of dividing lines or other intervals in a drawing into a desired number of parts. However, what if the line you wish to divide into parts is a curve—or worse—a polyline? Dividing the line would be extremely difficult and inaccurate if the line were irregular.

AutoCAD gives you a powerful tool for dividing lines of any kind into any number of parts. With the DIVIDE command, you can place a series of Point entities along the line you wish to divide. Lines can be divided into any number of parts from 2 to 32,767.

To see the DIVIDE command in action, refer to Figure 2-17. Enter the DIVIDE command on the command line. The prompt "Select object to divide:" is satisfied by your selection of the object using the crosshairs. The object must be a single line, polyline, arc, or circle; otherwise you will see the message "Cannot divide that entity." In Figure 2-17, a line has been drawn and divided into six parts.

After selecting the object to divide, you must indicate the number of segments into which you wish the object to be divided. Remember, the object is not actually broken up into parts. Points are placed along the object at equal intervals. You can later snap to these points to work at these precise divisions. If the "Block" option is used, as described in the following section, you can skip the step of snapping to the division points.

When you try to divide an object, you may notice the points (called *nodes*) where you want to divide get lost in the line. You can change the points to crosses for better visibility by using the SETVAR command to change the PDMODE value. See "SETVAR" in Chapter 16, "AutoCAD Command Reference," for more information on PDMODE.

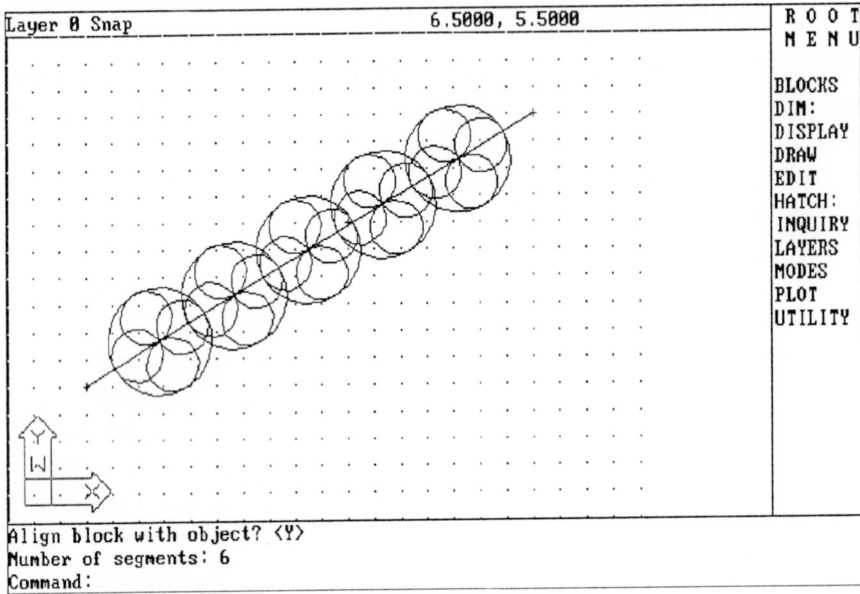

Figure 2-17. The DIVIDE command in action

Dividing with Blocks

A *block* is a grouping of entities that have been stored together with the BLOCK command. You can select a predefined block that you wish to be placed at each division point. You can read all about blocks in Chapter 4, "Working with Blocks." See Figure 2-18*a* for an object that has been divided; a block is repeated for each division but is not aligned with the object. An object is considered to be aligned with another object when its rotation angle matches the rotation angle of the object to which it is aligned.

When you store a drawing or define a part of a drawing as a block, the orientation of the object to the AutoCAD coordinate system is part of the object's definition. You can choose to have the orientation of the object match the current AutoCAD default coordinate system, or have the orientation of the object match the orientation of the object.

Figure 2-18*b* shows the same object divided with a repeated block aligned with the object. Note that a block repeated in this

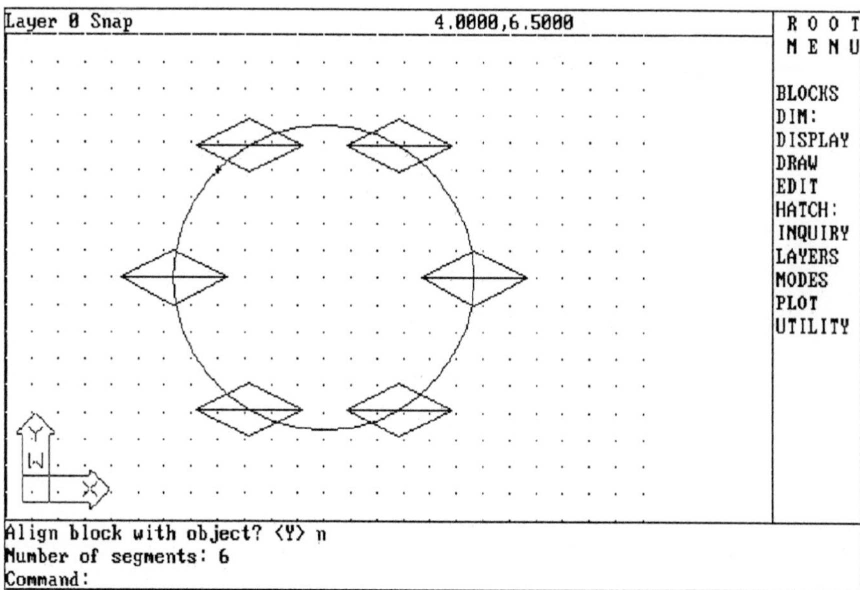

Figure 2-18*a*. A divided object using blocks not aligned

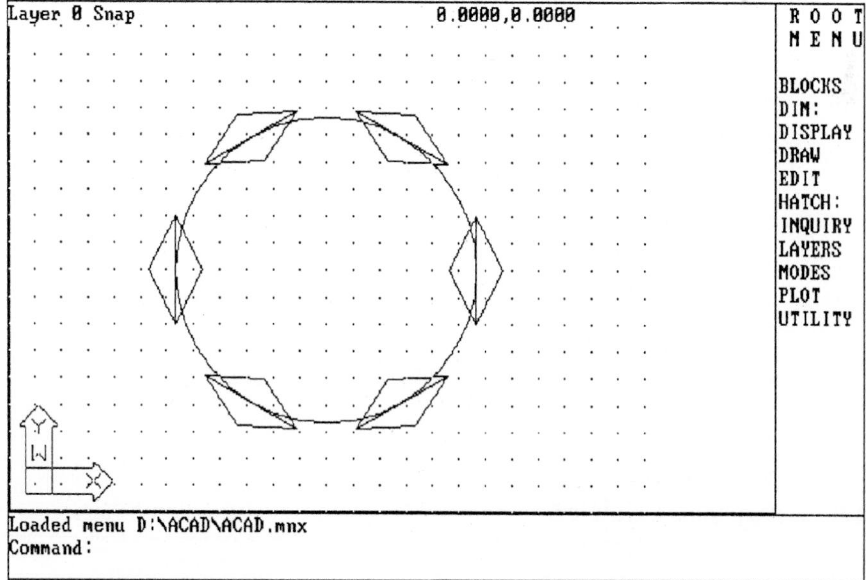

Figure 2-18*b*. A divided object using aligned blocks

way can be any combination of lines. Although simple shapes are shown here, there is really no limit to the possibilities. Imagine, for example, the repetition of gear teeth spaced evenly around the circumference of a circle.

Note that the block you choose must be defined within the current drawing as opposed to being defined as a separate drawing file on the disk.

Using Measures

What if you wish to measure out a series of equal distances along the object? Remember, CAD work is not done to scale, as with manual drawings. Instead, the CAD drawing is done using actual "real world" dimensions. One offshoot of this difference is that you can actually treat the drawing as a model of the real thing. You can measure distances just as though you were measuring an object in the real world.

You can measure off distances along an object by using the MEASURE command. Figure 2-19*a* shows an object and the MEASURE command entered at the command prompt.

Just as with the DIVIDE command you will need to "Select object to measure:". The MEASURE command has the same set of options as the DIVIDE command, except that the *segment length* rather than the number of segments is used to define the measured parts. The segment length is the distance in currently defined units that AutoCAD is to lay out repeatedly along the object's length. Figure 2-19*b* shows a polyline with measured intervals.

Now take a little time to think how difficult it would be to do divisions such as were done in the preceding examples with manual methods. There is really no doubt as to the value of AutoCAD as a drafting tool.

Drawing with Circles

After lines, in ascending order of complexity, circles and arcs are the next most useful entities to draw. While lines simply have

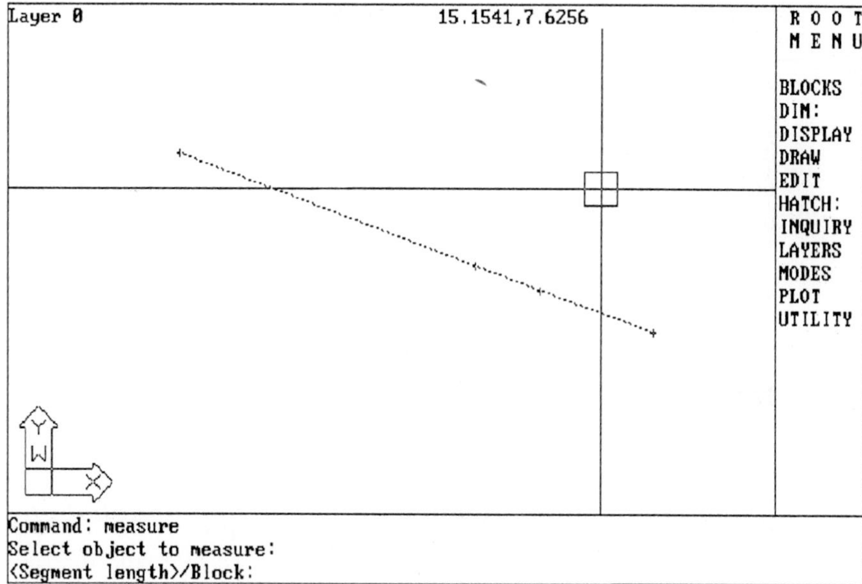

Figure 2-19*a*. An object and the MEASURE command

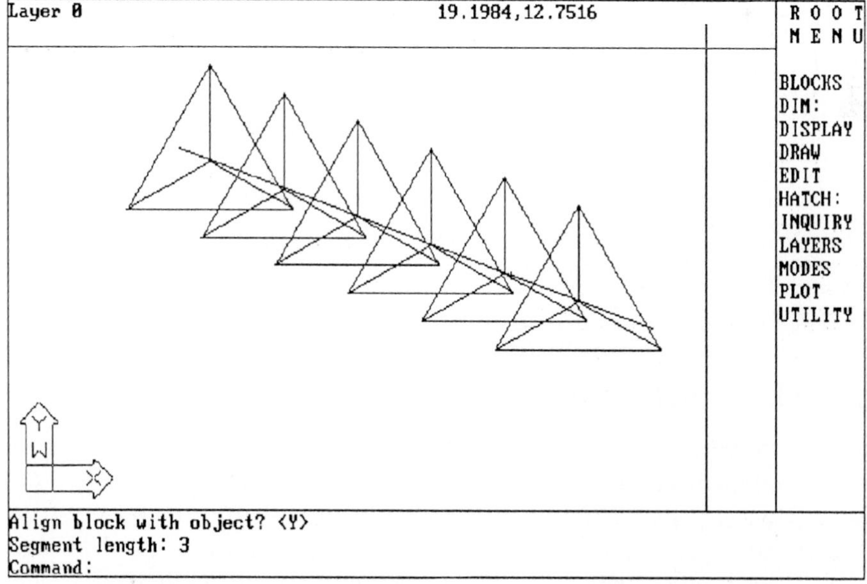

Figure 2-19*b*. A polyline with measured intervals

beginnings and endings, circles and arcs have more parameters.

A *circle* is defined as all points that are equidistant from a single point taken as the center. You will often wish to draw circles as extensions of straight lines or as tangent to straight lines. To handle all the possible combinations, you need as much flexibility as possible. As you will see, AutoCAD gives you a feast of interactive techniques.

An *ellipse* in AutoCAD is a subset of the circle. As you may already know, an ellipse is a circle that has been rotated out of its plane or "squashed."

An *arc* is part of a circle. Arcs come in handy when civil engineers need to draw curves for highway alignments. Architects often draw door swings using arcs. Mechanical engineers and machine tool engineers often use arcs to define parts of assemblies such as bearing housings and enclosures. Arcs can be drawn manually by placing the pin of a compass at the desired center of a circle and swinging an arc through as many degrees as you desire. The manual method of drawing arcs, however, has many limitations.

There are 11 ways to draw arcs using AutoCAD. You can specify arcs by included angle, center point, starting point, end point, length of chord, and radius. Using these 6 basic options, you have a total of 11 distinct ways to draw arcs. AutoCAD is particularly good at dealing with arcs and circles in combination with tangents. The tangent, because it has zero rate of change in its instantaneous slope at the point of tangency, is the best way to make smooth transitions between lines and curves. For more information on tangents, see the section "Working with Tangents" later in this chapter.

Drawing Fillets

A *fillet* (rhymes with "skillet") is a cylindrical arc that is installed within the vertex of two intersecting planes. Fillets are essentially "rounded corners." Fillets are often found in structural, civil, and mechanical engineering drawings. In drawings, such planes are viewed in section and appear as lines. The fillet smooths the transition of stresses in materials. It does this by eliminating the abruptness of the change in direction of those stresses. Two pieces of steel meet abruptly at right angles and are held rigidly in place. When they are bent, the tension and compression in them is brought together at one small point. This point could easily become fatigued and break. When a fillet is added, however, the tension and compression stresses are smoothed out.

Although fillets were invented by structural engineers, the term has come to be used wherever a curve is to be inserted at the intersection of two lines. You can, of course, use fillets to round the corners of any object.

As is usual with AutoCAD, you might expect that the name of the command to do fillets would be FILLET. AutoCAD commands are almost always named to help you understand immediately what they do. Figure 2-20*a* shows the command line for the beginning of a fillet and two lines that will be used as the basis for the fillet.

Using the Fillet Radius Option

When you select the FILLET command, you will see the following prompt:

```
Polyline/Radius/<Select two objects>:
```

At this time, select the "Radius" option to choose the fillet radius. Then re-enter the FILLET command by pressing the spacebar and select the two objects (in this case, two lines) that you wish the fillet to connect. Figure 2-20*b* shows the finished fillet.

Notice that AutoCAD knows automatically that the fillet is an arc that must be tangent to both lines. Almost all fillets used in engineering drawings are done as arcs tangent to lines. In the few instances where you do not want tangency, you will find it quite easy to create the fillet by using the ARC command, editing the portions of the intersecting lines from the point of intersection back to the points on the arc that connect with those intersecting lines.

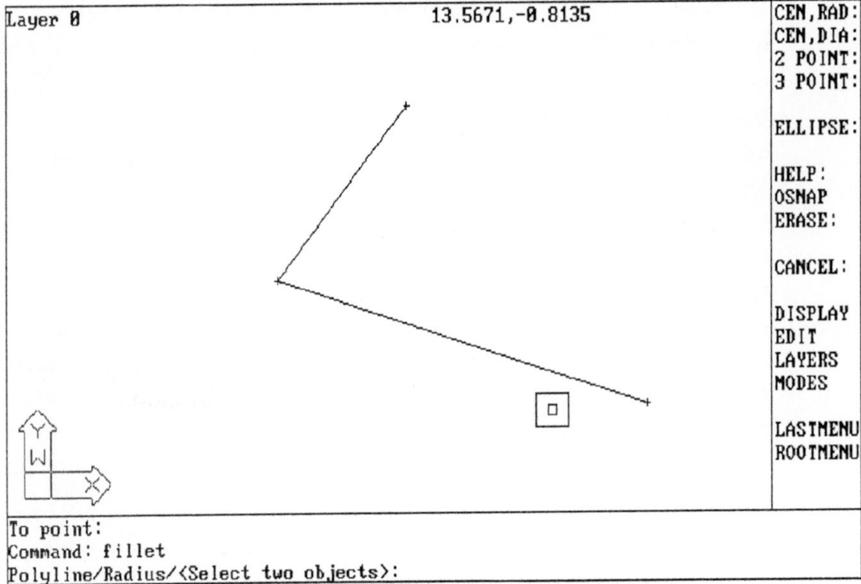

Figure 2-20*a*. Two lines and the FILLET command

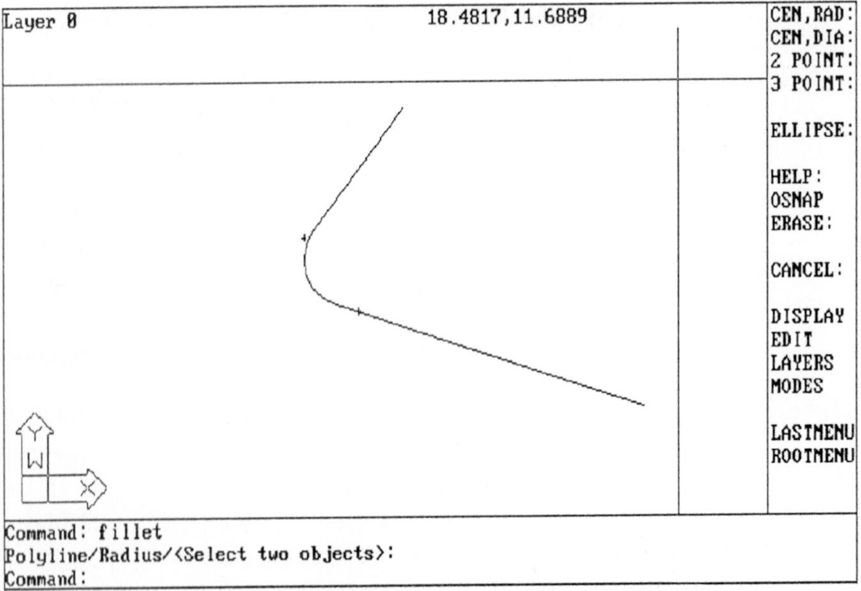

Figure 2-20*b*. The finished fillet

Drawing Ellipses

You can draw an ellipse if you choose the ELLIPSE menu item. Figure 2-21 shows an ellipse that has been drawn by selecting from the menu. Note the contents of the command line. The ellipse, unlike the circle, requires more information to construct. The circle is symmetrical. No matter how you rotate it, the circle looks the same. The ellipse is bilaterally symmetrical. When you rotate it in its plane, it looks different. The ellipse is "squashed," so its height and width are different.

When you draw the ellipse, drag the ellipse until its height and width are what you want. Then drag the ellipse around the insertion point until it is oriented at the desired angle.

Working With Tangents

One of the more powerful features of AutoCAD is its ability to define circles by specifying tangents. A *tangent* is a line drawn

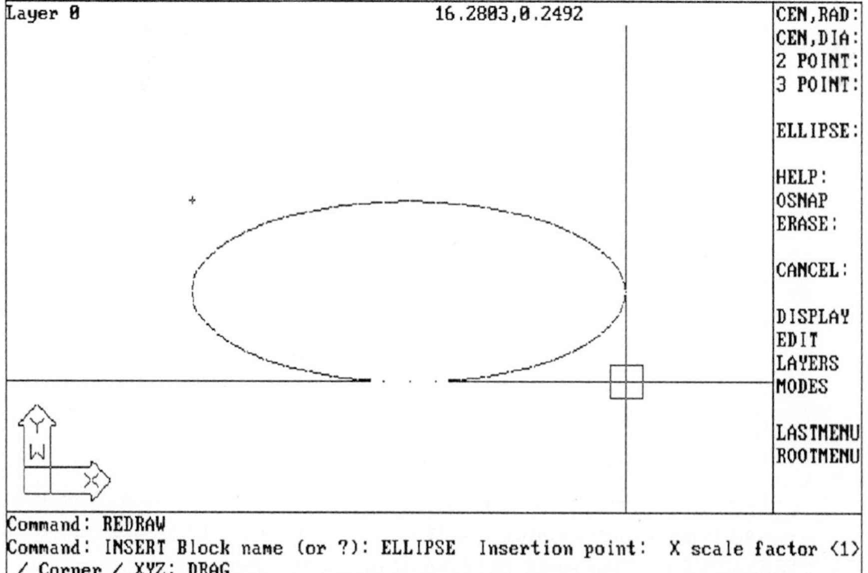

Figure 2-21. An ellipse drawn by sidebar menu selection

through a single point on the circumference of a circle perpendicular to the radius at that point. Other kinds of curves can, of course, have tangents.

Constructing tangents is very common in mechanical and civil engineering drafting. Mechanical engineers are always working with rotating shafts, spindles, and other round objects. Civil engineers are always dealing with center lines of roadways that curve in various directions. The point of *tangency* to a curve is the point where the slope of the line matches the slope of the curve and thus allows a smooth transition from the curve to the line (or to another curve). This keeps cars from careering off the road and driveshafts rotating smoothly.

AutoCAD enables you to construct tangents in a variety of ways. The following are a few common instances encountered in typical drafting work taken from the point of view of the drafting task to be performed.

Using Tangent Radius

Imagine that you need to find out where a sphere will rest when you drop it into a cone. The place where it contacts the inner surface of the cone is the point of tangency to the sphere. The problem can be reduced to a planar expression by taking a section through the cone parallel to the center of the cone. The sphere then can be treated as a circle of known radius and the cone can be treated as two intersecting lines. There are many instances in mechanical engineering where this type of problem needs to be solved. Designing belt drives is one example. Designing ball backflow preventers might be another. By using AutoCAD, you can construct a circle that is simultaneously tangent to two lines or even to two other circles.

To construct a circle tangent to two lines or circles you need to use the CIRCLE command with the "TTR" option. See Figure 2-22 for an example of two lines used to specify a circle with the "TTR" (Tangent Tangent Radius) method.

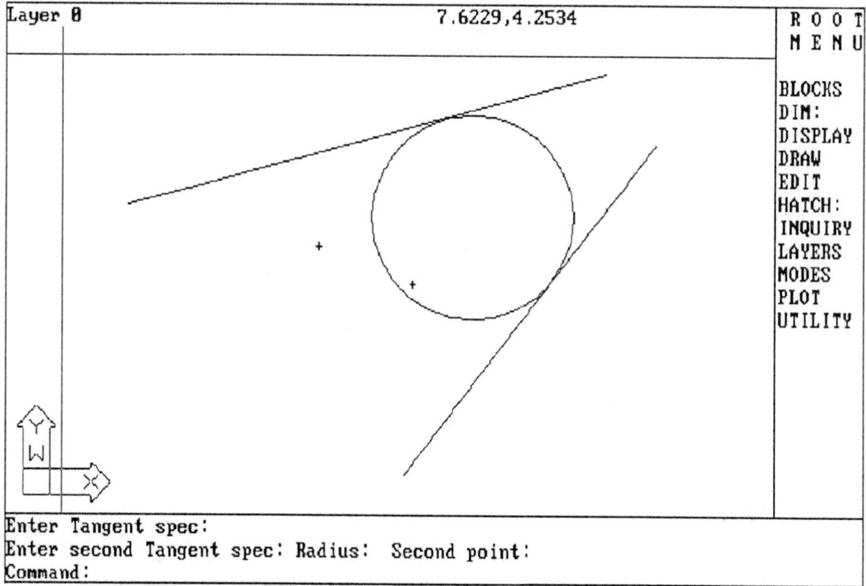

Figure 2-22. Two lines drawn to specify a circle

Drawing a Line Tangent to Two Circles

Figure 2-23 shows circles that have been drawn with tangents that do not intersect within their points of tangency. The drawing looks like two wheels with a drive belt arranged so that both turn in the same direction. Application for tangents common to circles are numerous in mechanical and machine tool engineering. There are actually two ways to draw tangents to most combinations of two circles. You can draw tangents that cross between the centers of the circles or that do not cross between the centers.

The construction in Figure 2-23 can be done with the following command sequence:

Command: **line**
From point: **tangent**
to
To point: **tangent**
to
To point:

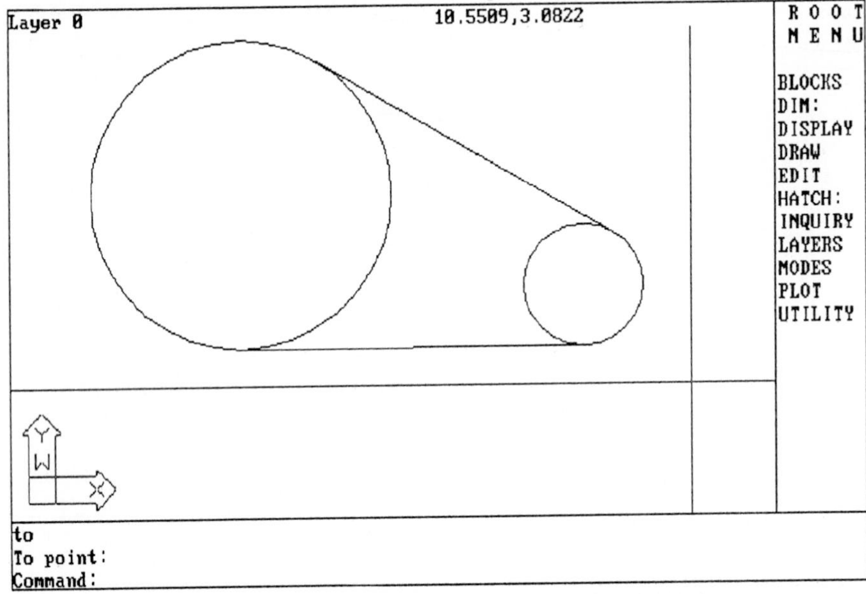

Figure 2-23. Two circles drawn with exterior tangents

First specify the entity type, in this case **line**. Respond to the "From point:" prompt with the AutoCAD key word **tangent** (or the abbreviation **tan**), thus specifying that the point is to be the tangent point on the object you select. In response to the mysterious "to" prompt, pick one of the circles. Respond to the "To point:" prompt again with the word **tangent**. In response to the "to" prompt, pick the second circle. After this the line will be drawn tangent to both circles. Terminate the command by pressing ENTER in response to the last "To point:" prompt. Notice that the tangent point closest to the pick point is used to determine which of the two possible points of tangency will prevail.

Figure 2-24*a* shows circles with common tangents that intersect within their points of tangency. AutoCAD enables you to specify common tangents in several ways. The drawing looks like two wheels with a drive belt arranged so that each turns in the opposite direction.

Drawing a Circle Tangent to Two Circles

The concept of tangency extends beyond the tangent of a line to a circle. Circles can share points of tangency such that at the tangent point the change in slope is zero. In fact, as long as the curve can be defined mathematically, you can construct a tangent at any point on the curve.

A good reason to be concerned about common points of tangency for circles and other curves is the need to reduce friction in moving parts. Cams, bearings, and gears must usually be designed so that their surfaces come in contact at a point where the change of slope is zero. This reduces friction which in turn reduces wear and increases efficiency.

Figure 2-24*b* shows two circles to which you wish to construct the tangent circle. Figure 2-24*c* shows the location of the new circle and the specification of radius. The tangent circle is then drawn. AutoCAD automatically generates the circle required for the two curves to be tangent at the desired point.

Because of the open-ended nature of many of AutoCAD's commands, it is possible to extend commands to perform complex tasks. You can construct circles tangent to any number of lines or circles in combination. Figure 2-24*d* shows the beginning of a circle defined tangent to three lines. To perform this task, you would enter the CIRCLE command, specify the three-point circle (3P) and, instead of specifying only the three points, you would let AutoCAD derive the locations of three tangent points on three lines.

Drawing Polygons

Polygons are drawn in AutoCAD either *inscribed* within a circle or *circumscribed* around a circle. A polygon in AutoCAD can have from 3 to 1024 equal sides. The POLYGON command invokes the drawing of polygons.

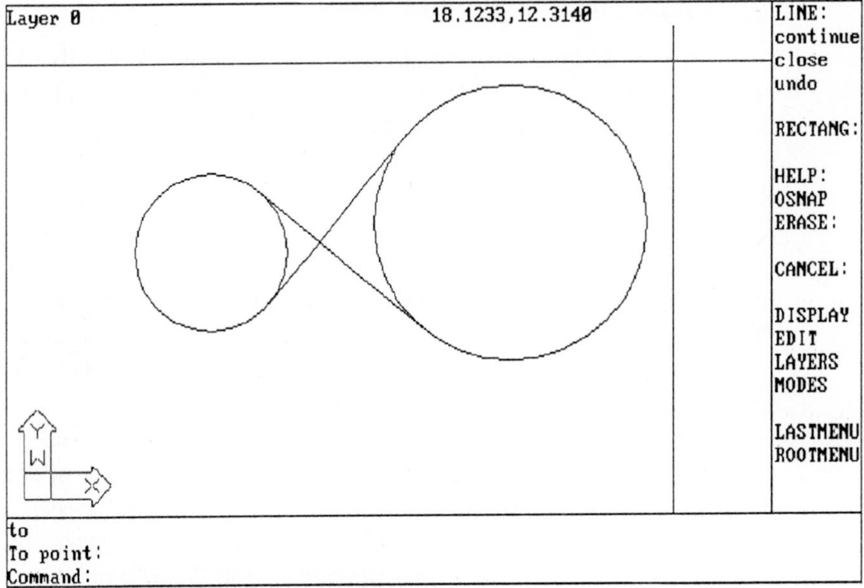

Figure 2-24*a*. Two circles with internal tangents

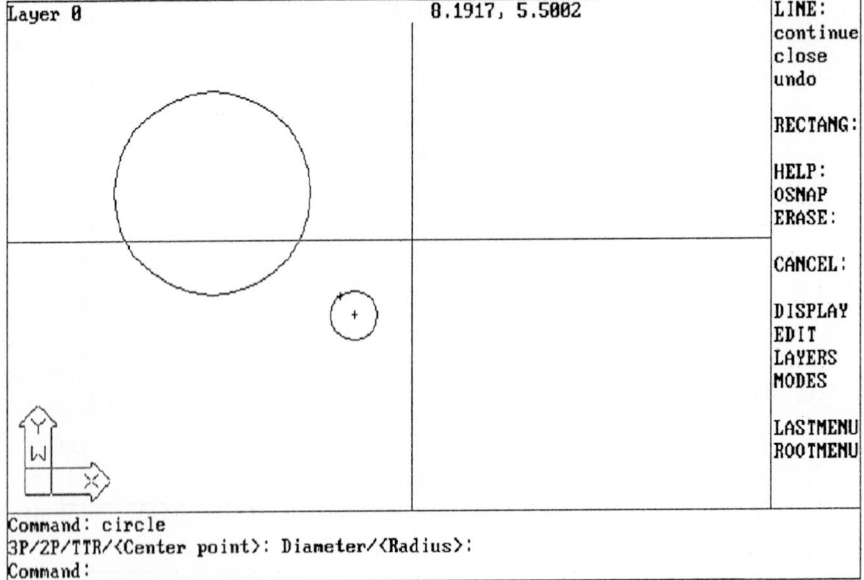

Figure 2-24*b*. Two circles drawn for the tangent circle

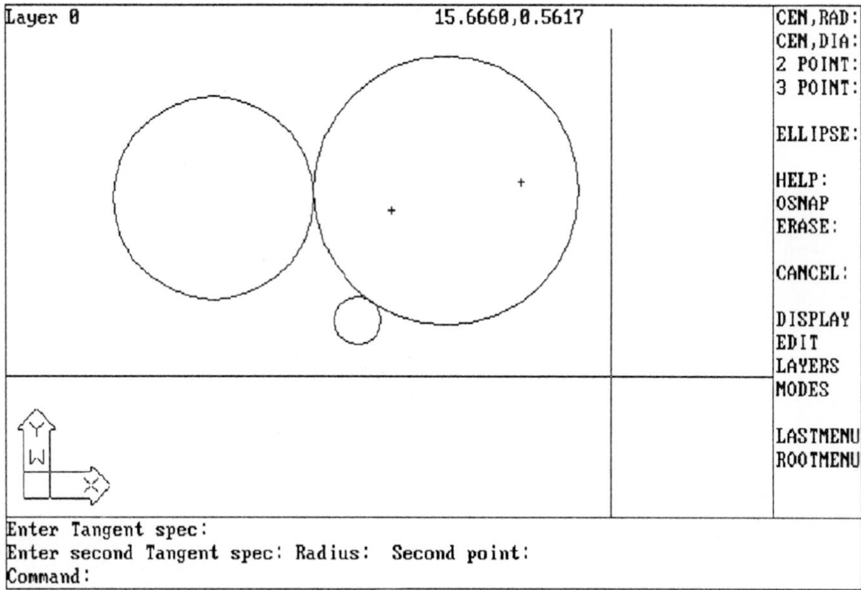

Figure 2-24*c*. The new circle and radius specification

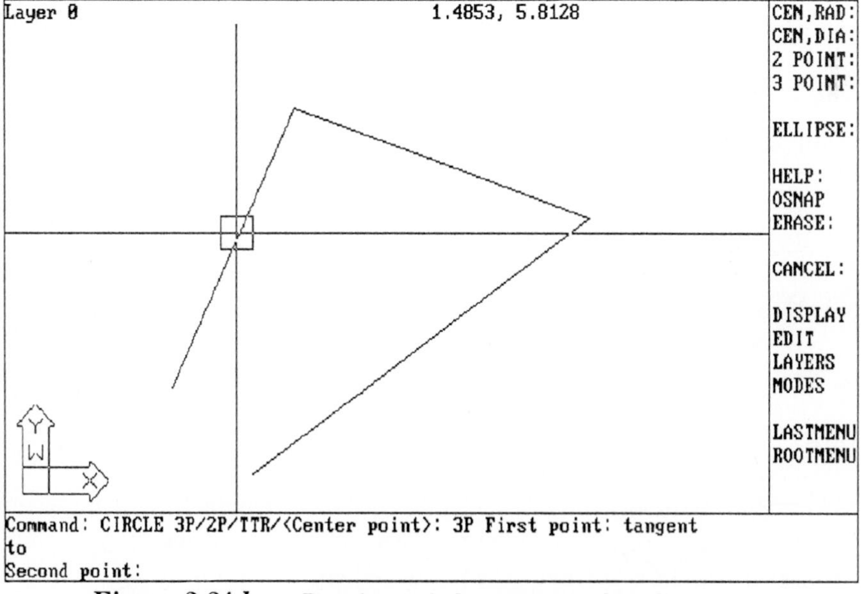

Figure 2-24*d*. Drawing a circle tangent to three lines

The command sequence for the POLYGON command with responses for a hexagon follows:

Command: **polygon**
Number of sides: **6**
Edge/<Center of polygon>:
Inscribed in circle/Circumscribed about circle (I/C): **i**
Radius of circle:

You will first be asked for the number of sides, then the "Edge/<Center of polygon>:". If you choose "Edge," the polygon will be drawn starting with the point you select on its edge. If you choose "Center," the polygon will be drawn around the point you select as the center. After choosing the "Edge" or "Center" option, you must indicate whether the polygon is to be drawn inscribed within or circumscribed around the circle. Figure 2-25*a* shows a command line specifying the start of a polygon.

Figure 2-25*b* shows the polygon after it has been drawn with the "Center" method. If the "Edge" method were used, you would be asked for the starting point and the ending point of one edge. This edge would be used to define the entire polygon.

User Coordinate Systems

Release 10 of AutoCAD adds the ability to define an unlimited number of "User Coordinate Systems" (UCS). As described earlier in this chapter, AutoCAD makes heavy use of coordinate systems. If you never change coordinate systems by defining your own UCS, you will be working in the standard AutoCAD World Coordinate System (WCS). This system is always the same. It acts as a frame of reference for the definition of your own User Coordinate Systems.

Why are User Coordinate Systems valuable? By using them you can draw anywhere in space, just as though you were drawing on the flat drawing area represented by your computer display surface.

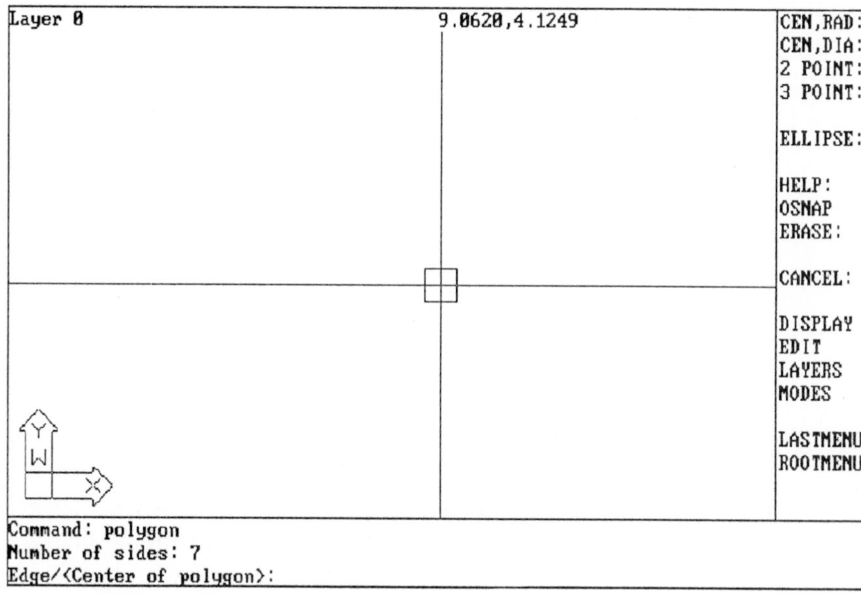

Figure 2-25*a*. Starting to draw a polygon

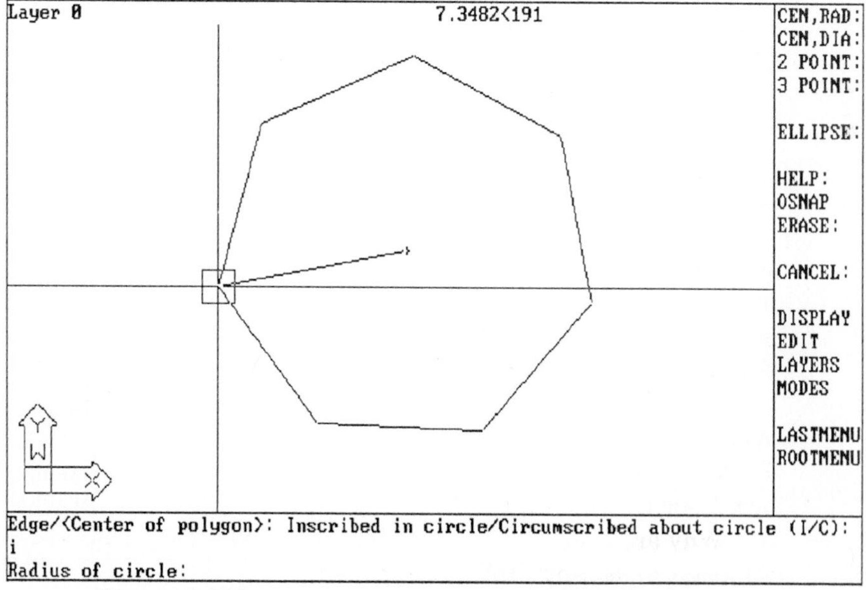

Figure 2-25*b*. The finished polygon using center method

Defining User Coordinate Systems

The User Coordinate System can perhaps best be explained by comparing it to a mechanical device. Imagine the UCS as a flat drawing board strapped to the palm of your hand. You can rotate your hand to any angle in space. You can raise, lower, and move your hand sideways. The drawing board follows each movement of your hand. The room that contains your hand and the drawing board is like the World Coordinate System. The surface of the drawing board is like the User Coordinate System.

The origin of a coordinate system is where the X, Y, and Z distances are all zero. In AutoCAD, the default origin is at the lower left corner of the drawing area on the display.

See Figure 2-26 for the small arrow icon in the lower left corner of the display. It shows the current orientation of the User Coordinate System. The UCS shown is rotated 30 degrees around the X axis, 30 degrees around the Y axis, and 30 degrees around the Z axis. The angles used are arbitrary and are only intended to show that the UCS icon changes when you redefine the UCS.

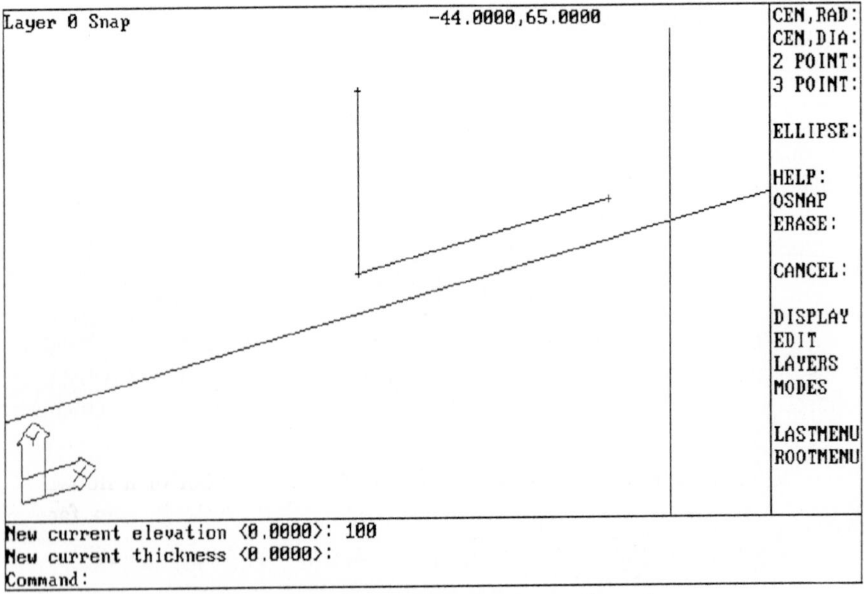

Figure 2-26. The UCS icon and current orientation

The ability to redefine your own coordinate system flexibly gives you much greater control over where you can do your drawings. By using your own UCS, you can treat any plane oriented any way in space as a drawing surface.

Changing the UCS

To change the User Coordinate System to be other than the World Coordinate System, use the UCS command. The following is the command sequence that generated the UCS icon that shows the new origin and orientation of the X, Y, and Z axes in Figure 2-26.

Command: **ucs**
Origin/ZAxis/3point/Entity/View/X/Y/Z/Prev/Restore/
Save/Del/?/<World>:
x
Rotation angle about X axis <0.0>: **30**
Command: **ucs**
Origin/ZAxis/3point/Entity/View/X/Y/Z/Prev/Restore/
Save/Del/?/<World>:
y
Rotation angle about Y axis <0.0>: **30**
Command: **ucs**
Origin/ZAxis/3point/Entity/View/X/Y/Z/Prev/Restore/
Save/Del/?/<World>:
z
Rotation angle about Z axis <0.0>: **30**

For an example of what you can do with the new UCS, see Figure 2-27. Notice how objects that would normally be drafted on the "tabletop" of the display surface can now be drawn directly on a planar surface at any orientation. You might want to do this to draw a skylight on the sloping roof of a house, for example. You might want to draw a bolt hole in one face of machine tool part. Whatever the purpose, this new capability of AutoCAD opens up a world of possibilities.

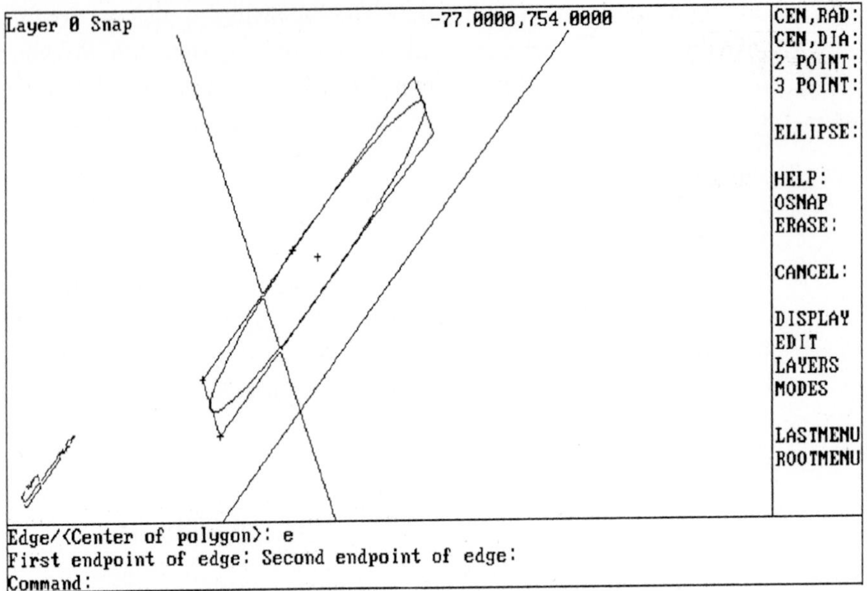

Figure 2-27. Objects drawn on a rotated planar surface

The objects shown in Figure 2-27 consist of a circle inscribed in a square shown rotated 30 degrees around the X axis, 30 degrees around the Y axis, and 30 degrees around the Z axis. Any two-dimensional drawing you could do in the World Coordinate System can be done in a rotated User Coordinate System.

When doing "path curves" for use with AutoCAD's new TABSURF and REVSURF commands (as well as with for other commands), you can use the User Coordinate System to temporarily draw on planes that are oriented at any position in space. Often such curves, used to generate surfaces of revolution, must be constructed in strange locations indeed. The potential for creative use of the UCS capability of AutoCAD is limitless.

Using the PLAN Command

If you define a User Coordinate System and draw something in it, you can use the PLAN command to make the current UCS the plan view. In other words, the UCS will be made to correspond with the plane of the drawing area.

To help illustrate the power of the PLAN command in concert with the UCS command, the design of a simple lighting fixture will be presented here. The PLAN command will then be used to create a pattern of one of the elements of the lighting fixture. In this way you will see how the PLAN command can be used to "take apart" a complex three-dimensional object and to create patterns. With the patterns, you can actually cut materials and construct models by pasting them together. Since this example is intended to give you a feeling for the capabilities of the PLAN command and not to teach how to replicate this example, details concerning the commands involved would obscure this discussion, so they are not presented here. You should consult Chapter 16, "AutoCAD Command Reference," if you want to know more about the commands.

In order to construct the lighting fixture, the REVSURF command will be used. First, a shape is drawn as the generating curve, followed by an axis around which to revolve the curve. Figure 2-28*a* shows the generating curve and the axis of revolution.

After the path curve and axis have been drawn, the REVSURF command creates the surface of revolution shown in Figure 2-28*b*. The VPOINT command has been used to set up a viewpoint that shows the resulting surface of revolution that makes the lighting fixture. In addition, hidden lines have been removed with the HIDE command. In Figure 2-28*c*, the EXPLODE command has been used to explode the block created by the REVSURF command. A few mesh entities have been selected and moved away from the fixture to isolate them. The current UCS is made parallel to a selected mesh element with the UCS Entity command. Finally, in Figure 2-28*d*, the PLAN command has been used to orient the UCS to show one of the mesh entities in plan view. The selected entity is shown hatched with the HATCH command. This pattern piece could be "cut out" of the screen. It is oriented so that all of its dimensions are "flat" as though the curved band were resting on it on your drawing board.

By using the PLAN command to isolate each mesh entity in the row of entities that make up one band in the lighting fixture, you could derive patterns for each part of the fixture. If you

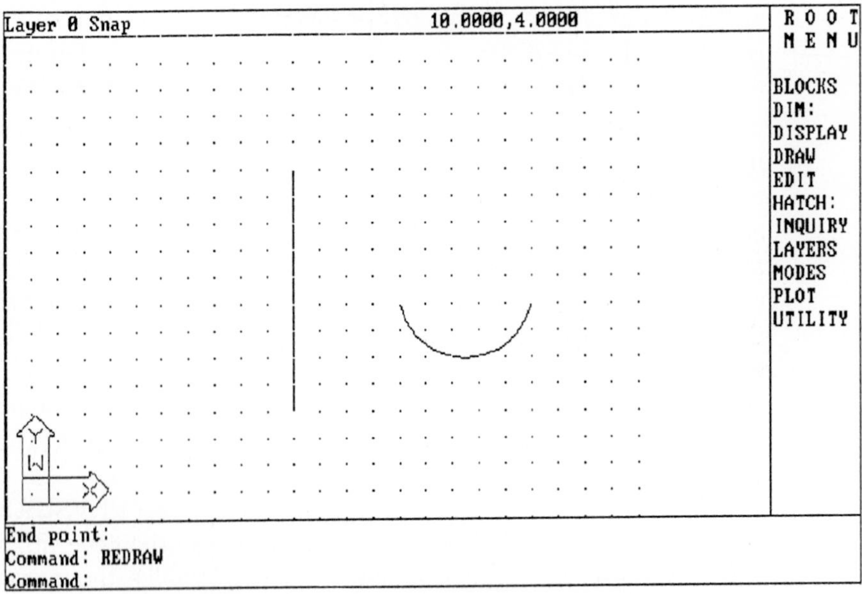

Figure 2-28*a*. A path curve and axis of revolution

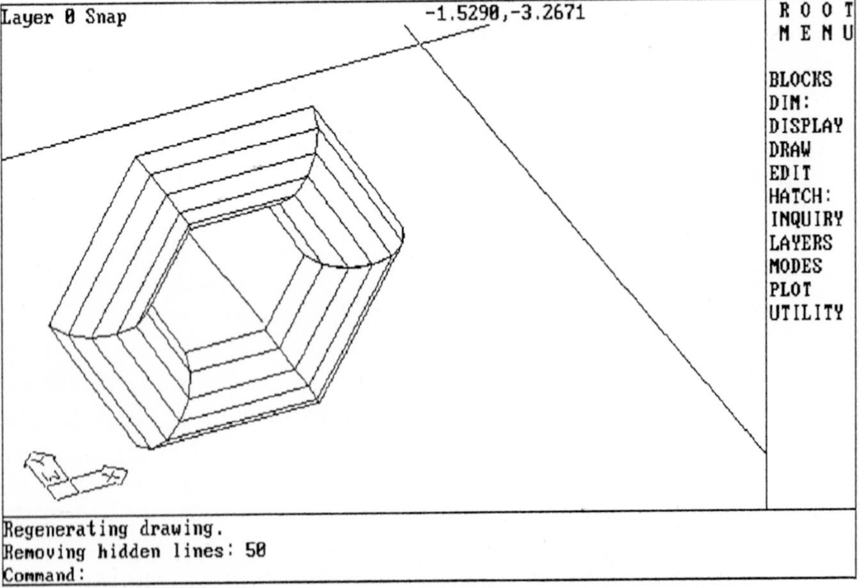

Figure 2-28*b*. The finished surface of revolution

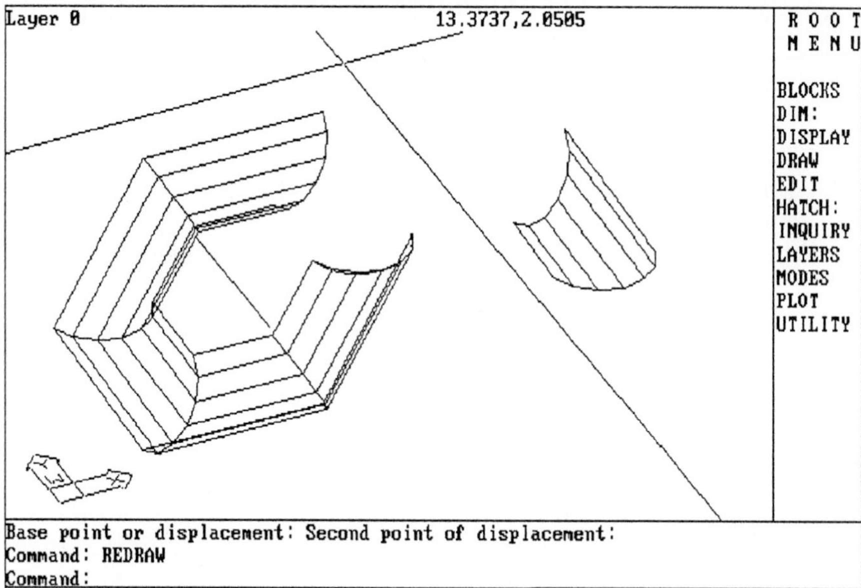

Figure 2-28*c*. The surface of revolution is taken apart

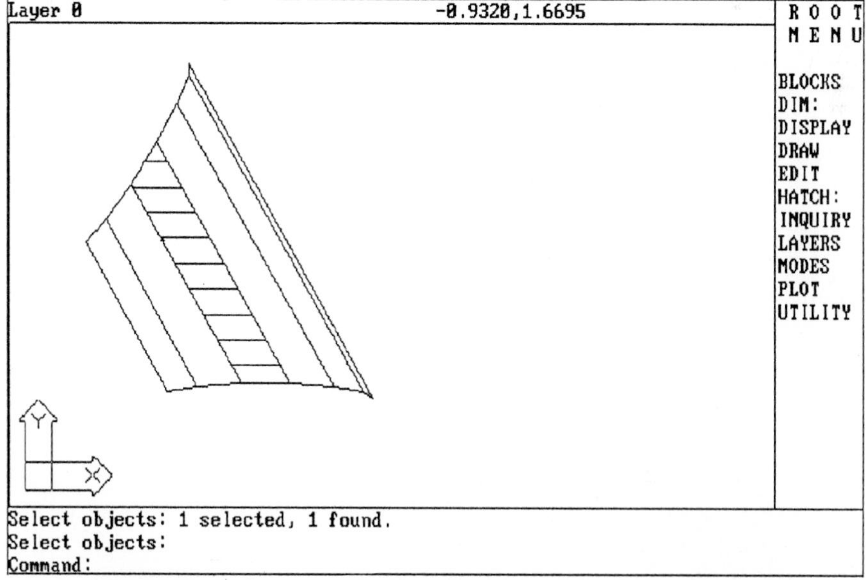

Figure 2-28*d*. The PLAN command makes a pattern element

were to cut each part created in this way out of cardboard and paste each of them together at their edges, you could create a model of the actual lighting fixture.

AutoCAD can be used very effectively to create models of anything you can imagine. User Coordinate Systems and the PLAN command make AutoCAD useful in ways that go beyond drawing. Product designers, architects, engineers, and even sculptors can now make their designs into solid models.

Editing

THREE

Erasing, Trimming, and Extending
If You Make a Mistake
Rotation, Translation, and Scaling
Layers

When you draw manually, you often need to erase lines with an eraser made of rubber or another material. You can be selective, of course, by using an "erasing shield," which is nothing more than a piece of sheet metal with holes in it. You position the erasing shield over the part of the drawing you wish to erase and rub the eraser over it. Your linework is erased, but sometimes the tracing vellum is erased along with it.

AutoCAD, as you might suspect, enables you to erase entire lines as well as parts of lines. With AutoCAD's many editing options, you can achieve the same effect as with an erasing shield, and more.

You can trim and extend objects, rotate, move, and scale entities, and work with different combinations of layers. Additionally, AutoCAD gives you many ways to undo any mistakes you have made. This chapter describes these various operations.

Editing is not limited to simple erasures but includes so many possible ways to change a drawing that functions are sometimes hard to classify. It can be hard to tell whether a given operation is appropriately labeled a drawing or an editing function. For example, when you crosshatch an area in a drawing, you are drawing lines spaced at intervals across the area, but you are also editing the lines that form the area boundary.

The use of AutoCAD's drawing and editing commands in combination gives you complete control over the creation of your drawing. Don't be afraid to experiment. Unlike the manual drawing, the AutoCAD drawing is very forgiving. If you make a mistake, you can use the UNDO, REDO, and OOPS commands to reverse the effects of what you have just done. With manual drafting methods, you have no choice but to draw it all again.

Erasing, Trimming, and Extending

When you draw entities with AutoCAD, you can erase, break, trim, and extend them as required. To *erase* an entity, you pick the entity and AutoCAD removes it from the drawing. To create an opening in a line or in another AutoCAD entity, you can *break* the line or other object. You can *trim* an object as well, in which case only the trimmed portion of the entity is removed from the drawing. When you *extend* an object, you change the object's description to add, rather than remove, the distance over which the entity is drawn.

With these tools, you can make openings in continuous lines and modify your drawing to add entities that interrupt an already-drawn object. For example, in a drawing of a floor plan, you can add a window to a wall by breaking the lines that define the wall. You can use the EXTEND command to lengthen a wall. Or you can erase all or part of the drawing within the AutoCAD window.

Erasing

If you wish to erase entire entities from your drawing you can use the ERASE command. As with many other commands in AutoCAD, you can select objects to erase by picking them with the pointing device. When you use the ERASE command, you have other options in addition to picking the object to erase. For example, you can specify the "Last" object you drew to quickly erase your work until all of the most recent changes have been erased. Another option, "Window," enables you to select the entire drawing or any rectangular area within which you can choose objects to erase.

Picking Objects to Erase

Figure 3-1 shows a series of objects that have been drawn with AutoCAD. The entities were drawn in the following order: first the triangle, then the square, the pentagon, the hexagon, and finally the ellipse.

The first objects to be erased will be the pentagon and the hexagon. As neither of these objects was the last object drawn, it will be necessary to pick each of them with the pointing device. In order to start the command sequence, prepare your command line as follows:

Command: **erase**
Select objects:

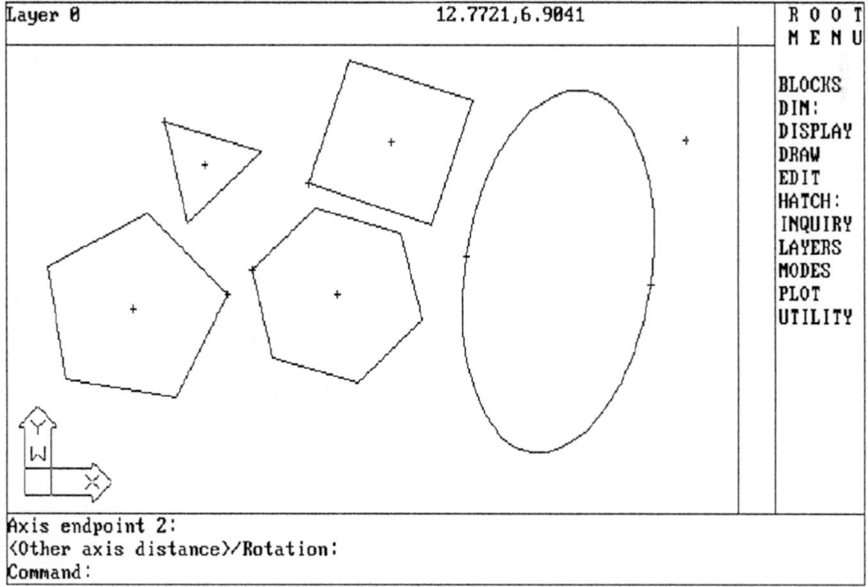

Figure 3-1. A series of objects that will be erased

You can now select the object or objects that you wish to erase. Note that the crosshairs now appear as a small box. You move the box so that it contains part of the object you wish to select. As long as any part of the object appears in the area of the box, the entire object will be selected when you "pick" the object.

Note: If you want to enlarge the pick box, you can use the APERTURE command. Or you could set the PICKBOX system variable with the SETVAR command, AutoCAD's general command for setting system variables. The PICKBOX variable stores the size of the box used to pick objects. Refer to Chapter 16, "AutoCAD Command Reference," for more information on these topics.

See Figure 3-2 for the appearance of the display after the pentagon and hexagon have been selected. Note that the pentagon and hexagon are now highlighted by dotted lines. At this point, the objects have only been selected. To actually complete

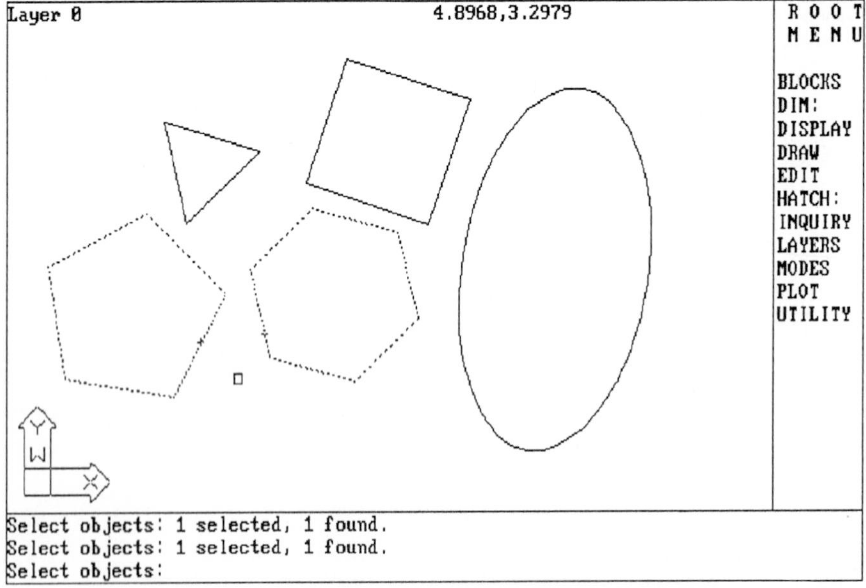

Figure 3-2. After selecting the pentagon and hexagon

the command, you must press ENTER or use a button on the pointing device that effectively presses ENTER, such as the center button on a mouse. When you press ENTER, the objects you have selected will be erased. If you decide that you don't want to finish the command, press CTRL-C or select CANCEL from one of the menus. The right button on the mouse will express the cancel as well. AutoCAD often gives you several ways to accomplish the same thing.

Note that you can use the SETVAR command to turn highlighting on or off. To turn highlighting off, for example, you would use the following command sequence:

Command: **setvar**
Variable name or ? <ELEVATION>: **highlight**
New value for HIGHLIGHT <1>: **0**

If you turn highlighting off, you will not see entities highlighted at all when you pick them. This can be confusing, especially if AutoLISP programs or macros have turned highlighting off without your knowing it. If you find that you don't see entities highlighted when you pick them, you can turn highlighting on by using the SETVAR command to set HIGHLIGHT to 1. Use the preceding command sequence, but enter a **1** rather than a 0 at the last prompt.

Using the "Last" Option

If you wish to erase the last drawn object in the drawing, the ellipse, rather than pick objects to erase, you can use the ERASE command's "Last" option. You would follow the same approach as in the preceding section, except that you would enter **L** in response to the "Select objects:" prompt.

Note that if you select the "Last" option in response to the ERASE command, the object just disappears. It is not ghosted as when you pick objects to erase. This can be disconcerting. If you accidentally erase the last object, it seems to disappear forever. You can always get it back by executing the OOPS command explained in the "Oops" section later in this chapter.

Using "Windows" to Erase

As mentioned earlier in this chapter, the "Windows" option of the ERASE command allows you to erase every object entirely contained in a window you define. You can select the "Window" option with just the letter "W," the first letter, as with other AutoCAD command options. When you specify this option, you will be prompted for the first corner of a rectangle and then the opposite corner. The rectangle defines the portion of the drawing area that will be enlarged so that all of the contents of the rectangle will occupy the entire drawing area of the AutoCAD display. The window rectangle is shown with a solid line to remind you that you are using this option.

Figure 3-3 shows the ERASE command with the "Window" option in action. Notice the command area. The ERASE command has been picked from the sidebar menu, and the "Window" option has been selected from the sidebar menu in response to

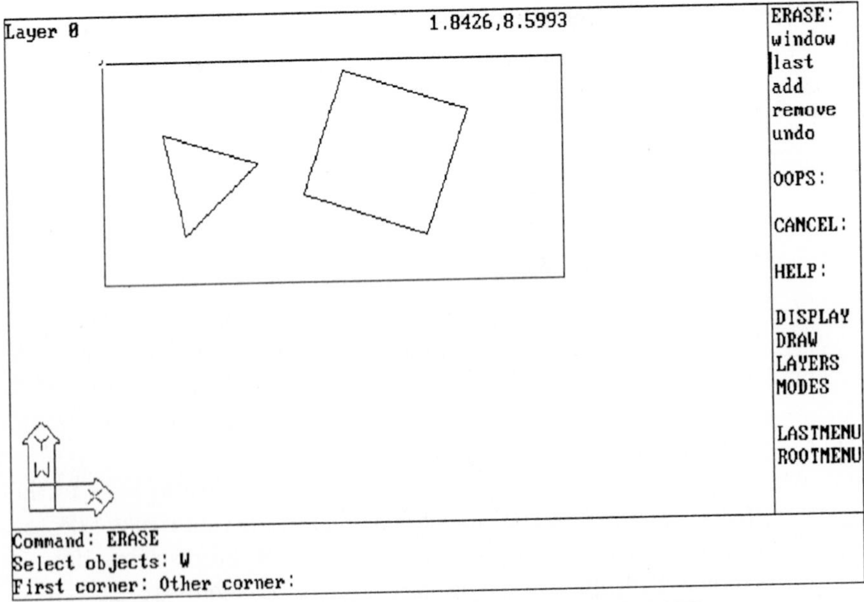

Figure 3-3. Using the "Window" option with ERASE

the "First corner:" prompt. AutoCAD has prompted for the first corner of the window rectangle, and the user has picked a location. The "Other corner:" is about to be picked.

After the window has been defined, the number of objects selected within the window will be reported by AutoCAD. The objects you select will be "ghosted" to indicate that they will be erased. The AutoCAD display will look something like Figure 3-4. Notice that the pick points for the corners of the window remain, as well as the pick box to enable you to continue selecting objects to erase. You can finish the ERASE command (rather than pick more objects) by pressing ENTER.

Although the ERASE command is very helpful, it can only erase entire entities. Fortunately, there are other AutoCAD commands—the TRIM and BREAK commands—that enable you to erase parts of objects.

Using the Crossing Option

The "Crossing" option is similar to the "Window" option in that you are prompted to pick the first corner, then the opposite corner of a rubber-banded rectangle. When you specify the

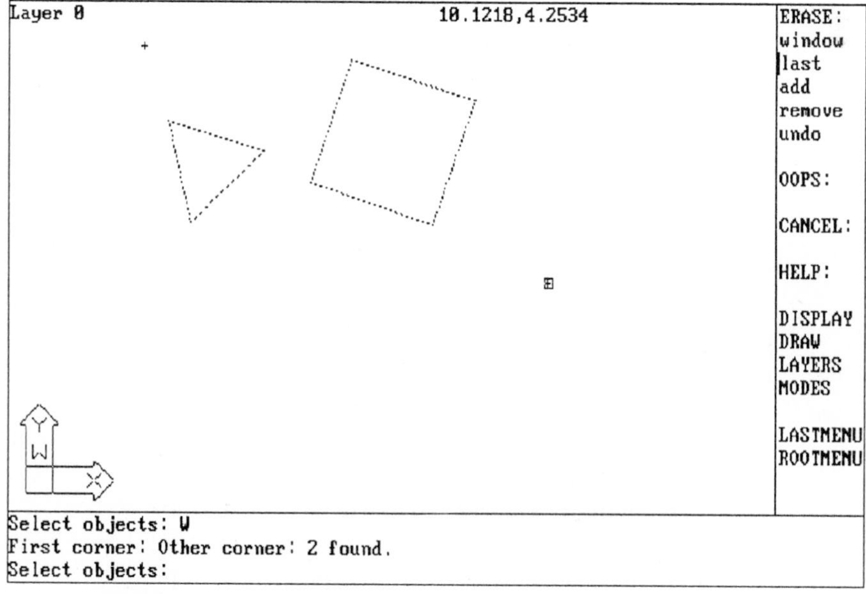

Figure 3-4. Objects ghosted to show they are selected

"Corner" option, however, the entities that are entirely contained within the rectangle are selected, but so are any entities that are *crossed* by the rectangle. You can select this option by pressing C. When you are in the process of using the "Crossing" option, the rubber-banded rectangle will appear with a dotted line.

Trimming

The value of the TRIM command is its ability to cut the drawing along the edges of predefined entities. For example, you could make part of your drawing appear within a "frame" composed of circles, ellipses, lines, and any other entities allowed by AutoCAD. Using this command is like using a paper cutter to "crop" your drawings, except that the paper cutter only allows you to cut along straight lines. With the AutoCAD TRIM command, you can cut along any lines you can define with AutoCAD entities.

Selecting Cutting Edges

Figure 3-5*a* shows a sample drawing that was drawn with a combination of AutoCAD commands. The circle around the hexagon, which is part of the original drawing, shows the outline of a large spindle that is part of the lathe assemby. In order to create cutting edges for this drawing, a hexagon will be drawn. A hexagonal shape is required to illustrate a very large hex screw that will penetrate the lathe bed and thread into the spindle in the background. Figure 3-5*b* illustrates a hexagon drawn in the position required for the trim. Any lines that pass through the lines that define the edges of the hexagon will be truncated at those edges.

Figure 3-5*c* shows an in-process view of the TRIM command. The display shows the prompts that are generated by the TRIM command. The first thing you pick is the entity that will be used for the trim edge. In this example, the hexagon has been picked in response to the TRIM command's prompts.

The next step is to pick the objects that are to be trimmed. Figure 3-5*d* shows the display that results from the successful execution of the TRIM command. Note that the predefined drawing has been competently truncated, line by line, at the hexagonal edge. Since the remaining lines were not included in the responses to the TRIM command, they were not removed.

Extending

What if you need to make objects continue from a predefined point to stop at a desired point? AutoCAD has a command, the EXTEND command, that has been specifically designed for the purpose of extending entities until they intersect other entities.

As shown in Figure 3-6*a*, you may have a pre-drawn set of entities that do not intersect. It's a shame, too, because the drawing would look much better if the lines connected with each other. If you had created this drawing manually, you would need to spend a lot of time reconstructing everything to make the lines meet. With AutoCAD, however, you can accomplish the same thing in one operation.

You execute the EXTEND command by typing the command at the "Command:" prompt as follows:

Command: **extend**
Select boundary edge(s). . .
Select object to extend:

As usual, when AutoCAD prompts you for the edges to be used as the boundary, you pick the desired objects. Likewise, you pick the objects that are to be extended in response to the "Select objects:" prompt. You are limited to the selection of open polylines, lines, circles, and arcs. No other AutoCAD entity types will be recognized. If you happen to select a closed polyline, the EXTEND command will respond with "Cannot extend a closed polyline."

In response to the EXTEND command's prompts, you are limited to a simple pick without the "Last," "Window," or "Crossing" options. Be sure when picking to select the correct

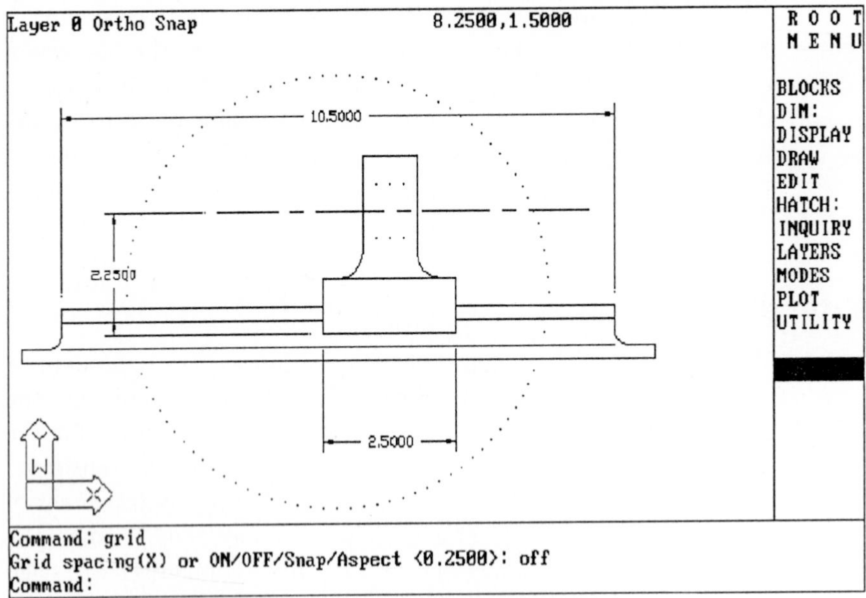

Figure 3-5*a*. A sample drawing to trim

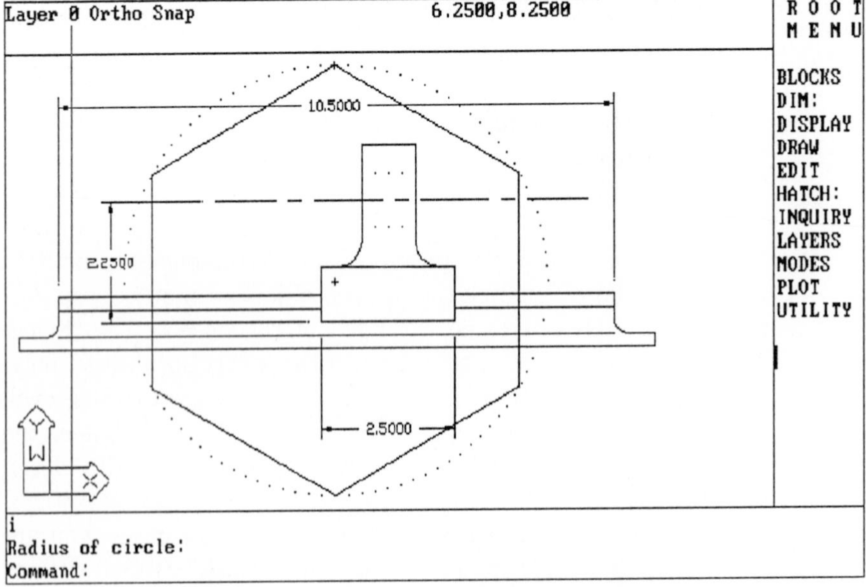

Figure 3-5*b*. The hexagon will provide trim edges

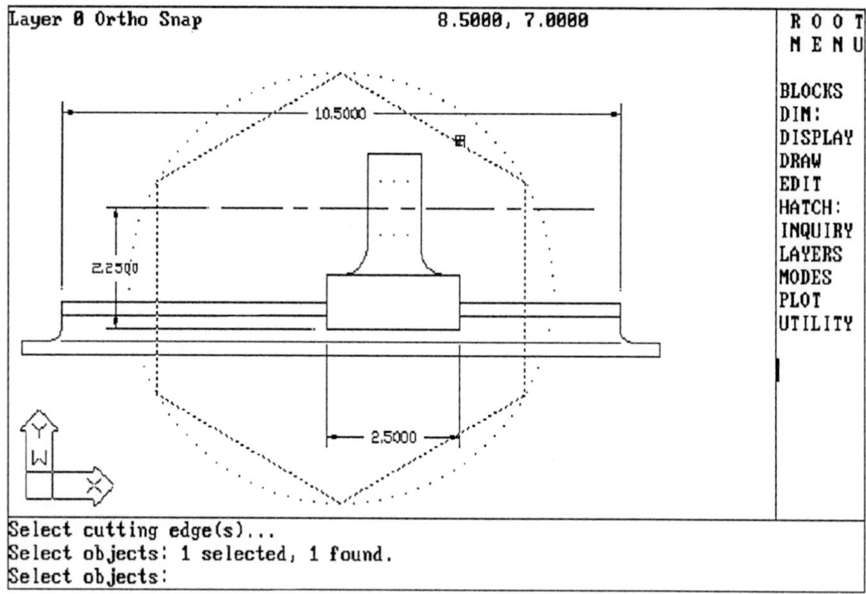

Figure 3-5*c*. The TRIM command at work

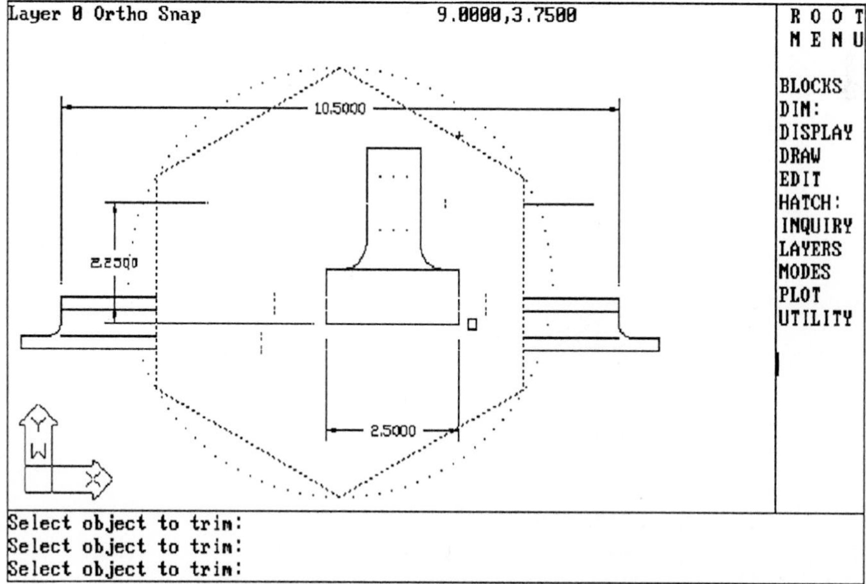

Figure 3-5*d*. A successful trim

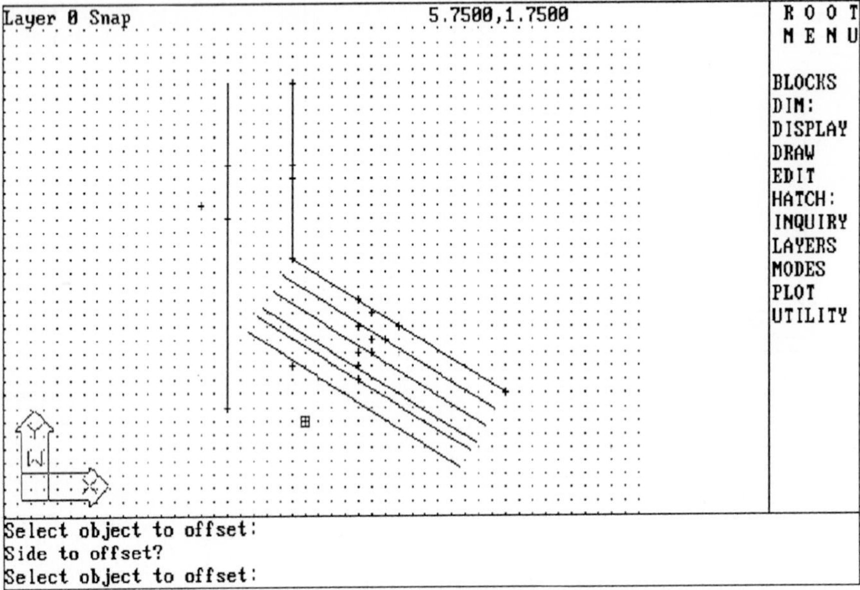

Figure 3-6*a*. Entities that do not intersect

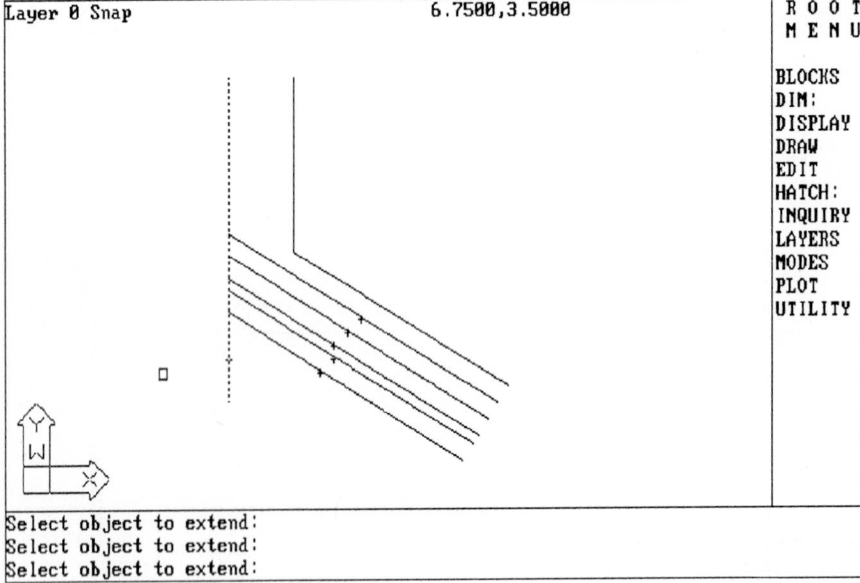

Figure 3-6*b*. Extended entities

part of the object to extend. For example, a hexagonal shape has six possible lines to extend. You want the one that will extend to intersect the boundary. If you pick one of the others, you will be surprised by the result.

In Figure 3-6*b*, the desired objects have been selected and AutoCAD has responded by extending them until they meet the line that defines the specified boundary.

Breaking

If you were to do a measured drawing of your house or apartment, you would certainly need to draw door and window openings. Yet "breaking" your wall lines requires a command other than ERASE, because the ERASE command erases entire lines, not parts of lines.

Because building designers were among the first users of AutoCAD, the problem of breaking lines for openings was one of the first special command requirements. The BREAK command accomplishes this task. With it, you can easily break a line, polyline, trace, circle, or arc.

As with other AutoCAD commands, you enter the BREAK command on the command line:

Command: **break**
Select object:
Enter first point:
Enter second point:

Figure 3-7*a* shows a sample drawing of a partial building plan. See Figure 3-7*b* for a finished break and the construction of a wall opening. Note that in addition to the break, the door jambs must be drawn. If you draw such wall openings frequently, you should construct a macro or AutoLISP function that will automatically break the wall and insert the door (or window) and the jambs. See Chapter 10, "Working with Menus," Chapter 11, "Introduction to AutoLISP," and Chapter 12, "Programs in AutoLISP," for extensive instructions in writing the necessary functions to do this. You can also obtain several excellent toolkits that will customize AutoCAD for you.

Changing Entities

After you draw an entity, you can still change the entity without having to erase it and draw it again. The CHANGE command enables you to modify objects by changing certain aspects of their records in the drawing data.

Each entity you draw with AutoCAD is stored with its own data record in the drawing file. Of course, you can't see what is in the drawing file directly. You can, however, change the information in the drawing file by using commands that enable you to change entity records. For example, AutoCAD provides you with the ability to change either the coordinates in the drawing or the properties of the object so you will have the maximum control over the drawing file.

Changing Points

If you wish to change the point where an entity is inserted, you can select the CHANGE command's "Change point" option. To use the CHANGE command, you enter the following command sequence:

Command: **change**
Select objects:
Properties/<Change point>:

To merely change a point on the object to become the new point for the object's termination or insertion point, you pick a point. The new point will then be made a part of the entity record.

Changing Properties

You may wish to change an object's color, elevation, layer, linetype, or thickness. These are the object's properties. You can select the "Properties" option of the CHANGE command. When you do so you will see the following prompt:

Change what property (Color/Elev/LAyer/LType/Thickness)?

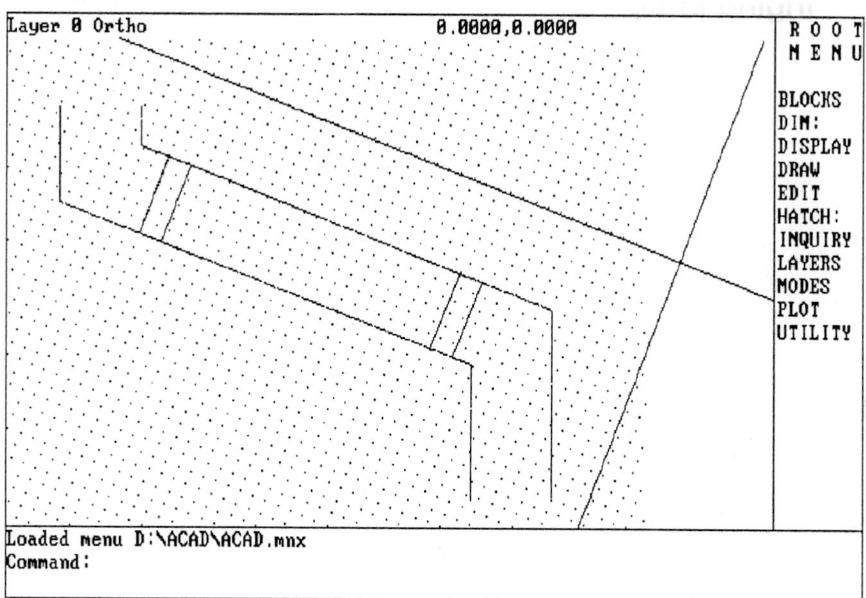

Figure 3-7*a*. A wall in plan needs to be broken

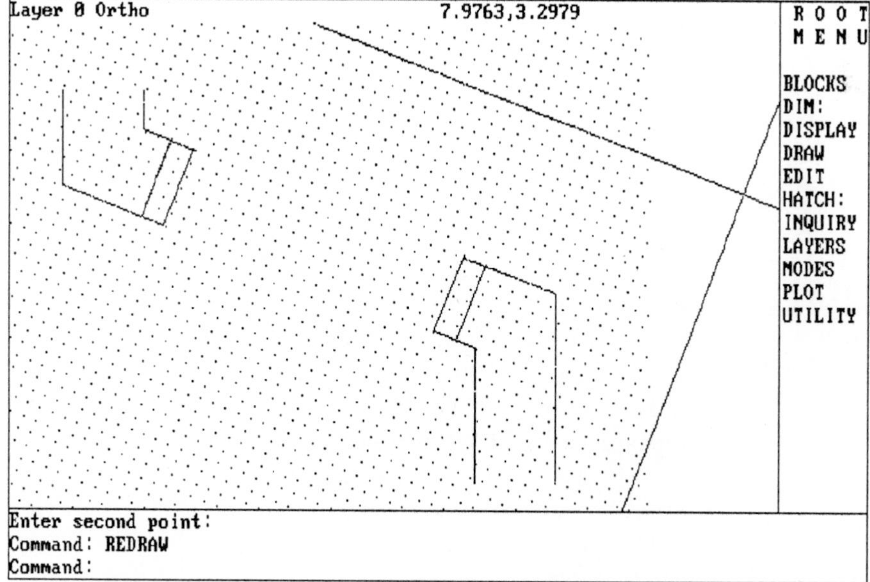

Figure 3-7*b*. The finished break in the wall

As usual with AutoCAD command prompts, you can select the option by using only the capitalized letter (or letters) in the option name. Be careful, though, because the "LAyer" and "LType" options each begin with the letter "L." Note that in this instance, you must specify the additional capitalized letter so AutoCAD can discern the difference.

Changing Color If you specify the "Color" option, you will be prompted for the new color. If you want to keep the same color, just choose the default by pressing ENTER. To change the color, use any of the color names allowed by your configuration of AutoCAD. For example, the color blue can be specified by the word "blue" or by the number 3. You can specify that the color of the object's group is to be used for the object if the object is indeed part of a group. Use the "BYGROUP" key word to do this. You can also choose to pass on the color or the object's layer to the object by using the "BYLAYER" key word. Read about "BYGROUP" and "BYLAYER" under "LAYERS" in Chapter 16, "AutoCAD Command Reference."

Changing Elevation Because AutoCAD's Release 10 uses a full three-dimensional coordinate system, it is possible to define an object not only in plan but in elevation as well. If you wish to change the elevation of an object, you can choose the "Elev" option.

Remember, an object can exist not only in the X,Y plane but can have an additional Z coordinate. When you change the elevation of the object, you redefine its position in the direction of the Z axis. Figure 3-8 shows two objects. The objects were drawn at elevation 0.0000. The elevation of one of them was changed. The objects are shown in perspective for clarity. One object appears to be above the other. The command sequence used to change the object that was moved is as follows:

```
Command: change
Select objects:
Properties/<Change point>: p
```

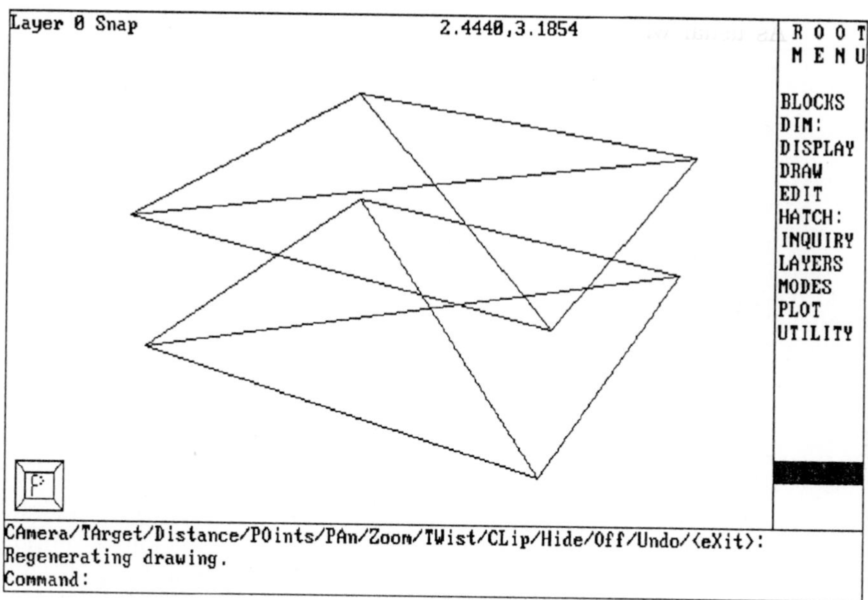

Figure 3-8. One object's elevation has been changed

> Change what property (Color/Elev/LAyer/LType/Thickness) ? **e**
> New elevation <0.0000>: **2**

In the preceding command sequence, the CHANGE command will change the Elevation property to 2 units.

Note that all the points contained in the object must have the same elevation, even if the object is a three-dimensional polyline, a three-dimensional face, or a line. Refer to the section on the MOVE command in Chapter 16, "AutoCAD Command Reference," to see how to move an object that is defined with varying elevations.

Changing Layers To move an object to another layer from the one for which it has been defined, you must first have defined and named the new layer. Then, when you want to change layers, you use the name of a layer that exists in the drawing in response to the prompt for the "LAyer" option. To learn more about layers, read the section "Layers" later in this chapter. Also, see Chapter 16, "AutoCAD Command Reference," for a description of how to use the LAYER command to create new layers.

Changing Line Types In order to define a new line type for an object, you must use a currently valid linetype name. See the section on the LINETYPE command in Chapter 16, "AutoCAD Command Reference," for a description of how to create and use line types. You can use the "LType" option to change line types for polylines, lines, circles, and arcs.

Changing Thickness AutoCAD will extrude an object into the third dimension if that object has a thickness property. You use the ELEV command to set a new object's elevation and thickness. To change the thickness, use the "Thickness" option of the CHANGE command. You will be prompted for a number that indicates the distance from the "top" of the object to the "bottom" of the object in the direction of the Z axis. Figure 3-9 shows an object that has thickness. In this case, the object happens to be a text entity (the word "THICKNESS"). Text entities in AutoCAD can have thickness like any other entity, a fact that will come in handy when you want to produce special effects in drawing annotations.

If You Make a Mistake

If you make a mistake when you draw manually, it can be very frustrating. Sometimes you erase holes in your tracing vellum. Sometimes you erase an entire part of your drawing only to find that it was the wrong part. No one and nothing is perfect.

If you make a mistake using a CAD system, you are much better off. AutoCAD enables you to correct your mistakes with a minimum of effort because the system "remembers" what you are doing as you are doing it. When you realize that you have just erased the entire valve assembly instead of just the bolt

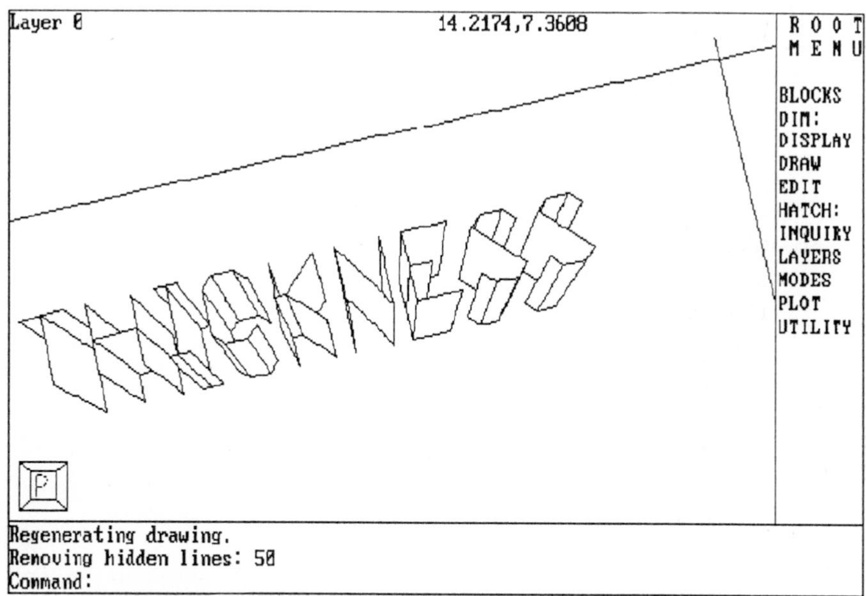

Figure 3-9. A text entity that has thickness

circle, you don't need to scream and shout—just activate any of AutoCAD's several lifesaving mechanisms.

Undoing Commands

Because AutoCAD keeps a running log of the commands you enter, it is possible to work your way back through the steps you took to create the drawing. You can undo any number of commands, right back to the beginning of the current session.

The UNDO command permits you to reverse the effects of entering most of the AutoCAD commands. It is not possible to undo all commands because some commands create things that are impossible to do in reverse. But in general, almost everything you do can be undone.

When you invoke the UNDO command, you will see a command box that looks something like this:

Command: **undo**
Auto/Back/Control/End/Group/Mark/<Number>:

To simply undo the last command you entered, type **U** in response to the "Command:" prompt. This U command is simply a shorthand way to execute an UNDO 1 command. Experiment with doing and undoing things to get a feel for the command.

One difference between the U command and the ERASE command is that when you use the OOPS command you cannot bring back something that has been undone, but you *can* bring back an object that has been erased. See the "Oops" section later in this chapter for information on that command.

Undoing "Auto"

If you select the "Auto" option of the UNDO command you will be able to undo entire menu item selections, not just single commands you have entered. The "Auto" option can be either ON or OFF. You select the ON or OFF options following the "ON/OFF <current>:" prompt.

Setting Marks

To undo back to a set place in the sequence of commands that made your drawing, you must first have set a mark or marks. To set a mark, you use the following command sequence:

Command: **undo**
Auto/Back/Control/End/Group/Mark/<number>: **m**

This invocation of the UNDO command sets a mark at the current status of the drawing. The mark is not visible but is stored in the drawing data. When you then use the "Back" option of the UNDO command, the drawing will be undone only until the command gets to the place in the sequence of drawing operations where you set the mark. You can set any number of marks in your drawing.

To undo back through the drawing to a mark, you must execute the UNDO command and select the "Back" option. If there are no marks in the drawing, AutoCAD will assume that you wish to un[illegible] way back to the beginning. You will be prom[illegible] this is what you really want to do, [illegible] rk is undone.

[illegible] command with a specified number [illegible] the following command sequence [illegible]:

[illegible] up/Mark/<number>: **10**

If y[illegible] fifth command, however, only the [illegible] ne.

Undoi[illegible]

If you w[illegible] ommands, you must tell AutoCAD [illegible] ere it ends. You do this by enterin[illegible] the start of the work you think y[illegible] e end of the group of commands, [illegible] ommand. After you identify the [illegible] y, use of the U or UNDO <num[illegible] lly undo the entire group as thoug[illegible]

The UND[illegible] e used with the AutoCAD menu [illegible] of menus under the MENU com[illegible] Command Reference."

Controlling UNDO

The UNDO command is flexible in the way it operates. You can remove the UNDO command entirely from the executing AutoCAD code to make more room for drawing information. Or you can limit the UNDO command to only a single operation. Finally, you could also enable the full UNDO command with all of its features. To do this you enter the UNDO command and select the "Control" option.

When you select the "Control" option of the UNDO command, you will see the "All/None/One <All>:" option list. If you select "All," you will enable all of the UNDO command. If you select "None," you will disable the UNDO command entirely. If you select the "One" option, you will enable UNDO only for one command at a time. This gives you control over the space you need for your drawings by removing most or all of the code that makes elaborate undoing possible.

Redoing Commands

REDO If you use the UNDO command too aggressively, you may accidentally remove too much of your work. The REDO command is intended to serve you under just these circumstances. You must enter the REDO command as the very next thing you do after the offending UNDO command. The REDO command exactly reverses the effect of the UNDO command.

OOPS If you accidentally use the ERASE command, the BLOCK command, or the WBLOCK command to remove a set of commands from the drawing, you can use the OOPS command to bring everything back again. OOPS only works for the last such command entered, however. If you erase the last entity, for example, you can bring it back with OOPS. If you erase the last entity and then erase the one before it, only the one before it will be brought back with OOPS.

Rotation, Translation, and Scaling

Objects in the real world can be rotated, translated, and scaled. In the simplest sense, these three operations also work in the world of the three-dimensional CAD system. The world of the CAD system is the good old-fashioned world of Descartes and Newton – the dimensional world of our everyday lives.

When you give it some thought, you will see that an object can be moved (*translated*) along any of the three-dimensional axes (X, Y, and Z). The object can also be changed in size (*scaled*), or *rotated* about a single point in space. Rotation, translation, and scaling are all the operations you need to move an object and change its size for most purposes. These simple *transformations* are very useful in the CAD environment. After you draw something, you can easily move it into position and/or change its size. Such transformations are particularly difficult to make with manual drafting methods. The CAD system is cost-justified by these transformational capabilities alone.

AutoCAD implements rotation, translation, scaling, and distortion for both two-dimensional and three-dimensional objects. The commands that do most of the work are the MOVE, COPY, ARRAY, ROTATE, SCALE, MIRROR, EXPLODE, and STRETCH commands. The MOVE command moves objects. The COPY command is like the MOVE command, but it leaves the original rather than erases it. The ARRAY command creates multiple copies of objects the same distance apart. The ROTATE command rotates an object and the SCALE command changes the size of the object without distorting it. The MIRROR command creates the object's mirror image and the STRETCH command changes its length. The EXPLODE command breaks down blocks with more than one line into single-line elements.

Rotating

With the ROTATE command, you can rotate a pre-existing object. You might want to rotate an object in a drawing to more accurately fit it into an assembly. Perhaps the windshield of a car you are designing needs to be raked back at an angle more appropriate for a racing machine.

When you enter the ROTATE command, you have several options. The command line after entering the ROTATE command might look like this:

Command: **rotate**
Select objects:

Base point:
<Rotation angle>/Reference:

Figures 3-10*a* through 3-10*d* show how the ROTATE command can be used with a simple object. The NORTH arrow shown in Figure 3-10*a* can be rotated by first selecting all objects that make up the symbol. Figure 3-10*b* shows the NORTH arrow after all of its parts have been picked. The selected entities are shown with dotted lines. A prompt will appear asking for the "Base point:". The base point is the point about which the selected objects will be rotated. After the base point is selected, there will be a prompt for the "<Rotation angle>/Reference:". If the "Rotation angle" (default) option is selected, a drag line will extend from the base point to the crosshairs. This drag line defines the angle through which to rotate the object. In Figure 3-10*c*, the NORTH arrow is in the process of being rotated. Note that the objects are repeatedly shown at their new locations as the drag line is rotated. Picking the new orientation of the drag line will freeze the object in its new rotation angle. Figure 3-10*d* shows the finished rotation operation.

Moving

After you have drawn a significant part of your drawing, you may wish to move objects around. For example, you may want to relocate a word in a drawing from one place to another. Or you may want to move the entire kitchen area in a house you are designing. You can make these changes in location with the MOVE command.

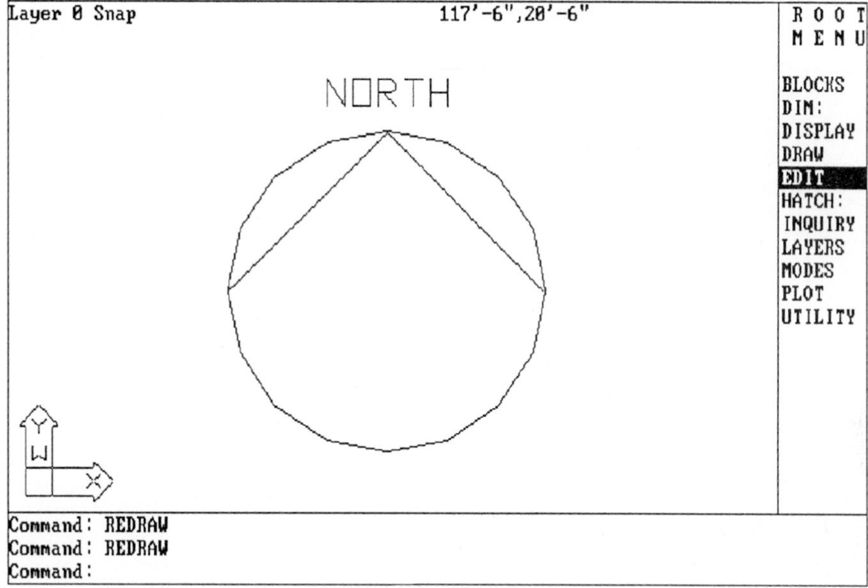

Figure 3-10*a*. A NORTH arrow that will be rotated

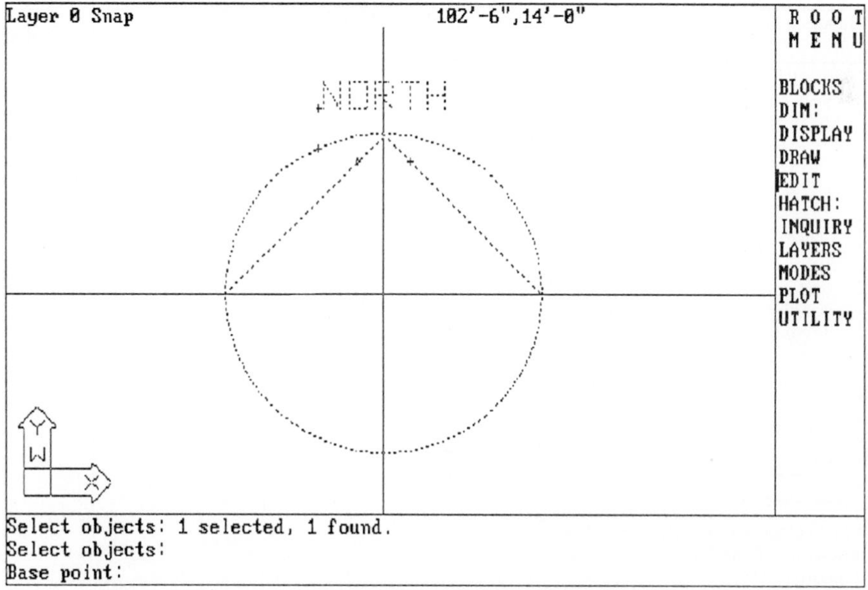

Figure 3-10*b*. All the parts have been picked

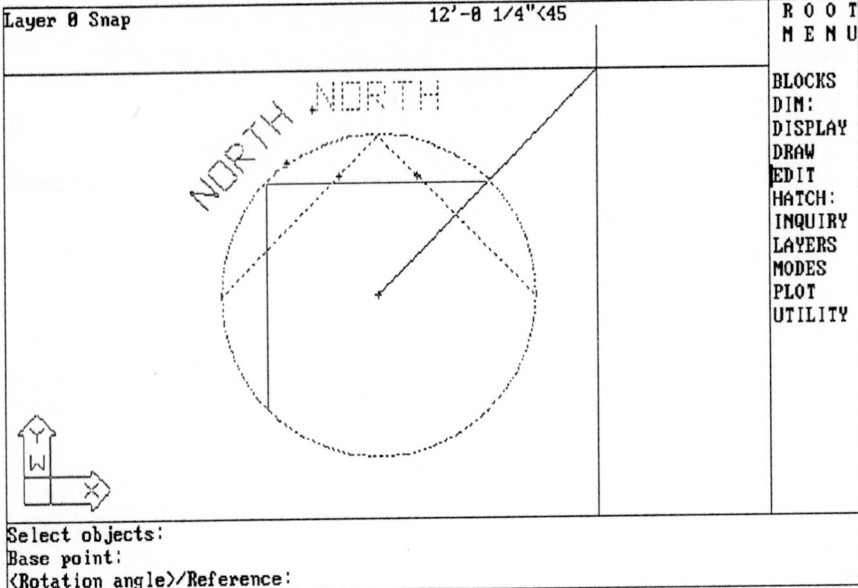

Figure 3-10*c*. The objects in the process of being rotated

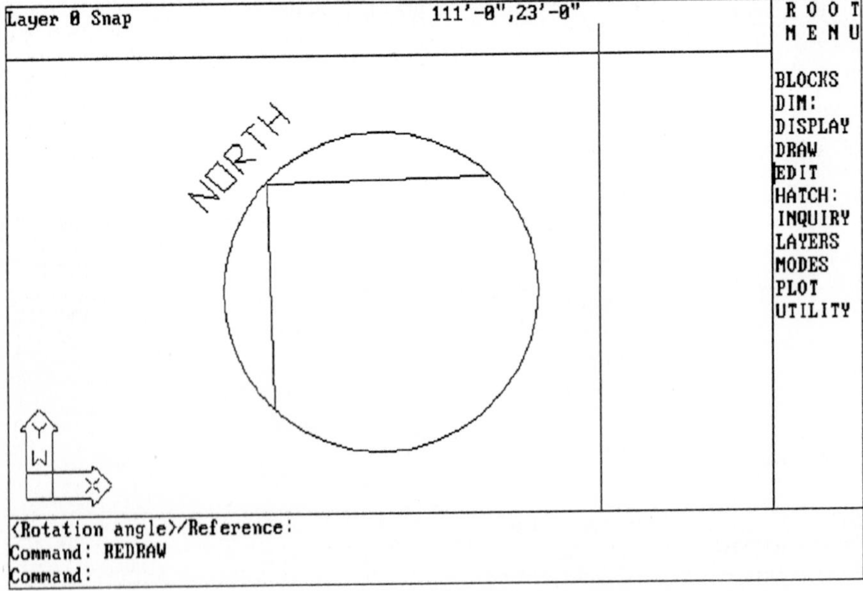

Figure 3-10*d*. The finished rotation operation

The floor plan of a house is shown in the process of being drawn in Figure 3-11*a*. The kitchen area needs to be moved from its current location. In Figure 3-11*b*, the objects to be moved have all been selected. Figure 3-11*c* shows the objects being dragged into position. You can see the final result in Figure 3-11*d*. After the objects are moved, various lines will need to be extended.

Copying

The COPY command works almost the same as the MOVE command. The only exception is that the original objects remain where they were and a copy of them appears at the new distance offset. The COPY command sequence appears as follows:

Command: **copy**
Select objects:
<Base point or displacement>/Multiple:

You can choose the "Base point or displacement" default as was done in the preceding sequence, or you can choose the "Multiple" option. If you choose the "Multiple" option, you will be prompted for a base point and a second point as follows:

Base point: Second point of displacement:

The difference is that you will be repeatedly prompted for a "Second point" and a new copy will be created as long as you pick new points. In this way, you will be able to create multiple copies without needing to re-enter the COPY command each time. When you wish to stop multiple copies, you can press ENTER, the spacebar, or CTRL-C.

Scaling

It is easy to get confused when you compare the ZOOM command and the SCALE command since each command, in its own way, changes the apparent size of the drawing. Unlike zooming, scaling involves a change in the size of a given object. The scale

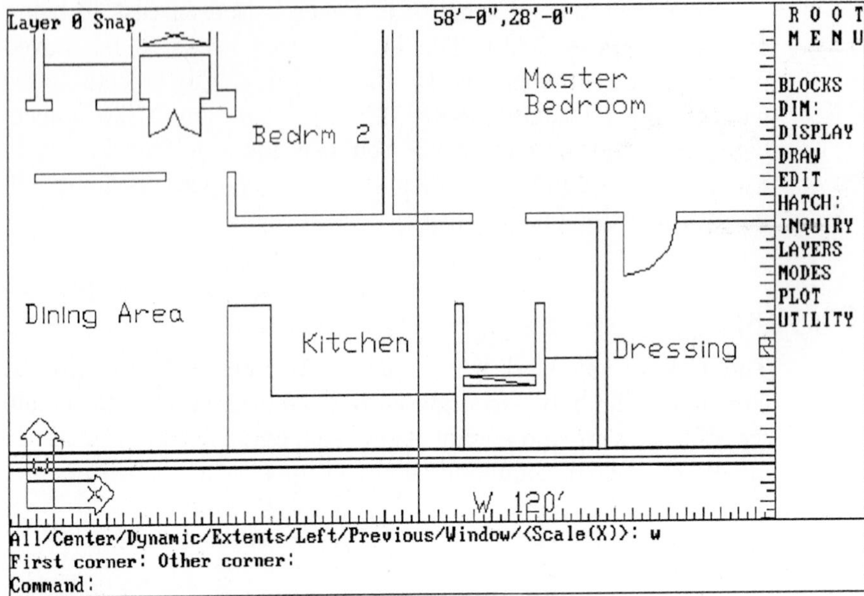

Figure 3-11*a*. An unfinished house floor plan

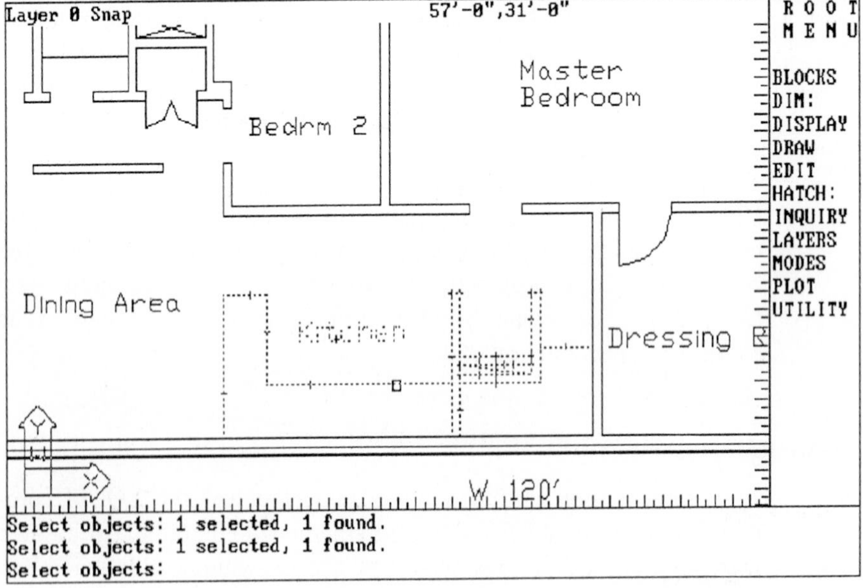

Figure 3-11*b*. Objects to be moved have been selected

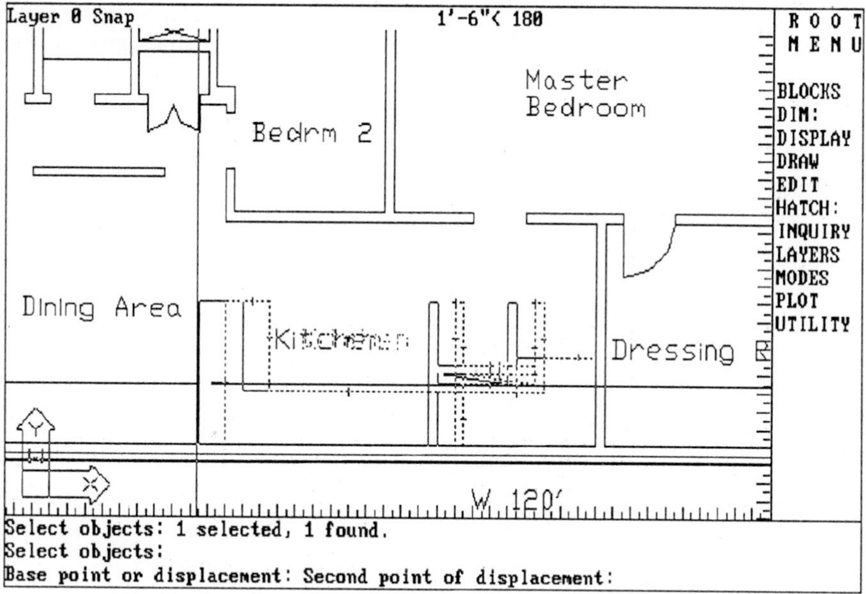

Figure 3-11*c*. Selected objects being dragged into position

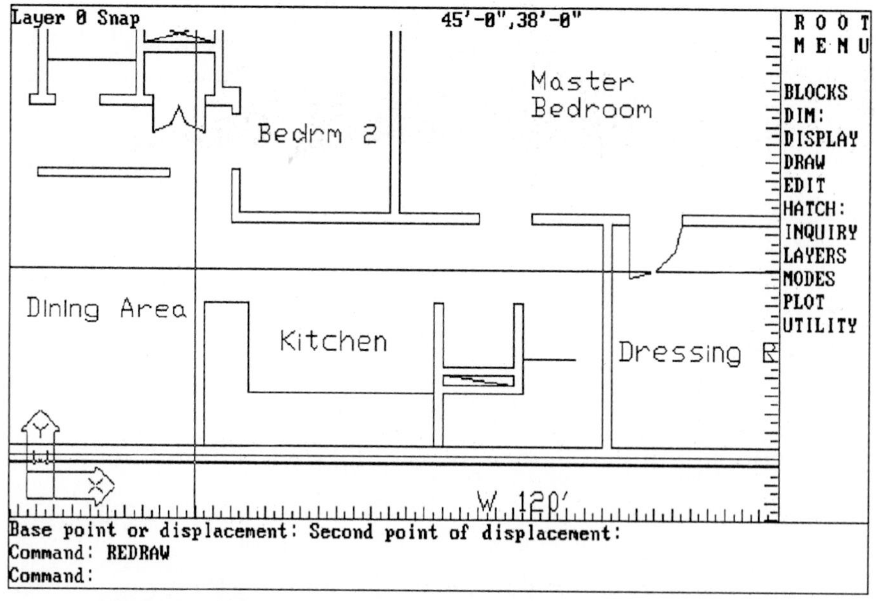

Figure 3-11*d*. The selected objects have been moved

change is made for those objects only, rather than for the drawing as a whole. In addition, the scale is made part of the drawing file.

You can change the scale of any object by using the SCALE command. You would prepare the command line as follows:

Command: **scale**
Select objects:
<Scale factor>/Reference:

You can enter a scale factor as a number or you can drag the crosshairs to a new scale factor for the objects you selected. If you choose the "Reference" option, you will be prompted for the current length and the new length. The first length is a distance as it appears now. The second length is what you would like that distance to be for all of the objects you have selected.

Making Arrays

Arrays in AutoCAD are regularly-spaced repetitions of objects. A typical array would be the windows in a building. Each window is roughly the same in size and all of the windows are arranged in rows and columns, perfectly aligned. An array such as this can be made by using the ARRAY command.

Figures 3-12*a* through 3-12*d* show a single window being propagated into an array of 15 windows to make a window wall. You enter the ARRAY command sequence as follows:

Command: **array**
Select objects: 1 selected, 1 found.
Select objects:
Rectangular or Polar array (R/P): **r**
Number of rows (---> <1>: **3**
Number of columns (¦¦¦) <1>: **5**
Unit cell or distance between rows (---): **−9**
Distance between columns (¦¦¦): **5**

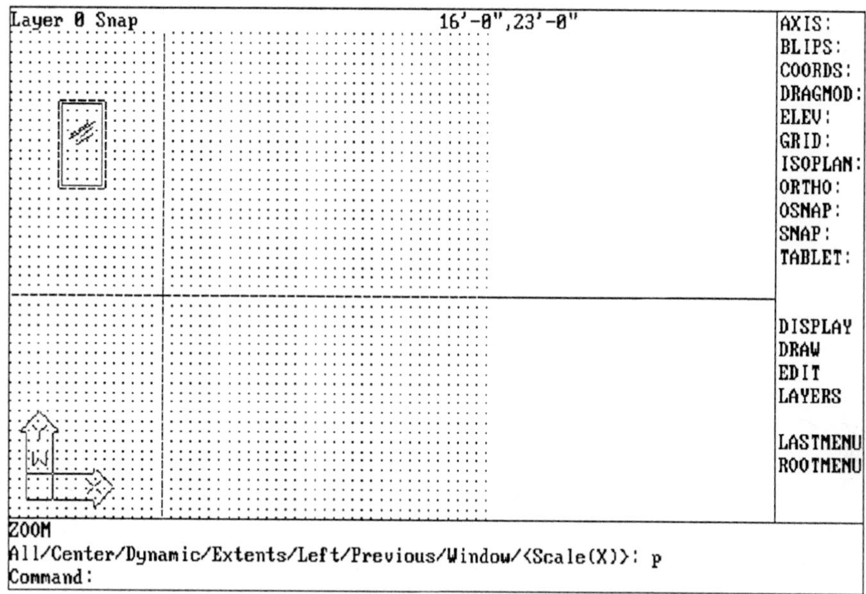

Figure 3-12*a*. A modular window element

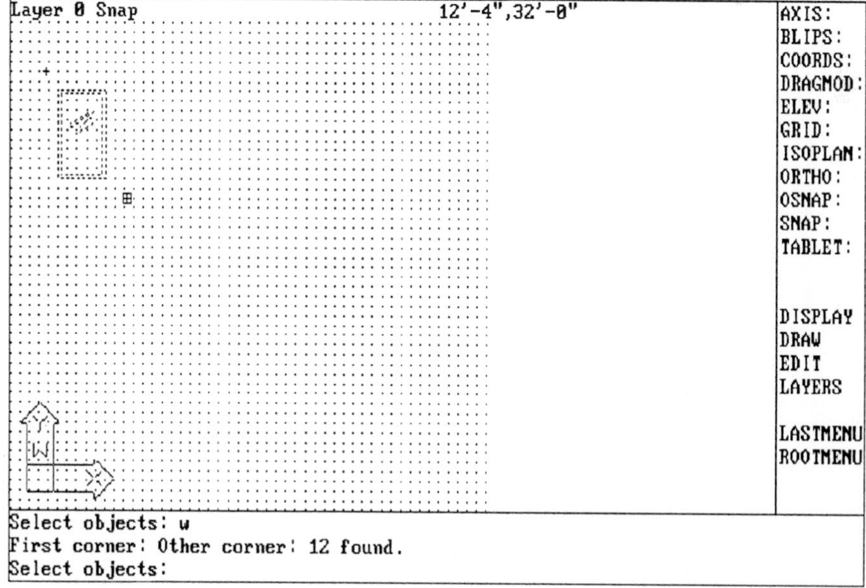

Figure 3-12*b*. The invocation of the ARRAY command

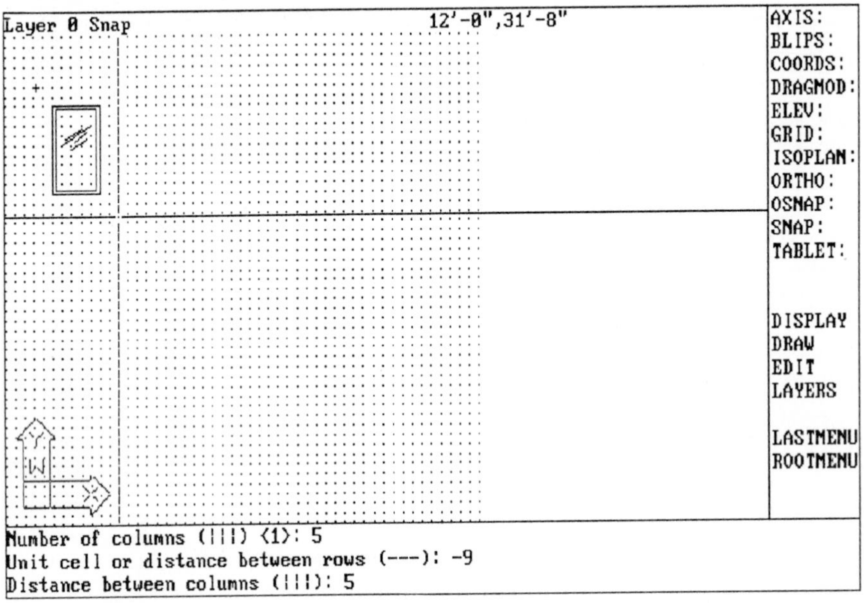

Figure 3-12c. A rectangular array has been specified

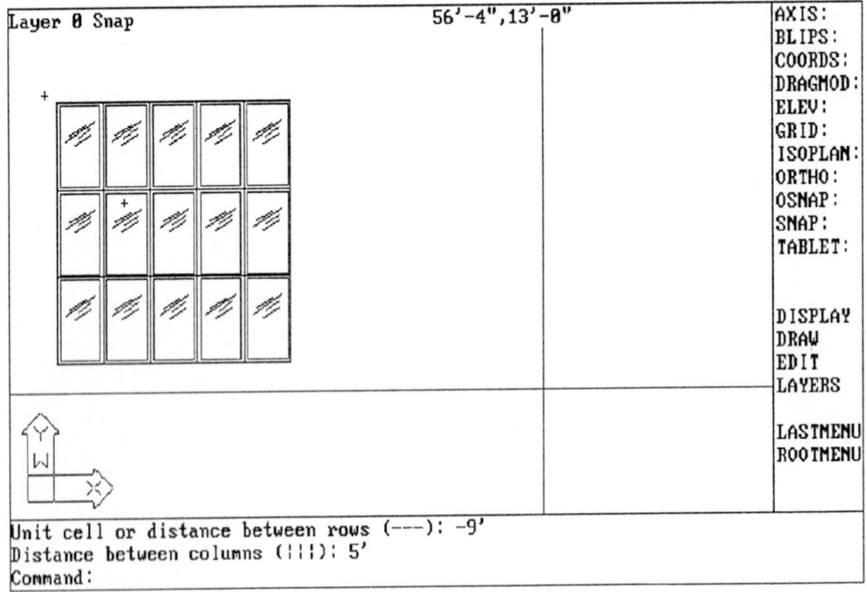

Figure 3-12d. The finished array of window elements

Note that you first select the objects to be propagated into the array. You then select a rectangular or polar array. If rectangular (as in this case) you will be prompted for the number of rows and columns. The *unit cell distance* is the distance in the X and Y directions, defined by a single cell in the array, that the array elements will be propagated for each row and column. If you pick in response to the "Unit cell" prompt, you will be prompted for the "Other corner:" of a rectangle that represents one *cell* in the future array. The array is made up of repetitions of the cell you pick. If you respond with a number to the "Unit cell" prompt, it will be taken as the vertical distance between rows, and you will be prompted, as above, for the horizontal distance between columns.

Stretching

The STRETCH command is very valuable when you want to place an object after you have drawn it in one location, but also want to preserve its connections to other objects. You first identify the objects to be moved, then you specify the displacement. When the objects are moved, anything that connects to them will be rubber banded into the new location.

The stairway shown in Figure 3-13*a* can be moved farther into the building with the STRETCH command. Figure 3-13*b* shows the stairs after the desired objects have been selected. Figure 3-13*c* shows the stairway displacement. Finally, Figure 3-13*d* shows the end result of moving the stairs. The walls have been stretched to accommodate the new position.

The "Crossing" option must be used with the STRETCH command or entities to be stretched will not be selected. When you choose the STRETCH command from a menu, the "Crossing" option is automatically used. If you enter the STRETCH command from the command line, you must select the "Crossing" option by entering the letter "C" where the first pick is required. Stretching of a line does not work unless both endpoints are selected and stretch does not work with blocks.

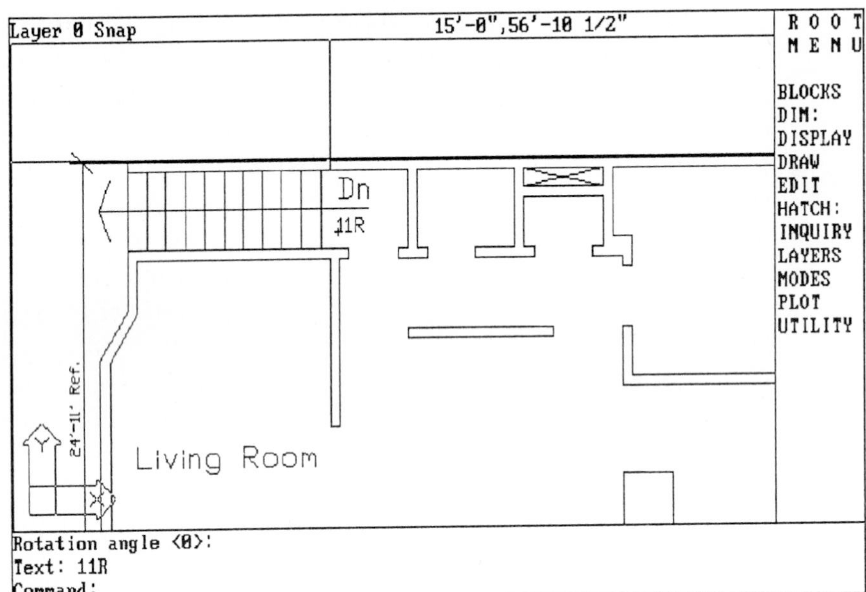

Figure 3-13*a*. A stairway whose connections will be stretched

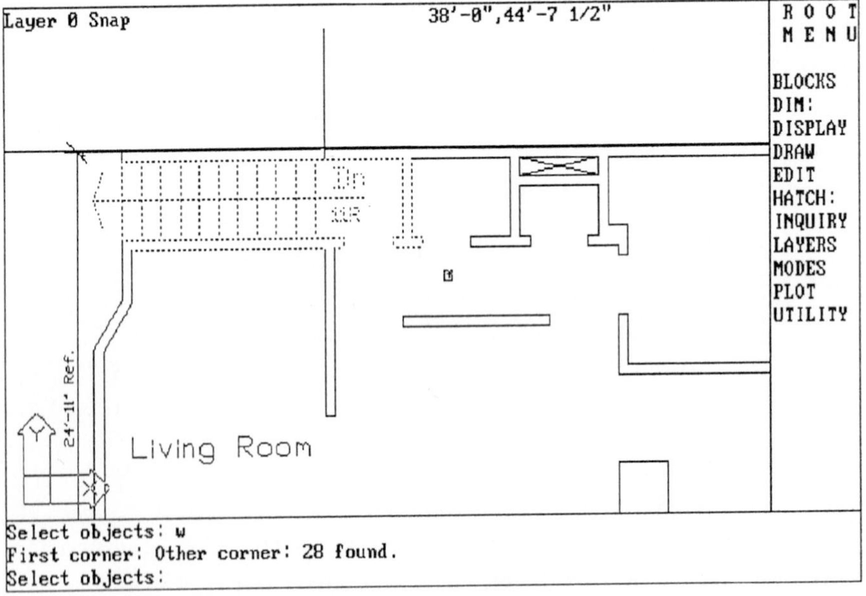

Figure 3-13*b*. Objects to be stretched have been selected

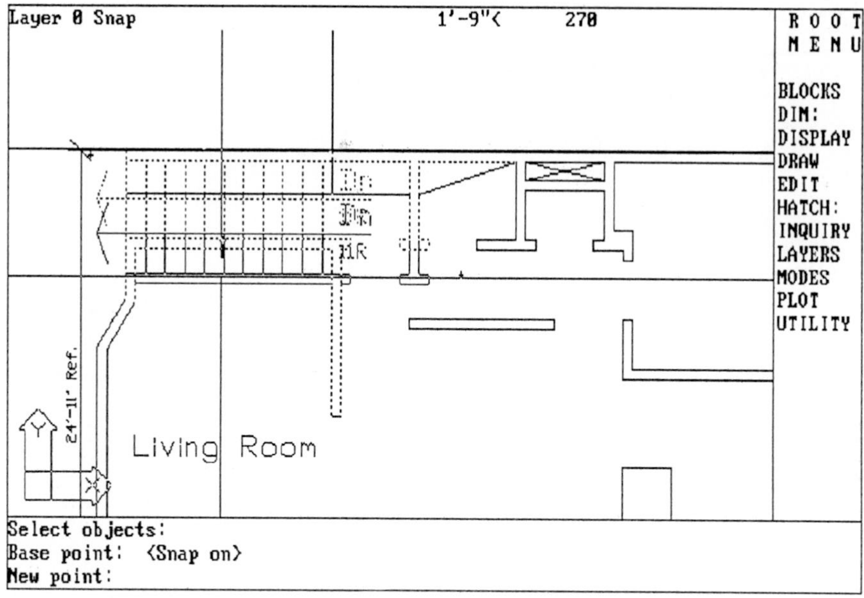

Figure 3-13*c*. The stairway in the process of being stretched

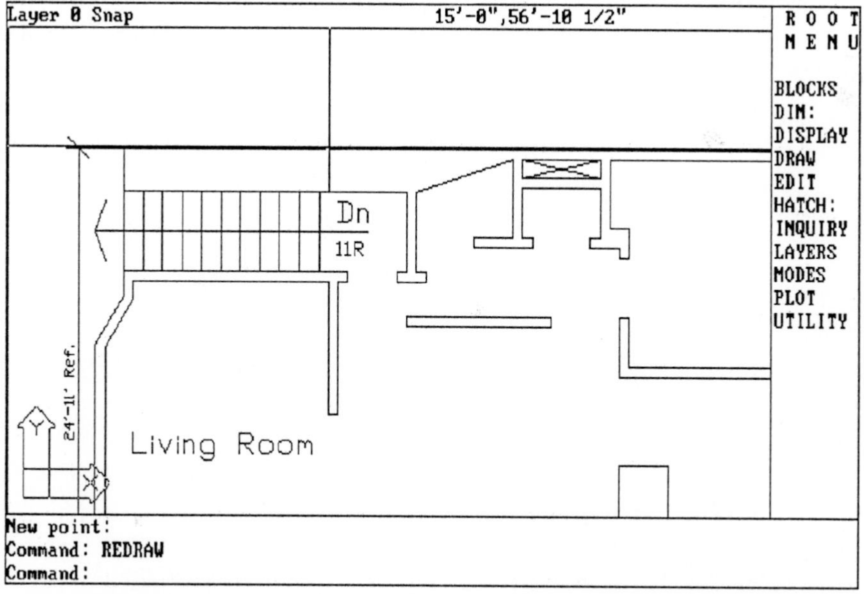

Figure 3-13*d*. Walls have been stretched or moved as required

Mirroring

You can generate the mirror image of an object by using the MIRROR command. Mirroring is useful for generating symmetrical parts of drawings. Many machine tool parts, for example, are bilaterally symmetrical. This means you need draw only half of the object and then you can mirror the first half to get the second half. Mirroring can thus save you a great deal of time if used wisely.

The object shown in Figure 3-14*a* is the left half of a spindle. Since spindles are symmetrical, you can generate the mirror image of the first half to finish the spindle as shown in Figure 3-14*b*.

The command sequence for the MIRROR command is as follows:

```
Command: mirror
Select objects:
First point of mirror line:          Second point:
Delete old objects? <N>
```

If you choose to "Delete old objects," the original objects being mirrored will disappear. If you choose not to delete the old objects, you will see a bilaterally symmetrical object formed from two mirrored halves. Note that the mirror line determines whether the mirrored halves will be horizontally or vertically oriented. You can mirror at any angle as well as horizontally or vertically. Experiment with mirroring at unusual angles.

Exploding

Certain objects are defined and stored as single entity types. If you create a polygon, for example, and you wish to erase one of its sides, you will be unable to do so. The ERASE command will prompt you for the objects to erase and you will always be forced to select the entire polygon.

In order to break up blocks into their component entities, you must use the EXPLODE command. No, the computer won't explode when you enter the command, but any objects you select

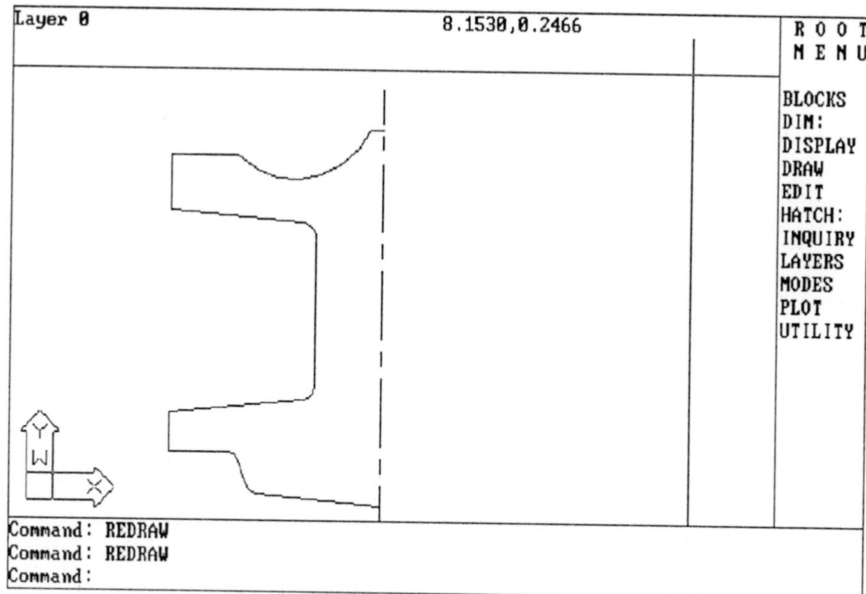

Figure 3-14*a*. The left half of a spindle

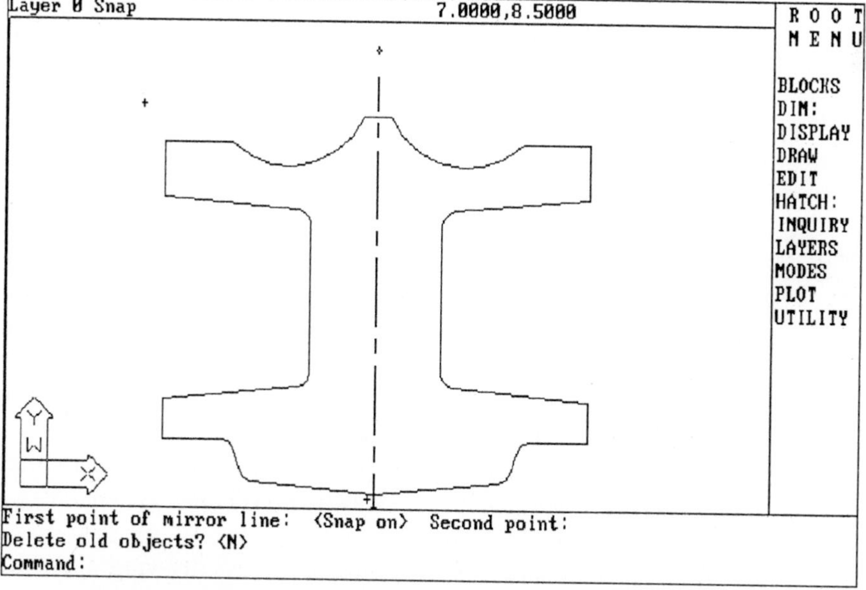

Figure 3-14*b*. The mirrored half makes the object symmetrical

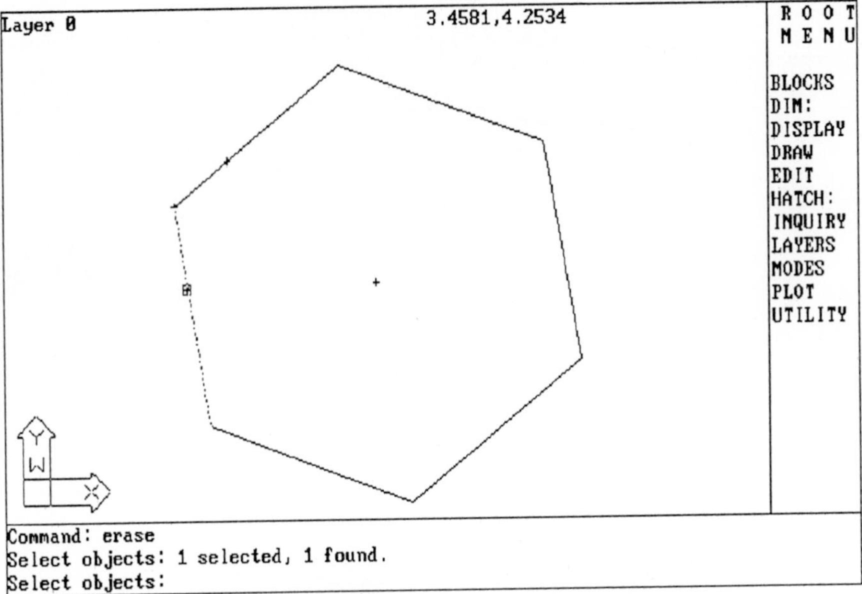

Figure 3-15. A hexagon that has been exploded

will be broken down into single-line elements. Figure 3-15 shows a hexagon that has been selected and exploded. One of the sides of the hexagon has been erased.

Layers

When you create your working drawings, you seldom rely on one sheet to describe an entire project. If you are an architect or an engineer, you use different sheets for different information. The plan of the first floor of a building will often be on a different sheet from the second floor plan, for example. Plumbing, structural, and electrical drawings will also often occupy different sheets.

AutoCAD synthesizes the function of the drawing sheet by providing you with layers in which to draw. Each layer can have a name or a number. Only one layer can be the "current" layer at any given time. Layers can be on and off in any combination that you desire.

For example, a piping designer in the chemical industry could make all of the piping on the cooling tower sheet be red and all the piping on the evaporator sheet be blue. An architect could have all the linework on the site plan be blue and all the linework on the first floor plan be black.

Using Layers

To control layers in AutoCAD, you use the LAYER command. To work with layers at any time when the "Command:" prompt is shown, just enter the LAYER command. The command sequence is as follows:

Command: **layer**
?/Make/Set/New/ON/OFF/Color/Ltype/Freeze/Thaw:

The question mark gives you a list of layers and their current status. Don't confuse this with the LIST command, however. Here, the currently defined layers are listed, not the entities in the drawing.

You can "Make" a layer and use it immediately. You can "Set" the current layer to be an existing (already made) layer. You can create a "New" layer. You can turn a given layer on or off. A "Color" can be associated with a layer. A linetype ("Ltype") can also be associated with a layer. When you use a given layer, the color and linetype associated with that layer become the defaults for the drawings on that layer. Finally, you can "Freeze" a layer, making it invisible to the system, or you can reverse the freeze by "Thawing" it. These options are described in more detail in Chapter 16, "AutoCAD Command Reference."

Listing

Two commands, LIST and DBLIST, enable you to list either the information about specifically identified objects (the LIST command) or about the drawing as a whole (the DBLIST command).

In addition to information about objects, you can obtain information about the location of a given point with the ID command. You can find the distance between two points by using the DIST command.

The LIST Command

The drawing shown in Figure 3-16*a* illustrates the use of the LIST command. A dimension callout has been selected in response to the "Select objects:" prompt. The selected object is shown with a dotted line. The information about that object is shown in Figure 3-16*b*.

The DBLIST Command

The entire contents of a drawing can be listed with the DBLIST command. The report produced by DBLIST is the same as for

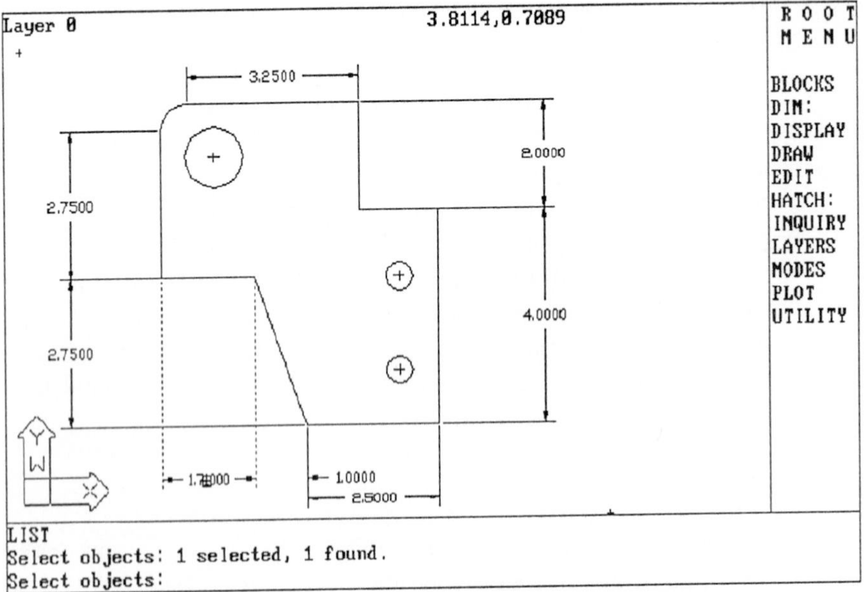

Figure 3-16*a*. An object is selected to list

```
DIMENSION Layer: 0

type: horizontal
extension defining point:          X= 3.0000  Y= 4.5000  Z= 0.0000
extension defining point:          X= 4.7500  Y= 4.5000  Z= 0.0000
dimension line defining point:     X= 4.7500  Y= 4.5000  Z= 0.0000
default text position  X= 3.8750  Y= 0.7500  Z= 0.0000
default text
```

Figure 3-16*b*. The resulting list of the object's properties

the LIST command, except that you do not need to identify the objects to report. The entire drawing is used instead.

The ID Command

The command sequence for the ID command is as follows:

Command: **ID** Point:
X = 3′ −4 1/2″ Y = 110′ −3 3/8″ Z = 15′ −7 1/8″

You just enter the ID command and pick a point, any point in three-dimensional space, to get the coordinates of that point. This command is helpful if you want to know the coordinates of a point to use as input to another command. You might also need the coordinates of a point to use in a mathematical formula that is external to AutoCAD.

The DIST Command

The DIST command is very handy for predicting the distances you wish to use in your drawings. For example, you might want to measure the size of a door or window opening in a wall.

To use the DIST command, you enter it as follows:

Command: **dist**
First point:
Second point:
Distance = 3.1416
Angle in X-Y plane = 130
Angle from X-Y plane = 12
Delta X = 32.7600 Delta Y = 1.2345 Delta Z = 1.1111

Computing Area

AutoCAD has built-in area computation capabilities. You can use the AREA command to obtain areas in several ways.

The drawing in Figure 3-17 shows an irregular figure. The AREA command has been entered and the edges of one of the objects have been selected. The area report that results when the area subtended by the picked points is computed is shown in the command box. In addition to the area, you see the distance around the perimeter.

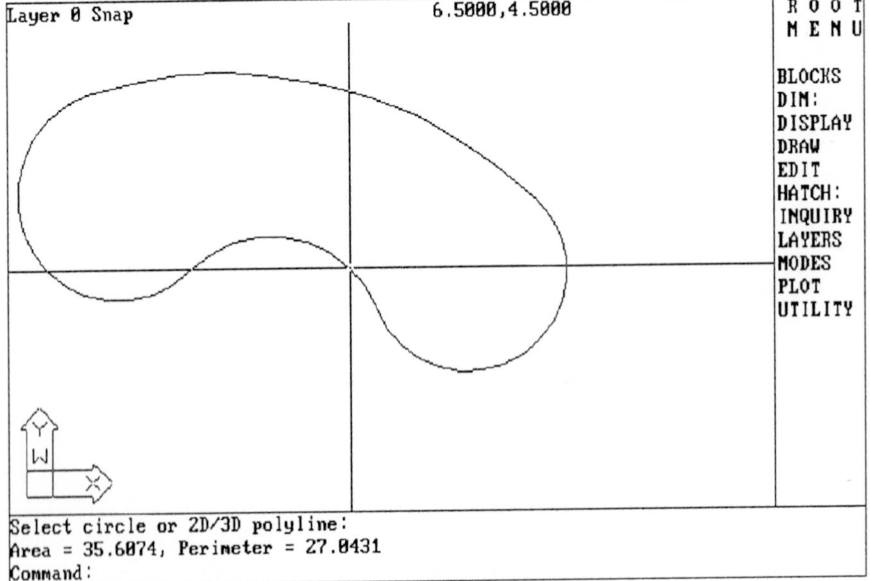

Figure 3-17. The area of a free-form polyline

The command options for the AREA command are as follows:

Command: **area**
<First point>/Entity/Add/Subtract:

The "First point" option determines area by using a series of points you enter as the area container. These points are considered to be connected by lines that define the area's extent. If you choose the "Entity" option, you must select either a circle or a 2D/3D polyline for the area to be computed. The "Add" option of the AREA command, when selected, makes subsequent area calculations accumulate. Finally, the "Subtract" option will make subsequent area calculations be removed from the accumulated area. You can read in detail about the AREA command in Chapter 16, "AutoCAD Command Reference."

PART TWO

Enhancing AutoCAD Drawings

Working with Blocks

Using the BLOCK Command
Using the INSERT Command

FOUR

You have now seen how to draw and edit individual entities with AutoCAD. Although this in itself gives you most of the power you need to do very sophisticated drawings, it is not nearly all there is to AutoCAD.

When you want to work on entities combined together in various ways, you can use *blocks.* A block is a grouping of entities under a single name. Think of blocks as drawings within drawings referred to by name. The BLOCK command enables you to specify a block that you can then insert in a drawing with the INSERT command.

The power you gain from defining and inserting blocks comes from the consolidation of all drawing information under a single name. A drawing file that contains numerous instances of the same block is much smaller than the same file would have been if you had just copied the same entities over and over. This is because only the block name is stored for each repetition of a defined block. You can change the contents of the block and all instances of that block will, in effect, instantly be revised.

Using the BLOCK Command

In order to illustrate the use of blocks, a special kind of drawing will be constructed. This drawing will be of a small printed circuit (PC) board. Even if you are not an electrical engineer, you can still understand how the symbols in a typical printed circuit board drawing are created and manipulated.

The printed circuit board drawing was selected to show you how to use blocks because such drawings use many repetitive symbols. To understand the symbols in the drawing, you must know what a *trace,* an *insertion hole,* and an *integrated circuit package* are.

A trace is simply a line of a certain width, usually solid. AutoCAD has a command, the TRACE command, that generates traces for you. The insertion hole is a small hole in the printed circuit board through which the wires, or "leads" (rhymes with deeds), are inserted and soldered in place. Each insertion hole is surrounded by metal to provide a connection point that will accept solder. Finally, the integrated circuit (IC) package is an electronic circuit etched in silicon and contained in a solid plastic enclosure with connecting wires extending out of it. The package is referred to as a "Digital Inline Package," or DIP. There are many other items, such as capacitors, resistors, and diodes, that are also inserted into the insertion holes and soldered into place on the PC board.

The drawing that will be constructed in this chapter is intended for use as a *mask* to etch the actual printed circuit. The mask is literally a photograph of the drawing. It is placed over a plate that contains a layer of photosensitive material, a layer of copper, and a "substrate" of resinous, non-conductive material. The positive transparency of the drawing is placed in contact with the plate and the plate is exposed for a certain time to light. The plate is developed just like any other photograph. Then the plate is immersed in a ferrochloride bath. The ferrochloride eats away any metal that is not covered by the photographic image of the drawing.

With this background, it will be easy for you to see how AutoCAD can be a boon to the printed circuit designer. The electronics industry has created standards for the sizes, tolerances, and construction of many integrated circuit components. With a library of standard parts symbols, the printed circuit mask can be constructed with ease. These symbols, stored as

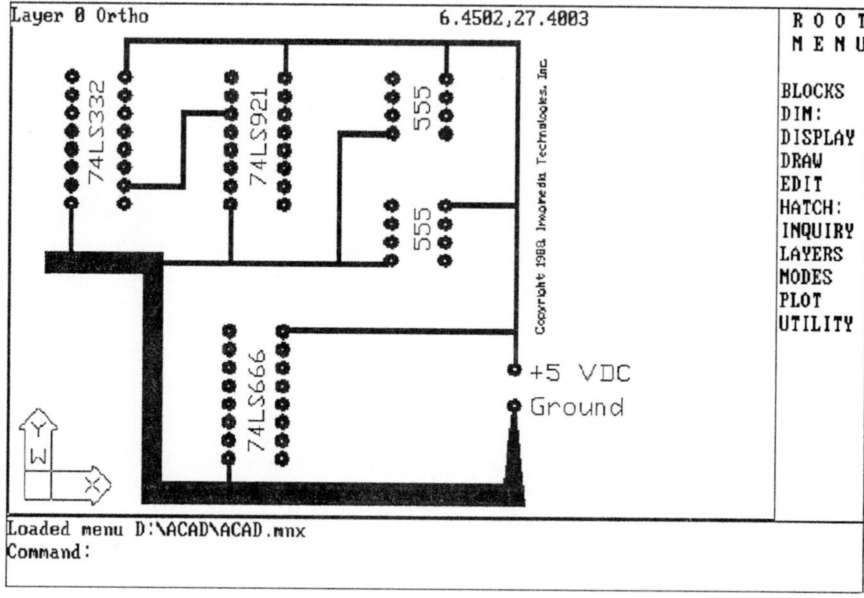

Figure 4-1. An unfinished sample PC board mask design

blocks, can be inserted in a drawing very easily so the designer does not need to redraw each part.

Figure 4-1 shows a printed circuit board mask drawing. The work is not complete. Do not try to use it for anything because it does not really function as an electronic circuit. In this chapter, the drawing in Figure 4-1 will be constructed, mostly with the BLOCK command.

Creating Blocks

Since components would need to be added to the printed circuit board, it will be necessary to create a symbol for making insertion holes. In order to do this, a prototypical insertion hole mask will be created. The DONUT command will be used to create a small, doughnut-shaped object. To begin the doughnut, you would prepare the following command sequence:

Command: **donut**
Inside diameter <default>: **.5**
Outside diameter <default>: **2**
Center of doughnut:

Locate the center of the doughnut by picking a point with your pointing device. Figures 4-2*a* through 4-2*d* show an "animated" version of the entire command sequence required to construct the doughnut.

Note that the UNITS command has already been used to set AutoCAD for decimal units (the AutoCAD default). The current ZOOM scale makes the screen only several millimeters wide. For the sake of simplicity, the AutoCAD defaults were used. With this combination of settings, you can work comfortably on this tiny object.

To make the doughnut into a block, you must select the doughnut entity into a block with its own name. To do this, enter the BLOCK command on the command line, then enter the name of the block. For this example, the name will be IH, for "insertion hole." The command sequence should look like this:

Command: **block**
Block name (or ?): **ih**
Insertion base point:
Select objects:

Picking the Insertion Base Point

After you name a block, you need to pick the insertion base point. This is the point that will align with the crosshairs when you insert the block into a drawing. You can use any point on the drawing that you are making into a block as the insertion base point.

In the case of the IH block, the base insertion point will be the center of the doughnut so pick that point in response to the "Insertion base point:" prompt.

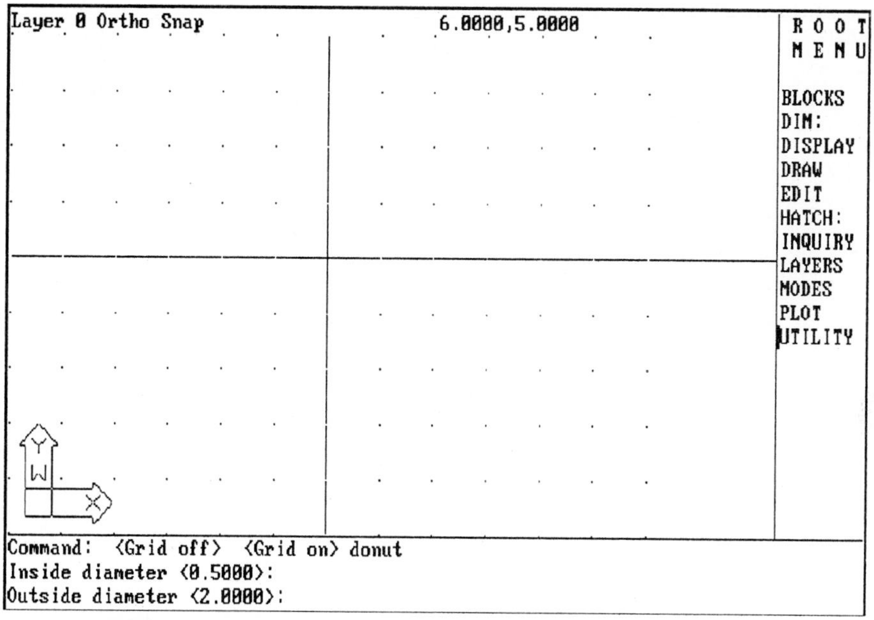

Layer 0 Ortho Snap 6.0000,5.0000

ROOT MENU

BLOCKS
DIM:
DISPLAY
DRAW
EDIT
HATCH:
INQUIRY
LAYERS
MODES
PLOT
UTILITY

Command: <Grid off> <Grid on> donut
Inside diameter <0.5000>:
Outside diameter <2.0000>:

Figure 4-2*a*. The DONUT command is entered

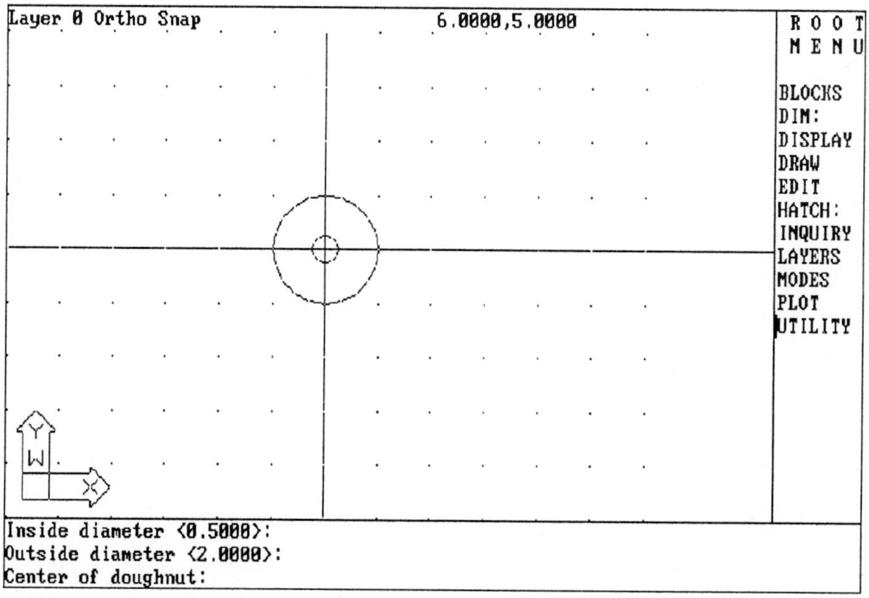

Layer 0 Ortho Snap 6.0000,5.0000

ROOT MENU

BLOCKS
DIM:
DISPLAY
DRAW
EDIT
HATCH:
INQUIRY
LAYERS
MODES
PLOT
UTILITY

Inside diameter <0.5000>:
Outside diameter <2.0000>:
Center of doughnut:

Figure 4-2*b*. The doughnut center is located

```
Layer 0 Ortho Snap                6.0000,5.0000            ROOT
                                                           MENU

                                                           BLOCKS
                                                           DIM:
                                                           DISPLAY
                                                           DRAW
                                                           EDIT
                                                           HATCH:
                                                           INQUIRY
                                                           LAYERS
                                                           MODES
                                                           PLOT
                                                           UTILITY
Outside diameter <2.0000>:
Center of doughnut:
Center of doughnut:
```

Figure 4-2*c*. The first doughnut is drawn, awaiting more

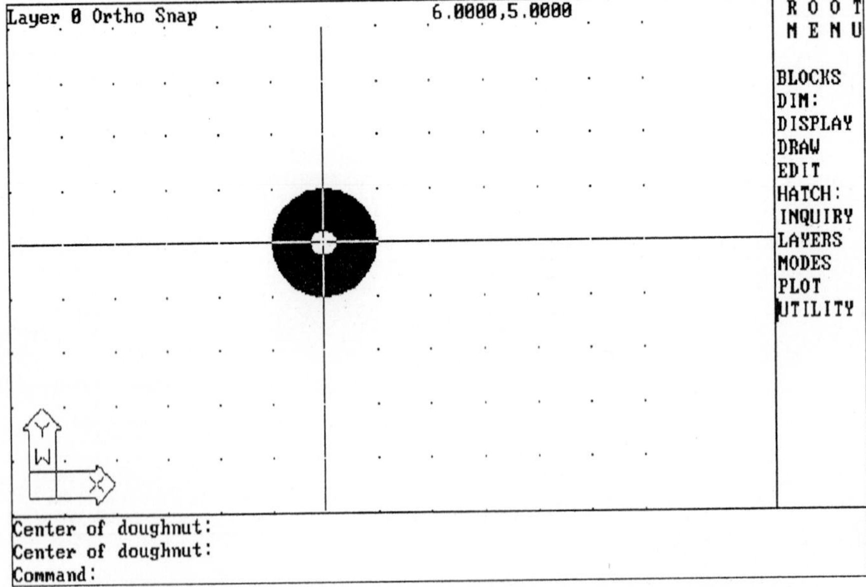

Figure 4-2*d*. The DONUT command is terminated using ENTER

Picking Objects to Block

In order to identify the objects that will make up the block, you pick them in the usual way with your pointing device. After you select your last object (or select all the entities or blocks by using a window), you press ENTER to terminate the selection process.

After all is entered satisfactorily, you will be able to refer to the doughnut, or more accurately the insertion hole, by its block name IH.

Adding Attributes to Blocks

When you are creating a block, you can include text information about the drawing in the form of an *attribute.* Like lines and points, attributes are AutoCAD entities that are included in a block. By reading the information in the attribute, you can learn about the block to which it is attached. This information is also accessible to database software outside of AutoCAD, which you can use to extract the attributes in order to create specifications such as parts lists.

For instance, if you wanted to prepare a list of the parts in your integrated circuit design, you could add descriptions of the parts directly to the drawing as attributes. Each integrated circuit, resistor, capacitor, and other component could be identified. Then, after the drawing was complete, you could easily read the attributes for each part into your database and use that data to prepare your list.

Attributes are stored in tag entities. Think of a tag entity as a container into which you can put information. The containers are labeled with tag names, which can be used to call the information when it is needed. However, the contents need not be the same each time the tag name is used. For instance, you could use the same block with the same tag name each time you needed a transistor represented in a drawing. But for every use of the block and tag name a different type of transistor could be specified and different information stored.

Chapter 9, "Attribute Management," deals thoroughly with

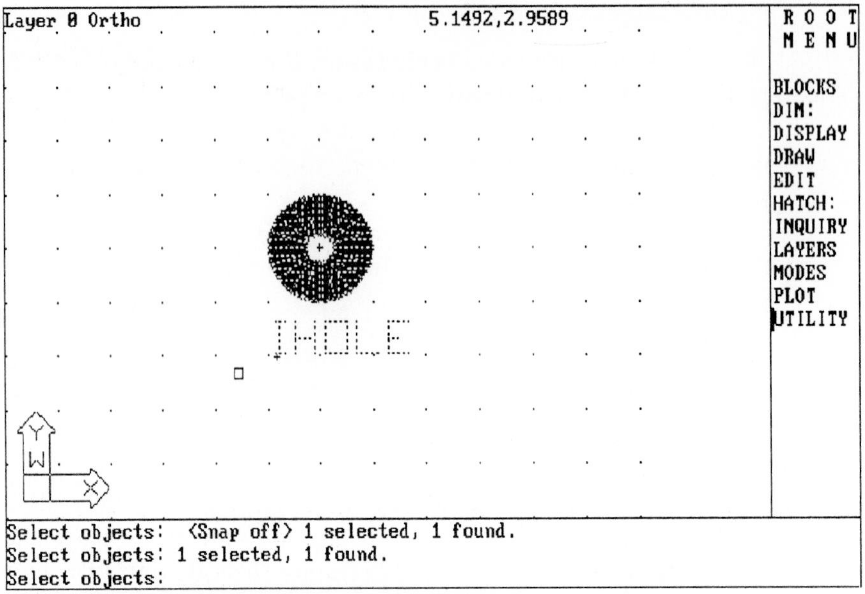

```
Layer 0 Ortho                    5.1492,2.9589
```

ROOT MENU
BLOCKS
DIM:
DISPLAY
DRAW
EDIT
HATCH:
INQUIRY
LAYERS
MODES
PLOT
UTILITY

IHOLE

```
Select objects:  <Snap off> 1 selected, 1 found.
Select objects: 1 selected, 1 found.
Select objects:
```

Figure 4-3. The inclusion of an attribute entity in a block

the database management of attributes and blocks. This information is important because attribute management is the link that brings drawings and text information together.

In Figure 4-3, a new block is being created. It is shown ghosted because an attribute entity is being included in it by selection. An attribute tag called "ihole" has been selected as part of the block. The block, when complete, will be called NEWIH.

Using the ATTDEF Command

In the drawing of the printed circuit board, you may want to identify each insertion hole with an attribute tag so that later on, by studying Chapter 9, "Attribute Management," you can manipulate the database. You could then count the number of holes in the printed circuit board and even identify what will be inserted into each hole.

You add attributes to a block by first using the ATTDEF

command to create an attribute entity. Then, when you select the objects you wish to include in the block definition with the BLOCK command, just include the attributes as well.

To add attributes to a drawing, you use the ATTDEF command:

Command: **attdef**
Attribute modes - - Invisible:N Constant:N Verify:N
Preset:N
Enter (ICVP) to change, RETURN when done:

Creating Attribute Tags

After you enter the ATTDEF command, you will be prompted "Attribute tag:." At this prompt you type the tag name by which the attribute will be identified within the drawing. Figure 4-4 shows the doughnut defined with an attribute tag. In this case

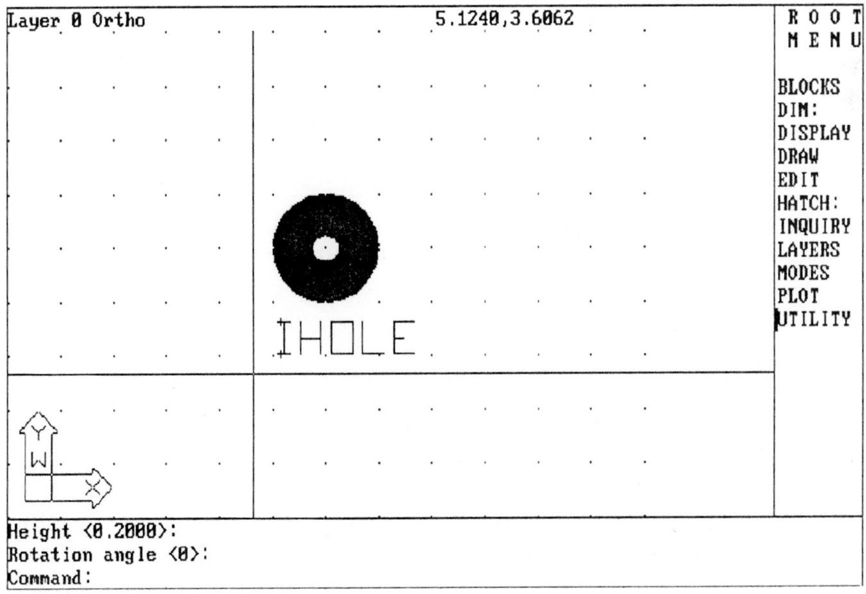

Figure 4-4. The definition of an attribute

the tag name is "ihole." The tag name serves as a placeholder for the attribute information until the block is actually inserted. When you insert the block, the tag name does not appear, only the tag's attribute information.

Defining the Attribute Prompt

After you enter the attribute tag, you will be prompted for the "Attribute prompt:". This is the prompt that will appear when you use the INSERT command to insert the block into a drawing. You type the words you want to appear as the prompt. In the case of the doughnut, the "ihole" tag allows you to specify a code that identifies the component you want to insert into this particular insertion hole. When you later insert the block, you will be prompted for this identification code so you might enter the prompt "Enter component ID."

Setting Attribute Values

Finally, you will be prompted for the "Default attribute value:". You use this to assign a default attribute to the tag. This is the value that will be entered when you press ENTER on an empty line. In the case of the IH block, the default identifier "no connection" has been entered.

Once the attribute has been added to the block, you can insert that block into any AutoCAD drawing and you will be prompted for its attribute with the "Enter component ID <no connection>:" prompt you have just invented. Each time the prompt appears you can enter a different value for the "ihole" attribute. The attributes that you enter stay with each instance of the block in the drawing. In other words, you create a template doughnut hole that you can use many times with different attributes.

Block Writing

If you just use the BLOCK command to identify a set of entities as a block object, the definition of the block will be contained only in your current drawing. This means that if you start another drawing and want to use a block from another drawing, you will be unable to do so. If, however, you use the WBLOCK command to write the block to disk as a separate file, you will be able to use the block in any other drawing. You use the WBLOCK command by entering the following command sequence:

Command: **wblock**
File name: **ih**
Block name: =

In response to the "File name:" prompt, you enter any name you choose in conformance with your operating system's rules. In MS-DOS, for example, you can use up to eight characters which will all be converted by DOS to uppercase. With UNIX, however, you must use lowercase. Other operating systems will have other restrictions. See your AutoCAD Reference Manual for specific information about the version of AutoCAD you are using.

After you enter the file name, you will be prompted to enter the block name you want placed in that file. You can use certain shorthand methods to specify the block name. If the block name has the same name as the file name you just entered, use the "=" (equal) character and you need not repeat the name. If you wish to save the entire drawing as a block, you can enter the "*" (asterisk) character.

If you press ENTER with nothing else in response to the "File name:" prompt, AutoCAD will ask you to select objects to write to the file as a block. If you choose this option, the objects you select will be removed from the drawing and placed in the file as a block.

Although the file to which you write the block will have a ".DWG" extension like other AutoCAD drawing file names, you must not include the extension in response to the "File name:" prompt. The block, when saved to disk, actually becomes a complete AutoCAD drawing in itself.

Understanding Blocks and Coordinate Systems

AutoCAD has two different coordinate systems, the World Coordinate System (WCS) and the User Coordinate System (UCS).

The WCS never changes. It is a stable frame of reference. When you begin a new drawing using AutoCAD, the World Coordinate System's origin is at the lower left corner of the drawing area. The X axis extends out from the origin to the right along the lowest extent of the drawing area. The Y axis extends upward along the farthest left extent of the drawing area. The Z axis extends directly outward from the screen toward you. You can view the World Coordinate System in many ways, but it is always the same and cannot be rotated or moved.

The UCS differs from the WCS in one very important way. Whereas the WCS is not changeable, the UCS can be changed relative to the WCS. The UCS can be defined to have its origin anywhere in the WCS, providing you a way of defining your own place to draw in the WCS. The UCS can be oriented by rotating around the X, Y, and/or Z axes. With a specific UCS, you can position the drawing area to draw on any surface at any orientation in space.

The two cubes in Figure 4-5 illustrate these two coordinate

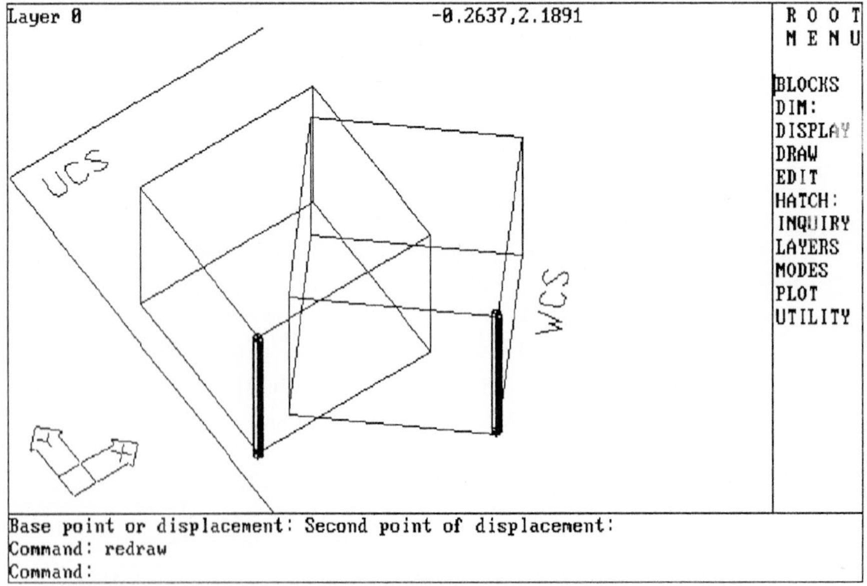

Figure 4-5. The World versus the User Coordinate Systems

systems. The WCS cube represents the World Coordinate System. The UCS cube represents a block that was created with the WCS cube and inserted at the then-current crosshairs location in a then-current UCS. Notice that the UCS cube is contained within the WCS cube, but with its origin (the thick line) at an entirely different location. Its rotation angle is also different.

When you write a block to a file, it is saved as though the current User Coordinate System were the World Coordinate System. The absolute position of the insertion base point is stored as the origin of the block's World Coordinate System. This is a very important point to keep in mind. When you insert the block into a drawing, it is inserted with its coordinate system oriented to the current User Coordinate System. The block's insertion base point, the World Coordinate System's origin for the block, is placed wherever you choose. You could, for example, create an advertising billboard that could be seen by airplanes. You could create the billboard as a new drawing and then insert it as a block so that it was drawn on the pitched roof of a barn.

In effect, if you save a block to disk, it can be brought back at any position or rotation angle that is currently defined by the User Coordinate System. Figure 4-6 shows an example of a single block that has been written to disk and inserted at several different positions and rotation angles.

You can change the insertion base point by using the BASE command. See Chapter 16, "AutoCAD Command Reference," for more details on the BASE command. Read about the World Coordinate System and the User Coordinate System in Chapter 2, "Drawing," and Chapter 16, "AutoCAD Command Reference." The AutoCAD Reference Manual also has an excellent section on coordinate systems.

Using the INSERT Command

In order to use the blocks you have defined, you must insert them into your drawings with the INSERT command. Depend-

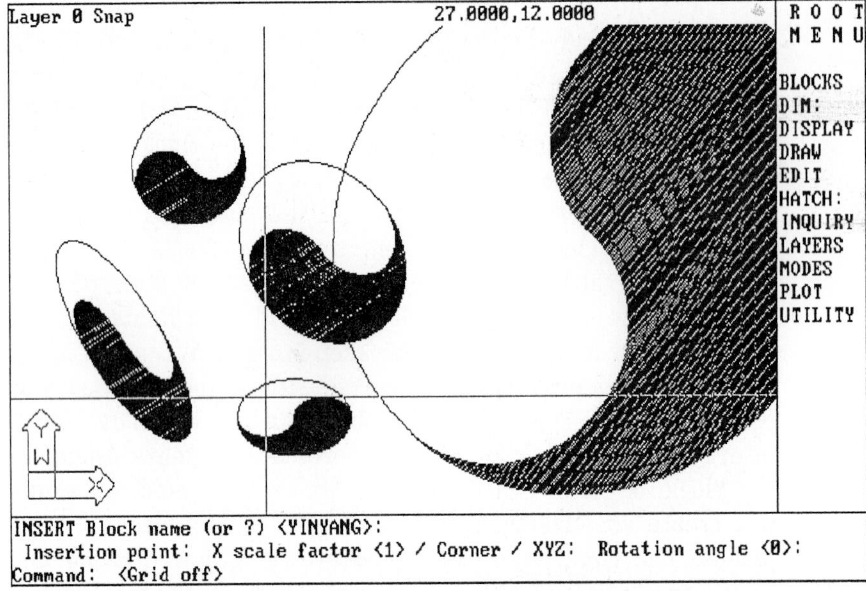

Figure 4-6. A single block inserted repeatedly

ing on what options you choose, the insertion process will be handled differently. Each block you insert into your drawing is actually an AutoCAD drawing in itself. Even though you use your own User Coordinate Systems to create AutoCAD drawings, they are always saved within the universal World Coordinate System.

A problem arises with respect to the insertion of blocks. How do you change the position of a block from the World Coordinate System when you insert it in your drawing? If blocks were inserted only in the same places and at the same rotation angles at which they were created, you would not be able to use blocks to build drawings. The value of blocks would be lost.

There are two basic rules about the locations of blocks when you insert them:

- AutoCAD uses the location of the crosshairs as a reference point when you insert a block. The insertion base point you picked when you created a block will be at the crosshairs location when you insert the block.

• The location of the crosshairs is always identified according to the User Coordinate System current at the time you insert a block. In other words, you can use the User Coordinate System to govern the placement of a block in the World Coordinate System of your drawing.

Understanding the Insertion Base Point

The *insertion base point* is a point in the User Coordinate System at the time a block is created that will be at the crosshairs location when a block is inserted in a drawing. In other words, the insertion base point is a "handle" that you attach to a block when you save it and grab with the crosshairs when you insert it.

There are essentially two ways to specify the insertion base point. You can specify it for the entire drawing with the BASE command, or you can specify it for a given block with the BLOCK command. You learned about the BLOCK command in the preceding section. If you want to know how to use the BASE command see Chapter 16, "AutoCAD Command Reference."

Using INSERT Options

Now you will see how the blocks you create can be inserted into drawings.

The INSERT command is invoked as follows:

Command: **insert**
Block name (or ?):
Insertion point:
X scale factor <1> / Corner / XYZ:
Y scale factor (default=?):
Rotation angle <0>:

After you enter the INSERT command, you will be prompted for the block name and its insertion point. Remember the "insertion base point" prompt of the BLOCK command described in the preceding section? This base point becomes the point of insertion of the block into your drawing.

Using Scale Factors

A scale factor can be specified for each of the X, Y, and Z axes. The simplest response to the "X scale factor" prompt is to enter the default (1). If you have created your symbol with a *unit grid*, however, you will probably want to use a scale factor to conform the units of the block with the units of the drawing. A unit grid is a grid that has been defined with one drawing unit per cell. In other words, a unit grid that measures ten units horizontally and ten units vertically will have ten grid cells in each direction. By using the unit grid approach, you standardize all of your blocks to be drawn so that one dimensional unit in the block can be converted to any other dimensional unit. For example, you could create a circle with a one-unit radius and store it as a block. When you wished to use that block in a drawing, you could insert a circle with a ten-unit radius by using a scale factor of ten in the X and Y directions.

The possibilities presented by scale factors make extremely complex geometry possible with AutoCAD. You can create prototypical ellipses, parabolas, hyperbolas, and a host of other mathematically defined curves that can be inserted as blocks and scaled appropriately. In fact, the ELLIPSE command generates just one such curve as a block in your drawing. By using AutoLISP, discussed in Chapters 11 through 13 and Chapter 15, you can probably create your own curve generators using blocks and scaling creatively.

Insertion Presets

You can specify scale and rotation by using various presets in response to the "Insertion point:" prompt. These presets are not intuitively obvious. Like commands within commands, they satisfy your need to dynamically place blocks in your drawings. With presets, you can specify the scale and rotation of a block *before* you drag it into position in your drawing. If you use any presets, you will not be prompted for scale or rotation angles before the block is inserted in your drawing.

To preset scale and rotation, you enter a valid name when AutoCAD asks you for the insertion point. You can enter any of the following: Scale, Xscale, Yscale, Zscale, Rotate, PScale, PXscale, PYscale, PZscale, PRotate. As always, the capitalized letters alone in each option's name will activate the options. Thus, the options are S, X, Y, Z, R, and any of these preceded by a P:—PS, PX, PY, PZ, and PR.

The "*Scale*" option permits you to enter a scale factor. The "*Xscale*" option enables you to preset the scale factor along the X axis only. The "*Yscale*" option enables you to preset the scale factor along the Y axis only. The "*Zscale*" option enables you to preset the scale factor along the Z axis only. The "*Rotate*" option prompts you for a rotation angle. In practice, you should think of these option names as "SXYZR."

If you precede the option name with the letter "P" (for position), you will be able to drag the block into position, but be prompted for the scale and rotation after you pick the position. You might wish to do this, for example, if you started doing presets but later changed your mind. The "P" option cannot be specified by itself, only as a prefix. If you try to request a normal series of INSERT prompts and cancel out your presets, you must use PS, PX, PY, PZ, or PR. You cannot, however, use the letter "P" by itself as an option to simply remove the effects of all presets.

A typical response to the "Insertion point:" prompt is

Command: **insert**
Block name (or ?): **yinyang**
Insertion point: **s** Scale factor: **2**
Insertion point: **r** Rotation angle: **30**
Insertion point: **pr** Rotation angle: **0**

In the previous example, the block yinyang is preset to a scale factor of 2 and a rotation angle of 30 degrees. The user has had a change of mind, however, and has used the "P" option to specify the rotation angle of 0. After having done this, the usual prompts for the INSERT command will resume.

Chapter 16, "AutoCAD Command Reference," and the AutoCAD Reference Manual have more information regarding the options available to you with presets.

Using the "Corner" Option

If you don't wish to specify scale factors numerically, you can use the "Corner" option to pick a box. The absolute dimensions of this box will then be used as the scale factors in the X and Y directions. You specify the "Corner" option by typing the word "corner" or just the letter "C" in response to the prompt

X scale factor <1> / Corner / XYZ:

You cannot enter negative numbers for the scale factors with the "Corner" option. If you enter negative numbers for scale factors, the effect is to reverse the block in that direction. You can create a "mirror" effect by using negative scale factors.

The drawings in Figures 4-7*a* through 4-7*d* show a block that has been inserted four times, with negative rotations enabling it to be reflected into four different orientations. Notice what has happened to the center lines in these drawings. The changes in the lines could have been avoided if the center lines had been erased or if they had not been included in the block that was inserted. Why did the center lines change? The center lines' short dashes now overlap each other slightly out-of-sync and have thereby created longer lines. Sometimes you will see unexpected effects like this, but with AutoCAD you can always correct what you do not want by erasing it and replacing it with something you do like.

Using the INSERT "XYZ" Option

The "XYZ" option enables you to set scale factors along all three coordinate axes, not just X and Y. If you select the "XYZ" option of the INSERT command, you will be prompted first for the X

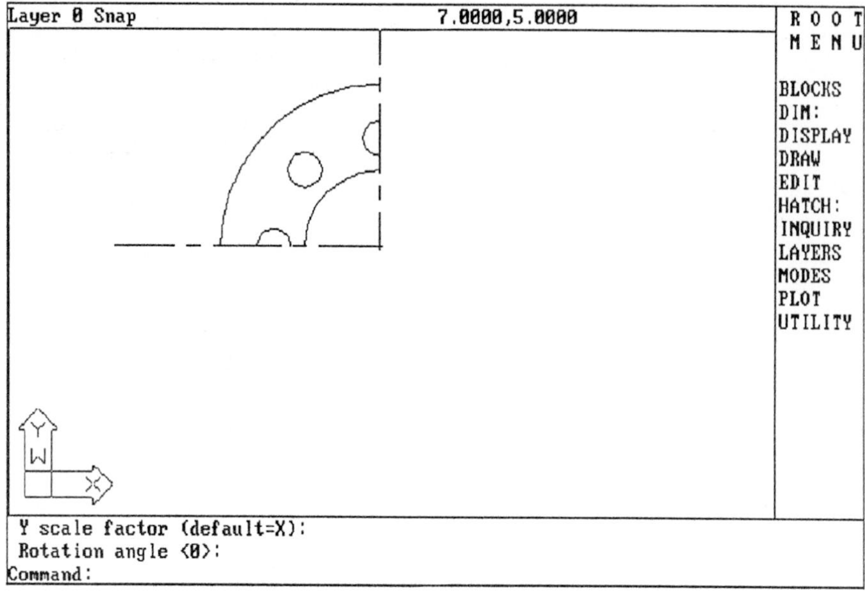

Figure 4-7*a*. The first of four quarters of a bolt ring

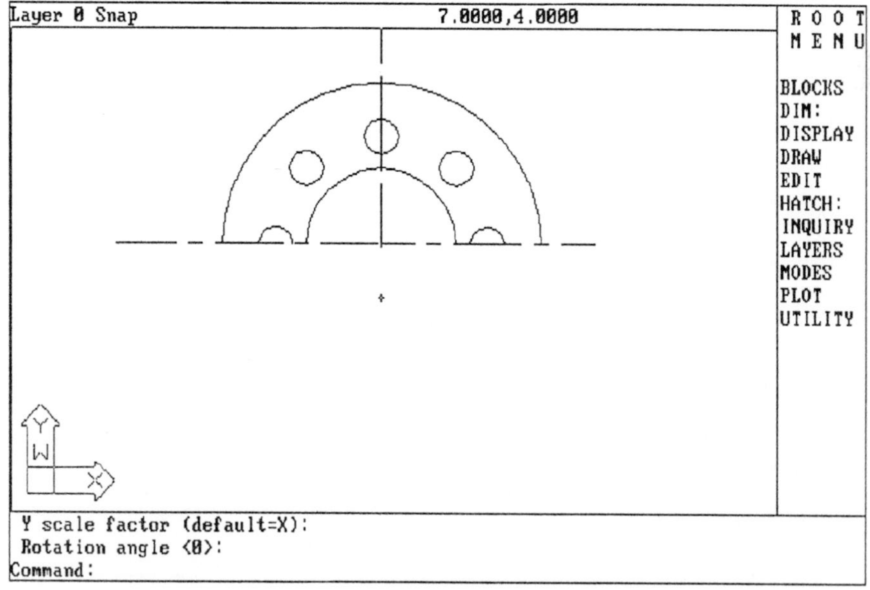

Figure 4-7*b*. The second insertion, rotated −90 degrees

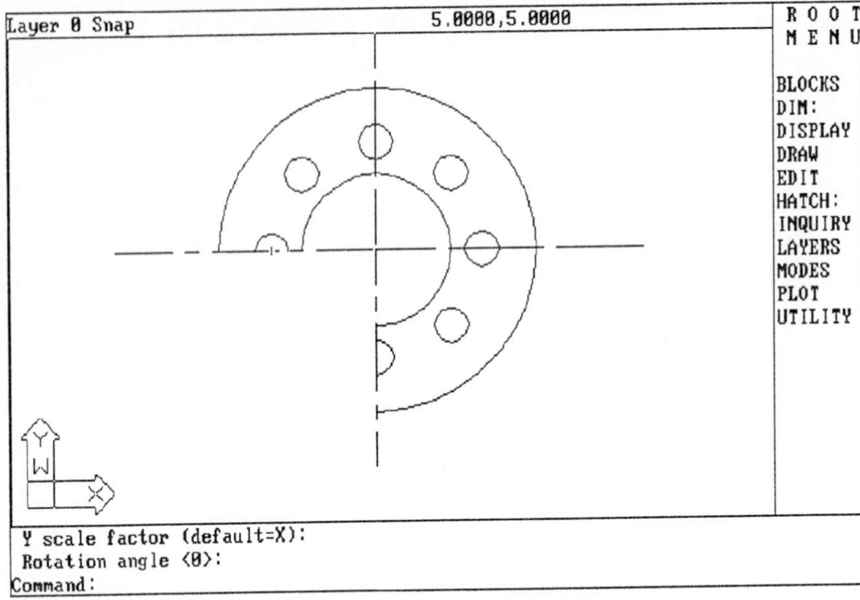

Figure 4-7*c*. The third insertion, rotated −180 degrees

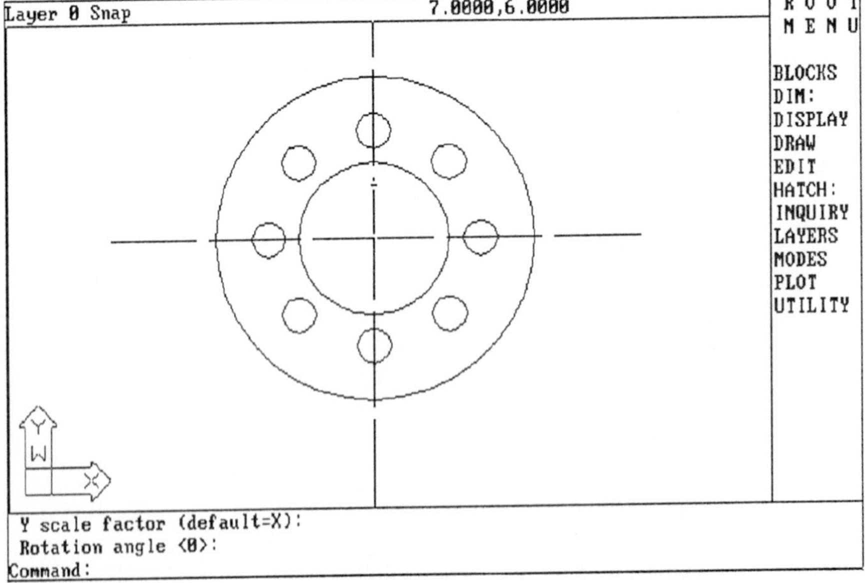

Figure 4-7*d*. The final insertion and the finished figure

scale factor, then for the Y scale factor, and finally for the Z scale factor. If you do not select the "XYZ" option and you wish to insert a block into a drawing at a specific elevation, you must later move the block to its proper elevation. Remember, the block is inserted with its World Coordinate System (with the origin at its insertion base point) identified with the current crosshairs location in the User Coordinate System.

Rotating a Block

You can rotate a block during the insertion process rather than wait and rotate the block later. The last option of the INSERT command enables you to do this. If you respond to the "Rotation angle <0>:" prompt with a rotation angle, the block will be inserted with its WCS rotated to the specified rotation angle rather than to the default angle of the UCS. You can also enter a reference point, rather than an angle, in response to the "Rotation angle" prompt. If you do, the angle from the insertion point to the point you specify, will be used as the rotation angle for the block. Figures 4-8*a* through 4-8*d* show some symbols created with the BLOCK command being inserted into a printed circuit drawing.

Using the DRAGMODE Command

As with other prompts in AutoCAD, when you are asked for a rotation angle number, you can substitute a pick with the pointing device. With the DRAGMODE command you can change AutoCAD's selection modes. Invoking drag mode is accomplished with the following command sequence:

> Command: **dragmode**
> OFF/ON/Auto <On>:

Dragging responses are those that allow you to use rubberband lines and rectangles rather than numerical values. If you

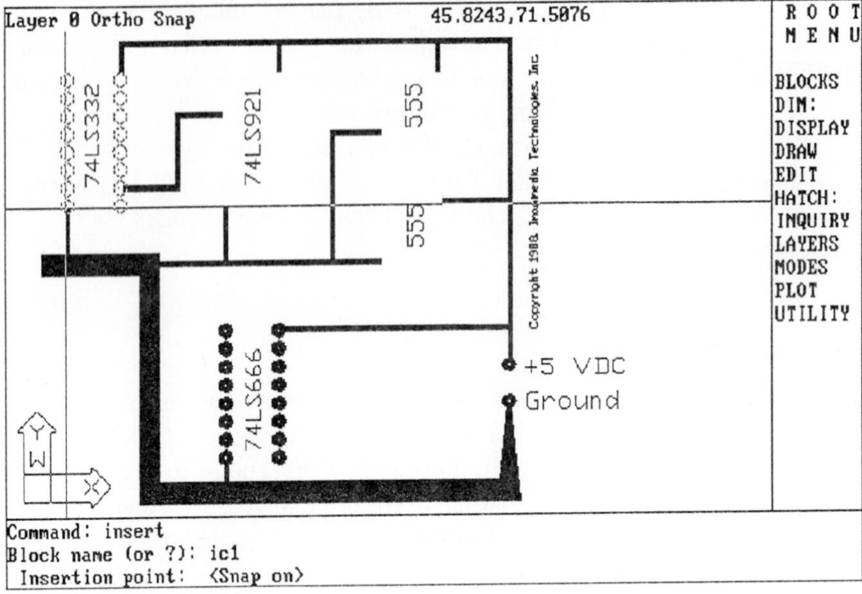

Figure 4-8*a*. The first DIP (IC1) is inserted

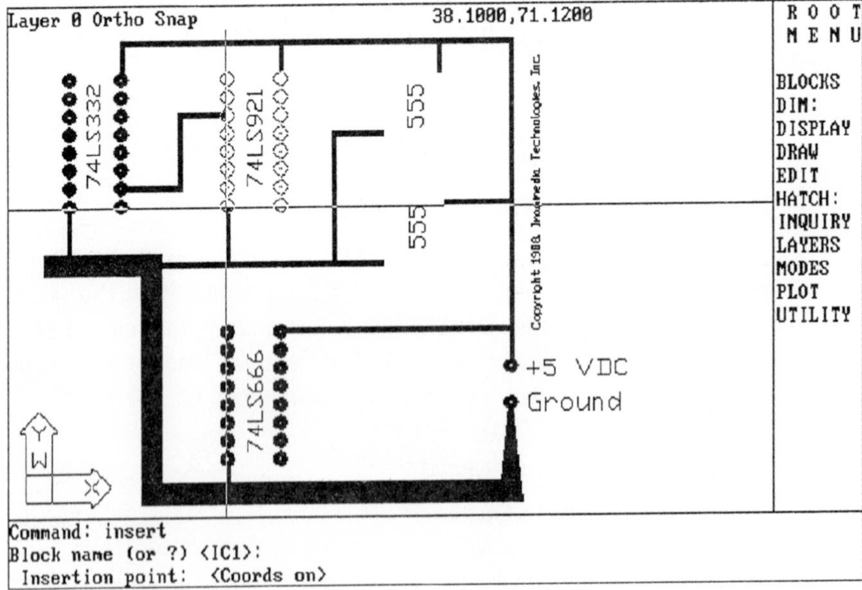

Figure 4-8*b*. The second IC1 block is inserted

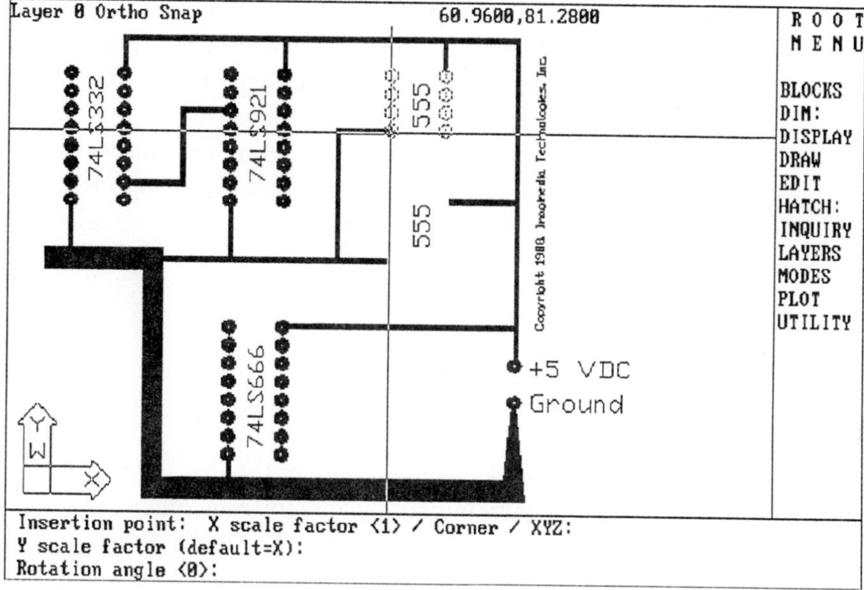

Figure 4-8*c*. The third DIP (IC2) block is inserted

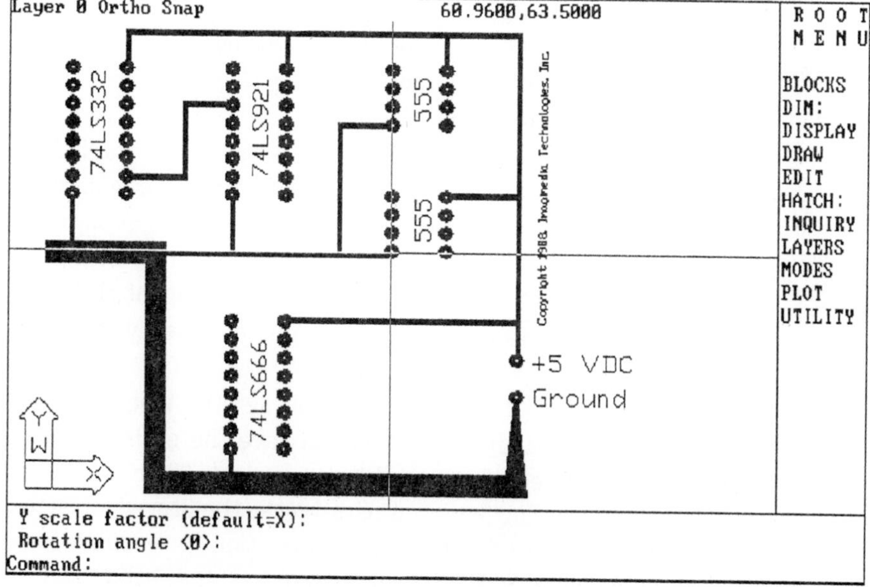

Figure 4-8*d*. The last IC2 block is inserted

select the "OFF" option, you will turn drag mode off entirely, meaning you will be unable to drag to pick values in response to prompts. If you select the "ON" option, you will be able to use drag mode for prompts that allow it. If you choose the "Auto" option, every prompt that permits dragging will automatically allow a drag response. If the "Auto" option is not selected, you enter the key word "drag" at a prompt that permits dragging in order to pick a value.

Inserting Drawings

Because AutoCAD blocks, when saved on the disk, become AutoCAD drawings and are indistinguishable from other AutoCAD drawings, you can treat entire drawings as blocks. When you do this, you use the drawing name as the block name for the INSERT command. You can use a path name, including a drive specifier, as the desired drawing name. The block name formed from the drawing name will not include the path. You can even assign a drawing name to a new block name by using the equal (=) sign. For example, you can add a block named "auto" made of a drawing named "edsel.dwg" by responding to the "Block name (or ?):" prompt with **auto=edsel**.

If you enter a block name in response to the INSERT command and that name cannot be found in the current drawing, AutoCAD will search for a drawing file with that name. If such a drawing is found, it will be made into a block within the current drawing. You can skip the actual drawing of the block on screen by canceling the INSERT command when you see the "Insertion point:" prompt.

With the BASE command, you can set the insertion base point for the current drawing. You can save the entire drawing after having changed the insertion base point. Then when you use the entire drawing later on as a block, the stored insertion base point will be used. The default insertion base point for a drawing in which the BASE command has *not* been used is X=0, Y=0, Z=0. You enter the BASE command as follows:

Command: **base**
Base point:

You can pick a point in response to the "Base point:" prompt, or you can specify a two-dimensional or three-dimensional point numerically.

Building a Drawing with INSERT

In order to add some insertion holes to a drawing, it will be necessary to insert some IH blocks. Insertion hole blocks will be inserted at the ends of traces to form connections for the integrated circuits and other electronic components that will be placed there. Figure 4-9 shows the PC mask drawing with some insertion holes installed. Traces have been extended to the holes.

Inheritance Rules

When you insert a block into a drawing, the block will be lower in priority than the drawing. The information in the block will

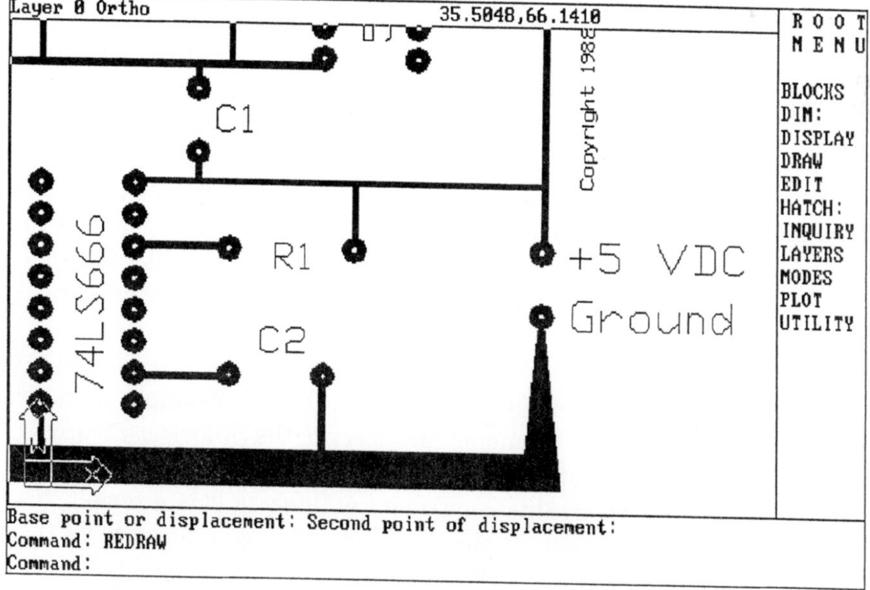

Figure 4-9. Some new IH blocks have been added

conform to information in the drawing, rather than the other way around. Any line types, layers, and text styles that were true for the block will be overridden by the current line types, layers, and text styles with the same names in the drawing. For example, a layer in the drawing may be called "MYLAYER" and a layer in the block may have the same name. If this is the case, the layer in the drawing will be used instead of the layer in the block. You may be surprised by this when the layer in the block changes for no apparent reason. If the current drawing has no line type, layer, or text style for a given name in the block, the current default will be used instead of those specified in the block.

In other words, if you want your inserted block to have the same text fonts, line types, and layers as were in the original block when it was made, you must make sure the current drawing also has these same definitions.

Exploding Blocks

When you *explode* blocks with AutoCAD, you break them up into their component entities. You can use the EXPLODE command to break up polylines and blocks. If you explode a block made up of several lines, you will be left with only the line entities themselves. Before you exploded it, the group of lines could be selected as a block and picking any one of the lines in the block would select all the others. After the block has been exploded, however, picking any line will only select that line and none of the others. Any time you explode a block, it will lose its identity, but then you will be able to select any entity separately that was formerly part of the block.

You can explode a block while it is being inserted if you precede the block name with an asterisk (*). For example, if you enter the INSERT command and answer the "Block name (or ?):" prompt with ***auto**, the auto block or drawing will be automatically exploded into its component entities as it is inserted. Normally, blocks exist in the drawing only by reference to their names but when a block is exploded, it is no longer referenced by its name. Instead, each entity that made up the block is kept separately in the drawing. This is why the exploded block takes up so much more memory than before it was exploded.

Combining Blocks Within Blocks

Blocks within an AutoCAD drawing may contain blocks, which in turn may contain more blocks, limited only by the space available on your drive. Blocks within blocks are said to be *nested.* The only thing you may *not* do is place a block within itself. For example, a block named RESISTOR cannot have any blocks named RESISTOR within it.

You can make prototypical symbols for complete integrated circuit packages by first creating a block that is a single insertion hole, then creating a block of several insertion holes. Figure 4-10 shows a complete DIP (Digital Inline Package) insertion symbol. This symbol was made by first defining a single block much like the IH block, but designed to allow proper placement

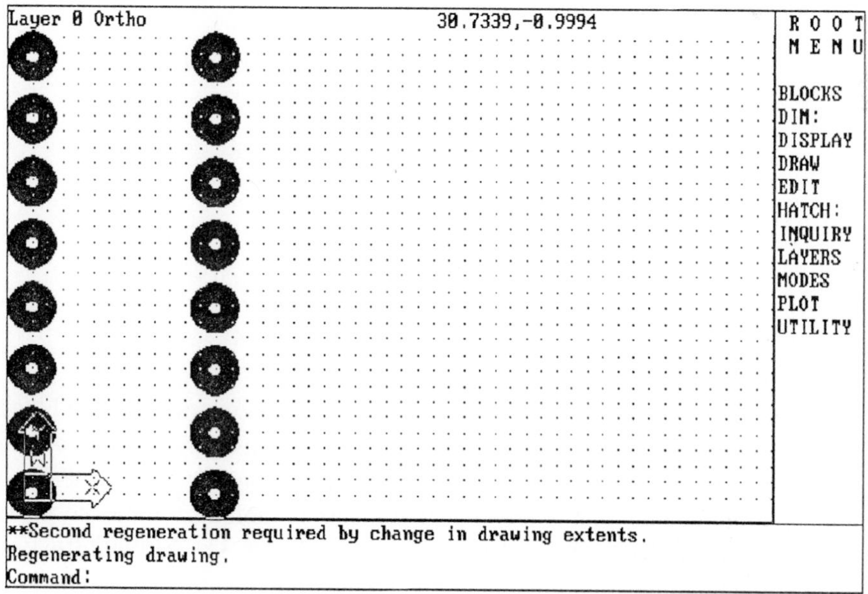

Figure 4-10. A DIP insertion symbol

within the array of insertion holes required by the DIP. Then a snap grid was set up to identify the locations of as many insertion holes as would be required for all the leads of the DIP. Each insertion hole symbol was placed on the grid with the INSERT command. The MINSERT command could have been used to do the same thing more quickly.

The MINSERT Command

You can save time when creating arrays of blocks by using the MINSERT command. The command is intended to allow multiple insertions of the block. It does this without requiring you to first insert the block and then use the ARRAY command. MINSERT is very useful for work in the electronics industry since many electronic components are designed as arrays of objects.

Like the INSERT command, the MINSERT command prompts for information about the block to be inserted into an array. The command sequence is as follows:

Command: **minsert**
Block name (or ?) <NEWIH>:
Insertion point: X scale factor <1> / Corner / XYZ:
Y scale factor (default=X):
Rotation angle <0>:
Number of rows(- - -) <1>:
Number of columns (¦¦¦) <1>:
Unit cell or distance between rows (- - -):
Distance between columns (¦¦¦):
Enter attribute values
Enter Component ID <no connection>:

The last prompt in this sequence is the one we defined for block NEWIH, "Enter Component ID <no connection>:". The entire sequence has been answered by simply entering each line. Each step in the command sequence has a default value, so it is possible to "default through" most AutoCAD commands like this.

Figures 4-11*a* and 4-11*b* show the MINSERT command in

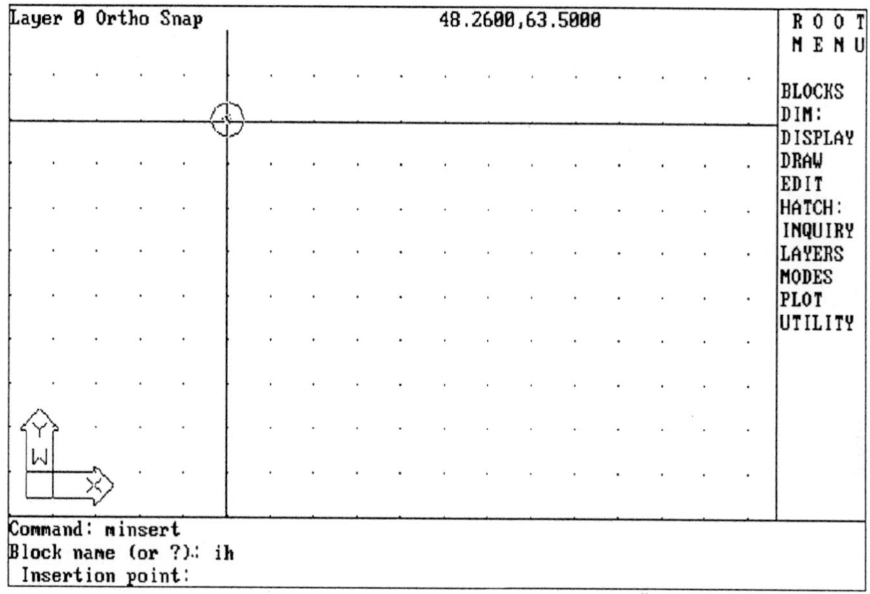

Figure 4-11*a*. The MINSERT command and first object for array

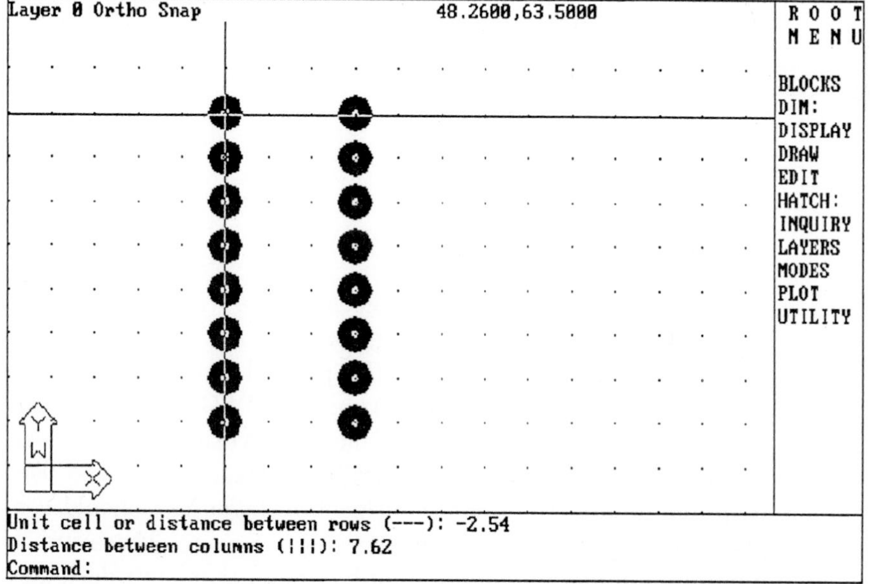

Figure 4-11*b*. The entire array that makes up a standard DIP

action. Notice that the distance between rows has been specified as negative. Otherwise, the rows of insertion holes that make up the DIP symbol would be propagated upward and off the screen.

Redefining Inserted Blocks

You can redefine a block that has been inserted into a drawing. It is important to remember that the only thing a drawing "knows" about a block is its definition in the drawing and its reference by name. The block is defined only once and its details are contained in only one place in the drawing. You call for it by name and it can appear any number of times at any number of different scales and rotations. The block usually originated as a drawing in itself.

If you wish to revise a block that was inserted from another drawing, you must change the original drawing. Changing the block in the current drawing will not change the original drawing.

In order to change the block, change the drawing it came from first. Then redefine the block by using the INSERT command to reinsert the drawing as the desired block. To do this, enter the INSERT command as follows:

Command: **insert**
Block name (or ?): **ih=**
Block IH redefined
Insertion point:

If you don't want to insert a block at the "Insertion Point:" prompt, cancel with CTRL-C. Figure 4-12 shows an example of a redefinition of the IH block in the printed circuit board mask drawing from Figure 4-1. The drawing IH.DWG was revised and the revision shows up in each instance of the use of the IH block.

You have seen how blocks can be defined, stored, and used as drawings within drawings within drawings. You should consider how you will manage blocks in your work. There are as many ways to manage the use of blocks as there are designers and drafters who use them. Yet for your given application, there

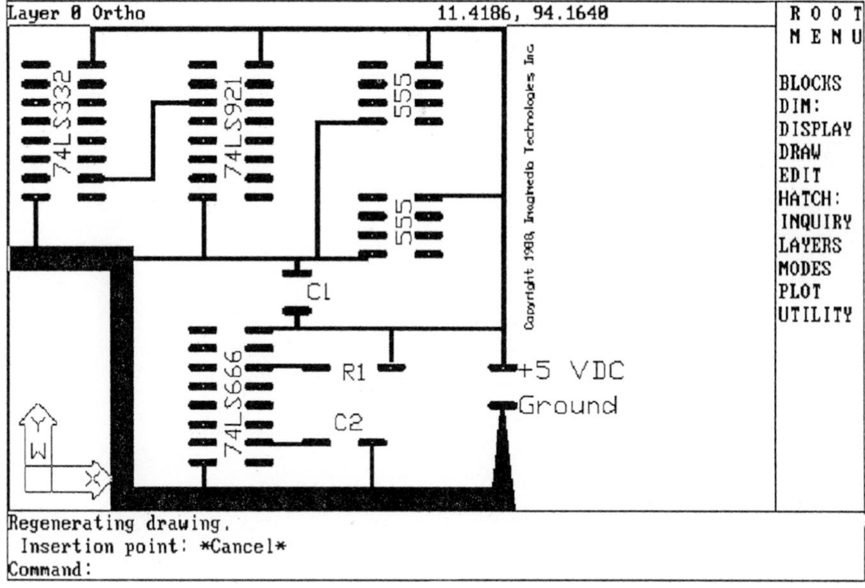

Figure 4-12. The PC board with IH block changed to NIH

are probably some methods that work better than others. For example, if you are an architect, you may want to organize your blocks according to the CSI (Construction Specifications Institute) standard. With this method, each block that represents a building component will have a number that is keyed into the CSI format. Better yet, read Chapter 9, "Managing Attributes," to find out how to assign specifications directly to blocks.

No matter how you use them, you will find that blocks are an indispensable part of AutoCAD. You should always look carefully at the repetitive aspects of your drawings and try to use blocks wherever repetition exists. It will save in the size of your drawing file and in the time it takes to redisplay your drawings.

Dimensioning

The DIM Command
Modifying Dimensions
Setting Dimension Variables
Dimensioning a Simple Drawing

FIVE

The dimensions in a drafted document or working drawing are the precise statement of angles and distances that are required to construct an accurate design object. The distances and angles in your drawing are presented in the form of dimension callouts which take many forms. Callouts usually use *extension lines* to "point" to the places where the measurements are meant to be taken. Extension lines, in effect, bring the dimension out to a place where it can be expressed. The string of characters that represents the dimension distance or angle is placed near the *dimension line.* This line connects two or more extension lines and indicates with arrowheads or "tick" marks precisely which extension lines call out the dimension.

Whether the object of your design efforts is a building, an automobile, or a highway, you do not want anyone to have to measure your drawings to find those angles and distances. Yet if your design does not have accurate dimension callouts, that is just what people will be tempted to do.

One of the most tedious aspects of the art of drafting is the creation and revision of dimension callouts. The draftsperson must often put more work into the expression of dimensions than any other part of the drawing. Mistakes are easy to make. Even if you create accurate dimensions, you will inevitably be required to change them when the design changes. Changes must always be viewed as "opportunities" to make mistakes.

AutoCAD enables you to create clear and accurate dimension callouts and also allows you to easily change dimensions as you change your drawings.

Dimensioning can be done in either a rectangular or an angular mode, with many options in each mode for the dimension style, placement, orientation, and much more. Read this chapter for examples of how to use most of AutoCAD's dimensioning options. For more detailed information regarding options with the DIM (or "dimensioning") command, refer to Chapter 16, "AutoCAD Command Reference."

In this chapter, you will see many examples of dimensioning. Although it is impossible to show you all of the possible combinations, if you follow the examples, you will quickly comprehend the principles involved in dimensioning. By using those principles and a little imagination, you will be able to save a lot of time and build better, more accurate drawings.

The DIM Command

The entire world of AutoCAD's dimensioning powers is accessed through the DIM command. To invoke the dimensioning capabilities of AutoCAD, you prepare your command line as follows:

Command: **dim**
Dim:

The dimensioning commands are, in fact, a secondary command set. You create and manage dimensions using an entire command language that is meant just for this purpose.

Returning to Command Prompt

To return to the normal command level from the "Dim:" command level, press the cancel button on your pointing device, press CTRL-C from the keyboard, or enter the EXIT command.

If you wish to create dimensions from the "Command:" prompt and return to it rather than to the "Dim:" prompt, use the DIM1 command instead of the DIM command. Everything the DIM command does is also done by the DIM1 command. The DIM command uses the "Dim:" prompt and the DIM1 command uses the normal "Command:" prompt.

Dimensioning Styles

There are many reasons to create drawings. You may be an electrical engineer, an architect, a civil engineer, a designer, a contractor, or an artist. In all of these fields, you use drawings to communicate your ideas to other people. Each profession, however, has its own standards and each professional has his or her own preferences. AutoCAD tries to accommodate these different needs by providing both a range of built-in functions and the ability to customize.

Figure 5-1 shows several *linear* dimension callouts. Linear dimensions are used to specify linear distances. Note the arrows

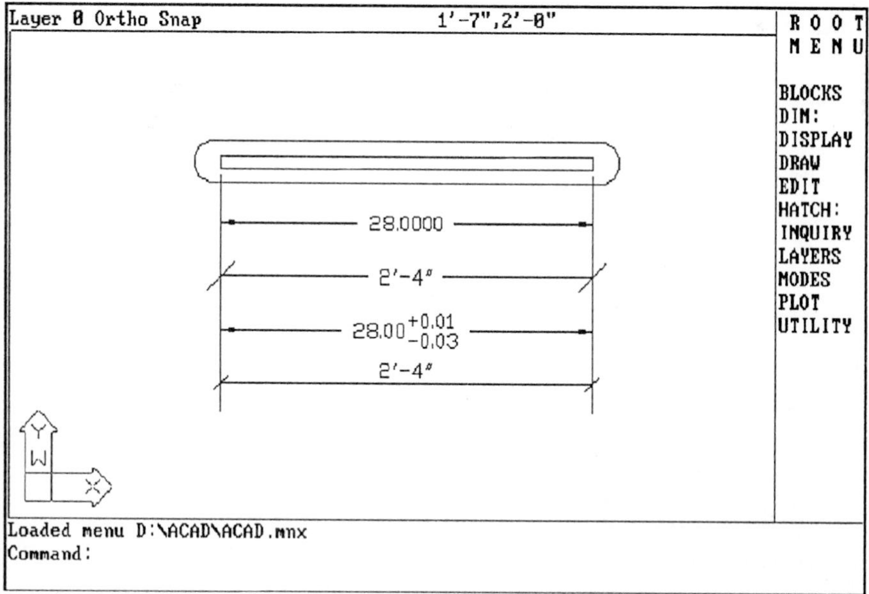

Figure 5-1. Linear dimension callouts

and tick marks that identify extension lines. (AutoCAD shows arrows at this scale as thickenings at the ends of lines.) Dimensions themselves can be placed above, below, or within the dimension line.

See Figure 5-2 for some examples of *diameter* and *radius* dimensioning styles. Arrows identify the extents of dimensions, but extension lines are not used.

You can use arrows, tick marks, or your own blocks to identify the extents of dimension lines. You can actually control many aspects of arrows used in dimensioning, including their scale and size. The arrow itself is a block. See Chapter 4, "Working with Blocks," for more information on the creation of blocks. Also, see Chapter 16, "AutoCAD Command Reference," for how to use the DIMBLK variable to control the appearance of arrows in your linear dimensions.

Some typical *angular* dimensions are shown in Figure 5-3. Extension lines are used in angular dimensioning, but you can remove them if you wish. The dimension line itself is an arc in

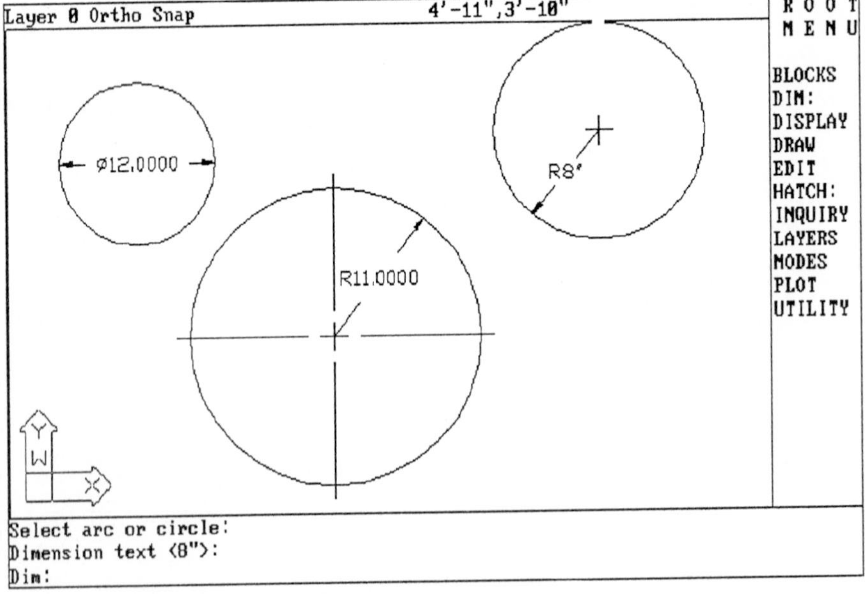

Figure 5-2. Diameter and radius dimension styles

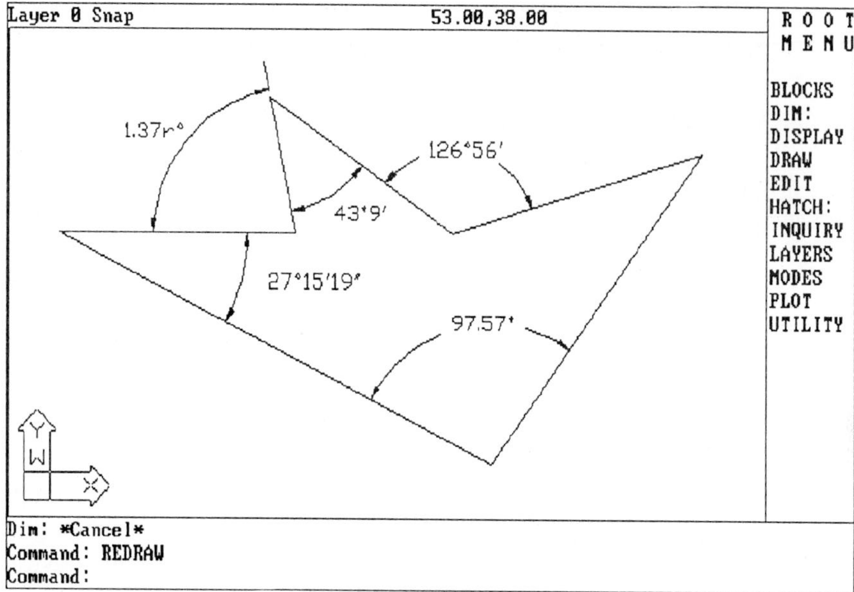

Figure 5-3. Typical angular dimensions

angular dimensioning, while it is a straight line in all other dimensioning styles.

As with all other types of dimensioning, if you are using angular dimensions, you can make the dimension interrupt the dimension line or you can place the dimension inside or outside of the arc. You can control these choices with system variables. For a complete list of system variables used in dimensioning, refer to the DIM command in Chapter 16, "AutoCAD Command Reference."

Extension Lines

AutoCAD gives you maximum control over the expression of extension lines. Extension lines extend the locations of the actual points you are dimensioning to a convenient location for the dimension line. How you draw extension lines will vary with how you need to draw dimensions in a particular drawing. With AutoCAD, you have the flexibility to use extension lines at the beginning *and* ending of the dimension line, or you can locate extension lines at only the beginning *or* ending of the dimension line. The extension line in Figure 5-3 appears only at the end of the dimension line.

Dimensions can be created either by manually selecting the beginning and ending points for the dimension, or by picking an entity (line, circle, or arc). If you pick an entity, the properties of the entity will be used to locate the extension lines. The property of a line would be the line length; the properties of a circle or arc would be its radius.

Automatic Extension Lines

When you enter a dimensioning command, you see the prompt "First extension line origin or RETURN to select:". When you press the ENTER key or the return button on your pointing device, you will be prompted to "Select line, arc, or circle:". If you are trying to dimension a line, an arc, or a circle, just pick the entity you wish to dimension and the dimension will be drawn automatically with the appropriate extension lines.

Manual Extension Lines

You may not be able to generate automatic extension lines because there is no line, circle, or arc entity to dimension in its entirety. Under these circumstances, when AutoCAD prompts "First extension line origin or RETURN to select:", you just pick the first origin. After you do this, you will see the prompt "Second extension line origin:". After you pick this point, the dimension will be drawn.

Suppressing Extension Lines

You may want to suppress extension lines if you are dimensioning from a point on one object to the face of another object. In architectural practice, for example, you might want to dimension to a finished surface rather than to the rough surface. When an architect dimensions to the rough, the dimension is understood to be approximate, not exactly as shown. When you dimension to a finished surface, the position of the extension line should be exact; therefore, you may want to suppress one of the automatic extension lines so you can add a more precise one later.

You can suppress the drawing of either of the two extension lines by using the DIMSE1 and DIMSE2 system variables. DIMSE1, if it is *on,* will suppress the first extension line. (The value for on is 1 and the value for off is 0.) DIMSE2 will suppress the second extension line.

Creating Vertical Dimensions

Vertical dimensions are a unique type of dimension in which the dimension line is oriented vertically. You can create a dimension like the one shown in Figure 5-4 by entering the following command sequence:

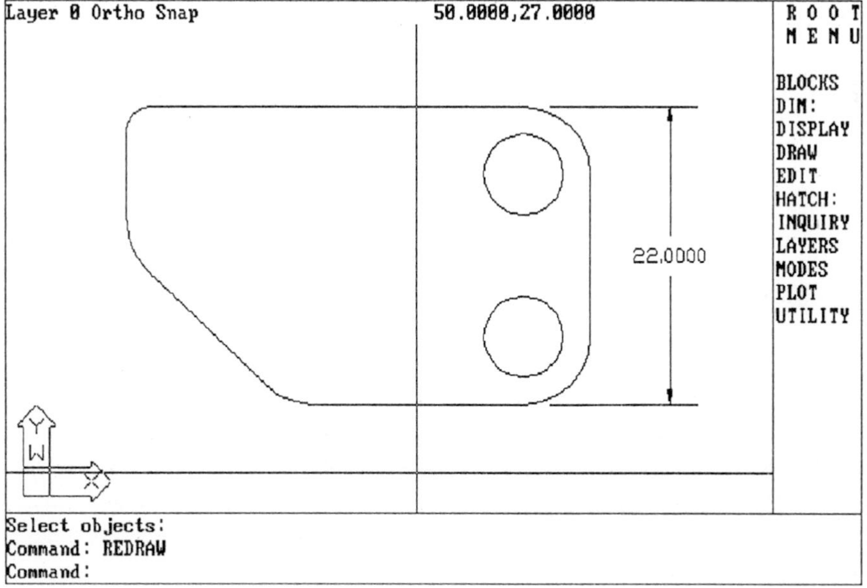

Figure 5-4. A vertical dimension

Command: **dim**
Dim: **ver**
First extension line origin or RETURN to select:
Second extension line origin:

Creating Horizontal Dimensions

To create horizontal dimensions, you use the HORIZONTAL dimensioning command. Only the first three letters of the command need to be entered. As with the vertical dimensioning sequence, you enter **hor** in response to the "Dim:" prompt and then pick the extension line origins.

See Figure 5-5 for an object that has been dimensioned using the HORIZONTAL dimensioning command.

One thing to observe when you create dimensions is that AutoCAD places a point at the origin when you select it. This enables subsequent object snaps to pick the exact point you selected for the origin. If, however, you pick a point on a line of

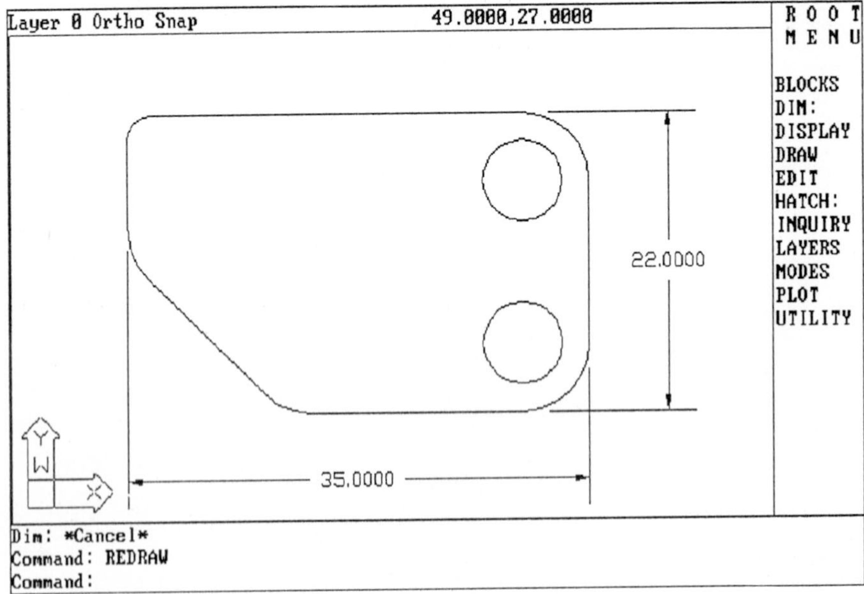

Figure 5-5. Typical horizontal dimensions

the object as the origin, you will not see it. The basic rule to follow is that you should pick the real origin, not a different point. If you want to keep the extension lines from touching the object, set the DIMEXO system variable. You can read about the DIMEXO variable in Chapter 16, "AutoCAD Command Reference."

Creating Aligned Dimensions

Dimensions sometimes need to be aligned with objects. You might wish to have the dimension line follow the line it is dimensioning in order to more clearly indicate the dimension. The drawing in Figure 5-6 shows an object with a component that is at an angle to the horizontal. The dimension line has been drawn to follow the line on the object and specify its length, rather than that of the horizontal or vertical component.

The endpoints of the line were found by using the OSNAP command to set ENDP on. When this is done, the identification

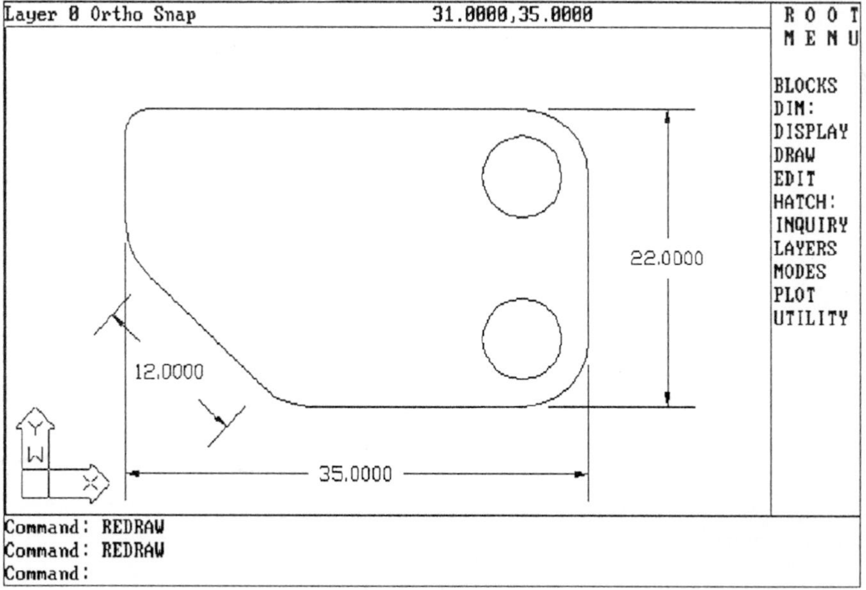

Figure 5-6. Creating aligned dimensions

of the object in response to the DIM ALIGN command sequence also automatically picks the closest line endpoint. You can read about the OSNAP command in Chapter 16, "AutoCAD Command Reference."

Dimensioning the Diameter

Arc and circle entities can have their diameters dimensioned with the DIAMETER subcommand. Remember, you must first enter the DIM command unless the "Dim:" prompt is already displayed. The following command sequence was entered to add diameter dimensions to two circles on the object in Figure 5-7:

Command: **dim**
Dim: **dia**
Select arc or circle:

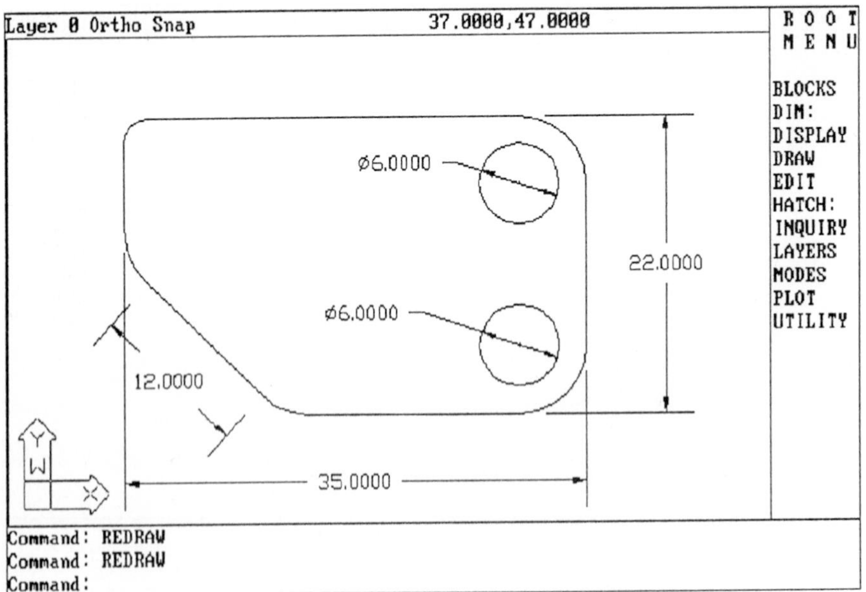

Figure 5-7. Diameter dimensions

Dimension text <6.0000>:
Text does not fit.
Enter leader length for text:

Note that AutoCAD has automatically determined that the text for the dimension will not fit inside the circle. A prompt asks for the length of the *leader* to the dimension text that will be drawn outside the circle. A leader is a line that "leads" from the dimension line to the dimension text. Figure 5-7 shows the leader and dimensions for each circle after the leader length was entered.

Dimensioning the Radius

Like the DIAMETER subcommand, the RADIUS subcommand will create radial dimensions. See Figure 5-8 for a radius dimension that has been added to the sample drawing.

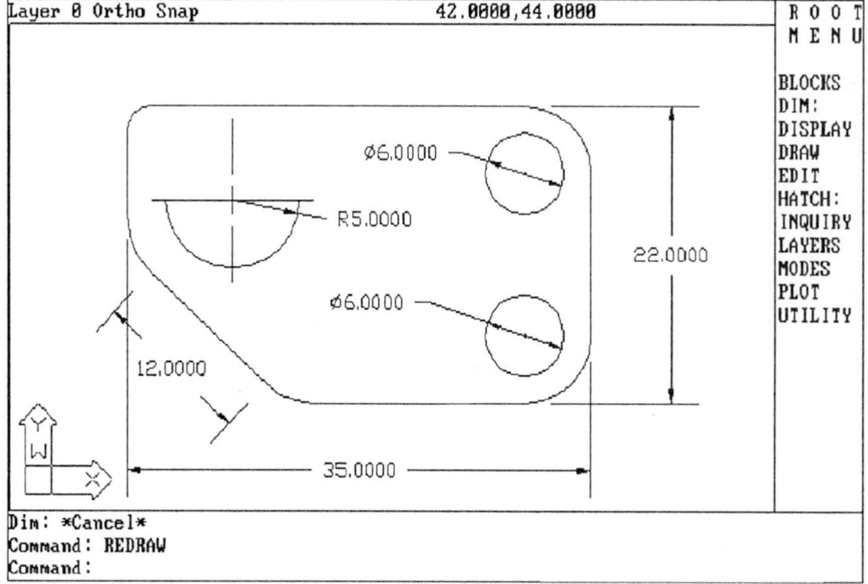

Figure 5-8. Radius dimension using center lines

After you have set the center line option, you create the actual radius dimension by entering the following:

```
Dim: rad
Select arc or circle:
Dimension text <5.0000>:
Text does not fit.
Enter leader length for text:
```

After your last response, the radius dimension will be drawn.

Creating Center Lines

The 5.0000 unit radius in Figure 5-8 was created with center lines. The center lines were automatically drawn when the radius dimension was drawn. In order to do this, the DIMCEN variable was used to invoke full center lines. A negative value was entered:

```
Command: dim
Dim: DIMCEN
New value: -1
Current value <0.0180>
```

By entering a negative number, you are stating that you want full center lines to be used. In this case, the size of the center mark was set at 1 unit, with full center lines extended.

Creating Center Marks

If you do not want full center lines, you can use a positive number for the DIMCEN variable. You would then only see a center mark of the specified size instead of full center lines.

Customizing Arrows and Tick Marks

With AutoCAD, you have full control over the appearance of your dimensions. The default is to use arrows that are predefined by AutoCAD but this setting can be changed. If you set the DIMTSZ variable to a non-zero value, you will set the tick size. Then, when you subsequently use dimensioning subcommands, tick marks will appear instead of arrows.

You can go beyond this change, however, if you want to use other symbols (defined as blocks) in place of arrows or tick marks. With the DIMBLK system variable, you can customize the symbols you use in dimensioning so they will be different from the standard arrowheads or tick marks.

One predefined block is available to you when you set the DIMBLK variable. If you use the name DOT, AutoCAD will create a DOT block for you. See Figure 5-9*a* for a simple drawing in which dots rather than tick marks identify the endpoints of dimension lines. In order to generate the drawing, the DIMBLK variable was first set.

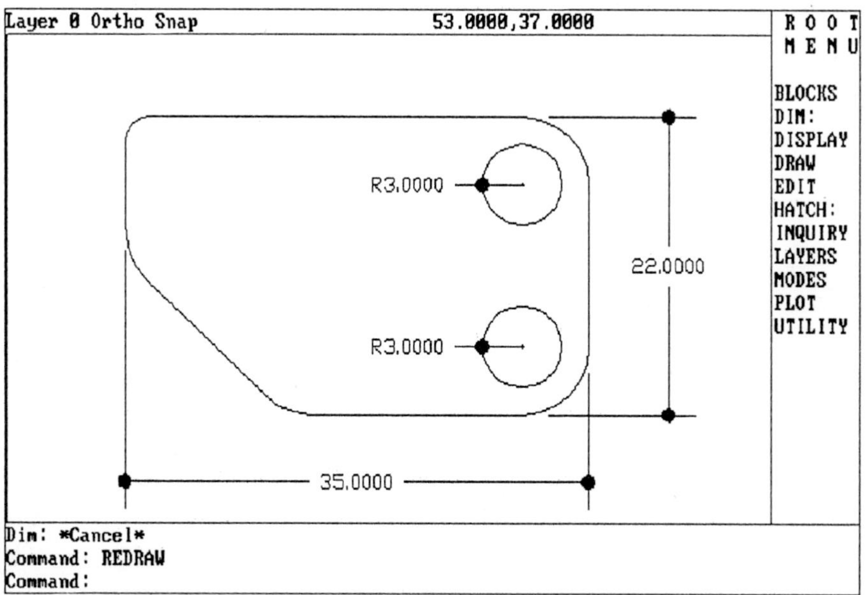

Figure 5-9*a*. Dots used instead of tick marks

If you use a block name other than DOT, and that block exists either in the drawing or on disk, that block will be used instead of arrows or tick marks.

Figure 5-9*b* shows the same drawing as in Figure 5-9*a*, but with a custom block set with the DIMBLK variable. This block now shows up at all ends of dimension lines.

Dimensioning Angles

You can express angular dimensions as well as diameter and radial dimensions. Angular dimensioning involves the use of an arc instead of a straight line for the dimension line.

Figure 5-10 shows a simple angular dimension. It was created by entering the following command sequence:

Command: **dim**
Dim: **ang**

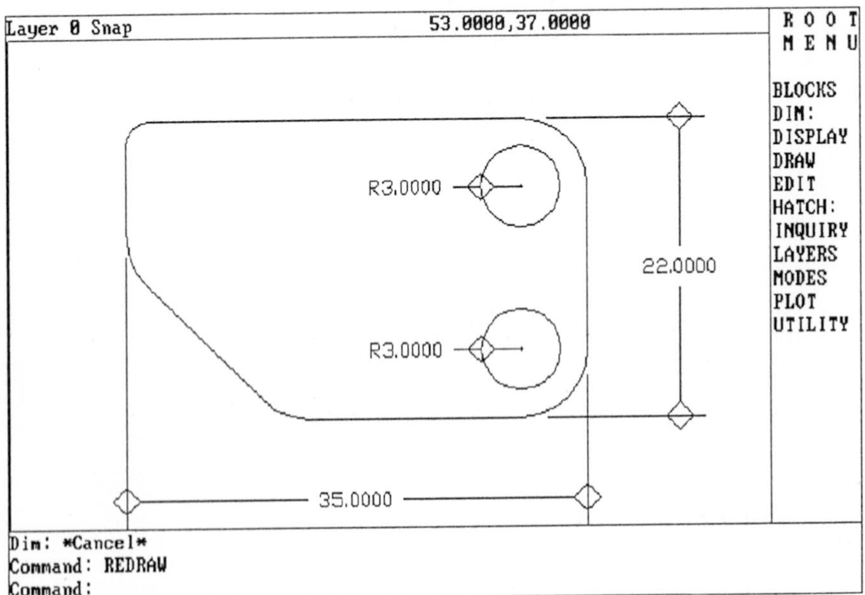

Figure 5-9*b*. A custom block used as an arrow

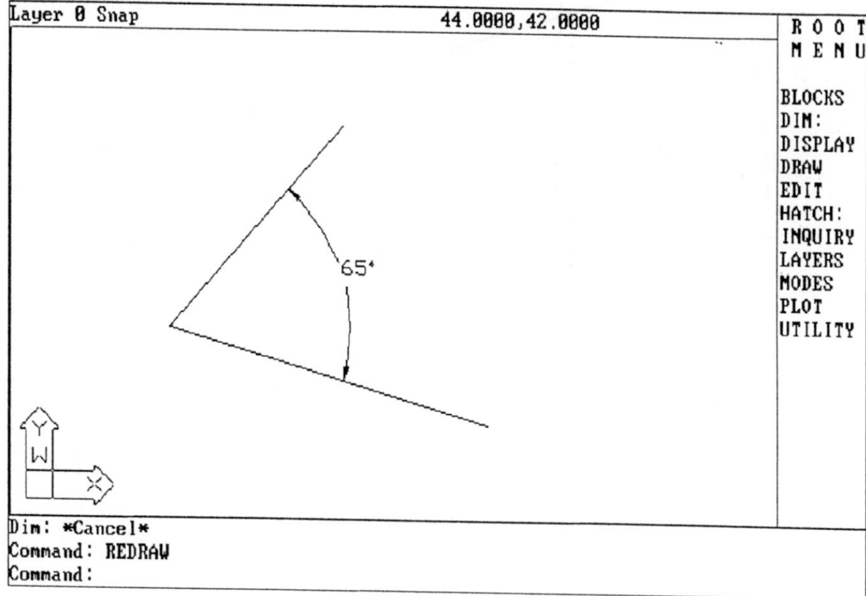

Figure 5-10. A simple angular dimension

Select first line: Second line:
Enter dimension line arc location:
Dimension text <65>:
Enter text location:

After you select the text location, you will see the finished angular dimension. Note that if you pick the same point for the dimension text as the point for the location of the dimension line, the text will be included in that line. The dimension line will be broken to admit the text. If, however, you select a point off of the dimension line for the text, the text will be placed there. The dimension line will then be unbroken.

Rotating Dimensions

So far you have seen how dimensions can be drawn horizontally and vertically, and aligned with entities. Most of your dimensioning needs will be satisfied with these techniques. Under some circumstances, however, you may wish to dimension a measured distance that is not horizontal, vertical, or aligned.

Look at Figure 5-11 for a fictional machine part with three bolt holes in it. The goal of dimensioning this part is to express the clearance between the centers of the three holes. Horizontal dimensioning won't work because the clearance is not horizontally oriented. Likewise, vertical dimensioning is inappropriate. You can't use aligned dimensioning because the distance does not align with anything. You can show the distance, however, with rotating dimensions.

You produce rotated dimensions by using the following command sequence:

Command: **dim**
Dim: **rot**
Dimension line angle <0>:
First extension line origin or RETURN to select:
Second extension line origin:
Dimension text <default>:

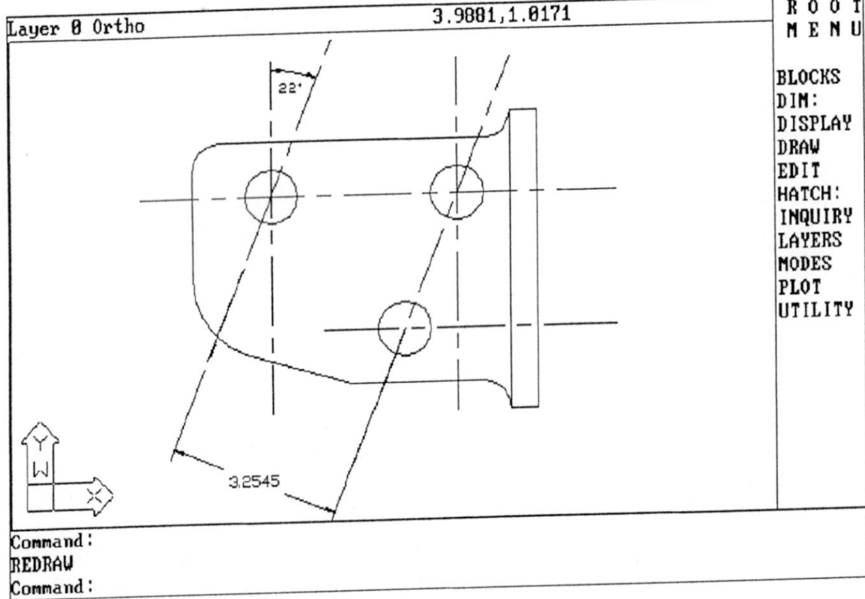

Figure 5-11. Rotating dimensions

The rotation angle of the dimension line is set to the angle made by two of the bolt holes to the vertical. The resulting dimension is the measured distance between two of the bolt holes and the third.

To rotate the dimension to the correct angle, 158 degrees was used as a response to the "Dimension line angle <0>:" prompt. The angle to the vertical is 22 degrees, as can be seen in the drawing. Subtracting 22 degrees from 180 degrees gives the desired rotation angle of 158 degrees. Remember, angles are expressed as counterclockwise unless you use the UNITS command to specify the clockwise sense of rotation.

Continuing

Very often you will need to express *strings* of dimensions rather than single dimensions. For example, a series of wall centers in a building design may need to be expressed one after the other. You do not need to reenter the HORIZONTAL command repeatedly to show this "string" of dimensions. Instead, you can indicate to AutoCAD that you wish to continue from one dimension line to the next.

Figure 5-12 shows dimensions put together into a continuous string. You start the string of dimensions by using the VERTICAL, HORIZONTAL, ROTATED, or ALIGNED dimensioning subcommands. When you want to continue after you have entered the first dimension, you enter the CONTINUE subcommand as follows:

Dim: **continue**
Second extension line origin:

Continuing can only be done with the DIM option—it will not work with DIM1. You can abbreviate the word "continue" as "con."

Of course, as with other AutoCAD commands, you can repeat the CONTINUE command by pressing the ENTER key or the enter button on your pointing device.

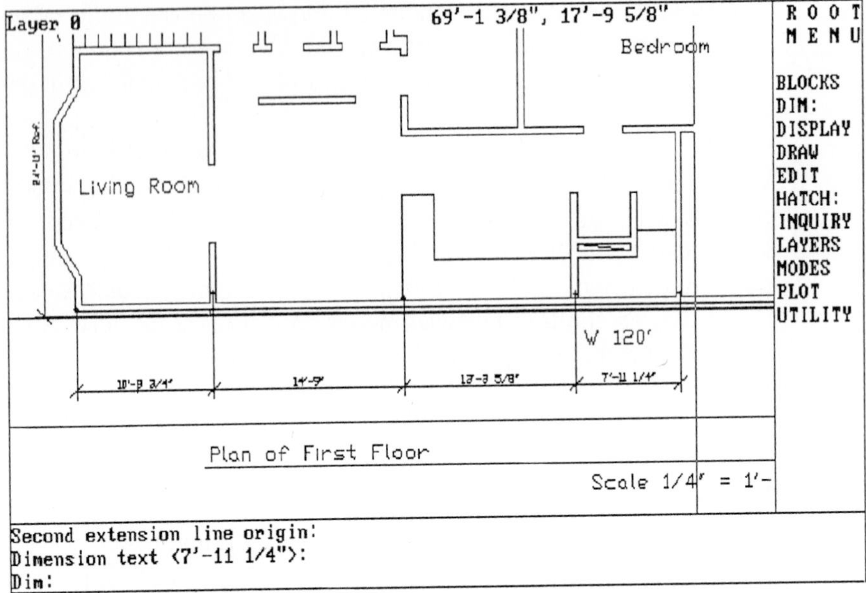

Figure 5-12. A continuous dimension string

Dimensioning by Base Line

The dimension string shown in Figure 5-12 uses center line locations for walls. The dimension string is drawn the way you would usually expect to find it (more or less) in a typical building plan.

Figure 5-13 shows the same plan as in Figure 5-12, but instead of showing a continuous string of dimensions, each wall center is called out by its own dimension. The BASELINE command was used to repeat the dimensions, but all of the dimensions were taken from the first point. The BASELINE command performs in much the same way as the CONTINUE command, except that separate dimensions are created, offset by a specified distance and referenced to a single starting point. When you enter the command, you can abbreviate "baseline" as "bas."

In order to use the BASELINE command, you must set the DIMDLI system variable to the desired value of the dimension line offset distance. In Figure 5-13, the break distance is two feet.

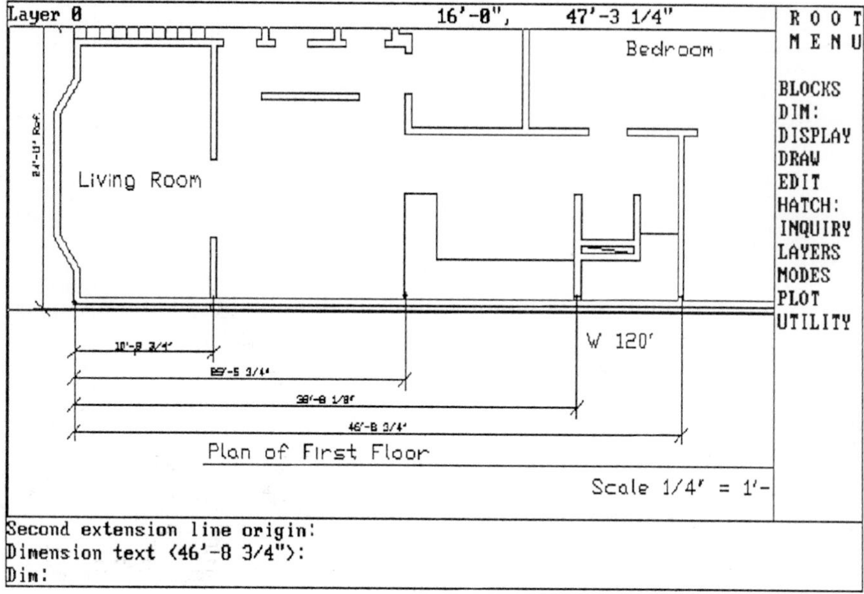

Figure 5-13. Dimensions by base line

Drawing Leaders

You can use a leader to draw text notes and to indicate what part of your drawing the text is intended to describe. As discussed earlier in this chapter, a leader is a line that has an arrow or tick mark on the end that points to the part of the drawing to be identified. Leaders are used so often in drawings that AutoCAD has a command, the LEADER command, for drawing them.

Look at Figure 5-14 for a leader that has been added to a text description. You use the following command sequence to enter the leader:

Command: **dim**
Dim: **leader**
Leader start:
To point:
To point:
Dimension text <3>: ***Cancel***

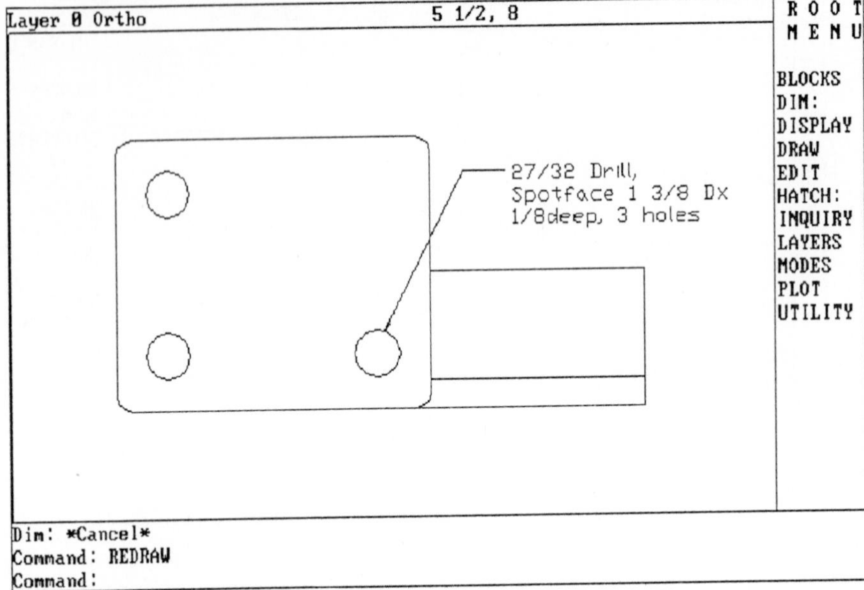

Figure 5-14. Adding a leader and text

You must cancel the "Dimension text <3>:" prompt if you want to supply several rows of text; otherwise, you can enter text immediately. In this case, the note consists of several lines of text, so the text was added by exiting from the DIM command level and by using DTEXT.

Text for Dimensioning

The text used in dimensioning is the same text used for the TEXT or DTEXT commands. The currently defined size, font, and other parameters are used to draw dimension text. Dimensions, however, are drawn with more options than you have with other commands that draw text.

When you have located your dimension line in response to any of the dimensioning subcommands, you will be prompted for the "Dimension text <default>:". You can change the text at this time or you can use the default by entering an empty command line.

If you want to change the text, you have several options. You can accept the default value and prefix or append to it. Think of the default as symbolized by the <> pair of characters. If you enter a response to the "Dimension text <default>:" prompt that includes the <> characters, the default will be substituted for them. For example, you could use a default of 3′ 5 3/4″ by prefixing "Make this" and postfixing "approximately." If you were to enter "Make this <> approximately." the result would be "Make this 3′ 5 3/4″ approximately."

Postfixing by Variable

The system variable DIMPOST enables you to automatically add a standard string expression to the end of your dimension. You could, for example, add the word "inches" to all instances of linear dimensions. Read about the use of the DIMPOST variable under the DIM command in Chapter 16, "AutoCAD Command Reference."

Dimensioning Tolerances

You can add standard tolerance specifications to your dimensions. In machine tool engineering, for example, you often need to express the tolerances required for fabrication of a part. It would be a chore to add such tolerances repeatedly, so AutoCAD provides you with an automatic way to do it.

Set the DIMTOL variable *on* and the DIMTP and/or DIMTM variables to the greatest and least tolerances you require. For example, the following command sequence sets DIMTOL, DIMTP, and DIMTM:

Command: **dim**
Dim: **dimtol** Current value <Off> New value: **on**
Dim: **dimtp** Current value <0> New value: **.01**
Dim: **dimtm** Current value <0> New value: **.03**

The effect of these settings is to produce a dimension string like the one in Figure 5-15. The dimension shown in this drawing

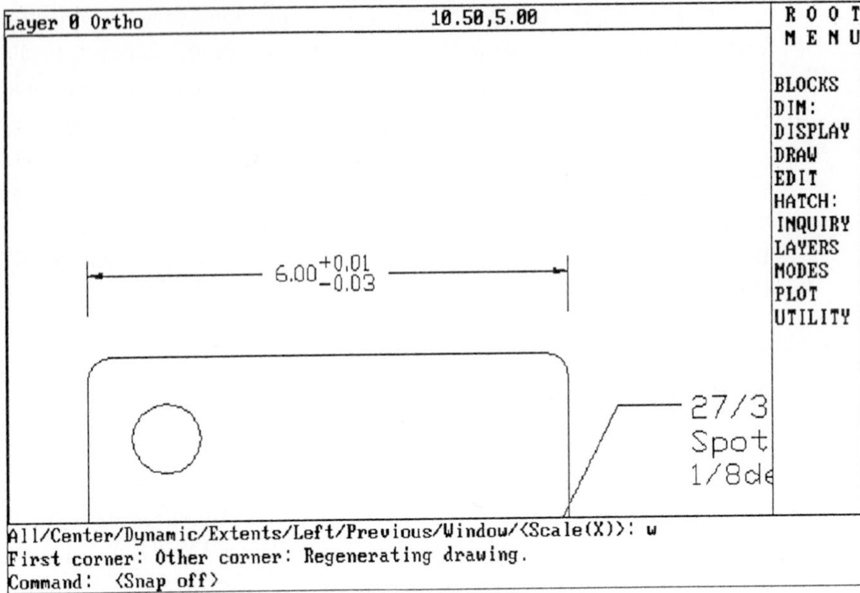

Figure 5-15. Dimensioning with tolerances

expresses the standard tolerances specified in the command sequence.

Using Alternate Units

Increasingly, as the world tries to standardize dimensional systems, you will need to express dimensions using feet-inches and metric notations. AutoCAD facilitates the creation of dimensions that have alternate units by providing the DIMALT, DIMALTF, and DIMALTD variables. See Chapter 16, "AutoCAD Command Reference," for details regarding these variables.

You can set AutoCAD to produce both feet-inches and metric dimensions with the following command sequence:

Command: **dim**
Dim: **dimalt** Current value <Off> New value: **on**
Dim: **dimaltf** Current value <25.4000> New value:
Dim: **dimaltd** Current value <2> New value:

The DIMALTF variable stores a value that is used as a multiplier to derive the alternate dimension. In this case (the default), you will convert from inches to millimeters. The DIMALTD variable stores the number of decimal places for the conversion. In this example, the default of two decimal places will be used.

The result of using alternate dimensioning on a typical drawing is shown in Figure 5-16. This is the same drawing as in Figure 5-15, but alternate units are now expressed *in addition* to tolerances. Note that the tolerances are also converted to millimeters. Of course, if you turn DIMTOL *off,* you will see only the original and alternate units.

Modifying Dimensions

When you make changes to a manually drafted drawing, you must often spend hours re-computing the various dimensions in

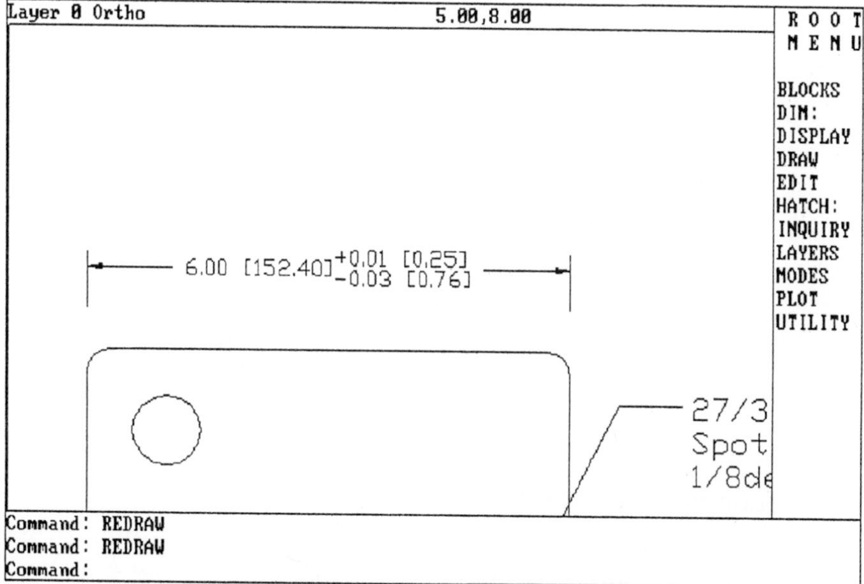

Figure 5-16. Alternate dimensioning plus tolerances

the drawing. The usual practice is to label dimensions "N.T.S." (not to scale) to identify dimensions that have changed where the drawing itself could not be changed conveniently. This practice is fraught with danger. Just changing dimensions may not be enough. The change in dimensions may have implications in the design that have not been dealt with in the drawing. Errors happen. Projects fail.

AutoCAD has been designed to make dimension changes quite easy. When you change a drawing, the dimensions can be updated automatically.

Although under most circumstances, this associative dimensioning is far superior to manual dimensioning, you should have a healthy respect for anything "automatic." If you don't check your dimension strings after updating them, you leave yourself open to unpredicted side-effects. The fact that things can be done automatically does not relieve you of the responsibility to check what the computer has done.

Associative Dimensioning

Most of the dimensioning entities you can create with AutoCAD are associative. The dimension entities "associate" with the objects they dimension. By association, they can be updated to reflect changes in the objects.

With *associative dimensioning,* you can automatically revise your dimension callouts when the design changes. Associative dimensioning is the linking of the contents of dimension callouts to the angular and distance properties of the entities you call out. When the entity's properties change, the dimensions can be automatically updated by reference to those properties.

Editing Associatively

When you identify objects to dimension associatively, you use *definition points.* Definition points are points you pick on lines, angles, circles, and arcs that define the extents of dimensions to be associated with these entities.

Dimension entities in AutoCAD are automatically associative. All you need to do is pick the dimension entities as well as the objects you wish to edit, and the dimensions as well as the objects will be modified.

See the AutoCAD Reference Manual for current editing commands supported by associative dimensioning. Chapter 16 of this book, "AutoCAD Command Reference," also contains information on associative dimensioning.

Trimming Dimensions

A good way to show how trimming works is to create a drawing and edit it. See Chapter 3, "Editing," for more information on editing drawings.

Figure 5-17*a* shows a room plan that is part of an architectural drawing. Figures 5-17*b* through 5-17*d* show the same room during the trimming operation for one wall. Note that the associated dimension entity is picked along with the wall object. After trimming, the dimension has been redrawn to show the change.

Extending Dimensions

See Figures 5-18*a* through 5-18*d* for an "animated" sequence of commands required to extend a wall in an architectural drawing. You can see how the EXTEND command is used by observing the command line in action. Note that the associated dimension entity must be selected here, as it was in the preceding trim operation.

Stretching Dimensions

Stretching involves the selection of objects by crossing. Read about stretching in Chapter 3, "Editing," and see the section on the STRETCH command in Chapter 16, "AutoCAD Command Reference."

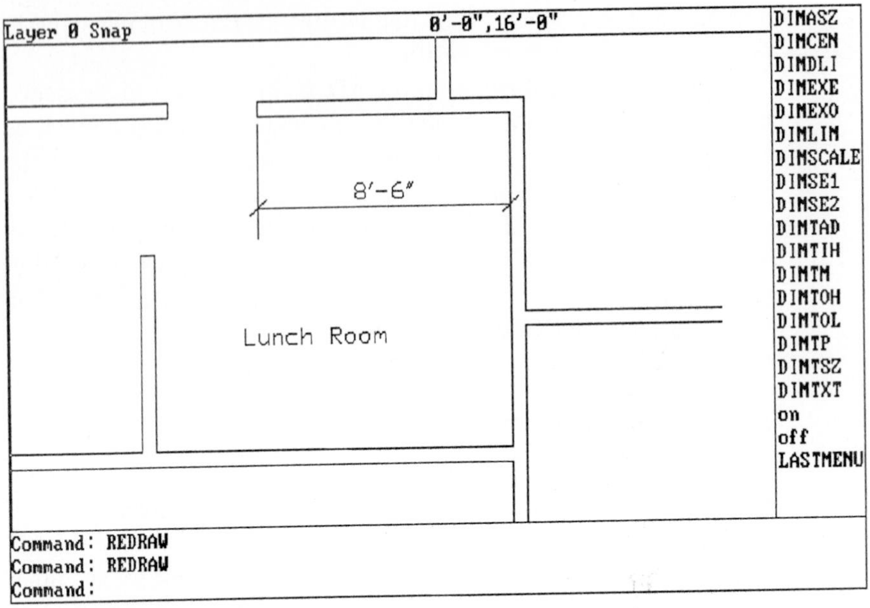

Figure 5-17*a*. The original drawing for trimming

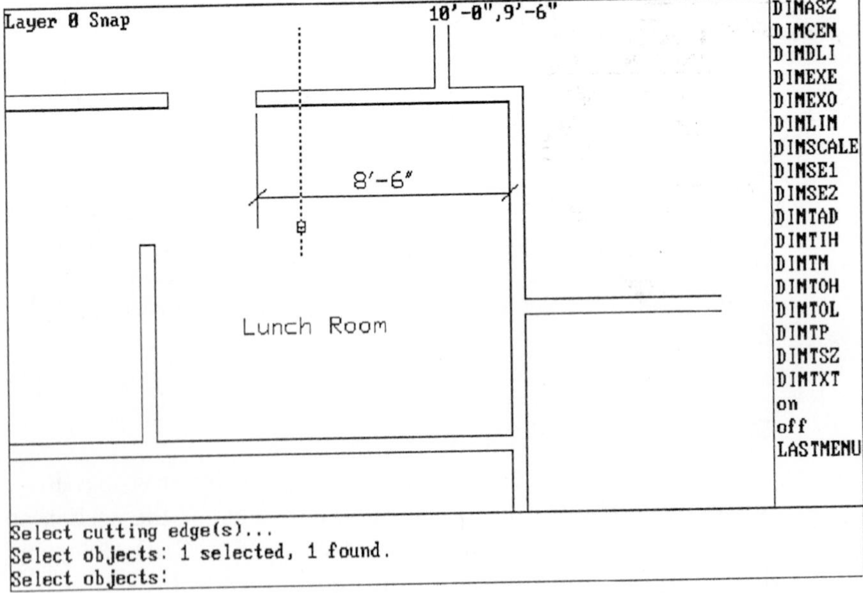

Figure 5-17*b*. Selecting the trim line

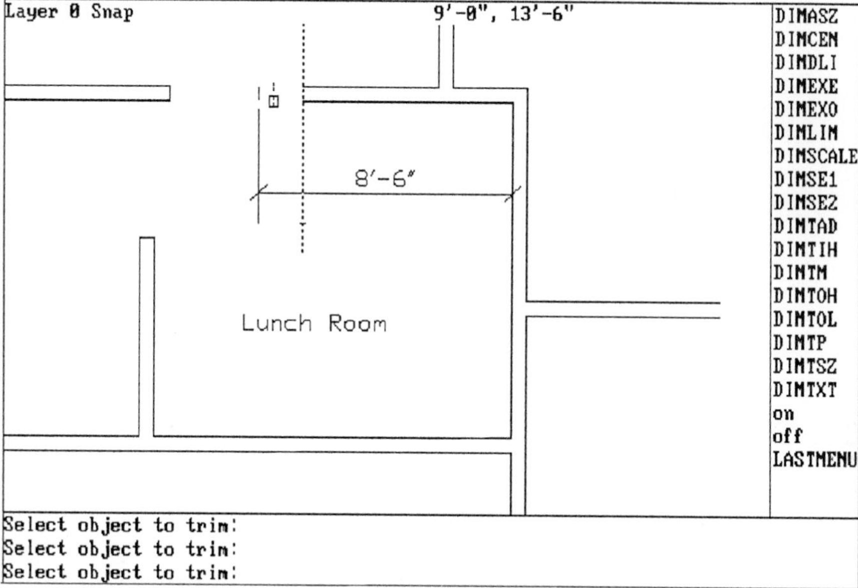

Figure 5-17*c*. Selecting objects to trim

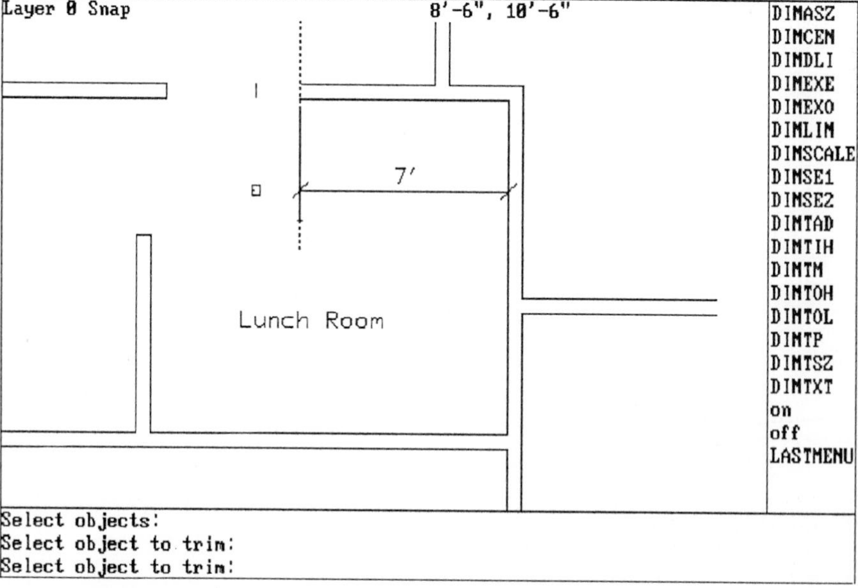

Figure 5-17*d*. The finished trim, including dimension

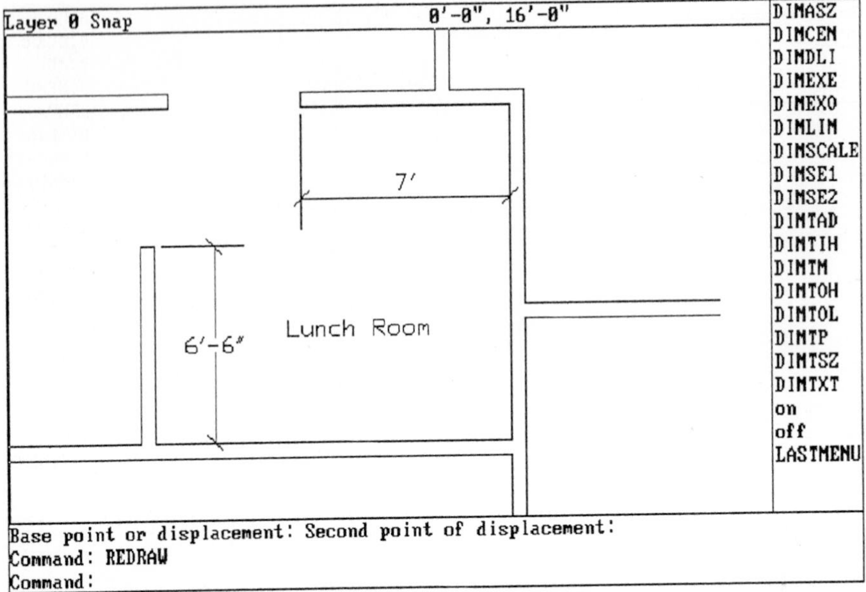

Figure 5-18*a*. The original drawing for extending

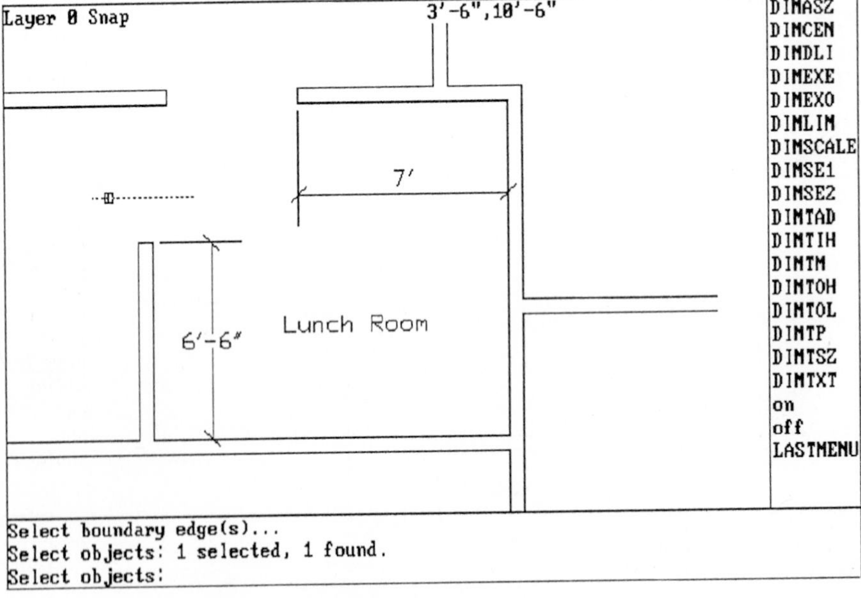

Figure 5-18*b*. Selecting the extend boundary

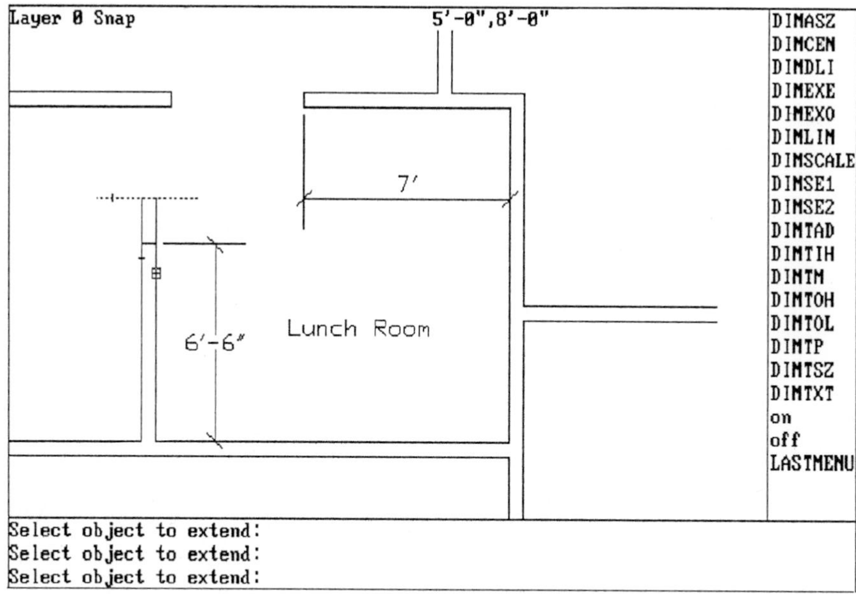

Figure 5-18*c*. Selecting objects to extend

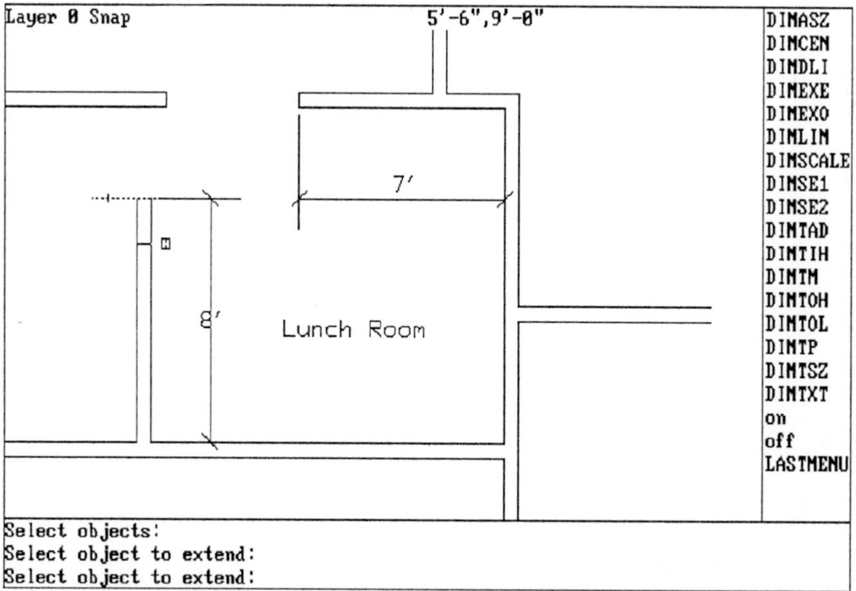

Figure 5-18*d*. The finished extension, including dimension

Figures 5-19*a* through 5-19*d* show the process involved in stretching wall lines to move a wall opening.

Updating Dimensions

You may want to change dimensioning variables during the creation of a drawing. If you do change variables, any new dimensions you create will use the new variables. But what about the dimensions you have already drawn?

AutoCAD provides a command, the UPDATE subcommand, that enables you to update your existing dimensions to use the new variable settings. To use UPDATE, you must have executed the DIM command. UPDATE must be entered at "Dim:", rather than "Command:". Figure 5-20 shows an architectural drawing that was dimensioned and updated with the UPDATE subcommand.

Setting Dimension Variables

You can control the general ways of expressing dimensions by setting certain systemwide (or global) variables. The actual string of characters that contains the dimension distance or angle can be placed in many different positions with respect to the dimension line. Although there are standards that govern all forms of drafting, you need flexibility in placing dimension strings. In some disciplines, the dimension string will be placed above the dimension line. In others, the string will be placed "within" the dimension line, interrupting it. Sometimes dimension strings are required to be horizontal; yet at other times the dimension strings must follow the same angle as the dimension line.

Using Variables With Dimensioning

You have already seen variables used in creating dimensions, such as the DIMTOL, DIMPOST, and other variables. There are many more variables you can use to customize the appearance of dimensions for specific applications. See Chapter 16, "AutoCAD Command Reference," for a complete list of dimensioning variables. An interesting project would be to create a special menu system to handle the setting of these variables since it is particularly time consuming to type the variable names. With the AutoCAD standard menu, you can select the variables you wish to change.

Dimensioning a Simple Drawing

After you have drawn an object with AutoCAD, you will have defined it entirely in terms of AutoCAD's World Coordinate System. This means that the distances used are usually the exact measurements that would describe the object in the real world. Fifteen feet, three and one-half inches in AutoCAD's drawing space is exactly fifteen feet, three and one-half inches in the real world.

When you make a drawing using AutoCAD, you must think in terms of real world dimensions, not the dimensions of architectural or engineering scales. Your dimensions in AutoCAD will be very large. For instance, where you would draw a line 3 inches long on a piece of paper to express a dimension of 30 feet, in AutoCAD that line would be 30 feet long. Thus, text used in a drawing might be 1 foot high. Keep this in mind as you prepare dimensions in AutoCAD. The simple drawing in Figure 5-21 shows a machine-like object that will be dimensioned in several different ways with AutoCAD's dimensioning capabilities.

Adding Horizontal Dimensions

A horizontal straight line dimension will be the first dimension string that you will add to the drawing. Working from the sidebar menu, you can select the DIM menu item. You will then see some of the dimension choices available to you. The one to use for this example is LINEAR.

Layer 0 Snap 0'-0",16'-0"
DIMASZ
DIMCEN
DIMDLI
DIMEXE
DIMEXO
DIMLIM
DIMSCALE
DIMSE1
DIMSE2
DIMTAD
DIMTIH
DIMTM
DIMTOH
DIMTOL
DIMTP
DIMTSZ
DIMTXT
on
off
LASTMENU
5'-6"
4'-6"
7'
8'
Lunch Room
Command: REDRAW
Command: REDRAW
Command:

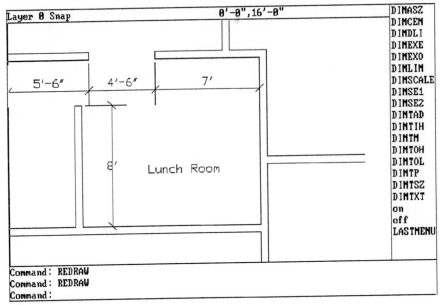

Figure 5-19*a*. The original drawing for stretching

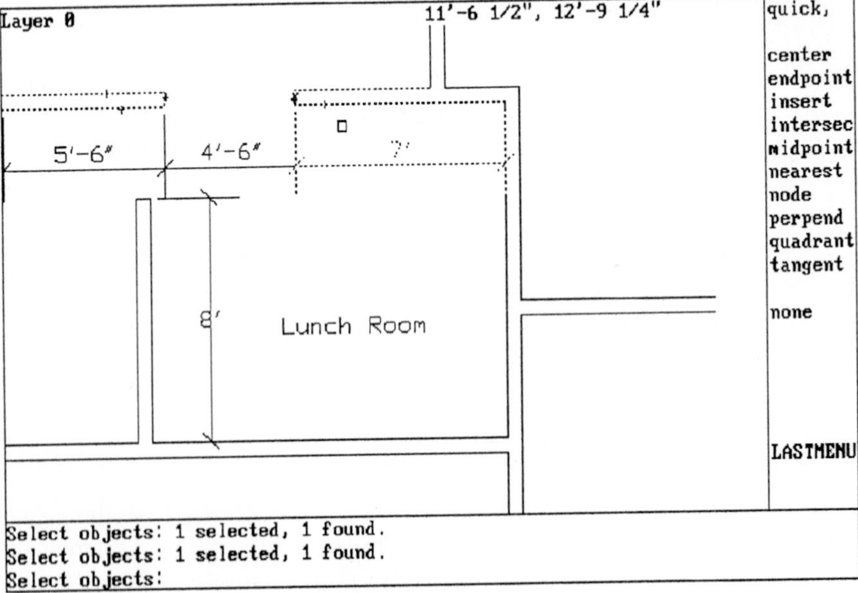

Figure 5-19*b*. Selecting objects to stretch

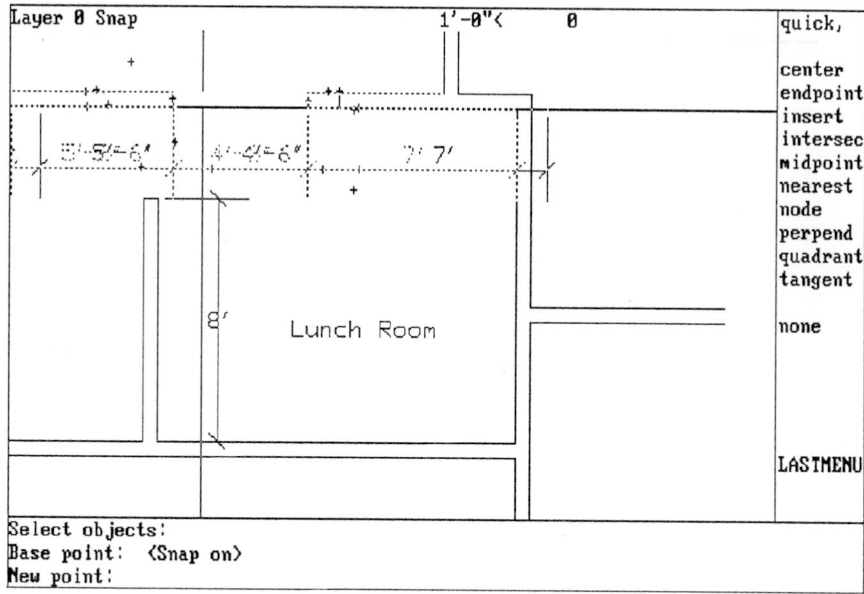

Figure 5-19*c*. Selecting dimensions to stretch

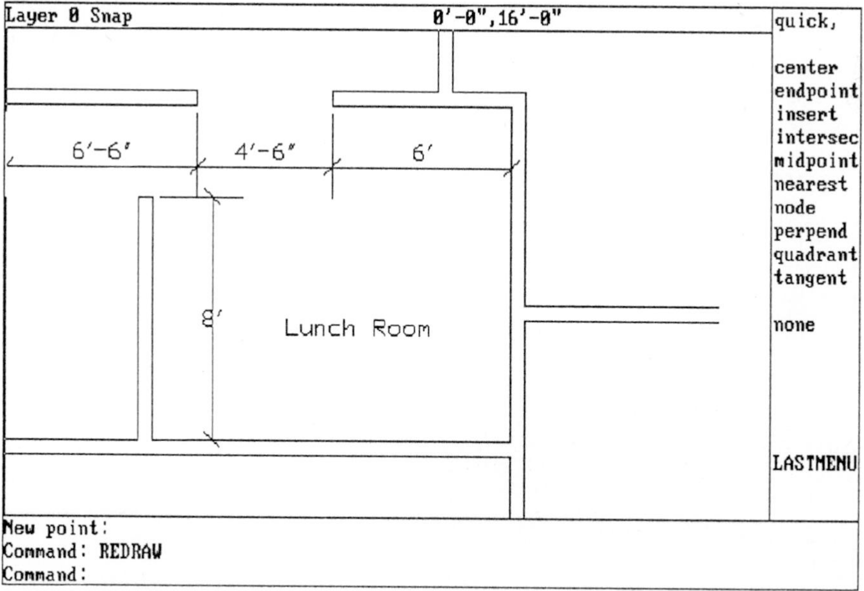

Figure 5-19*d*. The finished stretch, including dimension

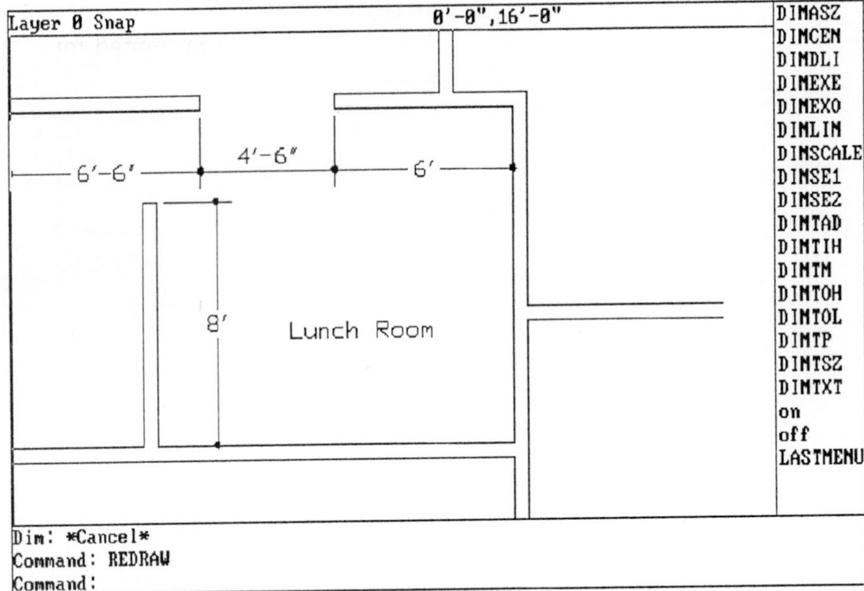

Figure 5-20. A drawing with updated dimensions

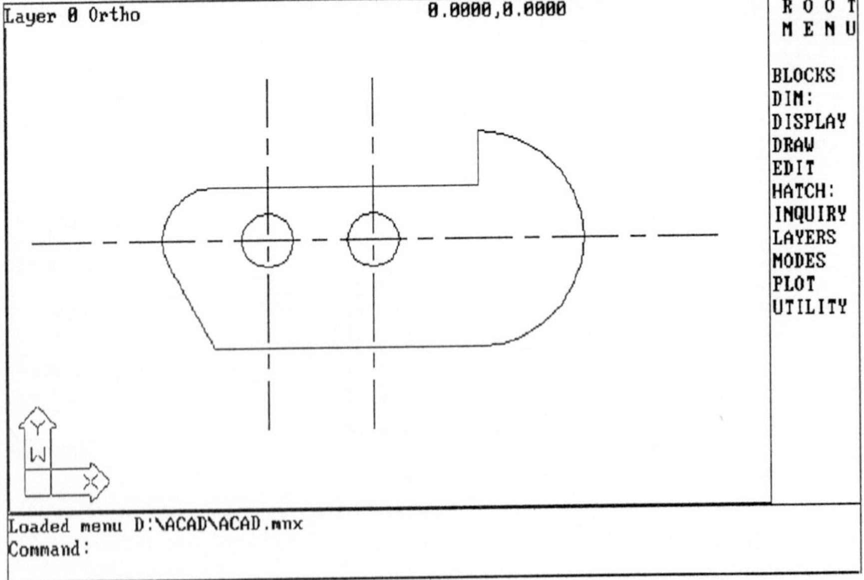

Figure 5-21. A machine-like object that will be dimensioned

When you select LINEAR, you will see a series of sub-options. If you then select HORIZ, you will be prompted for the "First extension line origin or RETURN to select:". Although this prompt seems cryptic at first, it is really asking you to choose between two options. You can either pick an origin for the extension line directly from the display, or you can press ENTER and select an entire entity that will be measured automatically. In this case, press ENTER to enable you to select an object. Select the horizontal line shown in Figure 5-22.

Note that you must keep your selection to a line, arc, or circle. Other entities cannot be directly dimensioned with this technique. In special circumstances, you can always select extension line origins rather than objects.

Selecting Dimension Line Location

When you have selected the object to dimension, you will be prompted for the "Dimension line location:". You respond to this prompt by picking a location through which you want the dimension line itself to pass. In this case, the dimension line will be horizontal and above the object.

Entering Dimension Text

After you pick the dimension line location, you will be prompted for the "Dimension text <5.0000>:". This prompt gives you the default measurement of the line. You can enter this or you can enter a new string. See Chapter 16, "AutoCAD Command Reference," as well as the AutoCAD Reference Manual for the many options you have for the text that you enter on this line. Global variables that govern the expression of dimension text can also be changed.

See Figure 5-23 for the finished dimension string. Note that there are arrowheads at the ends of the dimension line and that the dimension text is located within, rather than above or below, the dimension line.

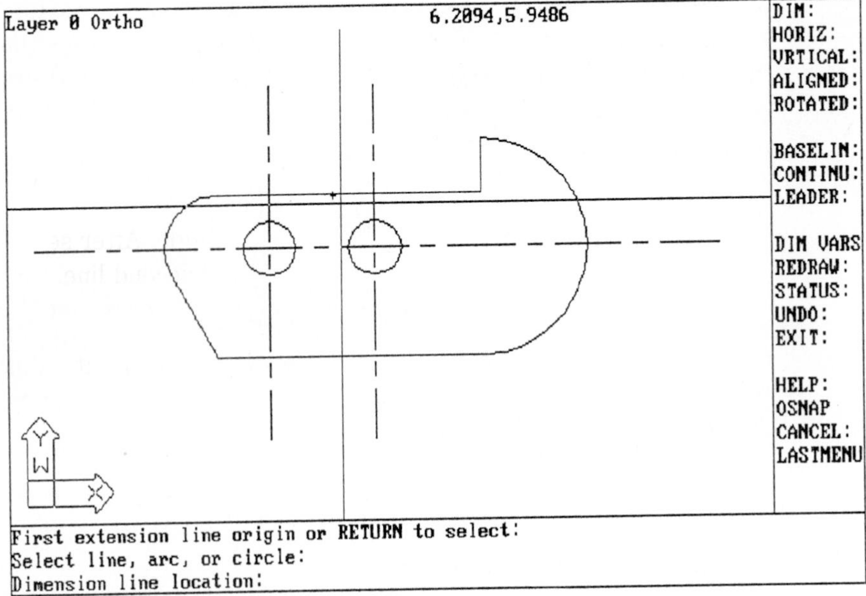

Figure 5-22. Selecting an object to dimension

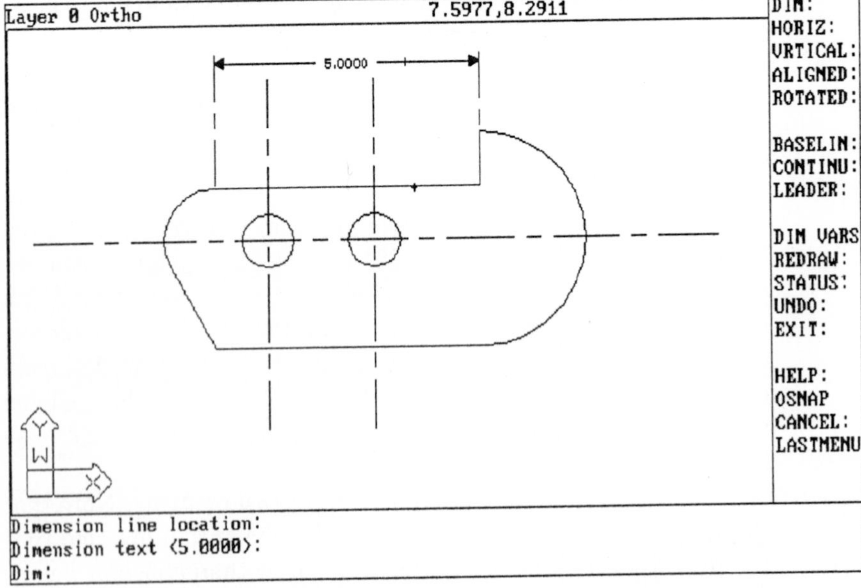

Figure 5-23. The finished horizontal dimension string

Adding Angular Dimensions

In addition to horizontal dimension strings, you can create vertical, aligned, and rotated dimension strings of the linear type. You can also create angular dimensions.

To create an angular dimension, select ANGULAR from the sidebar menu. You will be prompted to "Select first line:". Respond by picking the first line that forms the angle. After selecting the first line, you will be asked to select the second line, then the dimension line arc location. After you select the dimension line arc location, you will be prompted for the "Dimension text <120>:", which expresses the default value AutoCAD has computed from the angle subtended by the two lines. You can press ENTER at this time to accept the dimension angle as expressed, or you can enter your own string.

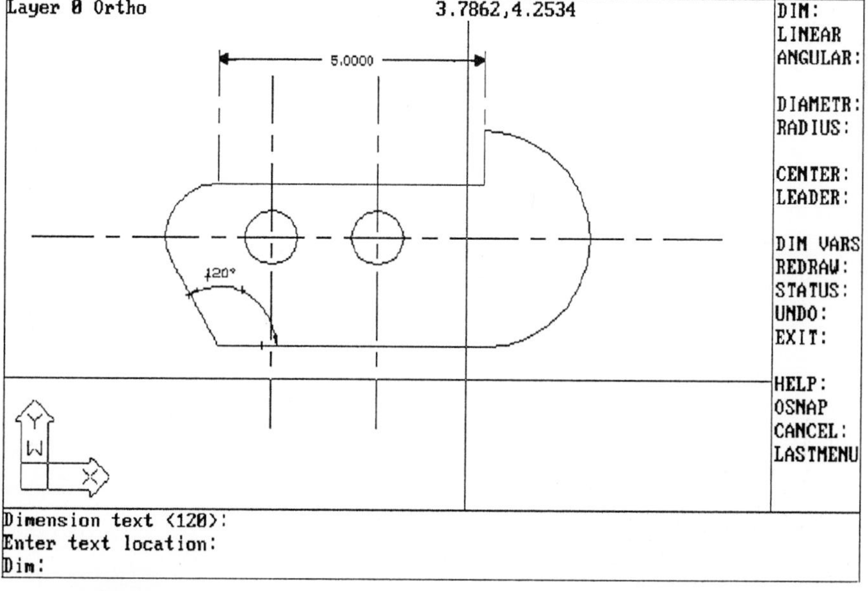

Figure 5-24. The finished angular dimension callout

Locating the Dimension Angle

After you have responded to the preceding series of prompts, you will be asked to show where you want the dimension angle itself. Respond to this prompt by picking the location you desire. See Figure 5-24 for the finished angular dimension callout.

You now have a start in using AutoCAD's powerful dimensioning capabilities. To study the AutoCAD DIM command subset in more detail, refer to Chapter 16, "AutoCAD Command Reference."

Crosshatching Techniques

Working with the HATCH Command
Making Your Own Crosshatch Patterns
Hatching a Typical Drawing

SIX

Crosshatching patterns are often used in drawings to symbolize materials and other features. Architectural drawings use crosshatching to show finishes, solid areas, translucency, and transparency. Crosshatching symbolizes steel, aluminum, and other materials in structural engineering drawings. Cartographers use crosshatching and *pattern filling* to show marshes, woodlands, rivers, and other land features.

Both crosshatching and filling are ways of covering areas with lines. Filling, by contrast, is the technique used to fill an object in solidly. Crosshatching is performed with the HATCH command. Filling can be done with either TRACE or PLINE (see Chapter 2, "Drawing," for information on filling with these commands).

Manual crosshatching can be extremely tedious since you must draw many lines across areas, being careful to match line endpoints with intersections. Fortunately, crosshatching is an activity that a computer can do very well. AutoCAD provides a variety of well-implemented crosshatching mechanisms. It is possible not only to draw lines that crosshatch areas, but also to draw repetitive symbols across areas. Where the symbols meet lines that define the area boundaries, they are clipped just as though they were applied and cut with a knife. You can design your own symbols for pattern fills or you can choose from a library of such symbols provided by AutoCAD.

This chapter will show you how to use AutoCAD's powerful crosshatching and pattern filling capabilities. Throw away your matte knife and forget about drawing line after line after line. Sit back and watch AutoCAD do it for you.

Working with the HATCH Command

There are two keys to understanding the HATCH command. The first key is the *boundary* and the second is the *hatch pattern.* If you fully understand how hatch patterns work and how to define "legal" boundaries, you will find crosshatching very easy. Most mistakes in crosshatching come from misunderstanding how boundaries are defined and used.

Creating Boundaries

The drawing shown in Figure 6-1 was supposed to be partially filled. The user wanted to contain the crosshatching within the left side of the figure, without affecting the right side of the figure, the circle, or the line trailing off to the left. Instead, the crosshatching went outside of the boundaries intended by the user. The wrong lines were selected and the hatching pattern (in this case, an AutoCAD pattern named ESCHER) was drawn incorrectly. Note that it was crosshatched incorrectly only in terms of what the user expected, not according to AutoCAD's rules. AutoCAD "thinks" the drawing in Figure 6-1 looks just fine.

If you are to use the HATCH command effectively, you must first understand that disasters such as the one in Figure 6-1 are easy to create. Avoiding them is your responsibility because AutoCAD cannot read your mind to know what you intended to do. All AutoCAD knows is which objects you selected and how those objects were *strictly* defined.

Selecting Boundaries

Drawing correct boundaries means that you must draw "closed" figures. That is, you must begin and end the series of lines that

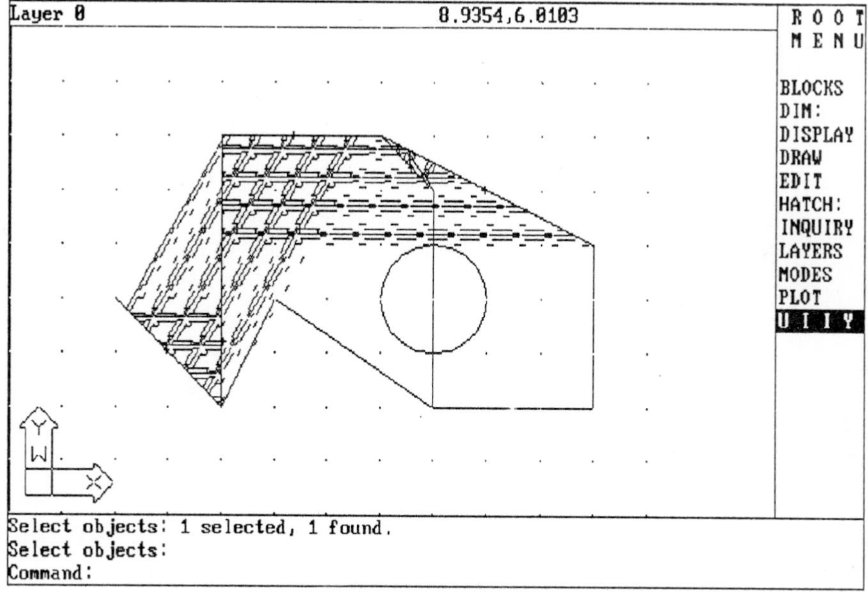

Figure 6-1. A crosshatch "monster"—the wrong way

define your boundaries at the same points. If you do not do this, the hatching pattern will "leak" through the gaps or will leave open spaces.

In addition to drawing closed boundaries, you must accurately select the boundaries when you use the HATCH command. AutoCAD, in its reference manual, recommends that you select boundaries by using windows. This way you will be sure to select all of the parts of the object you wish to crosshatch. If you select with windows, you have access to three basic hatching styles that enable you to determine how the window-selected objects will be crosshatched.

Entering the HATCH Command

To do the crosshatching correctly in the drawing in Figure 6-1, you would enter the HATCH command as follows:

Command: **hatch**
Pattern (? or name/U,style) <ESCHER>: **escher,o**

<0.5000>:
Scale for pattern
Angle for pattern <0>:
Select objects:

The "o" (for "outermost") has been entered after "escher" in order to produce the results shown in Figure 6-2. The "N," "O," and "I" options are explained in the next section, "Hatching Within Boundaries." When you select your objects, choose the ones shown in Figure 6-2. Note that the "circle" is really two arcs placed side by side. The "line" that bisects the "circle" is really three line segments.

Sometimes you must change the way you draw in order to accommodate the HATCH command, but there is usually a way to put the parts together so you get the desired effect. Circles

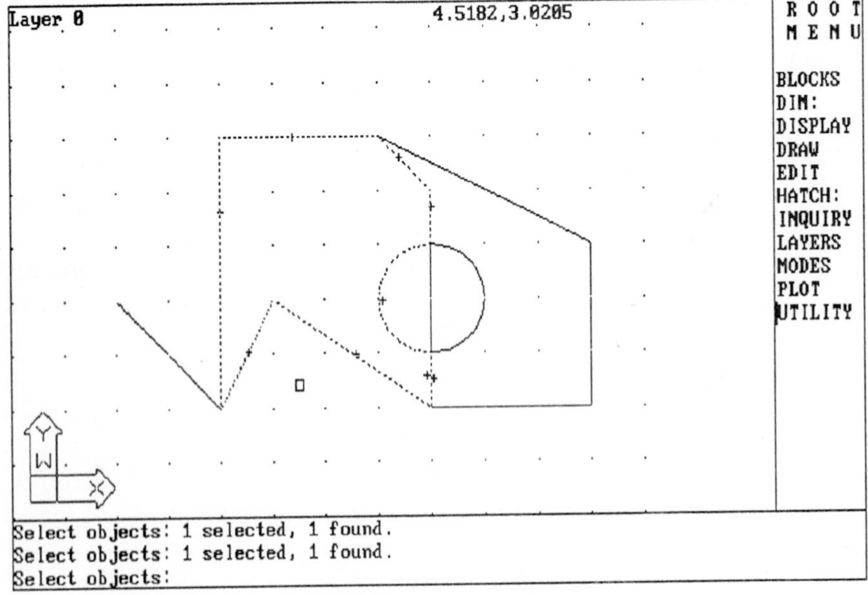

Figure 6-2. Choosing the correct boundary

can always be made up of arc segments. Lines can always be redrawn in segments. Count on experimenting until you know the rules.

Figure 6-3 shows the finished hatching exercise. The desired result has been achieved and now the design makes sense, even though it is still only a random set of lines and arcs. As long as you create boundaries that work, you can crosshatch almost anything.

Hatching Within Boundaries

The HATCH command has a few simple options. If you enter the HATCH command and a question mark, you will see the

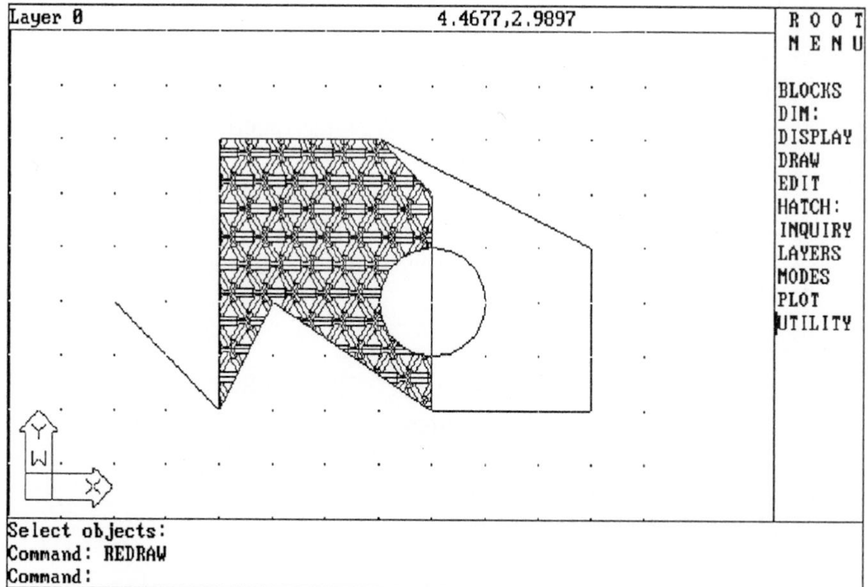

Figure 6-3. The finished crosshatch

large collection of hatch patterns contained in AutoCAD's ACAD.PAT file.

If you enter the HATCH command and the name of a valid hatch pattern (like the name ESCHER above), you can use that pattern for hatching. The prompt "Pattern (? or name/U,style) <ESCHER,O>:" shown in the preceding command sequence tells the story. The hatch pattern's name can be followed by a comma and then by a letter that determines one of three sets of rules that can be used for hatching. The *style* of the hatch refers to the "Normal," "Outermost," or "Ignore" options.

"Normal" Hatching

If you choose the "Normal" hatching option, you will be using the default hatching style. This style implies that the pen is alternately lowered and raised as it crosses lines that have been selected for hatching. Figure 6-4 should help you to understand how this works. This simple figure contains several "holes" that must remain devoid of hatching patterns.

You can select the "Normal" hatching style by following the hatching pattern's name with a comma and then the letter **N**. Use this only if you have set the "Outermost" or "Ignore" options (described in the following sections) because the "Normal" style is the default.

Rather than selecting a named hatching pattern, you can select the "U" option to use straight lines. The following command sequence was used to crosshatch Figure 6-4:

Command: **hatch**
Pattern (? or name/U,style) <ESCHER,O>: **U**
Angle for crosshatch lines <0>:
Spacing between lines <1.0000>: .5
Double hatch area? <N>
Select objects:

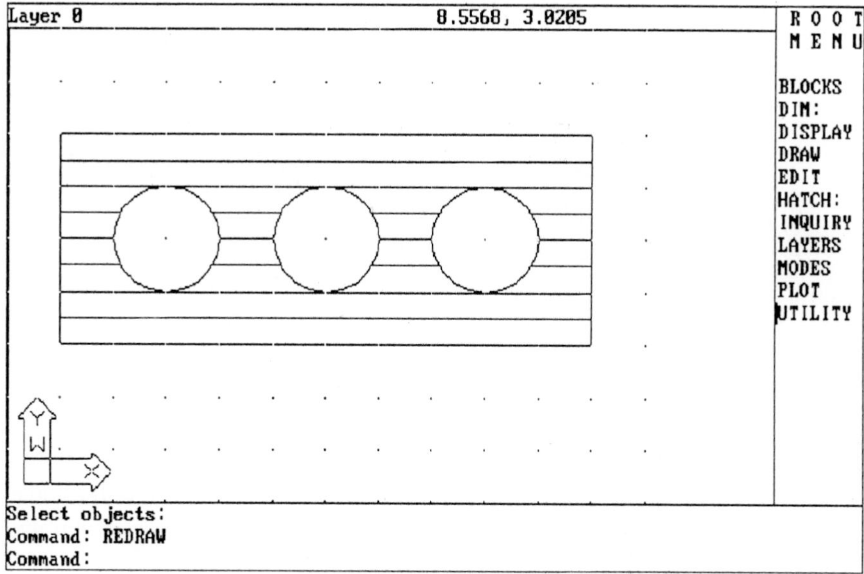

Figure 6-4. "Normal" style crosshatching

It is an interesting property of the topology of closed bounded planar surfaces that they can be divided into regions and filled by following a simple process. The software starts with the pen down and alternately raises and lowers the pen when it intersects boundaries. The regions of the bounded area in Figure 6-4 consist of the outermost boundary itself and the boundaries of the three circles. As you can see, applying this method creates the effect of crosshatching around the circles.

The "pen-up, pen-down" algorithm has many applications in computer graphics, including the processing of drawings to remove hidden lines. You can find out about hidden lines in Chapter 1, "Quick Start," Chapter 10, "Working with Menus," and Chapter 13, "Putting It All Together in 3D." Chapter 16, "AutoCAD Command Reference," also contains some information on AutoCAD's removal of hidden lines.

Using the "U" Option

In addition to showing crosshatching around circles, the command sequence that generated Figure 6-4 illustrates the "U" option of the HATCH command. If you enter the letter **U** in place of a hatching pattern name, straight lines of infinite length will be used to crosshatch. You can specify the angle to be used to draw the lines in response to the "Angle for crosshatch lines <0>:" prompt.

The prompt "Spacing between lines <1.0000>:" is unique to the "U" option. It enables you to specify a distance between lines that will be used to create the crosshatch spacing. The "U" option does not draw hatching patterns, only straight lines.

Finally, before you select the objects to crosshatch, you see the "Double hatch area? <N>" prompt. Usually, you will choose the No default. If you specify Y, however, the hatch pattern will

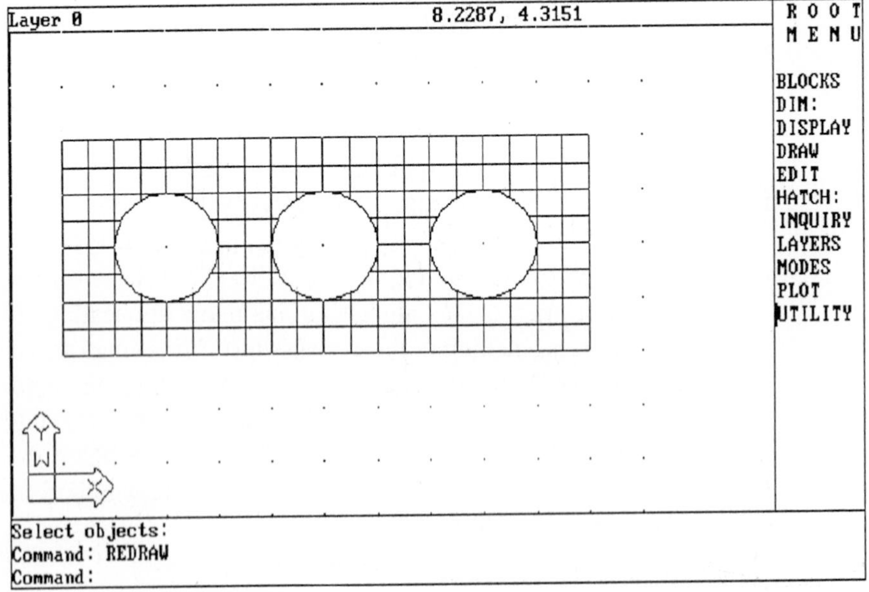

Figure 6-5. The "U" option used to crosshatch

be repeated at a rotation angle of 90 degrees. This will generate a hatching pattern like the one shown in Figure 6-5.

"Outermost" Hatching

With the "Outermost" style of hatching, you confine hatching only to the outermost region of the figure. You might use this option to crosshatch a border area, keeping everything inside the border free of crosshatching. You can choose this option by following the name of the hatching pattern with a comma, then the letter "O."

See Figure 6-6 for an example of crosshatching with the "Outermost" style. Think of "Outermost" crosshatching as "Normal" crosshatching where the pen is lowered, raised at the first intersection, and not lowered again until the next-to-last line intersection.

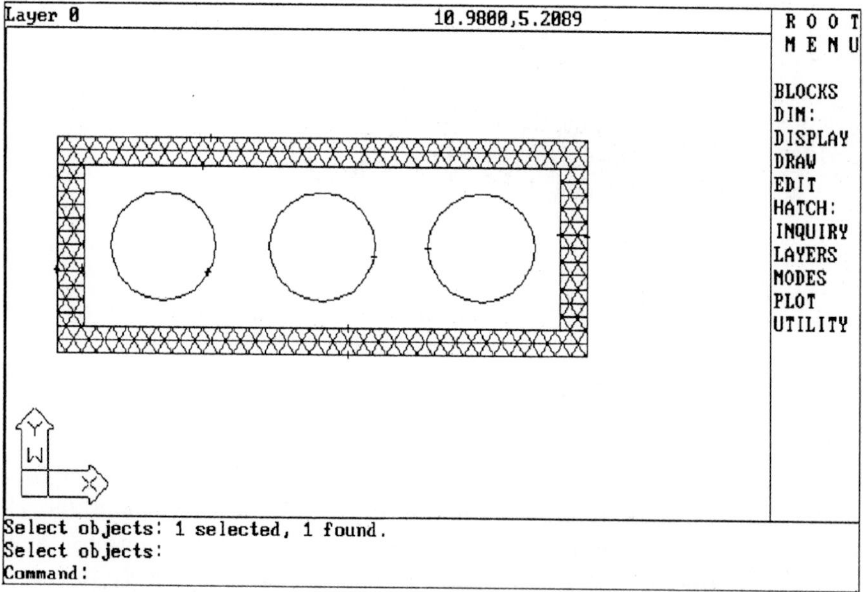

Figure 6-6. "Outermost" style crosshatching

The result in Figure 6-6 was achieved with the following command sequence:

Command: **hatch**
Pattern (? or name/U,style): **net3,o**
Scale for pattern: 2.0000
Angle for pattern <0>:
Select objects:

All the objects were selected, but only the border area was crosshatched.

"Ignore" Hatching

The final style option you can choose for crosshatching is the "Ignore" style. This method uses only the outermost boundaries of a figure, no matter what else you select. Entering the following command sequence will crosshatch the entire figure:

Command: **hatch**
Pattern (? or name/U,style) <NET3,O>: **honey,i**
Scale for pattern <2.0000>:
Angle for pattern <0>:
Select objects:

Select all the objects in the figure and you will see something like the result shown in Figure 6-7. Note that you can achieve the same effect by selecting only the outermost boundary. AutoCAD will ignore any objects you do not select, covering them with the hatch pattern if they lie within the outermost boundary.

The "Normal," "Outermost," and "Ignore" hatching options are essentially superfluous since you can achieve the same effects by selecting objects carefully. These style options were intended to speed and simplify your selection of objects to crosshatch. If you use these style options carefully, you can select all objects with a window.

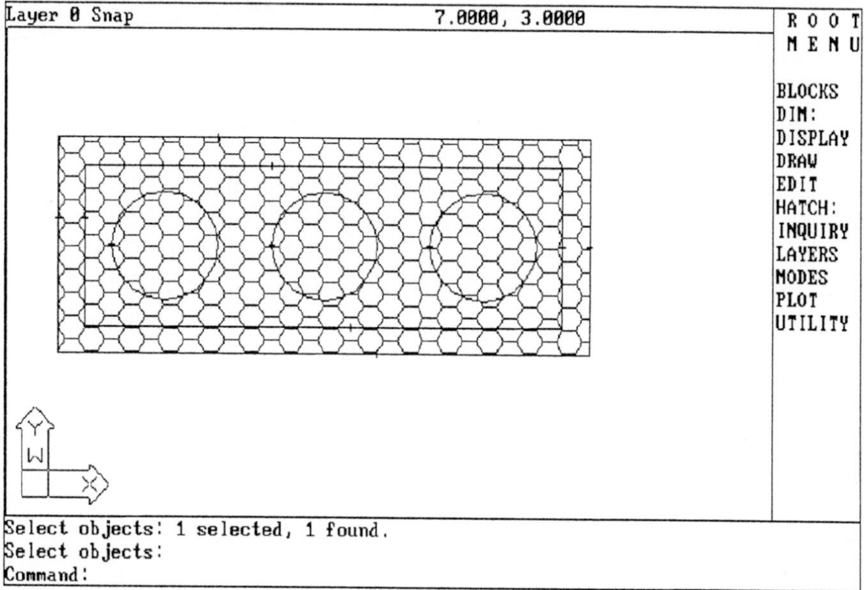

Figure 6-7. The "Ignore" crosshatching style

Crosshatching Blocks

If you select a block in an AutoCAD drawing, it is as though you used the "Window" option in response to the "Select objects:" prompt. All the entities in the block will be treated separately. Since you do not have any control over the selection of separate objects within the block, you can use the style options to gain some selectivity.

Because you cannot completely control the selection of objects, it is probably a good idea to crosshatch blocks and then reinsert them in the drawing. You can do this with the BLOCK command. See the description of the BLOCK command in Chapter 4, "Working with Blocks," for more information on redefining blocks.

Setting the Pattern Base Point

When crosshatching patterns are drawn, each line definition within the pattern is drawn in turn, in the order you specify in the pattern file. The starting point for each line is the origin of the snap grid as currently defined. Each line is drawn from this origin, offset by the delta distances, outward toward infinity. Each crosshatching line intersects lines in the drawing. As it crosses these other lines, the crosshatching line is treated according to the style you selected ("Normal," "Outside," or "Ignore") for the HATCH command.

Because each line in the crosshatching set begins at a common origin, the origin for the entire system of lines is the same. If this origin is moved, the entire set of crosshatching lines is moved accordingly.

You can use the SNAPBASE system variable to set the origin of the entire crosshatching pattern. With the SETVAR command, you can change the SNAPBASE variable to be wherever you want it to be. For example, you might wish to align a brick pattern with a wall elevation. See Figure 6-8*a* for a brick wall that has unaligned bricks. Figure 6-8*b* shows the masonry aligned differently. The alignment was changed with the following command sequence:

Command: **setvar**
Variable name or ?: **snapbase**
New value for SNAPBASE <0.0000,0.0000>:

In response to the "New value" prompt, you pick the lower left corner of the wall. Note that the alignment now places full masonry units at the base and the left edge of the wall, instead of requiring special masonry cuts for all edges.

Making Your Own Crosshatch Patterns

You can use the standard AutoCAD hatching patterns contained in the ACAD.PAT file for many things. Inevitably, though, you

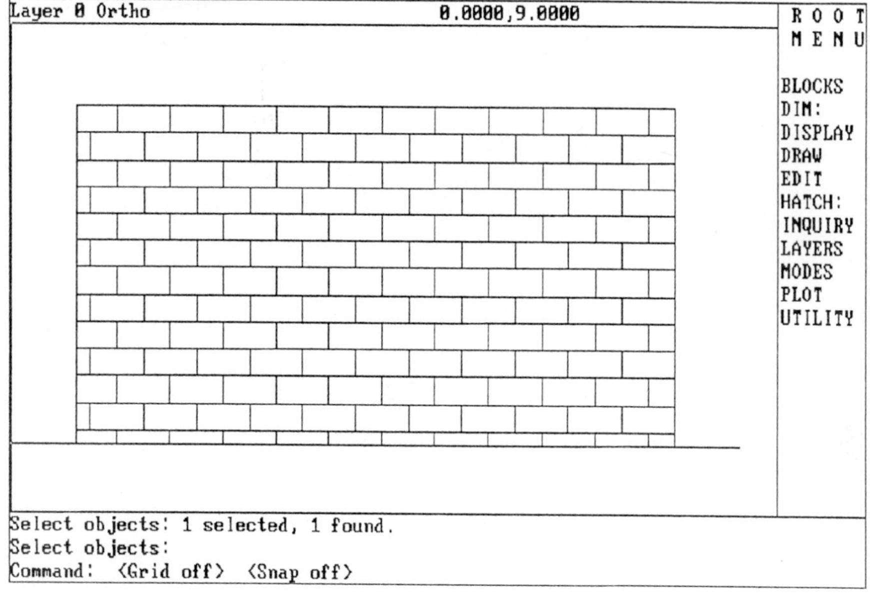

Figure 6-8*a*. An improperly aligned masonry wall

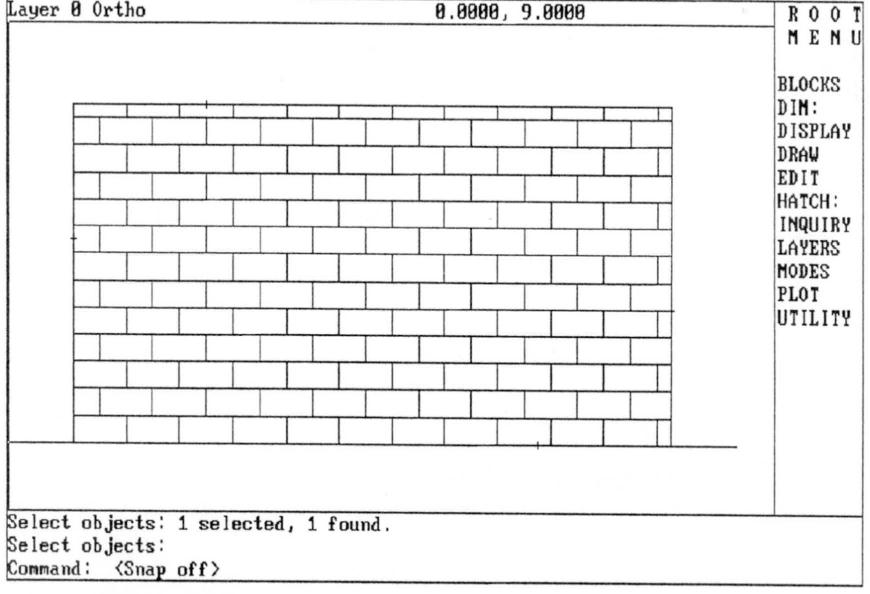

Figure 6-8*b*. The masonry wall properly aligned

will want to create your own crosshatching patterns to do exactly what you want to do. AutoCAD is very accommodating in this respect, though it is not easy to master the pattern "language."

The creation of hatching patterns involves the use of a somewhat obscure language. You may find the pattern language easier to learn if you understand how AutoCAD performs crosshatching.

Understanding the Hatching Mechanism

Crosshatching patterns are created in a very simple way. Think of a crosshatching pattern as being made up of line segments drawn at various intervals and in various directions. If you observe carefully when a standard AutoCAD hatching pattern is drawn, you will see that AutoCAD makes the pattern by drawing one set of lines after another, *not* by drawing each cell of the pattern at a time. The "honey" pattern drawn in Figure 6-7 is an example. It was drawn in three passes. First the horizontal elements were drawn, then the lines oriented at 120 degrees, and finally, the lines oriented at 60 degrees. The result appears to be a honeycomb made up of hexagons.

Crosshatching patterns are *always* drawn in the way just described—line by line. Because the patterns are always composed of lines, it is easy to see how AutoCAD can always guarantee that the patterns will be clipped neatly at boundaries. Each line element is clipped at each intersection point, with the effect that the pattern itself is neatly cut at the boundaries.

Designing the Pattern

The preceding explanation should help you understand how to specify the patterns. If you want to create your own pattern, you must first break up your pattern into lines. You can, of course, use AutoCAD to create the pattern prototype. Take, for example, the pattern "cell" shown in Figure 6-9, in which the entire

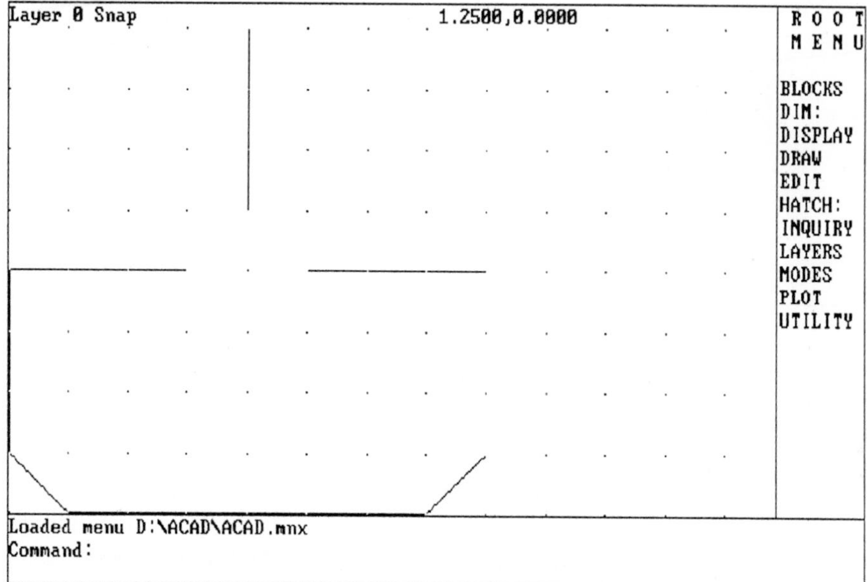

Figure 6-9. Designing a crosshatching pattern "cell"

drawing area is one cell. The snap grid is set up for 0.125 unit. You can draw the pattern element easily within this unit cell.

Listing the Design

With the LIST command, you can list the origin, angle, and delta values for each line entity that makes up the pattern. If you do so, you will be able to create the list shown in Figure 6-10. Note that the listing would be inappropriately long to show, so only the relevant information regarding the listing is extracted here. You will see how it is used later.

It is not difficult to transform the information in listings to a series of instructions that will create new hatching patterns. The listing gives you the origin for each line, the length of the line

Angle,	Origin,	Delta,	Dashes
90,	0,.125,	1,1,	.375, −.625
0,	.125,0,	1,1,	.75, −.25
0,	0,.5,	1,1,	.375, −.25,.375, −0
90,	.5,.625,	1,1,	.375, −.625
135,	.125,0,	.707,.707,	.1768, −.5303
45,	.875,0,	.707,.707,	.1768, −.5303

Figure 6-10. Listing of CEDAR hatching pattern

(the dash length), and the rotation angle. You must derive other information yourself. For example, you must compute the delta, which is the distance that each line will be offset along its length (for dashed lines) and perpendicularly. Delta X is the offset perpendicular to the line and Delta Y is the offset normal to the line (along its length). If your lines have no dashes in them, Delta Y is meaningless.

Entering the Pattern Name

The pattern for the prototype in Figure 6-9 will be named CEDAR. It will symbolize cedar shingles used as a siding material in buildings.

To create the actual crosshatching pattern, you must use a "straight ASCII" text editor. The standard editor supplied with your operating system may suffice, but there are many editors used by programmers that are very easy to operate. You can also use a word processor, but be careful that it doesn't add "extended" characters, formatting blocks, or other peculiarities to the text. Most word processors have a mode that enables you to generate straight ASCII text. The only characters that will be acceptable for use by AutoCAD include the letters of the alphabet (upper- and lowercase), the comma, the asterisk, and the period. Invisible characters such as the space character, the carriage return, and the line feed are also required.

At this time, you may wish to examine the contents of the ACAD.PAT file. You can read this file with your straight ASCII text editor. When you read the file, the first five lines look like this:

```
*angle,Angle steel
0, 0,0, 0,.275, .2,-.075
90, 0,0, 0,.275, .2,-.075
*ansi31,ANSI Iron, Brick, Stone masonry
45, 0,0, 0,.125
```

The last two lines are of interest for this discussion because what they produce is a simple hatching pattern. The first line looks like this:

```
*ansi31,ANSI Iron, Brick, Stone masonry
```

This line contains the name of the hatching pattern ("ansi31") and a description of the pattern following a comma. Note that an asterisk precedes all hatching pattern names in the ACAD.PAT file.

Creating Custom Names

In the case of the CEDAR pattern being created here, you could prepare a text line for the pattern file as follows:

```
*cedar,Cedar shake pattern for siding material.
```

Note that you are using the techniques in ACAD.PAT to create your own patterns. It is often valuable to have working examples from which to learn. When making your patterns, always remember to precede the pattern name with an asterisk.

Entering the Pattern Description

The pattern generator depends on a description that follows certain rules. Each line in the pattern is described on its own text line in the pattern file. The "ansi31" pattern consists of only one line repeated at a distance of 0.125 unit. The line specification appears as follows:

```
45, 0,0, 0,.125
```

Notice that this line consists of numbers delimited by commas. The first number, 45, indicates the rotation angle of the line. The second two numbers are the origin of the pattern. In this case, the origin is the same as the origin of the snap grid. All hatching patterns are automatically aligned with the origin of the snap grid when they are brought into AutoCAD by the HATCH command. The third pair of numbers (0,.125) indicates the amount this line will be offset in the normal and perpendicular directions with respect to the hatching line. With this unbroken line, there is no meaning to an offset in the direction normal to the line. With dashed lines, however, there would be a need to express the offset normal to the line. The direction perpendicular to the line contains the line spacing of .125 unit. The result of using this pattern appears in Figure 6-11.

Creating the Custom Pattern

Like the "ansi31" pattern, you can create your own patterns. Just follow the same rules: angle, x_origin, y_origin, delta_x, delta _y, and dash lengths. With the information in Figure 6-10, you can create your own cedar shingle pattern. The information in Figure 6-10, extracted from a list of the drawing in Figure 6-9, can be used as is. The finished specification for the CEDAR pattern is shown in Figure 6-12. Note that positive numbers for the "Dashed" values mean "Hold the pen down for this

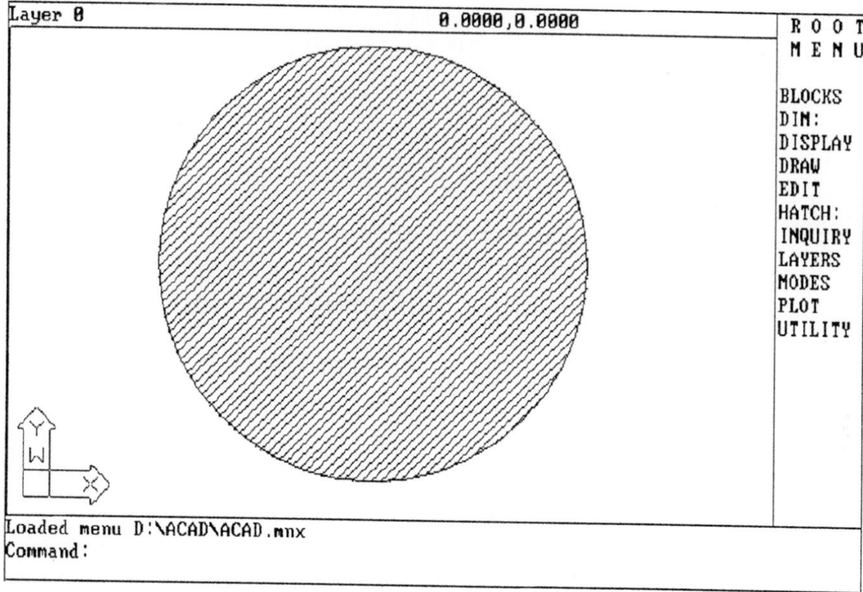

Figure 6-11. A sample of the "ansi31" pattern

```
*cedar,Cedar shake pattern for roofing material.
90, 0,.125, 1,1, .375,-.625
0, .125,0, 1,1, .75,-.25
0, 0,.5, 1,1, .375,-.25,.375,-0
90, .5,.625, 1,1, .375,-.625
135, .125,0, .707,.707, .1768,-.5303
45, .875,0, .707,.707, .1768, -.5303
```

Figure 6-12. Specification for CEDAR hatching pattern

distance," and negative numbers mean "Raise the pen for this distance." See Figure 6-10 for an identification of the Dashed values.

Putting Patterns in Files

You could append the information in the listing for the CEDAR pattern directly to the ACAD.PAT file or create your own pattern file under any other legal file name. AutoCAD first looks for patterns in the ACAD.PAT file. If it does not find the pattern name there, it looks for a file with the exact pattern name, assuming it has the extension .PAT. If the pattern name includes a period followed by up to three letters, the exact file name is used for the pattern, assuming the file exists. For example, if you were to put the information from Figure 6-12 in a file called "cedar.pat", AutoCAD would look for the cedar name in ACAD.PAT and, not finding it, would then open the file CEDAR.PAT and read the pattern definition from it.

Figure 6-13 shows an object that was crosshatched with the CEDAR pattern just created.

The AutoCAD Reference Manual contains descriptions of the standard patterns available in ACAD.PAT. Consult the AutoCAD documentation for current descriptions of these patterns.

Hatching a Typical Drawing

To illustrate crosshatching in a typical application, a sample detail drawing was developed. Figure 6-14*a* shows the drawing that will be crosshatched. The drawing attempts to describe an angle plate with two mounting holes and a bushing for a pipe with a three-inch inside diameter. As shown, the drawing is very hard to read because the pipe is drawn in section but is not shown that way. The bent portion of the angle plate should also be shown in section, but no crosshatching denotes the part where the section was cut.

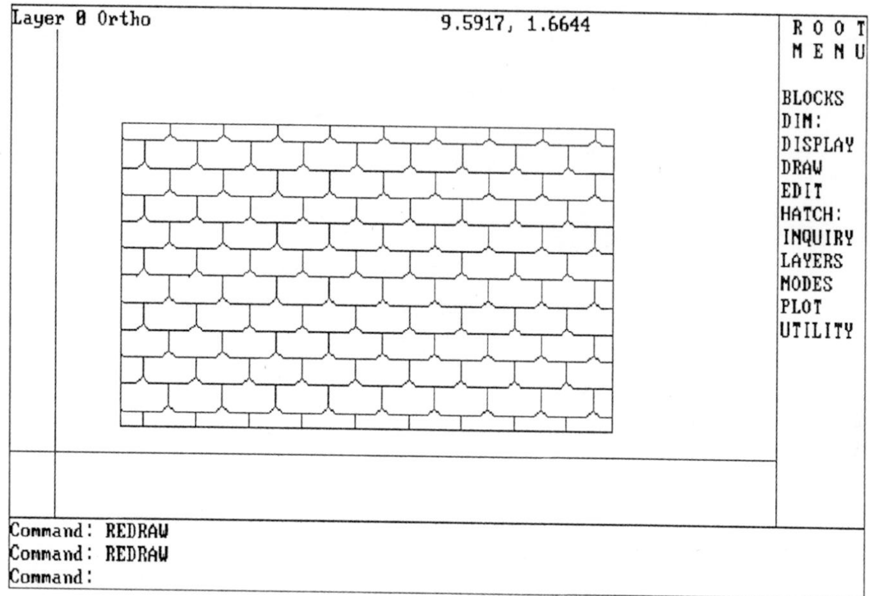

Figure 6-13. Crosshatching with the new CEDAR pattern

First, the pipe section will be crosshatched. The following command sequence was used to start the crosshatching process:

Command: **hatch**
Pattern (? or name/U,style) <ANSI32>:
Scale for pattern <1.0000>:
Angle for pattern <0.00>:
Select objects:

The objects selected were the two centermost circles of the pipe object. After the two boundary circles were selected, the crosshatching pattern (symbol for steel) was drawn. See Figure 6-14*b* for the finished pipe crosshatch. After the pipe was crosshatched, the cut portions of the angle plate were crosshatched. The command sequence involved the selection of the lines shown in Figure 6-14*c*.

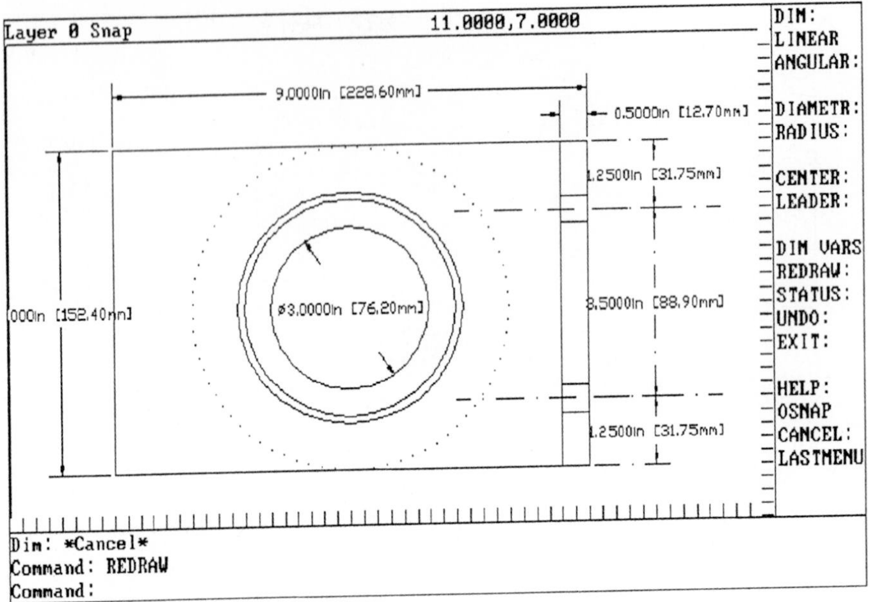

Figure 6-14*a*. A sample drawing to be crosshatched

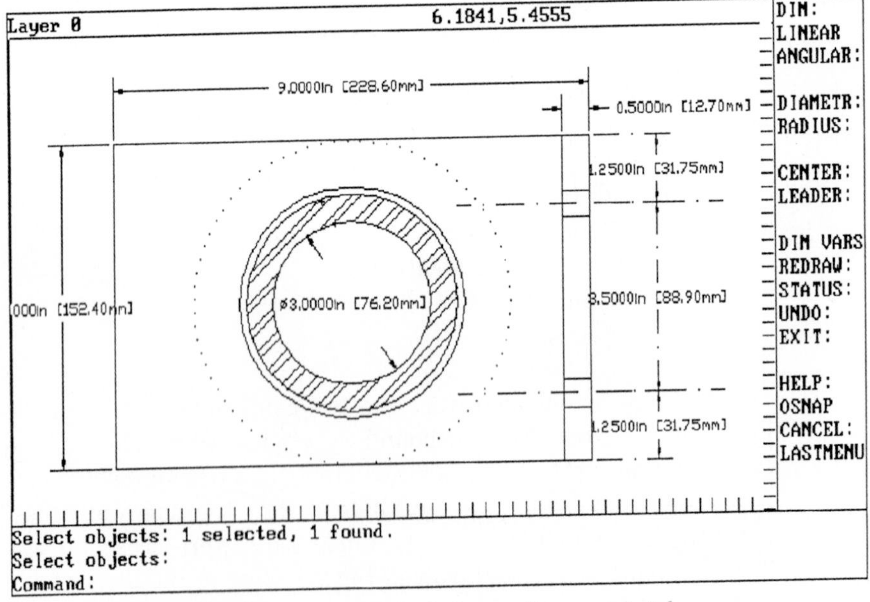

Figure 6-14*b*. The finished pipe section crosshatch

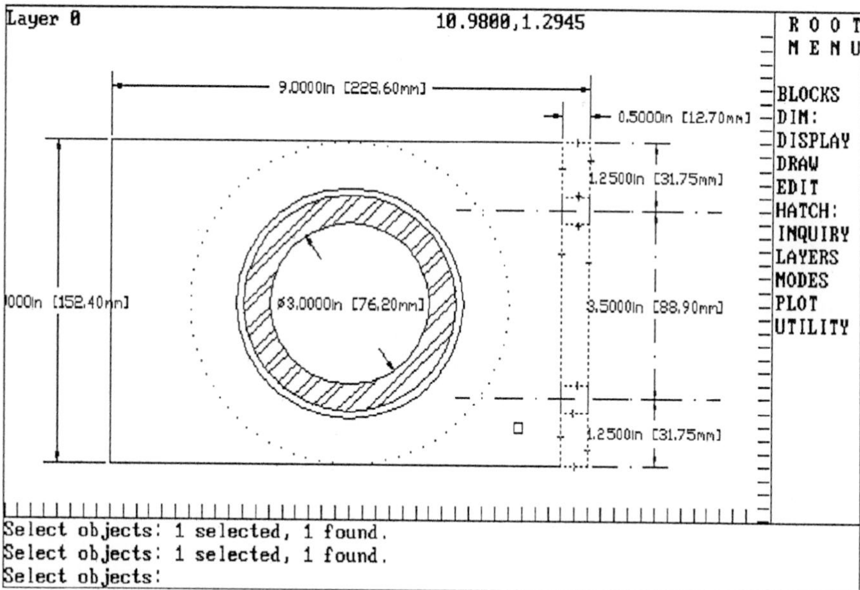

Figure 6-14*c*. Lines selected for crosshatching

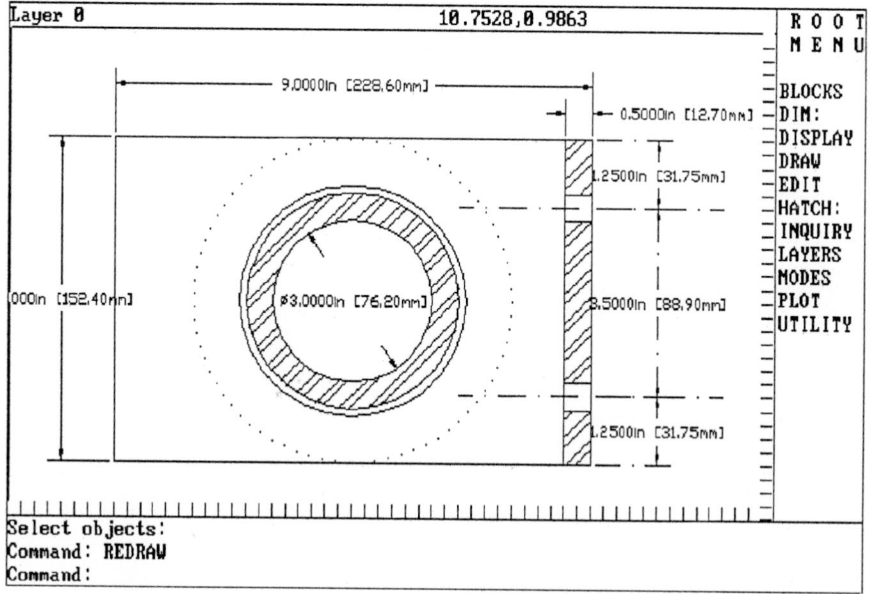

Figure 6-14*d*. The finished crosshatching job

The finished crosshatching job is shown in Figure 6-14*d*. It is now much easier to see what the drawing was meant to convey, and the fabricator knows that the material to be used is steel.

Text and Fonts

Working with Text
Understanding Shapes

SEVEN

The text in engineering drawings is as important as the graphics. Engineering drawings are usually *contract documents,* which means they are legally part of the contract to manufacture or build something. As such, it is often crucial that information be accurately conveyed by text. Written descriptions are less subject to arbitrary interpretation than purely graphic descriptions. The graphic and textual parts of a set of contract documents work together, with each having something essential to contribute to a successful project.

A CAD system would not be worth very much without the ability to use text. AutoCAD has very sophisticated text capabilities. You can use text *fonts* that are provided by Autodesk. Fonts are designed expressions of the letters of the alphabet, numbers, and special characters. A font gives each letter in the alphabet its own unique expression. Just as in this book, the font is responsible for the legibility and artistic appearance of text. AutoCAD has a rich collection of standard text fonts for you to use. With AutoCAD, you can also create your own text fonts, though most users will not have the time to do this.

Using the proper font in a drawing can be very important for the legibility of the text. There are engineering standards regarding the appearance of fonts. Each project will be different, but you should always choose your fonts carefully to match the requirements of the work you will perform.

In addition to fonts, text can be varied in size, slant, and orientation. These aspects are the *style* of text. The combination of font and style accounts for the wide variety of text expressions in an AutoCAD drawing.

Working with Text

Text is controlled with several commands and system variables. The primary command for creating text is the TEXT command. To create the style of your text, you will use the STYLE command. The TEXT command and its options, in combination with style and system parameters, are all you need to do most of your work with text.

Entering the TEXT Command

To begin to create a line of text in your drawing, you first invoke the TEXT command. A typical command sequence follows:

Command: **text**
Start point or Align/Center/Fit/Middle/Right/Style:
Height <0.2000>: **1**
Rotation angle <0>:
Text: **Sample text.**

Note that the height of the text has been changed from the default to 1 unit. If this were not done, the text would be very small in the drawing area. If this invocation is the first time you have entered the TEXT command during the current session, you must pick a point in response to the "Start point. . ." prompt. If you press ENTER, you will see the message

Point or option keyword required.

If, however, the invocation was *not* the first in the current session, you can skip everything except the "Text:" prompt and the default values from the first invocation will be used.

If you only press ENTER in response to each prompt, you will set the text height to 0.2000 unit and the rotation angle to 0 degrees. Of course, you must enter the actual text that you wish to appear at the start point.

Figure 7-1 shows the results of entering the TEXT command as the first command in a new drawing. The default text height makes the text appear to be rather small, but you can enter any height you desire, as shown below.

Figure 7-1 illustrates a simple case of text entry. You will want more control over your text than this. AutoCAD gives you several options that are summarized in the prompt

Start point or Align/Center/Fit/Middle/Right/Style:

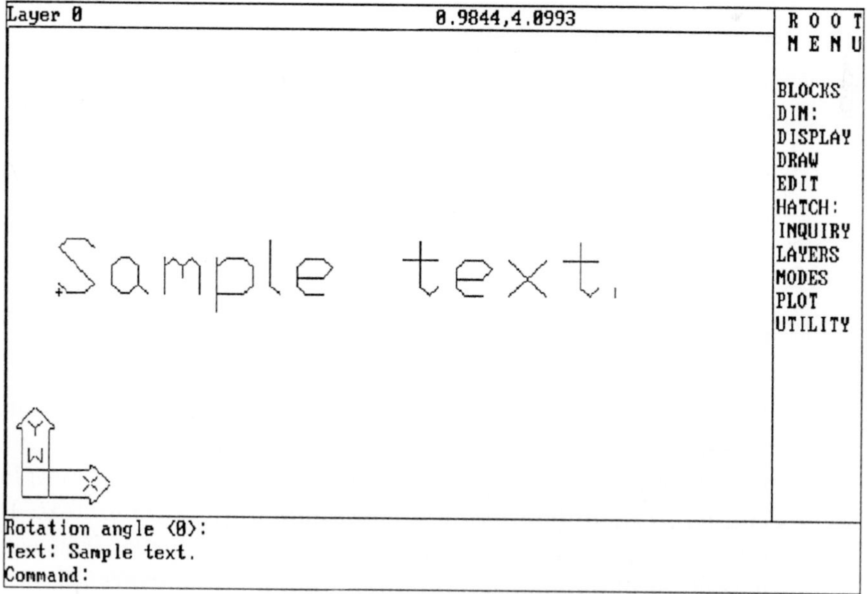

Figure 7-1. Sample text entered using the TEXT command

Each of the words (such as "Align" and "Center") is an option of the TEXT command. You can place text to fit between two points with the "Align" option. You can center your text on the start point by using the "Center" option. With the "Fit" option, you can fit your text in the same way as with the "Align" option, but the text will maintain its height, varying only its width. The "Middle" option centers your text both horizontally and vertically, while the "Center" option only centers text along its length. Unless you specify the "Right" option, the text will be left justified. Finally, the "Style" option enables you to choose a style you have prepared with the STYLE command.

Positioning Text

The first option in the series of TEXT options asks for the "Start point" for your text. If you pick a point with your pointing device, your text will begin at that point. The point identifies the lower left corner of an imaginary box that surrounds the text string you will enter as the last response in the TEXT command's sequence of prompts.

If you do not enter a point's coordinates or pick a point, you must enter one of the other options from the series of options specified, press ENTER, or cancel the command with CTRL-C. The only way to position your text other than to move or copy it is to pick a starting point.

Left and Right Justifying Text

Modern word processor systems permit you to left or right justify your text. Left justified text always starts at the left margin. This is the usual way you expect to see text, and it is the default for AutoCAD. With right justification, the right margin is used to align the rightmost characters of each line of text. If you select the "Right" option of the TEXT command, you can make your text line up with its rightmost characters aligned with a point you pick.

When you select the "Right" option, you will be prompted for the "End point:" rather than for the "Start point:". After you pick the endpoint, you enter your text as usual. Each row of text characters will be aligned with the endpoint you picked. Figure 7-2*a* shows text that has been left and right justified.

Centering Text

If you choose the "Center" option of the TEXT command, you can center your text around a point you pick. When you select this option, you will be prompted for a "Center point:", and the point you pick will be used to center each line of text you enter. Remember, you must re-enter the text command for each line of text and default (press ENTER) at the "Start point" prompt to continue centering subsequent text lines. If you choose any other option, you must start by picking a new point. Figure 7-2*b* shows text that was entered with the "Center" option.

Mirroring Text

When you use the MIRROR command, you will create a mirror image of all of the selected objects in your drawing. Often, however, you will not wish to mirror your text as well. You can control the mirroring of text with the MIRRTEXT system variable.

When you use the SETVAR command to set the MIRRTEXT variable to 0, text entities will not be mirrored. Use SETVAR as follows to change the MIRRTEXT variable to 0:

Command: **setvar**
Variable name or ?:
New value for MIRRTEXT <1>: **0**

If you do not change the MIRRTEXT variable, it will be set to the default value of 1, meaning text will be mirrored along with other entities.

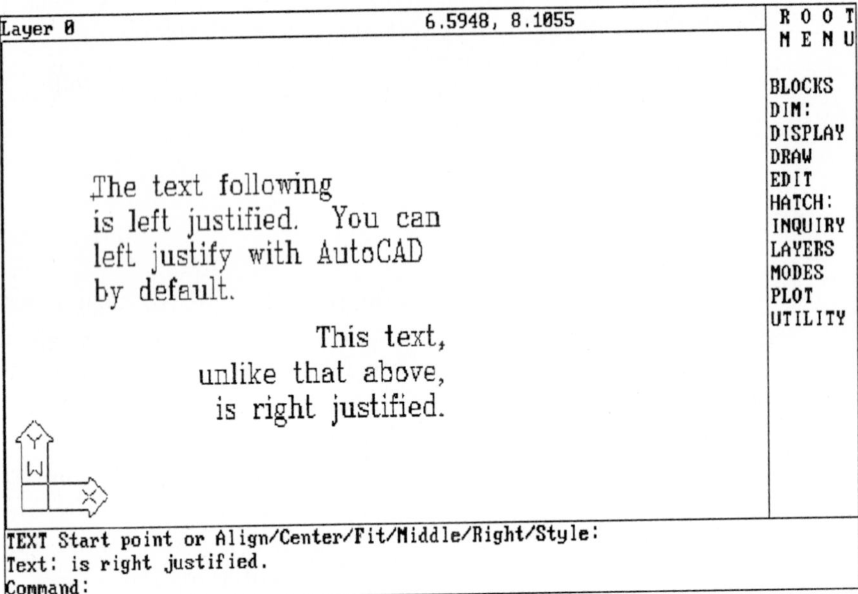

Figure 7-2*a*. Left and right justified text

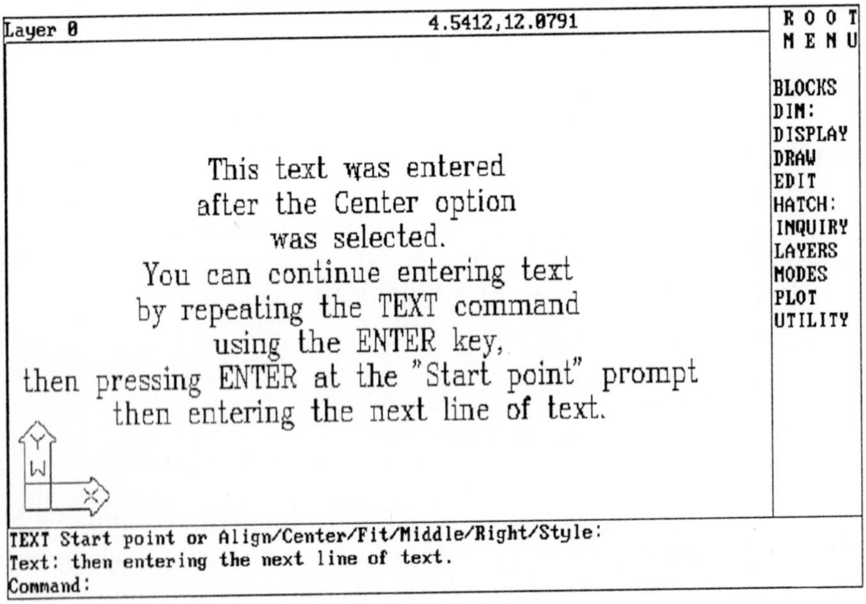

Layer 0
4.5412,12.0791
ROOT MENU
BLOCKS
DIM:
DISPLAY
DRAW
EDIT
HATCH:
INQUIRY
LAYERS
MODES
PLOT
UTILITY

This text was entered
after the Center option
was selected.
You can continue entering text
by repeating the TEXT command
using the ENTER key,
then pressing ENTER at the "Start point" prompt
then entering the next line of text.

Y
W
X

TEXT Start point or Align/Center/Fit/Middle/Right/Style:
Text: then entering the next line of text.
Command:

Figure 7-2*b*. Text drawn using the "Center" option

Fitting Text

Text can be fitted between two points. If you choose the "Fit" option of the TEXT command, you will be prompted as follows:

First text line point:
Second text line point:
Height <default>:
Text: **My text string.**

Each character in the text string you enter will be stretched so that the entire string fits between the two points you pick. The height you specify will be used, and must be selected, so that the characters look appropriate to you. A small value for height will produce characters that appear stretched horizontally. You can pick the height, so you can control the proportions.

Understanding Text Fonts and Styles

AutoCAD provides you with a default text font that you can use very easily. The standard default font is named "txt" and is the one you will see if you do not change the default font. This font is designed to enable you to draw legible text with a minimum of lines. Because it is simple, it can be drawn quickly.

Do not limit yourself to the standard "txt" font, but take the time to use one of the many available fonts to make your text more interesting. Then when you use text, your drawings will be more attractive because you will have learned how to best use the text fonts available to you.

Adding Style to Text

To use an alternate font, you must first load it into memory. To do this, AutoCAD provides you with the STYLE command. A font file is a special form of *shape* file. Shape files contain special shape definitions which, like blocks, are drawings that can be read from disk into your drawing workfile. A shape file can be recognized by its ".shx" extension. When you use the STYLE command, however, you will specify a font name without adding the ".shx" extension.

To load a new font, you must first enter the STYLE command on the command line or pick it from a menu. The STYLE command sequence is as follows:

Command: **style**
Text style name (or ?) <STANDARD>:
Existing style.
Font file <txt>: **romanc**
Height <0.0000>: **1**
Width factor <1.00>:
Obliquing angle <0>:
Backwards? <N>
Upside-down? <N>
Vertical? <N>

In the preceding invocation, the font named "romanc" was entered by using the "standard" style with a height of 1 unit, a width factor of 1, and an obliquing angle of 0. Text will be drawn in the normal way, forward, right-side-up, and horizontally oriented. All of these prompts will be explained in detail in the following sections.

In addition to entering the font name, you had to answer a few questions regarding the standard appearance of text in your drawings. Your answers determine how existing text in your drawing as well as future text you will enter will be drawn.

If you had entered the text in Figure 7-1 with the default "txt" font, and then you change the font as just described, you will see the font change for the existing text. All text in a drawing is drawn using the current font and all text is changed if the font is changed. Figure 7-3 shows what happens to the text shown in Figure 7-1 when the STYLE command is used to load the "romanc" font with "standard" style. Notice how much smoother the curves in this font are and how much easier the text is to read.

Text Styles

The STYLE command permits you to create new styles or use existing styles. The first prompt you will see when you enter the STYLE command is

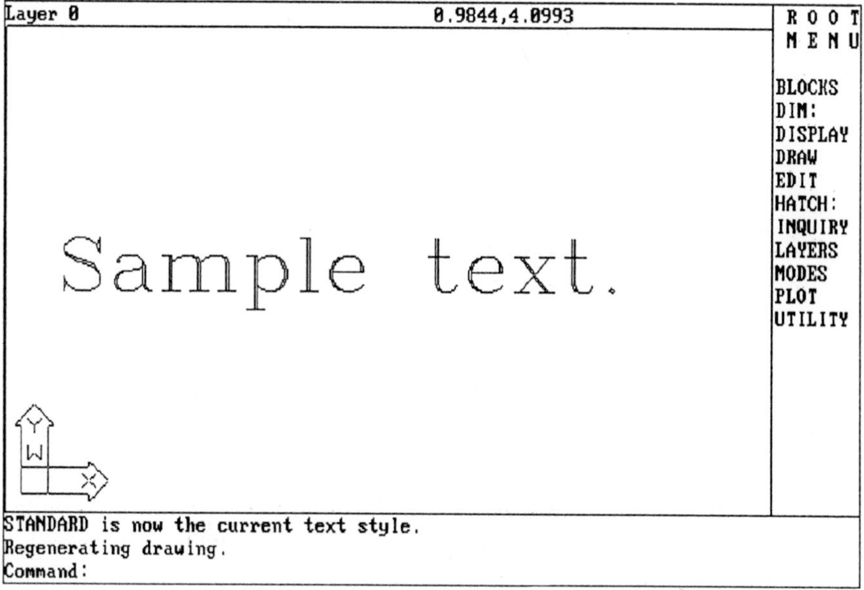

Figure 7-3. Text font changed from "txt" to "romanc"

Text style name (or ?) <STANDARD>:

If you respond to this prompt with a press of the spacebar or the ENTER key, you will use the default style (in this case "standard"). If you enter a question mark (?), you will see a list of available styles. If you enter a style name that is in the list of available styles, that style will be loaded. If, however, you enter a style name that is *not* in the list of available styles, the message "New style" will appear. The new style will then be added to the list of available text styles, and you will be prompted for the style parameters that will characterize it. These parameters include the font, height, width factor, obliquing angle, and text orientation (generation).

Text Height

The text height, in drawing units, is the distance from the bottom to the top of a capital letter in the text font. You can specify the height in response to the "Height" prompt of the STYLE command, by using the SETVAR command to set the TEXTSIZE system variable, or by specifying the height in response to the "Height" prompt of the TEXT command. In all cases, though the text height is made available to you in three different ways, it is stored in just one place in AutoCAD. By allowing you to change the text height in several ways rather than just one, AutoCAD gives you maximum control over this important variable.

Width Factor

The width factor is a number that is used to multiply the width of a string of text. If the width factor is 1, the normal appearance of the text font will be used. If the width factor is less than 1, the text string will be shorter than normal and compressed in length. If the width factor is greater than 1, the text string will appear longer than normal.

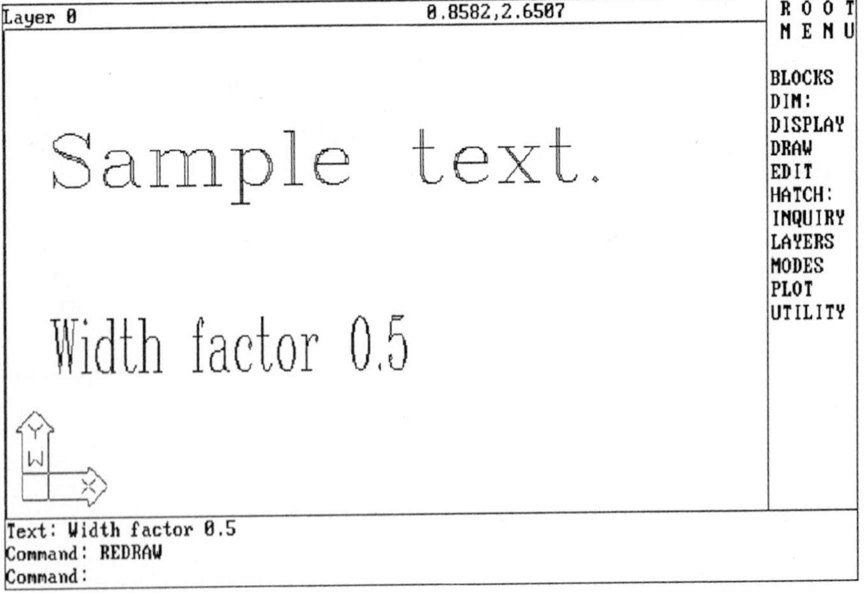

Figure 7-4. Using a width factor of 0.5 to compress text

Figure 7-4 shows a text string that has been compressed by changing the style width factor to be less than 1. The same font was used ("romanc"), but the width factor is now 0.5 instead of 1.

Obliquing Angle

You can change the style of your text so that each character is drawn at an angle to the vertical. If you enter a zero for the obliquing angle in response to the "Obliquing angle" prompt, all characters will be vertical. If you enter a positive angle, each character will be drawn leaning to the right. If negative, the angle will produce characters that lean to the left. Figure 7-5 shows text that is vertical, leans to the left, and leans to the right.

You can use a positive or negative angle of up to 85 degrees, but for larger angles the characters in your text will be illegible. Angles from 0 to 30 degrees or so work very well.

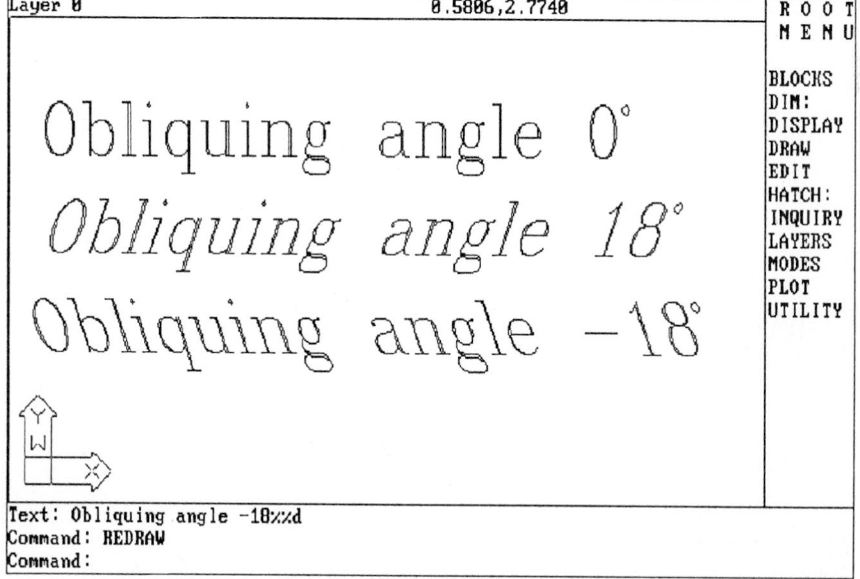

Figure 7-5. Obliquing angle options

Text Orientation

In addition to controlling the appearance of the characters in your text, you can control some aspects of the orientation of groups of characters. You can make your text appear backwards, upside down, or vertically.

Backwards Text Sometimes you will use your drawings to make direct positive prints, in which case the drawing itself acts as a kind of photographic negative. Since a negative reverses characters, creating a "mirror image," you must be able to draw your text so that characters are drawn in reverse. The direct positive print will then have the characters drawn normally.

To draw your characters in reverse, you just specify **Y** in response to the "Backwards?" prompt. Then any characters you draw will be drawn backwards. Figure 7-6 shows a text string that was drawn backwards.

Upside-down Text For the same reasons you might wish to use backwards text, you could use upside-down text. You can

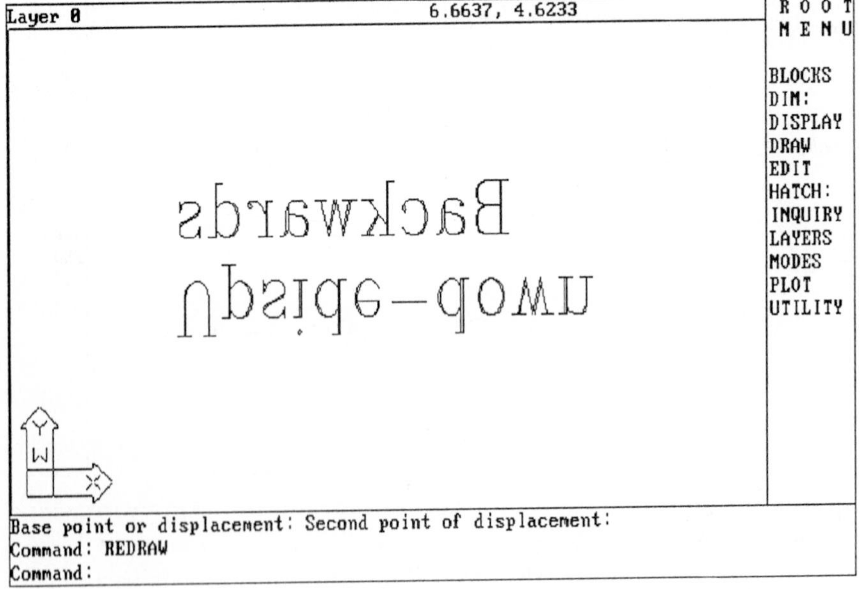

Figure 7-6. The "Backwards" and "Upside-down" options

achieve the same results, except that your entire drawing would need to be drawn upside down as well. You might also draw your text upside down to produce special effects for mechanical drawings in which you want to see text engraved on the other side of a transparent object.

To draw your text upside down, all you need to do is respond to the "Upside-down?" prompt by entering a **Y**. When you do this, all subsequent text will be drawn upside down. Figure 7-6 shows upside down text.

Vertical Text Many books have titles on their spines that are drawn vertically. With vertical text, each character is drawn in its normal orientation, but directly under (or above) the character adjacent to it. The effect is to produce a vertical stack of characters rather than a horizontal row.

You can set AutoCAD to draw characters vertically by responding to the "Vertical?" prompt with a **Y**. Figure 7-7 shows

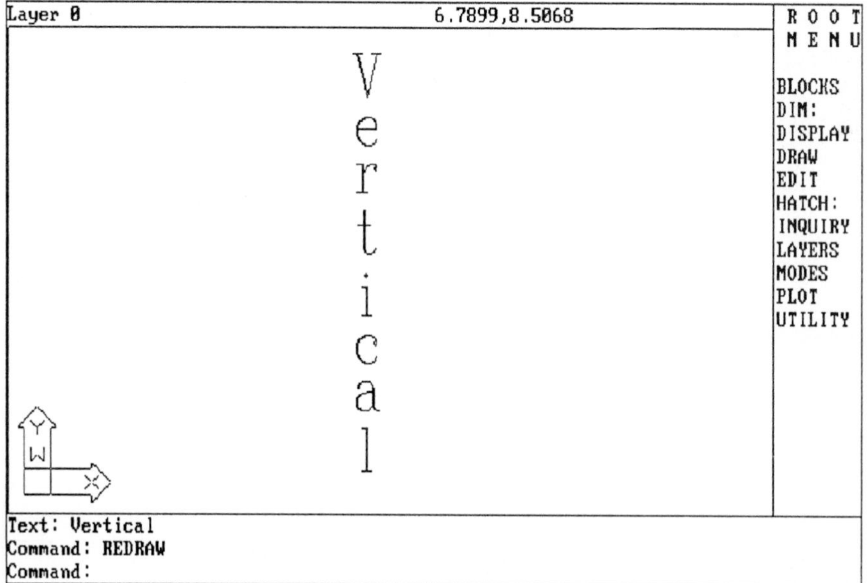

Figure 7-7. Text drawn vertically

text that has been drawn vertically. Note that the "Vertical" option governs all existing text, not just future text.

Mixed Orientations You can combine these orientation options in several ways. For example, "Backwards" and "Upside-down" can be *on*, while "Vertical" is *off*. Figure 7-8 shows what happens when "Backwards" and "Upside-down" are both in effect, and "vertical" is not. By turning "Vertical" *off*, the word "Vertical" from Figure 7-7 has become horizontal, but "Backwards" and "Upside-down" are now correctly shown. You could rotate the string "Backwards and upside-down" 180 degrees with the ROTATE command and see normal text. This method of entering normal text is not, of course, recommended.

Proportional Spacing

Word processing systems usually give you the option of spacing your text *proportionally*. Proportional spacing is the placement

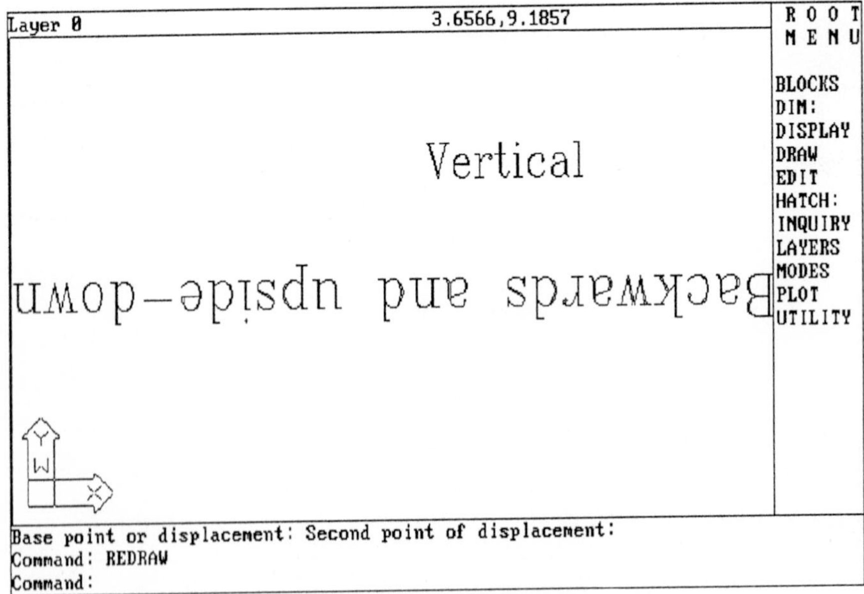

Figure 7-8. Text drawn upside-down and backwards

of characters in such a way that the width of each character determines the amount of space between characters. Without proportional spacing, each character is placed at a fixed distance from each other in the text. Such fixed-distance characters are said to be monospaced. Proportional spacing creates text that is much more pleasing to the eye and is easier to read than monospaced text. For example, in proportionally-spaced text, the letter "I" is given much less space than the letter "M" because of the respective widths of the letters. The space between these two letters in a line of text will be much less in a proportionally spaced line than in a monospaced line.

All AutoCAD fonts supplied by Autodesk are proportionally spaced. The only font that is not is the "monotxt" font, which is monospaced. There are some circumstances, such as in charts and tables of data, where you may wish your text to line up in vertical rows. The "monotxt" font is useful for such aligned text. Whether a font is proportionally spaced or not depends on the contents of the font's ".shx" file. Proportional spacing is part of the design of a given font, not a style parameter.

Using Special Characters

When you enter text in response to the TEXT command, you can use all of the alphabet, the numbers from zero through nine, and all the characters that appear on your keyboard, including the following:

abcdefghijklmnopqrstuvwxyz
ABCDEFGHIJKLMNOPQRSTUVWXYZ
0123456789
!@#$^&()_ + − =|<>?\,./*

In addition to these characters, you can use AutoCAD's *special characters,* including underscore, overscore, degrees, tolerance, circle diameter, percent, and ASCII.

Note that the only character you see on your keyboard that cannot be used directly in response to the "Text:" prompt of the TEXT command is the percent (%) character. This character must be entered by using three percent characters (%%%).

Figure 7-9 shows examples of AutoCAD's special characters. Each line of text was created by entering the following in response to the "Text:" prompt:

Circle diameter dimensioning symbol: **%%c**
Degrees symbol: **%%d**
%%uUnderscore mode on.
%%oOverscore mode on.
%%o%%uBoth underscore and overscore on.
Plus/minus symbol: **%%p**
Single percent sign: %%%
Character by ASCII number: %%38

Layer 0 -3.0728,12.2334
ROOT MENU
BLOCKS
DIM:
DISPLAY
DRAW
EDIT
HATCH:
INQUIRY
LAYERS
MODES
PLOT
UTILITY
Circle diameter dimensioning symbol: ⌀
Degrees symbol: °
Underscore mode on.
Overscore mode on.
Both underscore and overscore on.
Plus/minus symbol: ±
Single percent sign: %
Character by ASCII number: &
Start point or Align/Center/Fit/Middle/Right/Style:
Text: Character by ASCII number: %%38
Command:

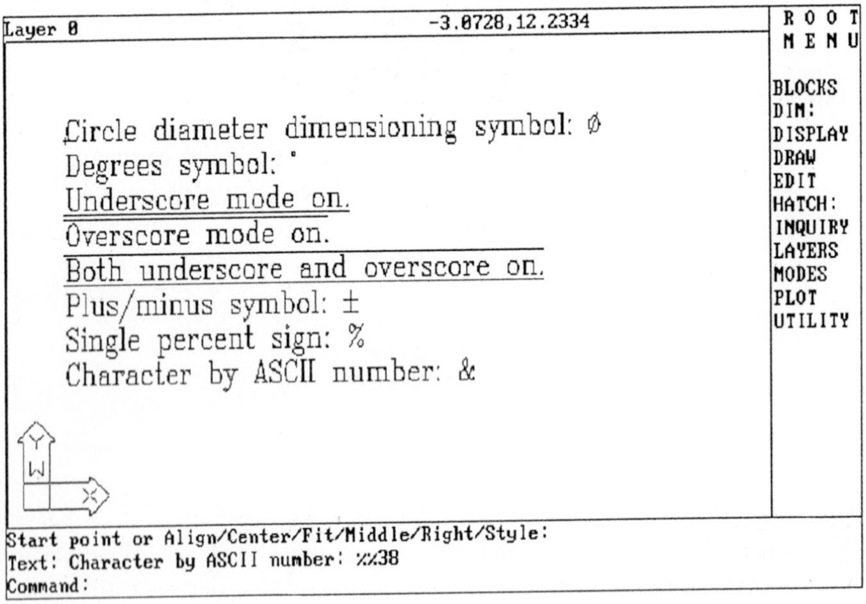

Figure 7-9. Special characters, overscore and underscore

Special characters are always invoked by two percent characters (%%) known as *control codes.* In the case of underscore and overscore, the %%u and %%o special characters toggle the modes *on* and *off* rather than being characters you can see in the drawing area. If you toggle underscore or overscore *on* for a given line of text, they will be toggled *off* automatically at the end of the line. Each line of text you enter starts with underscore and overscore *off,* so you do not need to worry about turning them *off* at the end of each text line.

If the font you are working with does not have a character for the ASCII code used (as in %%38 above), you will see a question mark instead of the character. ASCII codes are used in the computer industry to identify characters in a standard way. The ASCII acronym stands for "American Standard Code for Information Interchange." With this code, each character in the alphabet has its own unique number. For example, the ampersand character (&) has the number 38.

In some special fonts (such as "symath" and "symusic"), you may select mathematical, musical, or other special symbols by their ASCII numbers. In these fonts, the ASCII codes are used unconventionally to call up such special characters.

Figure 7-10*a* shows the letters of the alphabet in the "romanc" font. These characters, in the same positions, are shown in Figures 7-10*b* through 7-10*d* in different symbolic fonts.

Figure 7-10*b* shows the "symath" symbols. In order to make these symbols available, the STYLE command was used to load the "symath" font. The characters in Figure 7-10*a* now appear as mathematical symbols in the same positions.

Figure 7-10*c* shows the "symusic" symbols. Note that the same characters that appear as the alphabet in Figure 7-10*a* now appear as musical symbols.

In Figure 7-10*d*, the "symap" font shows mapping symbols. Cartographers use these symbols to produce various kinds of maps. Note the symbols for state and interstate highways, for example. As with the "symath" and "symusic" fonts, the symbols correspond to letters of the alphabet in the same positions as shown in Figure 7-10*a*.

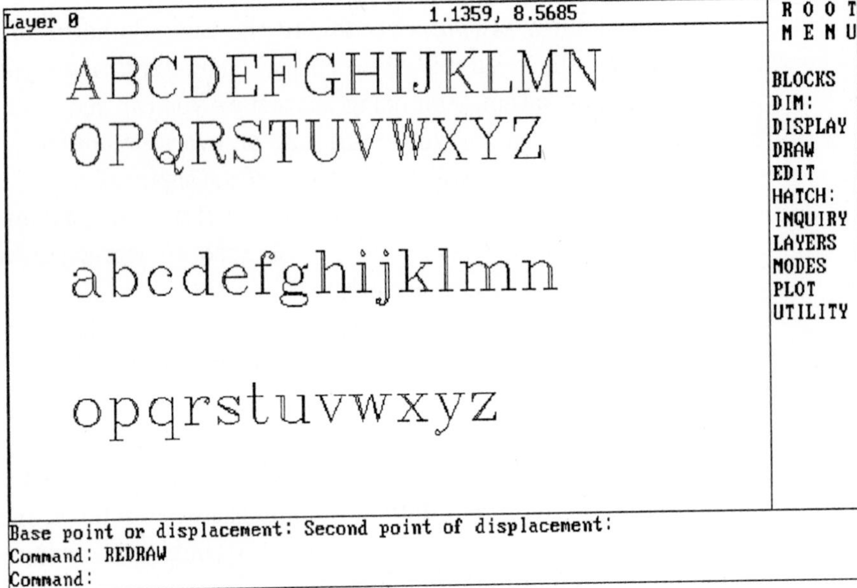

Figure 7-10*a*. The alphabet shown in the "romanc" font

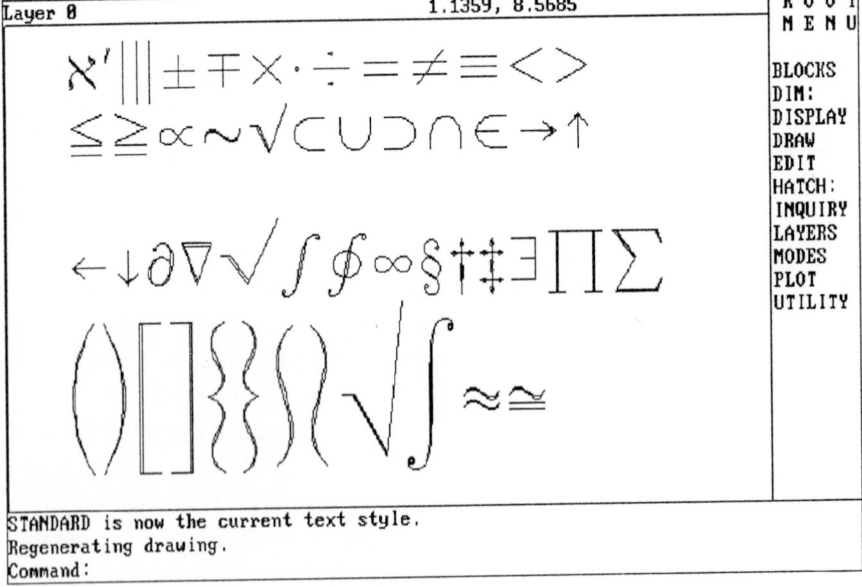

Figure 7-10*b*. The alphabet shown in the "symath" font

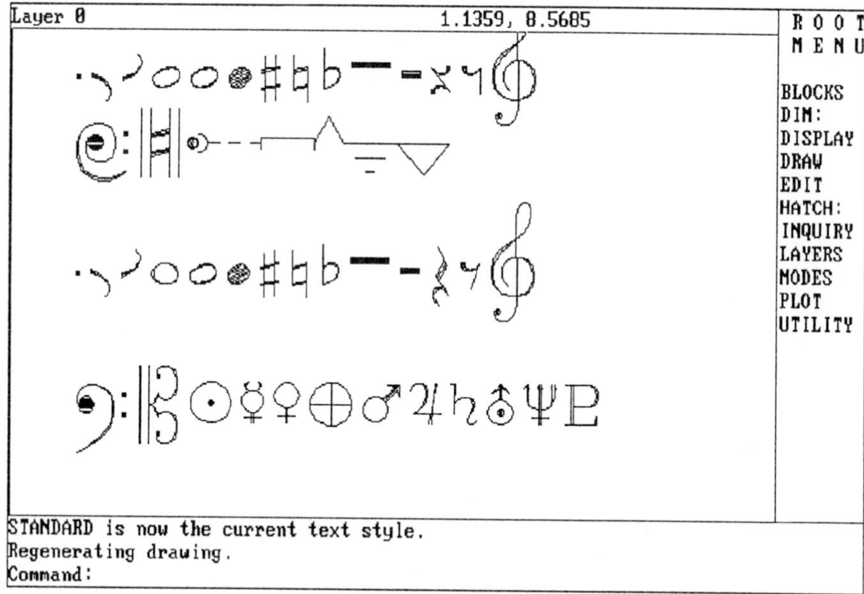

Figure 7-10*c*. The alphabet shown in the "symusic" font

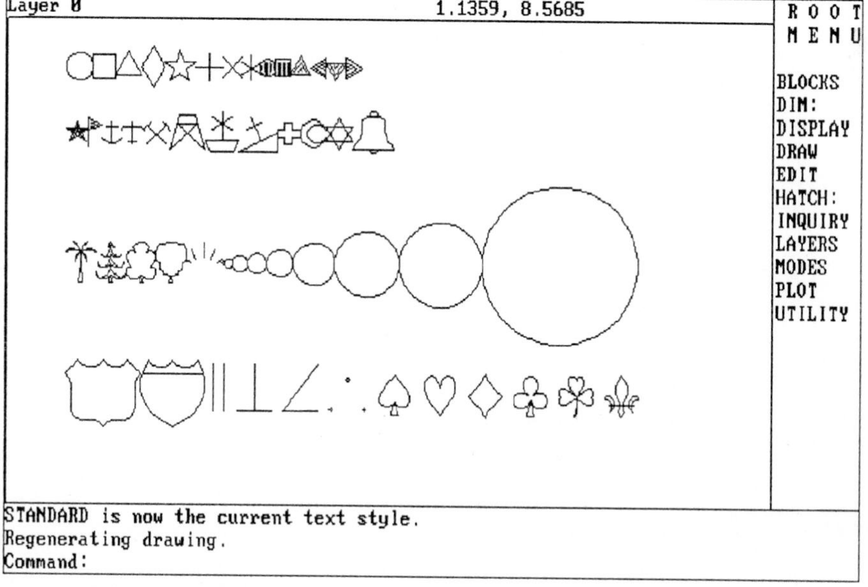

Figure 7-10*d*. The alphabet shown in the "symap" font

Setting Quick Mode

Depending on the font used, it can take more or less time to regenerate text. If you have a lot of text in your drawing, you may find that it takes too long to regenerate. AutoCAD provides a way to speed up this process. With the *quick text* mode, you can reduce all text drawing to the display of outline rectangles. When quick text mode is *on*, you will not see your text after each regeneration, only rectangles that show the location of the text.

To turn quick text mode *on*, you must use the QTEXT command with the following command sequence:

Command: **qtext**
ON/OFF <Off>: **on**

Figure 7-11 shows the same display as Figure 7-9, except that quick text mode is on. Note that the drawing must be regenerated, not simply redrawn, to show the effect of quick text mode.

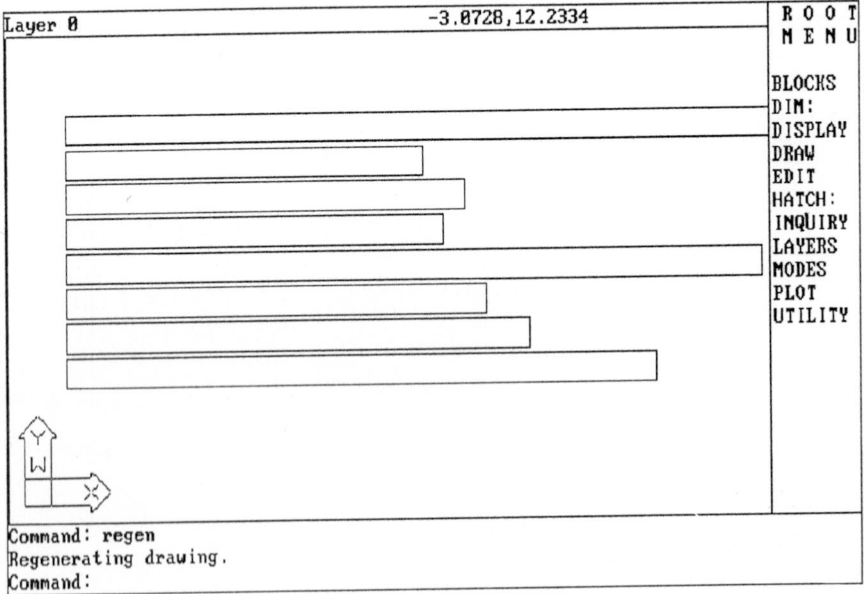

Figure 7-11. A text paragraph shown in quick text mode

Working with Dynamic Text

You can enter and edit entire paragraphs of text with the DTEXT command. Perhaps the best way to explain DTEXT is by contrast with the TEXT command. The TEXT command explained in this chapter enables you to enter one line of text at a time. Each time you enter your text, you must go back to the command line and re-enter the TEXT command. Fortunately, this is easy to do because simply pressing ENTER will repeat an AutoCAD command. In addition to entering the TEXT command, though, you must press ENTER again to respond to the "Start point" prompt:

Command: **text**
Start point or Align/Center/Fit/Middle/Right/Style:
Text:

At the "Text:" prompt you can then enter the next line of text. Each line of text will be below the one above it until you choose a new start point. This sequence is fine for entering a few lines of text, but what about whole paragraphs? The process can be tedious for multiple text lines. You can make mistakes, like pressing the pick button accidentally when you really wanted to continue on to the next line of text. If you accidentally press the pick button instead of the enter button, you will select a new start point. This voids your text alignment, often requiring you to undo your text, rather than make a mistake in picking a new start point.

There is a way you can draw text as though you were using a word processor, one paragraph at a time. You can even edit your text dynamically. You can accomplish all of this with the DTEXT command. The command sequence for the DTEXT command follows:

Command: **dtext**
Start point or Align/Center/Fit/Middle/Right/Style:
Rotation angle <0>:
Text: **This is dynamic text**

Note that the DTEXT command so far is just like the TEXT command. This is where the similarity ends.

Figures 7-12*a* through 7-12*d* show dynamic text in action. Figure 7-12*a* shows the invocation of the command and the picking of the start point. Figure 7-12*b* shows the words "This is" being entered, as well as the rectangular cursor that shows the size of the character you specify with the STYLE command. Figure 7-12*c* shows the entry of two lines of dynamic text and the new location of the text cursor. Note that the DTEXT command has automatically prepared the next "TEXT:" prompt without going back to the command line.

In Figure 7-12*d*, the backspace key has been used to backspace over the words "text in action." and the character "c" of the word "dynamic." The characters "te." have been added, turning the word "dynamic" into the word "dynamite." Note that the "Text:" prompts at the bottom of the screen have been automatically managed by the DTEXT command. When the words "text in action." were deleted by the BACKSPACE key, the text line was "*Deleted*" from the "Text:" prompt. The text cursor automatically went back to the previous line which was then redisplayed at a new "Text:" prompt.

You can now see why it is easier to create and edit entire text paragraphs with the DTEXT command than with the TEXT command. As you gain proficiency, you will be able to decide when to use each method.

Understanding Shapes

AutoCAD produces text fonts by using shape files. These files, which have the extension ".shp", actually have a more general purpose. They are used to store shapes. Fonts are specialized

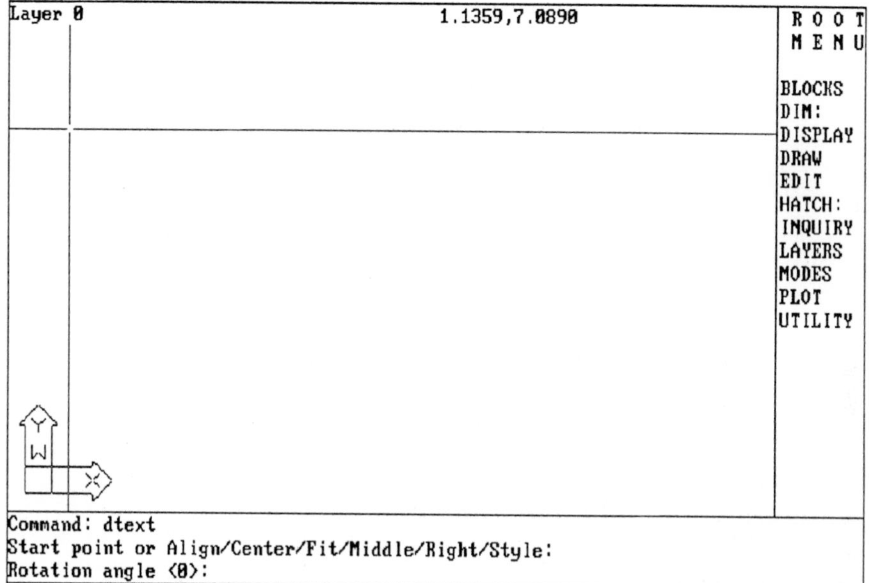

Figure 7-12*a*. The invocation of the DTEXT command

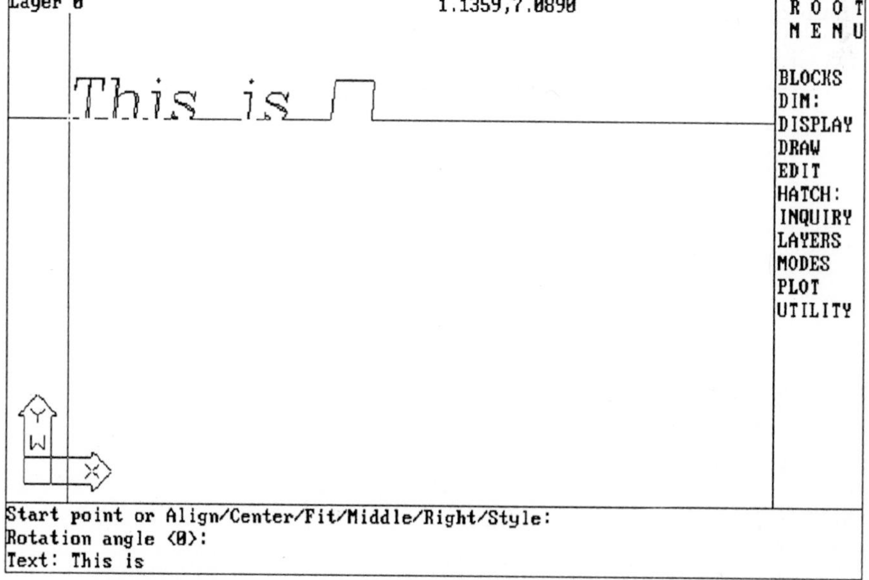

Figure 7-12*b*. Entering dynamic text

Layer 0 1.1359,7.0890

ROOT MENU

BLOCKS
DIM:
DISPLAY
DRAW
EDIT
HATCH:
INQUIRY
LAYERS
MODES
PLOT
UTILITY

This is dynamic
text in action.

Rotation angle <0>:
Text: This is dynamic
Text: text in action.

Figure 7-12*c*. The next line of dynamic text

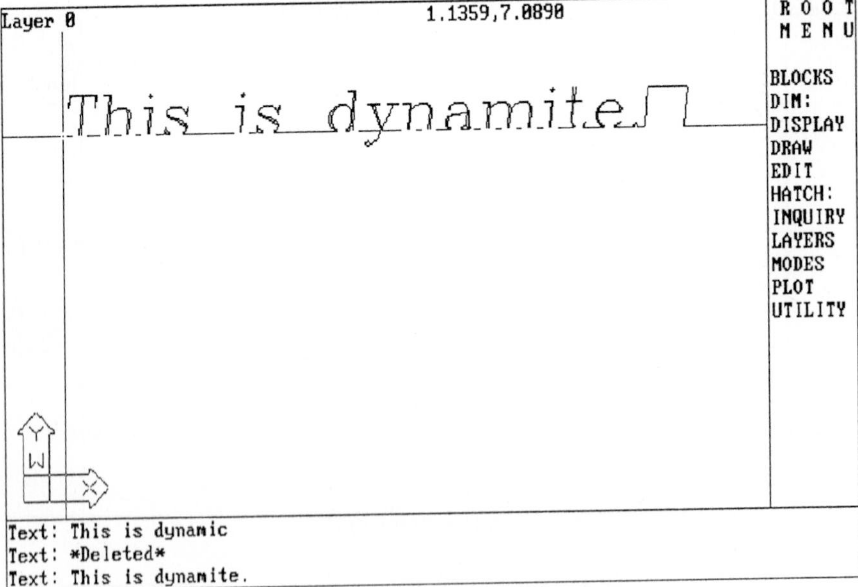

Figure 7-12*d*. Editing dynamic text using BACKSPACE

shapes that can be called up with the TEXT and DTEXT commands. You can use other kinds of shapes by using the LOAD command.

Shape files have the advantage that they can be drawn much more quickly than blocks. Although they can be brought into a drawing like blocks, they are much more compact and efficient. You should use blocks rather than shapes for most of your work, however, because shapes are much more difficult to define. The shape capability of AutoCAD is provided primarily as a way to produce repetitively used symbols in the fastest way possible. Unless you need many such symbols in your drawings and you have a lot of time to spend creating shapes, it is best to use blocks rather than shapes in your work.

Shapes and Fonts

Shapes are very much like fonts. In fact, a font is a special instance of a shape file. The STYLE command as described earlier in this chapter allows you to use fonts in your drawings. To use a shape file, however, you must use the LOAD command. The STYLE command loads a special shape file with shapes that are called up by their ASCII codes when you work with the TEXT or DTEXT commands. The LOAD command loads a general shape file that contains shapes that can be used by name when you invoke the SHAPE command.

Loading Shape Files

AutoCAD provides a sample file, "pc.shp", that can be used to illustrate the use of shapes in your drawings. Before you can use the "pc.shp" file, you must compile it into a ".shx" file. You do this by selecting option 7 on the main menu:

7. Compile shape/font description file

When you select this option, you will see the following prompt:

Enter NAME of shapefile: **pc**

Do not include the ".shp" extension. The ".shp" file will be converted into an ".shx" file of the name you selected.

You can load this sample file with the following invocation of the LOAD command:

Command: **load**
Name of shape file to load (or ?): **pc**

You have not used any of the shapes available in the file. The LOAD command only loads the shape file so you can gain access to the shapes within it.

The following is an example of the improper use of the LOAD command. The "txt" font is AutoCAD's default font. In this case, an attempt has been made to load it as though it were a shape file:

Command: **load**
Name of shape file to load (or ?): **txt**
txt is a normal text font file, not a shape file.
Enter another shape file name (or RETURN for none):

Using the SHAPE Command

The SHAPE command allows you to use shapes in your drawings. You can see the names of the shapes contained in the "pc.shp" file you have just loaded by choosing the question mark option of the SHAPE command as follows:

Command: **shape**
Shape name (or ?): **?**
Available shapes:
File: **pc**

FEEDTHRU	DIP8
DIP14	DIP16
DIP18	DIP20
DIP24	DIP40

The "pc.shp" file contains symbols for use in printed circuit (pc) boards. A feedthru is a hole in a printed circuit board that enables electrical connections through the board to the other side. The various "DIP" symbols, such as DIP8, DIP14, and DIP16 refer to "Digital Inline Package" insertion hole patterns. Each name shown above invokes a unique shape. In this case, the shapes can be used, as in Chapter 4, "Working with Blocks," to create printed circuit boards. The same work that was done in that chapter with blocks will now be done in the following example with shapes.

Figure 7-13 shows a printed circuit board drawn with the shapes in the "pc.shp" file. The shape "DIP8" appears in the upper left corner. Below it are two "DIP16" shapes. To the right is a "DIP24" shape. Note that the insertion holes are simple squares, not doughnuts as in Chapter 4. You could, however, use any shape you want by defining your own shapes, though this is not as easy as defining blocks.

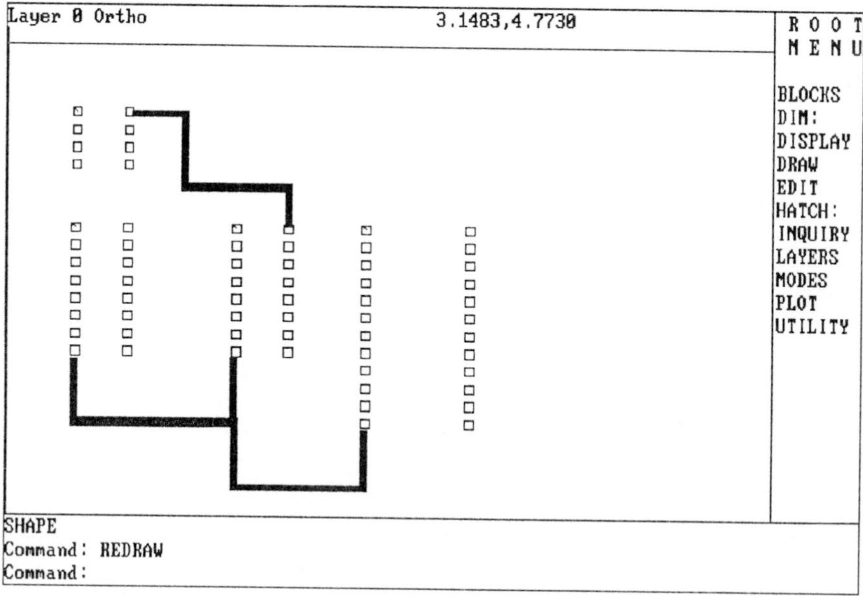

Figure 7-13. Sample drawing with shapes

To place one shape in your drawing with the SHAPE command, you would use the following command sequence:

Command: **shape**
Shape name (or ?) <DIP16>: **dip24**
Starting point:
Height <1.0000>:

This invocation of the SHAPE command would permit you to use the 24 pin DIP shape ("DIP24") as shown in Figure 7-13.

Shapes can be very useful because they are drawn quickly by AutoCAD, but they are limited by the difficulty you will encounter in creating them. In earlier versions, shapes occupied the place blocks now have in the AutoCAD pantheon of objects. Although shapes can be useful, most of your work will be more easily accomplished by using blocks.

Working with Plotters

EIGHT

Creating a Calibration Plot
Configuring Plotters
Configuring Printers
Plotting a Drawing

In the late seventies and the early eighties, a true phenomenon occurred in the computer industry. Until that time, it was virtually impossible for an individual or small company to own computer graphics hardware. It was just too expensive. For example, a typical *plotter* cost in the neighborhood of fifty thousand dollars. Plotters in those days were huge devices, often as large as cars, consisting of flat horizontal surfaces over which pens would travel. The pens would draw in much the same way as people would, except that the pens were guided by electromechanical linkages under computer control.

There were two basic types of plotters, the *flat bed* and the *drum*. Flat bed plotters, as the name implies, would hold the drafting sheet on a horizontal bed much as the sheet would be placed on a manual drafting table. Drum plotters used a large belt that held the drafting sheet. The belt would move the drawing under the pen. The pen moved on a rail, generating the X axis, while the drawing moved under it, generating the Y axis. Most of the plotters you can buy today follow the drum model, but there are also more than a few small ones that use the flat bed design. There are even designs, such as electrostatic and photographic, that have become available. Add to this the emergence of dot matrix and laser printers that double as plotters, and you have a rich source of hardware indeed.

In the first five years of the personal computer revolution that began circa 1978, a frenzy of development brought many inexpensive plotting devices to market. AutoCAD was introduced during this period of fast change and incorporated software *drivers* to work with almost all of these devices. The list of devices supported today includes the names of almost all of the plotters that were the products of that period in personal computer history. Each device on the list has its own driver, written by Autodesk in close cooperation with hardware manufacturers.

AutoCAD must be configured to work with your plotter. You probably already know this and may even have gone through the configuration process. This book does not attempt to tell you how to set up AutoCAD to use specific devices. Such an effort would be futile, because the device configurations change with each AutoCAD release. Instead, this chapter will focus on characteristics that are general to all devices.

There are two basic types of graphic output devices that can be used with AutoCAD: plotters and printers. AutoCAD breaks these devices down into two categories based on their input requirements. If a device accepts *vector* commands, it is configured as a plotter. Vectors are like straight lines. They have distance and direction. A device that accepts vector input needs to know the starting and ending points of vectors, but not every point along the vectors. If the device accepts *raster* commands, it is generally configured as a printer. A raster is an array of dots. Any dot in the raster can be changed in color by reference to its position in the array. Your computer screen is a raster. When you draw a line on a raster, you must change the color of each dot on the line. You cannot just give the endpoints of the line and expect the raster device to draw the line for you.

Among the many plotters and printers available, there is almost every conceivable combination of ways to communicate graphic information. Some raster devices also accept vector input. Some vector devices also accept raster input. So it is sometimes difficult to decide whether to treat a device as a printer or a plotter. Fortunately, AutoCAD has made that decision for you. All you need to do is buy your favorite compatible hardware and answer a few simple questions to configure AutoCAD to use it.

Creating a Calibration Plot

Plotting and printing devices are not always perfectly accurate. It is not that the manufacturers are less than diligent in quality control. Plotters and printers are mechanical devices with moving parts that wear over time or respond to atmospheric changes. Even in an imperfect world, however, you want your plotted drawings to be as accurate as possible. Plotters are often accurate enough to require no calibration; still, you may wish to achieve the highest accuracy possible by carefully configuring your plotter. Printers are often much less accurate than plotters, and so you will usually need to calibrate a printer.

To correctly complete the configuration of AutoCAD, you must do some homework. Go through the appropriate configuration without doing any calibration. Then use AutoCAD to do a calibration drawing. The configuration procedures are intended to be run repeatedly as you change plotting or printer plotting parameters, so you can partially configure the system at least to get the plotter or printer to work until you calibrate it.

To get around the problem of configuring your device twice, you can often use your plotter or printer in its "test mode." Most plotters have a mode you can select from the plotter control panel. If the test plot is a good one, it will contain measured line lengths. These test lines will be drawn with tick marks or with some other indication of what their lengths *should* be. You should measure these lines with a drafting scale or other accurate measuring device.

Figures 8-1*a* and 8-1*b* show a typical test plot with calibration lines drawn to scale. The test plot was created with AutoCAD by configuring the plotter without calibrating it. You could also make a similar plot with your printer. The test drawing was done by simply drawing a ten-unit square. The sides of the square were then measured and the results are shown in Figure 8-1*b*. The dimensions of the sides as they *should* be are shown outside the square. The measured dimensions are shown inside.

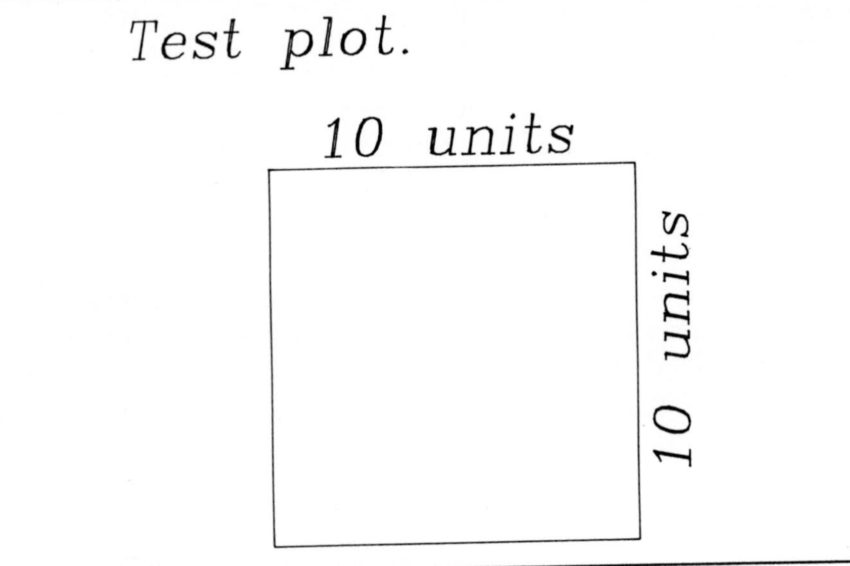

Figure 8-1*a*. A ten unit test plot

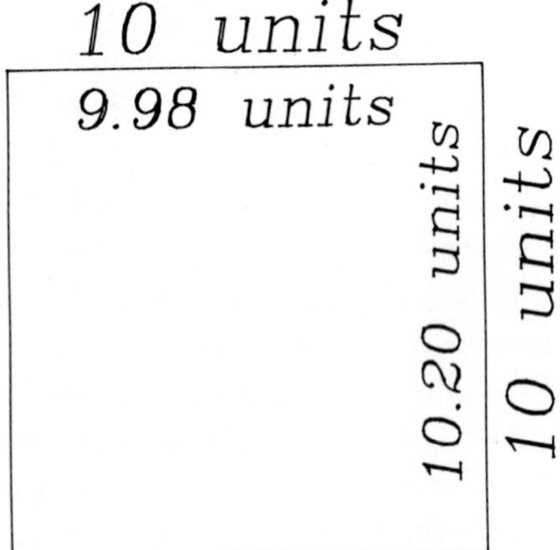

Figure 8-1*b*. The measured lengths of the test plot

Note that the plotter used to do this drawing is not indicated, so the inaccuracy is not to be ascribed to any particular brand of plotter.

When making your test plot, measure one horizontal line and one vertical line, and write down the lengths the lines should be, as well as the lengths you actually measured. For example, you might write the following notes based on your observations:

Horizontal measured: 10.72
Horizontal should be: 10.00
Vertical measured: 9.34
Vertical should be: 10.00

If your plotter or printer does not have a test mode or its test pattern has no measured lines, you can configure AutoCAD to use your plotter without calibrating it. During the configuration, you will see the following prompt for plotters:

Would you like to calibrate your plotter? <N> **n**

You will see a similar prompt for printers:

Would you like to calibrate your printer? <N> **n**

By answering with a letter **n** (no), you will avoid the calibration prompts. You then can create a drawing with a single horizontal line of, say, ten inches in length and a single vertical line of the same length. You then plot those lines with the PLOT command (described later in this chapter) and measure the actual lengths of the plotted lines. Keep a record of the desired and actual lengths of both of these lines.

If you know how to create ASCII text files with EDLIN or another text editor, you can calibrate your plotter or printer by using your device's command language directly from the instruction manual. You can create an ASCII text file with the commands to draw a horizontal and a vertical line of a desired length. Use the DOS COPY command to copy that file directly to the communications port to which the plotter or printer is connected. Of course, you must use the DOS MODE command to set the communications parameters, including the baud rate, parity, data, and stop bits for serial ports. This procedure is not for the inexperienced, but if you are an advanced user it can be a quick way to plot calibration lines. Read your DOS manual for information on the COPY and MODE commands.

For example, you could plot a horizontal calibration line ten inches long and a vertical line ten inches long. If the horizontal line, when measured, is 10.72 inches long and the vertical line, when measured, is 9.34 inches long, you should definitely calibrate your plotter. The discrepancies are great enough to create drawings that will be very inaccurate. Fortunately, most plotters are much more accurate than this. If you plot lines that are supposed to be 10 inches long, and actually are 10 inches long when measured, you do *not* need to calibrate.

Configuring Plotters

Pen plotters are perhaps the most popular graphic output devices for use with computer-aided design. This is because they are capable of accepting large sheets of drafting paper, they produce smooth linework, and they do so at a relatively low cost.

Economical pen plotters are almost always of the drum type. Low cost drum plotters generally grip the drawing sheet by the edges of its narrowest dimension. Rollers pinch the edges and the sheet is moved between them. Because the rollers require less material to manufacture than the surface of a flat bed, drum plotters have an automatic economic advantage over flat bed plotters. In addition, the footprint of a drum plotter is much smaller than that of a flat bed plotter.

Pen plotters vary greatly in size. The smallest pen plotter is generally of the A size, with a plotting area (not a sheet size) of 8 inches by 10 1/2 inches. The largest pen plotters are generally capable of working with D size sheet, or 21 inches by 33 inches.

Government work often involves the use of E size plotting areas (33 inches by 43 inches), but plotters that accommodate this large size are fewer and somewhat more expensive. AutoCAD enables you to set the plotting area to any size you want during the configuration process. You are not confined to standard sizes.

Depending on which plotter you have selected in the configuration procedure, AutoCAD will give you a range of permitted sizes. If you select a size greater than the device can handle, AutoCAD will still let you do it, but will warn you about it.

Setting Configuration Parameters

To use your plotter with AutoCAD, you must first configure it. AutoCAD comes with a list of currently supported plotters. Configuration, in its simplest sense, consists of selecting your hardware from that list.

Configuration is more than merely selecting the driver AutoCAD will use to send output to your plotter. There are many other factors to consider. In other words, the selection of the output driver is a simple process that depends on what is currently available. The selection of configuration parameters that apply to all drivers, however, is much more complex.

During the configuration process, you will be asked to provide certain information that AutoCAD will store and use when you plot your drawings. Many of these values can be changed when you actually plot a drawing. These *default* values will save you time since you will not have to type those values when you want to use them.

Using the Configuration Menu

To configure your plotter, you must first run AutoCAD as usual from the DOS command line. You do this by entering "acad" as in Chapter 1, "Quick Start." When you see the Main Menu, select option 5, "Configure AutoCAD." You will then see a list of the current devices for which AutoCAD has been configured.

The current video display, digitizer, plotter, and printer plotter will be shown. At the bottom of the screen you will see the following prompt:

Press RETURN to continue:

If you press ENTER at this time, you will see the configuration menu. Choose option 5 of the configuration menu by typing the number **5** at the "Enter selection <0>:" prompt. Notice the following:

Your current plotter is: None
Do you want to select a different one? <N> **y**

After you answer with a **y** (for yes), you will see a list of plotters supported by AutoCAD. The following prompt appears at the bottom of the screen:

Select device number or ? to repeat list <1>: 8

Select the numbered option that corresponds with your plotter. In this case, the number 8 was chosen. This will select the Hewlett Packard models. You will see a list of the models that are supported by AutoCAD. Notice the prompt at the bottom of the screen:

Enter selection 1 to 10 <1>: **10**

This selection will choose the Hewlett Packard DraftMaster plotter.

After you select the plotter manufacturer and model, the following prompt appears:

Connects to Asynchronous Communications Adapter port.
Standard ports are:
COM1
COM2
Enter port name, or address in hexadecimal <COM2>: **COM2**

If you have installed two serial adapters in your computer and have set the switches appropriately (see "Common Sources of Frustration" later in this chapter), you can use one of them for the pointing device and one for your plotter. In this case, the pointing device is using COM1, so you will want to use COM2. Be sure you have plugged your devices into the proper ports.

Plotter Calibration After you enter the name of the port to which your plotter is connected, you will see the following message: "If you have previously measured the lengths of a horizontal and a vertical line that were plotted to a specific scale, you may use these measurements to calibrate your plotter." This message will be followed by this prompt:

> Would you like to calibrate your plotter? <N> **y**

If you have not yet created a calibration plot, you will want to respond to this prompt with the letter **n** (no). This will result in configuration for an uncalibrated plotter. Without calibration, you can then proceed to create a calibration plot and run the configuration process again to complete the calibration.

If you answer with a **y** (yes), you will be asked for two measured lengths and two actual lengths. The prompt sequence appears as follows:

> Enter measured length of horizontal line <1.0000>: **10.72**
> Enter correct length of horizontal line <1.0000>: **10**
> Enter measured length of vertical line <1.0000>: **9.34**
> Enter correct length of vertical line <1.0000>: **10**

Refer to the calibration plot suggested in the preceding section, "Creating a Calibration Plot," to provide the required calibration information. If the horizontal line you plotted was 10 units long and the plotted line measured 10.72 units, you would use 10.72 units as the measured length and 10 units as the correct length. You would follow the same procedure for the vertical plotted line. If it was supposed to be 10 units long, but measured 9.34 units, you would use 9.34 units for the measured length and 10 units for the correct length.

Writing the Plot to a File Sometimes you may wish to *spool* your plots so that they can be plotted on a slow plotter overnight or be sent to a service bureau for plotting. You can configure AutoCAD so that the same information that would be sent directly to a plotter will be sent instead to a designated file. After you calibrate your plotter you will be prompted as follows:

Write the plot to a file? <N> **y**

If you respond to this prompt by entering a **y** (yes), your plotter output will be directed to a file with the same name as the drawing, but with a ".plt" extension. You can change this configuration in response to the PLOT or PRPLOT command discussed later in this section.

Selecting Size Units After you choose whether or not you will plot to a file, you will see the following prompt:

Size units (Inches or Millimeters) <I>:

If you select "Inches," each unit of length in your drawing will be plotted as an inch on the plotter. If you select "Millimeters," each unit of length in your drawing will be plotted as a millimeter on the plotter. Since there is a big difference between the sizes of these two units of measure, a wrong answer to this prompt will produce a drawing that is much too small or much too large. Make sure that the units you select here are the same as the units you plan to use in the drawing you will plot.

Setting the Plot Origin You can choose to have the origin of the coordinate system for your plotted drawing anywhere in the plotting area, not just in the lower left corner. Since your drawing probably will have a border and will not be drawn all the way to the edge of the sheet, you will probably want to set the origin.

The default plotting origin is aligned with the lower left corner of the plotter's drawing area, not with the lower left corner of the physical sheet. The actual location of the plotter's drawing area varies from manufacturer to manufacturer, so you may need to do some research. The plotter manual will usually tell you the limits of the drawing area.

The origin will be measured in the plotting units you selected with the preceding "Size units" prompt (either inches or millimeters). You will see the following prompt:

Plot origin in Inches <0.00,0.00>: **1.5,3.0**

The response shown for this prompt will place the plot origin 1.5 inches from the left extent of the plotting area and 3.0 inches from the bottom extent.

Setting Plotting Size After you set the plot origin, you will be prompted to select the plotting size you want. The range of sizes available depends on the plotter you are using. Some plotters have small plotting areas, others have large areas. Some plotters allow you to plot with a range of sheet sizes. Others permit only one sheet size. First you will see a list of standard values, then you will be prompted for the plotting size you want:

Standard values for plotting size

Size	Width	Height
A	10.50	8.00
B	16.00	10.00
C	21.00	16.00
D	33.00	21.00
E	43.00	35.31
MAX	44.72	35.31

Enter the Size or Width,Height (in Inches) <MAX>: **D**

You can select the desired plotting size by letter (upper- or lowercase), or you can enter a desired width and height separated by a comma:

Enter the Size or Width,Height (in Inches) <MAX>: **22,11**

If you enter a size that exceeds the "MAX" value, you will be warned, but AutoCAD will not prevent you from using it. If you try to plot beyond your plotter's mechanical limits, usually no harm will be done to your plotter, but you will not see part of your drawing. Modern equipment is generally protected from mechanical damage caused by bad data.

Setting the Default Rotation After you select your desired plotting size, you will be asked whether or not you want to rotate your plots 90 degrees. Sometimes you will do a drawing that has its longest dimension oriented vertically even when the sheet on which you will plot it is oriented with its longest dimension horizontally. To obtain the largest drawing using the entire sheet, you may want to rotate the drawing 90 degrees. You will see the following prompt:

```
Rotate 2D plots 90 degrees clockwise? <N>
```

If you answer with a **y** (yes), your drawings will be rotated 90 degrees in a clockwise direction. In this example, the plotting origin will be measured from the upper left corner of the plotting area rather than from the lower left corner.

Figure 8-2*a* shows a drawing that was plotted in the normal orientation. Figure 8-2*b* shows the same drawing plotted with the rotation 90 degrees clockwise.

Setting the Pen Width Plotting pens have many different widths. When you plot an area fill, the actual filling is done with many lines drawn side-by-side. A large pen will need fewer passes to fill the same area than a small pen. You should set the pen width to be a little narrower than the width of the smallest pen your plotter uses. This will reduce the amount of time it takes AutoCAD to fill areas in your plots. You set the pen width in response to the following prompt:

```
Pen width <0.010>:
```

Adjusting Fill Boundaries If the pen is too large, a line will appear to end at a given point in the drawing, but when plotted will overlap slightly. This often happens when crosshatching is

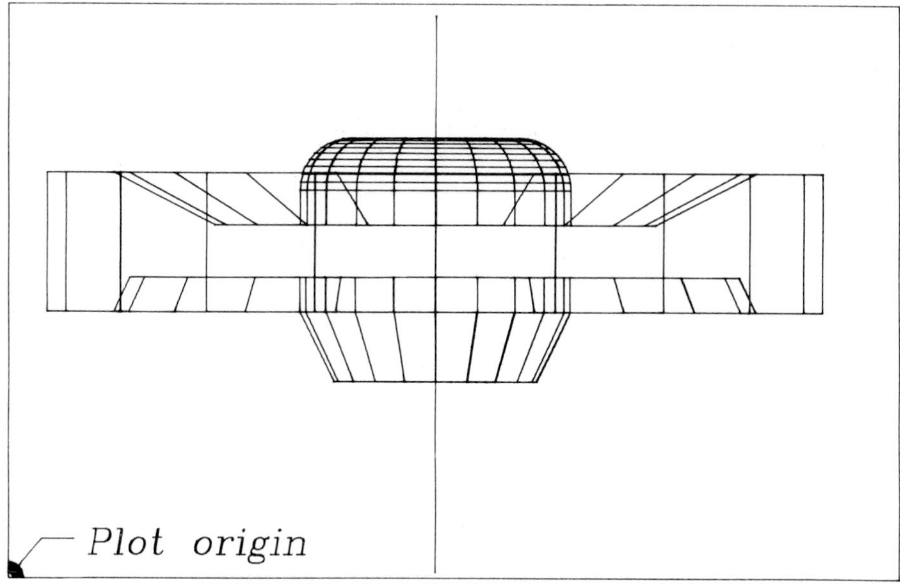

Figure 8-2*a*. A plot shown in normal orientation

used without consideration for the pen width. When the cross-hatch line reaches a boundary, the pen is made to stop exactly at the intersection point. If the pen is too large, however, it actually draws beyond the intersection point. You can instruct AutoCAD to automatically compensate for pen width when drawing fills to boundaries by answering the following prompt with a **y** (yes):

Adjust area fill boundaries for pen width? <N>

Removing Hidden Lines If you would like to have your drawing automatically processed to remove hidden lines, you should answer **y** (yes) to the following prompt:

Remove hidden lines? <N>

If you wish to remove hidden lines by default, any drawing that has three-dimensional surfaces in it will appear solid rather than as wire frame. Wire frame drawings are, as the name implies, composed of lines in space that connect points together. Since the wire figure is not composed of solid areas, but only of lines, there is nothing to block your view right through the figure.

The hidden line removal process takes much more time than simply plotting your drawing without hidden line removal. For simple two-dimensional drawings, you should definitely not use hidden line removal.

Specifying Scale You can plot your drawings so that an inch in the drawing (one drawing unit) appears as an inch in the plot.

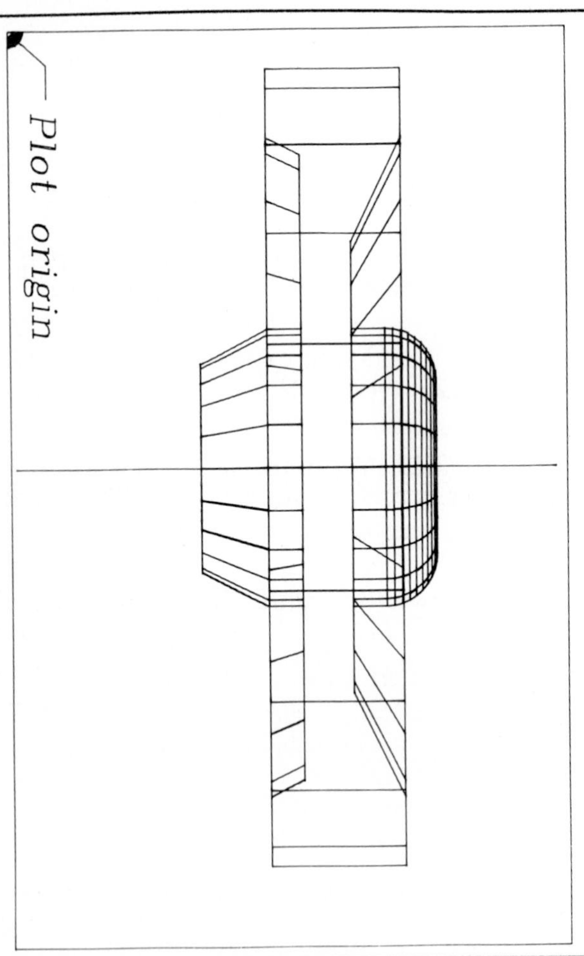

Figure 8-2*b*. A plot shown rotated 90 degrees clockwise

You can also change the scale so that an inch in the drawing is any size you want in the plot. You specify the scale factor in response to the following prompt:

Plotted Inches = Drawing Units or Fit or ? <F>: **1 = 1**

If you were to design a machine tool part that was three inches wide in drawing units and you wanted to plot the part at actual size, you would enter **1 = 1** as in the preceding example. If, however, you wanted to see the part take up the entire plotting area, you would use the "F" response to "Fit" the drawing, making it as large as possible to still fit in the plotting area.

If you were to use a **2 = 1** response to the above prompt, each drawing unit would be two inches in the plot. You can use scaling to create scale drawings for many drafting purposes. For example, an architectural drawing with a scale of 1/4 inch to a foot would require a response of **1 = 48** to the above prompt. This way 1/4 inch in a plot would be equivalent to 12 inches (1 foot) in the drawing, since 1 inch is 1 drawing unit.

Common Sources of Frustration

You should be aware of two common sources of frustration that you will almost certainly encounter in the configuration process. Over the years, these two problems have appeared time and again in dealing with plotters. Being aware of them will save you a great deal of misery when you are confronted with the unexplained. The problems are completely external to AutoCAD and to your specific plotter. The problems have to do with what goes on *between* your computer and your plotter hardware. Because the solutions to these problems are extremely device dependent, you must work out the solutions yourself, but just knowing what the source of the problem is should help a great deal.

Confronting Bus Contention AutoCAD makes it as easy as possible for you to configure your plotter. You may still have problems, however, because there are many combinations of hardware with which you can run AutoCAD. For example, a problem that often appears is *bus contention.* Bus contention occurs when two adapter cards have their switches set so they appear to the computer to be the same device. Since both cards are plugged into the computer at once and they both tell the computer they are one device, they must compete or "contend" for the computer's attention. The result is chaos and the computer may stop working (lock up). Bus contention often happens when you have two serial adapters plugged into your computer at once without having set their switches appropriately.

Confronting Cantankerous Cables The other major source of difficulty in successfully configuring your plotter has to do with the cable that connects your plotter to your computer. Plotters, with a few exceptions, are *serial* devices. Serial devices communicate with the computer by using one wire to receive data. The data consists of *bytes,* each of which is a combination of eight *bits,* each of which is either on or off. If there were eight wires, each bit in a given byte could have its own wire. This would be *parallel* data communication. But, since there is only one wire, the bits must be sent one after another, in serial mode.

The requirements for serial transmission are much more complex than for parallel. There is, for example, the problem of the speed at which the bits are to be sent. There is also the problem of synchronization; how do you know when you have received eight of them? These factors, among others, make serial *interfacing* very difficult. Unless you hook up all the wires in your cable just right, the plotter will not work. Sometimes the plotter will appear to work for a while, and then stop for no apparent reason. Sometimes you will see a tangle of lines instead of the drawing you expected. Therefore, you must be extremely careful that the cable you use with your plotter is wired correctly. Do not be surprised if your plotter does not work just by plugging it in.

Configuring Printers

In addition to supporting plotters, AutoCAD supports a wide range of printers that can be used as graphics output devices.

These devices produce graphics by means of a matrix of dots (a raster) rather than by means of pens. Printers sometimes produce their images by using a print head with a row of pins that strike the paper through a ribbon, much like an old-fashioned typewriter. Laser printers use an entirely different technology. They produce images by electrostatically energizing a row of pins that, much like an electrostatic copy machine, cause the paper to attract carbon particles. In either case, the key to understanding printer plotting is to know that arrays of dots, rather than ink lines, produce the final images.

As far as the user is concerned, printer plots are created in much the same way as are pen plots. You configure AutoCAD to use your printer hardware in much the same way as you configure it to use your plotter hardware.

Setting Configuration Parameters

To configure AutoCAD to work with your printer, you must first run AutoCAD from the DOS command line. When you see the Main Menu, you select option number 6, "Configure printer plotter," and AutoCAD shows you your current configuration in the following message:

Your current printer plotter is: None
Do you want to select a different one? <N> **y**

You respond with a **y** (yes) to indicate that you wish to select a different printer plotter. When you do, you will see a list of the currently available printer plotters. You choose one of them in response to the prompt that appears at the bottom of the screen:

Select device number or ? to repeat list <1>: **5**

In this case, printer number 5 was chosen. After you choose the printer manufacturer in this way, you will see a list of available models. You then choose the model that you plan to use.

Printer Calibration

After you enter the name of the port to which your printer is connected, you will see the following message: "If you have previously measured the lengths of a horizontal and a vertical line that were plotted to a specific scale, you may use these measurements to calibrate your printer." This message will be followed by this prompt:

Would you like to calibrate your printer? <N> **y**

If you have not yet created a calibration plot, you should respond to this prompt with the letter **n** (no). This will result in configuration for an uncalibrated printer. Without calibration, you can then proceed to create a calibration plot and run the configuration process again to complete the calibration.

Calibration is usually more important for printers than for plotters. Printers are not usually expressly made for the high resolution graphics that are required by computer-aided design. They are capable of producing graphics quickly, however, and can be used very effectively to produce test plots. You will find that your plotter may not need calibration at all, but your printer may need to be calibrated.

If you answer the preceding prompt with a **y** (yes), you will be asked for two measured lengths and two actual lengths. The prompt sequence appears as follows:

Enter measured length of horizontal line <1.0000>: **10.72**
Enter correct length of horizontal line <1.0000>: **10**
Enter measured length of vertical line <1.0000>: **9.34**
Enter correct length of vertical line <1.0000>: **10**

To provide the required calibration information, refer to the calibration plot suggested in the earlier section, "Creating a Calibration Plot." If the horizontal line you plotted was ten units long and the plotted line measured 10.72 units, you would use 10.72 units as the measured length and 10 units as the correct length. You would follow the same procedure for the vertical plotted line. If it was supposed to be 10 units long but measured

9.34 units, you would use 9.34 units for the measured length and 10 units for the correct length.

Printer and Plotter Options

After calibration, you will see the same prompts as for the plotter configuration "Configuring Plotters" with the exception that pen width is not included. Because printers do not use pens, the pen width is irrelevant. The printer driver automatically produces attractive plots based on what is known about the dot matrix that the device produces.

You can set the configuration of your printer, as for your plotter, to write the plot to a file, to use inches or millimeters, to have a special plot origin, to use standard or special sheet sizes, or to rotate the plot 90 degrees. You can also choose to remove hidden lines and set the default scale of the plot.

Plotting a Drawing

After you have configured your plotter or printer, you can begin to plot a drawing you have created with AutoCAD. You plot a drawing on your plotter with the PLOT command. Similarly, to plot a drawing on your printer, you must use the PRPLOT command.

Pen plotters are very accurate and produce smooth line work, but they are sometimes very slow. When working with a drawing, you may wish to see what the drawing will look like when it is plotted. If you were to plot it on your plotter, it would take a long time and use up your ink supply. This is where the printer can be handy. Instead of plotting your drawing, you can printer plot it in much less time.

Printer plots are also helpful for producing progress prints for use in job correspondence. You can include printer plots with your letters to clients and associates much more quickly than if you pen plot them.

Pen Plotting

The PLOT command is the gateway to AutoCAD's sophisticated plotting capabilities. You have already seen how to set up the default parameters for plotting. Now you will see how actual plotting is accomplished. You can change the default parameters during the plotting process.

Entering the PLOT Command

You enter the PLOT command, like other AutoCAD commands, in response to the "Command:" prompt. Of course you can also select the command from the sidebar, popup, or tablet menus if you have configured AutoCAD to use them. When you invoke the PLOT command, you will see the following command sequence:

Command: **plot**
What to plot – Display, Extents, Limits, View, or Window <E>:

You see a series of options. You can plot the display contents, the extents of the drawing, the drawing limits, a specified view, or the contents of a window.

Plotting the Display With the "Display" option of the PLOT command, you plot only what appears on the current display. This is an easy way to plot what you are working on to see how it will look or to share the information with someone else. You choose the "Display" option by entering the letter **D**, either upper- or lowercase. Remember, you can select any command option by entering its uppercase letters only. You do not need to type the whole word.

Figure 8-3*a* shows the display that was used to produce the plots in Figures 8-2*a* and 8-2*b*. When you choose the "Display" option of the PLOT command, you will plot only the contents of the drawing area.

Plotting the Extents The drawing extents are the outer most reaches of the drawing itself. In the case of a circle, for example, the extents would be four points farthest to the left, right, top, and bottom. If you choose to plot the drawing extents, the part of the drawing outside of any drawing information will be ignored.

Figure 8-3*b* shows the extents of a drawing that will be plotted. When plotted, the object shown within the dotted lines will be the only thing plotted. If you set the scale to "Fit," the object will take up the entire plotting area; otherwise, the scale you designate will be used.

Plotting the Limits The drawing limits are the limits you select with the LIMITS command. They are equivalent to the size of the sheet of paper you tell AutoCAD you are using while drawing. This is not to be confused with the actual size of the sheet of paper you will use in your plotter, however. If you select the "Limits" option, you will see the entire drawing, not just what you see on your display.

Figure 8-3*c* shows the drawing limits and the amount of the drawing that will be plotted within the plotting area if you select the "Limits" option of the PLOT command. As with the "Extents" option, the scale you request will determine how much of the drawing you will see. If you set the scale to "Fit," the entire drawing limits will be forced to fit into the plotting area.

Plotting the View If you choose the "View" option, you will be prompted for a "View name:" that must be a previously created view. You create views with the VIEW or DVIEW command. You can find out more about the VIEW and DVIEW commands in Chapter 2, "Drawing." After you enter a validly named view, you can proceed with your plot.

Plotting a Window If you choose the "Window" option of the PLOT command, you will be prompted for a window in the usual way, by corners. You will see the "First corner:" prompt to which you respond by picking the location you desire for the

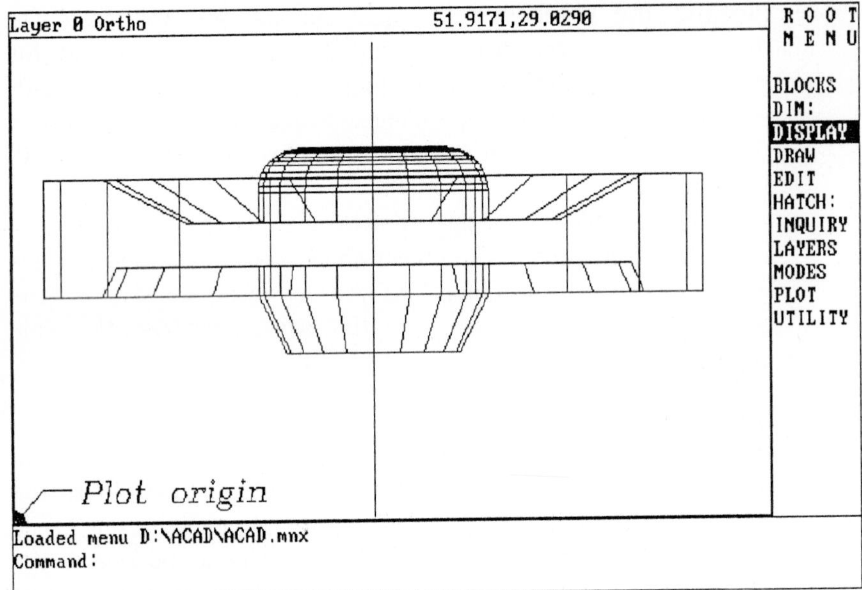

Figure 8-3*a*. The "Display" option will plot this view

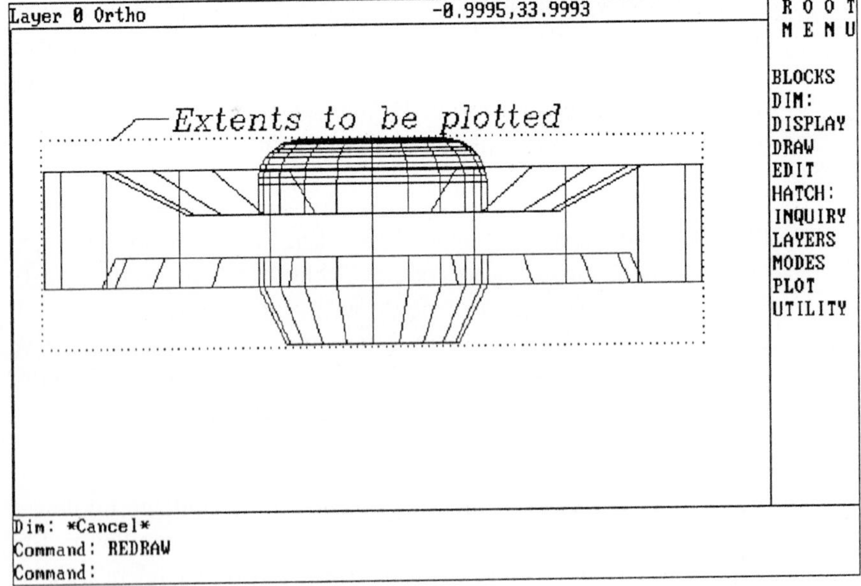

Figure 8-3*b*. The extents of a drawing to be plotted

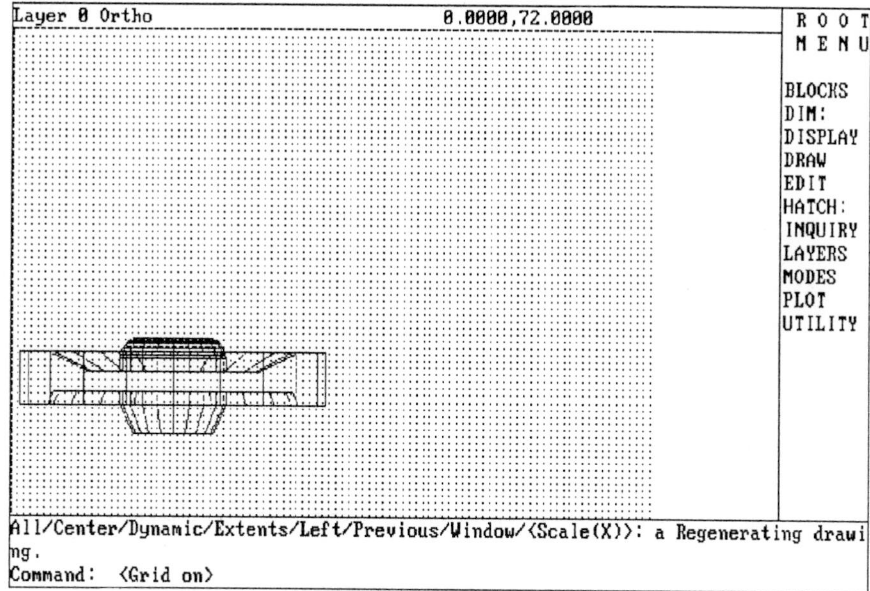

Figure 8-3*c*. The drawing limits that will be plotted

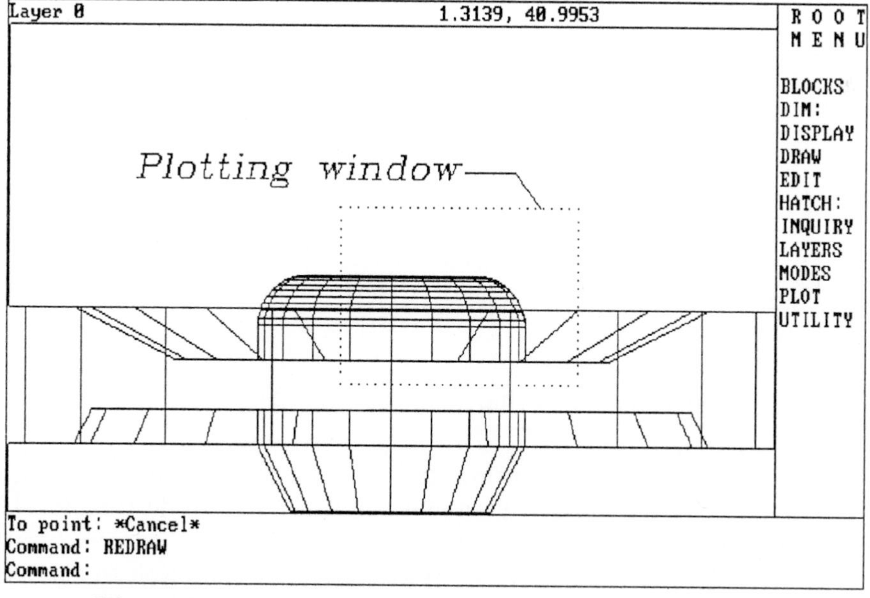

Figure 8-3*d*. The plotting window

first corner of the rectangle that will define the window. After picking the first corner, you will see the "Other corner:" prompt. After you select the other corner, you will be able to go on to plot whatever appears in the rectangular window you defined.

Figure 8-3*d* shows the part of a drawing that will be plotted if you select the "Window" option of the PLOT command. The window is shown dotted in the drawing. The contents of the window will be the only thing plotted. If you set the scale to "Fit," the entire contents of the window will be forced to fit the plotting area.

Changing Plot Parameters

After you choose a desired option from the list of options that appears for the PLOT command, you will see the following messages:

```
Plot will NOT be written to a selected file
Sizes are in inches
Plot origin is at (0.00,0.00)
Plotting area is 24.00 wide by 12.00 high (MAX size)
2D Plots are rotated 90 degrees clockwise
Pen width is 0.010
Area fill will NOT be adjusted for pen width
Hidden lines will NOT be removed
Scale is 1=1
```

These are the default plot parameters you set from the preceding Configuration Menu. After these messages, you will see the following prompt:

```
Do you want to change anything? <N>
```

Changing Pen Assignments If you do not want to change anything, just press ENTER and you will go on to do the plot. If you wish to change any of the parameters shown, enter **y** (yes). You will then see a series of prompts that allow you to change entity colors and line types. You will see a screen that shows which colors are assigned to which pens and/or line types. You will also see a list of pen speeds associated with each pen and a list of line types. The following prompt will will appear at the bottom of the screen:

Do you want to change any of the above parameters? <N>

If you respond to this prompt by pressing ENTER, you will be able to go on with the rest of the plot session. If you respond with a **y** (yes), however, you will see a series of prompts, one for each layer color, enabling you to select pens by layer. For example, the first such prompt will be

Layer Color	Pen No.	Line Type	Pen Speed	
1 (red)	1	0	36	Pen number <1>: 2

By responding with the number 2, you are telling AutoCAD that you want pen number two on your plotter to plot all colors designated as red. After you select the pen number (or press ENTER to select the default), you will see the "Line type <0>:" prompt. You can select any of the numbered line types shown on your display. After selecting the line type to be associated with layer 1, you will be prompted for the "Pen speed <36>:", to which you can respond with a desired pen speed as permitted by your hardware. AutoCAD will allow you to select only the parameters permitted by your hardware.

After selecting the pen speed, you will go through this same sequence for each layer color allowed, from 1 through 15. In this way, each AutoCAD color can be associated with a pen and/or a line type. You must, of course, carefully coordinate these layer colors with the pens and line types you actually use in your drawings. In order to do high quality drafting, you need to know how AutoCAD's colors relate to layers and line types.

Changing the File Plot Parameter After you have assigned the appropriate colors to the appropriate pens and line types for your drawing, you must stop the selection process. You do this by entering the letter **x** (upper- or lowercase) at any time. You will then see the following prompt:

Write the plot to a file? <N>

The default you selected when you configured your plotter will be shown and you can select it by pressing ENTER. If you choose to change the default, you may do so by entering a letter **n** (no) or a letter **y** (yes) as appropriate. If you choose to write the plot to a file, you will be prompted for the file name.

Changing Size Units You selected the size of your units when you first configured your plotter, choosing inches or millimeters. After you decide whether or not to write the plot to a file, you will see the following prompt:

Size units (Inches or Millimeters) <I>:

You now have the opportunity to change the default for the units you want for your plots. You can accept the default by pressing ENTER or you can enter **i** (Inches) or **m** (Millimeters) at this time.

Changing the Plot Origin You can change the plot origin from its default setting (the one you selected when you configured your plotter) by entering a new origin. You will see the following prompt:

Plot origin in Inches (0.00,0.00):

You now can change the plot origin from the default value you set when you configured the plotter.

Changing the Plot Size After you respond to the prompt for the plot origin, you can change the plot size. You will see the following prompt:

Enter the Size or Width,Height (in inches) <MAX>:

In this case, the default value, MAX, was selected during the plotter configuration process. You can now change it or you can accept the default by pressing ENTER.

Changing the Plot Rotation Like the plotting size, the rotation of the plot can also be changed from its default setting. You will see the following prompt:

Rotate 2D plots 90 degrees clockwise? <Y>

In the example shown, the default value is to rotate plots 90 degrees. You can choose to accept the default by pressing ENTER or you can enter the letter **y** (yes) to change it.

Changing the Pen Width The pen width can also be changed. You will see the default value in the prompt as follows: "Pen width <0.010>:." As with the other plot options you set during the configuration process, you can now change the pen width. If you choose to keep the default value, you can press ENTER now. If you choose to change the pen width, you can enter a new value.

Changing Fill Boundary Adjustment After you select the pen width, you can change the way the pen interacts with fill boundaries. You will see the following prompt:

Adjust area fill boundaries for pen width? <N>

If you choose to keep the default value you set during the plotter configuration, you can just press ENTER. To change the parameter, enter **n** (no) or **y** (yes) as appropriate.

Changing Hidden Line Removal You can indicate whether or not you want hidden lines to be removed. To remove hidden lines before plotting the drawing, respond appropriately to the prompt

Remove hidden lines? <N>

The default value is shown. You can accept the default value by pressing ENTER or enter **y** (yes) or **n** (no) to change the default.

Changing Plotting Scale You can change the default plotting scale you entered during the configuration process. The following prompt will enable you to do this:

```
Specify scale by entering:
Plotted Inches=Drawing Units or Fit or ? <1=1>:
```

The default shown is the setting you selected when you configured your plotter. You can accept it by pressing ENTER or change it by entering a new value. Read about the options in the "Configuring Plotters" section earlier in this chapter.

Permanence of Changes If you change any of the preceding default parameters, the changes will be permanent. If you want to re-configure your plotter, you must go through the configuration process from the configuration menu or perform another plot.

Preparing to Plot

After you either accept the default configuration or change some or all of the plotting parameters, you will see the following prompt on the screen:

```
Effective plotting area: 3.14 wide by 2.90 high
Position paper in plotter.
Press RETURN to continue or S to Stop for hardware setup
```

If you press ENTER, you will continue to plot and, if everything is hooked up correctly, your plotter will spring into action. If you wish to set any switches on your plotter or change any hardware settings at the last minute, press the S key to allow this.

Printer Plotting

If you want to use your printer to plot a drawing, you can do so with the PRPLOT command. Printer plotting is quite similar to plotting with a pen plotter. The PRPLOT command sequence is as follows:

Command: **prplot**
What to plot – Display, Extents, Limits, View, or Window <L>:

After you select one of the options, which mean the same as for the PLOT command, you will see messages that show the default parameters you set when you configured you printer. They appear as follows:

Plot will be written to a selected file
Sizes are in inches
Plot origin is at (0.00,0.00)
Plotting area is 7.99 wide by 10.29 high (MAX size)
Plot is NOT rotated 90 degrees
Hidden lines will be removed
Plot will be scaled to fit available area

Depending on the parameters you selected when you configured your printer plotter, you will see something like the messages shown. Note that in the case of the printer plotter, you have no option to change the pen width or to adjust area fills for pen width. This is because printer plotting does not use pens. With these exceptions, all the prompts are the same as for the PLOT command. After you change the default plotting parameters or choose not to change them, the printing will begin.

Plotting by Layer

To plot a single layer, you must use the LAYER command to select layers. In order to be plotted, a layer must not be frozen and it must be turned *on*. You assign pens and line types to layers as described earlier in the section "Changing Pen Assignments." The pens and line types you select will be assigned to layers either by default or according to the values you select when you choose to change values for the plot. For more information about layers, see the LAYER command in Chapter 16, "AutoCAD Command Reference."

Attribute Management

NINE

Using the Attribute Commands
Using Attributes
Extracting Attributes

Computer-aided design opens up a world of possibilities that did not exist before computers became widely available. The potential is only beginning to be explored. One of the most promising new capabilities of affordable CAD is the integration of graphic and non-graphic information.

Think back to the days before affordable computing. If you were drawing then, you had no choice but to do a drawing on your drafting table and a *specification* on your typewriter. The two activities were totally separate. The specification, a document that describes the contents of the drawing, would often be inaccurate. Errors have a way of creeping in when tasks are not all of one piece, or *integrated.*

When drawings are done on computers, the information in them can take many forms, not just points and lines. If the CAD system is well designed, you can store any kind of information along with the entities in the drawing. AutoCAD is especially designed to incorporate non-graphic information in drawings through the use of the *tag* entity. The tag entity, created with the ATTDEF command, is used to store non-graphic information. With the BLOCK command, you can combine tag entities with any other entities, and create very complex, information-rich objects.

This chapter will show you how to use AutoCAD to combine your specifications with your drawings. A system for extracting attributes will also be introduced. You will see how a drawing can be used to contain all the information about a project. You will see how reports can be derived from drawings to automatically count objects, generate specifications, and assemble prices.

The use of attributes in blocks was discussed briefly in Chapter 4, "Working with Blocks." Since you must use attributes in blocks and insert the blocks into your drawings, refer to Chapter 4 before you try to fully understand this chapter. This chapter contains a more thorough treatment of the ATTDEF command.

After reading this chapter, you will see why attribute management is so important to the future of CAD. It offers a way to move forward in creating efficient, accurate, and inexpensive fabrications.

Using the Attribute Commands

Autodesk has done a great job of providing a way to store non-graphic information in drawings. The method is ingeniously simple. All that it involves is the use of a special new entity, the tag entity.

Like the line, circle, ellipse, and other AutoCAD entities, the tag entity can be used in a drawing. A tag entity stores text that can either appear in the drawing or be hidden from view. Each specific attribute is identified by a tag. Think of a tag as being similar to a name tag worn by organization members at a meeting. You can attach the tag to your lapel to identify yourself to others. On the tag, you will see your name and the name of the organization to which you belong. Everyone else at the meeting may belong to the same organization, or they may represent many other organizations, each with its own type of name tag. The organization name is the tag name. Your name is the attribute data associated with the tag. In this analogy, you are the "block" of entities identified by the tag.

Creating Tags

Tag entities are created and manipulated with a family of commands that all begin with or contain the three letters "ATT." The attribute definition must first be created with the ATTDEF command. That attribute definition can then be specified as part of a block with the BLOCK command. When you insert the block into your drawing, you are prompted for the specific attribute information for that instance of the block. This is how the attributes for each use of the block can be different.

It is important to differentiate between attributes and text information. Although attributes are text strings, they are not text entities. You enter attributes in response to prompts you create with the ATTDEF command. You enter text in response to the TEXT command. Text entities are not tagged.

There are four modes under which you can create attributes. Depending on which combination of modes are in effect during the creation of an attribute, the insertion of the attribute will be handled differently by AutoCAD. You have the options of making the attributes "Invisible," "Constant" (unchangeable), "Verified," or "Preset."

Using the ATTDEF Command

You use the ATTDEF command to define attribute tags. The best way to illustrate the ATTDEF command is with an example. The following is an invocation of the ATTDEF command for the creation of a simple tag entity:

Command: **attdef**
Attribute modes – Invisible:N Constant:N Verify:N
Preset:N
Enter (ICVP) to change, RETURN when done:
Attribute tag: **tag1**
Attribute prompt: **Enter attribute**
Default attribute value: **nothing**
Start point or Align/Center/Fit/Middle/Right/Style:
Height <0.2000>: **.5**
Rotation angle <0>:

When you enter the ATTDEF command, you will first have the option of changing the four modes for the display of attributes. You can set any of these modes by *toggling* it *on* or *off* (Y or N). For example, to turn "Invisible" mode *on* you would respond to the "Attribute modes" prompt by entering the letter **I** (upper- or lowercase). Each time the letter "I" is entered, you will see the "Invisible:" message switch from N to Y and back again. The following is a series of changes to the "Invisible" attribute mode:

```
Attribute modes – Invisible:N Constant:N Verify:N
Preset:N
Enter (ICVP) to change, RETURN when done: i
Attribute modes – Invisible:Y Constant:N Verify:N
Preset:N
Enter (ICVP) to change, RETURN when done: i
Attribute modes – Invisible:N Constant:N Verify:N
Preset:N
Enter (ICVP) to change, RETURN when done:
```

You can continue toggling modes until you get the right combination of them. Each mode has very specific effects on the nature of the attribute tag you will create. When you are finished setting modes, just press ENTER and you will go on to the prompts necessary to create an attribute tag.

The modes you set are immortal—they are set for the drawing and can only be changed with the ATTDEF command. Even if you use the END command to end the drawing session and later go back to work on the drawing, the modes you changed will retain their values. If you only want to change modes without creating an attribute, cancel with CTRL-C when you see the "Attribute tag:" prompt.

Selecting "Invisible" Mode If you select the "Invisible" option, tagged data will not be displayed. You will see only the graphic and text information in the drawing. You might wish to make attributes invisible if there are so many of them that your drawing would be cluttered. Attributes can contain information that is intended to be used as computer code and not to be read by people. If your attributes are not meant to be read by humans, you can make them invisible. If your attributes are numerical codes for controlling machine tools, for example, you may have no need to see them except when they are edited.

Selecting "Constant" Mode If you select the "Constant" option, the value of the tag for all future insertions of the tag in your drawings will be constant. You can never change it. You can choose this option to create a tag that identifies a block when you want to make sure that the attribute cannot be changed, insuring that the block will always be correctly identified. Since you can have any number of attribute tags in a block, some of them can be constant and some of them variable. You will not see a prompt for a constant value.

Selecting "Verify" Mode If you select the "Verify" option of the ATTDEF command, you will be shown the value of the attribute when the block is inserted in the drawing. To keep the value the same as the default, you must type it exactly as shown, repeating it completely. If you try to use the default value as is by pressing ENTER, you will see the message "Verify attribute values." You will then see a repeat of the tag prompt and the default value. If you then press ENTER, the default will be used. If you enter a new value, the new value will be used.

You can use this mode to make sure the operator checks each time an attribute value is requested. The temptation to just "default through" the prompt by pressing ENTER will be reduced if the operator sees the "Verify attribute values" message and is forced to pause. The "Verify" option should not be used for all tags, only for those that are especially important. If this option is always selected, the operator will subconsciously learn the response pattern and the verification will be ineffective.

Selecting "Preset" Mode If you choose the "Preset" mode, the attribute you create will be changeable, unlike "Constant" mode, but you will not be prompted for the value when the block is inserted in your drawing. The attribute used will be the default value.

You might want to select this mode to create attributes when the value of an attribute must be the same for most insertions, but should still be changeable from time to time. You must use the ATTEDIT command to modify the attribute if the attribute has been created with the "Preset" mode. With the ATTEDIT command, you can modify entire groups of attributes. The "Preset" mode makes working with attribute-laden blocks much easier, especially when most attributes will remain as their default values.

Modes Act Together Remember, the modes you select act together. More than one mode can be active at a time. In this way, you can, for example, have attributes that are invisible and verifiable or invisible and preset.

Entering the Attribute Tag The attribute tag is the tag name (not the attribute itself) by which the attribute will be identified in the drawing. It is like the organization name on your name tag at a meeting. When you later read the drawing database for attribute information, it will be organized under tag names. For example, a drawing might show ten machine screws. Each screw is slightly different in length and width. You could describe the length and width of each screw separately by creating a tag called "screw" and combining it into a block with the symbol of a screw. Then, whenever the screw symbol was inserted into your drawing, you would be prompted for the attributes of that particular screw. In the case of the invocation of the ATTDEF command shown earlier, the tag "tag1" was used.

Entering the Attribute Prompt The attribute prompt is the prompt you create and will see when the tag entity prompts you for attribute information. In the earlier example of the use of the ATTDEF command, the prompt "Enter attribute:" appears when you insert the block containing this tag entity, "tag1," into your drawing. It is important to understand that you are actually creating an AutoCAD prompt in response to "Attribute prompt:".

You can use almost any combination of characters to create the prompt. However, if the first character you enter is a space character, you will unintentionally enter a null prompt string. Remember, the spacebar acts like the ENTER key. Also, if you enter a backslash character (\) as the first character in the prompt string, it will be ignored and any following space characters will be accepted in the prompt. If you want the first character to be a backslash, you must enter two backslash characters. For example, the prompt string "\ Enter value" will look like "Enter value: " when it appears as a prompt. Similarly, the prompt string "\\ Enter value" will appear as "\ Enter value: ". The string " Enter value" cannot even be entered because it is preceded by a space character.

Setting the Default Attribute Value The default attribute value is a text string that will be used if you press ENTER in response to the prompt you have created. The default value will be shown when you insert a block containing the attribute into your drawing. In the preceding example of the ATTDEF command, the word "nothing" will be used as the default.

Placing the Attribute The last thing you do to create a tag entity is to place the entity in the drawing. This is done in much the same way that a text entity is placed. To find out more about text parameters, read Chapter 7, "Text and Fonts." You can select the usual text options:

```
Start point or Align/Center/Fit/Middle/Right/Style:
Height <0.2000>: .5
Rotation angle <0>:
```

In this case, a start point has been picked and the height has been set to 0.5 unit. The default rotation angle of zero degrees has been entered.

Figure 9-1 shows an attribute tag that was created with the described ATTDEF command sequence. Note that the "TAG1"

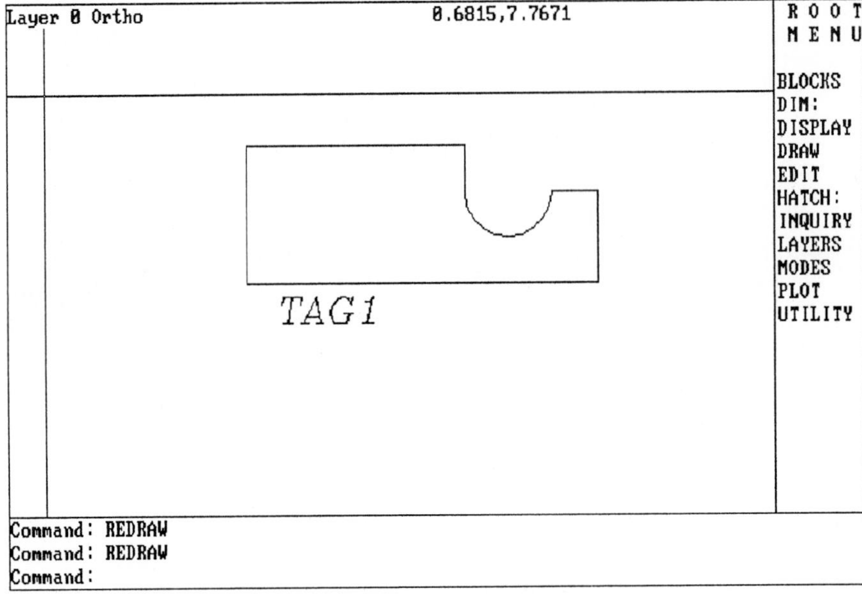

Figure 9-1. An attribute tag defined in a drawing

tag appears in the same position as the future attribute information. It is important to understand that the tag code itself will not appear when you insert a block containing it in your drawing. Instead, you will see the attribute information for which you are prompted during the insertion process. Tag entities, when included in blocks and inserted in drawings, invoke the prompts you associated with the entities.

Including Attributes in Blocks As in Chapter 4, "Working with Blocks," an entity must be included in a block and the block inserted in a drawing. You must create a block to finish the creation of a tag entity. The command sequence for the creation of a block that will store the two entities (a polyline and an attribute) shown in Figure 9-1 is as follows:

Command: **block**
Block name (or ?): **block1**
Insertion base point:
Select objects:

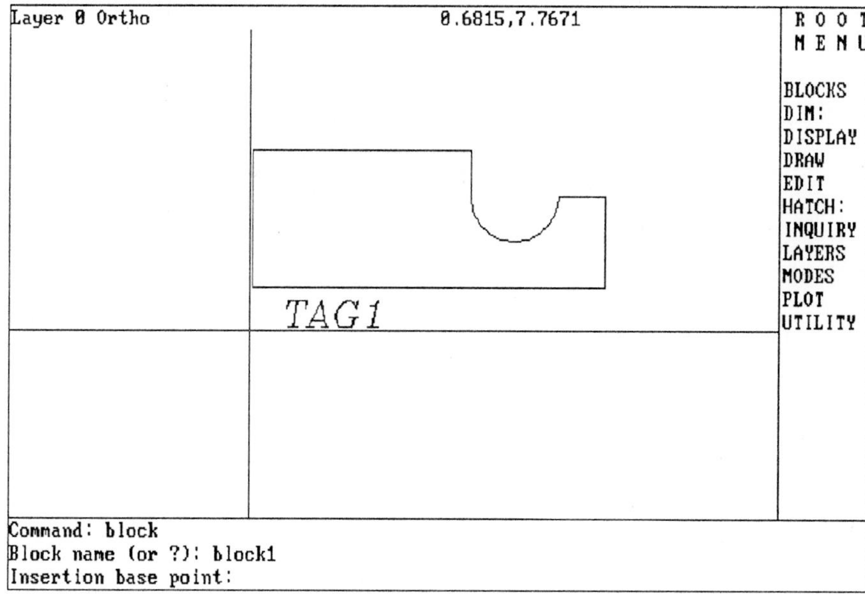

Figure 9-2. Beginning to make a block for an attribute

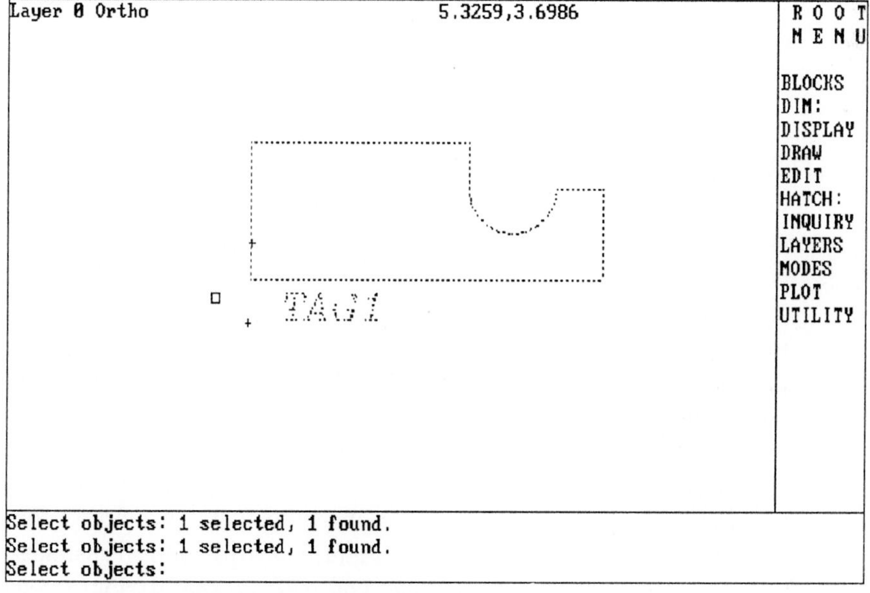

Figure 9-3. Selecting entities for a block

The name of the block will be "block1." When the block is inserted in a drawing, the point identified by the crosshairs in Figure 9-2 will align with the crosshairs in the drawing. The objects shown dotted in Figure 9-3 will be included in the block. After you select the last object, you press ENTER to complete the command. You can read more about the BLOCK command in Chapter 4, "Working with Blocks."

Inserting Blocks with Attributes After you have created the block with its included graphic and tag entities, you can insert it into your drawing by using the INSERT command. To do so, you create the following command sequence:

```
Command: insert
Block name (or ?) <TEST>: block1
Insertion point: X scale factor <1> / Corner
/ XYZ:
Y scale factor (default=X):
Rotation angle <0>:
Enter attribute values
Enter attribute <nothing>: my value
```

The block named "block1," created earlier, is inserted at the insertion point identified by the crosshairs using the default scale factors. The rotation angle is defaulted to zero. Figure 9-4 shows the block in the process of being inserted. Finally, because there is a tag entity in the block, you see the "Enter attribute values" message. After this message you see the prompt already created, "Enter attribute," with the default value "nothing." The value "my value" is used instead of the default. The result is shown in Figure 9-5. Note that the block has been placed in almost the same location in which it was created. This shows that the base insertion point prompted for when the block was created is identified with the crosshairs location picked on insertion. Also, you will see the attribute you

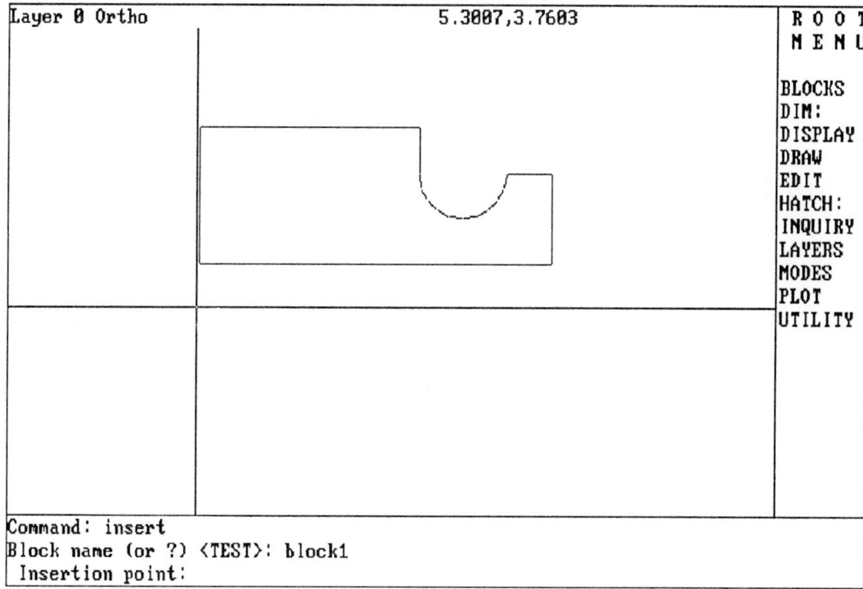

Figure 9-4. Picking the point of insertion for the block

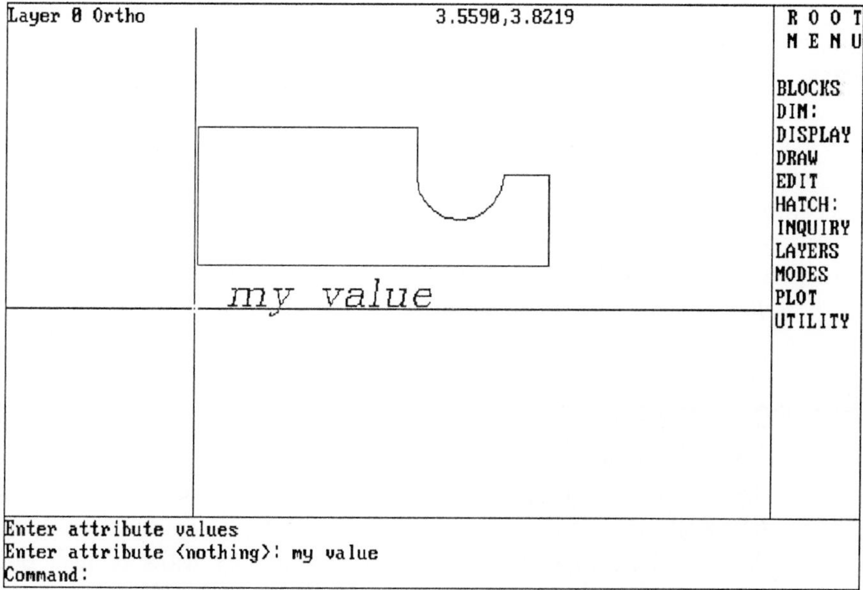

Figure 9-5. The inserted block showing the attribute value

entered to use with this particular block insertion. The value of the tag "tag1" is shown rather than "tag1" as when the attribute tag was created.

Using Dialog Box Attribute Entry

You can, if your hardware supports it, use a dialog box to enter your attributes. To enable dialog boxes for attributes, you must set the ATTDIA system variable. As with all system variables, you do this with the SETVAR command. The SETVAR command sequence for setting the ATTDIA variable follows:

Command: **setvar**
Variable name or ?: **attdia**
New value for ATTDIA <0>: **1**

If you set the ATTDIA system variable to 1, you will see a dialog box when you insert your blocks with attribute entities in them. Figure 9-6 shows a dialog box that accompanies the insertion of the "block1" block shown in Figure 9-5. You can change the value, cancel the command, or accept the value (OK) by moving the arrow to the desired box. When the arrow is placed over a desired box, the box will be highlighted and you can either pick it or change its contents. For example, when the "Enter attribute. . ." box is highlighted, you may change the contents from the shown default value. When the "OK" box is highlighted, a pick will result in completion of the INSERT command. When the "Cancel" box is highlighted, a pick will cancel the INSERT command.

Editing Attributes

After you have created attributes and used them in your drawing, you may edit them. There are many different circumstances in which you will want to edit attributes. You may wish to change attributes after the fact, or you may want to use, but alter, attributes that have been created with the "Preset" mode

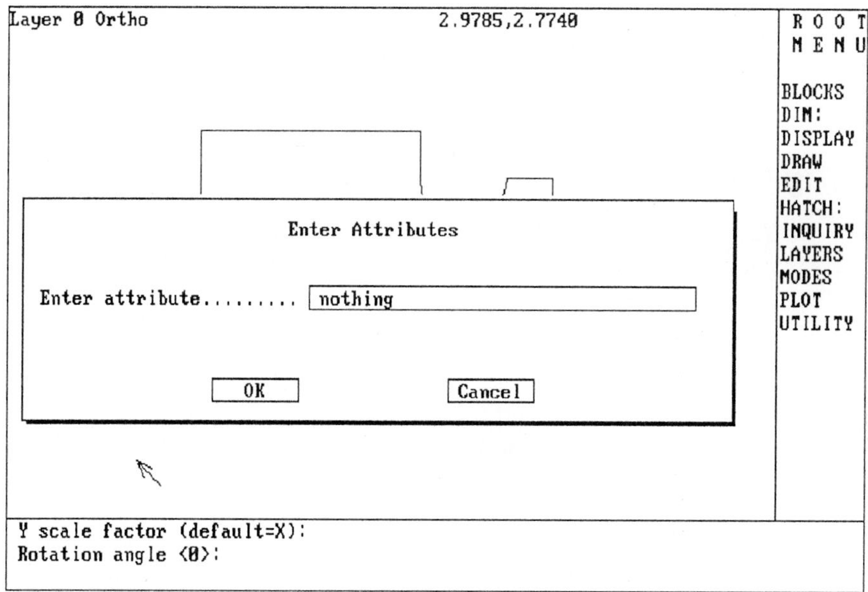

Figure 9-6. Using the attribute dialog box

of the ATTDEF command. In the latter case, you will not be prompted for attribute values when you insert blocks containing such attributes in your drawing. This makes the block insertion faster, and you can make changes later. You may also not want the person who inserts the blocks to be the one who adds attributes. If the person who inserts the blocks inserts only blocks containing "Preset" attributes, another person responsible for the attributes can then use the ATTDEF command to change the attributes for selected blocks.

Editing One Attribute at a Time

You can edit attributes in your drawings with the ATTEDIT command. This command enables you to change either the visible attributes that appear in the drawing area, or all of the attributes in the drawing, whether visible or invisible. The ATTEDIT command sequence appears as follows:

```
Command: attedit
Edit attributes one at a time? <Y>
Block name specification <*>:
Attribute tag specification <*>:
Attribute value specification <*>:
```

When you answer by entering **y** (yes), you will be prompted for the specifications of the block name, attribute tag, and attribute value. The default shown here is the single wildcard asterisk. A single asterisk indicates that any name will match. In other words, in this example, any block name, attribute tag, or attribute value will be edited.

Wildcards can also be applied to single characters in names. The question mark (?) character can be used to stand for any character in the position occupied. For example, the attribute tag "tag1" would be found, along with "tag2", "tag3", and any others that matched if the specification were "tag?". The use of wildcard characters is the same as in DOS, except that the names are not DOS file names. If you wish to select names that have no entries for attributes, you can use the backslash character (\) to specify this.

After you select the specifications for the attributes you wish to edit, you will be prompted to select the attributes as follows:

```
Select Attributes:
1 attributes selected.
```

You will see a message that confirms how many attributes were actually selected. If you press ENTER in response to the "Select attributes:" prompt, you will select the range of names that qualify under the list of specifications of block names, attribute tags, and attribute values you entered.

The parameters of the attribute you are allowed to edit are shown in the next prompt:

```
Value/Position/Height/Angle/Style/Layer/Color/Next <N>:
```

You can change the value, position, text height, text angle, text style, layer, color, or go on to the next attribute. In the case of "Value," you will be asked to choose "Change" or "Replace." If you select "Change," AutoCAD will prompt you for the "String to change:". You can enter a string of characters that will be searched for in the attribute value. You then will be prompted for the new string. This new string will replace all instances of the string you indicated in the "String to change:" response. If you choose "Replace," you will be prompted for the "New attribute value:". This value will replace the value of the selected attribute.

The "Position," "Height," and "Angle" options are the same as the options you encountered when you created the attribute, except that you were not then prompted for the "Style," "Layer," or "Color." Nevertheless, each attribute contains information about the text style, layer, and color that were current when the attribute was created.

Editing Attributes Globally

If you elect not to edit attributes one at a time, you will use the following command sequence:

Command: **attedit**
Edit attributes one at a time? <Y> **n**
Global edit of attribute values.
Edit only attributes visible on screen? <Y>
Block name specification <*>:
Attribute tag specification <*>:
Attribute value specification <*>:

Note that you now have the additional choice of editing only attributes visible on the screen. If you enter **y** (yes) in response to this prompt, you will only be able to edit attributes that are visible on the screen. If you enter **n** (no), you will be able to edit all attributes in the database that match the specifications you select.

If you chose to edit only those attributes that are visible in the drawing area, you will be prompted in the same way as for the "one at a time" option in the earlier example. If you chose to edit not only those attributes visible on the screen, but all attributes in the drawing database, AutoCAD will skip the "Select attributes:" prompt. You will be prompted for the "String to change:" and allowed to enter a new string value for each instance of the string found in the specified instances of blockname, attribute tag, and attribute value. The string itself will be the attribute string.

Using Dialog Boxes to Edit Attributes

You can use the DDATTE command to edit attributes. This feature may make you more comfortable than the ATTEDIT command because you edit in a dialog box. Dialog boxes are valuable in that they show the default value and permit you to change it in a more natural way than do command prompts. To use the DDATTE command, you enter the following sequence:

Command: **ddatte**
Select block:

When you select the block with attributes you wish to edit, you will see something like the display shown in Figure 9-7. As with the dialog box shown in Figure 9-6, you move the arrow to the box you want to edit. The box is highlighted. You then change the text by typing or by picking the box. When you are finished, you can enter the new attribute value by picking the "OK" box or you can cancel the command by picking the "Cancel" box.

If you want to select one block after another and see a dialog box for each one, you can use the MULTIPLE prefix for the DDATTE command as follows:

Command: **multiple ddatte**
Select block: DDATTE Select block: DDATE Select block:

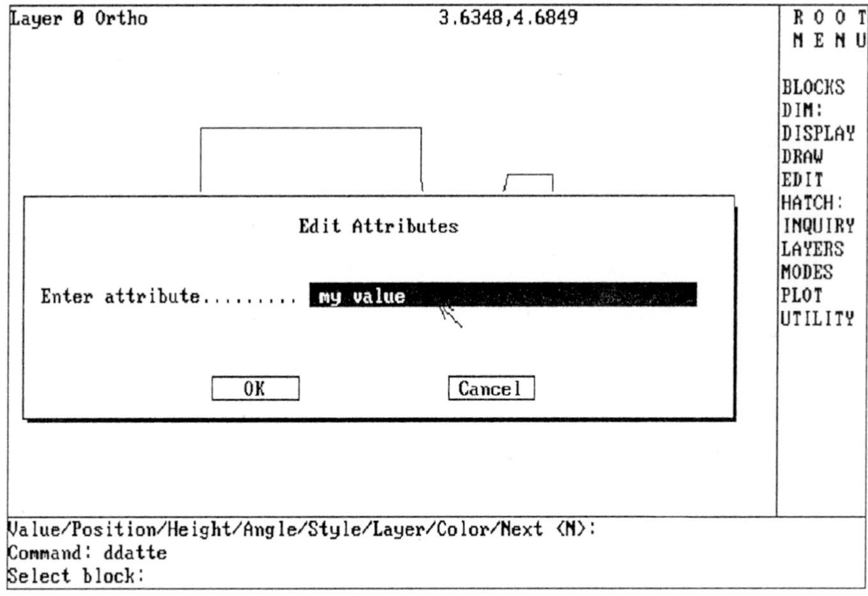

Figure 9-7. Editing an existing attribute value

If you enter the MULTIPLE DDATE command you will be prompted as shown. As you leave each dialog box, either by picking "OK" or by picking "Cancel," the DDATE command will be automatically reentered, and will then be followed by the "Select block:" prompt. Cancel the command with CTRL-C.

Controlling Attribute Visibility

If you choose the "Invisible" option of the ATTDEF command, you can create attributes that are invisible. You can also control attribute visibility with the ATTDISP command. You can even use the ATTDISP command to reverse the invisibility of an object that has been defined as invisible. You invoke the ATTDISP command sequence as follows:

Define: **attdisp**
Normal/ON/OFF <Normal>:

If you choose "Normal" mode by entering **N** (upper- or lowercase), the attributes in your drawing will appear as they were defined. If defined as invisible, they will be invisible. If defined as visible, they will be visible. If you choose the "ON" option of the ATTDISP command by entering the word **on** (upper- or lowercase), you will force all attributes to be visible. If you choose the "OFF" option, you will force all attributes to be invisible. You must regenerate the display to see the effects of the ATTDISP command.

You can also change the ATTMODE system variable with the SETVAR command. This will achieve the same effect as using the ATTDISP command. If you set ATTMODE to 0, it will be the same as forcing all attributes *off*. If you set ATTMODE to 1, it is the same as "Normal." If you set ATTMODE to 2, you will force all attributes to be *on*. You must regenerate the display to see the effect of the ATTMODE system variable after you change it.

Using Attributes

You can use attributes for a wide range of applications, from project management to direct control of machine tools. Attributes can convey information about symbols that cannot be contained in the symbols themselves. Furthermore, attributes can be *extracted* from drawings by reference to their tag codes. In this way, you can count the number of screws in the drawing of a dishwasher with AutoCAD, rather than relying on your own eyes, which might be tired from late night work. As you place each screw in the drawing, you fill out the attributes for each screw. When you are finished with your drawing, you can either use AutoCAD's built-in reporting capabilities or specially designed software to automatically report the quantities of objects. The result is a very accurate indication of the materials in your design.

It is impossible to present all the details about the various applications that follow. The companion software and documentation are intended to amplify this discussion, as well as cover other aspects of attribute management possible with the extended commands you can add to AutoCAD. This chapter will, however, present examples of a few areas of application. You should view the following applications as food for thought in creating your own uses for attributes. You will find that attributes open up a whole world of applications because they are one important way that AutoCAD can communicate with the outside world.

Attributes in Building Design and Construction

Imagine that the drawing in Figure 9-1 is a special countertop for a kitchen. Imagine you are looking down on it from the top, in plan. You could create a tag called "tag1" precisely as was done in the figure. More appropriately, you could call the tag "countertop." In either case, you could use the following string as an attribute:

Color: blue, Material: plastic laminate, Price: 250.00

If you were to include all of this information in a single tag, you would need to type a long string like this for each instance of the block in your drawing. Later on, when you wanted to extract the information, it would be very hard to extract each piece of information separately. For example, it would be difficult to extract only the prices of countertops and add them up. The word "Price:" in the string is the only way you would be able to isolate the price information. What if the word were misspelled? You would miss that particular price record and your total would be inaccurate.

Fortunately, you can avoid the problem of typing long strings as attributes by including multiple tags in the block. If you create separate tags called "color", "material", and "price", you would be much better off. Not only would you avoid the need to type the words "Color:", "Material:", and "Price:", but you would be able to extract only the information you needed. Your extraction software would only extract the tags you specify. The following is an example of a set of tags that would appear on the screen if you used separate tags to store the attribute information for the "countertop" in Figure 9-1. The following would appear in place of "TAG1":

COUNTERTOP
blue
plastic laminate
250.00

The word "COUNTERTOP" is a constant value, created with the "Constant" mode described earlier. It is made constant because then you would not have to be prompted for it or change it. The block will always show a countertop. The "color" and "material" tags could be created with all modes turned *off*. This would provide the normal prompt sequence. The "price" tag could be created with "Verify" mode *on*. This would result in a "Verify attribute values." prompt if the operator did not exactly copy the price amount. In this way, you could help to insure that prices were accurately entered.

Changing Methods of Building Design

The nature of the process of architectural design is such that many combinations of building materials must be dealt with. Traditionally, a builder would take an architect's drawings and run a *takeoff wheel* over them to measure the lengths of walls and partitions. A takeoff wheel is a device which has a small metal wheel with an abrasive edge that rolls over a drawing. Depending on the number of revolutions the wheel makes, a dial on the device indicates the distance the wheel has traveled. In addition to the takeoff wheel, a builder often uses a mechanical counting device that, when pressed against a drawing, will increment a counter. Devices such as the takeoff wheel and mechanical counter are simple in concept and have been used for many decades in the construction industry.

As designers and builders of buildings work more closely together, their roles are changing. Often, the designer works on the same team as the builder. This liaison, much feared because of a perceived conflict of interest, is now working quite well in many circumstances. AutoCAD helps to encourage such teamwork, since a design can now be created and "costed" in an integrated way. In other words, the designer can create a drawing to which detailers and estimators can directly add information.

Instead of using printed drawings (which often are inaccurate in scale) to measure lengths of building elements, the estimator can now automatically measure such elements with AutoCAD. The results can be entered as attributes and these attributes can then be extracted into reports that the designer and client can analyze. The designer and client thus receive an accurate picture of the impact of costs and can change the design in more informed ways.

The appropriate use of computers in design is a topic undergoing lively debate. Some see a danger in making design decisions automatic. However, if the computer is perceived and used as a tool, rather than as an automaton, there can be little harm and much good in design automation. It is unlikely that designers and estimators will ever be replaced by computers. Instead, they will use computers, and software like AutoCAD, to amplify their effectiveness.

Building design and construction are undergoing rapid evolution in today's technological environment. Used responsibly, the computer can help to integrate the process of building. The computer can act as the glue that binds the building team together.

Interior Design Attributes

Interior designers work with AutoCAD in much the same way as other building professionals. For the most part, the interior designer's task is to provide moveable, rather than fixed, building features. But interior design also involves the application of materials to fixed surfaces and the addition of lighting elements that are more or less fixed. Many of the techniques used by architects, engineers, and builders are used in the same way by interior designers. The "countertop" shown in Figure 9-1 might be a special kind of desk in an interior design plan. The attributes would be much the same, as would the reporting of them.

Interior designers have the same need as building designers to quantify and estimate the costs of materials. There is no simple way to automate this process since almost everything about it is subjective. Actual costs of furnishings are almost never the same as the prices shown in manufacturers' catalogs. This means that, like the building designer and builder, the interior designer and furnishings contractor must work together to arrive at accurate prices. The real value of AutoCAD in this process is in the integration of price information directly in the drawing. In this way, the removal of a desk by the designer is instantly reflected in the removal of the price as well.

Attributes in Facilities Management

After the interior designer has completed the design, and the furnishings have been ordered and installed, it becomes the job of the facilities manager to keep track of furnishing as the building is used. One of the unique aspects of interior design is that furnishings can be moved. Chairs are easily moved from office to office, and desks can be moved to accommodate changes in organizational structure. The facilities manager is responsible for protecting the company's costly furnishings and using them appropriately and economically.

In most modern organizations, the role of the facilities manager is beginning to be seen as a separate discipline in itself. Personal computers can be very effective tools for facilities managers because they can keep track of extremely complex databases. Each item of furniture can be numbered and entered into the management database. The numbering system itself can be expressed in *bar codes* and read by special hand-held hardware directly from labels (tags) that are attached to furniture. Bar codes are special combinations of lines drawn side by side that can be read by reflecting light off of them. Because the lines vary in width, a light beam passing over them will reflect light in a distinct sequence of long and short pulses. These pulses are then decoded with digital logic to form a number. You have probably seen bar codes at work in your local supermarket checkout stand.

The tag that is glued to the desk in an office can have a corresponding tag in a drawing of the desk stored in the AutoCAD database. The tag in AutoCAD contains the unique number assigned to the desk as an attribute. Whenever a facilities manager wants to know where all the desks are, the manager simply uses a bar code reader to read all the necessary labels. Each room has a label just as each desk has a label. The bar code reader stores the desk numbers under the room numbers and is connected directly to the computer that runs AutoCAD. Software running under AutoCAD then reads the bar codes and produces a report that shows where the furnishings are as opposed to where they ought to be.

Numerical Control Attributes

You can use attributes very creatively *indeed*, even in ways that you might not expect. For example, you can control machines with attributes. Although objects in drawings are symbolic of objects in the real world, they often do not contain all of the information required to produce real world objects. With attributes, however, you can thoroughly describe symbols in drawings. For example, machine tools can be digitally controlled with special codes called *G codes*. You can draw a symbol of a part in a drawing and, for each such symbol, accompany it with an attribute that contains the G codes required to machine the part associated with that symbol. All you need is software that can read the drawing and extract the G codes, sending them on to control your machinery.

A Simple Numerical Control Application

Numerically controlled machine programming began three decades ago with the use of punched tape input. Over the years, many variations on G codes have been implemented. There is no absolute standard. The actual codes will depend on your specific hardware.

The following example uses CAMM-GL1, the language used by the sophisticated CAMM-3 computer-aided modeling machine by Roland DG. It is capable of milling three-dimensional as well as two-dimensional shapes. This machine is a good example because it is an affordable product you can use with your personal computer. You can control much larger machines with personal computers. There is really no limit to the possible combinations in the modern factory or workshop.

Imagine that the drawing shown in Figure 9-1 is a part to be produced on a numerically controlled milling machine. The attribute string required to mill it might appear as follows:

```
M 361, 718 D 772,718 D 772, 632 M 854, 632 E 82,
772, 718, 180 D 936, 632 D 1022, 632 D 1022, 462
D 361, 462 H
```

This example is not meant to be precise in milling the exact shape, only to show the principles of how it might be done, so do not use the codes exactly as they are. Do not include the linefeed characters necessary to print the text for the above code example. The character string should be as shown, but should be one unbroken string. You would enter something like this as the attribute for "tag1," the tag associated with "block1" in Figure 9-1. When you extract the codes and direct them to the modeling machine, the machine should lower the spindle, mill approximately the shape shown in Figure 9-1, and then return to the home position.

When you use attributes to control machines, you have great power at your disposal. For example, you could control entire industrial processes directly from drawings. All you need is the software to interpret codes you place in the drawings, and to direct output to each necessary machine in the manufacturing process.

Instrumentation Attributes

Instrumentation engineering involves the construction of circuits that convey information about a wide variety of devices. The instrumentation engineer uses AutoCAD both to design instrumentation circuits and to design instrumentation displays. A typical electrical generating plant will have an enormous instrumentation panel that displays the current status of every system in the plant. The instruments that display the status information vary with the requirements of the systems being monitored.

Instrumentation design itself often involves many engineering skills, depending on the combination of measuring and reporting devices used. AutoCAD functions as an integration tool to allow the same drawing to be used by professionals in many disciplines. Because everything is in one place there is less likelihood of confusion.

AutoCAD can also be used directly as a display panel. In some applications, a process to be monitored may change so often that the usual techniques of instrumentation are not flexible enough. For example, an industrial process using robots may need to be customized radically for each job, and the assembly process carefully monitored. It would be difficult to build hard-wired panels with the usual bells and whistles screwed in place, but it would be relatively easy to use blocks with attributes to simulate such panels.

AutoCAD's *open architecture* enables almost everything about it to be easily customized. Open architecture has the nature of being intentionally designed to accept modifications, rather than be fixed. You can change menus and use AutoLISP to write your own programs. You can create *extended commands* to add your own features that work with almost any part of your computer. Because of this open architecture, you can make AutoCAD update itself based on information provided through your computer's bus (through plug-in adapter boards), its serial and parallel ports, and even its keyboard port. With the right combination of hardware and software, you can use AutoCAD to automatically update the attributes of blocks that act as instrumentation displays. Such a use is particularly suited to the laboratory, where experiments change rapidly.

Electrical Engineering Attributes

Electrical engineers create electrical circuits with devices as small as digital integrated circuit packages (discussed in Chapter 4, "Working with Blocks"), and as large as the electrical transformers at a hydroelectric power plant. AutoCAD finds its place everywhere in this range.

Attributes in electrical engineering applications can be used to report quantities, just as in architecture, interior design, and facilities management. The parts of complex circuits each have their cost and must be accounted for.

There are, however, more creative ways to work with attributes in electrical engineering drawings. The components in an electrical or electronic circuit are connected together by conductors that carry electromagnetic forces from connection to connection. The conductors are drawn with polylines or traces. Each conductor can have its own attribute to indicate its material, color, and electrical characteristics, and each electrical component can be similarly tagged.

Circuit Simulation

The electrical engineer often relies on complex formulas to design circuits. After the design is complete, it must be breadboarded—built using actual components—an often tedious process involving considerable time and materials cost. With the right software, however, a tagged drawing can simulate the circuit. Graphs created by the software can show the performance of the circuit. This can save time and lead to better performance because it increases the number of design alternatives.

Autorouting

When circuits are designed, they can be laid out by hand, with the traces that connect each device carefully drawn. This process takes time and is prone to errors. Instead of doing everything manually, an electrical engineer can rely on *autorouting* software to draw the connections. Autorouting software is specially designed to interpret a list of connection specifications, identify the components, and determine the most efficient route for each conductor. By simply listing the connection requirements, rather than drawing each connector, an engineer saves time and is less likely to make the wrong connections. After the software does its work, the process of routing the conductors is reduced to one of checking to make sure the software interpreted the list correctly.

Finite Element Analysis and Attributes

Structural engineers use a technique called *finite element analysis* to simulate the effects of loads on materials in various arrangements. While materials in the real world are composed of elements that are made of materials whose properties are smooth throughout, the computer is not capable of directly processing these smooth, analog properties. Because the computer is a digital device, it is necessary to break the elements up into discrete, *finite* chunks—hence the term "finite element."

For example, the steel frame of a building can be designed with AutoCAD. Each member of the frame can be given an attribute that records how its material changes under stress. By extracting information from the drawing database and using appropriate software, the structural engineer can simulate the effects of forces acting on the frame. A new drawing showing the deformations of the structure can be drawn automatically so the engineer can see how the structure reacts under loading.

A World of Applications

The above suggestions only touch the surface of existing and potential applications for AutoCAD's attributes. Several themes run through them all. One theme is that of integration. AutoCAD's tag entity is one of the features that brings many disciplines together, integrating the design with its environment. Another theme is that of modeling. AutoCAD can be used to simulate and report on the status of a design even after it has been built. The tag concept is one of AutoCAD's most powerful aspects because of its flexibility. Used in concert with creative menu designs, specially designed external commands, and AutoLISP code, it can greatly increase your effectiveness as a designer.

Extracting Attributes

Attributes are valuable within AutoCAD when they visibly identify blocks in drawings, but then they are of little more use than text would be. The real power of attributes, and their intended purpose, is their ability to be used *outside* of AutoCAD. AutoCAD provides the ATTEXT (ATTribute EXTract) command for this purpose. You have a choice of four unique extraction modes, with your choice of mode depending on the requirements of the software you will use to process the extracted data.

If you are familiar with programming languages like BASIC, Pascal, or C, you can read AutoCAD's export files directly and translate them. If you are familiar with dBASE or other database management systems, you can use data extracted from AutoCAD directly. If you are not familiar with programming languages, you can purchase software that is designed to handle a wide range of specialized data extraction and reporting tasks. One such software toolkit is available as a companion disk for this book.

Using the ATTEXT Command

The ATTEXT command will process the current drawing database to extract attributes in various ways. The ATTEXT command sequence is as follows:

Command: **attext**
CDF, SDF or DXF Attribute extract (or Entities)? <C>:

You are prompted for one of four possible processing strategies. You can select any of them by entering its first letter. For example, the default in this case is C, which stands for "CDF."

Using Format Files

In the case of the "CDF" and "SDF" extraction options, you will be prompted for a "Template file:". You must supply one. If you do not, you will see the "Invalid file name" message and will be prompted again for the name of the template file. If you wish to cancel at this point, just press CTRL-C. The template file contains specially formatted information that tells AutoCAD how to format the extracted data.

The template file requires a very specific construction. When you prepare your template file with your straight ASCII text editor, you give it the ".txt" extension. You cannot use any tab characters in preparing your template file. Sample template files are on the companion diskette for this book. These files will help you write your own templates and are designed to handle a range of common formatting needs.

Using "Comma Delimited Format"

If you respond to the first prompt of the ATTEXT command with the letter "C" (upper- or lowercase), you will begin extracting to a *CDF* file. The screen will be converted to text mode, and you will see the "Template file:" prompt. A template file can be used to format the output as stated above.

The letters "CDF" stand for "Comma Delimited Format." In this format, you will see each block in the drawing identified by name. After the block name, you will see fields separated by commas. Each field will contain data extracted from the drawing attributes, or other information as required by the template file.

In order to extract to the "CDF" format with the ATTEXT command, you must first prepare a template file. The following are the contents of a simple template file you could call "template.txt":

```
bl:name C030000
tag1 C030000
```

In this case, the sample drawing shown in Figure 9-1 was used. Since it has only one attribute tag ("tag1"), only one attribute value should be extracted.

You can prepare this file with EDLIN, the simple text editor that comes with DOS. Copy the EDLIN.COM file into your AutoCAD directory or use the DOS "set" command to set a path to it. If you are running AutoCAD now, use END or QUIT, and select the 0 option of the Main Menu to get back to the DOS command line. Just type the following at your DOS command line (not from within AutoCAD):

```
C>edlin template.txt
New file
*i
          1:*bl:name C030000
          2:*tag1 C030000
          3:*^C
          *e
C>_
```

Where you see the ^C characters in the above example, it means the CTRL-C keys were pressed. As in AutoCAD, CTRL-C here is used to cancel the entry of text.

The text entered in the preceding example shows that the block name ("bl:name") is to be extracted as a type of character (C), with a width of 30 characters (030) and no numeric information (000).

You have just created a simple text file containing the template information to extract attribute data according to the "CDF" format. Now get back into AutoCAD so you see the AutoCAD command line. Enter the ATTEXT command as follows:

```
Command: attext
CDF, SDF or DXF Attribute extract (or Entities)? <C>:
```

Template file: **template**
Extract file name <ATTRIB>:
1 record in extract file.

You first enter the default (C) to select the "CDF" option. Then you enter the name of the template file (which must previously exist on your disk). The extract file name is the same name as the drawing. In this case, the default drawing name was used. Finally, the extraction is performed and a message appears showing how many records were extracted.

If you entered everything exactly as in this example, you will now have a file called "attrib.txt" in your AutoCAD directory. It is given the ".txt" extension because it is a text file. You can edit it with your text editor, or with EDLIN if you do not have a text editor. The contents of the "attrib.txt" file appear as follows:

'BLOCK1','my value'

Figure 9-5 shows that the extracted attribute value is accurate. The same data you see in the drawing has been extracted into the "attrib.txt file". Note that the name of the extracted block as well as the attribute in that block are shown, delimited by a comma. This is the way output data appears in a typical "Comma Delimited Format," as requested by the template file.

Using "Space Delimited Format"

The *SDF* file is an attribute extract file produced in "Space Delimited Format." With this option, fields are not delimited by commas, but are shown at the fixed lengths required by the template file. As with "CDF" files, a template file is required.

To use the "SDF" option of the ATTEXT command, you must enter the following command sequence:

Command: **attext**
CDF, SDF or DXF Attribute extract (or Entities)? <C>: s

Template file <TEMPLATE>: **template**
Extract file name <ATTRIB>:
1 record in extract file.

The same template file is used in this example as was used in the "CDF" example. The output is much different, however. The following is the contents of the "attrib.txt" file produced by the above command sequence:

BLOCK1   my value

Note that the single quote characters no longer appear. The block name and attribute value are shown placed within fields that are 30 characters long. The "template.txt" file was constructed with the number 030 which is the field width.

Extracting to a "DXF" File

A *DXF* file is a file in AutoCAD's "Drawing eXchange Format." In the case of attribute extraction, however, the complete "DXF" file is not produced. Instead you will extract "Attribute," "Block Reference," and "End of Sequence" entities only. You can use the extracted data with programs that interpret "DXF" files. Many other CAD systems have adopted AutoCAD's "DXF" interchange format so data can be exchanged with AutoCAD.

To prepare a "DXF" extraction file, you use the ATTEXT command much as with the other formats. The command sequence is as follows:

Command: **attext**
CDF, SDF or DXF Attribute extract (or Entities)? <C>: **d**
Extract file name <ATTRIB>:
3 entities in extract file.

You select the "DXF" option by entering **D** (upper- or lowercase). In this case, the extract file name is the same name as the drawing, though you can use another name if you wish. After you enter the extract file name, the extraction process begins.

When the extraction is complete, you will see a message that shows how many entities (not records) have been extracted. Because you are not required to provide a template file for this option of the ATTEXT command, the extracted data will not be formatted, except as required by the standard "DXF" file. You also have no control over the extraction. Only the entities allowed by this option of the ATTEXT command will be extracted. You can see that three have been extracted here.

If you choose the "DXF" option, the file extension of the file that contains extracted data will be ".dxx" rather than ".dxf". The "attrib.dxx" file produced by this invocation of the ATTEXT command contains a specially formatted series of characters. Any software you use that allows input of a "DXF" file (even though this is technically a "DXX" file) will read the file.

Extracting "Entities"

If you choose the "Entities" option of the ATTEXT command, you will be prompted to select the entities you wish to include in your extraction. Then you will be prompted to choose one of three options (CSD) to control the output format:

Command: **attext**
CDF, SDF or DXF Attribute extract (or Entities)? <C>: **e**
Select objects: 1 selected, 1 found.
Select objects:
CDF, SDF or DXF Attribute extract? <C>:

You enter **E** (upper- or lowercase) to select the "Entities" option of the ATTEXT command. You are then prompted to select the objects to include in the extraction. After you select your last desired object, you press ENTER to terminate the selection prompts. You are then prompted for one of the three attribute extraction options illustrated earlier. You can choose "CDF," "SDF," or "DXF" extraction output.

The Companion Diskette

The software required to extract attribute information from AutoCAD drawings is too complex to describe here in detail. To write such software for advanced purposes requires competence in software development with languages like C and assembler. Instead, the general principles of attribute extraction are covered here.

Software has been written that greatly enhances AutoCAD's extraction capabilities and can be customized for many applications. You can even run the software from within AutoCAD, without ending your AutoCAD session. You can direct attribute information to serial and parallel ports in various ways. You can easily format reports in response to a sophisticated menu system and programming language. Many of the topics covered in this chapter can be handled by the companion software.

You can obtain a companion disk for this book that contains software for use in extracting attribute information from AutoCAD drawings. You will find a coupon in this book with which you can order the companion disks.

Creating External Commands

To understand how to use the companion software and to work with *external commands* in general, you must know how to edit the "acad.pgp" file. AutoCAD supplies you with a standard "acad.pgp" file. You can view it with EDLIN, the DOS text editor, by entering the following at your DOS command line:

```
C>edlin acad.pgp
End of input file
*l
          1:*CATALOG,DIR /W,27000,*Files: ,0
          2: DEL,DEL,27000,File to delete: ,0
          3: DIR,DIR,27000,File specification: ,0
          4: EDIT,EDLIN,42000,File to edit: ,0
          5: SH,,27000,*DOS Command: ,0
          6: SHELL,,127000,*DOS Command: ,0
```

```
        7: TYPE,TYPE,27000,File to list: ,0
*8i
        8:*REPORT,REPORT,64000,*Report options
        (if any): ,4
        9:*^C
*e
```

Note that the letter "L" is used in "*l" above, not the number "1." As shown, all the default AutoCAD external commands for a typical DOS system are in the "acad.pgp" file. The file can be changed with EDLIN or almost any straight ASCII text editor. In this example, a line of text has been added. The line adds an external command called "REPORT" to AutoCAD.

When you purchase the companion disk, you will receive a special ".pgp" file that adds the necessary set of commands to AutoCAD. You can use the supplied file directly or edit it to append the new commands to your existing "acad.pgp" file. You may have added new external commands of your own, or Auto-CAD's standard "acad.pgp" file may have changed. In either case, you will be able to preserve your existing AutoCAD configuration if you choose to append to the existing "acad.pgp" file rather than replace it.

In addition to attribute extraction software the companion disk contains a text editor specially designed to prepare files for use with AutoCAD. You may find that this editor is easier to use than EDLIN.

Working with Menus

How Menus Express Commands
Calling Menus from Menus
Using Menu Sections

TEN

AutoCAD is an extremely flexible system for many reasons. You can program AutoCAD with AutoLISP. You can add external commands that look as if they were added by Autodesk. You can also add your own menus that completely change the appearance of the program.

When you run the system for the first time, you will see AutoCAD's standard menus. If you have special needs that are not satisfied by the software, you can create your own menus or modify AutoCAD's standard menu file.

AutoCAD has several menu types that you may have already used. There is the sidebar menu that appears at the right side of the screen. If you are using the advanced user interface, you can work with *pull-down* menus. Pull-down menus are menus that you can pull down from a menu bar that appears at the top of the screen. Your menus can also use *icons,* which are pictures that you can associate with commands. Used appropriately, such pictures can allow you to work more quickly since icons provide a highly visual way to select commands. Finally, you can use tablet menus that are plotted on your plotter and secured to your digitizer tablet. Tablet menus show all the commands at once, so you know at a glance which command combination to use.

To control the menu system, you must learn to edit one type of file. This single menu file that contains all of AutoCAD's menu instructions has the extension ".mnu." AutoCAD's standard menu file is called "acad.mnu" and is normally found in your ACAD directory.

You must use a text editor to see what is in the "acad.mnu" file. Do not try to use your word processing software to do this unless it has a special mode that permits you to edit straight ASCII text. Such text uses no special formatting codes or characters that could confuse AutoCAD. If you purchase the companion disk for this book, you will receive a simple ASCII text editor with which you can edit AutoCAD's menu file. The text editor also has some built-in features that will help you write AutoLISP code. You can, of course, use EDLIN, the DOS text editor. This is not recommended because the editor is not very powerful.

You may wish to edit the "acad.mnu" file now, so you can familiarize yourself with it. Be careful not to change the file accidentally. Make a backup copy of "acad.mnu" by using the DOS COPY command to copy it into a file called "acad.bak," or some other appropriate name. You will then be protected if you incorrectly change the "acad.mnu" file. If that happens, you can just copy the "acad.bak" file to the "acad.mnu" file to get back to the original.

How Menus Express Commands

The text in a ".mnu" file can do two fundamental things. First, it can be displayed in the form of a menu on the screen. Second, it can contain commands and responses to prompts that will be fed to the command line when a menu item is picked. See Figure 10-1 for the standard implementation of the LINE command as shown in the "acad.mnu" file.

Although you may not know the specific meanings of the characters, you can recognize some of the characteristics of the LINE submenu as it appears on your AutoCAD display:

LINE:
continue
close
undo

This is not all that appears on the screen in the sidebar menu box, however, when you see the menu for lines. You will also see other menu items. These lines are the part of the menu that is influenced by the codes from the "acad.mnu" file, shown in Figure 10-1. Notice the similarities between the menu codes and the menu itself. They share certain words like "LINE," "continue," "close," and "undo." Certain other characters appear in the menu file, but do not appear on the menu itself. The square brackets ([]), for example, do not appear on your display, nor does the text that reads "**LINE 1."

You use special characters like square brackets and asterisks to tell AutoCAD the meanings of text strings in the context of your menu. For instance, in the preceding example, you tell AutoCAD that the menu at the second submenu level will contain the text that follows. That is what the two asterisks are for. They indicate that you are specifying a submenu, of which the text that follows will be the first part.

The Submenu Label

In addition, this part of the submenu will have the name "LINE." This is a *submenu label.* AutoCAD uses submenu labels to identify submenus in the menu, in this case the "LINE"

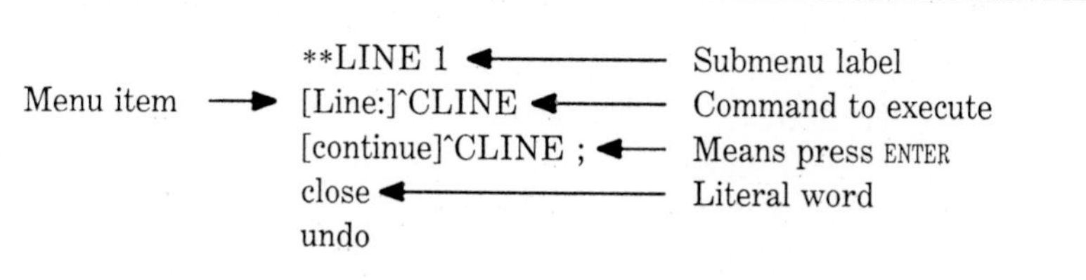

Figure 10-1. The LINE command from the "acad.mnu" file

submenu. This submenu label also has a number (1) which indicates that the submenu is to begin display of the menu entries at the first position in the screen menu.

Menu Items

After the section name, you see the first menu item, in this case "[LINE:]". Note that the item is surrounded by square brackets, which is a way of representing the command that will be sent to the command line. The actual command is shown following the menu item. In this case, it is "^CLINE". In other words, when you pick the menu item "LINE:", you will send "^CLINE" to the AutoCAD command line. This will first perform a Cancel (^C means CTRL-C) and then will enter the LINE command. Note that a semicolon used in a menu file command means that you want the command to be entered automatically, without your finger pressing the ENTER key. A semicolon appears in "^CLINE;".

The menu items that are not enclosed in square brackets, such as "close" or "undo," will simply be sent to the AutoCAD command line as though they were typed from the keyboard at the time they were picked. In other words, if you pick the literal word "continue" from the menu, it will be typed as though from your keyboard.

Calling Menus from Menus

It may be interesting that you can create a submenu, but how does the submenu fit into the menu structure? The answer has to do with the use of submenu names.

To activate menus from menus to create a "tree" of submenus, you must refer to submenus by using the special "$" character. For an illustration of this usage, take a look at the menu code from "acad.mnu" shown in Figure 10-2. Note that if you use EDLIN it will be hard to find this text and it will look different on your screen.

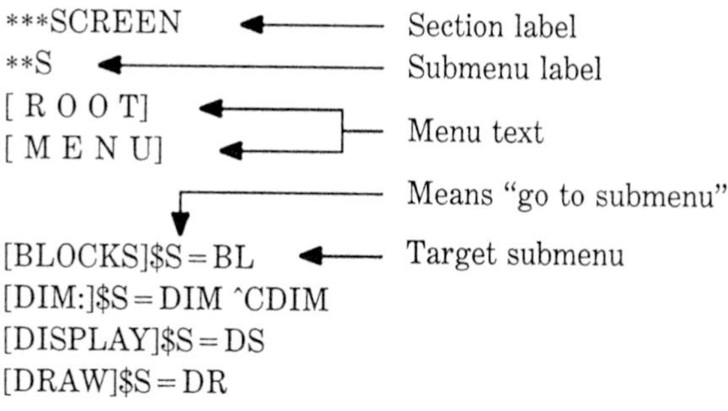

Figure 10-2. The SCREEN menu from "acad.mnu"

The section label "***SCREEN" indicates that this is the start of the screen menu. The submenu label "**S" indicates that the "S" submenu definition follows. After the submenu label, you see the first line of text that will appear in the sidebar menu box, "[R O O T]". Note that in the text lines that follow, you see the "$" character used repeatedly. As in the definition of a menu item, you see the menu item name enclosed in square brackets, followed by a series of characters. In the case of a simple menu item, this series of characters would be sent as though from the keyboard. If any character is a "$" character, however, the characters that follow mean something entirely different. These characters will be sent to the menu control system rather than to the command line. They will cause the display of a labeled submenu.

In the case of the last item, "[DRAW]$S=DR", when you pick the "DRAW" menu item from the root menu, the submenu "DR" will be displayed. Look at the code for the "DR" submenu contained in the "acad.mnu" file:

```
**DR
[ARC]$S=ARC
[CIRCLE]$S=CIRCLE
[INSERT:]^CINSERT $S=INSERT
[LINE:]^CLINE $S=LINE
```

You see that the "DR" submenu exists elsewhere in the "acad.mnu" file, and that the code "$S=DR" was used from the root menu to get there. Likewise, the code "$S=LINE" will get from the "**DR" submenu to the "**LINE" submenu, the code for which looks like this:

```
**LINE 1
[LINE:]^CLINE
[continue]^CLINE ;
close
undo
```

Do you recognize this code from the example shown in Figure 10-1? Now you know how the entire screen menu system works. You know how to construct a menu to send characters from an item picked from the screen menu to the command line. You also know how to call a submenu from another menu. There is a great deal you can do to customize AutoCAD for your own use with this simple knowledge.

There are many other types of menus in addition to the screen menus that have been discussed. There are many subtle combinations of menu items that can be created, not just in the screen menu area, but on tablet, pull-down, and icon menus as well.

Calling Submenus

When you follow a menu item designation with a "$" character, a section name, an equal sign (=), and a submenu name, that submenu will then be displayed. There are only a limited number of section types that AutoCAD will recognize.

It is not enough to call a submenu name. You must tell AutoCAD what type of submenu it is. To call a screen menu, you must use "$S=submenuname". A button menu is called with "$B=submenuname". To call pop-up menus, you use "$Pn= submenuname", when "n" is a number from one through ten. Tablet menus 1 through 4 are called with "$Tn=submenuname".

If you wish to call an icon menu, you must enter "$I=submenuname". Finally, the auxiliary menu is called by using "$A1=submenuname".

Using Menu Sections

A menu file contains sections, each of which pertains to a specific menu device. Each section is identified by three asterisks followed by a section name. The section names are very specific key words known to AutoCAD. You cannot make them up yourself.

Screen Menus

Screen menus like the one in the preceding examples can be defined with the "***SCREEN" section label. Only one screen menu can be active for a given menu file. Screen menus always appear in the right sidebar, as do the standard AutoCAD menus contained under the "***SCREEN" section in "acad.mnu".

Menus for Buttons

You can program the buttons on your pointing device with the "***BUTTONS" section label. The buttons, in a special numeric order, will send the commands that follow the label. When the driver for the device is written, the positions of each command by number are known. These numbers are *mapped* onto buttons as desired for the specific device. Thus sequence number 1 may be mapped to button number 4. The appearance of the commands in their sequence in the button section may thus appear to have nothing to do with the sequence of buttons on your device. This is because the mapping of the sequence in the menu file is handled by the pointing device driver. The following is part of the button definition for the standard "acad.mnu" file:

```
***BUTTONS
;
^CREDRAW
^C
```

Depending on the nature of your pointing device, the various control codes shown will do different things. The usual configuration on a three-button mouse, for example, is to pick with the left button, enter with the middle button, and cancel with the right button. The AutoCAD mouse driver will determine which codes are activated from the selection shown. You can change the order of the codes shown to change the functions of the pointing device's buttons. Experiment with different combinations.

You can use a backslash character (\) in button menus to skip prompts of commands that require you to pick points with the crosshairs. If you place the POINT command in a button menu followed by a space and a backslash character, when you press the appropriate button, the crosshairs location will automatically be used to draw the point. This saves you from needing to use the pick button after you use the button you have assigned to the POINT command.

Tablet Menus

You can have up to four tablet menus active at once. To call for any of them in your menu file, you use "***TABLETn". In this case "n" refers to the tablet number. Thus you could define tablet menu 4 by using "***TABLET4".

The standard tablet menu in AutoCAD, contained in the "acad.mnu" file, shows how the standard tablet menu works. The following is a listing of the first part of the tablet definitions:

```
***TABLET1
[< GO >];
[^Snap]
[^Ortho]
LINE
ARC
CIRCLE
```

Like the button section already described, the tablet commands are shown in a specific sequence in the menu file. The mapping of commands from the menu file sequence to the sequence required by the tablet menu is handled by the specification of the tablet menu. The TABLET CFG command is used to break the tablet up into a number of rows and columns. These rows and columns are identified sequentially from top to bottom, left to right. See Figure 10-3 for the mapping of the menu sequence to the tablet surface.

Pull-down Menus

Up to ten pull-down menus can be active at once. You specify a pull-down menu section by using the "***POPn" section label. The letter "n" refers to a number from one through ten. Thus you could specify pull-down menu 8 by including "***POP8" in your menu file. The following is a pull-down version of a menu that permits you to draw lines:

```
***POP1
**P1a
[Draw]
[Line ]$p1=p1b
**P1b
[Line]
[LINE:    ]^CLINE
[continue]^CLINE ;
[close]c
[undo]undo
[Exit]$p1=p1a
```

The submenus are named "P1a" and "P1b." Notice how "$p1=p1b" is used to call "**P1b" when the "LINE" menu item is picked. You can, of course, use any names you want for your submenus.

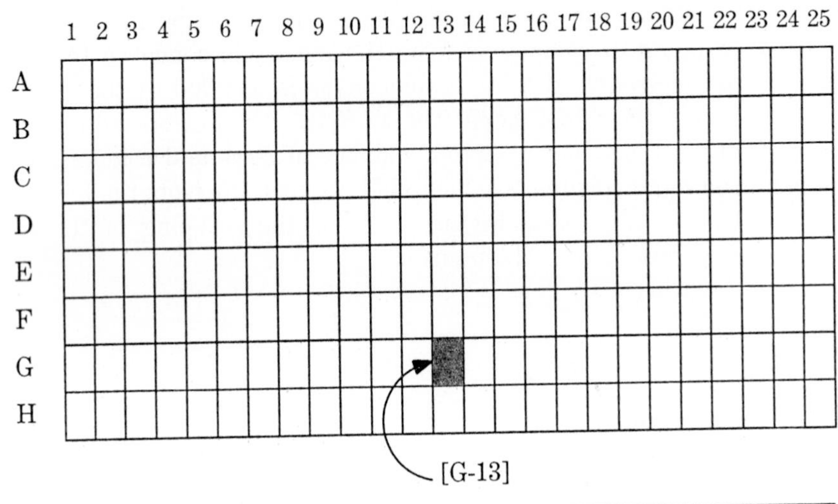

Figure 10-3. The user area of the tablet menu

Icon Menus

Icon menus use AutoCAD slide files, files that contain abbreviated images that can be drawn quickly to display as menus. You specify the icon menu section by using the section label "***ICON". The following is a simple icon menu that will draw an icon that represents the line drawing function. The symbol does not actually exist. The following is only an example of how such an icon would be called into the menu:

```
***ICON
**LINE
[Drawing Lines:]
[line]^Cinsert line
[pline]^Cinsert pline
```

You can prepare your own slide files for use in icon menus by using the MSLIDE command. You can include slides in libraries and extract them from libraries into menus. If you want to use a slide from a library, you precede the slide name with the library name and enclose the slide name in parentheses. For example, the "line" slide in the preceding example would be pulled from a library called "lines" by using "[lines(line)]" instead of "[line]" as was used.

Auxiliary Menus

You can create on-screen "buttons" for function boxes with the auxiliary menu section. You specify the auxiliary menu section with the "***AUX1" section label. On-screen buttons and function boxes were used in Chapter 9, "Attribute Management," to illustrate commands that use dialog boxes.

Using Commands In Menus

Any command sequence that you can type from the keyboard can be used in menus. The best way to prepare such menu commands is to run through the command sequence and record your exact responses. Every character you enter from your keyboard is important. As a simple example, the following exercise is the command sequence to draw an equilateral triangle with simple lines:

Command: **point**
Point:
Command: **line**
From point: **@0,0**
To point: **@3<60**
To point: **@3<180**
To point: **@3<300**
To point:

First, you pick any point to act as a starting point for the triangle. Next, the beginning of the first line is drawn starting at the last point entered in your drawing. The "@" character means "Pick the distance shown from the last point entered." You can express distances as the coordinates of a point or as an actual distance, depending on the format you use. If you enter a coordinate pair, (0,0) in this example, the format is two or three numbers separated by commas. If you enter a linear distance, you must use a number and an angular deflection. The numbers "3<60" are in the format required for the expression of angular distance, meaning "A distance of 3 units at an angle of 60 degrees."

The command sequence shown draws three lines, each 3 units long, at angles of 60, then 180, and finally 300 degrees from their endpoints. The last action in the sequence is to enter or cancel at the last "To point:" prompt. Try entering the above sequence yourself to see what happens. You should see a display that looks something like Figure 10-4.

When you prepare a menu item, you must put the entire command sequence on one line following the menu item, unless the last character on the line is the plus (+) character. You

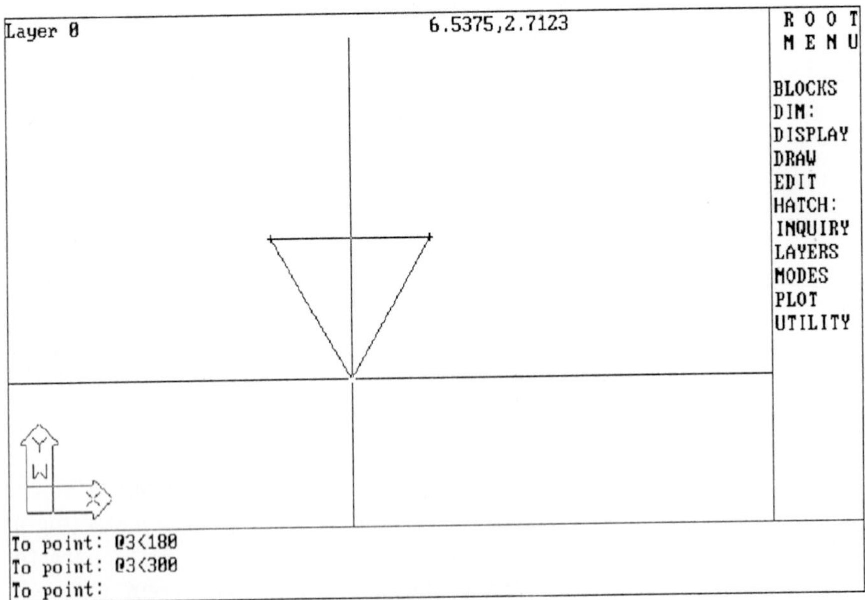

Figure 10-4. The creation of an equilateral triangle

could add a command to the root menu by adding the following code to "acad.mnu":

```
[TRIANGLE]^Cline @0,0 @3<60 @3<180 @3<300 ;
```

You could express the same sequence with two or more lines by using the plus (+) character. In the following example of the same command, the use of the plus character enables you to break the line in two:

```
[TRIANGLE]^Cline @0,0 @3<60 +
@3<180 @3<300 ;
```

You should precede your command sequences with the "^C" character (cancel) so that any commands that may be pending are canceled. You must be very careful to use the exact sequence

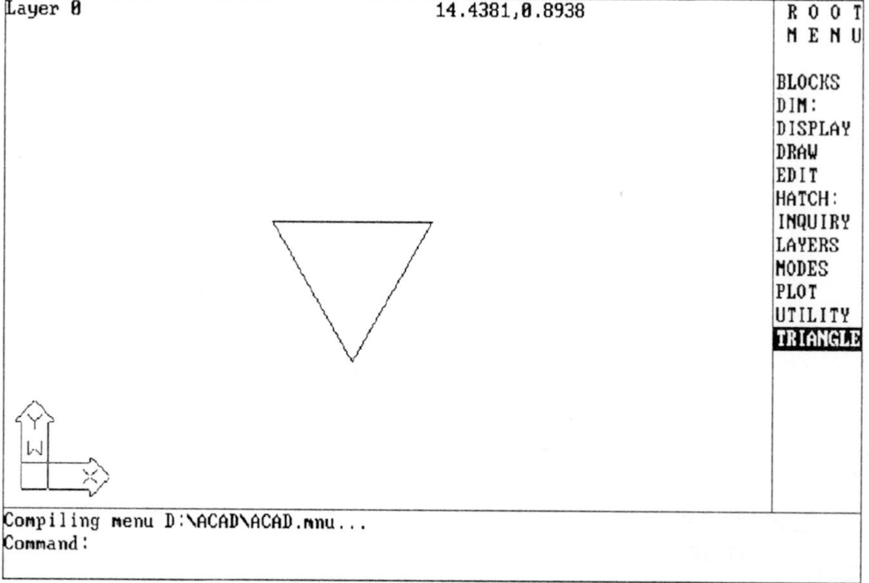

Figure 10-5. After the TRIANGLE menu item has been added

of characters you used to model the command sequence. Note that at the end of the command sequence, there must be a semicolon if you wish to simulate a press of the ENTER key. Figure 10-5 shows the display as it appears after the TRIANGLE menu item has been added to the "acad.mnu" file. Note that a message shows that "acad.mnu" has been automatically compiled. Figure 10-6 shows the display as it appears after a point has been entered and the new TRIANGLE menu item has been picked.

Waiting for Input

If you want to create an interactive command sequence that is executable from a menu item, you can include the backslash character anywhere to wait for user input. The command sequence will stop at the designated command prompt and you will be able to enter a value. After you enter a value, the menu-

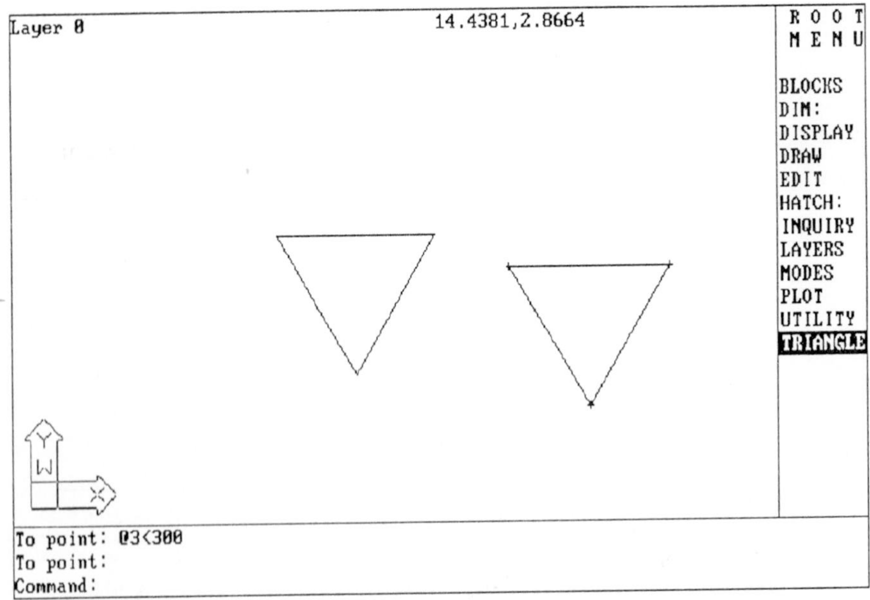

Figure 10-6. After the TRIANGLE menu item has been picked

activated command sequence will resume. You could modify the TRIANGLE menu item command sequence as follows to produce a different kind of geometry from the equilateral triangle.

[TRIANGLE]^Cline @0,0 @3<60 \ @3<300 ;

The command sequence will stop at the prompt for the second endpoint and you will be able to enter any value you wish. Be careful not to follow the backslash (\) character with a space unless you want to have the effect of typing a space character from the keyboard. In the following example, showing the *wrong* way to do it, the results will not be as you might have anticipated:

[TRIANGLE]^Cline @0,0 @3<60 \ @3<300 ;

What a difference a space makes. The space character in this instance will produce the following command sequence:

Command: **line** From point: **@0,0**
To point: **@3<60**
To point: **@3<200**
To point:
Command: @3<300 Unknown command. Type ? for list of commands.
Command:
LINE From point:

In this case the user entered "@3<200", followed by a press of the spacebar. The menu command sequence resumed with a press of the spacebar, terminating the LINE command, and the entry of "@3<300" as though it were a command. The ENTER key was pressed by the semicolon in the menu command sequence. This reentered the LINE command. The preceding is probably not a command sequence that would be useful to you. It shows how careful you must be when you create command sequences that are entered from menus.

Compiling Menus

The compiling of menus is very straightforward. When you make a change to a menu file, for example, the "acad.mnu" file, that file will be recompiled as soon as you try to use the menu. In the case of the "acad.mnu" file, compilation will be done automatically when you start AutoCAD. The file that results from the menu compile has the extension ".mnx". Compilation of a menu creates a file that AutoCAD can load much more quickly.

Advanced Techniques

PART THREE

Introduction to AutoLISP

ELEVEN

AutoCAD is usually thought of as a drafting program. You draw lines on the screen and transfer the lines to drafting vellum with a plotter. According to this point of view, AutoCAD is simply a way to increase productivity and avoid repetition.

In reality, however, AutoCAD is a powerful environment for manipulating graphical and non-graphical symbols and objects that can also be used for drafting. Drawing and editing are the most common ways to manipulate these graphic symbols in AutoCAD. There are also other ways to manipulate drawn objects with AutoCAD. You can create your own menus as discussed in Chapter 10, "Working with Menus." You can set AutoCAD's system variables as shown in Chapter 16, "AutoCAD Command Reference." The most powerful mechanism to change the AutoCAD environment, though, is by using the built-in programming language, AutoLISP.

Getting Acquainted with AutoLISP

AutoLISP is easy to use. Of course, because it is a real programming language, you must practice to be able to use it effectively. There are many ways you can begin to work with AutoLISP. Some people learn by following tutorials, while others learn by copying a program that someone else has written. Use whichever method is most meaningful to you. This book gives you a little of both—a tutorial and numerous code listings.

You will find that some of the code listings in this book are meant to teach and others are meant to be copied literally and used. In general, where a function is simple enough, it is spelled out in detail, with comments to help you fully understand it. Some functions are very complex and long and so are often "optimized" by the use of very short names for functions and variables. When optimized in this way, a function runs much faster.

Becoming Comfortable With AutoLISP

Computer languages are often much less intimidating than you expect. For example, the computer language Logo was invented in the 1960s as an easy language for elementary school children to use to learn computer programming. Logo is a language of symbol manipulation based on LISP. Logo contains all of the same conceptual features that make LISP a unique programming language, except that it does not make as extensive a use of parentheses.

You may feel much more comfortable about programming languages like LISP if you know that Logo is used very easily by small children. They proceed without preconceptions and enjoy working with the language. If you have a programming background, you may think about problems in terms of functions and mathematical formulas instead of symbol manipulation. In that case, unlike the small child, you may actually find it difficult to enter the world of symbol manipulation found in LISP. Do not let this discourage you, though. Just keep practicing, and it will become easy for you, too.

Putting Aside Preconceptions

The first thing you need to do when programming in AutoLISP is to put aside what you may already know about programming. You may have written programs with techniques that you learned in BASIC, Pascal, or C language, but as you become more attuned to AutoLISP, you will find it easier to manipulate symbols. Unlike languages that require *declarations,* LISP allows you to use symbols by simply naming them. When you use a language like C, all variables and functions in the program must be declared before being used. Everything must be predetermined. LISP is much different since nothing needs to be declared before being used.

LISP does use a lot of parentheses and it is very easy to get lost in them. Parentheses in LISP indicate the beginning and end of a *list.* In fact, the name "LISP" itself is indicative of the language's fundamental orientation. The language is used for LISt Processing. To keep lists separate from each other, some mechanism must be used, and parentheses work quite well for this. In LISP, the only expression separators are white space and parenthesis characters. White space is any combination of space, enter, linefeed, and tab characters.

Separators can be confusing in other computer languages as well. In C language, for example, you have to worry about such control separators as semicolons, braces, brackets, and commas, in addition to spaces and parentheses. These characters have very specific meanings that enable you to express program code tersely. C language is not a high level language, like LISP, and is used for an entirely different purpose. You use C language primarily to make your code easy to debug and independent of machine language, not to process lists. You could, for example, write a LISP evaluator in C, but you would certainly not write the C language in LISP.

At first, you will have a problem keeping track of all of the parentheses (you will see some new tricks later on), but it will become easier after you have gained some experience. At least with LISP, you only need to be concerned with one type of separator, the parenthesis characters.

Understanding Processing Speed

AutoLISP is slow compared to C language or Pascal, particularly when it uses lots of math functions. AutoLISP was tested with a benchmark program designed to test the speed of a computer language's floating point math operations. It was so slow in this respect that the results were discouraging. When AutoLISP is used as a symbol manipulation language, however, the results are quite different. A list of over 1000 symbols was put together and a routine was written to search that list for a specified symbol. AutoLISP accomplished that task in less than one second.

Poor programming techniques are another reason for a program that runs slowly. The new Extended AutoLISP, if used efficiently, should inherently speed up most AutoLISP applications. Even with Extended AutoLISP, however, you should be careful to write efficient code. Chapter 12, "Programs in AutoLISP," contains some helpful suggestions for accomplishing this.

AutoLISP is an excellent language for programming a CAD system. A CAD system is an environment for manipulating graphical symbols with a computer and AutoLISP is a language of symbol manipulation. AutoLISP and CAD thus go together because both the CAD system and the programming language have a similar purpose.

Evaluated, Interpreted, and Compiled Languages

LISP is usually a language that is *evaluated* rather than interpreted or compiled. Interpreted languages use the computer to read the same text with which you write your program, line by line. The interpreted language is very slow because each full word of the programming language must be read completely and converted into machine instructions. Compiled languages are very fast because all of the code you enter as text is converted into machine instructions when a program is compiled. An entirely new file containing a very efficient program is produced. After compiling, everything in the program is greatly abbreviated in machine language form and runs much faster.

An evaluated language is like an intermediate step between interpreted and compiled languages. The first time a block of code in an evaluated language is encountered by the evaluator, the entire block is converted into compact code. If that block is encountered again while the program is running, the evaluator knows the block has already been evaluated and simply runs it. This process is faster than interpreting but slower than compiling.

Although there are a few LISP compilers on the market, compiling an AutoLISP program tends to limit some of the inherent flexibility of the language. AutoLISP does not distinguish between data and instructions. For example, you could write an AutoLISP program that would permanently modify itself under certain circumstances. When you ran your program again, it would actually behave differently than it did before. When you use AutoLISP to manipulate an AutoCAD drawing, the drawing database (and the drawing itself) actually becomes a part of your AutoLISP program. If you want them to, changes in a drawing can cause very complex changes in the AutoLISP program. In this way, AutoCAD drawings can even be said to "learn" from changes you make in them. For example, the drawing can learn that whenever you add a certain type of line, some similar lines should be converted to that line type.

Every serious user of AutoCAD will profit from learning AutoLISP. For instance, if you devote three days to developing an AutoLISP routine that saves you thirty minutes a day of routine AutoCAD drafting, your efforts will be repaid in a little over a month. In addition, you can tailor your application to the way you actually work, instead of the way set up by someone else's application. Learning AutoLISP will be a struggle, but the rewards of increased productivity will be worth it.

What Is AutoLISP?

AutoLISP is a subset of LISP, a programming language also known as Common LISP that was developed in the 1950s by John McCarthy for Artificial Intelligence Research. It is one of the oldest computer programming languages still in use. LISP is considered to be important because it is a very flexible and extendable language. Many new features have been added over the years that have made it useful for many different applications.

AutoLISP adds a number of specialized built-in functions to LISP that are specially designed for manipulating AutoCAD drawings. Because AutoLISP is a true subset of an established programming language and still supports the concepts and constructions of the original language, it is in itself a "real" programming language, not a simple macro programming language.

Three features of LISP distinguish it from most other programming languages. LISP manipulates symbols rather than numbers, it is an object-oriented language rather than a procedural language, and it is a language that is evaluated rather than interpreted or compiled. These three features are what make LISP the language of choice for programming in the CAD environment.

How AutoLISP Works

LISP stands for LISt Processing, as stated earlier. The LISP language processes lists of symbols rather than numerical data. Most other programming languages are designed to process only numerical data. Computer languages such as FORTRAN, BASIC, and C are mathematically or numerically oriented, that is, they are used to manipulate numbers. A "word" in such a language has no meaning in itself, but is just a string of characters that are in themselves numbers. In fact the word "string" represents such strings of characters in most languages other than LISP.

Symbols

Symbols are simply representations of meaning. A word is one kind of symbol that communicates the meaning of that word from one person to another. For example, the word "simple" could, among other things, represent the dictionary definition of that word. The dictionary definition for the word "simple" is a list of symbols that imply other definitions.

If you were to look up the word "simple" in the dictionary, you would find, as a partial definition: "having or consisting of only one part." If you weren't familiar with the meaning of the word "consist(ing)," you could look that up in turn, and you would find that it means: "to be made up, formed or composed . . . ." If you still did not understand the meaning of the word "simple," you could look up more of the words contained in the definition until you were certain of the meaning.

In LISP, the definition of the word (or symbol) "simple" could look like this:

```
(setq simple '(having or consisting of only one part))
```

The word "setq" is a LISP function that tells the computer to set the meaning (or value) of the symbol "simple" to the meaning (or value) contained in the next element, the definition. Now, if you were to type **!simple**, AutoLISP would print

```
(HAVING OR CONSISTING OF ONLY ONE PART)
```

Although this is a trivial example of the assignment of values to symbols, it illustrates what is perhaps the most fundamental operation in LISP. Every language has its own ways of accomplishing assignment, of transferring information from one "container" to another. In AutoLISP, the assignment operation is performed by using "setq." In C language and BASIC, assignment is accomplished with the equal character (=). In Pascal, assignment is done with the colon and equal sign character combination (:=). If you know how to assign values, you can move information from one list to another in AutoLISP.

Symbols as Drawn Objects

A symbol does not have to be a word, but it can be almost anything to which a meaning can be attached. A symbol is simply something that refers to something else. A drawing of a chair, for example, is a symbol that represents a chair in the same sort of way that the word "chair" symbolizes a chair.

Visual representation may be a different medium than the printed word, but the purpose of the two media are the same. The purpose is to communicate something of value from one person to another.

There is nothing in the word "chair" that has the quality of "chairness." Attributes of a chair are only associated with the word because people have learned that the word "chair" is a symbol for that object. Likewise, a drawing of a chair is only a visual abstraction, a symbol of a chair. It contains none of the inherent qualities of the object that it represents. You cannot, for example, sit on a picture of a chair and obtain the same benefits as sitting on the chair itself. Pictures of chairs are usually too flat and too low to the ground to be any good for support.

How AutoCAD Uses Symbols

Letters of the alphabet standing by themselves have no inherent meaning until they are strung together into recognizable words, and those words are in turn manipulated into intelligible sentences and paragraphs. Similarly, lines, arcs, circles, points, polygons, and other entities are the drafter's alphabet. They are meaningless until they are selected and arranged into recognizable patterns. These basic recognizable patterns are combined to create a graphic symbol, such as the symbol for a chair.

Having created the drafted symbol for a chair, you can take the drawing (composed of lines and arcs) and save it as a block named "chair." Every time that you need a symbol for a chair in a drawing, you can insert that chair symbol.

Symbol Ambiguities

A problem may arise when you show this chair symbol to someone else. They may recognize your symbol as a chair, or they may only see an incomprehensible assemblage of lines and arcs. A graphical symbol can be either more or less ambiguous than a word symbol, depending on the context of that symbol. There is less agreement on the meaning of graphical symbols than on the meaning of word symbols. There are two ways to resolve the ambiguity of the chair symbol. The first is to draw a chair symbol detailed to the point where there is no chance that it will be mistaken for anything else. The second way is to attach to the symbol, with attributes, a textual description of the chair that is represented by that symbol. The graphical and textual description of a chair combine to form an object that represents a chair with a minimum of ambiguity. An "object," in this context, is just a symbol with the definition built into the symbol itself.

The attributes defining the chair can be very simple or very complex. It can be just a chair, or it can be a blue swivel chair, with arms, selling for $500. The object can be seen as a simulation of a real chair within the AutoCAD environment. The object called "chair" is still only the representation of a chair, but it has more of the substance of a chair than a simple line drawing of a chair.

Using Attributes in a Drawing

Here is a concrete example of how these objects can be manipulated in AutoCAD. Let's say that you have a floor plan of a house and it is your job to design a furniture layout for that house. If you did the layout in a traditional fashion, you would sketch out a pleasing arrangement of furniture, count and list all of the various pieces, and from that list develop a project cost. This could be both time-consuming and inaccurate.

Alternatively, you could use AutoCAD to create a more efficient and accurate result by creating "furniture objects." Each of these objects (called "blocks" in AutoCAD) could contain detailed information about each piece. Attribute information could include style, catalog number, and price. Then all you would need to do would be to insert and move these furniture objects around on the floor plan until you or your client was pleased with the results.

Instead of having a drawing consisting of a bunch of lines that someone would have to interpret as being an arrangement of furniture in a house, you would have a series of rooms containing objects that are defined as different types of furniture. You could query any of the rooms with a simple AutoLISP program (which you will learn how to write later) by asking, in effect, "What do you contain?" The room could then reply, "I contain 16 chairs and 5 tables, and it will cost $4000 to furnish me."

Object-Oriented Programming

Most computer languages, such as BASIC, Pascal, and C are known as procedural languages. A program written in a procedural language will have step-by-step instructions to do something with data usually (but not always) contained in an outside data file. A procedural program is normally divided into three parts. The first part says what information must be gathered, where to find it, and what it must look like. The second part tells how the data gathered in the first part must be manipulated. Finally, the third part instructs the computer on what to do with the manipulated data—for example, to put it into another file or print out a report. In such procedural-oriented languages, the sequence of operations is generally deterministic, in that it starts at one place and follows set rules to arrive at another place in the program. In general, the programmer avoids generating code that "changes itself."

In *object-oriented* programming, unlike in procedural-oriented programming, the language invests objects with information about themselves. The chair "knows" it is a chair. The chair may even "know" where it can and cannot be used. The programming language, instead of following fixed procedures regardless of what information is to be processed, asks objects about themselves.

Object-oriented programming is the latest buzzword among programmers. Much has been written about it, but the explanations all tend to be very abstract and difficult to understand. LISP in general, and AutoLISP in particular, do not meet all of the strict criteria for an object-oriented language, but they do contain enough features of this type of language to make certain object-oriented applications feasible.

An object-oriented program, as you might expect, deals with objects. Objects are self-contained modules that contain certain data as well as the functions necessary to manipulate that data within the same module. Although objects have other properties, this is the basic concept of objects most relevant to this discussion.

You could compare a procedural program to a recipe for baking a cake. The first part of the recipe tells you what ingredients (the data) are needed. The next part of the recipe is about what you should do with the ingredients (manipulate the data), and the final part of the recipe describes what the results of that recipe should be like. An object in an object-oriented program, on the other hand, is like a cake mix. Both the ingredients for the cake and the instructions for preparing it are contained in the same package.

The Versatility of AutoCAD

By now, you have probably had a chance to discover how AutoCAD works and have gained some proficiency in its use. You have undoubtedly also discovered two important things about AutoCAD:

- You can do almost any type of basic drafting operation with AutoCAD, from drawing a line to automatically generating a very complex hatch pattern. This makes AutoCAD very easy to use.

- AutoCAD is not set up to do any particular type of drafting, such as architectural drafting or mechanical drafting. This means that you must spend a lot of time and effort figuring out how to configure the program to serve your specific application. This setup requirement can make AutoCAD very difficult to use.

There are many CAD packages that are designed for specific drafting disciplines. One system is designed specifically for architectural drafting and another is intended for the layout of electronic printed circuit boards. You would have very little success in trying to lay out a printed circuit board with the architect's system. AutoCAD, on the other hand, can be used for both architectural drafting and printed circuit board layout, as long as it is configured appropriately.

AutoCAD is a general-purpose drafting system that can be configured and programmed to produce drawings that will conform to the specifications of almost any drafting discipline. This is both its strength and weakness. It is difficult to do much that is very productive within a specific drafting discipline with AutoCAD just "out of the box," and this can be very frustrating at first. But once AutoCAD is configured to perform a particular drafting task, it becomes a very flexible, powerful, and productive system. The advantage of such a general-purpose CAD system, as opposed to one designed for a specific application, is that it gives you the ability to make the system work in the way that you are comfortable with rather than having to adapt yourself to someone else's idea of how you should work.

There are many ways that AutoCAD can be configured into a discipline-specific drafting package, such as menus, symbol libraries, hatch patterns, and AutoLISP. In the next section, some ideas for how to expand the capabilities of AutoCAD with AutoLISP will be covered.

Extending the Utility of AutoCAD

Not all AutoLISP solutions require you to be a master programmer. Some are very simple. Perhaps you perform a series of the same operations over and over again. You could easily write a simple AutoLISP routine to execute this series of commands. Every time you execute your little routine, a whole series of AutoCAD commands will then be executed. Some of the most useful drafting utilities in AutoLISP consist of only a few lines of code.

You will learn how to write these simple routines in Chapter 12, "Programs in AutoLISP," the AutoLISP tutorial section. Here are a few ideas for simple AutoLISP applications that solve specific drafting problems:

- Transfer entities to a predefined layer by a single pick.
- Offset entities to a different layer.
- Rotate entities to a specified angle with a single pick.
- Manipulate all entities that have common properties (such as layer, color, entity type) in a particular way with a single command. For example, change the color of all text that is one-inch high to red.
- Highlight all circles that are of a user-specified diameter.
- Redefine existing AutoCAD commands so that they only require one or two keystrokes to execute.

The above ideas are simple applications, and most of them can be written with fewer than ten lines of AutoLISP code. The following examples are more complex, and each may take days to develop and require several pages of AutoLISP code to implement:

- Draw multiple parallel lines simultaneously (useful for drawing walls).
- Insert door symbols automatically into parallel wall lines.
- Generate three-dimensional objects from multi-view drawings.
- Generate double-line wall floor plans from single-line sketches.
- Generate three-dimensional solids automatically from user input.
- Generate dimensioning.

The applications are limited only by your imagination and perseverance.

Adding New Commands to AutoCAD

AutoLISP allows you to create your own personal AutoCAD commands that can be executed on the command line, like any other AutoCAD command. Most of the preceding examples might be defined as AutoCAD commands.

You can even redefine an existing AutoCAD command to do something entirely different from what it was originally intended to do. For example, suppose you had an application where you wanted the only valid type of line in a drawing to be a polyline. The people using the system might sometimes forget and use the LINE command. To prevent this problem from occurring, you could redefine the LINE command to mean PLINE.

Manipulating Graphics Directly

This is an area of AutoLISP programming that is very interesting, because you can see the drawing almost drawing itself on the screen as you sit back and watch. The best way to describe how this would work is with the following scenario.

Suppose your company makes custom cardboard boxes, and you are responsible for drawing the plan for each custom cardboard box according to the customer's specification. This plan is then used to set up the machinery that produces the box. Normally, you would make a separate drawing for each size box, but now you can simply type in the width, length, and height of the box, and an AutoLISP program will create a box drawing according to your specifications. This is called parametric programming and semi-automatic drafting.

Parametric Programming

A parametric program is one that will produce a drawing based on a series of parameters or variables that are passed to that program.

Parametric programming is basically a set of rules about how a specific object is constructed. For example, most boxes are constructed the same way, with the only difference between them being the dimensions for each size. If you had a set of rules that told what the length of each line that represented the box was in relation to the overall dimensions of that box, it would then be a simple matter to apply the dimensions of the box to the rules about the object box. This would create a drawing of a specifically dimensioned box. These rules could be expressed as a textual description pseudocode such as *If the height is X then Line 1 is X and line 2 is half of X.* Or the rules could be expressed graphically as a prototype drawing of a box.

Semi-Automatic Drafting in House Design

Semi-automatic drafting implies that a drawing is actually drawn on a CAD system by a program, not by a user. The program reads and interprets data that determine the specifications of that drawing.

The output of a parametric program, the drawing, is the result of semi-automatic drafting. Our programming tools can be used to design a system that is much more ambitious than the parametric program for a box. This system is conceptually the same as the program that developed the box, but is several orders of magnitude more complex. It is a house-design system.

The computer can be used with modular house designs because the parts with which a modular house will be built are predictable whereas the parts from which the framed house will be built are relatively unpredictable. Most tract housing today is quite similar in design. In an average three-bedroom, two-bath, single-family house, the rooms may vary in size and arrangement depending on the floor plan. The architectural detailing may vary from house to house, but functionally these houses will be identical.

If one were to design a program that contained all of the information about how a prototypical three-bedroom house is put together, then one could simply input all of the desired variables about a specific house design. When room dimensions and architectural style were specified, a set of construction drawings and specifications for that house could be automatically produced. Such house-design systems are now being used with some success in the modular housing industry in Japan. And a system like this was actually in operation in Australia in the 1960s.

There appears to be no system at this time that will produce a set of plans for a non-modular, conventional house. Non-modular houses are put together with assorted lengths of lumber that are cut onsite by the builders. Modular houses, on the other hand, are made up of panels that are assembled in manufacturing plants.

Parametric programming and semi-automatic drafting are two areas that are only now beginning to be explored. These areas will be extensively developed in the future since about 60% to 80% of all drafting being done is concerned with modifying existing designs for new applications. For example, a hydraulic cylinder may be available in a two-inch and a four-inch diameter, but an application has been found for a three-inch diameter. Normally, a drafter would have to draw a set of plans for a three-inch diameter cylinder from scratch before it could be manufactured. If, however, the manufacturer had the proper software along with data on hydraulic cylinder design, it would be a simple matter for a computer to generate the drawings. The new three-inch cylinder would be developed from the same design data as the two-inch and four-inch cylinders. In this way, the design process would be made more efficient, although a drafting job might also be eliminated.

Keeping Track of Items in a Drawing

AutoCAD is usually thought of as a drafting program. Another way of looking at AutoCAD is that it is a data entry program for adding and editing graphic data in a database. This database is called the drawing database. Since the drawing database contains information about everything in the drawing, you can use

AutoLISP to extract that information and format it in a useful way. For example, with AutoLISP, you can write a simple program to calculate the amount of paint required to paint a house given the floor plan of that house. You can also compute the length of two-by-four studs needed to frame the walls of that house.

The most common way of keeping track of things in the AutoCAD drawing is by extracting attribute data that is contained in blocks. Extracting and manipulating attribute information is covered in detail in Chapter 9, "Attribute Management."

Expert Systems

An *expert system* is an assembly of computer hardware and software that is capable of *inference* as well as mere data manipulation. An expert system is supplied with rules that are applied against information. Based on the rules, the expert system can come to roughly the same conclusions as would a human expert using those rules. Expert systems can be said to infer the conclusions from the data, by using methods that appear to be similar to human methods of inference.

Expert systems are becoming very popular. From reading some of the recent articles on the topic, one would think that a whole new basic science had been discovered. This is just not so. These "expert systems" have been around for a long time, but they are now finally being put on computers.

In almost every auto repair manual, you will find a troubleshooting chart, which is an expert system designed to assist you in getting your car running. The following is such a chart in an abbreviated form:

Symptom	Probable Cause	Remedy
Steering effort excessive	Low tire pressure	Inflate tire

Symptom	Probable Cause	Remedy
	Power steering pump	Check fluid Check belts Check pressure

If you were having difficulty turning your steering wheel, you would consult your automobile's manual. In it you would find the troubleshooting chart for steering. In the chart, you would find the reference to "excessive effort" and view both the probable cause and the remedy. The expert system, the chart, has enabled you to locate a symptom in a list of symptoms. Your intelligence has enabled you to relate the phrase "Steering effort excessive" to the problem you are having with your steering wheel. Once the symptom is identified in terms of the chart, the probable causes and associated remedies are easy to find.

The major leap of intelligence needed in the preceding example occurred in your ability to generalize about the difficulty you encountered in turning your steering wheel. In some way, you were able to associate the words "excessive effort" to a problem that could also have been described as a "sticky steering wheel" or a "steering wheel that is hard to turn." The major hurdle in expert system design that needs to be crossed, if the system is to be successful, involves the ambiguity of meaning exemplified in this simple example. The computer must be able to conclude that a steering wheel that is "hard to turn" also requires "excessive effort," in order to match your statement of the symptom to one meaningful element in a long list of possible symptoms.

A very important rule to keep in mind when you attempt to design an expert system is that the vocabulary used to specify symptoms must be no greater nor more complex than the vocabulary used to express the list of symptoms. The same recommendation applies to grammar. You must carefully limit the user's options in specifying symptoms to only those constructs that are stored in the list of possible symptoms. If the user expresses the symptom description in language that does not contain words or phrases that are available in the symptom list, the symptom, although there, will not be recognized from the description.

The Expert Design System

An *expert design system* is similar to an expert system, but it uses rules of design and assembly to either create or verify a design within a very narrowly defined discipline. For example, an expert design system could be created to check drawings for compliance with building codes. As the designer added doors, the system would check various building code criteria. The designer might wish a three-quarter-hour fire-rated door to be located at the end of a 30-foot corridor. The design system would warn the designer that such a door would require a two-hour rating if the building code required it. This way the designer would avoid the extra costs required by a contractor who installed an inadequate door only to be told to rip it out by the building inspector.

Many researchers have been involved in the development of expert design systems. Such systems, based on AutoCAD as well as other CAD software, already are available for facilities planners. Such systems have been developed for interior designers to design office layouts with *systems furniture.* These furnishings consist of panels, work surfaces, shelves, and other components which are assembled together in a systematic way to produce complex assemblies of workstations. Expert systems for systems furniture consist of collections of symbols and a set of rules for assembling the symbols into workstations.

Each component in a given system has a specific spatial and connectivity relationship with other components of the system. For example, panels of the same height can be connected together at their ends, and work surfaces and shelves can be hung from these panels.

The advantage of a system like this is that a designer can effectively design an office layout without an extensive knowledge of the furniture system being used. Some of these furniture systems can contain as many as 2000 different components, and sometimes the method of component assembly is not obvious to someone without a lot of experience with the particular system.

Expert Design System Shell

The systems furniture expert system described is a dedicated expert system. That is, all of the code and rules have been designed specifically for the assembly of systems furniture components. These same rules, however, would not be applicable to the design of sprinkler systems.

There is another way of designing an expert system called an *expert system shell.* An expert system shell consists of an inference engine which is a set of generalized procedures for the application of rules to a given problem. It also includes a method for linking the inference engine to the list of rules being used to solve a given class of problems. The advantage to using the shell over the dedicated method is that once the shell is developed, only the rules need to change when the class of problems changes.

Design Rule Checking

Another type of expert design system is called a *design rule checking* system. The rule checking system is used on a design after it has been completed and compares the drawing against a set of rules that specify how that type of object should be designed. Design rule checking is used extensively in the fields of electronics and integrated circuit design to make sure that the circuits do what they are designed to do.

Review of Rules Applications

A review of the methods of rule based systems shows that there are three ways that design rules can be implemented:

- The rules can be invoked interactively as the designer is creating the design.
- The problem can be stated explicitly at the beginning and the design can be generated automatically.

- The design rules can be invoked once the design has been completed to make certain that the designer has not violated any of the rules.

The method to use in implementing the design rules depends on the type of application being considered.

The examples in this chapter are a few of the possible ways in which you can use AutoLISP to expand the usefulness of AutoCAD. Some of these applications are fairly obvious and simple, while other examples could represent thousands of hours of development time. Some of these examples will be used in Chapter 12, "Programs in AutoLISP," to illustrate programming techniques that have been developed in working with AutoLISP.

Programs in AutoLISP

Using AutoLISP
An AutoLISP Programming Toolkit

TWELVE

AutoLISP, like any other programming language, has fundamental operational features. To write your own AutoLISP programs, you must understand how to use AutoLISP *syntax*. The syntax of a programming language, like the syntax of ordinary language, is the set of rules that governs the order in which you must place functions and variables. The theory of AutoLISP and how it employs functions to manipulate information stored in lists was described in Chapter 11, "Introduction to AutoLISP." In this chapter, you will read about some of the basic concepts of AutoLISP and go through a step-by-step tutorial that demonstrates a few basic AutoLISP functions. You will then learn how to write some helpful AutoLISP routines.

You do not need to have had any prior programming experience to use this AutoLISP tutorial section. You will start with some very basic programming concepts. You should, however, have a thorough understanding of how to use AutoCAD. Read the previous sections of this book and use the program before trying to write AutoLISP code.

Using AutoLISP

Anything that you type into AutoCAD on the command line is sent to the *command interpreter* routine. The command interpreter is a function in AutoCAD that reads the command you entered and compares it with all the commands that can be executed. If the command you entered matches any of the commands in the list of commands, AutoCAD figures out what to do next. For example, if you were to type the word "LINE", the command interpreter would then send a message to AutoCAD's Line routine and the LINE command would start to execute.

If the command interpreter finds an open parenthesis, it assumes that everything after that is an AutoLISP expression, until a matching closing parenthesis is found. It sends that expression to the AutoLISP evaluator for evaluation. In addition, if the command interpreter finds an exclamation point immediately followed by a word, it will search to see if that word has been defined as an AutoLISP symbol. It will then print the value that has been assigned to that symbol on the next line of the screen. For example, the following is the result of printing an AutoLISP variable called "cows":

```
Command: !cows
12
```

This assumes that the variable "cows" contains the number 12. As always, when you see a command line shown like this one, you must assume that the command is terminated by a press of the spacebar or the ENTER key. This will always be true, so it is unnecessary and confusing to show the word "enter" on the command line.

If no value has been assigned to the AutoLISP variable, printing it will return *nil*. The word "nil" in AutoLISP means the same as "nothing." It means the variable is empty, not that its value is zero. Most other LISPs will return an error if a symbol name has not been declared, and nil if the symbol has been declared, but no value has been assigned. AutoLISP will return nil in either case, which can sometimes lead to problems in debugging.

This ability to use AutoLISP interactively within AutoCAD is very useful because you can test expressions that you are unsure about to see if they are valid expressions and that they produce the expected result. For example, if you typed the following AutoLISP expressions in on the command line

Command: **(setq pets '(dogs cats))**

AutoCAD would then respond with

(DOGS CATS)

If you were then to type

Command: **!pets**

you would see the same thing:

(DOGS CATS)

The "car" operator in LISP will return the first *element* in a list. Lists are made up of elements, much as a shopping list is made up of the names of food products. For example, if you were to type the following on the AutoCAD command line

Command: **(car pets)**

AutoCAD would answer with

DOGS

The word "dogs" is the first element of the list pets. Lists can be extremely long, but the simple "car" function will always return the first element in a list.

Working with Lists

To proceed further in working with AutoLISP, you must understand the concepts behind the construction of lists and the use of symbols. Lists are always expressed as elements shown within parentheses and separated by spaces. Symbols have a more general usage than lists, as you will see in the following discussion.

There is only one kind of structure in AutoLISP and that is the list. A list can be made up of symbols (sometimes referred to as "words" or "atoms"), numbers, strings, or any of the other valid data types. A list can even be composed of other lists. Each element of the list must be separated by a space. The list has two basic types: the *standard list* (usually just called a list) and the *quoted list*. A quoted list is a list that is preceded by a quote symbol (usually an apostrophe). The quote symbol tells AutoLISP not to evaluate that list.

The basic rule about lists is that unless the list is a quoted list, the first element of a list must be a valid current AutoLISP function name followed by the correct number of arguments to that function. Here are some examples of regular lists:

```
(setq a b)
(car b)
(setq dog terrier cat siamese)
(setq pets '(cats dogs))
(member 'cat 'pets)
(* (+ 2 (- 6 4) 7) 6)
```

All of the preceding lists have as their first element the name of an AutoLISP function. A quoted list always starts with an apostrophe which is the AutoLISP symbol for QUOTE. Note that you can also use the AutoLISP symbol QUOTE (literally the word quote). The following are examples of quoted lists:

```
('(dogs cats birds fish))
('(a b c d))
('(xsdf cdwer ioumh uiop))
(quote (siamese persians American-shorthair burmese))
```

The Quoted List

If the AutoLISP evaluator sees a list that is preceded by the quote symbol (either the word "QUOTE" or an apostrophe), it will simply return the list without evaluation. For example, if you entered the previous example on the command line like this

Command: **(setq a '(+ 4 8))**

AutoLISP would just return the quoted list:

(+ 4 8)

The "setq" function, as you saw in Chapter 11, "Introduction to AutoLISP," simply stores the literal value "(+ 4 8)," a list, in the variable "a." This is a good way to store lists of symbols that are to be used as data within a function. You could achieve much the same result by entering the following, except that no assignment of value to "a" would occur:

Command: **(quote (+ 4 8))**

In this latter example, only the quoted information would be printed out. The result of printing the value of "a," for example, would be nil (unless it already contained something else) because "setq" was not used to cause the assignment of a value. A word or atom can also be quoted and the evaluator will return that word unevaluated. For example, the value of "a" in the preceding example was "(+ 4 8)," but the results of "(quote a)" would be, simply, "a."

There is an old joke you may have heard in school that may help you to remember how the quote operator works. Kay and Joe make a bet. Kay says, "I'll bet you I can say all fifty states in less than a minute." Joe makes the assumption that the symbol "all-fifty-states" refers to a list containing the names of all 50 states. Thinking that it must certainly take longer than a minute to recite such a list, Joe accepts the bet. Joe, thinking always in AutoLISP, sees the expression as follows:

Command: **!all-fifty-states**
(ALABAMA ALASKA ARIZONA ARKANSAS
CALIFORNIA COLORADO CONNECTICUT
DELAWARE FLORIDA GEORGIA HAWAII
IDAHO ILLINOIS INDIANA IOWA KANSAS
KENTUCKY LOUISIANA MAINE MARYLAND

```
MASSACHUSETTS MICHIGAN MINNESOTA
MISSISSIPPI MISSOURI MONTANA NEBRASKA
NEVADA NEW-HAMPSHIRE NEW-JERSEY
NEW-MEXICO NEW-YORK NORTH-CAROLINA
NORTH-DAKOTA OHIO OKLAHOMA OREGON
PENNSYLVANIA RHODE-ISLAND SOUTH-CAROLINA
SOUTH-DAKOTA TENNESSEE TEXAS UTAH
VERMONT VIRGINIA WASHINGTON
WEST-VIRGINIA WISCONSIN WYOMING)
```

In this bet, however, the symbol "all-fifty-states" is a quoted symbol, not a list. The statement of the bet can be expressed in LISP (or AutoLISP) as

```
Command: !'all-fifty-states
all-fifty-states
```

Kay says "all fifty states" and wins the bet.

Note that the states that have names made up of two words, such as New York and South Carolina, must use some character other than a space character to separate the words. Thus NEW YORK becomes NEW-YORK and SOUTH CAROLINA becomes SOUTH-CAROLINA. The hyphen character (-) is often used for this purpose. Since elements in lists are space separated, each word separated by spaces is an element in the list. NEW YORK, for example, would be separated into the elements NEW and YORK, which is clearly not what was intended.

Lists as Expressions

Lists are also known as expressions. A comparison is often made between LISP lists and grammar. The basic symbol (sometimes called an atom or word) is like a word, and, in fact, it usually is a word that has been assigned a specific meaning or value which may even be another list. A list or expression can be compared to a sentence in which the first word is always a verb, and the following words are subjects and objects. Sometimes LISP is referred to as Natural Language Programming (another favorite buzzword) because many times the programs can be read as if you were reading English prose. Consider this simple sentence:

John, throw the ball to Tony.

In this sentence, the subject is John, the verb is throw, the object is ball, and Tony is the object of the preposition. Let's assume that there is an AutoLISP function called "throw" that will pass (throw) an object (ball) from one object or location (John) to another object or location (Tony). The actual function call to the function "throw" might look something like this:

(throw ball John Tony)

The actual structure of the list that calls the function THROW would look like this (using pseudocode):

([function name] [object to pass] [from location]
[to location])

Admittedly, the phrase "throw ball John Tony" would not pass muster with your English teacher, but all of the essential information is there. All you have to do is to add the implied parts of speech and the sentence will read like this:

Throw the ball John, to Tony.

Note that this expression could have been written in several different ways:

Throw the ball to Tony, John.
(throw ball tony john)

Throw Tony the ball, John.
(throw tony ball john)

There are only two parts to LISP grammar: active verbs and objects (or nouns) that act or are acted on by the verb. Once you grasp this concept, you will find it easy to "read" AutoLISP expressions. Practice translating a few AutoLISP expressions into English, as follows:

(+ 3 2)
"Add to 3,2."

(− 3 2)
"Subtract from 3,2."

(− 16 4 2 3)
"Subtract from 16,4 and then subtract 2 from that result and then subtract 3 from that result."

(member 'cat pets)
"Is the symbol cat a member of the list pets?"

Note that in some dialects of LISP, the add function is named "add" rather than +. Also, many times the syntax of LISP is not directly translatable into English syntax (as in the third of the preceding examples); this just proves that computers are not always "smart."

Bindings

When you assign a value to a symbol, you are *binding* that value to the symbol. A binding is the pairing of a symbol with a value. When you assign a value to a symbol, that symbol is said to be bound to that value. The concept of bindings in LISP is subtly different from assigning a value to a variable name found in other computer languages. In BASIC, you would say "LET X%=27;" to assign the value of 27 to the variable name X%. The variable name X% then becomes 27 until the value is changed to something else. Even then, the variable X% will only accept another integer value. When you bind a symbol to a value in LISP, you are only referencing that value by the symbol name. In BASIC, the variable is literally a container for a value of a certain type. In LISP, the symbol only "stands for" the value. The value, not the symbol, determines the type of information that is represented.

Here is an analogy to illustrate the concept of binding. Joan is a person whose name is a symbol by which she is recognized. But the name "Joan" is not all there is to her. If she were to change her name to Martha, she herself would not change; only the symbol that identifies her would change.

Working with Symbols

A symbol is the basic object in AutoLISP. As stated earlier, it is sometimes referred to as a "word" or an "atom." The symbol in AutoLISP has two parts: the "symbol name" and the "symbol binding." Unlike Common LISP, an AutoLISP symbol is not capable of having a separate value binding and a function binding. A symbol can either be bound to a value or bound to a function, but not both at the same time.

Using the English grammar analogy, a symbol can either be a verb (a function name) or a noun. Just as the word is the basic building block of the sentence, the symbol is the basic building block of lists. A symbol can be bound to the values of any of the available data types including other symbols.

The AutoLISP evaluator always returns the value that is currently bound to the symbol. For example, you may enter the following on the command line:

```
Command: (setq a 68)
68
```

The return value, in this case 68, is printed on the next line. In most LISP environments, all you need to do is type in the symbol name to see what the binding value is for that symbol. If you did that in AutoLISP, AutoCAD would think that you were entering an AutoCAD command and you would get an error message. With AutoCAD, you must always precede the symbol name with an exclamation point (!) as mentioned earlier in this chapter.

A symbol name can be made up of any combination of printable characters with the exception of these characters:

```
( ) . ' " ;
```

In AutoLISP, you should avoid using a symbol name with more than six characters. You can use as many characters as you like, but symbol names that are longer than six characters use more memory. It has also been discovered that the shorter the symbol name (one or two characters), the faster the code seems to execute. It is very difficult to read and understand the code that you have written with one or two character symbol names, so you should usually write code with long symbol names that have some meaning for you, such as GETPART or FIND-BOLT. When the code has been debugged, you then use a search and replace feature in a text editor to change the symbol names to one or two characters. If you have done any programming in interpreted BASIC, this procedure should already be familiar to you.

Experimenting With Symbol Bindings

A symbol can be globally bound, meaning that it always retains its original binding unless it is declared or redeclared as a local symbol in the parameter list of a user-defined function. Here is an example of how a symbol can temporarily change its binding when it is redeclared within a function:

```
Command: (defun test (sample) sample)
TEST
```

This will define a function named "test" that takes the parameter (or argument) SAMPLE and returns that argument to the next line. You can run this function by typing

Command: **(test "this is a sample")**
"this is a sample"

AutoLISP has bound the symbol SAMPLE to the value of the string "this is a sample", and then returned the value bound to the symbol SAMPLE on the next line. You can check the binding of the symbol SAMPLE by typing

Command: **!sample**
nil

The symbol SAMPLE is not bound to any value because the symbol was only declared to be locally bound inside of the function "test." But maybe the function did not work properly and the symbol was never bound. There are two ways to check on whether or not the symbol was bound inside of the function. You could add the function "boundp" which would return true if the symbol were bound. Or you could add the function "type" which would return the type of data bound to the symbol. The second option can be illustrated by retyping the function on the command line:

Command: **(defun test (sample) (type sample)**)
TEST

Now run this function by typing the following:

Command: **(test "this is a sample"**)
STR

The returned symbol STR means that the symbol SAMPLE was bound to a string data type. The symbol STR always means this in AutoCAD. Now check the global binding of the symbol SAMPLE by calling the function "type" and passing the symbol SAMPLE to it:

Command: **(type sample)**
nil

Nil means that the symbol SAMPLE is not bound to anything. You can bind the symbol SAMPLE globally with "setq":

Command: **(setq sample 97)**
97

After binding the value 97 to the symbol SAMPLE, you can see the type of symbol it is by entering the following:

Command: **(type sample)**
INT

INT means that SAMPLE is bound to a value that is an integer. The symbol INT always means this in AutoCAD.

You can run "test" again to see what the binding for SAMPLE is while the function is running:

Command: **(test "a string")**
STR

What this tells us is that SAMPLE was bound to an integer before the function "test" was run, and bound to a string while the function was running. What do you think SAMPLE is bound to now? To find out, type

Command: **!sample**
97

The symbol SAMPLE is still bound to the value that was assigned to it globally with the SETQ function. Why is this so important? To answer that question you must first take a look at the "atomlist." You can see the "atomlist" by going into text mode (press the F1 key) and viewing the "atomlist" list command as follows:

Command: **!atomlist**

You will see a long list of words and symbols on the screen. Examine this list and you will see that it is a list of all of the AutoLISP function names. The list's first two words are SAMPLE and "test," a symbol and a function that were declared in the preceding examples. The "atomlist" contains the name of every symbol and function that has been declared during any given AutoLISP session. Every time a symbol is declared, it is added to the "atomlist." Every time AutoLISP sees a symbol name in any list that it is evaluating, it searches through the "atomlist," from top to bottom, to retrieve the value that is bound to that symbol. If you use a lot of different symbol names (which is very easy to do), and the evaluator is looking for a symbol name that is at the end of the list, AutoLISP will slow down. The longer the "atomlist," the more time is spent searching through the list. For this reason, you should use as few symbol names as possible in writing your code.

Data Types in AutoLISP

There are ten data types in AutoLISP. You can use integers (INT), floating point numbers (REAL), strings (STR), symbols (SYM), lists (LIST), files (FILE), subroutines (SUBR), selection sets (PICKSET), paging tables (PAGETB), and entity names (ENAME). LISP is designed to accommodate an unlimited range of data types. AutoLISP is only one example of a LISP system. The data types supported by a specific LISP system must be "hard wired" into the language by the programmers who create it. You cannot usually create your own data types.

AutoCAD has a data type for each of the major things it does. For example, you can express numbers in two forms: integer and floating point. Integers have no fractional parts and must be whole numbers. Floating point numbers may have fractional parts and may use decimal points. Strings are collections of characters that are enclosed in double quotes ("). Symbols and lists have already been discussed. It is interesting to see that files, with all of their contents, are also a data type. Think about the implications of the fact that a file—any file—can be used as an element in a list. This means that files can be used directly as sources for data in AutoLISP programs. In addition to the simpler data types, AutoCAD has types for its own internal functions and commands. Finally, entity names like LINE and CIRCLE can be expressed in their own type.

Now that you have used list and symbol data types, it is worthwhile to discuss the concept of data typing in general. In most other programming languages, you must predeclare the type of data that a given variable is to hold before you can assign actual data to that variable. That variable will only accept the type of data that has been declared for that variable. In AutoLISP, as mentioned earlier, you can assign any of the data types to a symbol without declaring what type of data that symbol should contain. You can even change the data type of a symbol by simply reassigning (or binding) a different type of data to the symbol. For example, you could set the value of the symbol "x" to an integer by simply assigning an integer to it:

```
Command: (setq x 7)
7
```

At a later time you could reassign the value of the symbol "x" to a string:

```
Command: (setq x "seven string")
"seven string"
```

You could even assign the value to a list:

```
Command: (setq x '(dogs cats))
(DOGS CATS)
```

It is crucial that you understand the basic concept involved in the use of symbols, which is why this information is repeated here in many ways. It is all too easy to think in terms of languages other than LISP and identify the symbol "x" (used in the preceding examples) as having a type of its own. *In LISP, the type of data (be it string, integer, or whatever) is a property of the data, not of the symbol used to refer to the data.*

The ability to reuse symbols with different data types can be very powerful because it allows the programmer a great deal of flexibility in writing code. The down side of this flexibility is that if you are not careful to keep track of the type of data that you are assigning to symbols, you could end up passing the wrong type of data to a function.

The Function Data Type

A function is a set of instructions in LISP that tell the computer to do something specific. It is the basic building block of a LISP program. There are two types of functions in AutoLISP, one type being the built-in functions that are a part of AutoLISP and functions you define yourself.

Built-in functions include math functions:

+, −, *, /

There are also list manipulating functions:

cons, car, cdr, list

There are unique AutoCAD handling functions such as

getpoint, entget, tblsearch, grread

Note that these built-in functions are called AutoLISP *primitives.* You can define your own functions, in addition to the built-in functions, if you use "defun."

There are no operators in AutoLISP, only functions. Most other programming languages have operators, procedures, functions, and commands. Each one of these structures must be handled differently when you write a program. AutoLISP only has functions, which are always handled in an identical way. This is what makes AutoLISP both easy to use and sometimes confusing.

A function in AutoLISP has four qualities:

- Most functions require *arguments* or *parameters.* An argument or parameter is an independent variable that determines the output of the function. The function +, for example, requires at least two variables that are summed to produce the result. The result of + depends upon the value of the arguments. For example, the function call (+ 4 8) will return a different value than (+ 9 8).

- A function always returns a value. Many functions return a value that is useful. The + function, for example, returns the sum of the arguments. Some functions are used for the "side effect" that they produce and the return value is usually ignored. In such cases, the return value is usually nil. The "(terpri)" function is an example of a function that takes no arguments, has a side effect, and returns nil. "Terpri" (TERminal PRInt) tells AutoCAD to print a blank text line on the screen (or terminal).

- Any symbols declared within a parameter list of a function are only bound to values while the function is in use. This is known as a local binding. If a symbol is bound to a value outside of a function (globally), and that same symbol is declared within a parameter list in a function, then that symbol is bound to a new value while the function is running. It reverts to the old value binding when the function is finished.

- A function always returns the value of the last symbol or list evaluated within that function. Examine the example function "test:"

```
(defun test (sample)
(listp sample)
(type sample)
)
```

The value returned by this expression is INT. You see that the return value of "test" was the result of evaluating the last function "type" and the return value of "listp" is ignored.

Understanding Side Effects

To understand the concept of *side effect*, consider the analogy of an automobile engine as a function. To operate, an engine requires certain things (parameters) supplied to it, such as gasoline and air. The direct result of supplying gasoline and air to an engine is that the engine produces heat and exhaust. The side effect of the engine is that it can turn the wheels of your car. You may think that the result of supplying gasoline and air to an engine is to turn the wheels of your car and heat and exhaust are side effects. However, the direct effect of burning gas and air is to produce heat energy, and this energy has to be translated into rotational motion.

How AutoLISP Evaluates Functions

When the AutoLISP evaluator encounters a list, the first thing it does is to look at the first symbol in the list. If it finds that the first symbol in the list is the name of a valid function, it then passes the rest of that list to the function to execute the code found in that function. When the function is complete, it returns the result of the function. Consider the following example by typing on the AutoCAD command line:

```
Command: (+ 4 8)
12
```

Here is what happens. The AutoLISP evaluator takes the list, looks at the first symbol in the list (the symbol "+"), and finds a function named "+." The code for the function "+" tells the evaluator to take the second symbol in the list (4), add any other symbols (8) to it, and then return the result (12). If you want to use the result (return value) of this function, you have to either attach that value to another symbol with an expression, or pass the value to a higher level function in a nested expression. For example, the following expression would assign the value of 12 to the symbol "a:"

```
Command: (setq a (+ 4 8))
12
```

The following expression, however, would use the result of "(+ 4 8)" to fuel another level of evaluation:

```
Command: (setq a (* (+ 4 8) 2))
24
```

LISP, like algebra, always evaluates the expressions from inner to outer. The preceding example might be expressed as "a = (4 + 8) * 2" in C language, for example. The only exception would be that the symbol "a" in LISP could later be assigned to a string, whereas the variable "a" in C language would always be an "int" (or whatever) and could not be easily used to store information about a string.

Creating Arithmetic Functions

AutoLISP contains all of the basic arithmetic functions. If you remember that these are functions and not operators, you will find it much easier to understand how these arithmetic functions work. Some references say that LISP uses prefix notation. This means that the operator is placed before the operand as in "(+ 4 8)." Normally, if you wanted to add 4 and 8, you would say "4 plus 8." If you look at this example and see that "+" is a function that sums the arguments presented to it and returns a result, you could say "add 4 to 8." Here are a few examples of arithmetic using AutoLISP:

```
Command: (- 17 2)
15
"Subtract from 17, 2."
```

Command: **(* 12 6)**
72
"Multiply 12 by 6."

Command: **(/ 18 3)**
6
"Divide 18 by 3."

Command: **(/ (* 3 (+ 6 9)) 5)**
9
"Starting with the innermost expression, add to 6, 9, take that result (15) and multiply it by 3 and take that result (45) and divide it by 5 and return the result (9)."

All of these arithmetic functions can take one or more arguments. If the "−" function is passed one argument, it will change the sign of the number like this:

Command: **(− 5)**
−5

Command: **(− −17)**
17

More than two arguments will work for all of the basic arithmetic functions:

Command: **(− 6 2 1 2 1)**
0
"Subtract from 6, 2 then 1 then 2 then 1."

Command: **(+ 17 14 3 15 4 2)**
55

Command: **(/ 190 8 4 3)**
1
"Divide 190 by 8, divide that result by 4 and divide that result by 3."

"But the answer is not 1," you say, as you whip out your calculator, "it is really 1.979167." This is integer arithmetic, and it works like this: Divide 190 by 8 and the answer is 23.75, but since we are dealing with integers, you drop the fractional part of the number (0.75), and the answer is 23, which you divide by 4. The answer to that is 5.75, and drop the fraction (0.75) to 5, which is divided by 3 for a final result of 1.6666667. Since you again must drop the fractional part, the final answer is 1. If you want the result to be a real number, one of the arguments must be a real number like this:

```
Command: (/ 190 8 4 3.0)
1.979167
```

Any other integers in the argument list will be converted to floating point numbers before the calculation is carried out within the function. It is particularly important that you do not use integer numbers when the result may be a real number or an integer greater than 32,767, since this is the largest integer value you can store.

All of the AutoLISP's math functions will be covered in great detail in the AutoLISP reference section at the end of this tutorial section.

Writing an AutoLISP Function

You are now almost ready to create some simple functions inside the AutoLISP environment. Once you have practiced with a few functions, you will see how to edit, save, and run larger AutoLISP functions.

There is a built-in AutoLISP function for incrementing a number passed to it by 1. It is called "1+" and it works like this:

```
Command: (1+ 7)
8
```

Let's say that you need a function that will increment a number by 2. Type in the following on the AutoCAD command line:

```
Command: (defun 2+ (input) (+ input 2))
2+
```

Remember, AutoLISP always returns the symbol name of the last function evaluated. You have used the built-in "defun" function and the "input" symbol to create a new function called "2+." You could say the function definition in these words: "Define a function called '2+', taking input from the keyboard, and adding the input and the number 2 together." Now you can call this function by typing

```
Command: (2+ 7)
9
```

Likewise, you can use your new function for the following:

```
Command: (2+ 98)
100
```

Now you can try writing your own function. Write a function that will multiply a number by ten. The function should work like this:

```
Command: (10× 10)
100
```

Use the function called "2+" as a template. Does it work? Congratulations, you have just written your first AutoLISP function. Just in case you are lost, here is the proper expression of the function definition for the "10×" function:

```
Command: (defun 10× (input) (* input 10))
```

If you leave the AutoCAD editor and return, you will notice that the functions that you just defined will disappear. AutoLISP will reset everything, so you either have to type in your functions again or load them from a file.

Writing an AutoLISP File

AutoLISP is able to load and evaluate LISP files so that the functions on those files can be executed at any time by the user. These files can be produced on almost any text editor or word processor that has a non-document or programmer's mode. A companion disk available for purchase with this book contains a specialized text editor you can use that has been specially designed to work with AutoCAD and AutoLISP.

It is strongly suggested that you format your AutoLISP code in a consistent way so that your code will be easy to read and understand. You might call this "pretty-printing."

The code below is perfectly acceptable to AutoLISP, but it is next to impossible for a person to read, much less understand.

```
(defun entlst ( / e) (setq e (entnext)) (while
e (print (entget e)) (terpri) (setq e (entnext e))))
```

Function 12-1 shows how much more clearly the same code is once it has been formatted. This formatting convention does not meet any particular standards. It is a merely a format that has been perfected over the past three years by one user of AutoLISP.

```
(defun entlst ( / e)
    (setq e (entnext))          ;sets e to the first entity
    (while e                    ;as long as there are entities
        (print (entget e))      ;print the entity list
        (terpri)                ;new line
        (setq e (entnext e))    ;set e to next entity
    )
)
```

Function 12-1. An example of formatted AutoLISP code

Here are a few descriptive rules for a simple method of "pretty-printing:"

- All arguments to the same function use the same amount of indentation. See lines 2, 3, and 5 of Function 12-1.

- The second line in a nest is indented one tab more than the first line. See lines 1 and 2 and lines 3 and 4 of Function 12-1.

- The closing parenthesis of a nested list is aligned vertically with the open parenthesis on its own line. See lines 1 and 8 and lines 3 and 7 of Function 12-1.

- Anything following a semicolon (;) to the end of the line is treated as a comment and is not evaluated. Comment profusely whenever possible, it will not slow down your program, and it may save a lot of time in the future when you need to revise old code.

These are only guidelines and not rules. AutoLISP will evaluate your code, if it is correct, no matter how it is formatted. The purpose in pretty-printing is to assist you in writing clear, understandable, and maintainable code.

To begin with, run your favorite text editor, and type in your desired code. When you have finished writing your program, save the file with any file name that you want with an ".lsp" extension (upper- or lowercase). Make sure that you have saved your file in an unformatted mode. If you use the text editor supplied with this book's companion software, you can be assured that your text will not contain characters that will interfere with the operation of AutoCAD.

For the sake of illustration, you may have copied the preceding AutoLISP function called "entlst," and you may have saved your file under the name of "entlst.lsp". If you have done this, load a drawing into the AutoCAD drawing editor, and type on the command line

Command: **(load "entlst")**
ENTLIST

Make sure that you type both parentheses and both quotes. Note that AutoCAD responds with the return value of the expression, "entlist," on the next line. This lets you know that AutoLISP has successfully evaluated your function. (Remember, AutoLISP returns the name of the last function evaluated.) Finally, press F1 to flip to the text screen and then type

Command: **(entlst)**

A list of all of the AutoCAD entities will scroll up your screen. Do not pay too much attention to this list right now. This is simply practice to familiarize you with the procedure for writing, saving, loading, and executing an AutoLISP program.

When you start writing your own programs, you will find that nine times out of ten, your program will not work right the first time (even the tenth time is not uncommon). If this happens, you must quit AutoCAD, load a text editor with your program, make any necessary corrections, save your file, reload AutoCAD, load your AutoLISP file, and try it all over again. You probably think this is tedious—there must be an easier way. There is, it is called the AutoCAD shell.

While you are in the AutoCAD drawing editor, enter the following at the command prompt:

Command: **SHELL**

The screen will clear, and you will see this message:

DOS command:

This means that AutoCAD has suspended operation, freed up 127,000 bytes of memory, and put you in the DOS environment. Now type in the name of a small text editor (something less than 100K in size). You should be able to work on a text file now. You are able to quickly get into your editor. When you exit your editor, within just a few seconds, you will find yourself back in AutoCAD exactly where you left off. But there is an even easier way to do this that involves modifying the "acad.pgp" file that came with AutoCAD.

You may remember that the "acad.pgp" file was used in Chapter 9, "Attribute Management," to add a command to AutoCAD. You can use the same technique to add the name of your text editor to AutoCAD. The "acad.pgp" file is supplied by AutoDesk and already contains the names of a few standard commands. You can find it in your AutoCAD subdirectory. Load the "acad.pgp" file into your text editor. One version of the "acad.pgp" file looks like this (yours may be slightly different):

```
CATALOG,DIR /W,27000,*Files: ,0
DEL,DEL,27000,File to delete: ,0
DIR,DIR,27000,File specification: ,0
ED,EDLIN,42000,File to edit: ,0
SH,,27000,*DOS command: ,0
SHELL,,127000,*DOS command: ,0
TYPE,TYPE,27000,File to list: ,0
EDIT,ET,127000,File to edit: ,0
```

Notice the sixth line. This is the line that controls the SHELL command used in an earlier example. Look at the eighth line. This is where a text editor called ET (which stands for Edit Text) has been implemented to run inside AutoCAD whenever the command "edit" is typed. ET is the name of the text editor that comes with the companion software for this book.

The first word, "edit," is the name that has been chosen for the AutoCAD command to load the text editor while AutoCAD is running. The second word, "ET," is the name of the text editor that you will use. The third item is the amount of memory that is reserved for running the text editor. This number must equal the size of the program (in this case about 50K), and the size of the largest file you might wish to edit (about 40K). Finally, you must reserve enough memory to run a copy of DOS inside AutoCAD (the file is "command.com", about 26K) plus a little more for good measure. The fourth word is the prompt that will appear after you type "edit" at the command prompt. You can respond with a file name (which is the same as typing "ET ENTLST.LSP" on the DOS command line and it is optional). The last item is a zero.

You make the appropriate modifications to your "acad.pgp" file and save it. Then you copy your chosen text editor to your AutoCAD subdirectory on your hard disk.

Whenever you want to create a text file from inside the AutoCAD drawing editor, simply type the EDIT command on the command line and type the name of a file in answer to the prompt, and you will enter your text editor. When you exit your text editor, you will find yourself back in AutoCAD exactly where you left.

An AutoLISP Programming Toolkit

To fully understand how to program in AutoLISP, it will help if you can see some complete programs that actually work. By using parts of these programs, you can quickly learn how to develop your own software.

As you use this section, you should refer to Chapter 15, "AutoLISP Function Reference," to find out about the functions that appear here. In that chapter, you will see a general explanation of the functions. If you combine that general explanation with the results of your own experimentation, you will find it easier and easier to understand the code. It helps a great deal to see AutoLISP code in a form that solves problems you are likely to encounter in your real work. Given a familiar context, code becomes more familiar.

This section contains many complete AutoLISP programs that add functions and commands to your AutoCAD system. For example, you will be able to draw and edit walls. You will see how to use AutoLISP to edit entire drawings, confining your edits to certain entities and excluding others. The functions fall into the following general categories:

- Utility functions and commands
- Association lists
- Converting circles and arcs
- Walls and intersections
- Drawing simplification
- Drawing generation

Many of the functions in this section have been used in actual practice. They are designed to solve real problems that crop up during the professional use of AutoCAD. (Because the large quantity of code may be difficult to copy by hand, companion software is available by mail order; see the Introduction.)

Utility Functions and Commands

The following functions are designed to serve simple purposes. With them, you can change text entities in an entire drawing, copy one file to another, draw a simple box, and delete all entities on a layer. You can also list all entities to a file, find a string in a file with a key, explode "mirrored" and "mincluded" blocks (which cannot normally be exploded), and delete and reinsert blocks as entities.

This collection of functions also enables you to delete an atom or sublist, find the position of an atom in a list, find the intersection of two lines, and change the starting and ending points of lines. In addition, you will be able to expand the number of user variables, close every polyline in a drawing, reset drawing limits, put offsets on a different layer, copy or move entities from layer to layer, and decompose (fracture) circles and arcs. The software also includes functions that round a number, and count all instances of named blocks.

Copying One File to Another

A common requirement of software is copying files. AutoLISP enables you to gain access to files. You can open, close, read, and

```
;This function illustrates how to copy one file to another.

(defun copy (in out)
       (setq ifp (open in "r"))
       (setq ofp (open out "w"))
       (while (setq s (read-line ifp))
              (write-line s ofp)
       )
       (close ifp)
       (close ofp)
)
```

Function 12-2. Copying one file to another

write them. Function 12-2 is a very simple program that opens one file in read mode, opens another in write mode, reads the first line by line, writes each line, and closes both files. You can see file access in operation in this example. With a little imagination, you can use the same commands to process data in files instead of just copying it.

Drawing a Box

Function 12-3 shows how to use AutoLISP to draw simple lines that form a two-unit square box. This function can be modified to

```
;This function draws a square box two units by two units in
;size.

(defun dbox (ip)
    (command "line" ip (list (+ 2 (car ip)) (cadr ip))
              (list (+ 2 (car ip)) (+ 2 (cadr ip)))
              (list (car ip) (+ 2 (cadr ip)))
              "c")
)
```

Function 12-3. Drawing a two unit square box

draw special shapes as required. Boxes are used for many purposes, including enclosing room numbers in building floor plans, enclosing part numbers in electronics drawings, and other applications.

Deleting All Entities on a Layer

You will often want to erase entities that exist on a layer rather than in the drawing as a whole. Function 12-4 creates a command that will erase all entities in a layer that you specify. In addition, you can see how the "entget" and "entdel" functions can be used to get and delete entities.

Listing Entities to a File

You may find it helpful to have a list of all of the entities in a drawing for reporting purposes. You may also want to use a file that contains a list of a drawing's entities as input to software that processes the list. You can generate a list of all entities in a drawing and put the entity names into a file by using Function 12-5. The command "blklst" lists all blocks in the file. To have all entities listed, use the command "entlist."

```
;Delete all entities on specified layer.
;This is a command.

(defun c:dellayer ()
   (setq L (strcase (getstring "\nEnter layer to delete: ")))
   (setq e (entnext))
   (while e
           (if (= L (cdr (assoc 8 (entget e))))
              (entdel e)
           )
           (setq e (entnext e))
        )
)
```

Function 12-4. Deleting all entities on a layer

```
;This command will list to a file all blocks in
;a drawing using a block table.  All names of blocks will be
;written to a file.
;
(defun c:blklst ()
 setq outfile (getstring
              "\nEnter file name for Block list: "))
       (setq outfile (strcat outfile ".txt"))
       (setq a (open outfile "w"))
       (setq blk (tblnext "BLOCK" t))
       (while blk
               (print blk a)
               (setq e (cdr (assoc -2 blk)))
               (while e
                   (print (entget e) a)
                   (terpri)
                   (setq e (entnext e))
               )
               (setq blk (tblnext "BLOCK"))
       )
       (close a)
)
;This command writes the association list format entity data
;to a file.
(defun c:entlst ()
 setq outfile (getstring
              "\nEnter file name for Entity list: "))
       (setq outfile (strcat outfile ".txt"))
       (setq a (open outfile "w"))
       (setq e (entnext))
       (while e
               (print (entget e) a)
               (print (entget e))
               (terpri)
               (setq e (entnext e))
       )
       (close a)
)
```

Function 12-5. Listing entities to a file

In the preceding functions, you see the use of a "while" loop to process a loop. As each block or entity name is encountered, it is printed to a file.

Finding a String in a File

You may want to use a file that contains coded strings to provide input to AutoCAD. This might be used in a custom help menu

```
; Given a filename and a string as x, finds the string in
; the file and prints it to the screen.  This version finds
; the first four characters and gives you the rest of the
; string.
;
(defun findline (fname x)
    (setq b (open fname "r"))
    (setq c (read-line b))
    (while (/= (substr c 1 4) x)
         (setq c (read-line b))
    )
    (print c)
    (close b)
)
```

Function 12-6. Finding a string in a file

system. In such a system, a file would contain help messages, each of which was preceded by a four-character code. Function 12-6 can be used to read such a file, compare the first four characters of each line in the file with a string of four characters, and print the string match found. The function, named "findline," is easy to understand. It uses a "while" loop, just as in the file copying function described earlier.

Exploding Unexplodable Blocks

Some blocks in AutoCAD drawings cannot be exploded with the EXPLODE command. If a block has been mirrored with the MIRROR command or inserted multiple times with the MINSERT command, you must modify it before you can explode it. Function 12-7 creates a command called "flatten" that reads your entire drawing and explodes everything except blocks that have been inserted with unequal X and Y scales.

Deleting and Reinserting a Block

Function 12-8 is used in Function 12-7. It is the part of the "flatten" command that gets information about a mirrored block, deletes it, and reinserts the block as its component entities. It then manipulates the entities to create the appearance

```
;This command will explode all blocks in
;a drawing including mirrored blocks
;and blocks that have been MINSERTED.
;This command will ignore blocks that
;have been inserted with an unequal X Y scale.
;No attributes are included.
;
;c=counter
;e=entity name
;ss=selection set to hold all insert entities

(defun c:flatten ( / e ss c)
    (setvar "cmdecho" 0)
    (setvar "blipmode" 0)
    (setq ss (ssget "X" '((0 . "INSERT"))))
    (while ss
        (setq c 0)
        (while (<= c (- (sslength ss) 1))
                (setq e (ssname ss c))
                (if (= (abs (cdr (assoc 41 (entget e))))
                       (abs (cdr (assoc 42 (entget e))))
                       (abs (cdr (assoc 43 (entget e))))
                    )
                   (cond
                       ((or
                            (> (cdr (assoc 70 (entget e))) 0)
                            (> (cdr (assoc 71 (entget e))) 0)
                        )
                                (fixmin e)
                       )
                       ((or
                            (< (cdr (assoc 41 (entget e))) 0)
                            (< (cdr (assoc 42 (entget e))) 0)
                            (< (cdr (assoc 43 (entget e))) 0)
                         )
                         (fixmir e)
                        )
                       (t (command "explode" e))
                   )
                )
                (setq c (1+ c))
        )
     (setq ss nil)
     (setq ss (ssget "X" '((0 . "INSERT"))))
     )
)
```

Function 12-7. Exploding mirrored and mincluded blocks

```
;This function gets the information about
;a mirrored block deletes the block
;and then reinserts it as entities.
;It then builds a selection set of those
;entities and manipulates them so that
;they will appear as the original
;mirrored block in the drawing.
;
;
;Variable names
;e=current entity name
;f=last entity in database before block entities are added
;g=insertion point of target block
;h=block name
;i=x scale of target block
;j=y scale of target block
;k=z scale of target block
;L=rotation angle of target block in radians
;ss=selection set made up of block entities
;
(defun fixmir (e / f g h i j k L ss)
    (setq f (entlast)
        g (cdr (assoc 10 (entget e)))
        h (cdr (assoc 2  (entget e)))
        i (cdr (assoc 41 (entget e)))
        j (cdr (assoc 42 (entget e)))
        k (cdr (assoc 43 (entget e)))
        L (cdr (assoc 50 (entget e))))
    (entdel e)
    (setq ss (ssadd))
    (command "insert" (strcat "*" h) g (abs i) 0)
    (setq f (entnext f))
    (while f
        (setq ss (ssadd f ss)
            f (entnext f))
    )
    (if (< i 0)
        (command "mirror" ss "" g (list (car g)
            (+ 10 (cadr g))) "Y")
    )
    (if (< j 0)
        (command "mirror" ss "" g (list (+ 10 (car g))
            (cadr g)) "Y")
    )
    (if (/= L 0) (command "rotate" ss ""
                 g (* (/ 180 pi) 1)))
    (setq ss nil)
)
```

Function 12-8. Deleting a block and reinserting as entities of the mirrored block. Note particularly the use of the "assoc" function. This function searches an *association list* for an item. An association list is a list of values that are associated with key names. For example, the following is an association list:

```
radius    10.234
height    5
length    10
```

If you wanted to know the radius for a particular element in a list, you could find it by the association between the word "radius" and the number 10.234. In AutoLISP, the association list shown would be expressed as follows:

```
'((radius 10.234) (height 5) (length 10))
```

Assuming the preceding list were named "lst," you would use the following expressions to return the radius, height, and length:

```
Command: (assoc 'radius lst)
(radius 10.234)
Command: (assoc 'height lst)
(height 5)
Command: (assoc 'length lst)
(length 10)
```

Deleting a MINSERTed Block

If the MINSERT command has been used to make multiple insertions of a block, the minserted blocks cannot be exploded with the EXPLODE command. Function 12-9 is called from

```
;This function gathers information about a
;block that has been placed by
;MINSERT, deletes that block and then
;inserts the correct number of blocks
;at the correct locations as individual blocks.
;
;
;Variable names
;e=current entity name
;g=insertion point of target block
;h=block name
;i=x scale of target block
;j=y scale of target block
;k=z scale of target block
;L=rotation angle of target block in radians
;m=column count for minsert
;n=row count for minsert
;o=column spacing for minsert
;p=row spacing for minsert
;
;
(defun fixmin (e / g h i j k L m n o p)
    (setq g (cdr (assoc 10 (entget e)))
          h (cdr (assoc 2  (entget e)))
          i (cdr (assoc 41 (entget e)))
          j (cdr (assoc 42 (entget e)))
          k (cdr (assoc 43 (entget e)))
          L (cdr (assoc 50 (entget e)))
          m (cdr (assoc 70 (entget e)))
          n (cdr (assoc 71 (entget e)))
          o (cdr (assoc 44 (entget e)))
          p (cdr (assoc 45 (entget e))))
    (if (equal n 0) (setq n 1))
    (if (equal m 0) (setq m 1))
    (entdel e)
;can't use array here to reinsert the
;blocks if the minserted block has
;also been mirrored
    (repeat n
        (repeat m
            (command "insert" h g i j (* (/ 180 pi) 1))
            (setq g (polar g L o))
        )
        (setq g (polar g L (- (* o m)))
            g (polar g (+ (/ pi 2) 1) p))
    )
)
```

Function 12-9. Deleting a minserted block

Function 12-7 to first gather information about the block and then delete that block, reinserting individual blocks at the appropriate locations.

Deleting Atoms or Sublists

You may wish to remove a single atom or sublist from a list. To do this, Function 12-10 uses a while loop on the search list, and copies each element into a temporary list (tl). If an atom or sublist matches the atom or sublist to be deleted, it is skipped over. Finally, the temporary list is reversed and returned as the result of the function using "(reverse tl)."

Finding the Position of an Atom in a List

Function 12-11, called "posit," finds the position of an atom in a list. Note that the position is an offset. As such, it is one less than the length of the list that starts at the atom's position, *after* the list has been reversed. For example, the following is a list of atoms:

(a1 a2 a3 a4 a5 a6)

```
;This function will delete an atom or
;sublist (LFI) from a list
;(LISTTOSEARCH).
;
(defun delete (lfi listtosearch / tl) ;general function
        (setq tl ())
        (while listtosearch
                (if (/= (car listtosearch) lfi)
                    (setq tl (cons (car listtosearch) tl)))
                    )
        (setq listtosearch (cdr listtosearch))
        )
        (reverse tl)
)
```

Function 12-10. Deleting an atom or sublist

```
;This function returns the position of an
;atom (VARNAME) in a list
;(LISTNAME) it is the opposite of
;the Autolisp NTH function.
;
(defun posit (varname listname) ;general function
        (1- (length (member varname (reverse listname))))
)
```

Function 12-11. Finding the position of an atom in a list

To find the position of atom 4, you reverse the list, making the list appear as follows:

(a6 a5 a4 a3 a2 a1)

Then you use the "member" function to refer to the list as though the member "a4" were the beginning of a new list. You use the "length" function to return the length of this new list, in this case 4. But this is not the position; this is the count of atoms in the new list. The position must be one less than the count. The positions of the atoms in the list are shown as follows:

```
(a1 a2 a3 a4 a5 a6)
 0  1  2  3  4  5
```

You can see that the *offset* of the atom "a4" is position 3, which is also the length of the reversed list starting at atom "a4" minus 1.

Finding the Coordinates of a Point on a Line

You can test if a point is on a line with Function 12-12. This function, named "pointinline," uses the "inters" function to find the intersection point from the current crosshairs location to the start of the line and the line "linename." If the lines are parallel, a result of nil is returned. The (null) function reverses nil to T. If

```
;This function will return T if the CHKPT is on the line
;LINENAME.
;
(defun pointinline (linename chkpt) ;general function
 (null (inters (cdr (assoc 10 (entget linename)))
               (cdr (assoc 11 (entget linename)))
               (cdr (assoc 10 (entget linename)
          )) chkpt nil))
)
```

Function 12-12. Testing if a point is on a line

they are not parallel (the point is not on the line), a point is returned from (inters) which (null) converts to nil.

Finding the Intersection of Two Lines

If you pass the names of two line entities to Function 12-13, "findinter," the intersection point (or nil) will be returned. The "inters" function is used to find the actual intersection.

Changing the Starting Point of a Line

The function "newst" will change the starting point of an old line entity "oldent" to a new starting point "new10." The number 10

```
;This function will find the intersection of
;two line entities (ENT1 and
;ENT2).  It is sometimes faster to use than inters because
;it requires less code.
;
;
(defun findinter (ent1 ent2) ;general function
        (inters (cdr (assoc 10 (entget ent1)))
            (cdr (assoc 11 (entget ent1)))
            (cdr (assoc 10 (entget ent2)))
            (cdr (assoc 11 (entget ent2)))
            nil)
)
```

Function 12-13. Finding intersection of two lines

```
;This function will change the starting
;point on an existing line (OLDENT)
;to a new starting point (NEW10).
;
(defun newst (oldent new10) ;general function
        (entmod (subst (append '(10) new10)
                       (assoc 10 (entget oldent))
                       (entget oldent)))
)
```

Function 12-14. Changing starting point of a line

refers to AutoCAD's DXF group code 10 for the line entity. AutoCAD uses a variety of group codes that identify entity properties. You can find out more about current group codes from AutoCAD's current file structure documentation in Appendix C of the AutoCAD Reference Manual. Function 12-14 shows how this is done. The "entmod" function is used to modify the line entity you specify.

Changing the Ending Point of a Line

You can change the ending point of a line with Function 12-15, "newnd." Like Function 12-14, this uses "entmod" to modify the

```
;This function will change the ending
;point on an existing line (OLDENT)
;to a new ending point (NEW11).
;
(defun newnd (oldent new11) ;general function
        (entmod (subst (append '(11) new11)
                       (assoc 11 (entget oldent))
                       (entget oldent)))
)
```

Function 12-15. Changing ending point of a line

entity, but uses AutoCAD's DXF group code 11 (line endpoint) rather than group code 10 (line startpoint).

Setting Each Digit of a Variable Separately

Occasionally, you will want to use flags in your code. Flags can be set or unset to save the status of a part of your code for later reference. For example, you could set a flag to indicate that a certain task has been performed so that future operations will not perform that task unnecessarily. Flags are great, but they use up your variables. With Function 12-16, you can use single digits in variables, rather than entire variables, as flags.

For example, you could use the number 1 as a flag. If a user variable were set to 1, the flag would be *on* and if the variable were set to 0, the flag would be *off*. By using the "codevar" function, you could set a number at a position in the variable, not only the entire variable. The number 1101, for example, would mean that position 3 was *off*. The number 1111 would mean that position 3 was *on*. You should never set the first digit of the variable to 2, because this will enable the number to grow too large for certain values.

All you need to do to use "codevar" is to pass the user integer variable name "intvar," the variable position "varpos," and the subvariable number "subvar." Do not use the number 0 to indicate the *off* condition. You can easily use any other number. For example, the number 1 could be used for the *off* and the number 2 could be used for the *on*.

This function also uses AutoCAD system variables such as USERI. You can find out about AutoCAD's current user variable list by consuting Appendix C of AutoCAD's Reference Manual. Since these variables may change in meaning, no attempt is made to discuss them in detail here.

Reading Variables Set by Position

The inverse of Function 12-16 is shown in Function 12-17. If you use "codevar" to set a flag, you can use "lkupvar" to get the flag by "looking it up."

```
;this function will take any USERI variable
;(intvar) and set each individual
;digit of that variable to a separate variable.
;This increases the number of
;user variables to 30: 5 real variables,
;5 variables from 1 to 2 and 20
;variables from 1 to 9.  These variables are
;very useful for setting flags.
;NOTE: You need to preset user variables in a
;prototype drawing for this function to work.
;A prototype is provided on the companion disk.
(defun codevar (intvar varpos subvar)
        (if (> varpos 1)
                (setq fststr (substr (itoa (getvar intvar))
                1 (1- varpos)))
        )
        (if (< varpos 5)
                (setq lststr (substr (itoa (getvar intvar))
                (1+ varpos)))
        )
        (if (> varpos 1)
                (if (< varpos 5)
                   (setvar intvar
                     (atoi (strcat fststr
                                  (itoa subvar) lststr)))
                   (setvar intvar (atoi (strcat fststr
                   (itoa subvar))))
                )
                (setvar intvar
                  (atoi
                    (strcat
                      (itoa subvar) lststr)))
       )
)
```

Function 12-16. Setting each digit of a variable separately

```
;this function reads the variables
;that have been set in CODEVAR.
(defun lkupvar (intvar varpos)
        (atoi (substr (itoa (getvar intvar)) varpos 1))
)
```

Function 12-17. Reading variables set one digit at a time

Removing Every Entity Not a Block or Polyline

Function 12-18 removes every entity from your drawing that is *not* a block or a polyline. You can use this function to clean up a drawing by putting everything you want to keep into blocks. Everything left over will be erased. In addition, with the structure of this function, you can make other kinds of global modifications, limited only by your imagination.

This function is also called the "cleanup" command. At the end of the execution of "cleanup," you will see that a number of entities have been removed.

Closing Every Polyline

You can create your drawings by carefully drawing polylines and closing them, or you can just quickly draw polylines that were

```
;this function removes every entity
;from the drawing that is NOT a block
;or a polyline.  The structure of this
;function can be used to look at and
;change any property of all selected
;entities in the drawing database.
(defun c:cleanup ()
        (setq e (entnext))
        (setq entcnt 0)
        (setq wlinecnt 0)
        (while e
                (setq blknm (cdr (assoc 2 (entget e))))
                (setq etype (cdr (assoc 0 (entget e))))
                (setq layername (cdr (assoc 8 (entget e))))
                (if (not (or (equal etype "POLYLINE")
                     (equal etype "INSERT")))
                        (entdel e)
                )
                (setq e (entnext e))
                (setq entcnt (1+ entcnt))
                (princ entcnt) (princ " Entities counted")
        )
)
```

Function 12-18. Removing every entity that is not a block or a polyline not closed and close them globally later. Function 12-19 will close all polylines, so you can work much more quickly. If you have not properly closed a polyline, commands such as the

```
;This function checks every POLYLINE
;in the drawing to make sure that they
;are properly closed.  If the polyline
;is not closed, or improperly closed,
;then this function will close the polyline
;or recreate an identical polyline
;that can be properly closed.
;
(defun c:closechk ( / e headl headlist vertlist firstvert
                firstvertpt
                vertcnt)
        (setvar "cmdecho" 0)
        (setq e (entnext))
        (while e
           (if (= (cdr (assoc 0 (entget e))) "POLYLINE")
             (progn
                (setq headl e)
                (setq lname (cdr (assoc '8 (entget e))))
                (setq headlist (entget e))
                (setq e (entnext e))
                (setq vertlist (list e))
;sets firstvert to the first vertex
                (setq firstvert e)
;sets firstvertpt to the coordinates of the first vertex
                (setq firstvertpt (cdr (assoc '10 (entget
                                                firstvert))))
                (setq vertcnt 0)
;adds all of the vertexes to a list
                (while (= (cdr (assoc '0 (entget e)))
                                "VERTEX")
                        (setq e (entnext e))
                        (setq vertlist (cons e vertlist))
                        (setq vertcnt (1+ vertcnt))
                )
                (setq lastvert firstvert)
                (setq ptlist (list (cdr (assoc '10
                (entget firstvert)))))
;adds all of the vertex coordinates to a list
                (repeat (1- vertcnt)
                        (setq lastvert (entnext lastvert))
                        (setq ptlist (cons (cdr (assoc '10
                        (entget lastvert)))
                             ptlist))
                )
```

Function 12-19. Closing every polyline in a drawing

```
;sets lastvertpt to the coordinates of the last vertex
                (setq lastvertpt (cdr (assoc '10 (entget
                lastvert))))
                (setq ptlist (reverse (cdr ptlist)))
;checks to see if the last vertex
;lies on the same coordinates as the
;first vertex, and if it does, it means
;that the polyline will look like it
;is closed but it will not be properly
;closed by setting the flag in
;group code 70.  If the two coordinates
;are the same, then this section will
;delete the polyline, and redraw it, properly
;closed, based on the coordinates
;contained in the ptlist.
                   (if (equal lastvertpt firstvertpt)
                        (progn
                            (entdel headl)
                            (setq cpt (car ptlist))
                            (command "pline" cpt)
                            (while ptlist
                                (setq ptlist (cdr ptlist))
                                (command (car ptlist))
                            )
                            (command "change" "l" "" "l"
                             lname)
                        )
                        (progn
;if the first vertex and the last vertex are
;not equal, then this section will
;set the group code 70 flag in the polyline
;header entity to 1 so that the
;polyline will be properly closed.
                           (setq headlist (subst '(70 . 1)
                             '(70 . 0) headlist))
                               (entmod headlist)
                        )
                   )
             )
           )
           (setq e (entnext e))
       )
)
```

Function 12-19. Closing every polyline in a drawing (*continued*)

HATCH command may cause lines to "bleed" through the unclosed breaks. The command created by this function is called "closechk."

Resetting Drawing Limits

You may have set your drawing limits to be very large and then decided to do a smaller drawing. Why use such large drawing limits when AutoCAD could run more efficiently with smaller limits? With Function 12-20, you can automatically reset your drawing limits to the extents of the current drawing, plus a margin that you can set in the code. After you run the "limtoext" command produced by this code, the display will be automatically zoomed, without going through an extra regeneration due to the change in drawing extents. This can save a lot of time with large drawings.

An Alternate BREAK Command

The normal BREAK command forces you to go back and re-pick the start point for the break because the current crosshairs location is assumed to be the start point. If you use Function 12-21, you will always be prompted to pick the entity to break,

```
;This function will reset the drawing
;limits to the actual extents of the
;drawing plus a small extra margin and
;execute a zoom all.  The advantage of
;this function is that you will not get
;the extra regen because of change in
;drawing extents.
;
(defun c:limtoext ()
        (setq maxtest (getvar "LIMMAX"))
        (setq maxset (getvar "EXTMAX"))
        (setq minset (getvar "EXTMIN"))
        (setvar "LIMMAX" (list (+ (car maxset) 0.01)
                               (+ (cadr maxset) 0.01)))
        (setq setmin (list (+ (car minset) -0.01)
                           (+ (cadr minset) -0.01)))
        (setvar "LIMMIN" setmin)
        (if (/= maxtest (getvar "LIMMAX"))
            (command "zoom" "a"))
)
```

Function 12-20. Resetting drawing limits to actual extents

```
;This is an alternate break command.
;It will always default to picking
;the entity and then picking the two break points.
;
(defun c:fbreak ( / ent)
        (setq ent (entsel "\nSelect entity to break: "))
        (command "break" ent "f")
)
```

Function 12-21. An alternate BREAK command

then the two break points. The command created by this function is called "fbreak."

Putting Offsets on a Different Layer

When you use the OFFSET command to offset polylines you put the new lines on the current layer by default. With Function 12-22, you can specify a new layer for the offset. The command created by this function is called "layeroff."

Moving Entities from One Layer to Another

You can use the CHANGE command to change an entity's layer. With Function 12-23, you can do the same thing, but much faster. The command created by this function is called "movelayer."

Copying Entities from One Layer to Another

You can move entities from one layer to another by using the "copylayer" command. Function 12-24 will not only move an entity from one layer to another, but it will leave a copy of the entity on the original layer. The copy will be located in the same position in your drawing, but there will be two copies, one on the source layer and one on the destination layer.

```
;This command is similar to the offset
;command, but it will put the new entity
;on a different layer (that you specify)
;from the original entity.  This
;command has defaults for both layer
;name and offset distance.
;
(defun c:layeroff ( / obj layno offdst side)
        (setq cmdmode (getvar "cmdecho")) (setvar "cmdecho" 0)
        (setq obj (entsel "\nSelect object to offset: "))
        (princ "\nEnter layer name for offset<")
        (if (null laynol) (setq laynol ""))
        (princ laynol) (setq layno (getstring ">: "))
        (cond ((equal layno "") (setq layno laynol)))
        (cond ((equal layno "") (setq layno
                                (getvar "CLAYER"))))
        (princ "\nOffset distance<")
        (if (null offdstl) (setq offdstl 0,0))
        (princ (rtos offdstl)) (setq offdst
                               (getdist (cadr obj) ">: "))
        (cond ((null offdst) (setq offdst offdstl)))
        (setq side (getpoint "\nSide to offset? "))
        (command "offset" offdst obj side "")
        (command "change" "l" "" "layer" layno)
        (setq offdstl offdst)
        (setq laynol layno)
        (setvar "CMDECHO" cmdmode)
        (princ)
)
```

Function 12-22. Putting offsets on a different layer

Rounding a Number

Function 12-25 shows a simple routine for rounding a number rather than truncating it. You can use "round" wherever you want to make sure your numbers round to the nearest whole number. This rounding is carried to eight decimal places.

Counting All Instances of Blocks

You can count all instances of blocks with desired names from your drawing with the "ssblkcnt" function shown as Function 12-26. The output from this function can be redirected to a file so the list of blocks can be used to prepare reports.

```
;This command will move entities from
;one layer to another.  It is a bit
;faster than using the CHANGE command,
;because you can set a default for the
;layer name and not have to type in the
;layer name each time that it is used.
;
(defun c:movelayer ( / objm layno)
        (setq cmdmode (getvar "cmdecho"))
                          (setvar "cmdecho" 0)
        (prompt "\nSelect object to change: ")
        (setq objm (ssget))
        (princ "\nEnter layer name for move<")
        (if (null laynol) (setq laynol (getvar "CLAYER")))
        (princ laynol) (setq layno (getstring ">: "))
        (cond ((equal layno "") (setq layno laynol)))
        (command "change" objm "" "layer" layno)
        (setq laynol layno)
        (setvar "CMDECHO" cmdmode)
        (princ)
)
```

Function 12-23. Moving entities from one layer to another

```
;This command will copy entities from
;one layer to another.  The new entities
;will appear in exactly the same position
;as the originals except they will
;be on a different layer.
;
(defun c:copylayer ( / start objc layno)
        (setq cmdmode (getvar "cmdecho"))
                          (setvar "cmdecho" 0)
        (setq start (getvar "LIMMIN"))
        (prompt "\nSelect objects to copy: ")
        (setq objc (ssget))
        (princ "\nEnter layer name for copy<")
        (if (null laynol) (setq laynol (getvar "CLAYER")))
        (princ laynol) (setq layno (getstring ">: "))
        (cond ((equal layno "") (setq layno laynol)))
        (command "copy" objc "" start start)
        (command "change" objc "" "layer" layno)
        (setq laynol layno)
        (setvar "CMDECHO" cmdmode)
        (princ)
)
```

Function 12-24. Copying entities from one layer to another

```
; This function rounds a number rather than truncating it.
;
(defun round (a)
  (fix (+ a 0.5)))
```

Function 12-25. Rounding a number

Reading and Writing Association Lists

You will find that it is often desirable to save association lists in files so you can have more space in your AutoLISP program. You can write such lists directly from the data in your running program, exit to DOS, and return later to load the list you saved. These two functions will read and write association lists that contain strings.

Writing an Association List

The association list concept was discussed earlier in this chapter in the section "Deleting and Reinserting a Block." You can write

```
;This function will count all instances of a list of block
;names in a drawing.  You can easily redirect the output to a
;file.
;
(defun ssblkcnt ( )
    (setq blklst '("ID1" "ID2" "SPACEID"))
    (while blklst
        (setq curblk (car blklst) blklst (cdr blklst))
        (setq etype (cons 0 "INSERT"))
        (setq ss (ssget "X" (list etype (cons 2 curblk))))
        (princ "there are ")
        (princ (sslength ss))
        (princ " blocks named ")
        (princ curblk)
        (princ " in this drawing")
        (setq ss nil)
        (terpri)
    )
    (princ)
)
```

Function 12-26. Counting all instances of blocks

an association list in a file by writing the association name, followed by the value of the association as follows:

nuts
23
bolts
54
screws
129

Function 12-27 will save an association list in a file. The function,

```
;This function writes an association list for use with the
;BLDLIST.LSP function.

(defun svlist ( / slist sublist fname l)
;prompt for name of a-list to save
    (setq slist (getstring "A-List to save: "))
;converts string to symbol
    (setq slist (read slist))
;links symbol name
    (setq slist (eval slist))
;prompts for a file name
    (setq fname (getstring "File name to write: "))
;opens the file
    (setq L (open (strcat fname ) "w"))
;as long as there is anything in SLIST do the loop
    (while slist
;sets sublist to the first sub-list in the a-list
        (setq sublist (car slist))
;return all but the first element in the list
        (setq slist (cdr slist))
;while there is anything in the sublist
        (while sublist
;write the first element of the sublist
            (write-line (car sublist) l)
;return all but the first element in the list
            (setq sublist (cdr sublist))
        )
    )
    (close l);close the data file
)
```

Function 12-27. Saving an association list

called "svlist," takes the name of a list from the user and prompts for a file name.

Reading an Association List

Function 12-28 will read a file such as the one just discussed into an association list. The comments in this function show how it works. The function is called "bldlist."

```
;If you create an ASCII file, consisting of data pairs at
;one item per line:
;
;      Key
;      Data
;      etc.
;
;an association list will be built.
;See SVLIST.LSP for a function that will save an association
;list for use by this function.
(defun bldlist ( / sublist dname L a)
;creates two empty lists to put the data in
    (setq alist () sublist ())
;prompts for a file name
    (setq fname (getstring "File name to read"))
;opens the file
    (setq L (open (strcat fname ) "r"))
;reads the first line in the file to A
    (setq a (read-line l))
;as long as there are lines in the file do the loop
    (while a
;read two lines for each list
        (repeat 2
;put the current line in sublist with cons
            (setq sublist (cons a sublist))
;read the next line of the file
            (setq a (read-line l))
        )
;when two lines are read reverse the order of sublist to
;put the key at the beginning of the list
        (setq sublist (reverse sublist))
;add the sublist to the alist with cons
        (setq alist (cons sublist alist))
```

Function 12-28. Reading an association list

```
;clear out the sublist
        (setq sublist ())
    );end of the while loop
    (close 1);close the data file
  (reverse alist)
)
```

Function 12-28. Reading an association list (*continued*)

Converting Circles and Arcs

Some other CAD systems do not have circle or arc entities. If you need to translate AutoCAD drawings so they can be used on such systems, you will find this code helpful.

Converting Circles to Polygons

Function 12-29 can be used to change drawings developed in AutoCAD that contain circles into drawings that contain only

```
;This function converts a circle to a polygon with 32 sides
;as a polyline.  Some CAD systems do not recognize circles.
;This function will enable you to translate circles so the
;data can be used by those systems.

(defun c:c2pgon ()
    (setq circ (car (entsel
                   "\nPick circle for conversion:" )))
    (if (equal (cdr (assoc 0 (entget circ))) "CIRCLE")
        (progn
            (setq rad (cdr (assoc 40 (entget circ))))
            (setq cen (cdr (assoc 10 (entget circ))))
            (setq lay (cdr (assoc 8 (entget circ))))
            (entdel circ)
            (command "LAYER" "S" lay "")
            (command "POLYGON" 32 cen "I" rad)
        )
        (princ "\nEntity picked is not a circle ")
    )
    (princ)
)
```

Function 12-29. Converting circles to polygons

polyline segments. The command created by this function is called "c2pgon."

Converting Connected Lines to Polylines

Function 12-30 converts circles to polygons as done in the conversion in Function 12-29. In addition, any series of connected lines will be converted to closed polylines. This function is intended to simplify drawings that have been made with multiple lines rather than polylines. Such drawing files are unnecessarily cluttered and this function will simplify them.

```
;This function takes a drawing that has lines, circles, arcs,
;etc. and creates closed polylines with them.  You can use
;this to convert such entities for use in a CAD system that
;does not have circle capabilities.  Other entities will only
;be flagged.

(defun c:convp ( / lstvrt e snlst cflag tstln
                   tstlay vrtlst ss ssall nxtss
                   nxtln lstln tpoint cnt erflag fln)
    (setq lstvrt nil)
    (setq e (entnext))
    (setvar "CMDECHO" 0)
    (setvar "BLIPMODE" 0)
    (setq snlst (getvar "SNAPUNIT"))
    (while e
        (cond
            ((equal (cdr (assoc 0 (entget e))) "CIRCLE")
                (c2pgon e)
            )
            ((equal (cdr (assoc 0 (entget e))) "ARC")
                (command "change" e "" "P" "LT" "DOT" "")
            )
            ((equal (cdr (assoc 0 (entget e))) "LINE")
                (setq cflag nil)
                (setq tstln e)
                (setq tstlay (cdr (assoc 8 (entget tstln))))
                (setq vrtlst ())
                (setq vrtlst (cons (cdr (assoc 10 (entget
                tstln))) vrtlst))
                (setq vrtlst (cons (cdr (assoc 11 (entget
                tstln))) vrtlst))
                (if lstvrt
                    (if (< (distance lstvrt
                              (cdr (assoc 11 (entget tstln))
```

Function 12-30. Converting circles and arcs to polygons

```
                  ))
                     (distance lstvrt
                  (cdr (assoc 10 (entget tstln))
                  )))
              (setq vrtlst (reverse vrtlst))
      )
  )
  (setq ss (ssadd))
  (setq ssall (ssget "X" (list (cons 0 "LINE")
  (cons 8 tstlay))))
  (setq ss (ssadd tstln ss))
  (redraw tstln 3)
  (setq nxtln tstln lstln tstln)
  (setq nxtss (ssadd))
  (setq nxtss (ssadd nxtln nxtss))
  (while (and ssall (> (sslength nxtss) 0))
      (setq tpoint (car vrtlst))
      (setq nxtss (ssget "C" (list
      (- (car tpoint) 0.01)
              (- (cadr tpoint) 0.01))
              (list (+ (car tpoint)
              0.01) (+ (cadr tpoint) 0.01)
              )))
      (if (ssmemb lstln nxtss) (setq nxtss
      (ssdel lstln nxtss)))
      (if (ssmemb lstln ssall) (setq ssall
      (ssdel lstln ssall)))
      (setq cnt 0)
      (while (< cnt (sslength nxtss))
          (setq nxtln (ssname nxtss cnt))
          (if (null (ssmemb nxtln ssall))
              (setq nxtss (ssdel nxtln nxtss))
          )
          (setq cnt (1+ cnt))
      )
      (setq cnt 0)
      (while (< cnt (sslength nxtss))
          (setq nxtln (ssname nxtss cnt))
          (if (and
                  (equal (cdr (assoc 0 (entget
                  nxtln))) "LINE")
                  (equal (cdr (assoc 8 (entget
                  nxtln))) tstlay)
                  (ssmemb nxtln ssall))
              (progn
                  (setq ss (ssadd nxtln ss))
                  (setq cnt (1+
                          (sslength nxtss)))
                  (if (< (distance tpoint (cdr
                  (assoc 10
                          (entget nxtln))))
```

Function 12-30. Converting circles and arcs to polygons (*continued*)

```
                                        (distance tpoint
                                        (cdr
                                        (assoc 11 (entget
                                        nxtln)))))
                                    (setq vrtlst (cons (cdr
                                    (assoc 11
                                        (entget nxtln)))
                                        vrtlst))
                                    (setq vrtlst (cons (cdr
                                    (assoc 10
                                        (entget nxtln)))
                                        vrtlst))
                                )
                                (redraw nxtln 3)
                                (setq lstln nxtln)
                            )
                        );end if
                        (setq cnt (1+ cnt))
                    );end while cnt
                    (if (> (length vrtlst) 190) (setq nxtss
                    (ssadd)))
                );end while nxtss
                (cond
                    ((equal (car vrtlst) (car
                                        (reverse vrtlst)))
                        (setq vrtlst (cdr vrtlst))
                        (setq fln nil nxtln nil)
                        (setq cflag t)
                    )
                    ((equal nxtln tstln)
                        (setq fln nil nxtln nil)
                        (setq cflag t)
                    )
                    ((> (length vrtlst) 190)
                        (setq ss (ssdel nxtln ss))
                        (setq vrtlst (cdr vrtlst))
                        (redraw nxtln 4)
                        (setq lstvrt (car vrtlst))
                        (setq fln nxtln nxtln nil)
                        (setq erflag T)
                        (setq cflag t)
                    )
                    (t nil)
                )
                (npoly ss vrtlst tstlay cflag)
                (print "return from polyline")
                (if erflag
                    (progn
                        (command "change" (entlast) "" "p"
```

Function 12-30. Converting circles and arcs to polygons (*continued*)

```
                        "LT" "DOT" "")
                        (setq erflag nil)
                    )
                )
                (setq vrtlst ())
            );equal line
        );end cond
        (if fln
            (setq e fln)
            (setq e (entnext e))
        )
    );end while e
    (setq ssall (ssget "X" (list (cons 0 "LINE"))))
    (if ssall
        (command "convp")
    )
)
(defun npoly (ss vrtlst tstlay cflag / n)
        (command "erase" ss "")
        (command "layer" "S" tstlay "")
        (if cflag
            (setq vrtlst (cons "C" vrtlst))
            (setq vrtlst (cons "" vrtlst))
        )
        (setq vrtlst (reverse vrtlst))
        (command "pline")
            (foreach n vrtlst (command n))
        (setq cflag nil)
)
(defun c2pgon (e / c r)
            (command "layer" "S" (cdr (assoc 8 (entget e)))
                                                         "")
            (setq c (cdr (assoc 10 (entget e))))
            (setq r (cdr (assoc 40 (entget e))))
            (entdel e)
            (command "POLYGON" 32 c "I" r)
)
```

Function 12-30. Converting circles and arcs to polygons (*continued*)

Walls and Intersections

AutoCAD has no built-in commands or functions that draw parallel lines to use for drawing wall outlines. Building plans have many such parallel lines that intersect. It is difficult to draw walls without a wall-drawing utility because you must do twice the work. You cannot just indicate a wall center line or edge and have AutoCAD draw the wall outline.

If you add the following functions to your AutoCAD armory, you will be able to do battle with the ubiquitous army of walls in your architectural drawings. Shown here are functions and commands that clean up wall intersections and corners, create walls parallel to each other, and draw wall outlines. You can even break openings in walls that already have been drawn. You can then "weld" those breaks together into a solid wall and clean up all of the wall intersections in your drawing.

Cleaning Up Wall Intersections

If you put your walls on a layer called ARWALL or a layer that has "AWALL" as its first five characters, you can make the walls intersect correctly. You may have drawn double lines that do not quite meet. This program will make them meet if they are within a fixed distance from each other. Function 12-31 shows the function that creates this capability.

```
;This function cleans up wall corner intersections where
;double wall lines have been used in a drawing.  All lines
;must be on a layer called ARWALL or a layer that has the
;first six character ARWALL.

(defun CNRCLN ( / b c d e f g h m n o p q r t u x y w z)
   (setvar "cmdecho" 0)
   (setq lstlay (getvar "clayer"))
   (setvar "osmode" 32)
   (setvar "blipmode" 0)
   (setvar "orthomode" 0)
   (setq b (getpoint "Pick the intersection: "))
   (setvar "osmode" 0)
   (setq c (mapcar '- b '(12 12))
         d (mapcar '+ b '(12 12))
         e nil f 0 g 0 n 0 o nil p nil q nil r (+ pi pi))
   (setq h (ssget "c" c d))
   (setq b (getpoint b
   "\nPick a point on the inside of the wall corner: "))
   (SETVAR "ORTHOMODE" 1)
```

Function 12-31. Cleaning up wall corner intersections

```
(while (setq e (ssname h g))
   (setq e (entget e))
   (cond
      ((or (equal "ARWALL" (cdr (assoc '8 e)))
            (equal "AWALL" (substr (cdr (assoc '8 e))
                                    1 5)))
         (setq f (1+ f))
         (cond
            ((= 1 f)
               (setq i (list (cdar e)(cdr (assoc 10 e))
               (cdr (assoc 11 e)))
                  w (cdr (assoc 8 e))
                  aa (cdr (assoc 39 e))))
            ((= 2 f)
               (setq j (list (cdar e)(cdr (assoc 10 e))
                              (cdr (assoc 11 e)))
                  t (cdr (assoc 8 e))
                  ab (cdr (assoc 39 e))))
            ((= 3 f)
               (setq k (list (cdar e)(cdr (assoc 10 e))
                              (cdr (assoc 11 e)))
                  u (cdr (assoc 8 e))
                  ac (cdr (assoc 39 e))))
            ((= 4 f)
               (setq L (list (cdar e)(cdr (assoc 10 e))
                              (cdr (assoc 11 e)))
                  z (cdr (assoc 8 e))
                  ad (cdr (assoc 39 e))))
         )
      )
   )
   (setq g (1+ g))
)
(cond
   ((= f 4)
      (cnrcln3 i j)
      (setq i x j y)

      (cnrcln3 i k)
      (setq i x k y)

      (cnrcln3 i l)
      (setq i x L y)

      (cnrcln3 j k)
      (setq j x k y)

      (cnrcln3 j l)
      (setq j x L y)

      (cnrcln3 k l)
      (setq k x L y)
```

Function 12-31. Cleaning up wall corner intersections (*continued*)

```
          (cond
             ((= 4 n)
               (setq p (cadr p)
                     q (cadr q))
                (cnrcln2 i w aa)
                (cnrcln2 j t ab)
                (cnrcln2 k u ac)
                (cnrcln2 L z ad)
                (eval (command "layer" "s" lstlay "")))
             ((< n 4)
                (prompt
             "\nFewer than 4 valid intersections were found"))
             ((> n 4)
                (prompt
           "\nGreater than 4 valid intersections were found"))
          )
        )
        ((< f 4)
           (prompt
           "\nFewer than 4 valid wall lines were found"))
        ((> f 4)
           (prompt
           "\nMore than 4 valid wall lines were found"))
      )
)
(defun cnrcln2(a v z / d e f g h i j k l)
;
   (setq d (cadddr a) e (car (cddddr a))
         f (cadr a) g (caddr a))
   (setq k (rem (+ (angle f g) r 1) r))
   (entdel (car a))
   (cond
      ((equal q d)
         (setq h d
               j (rem (+ (angle e d) r 1) r)
               L (- (max j k)(min j k))))
      ((equal q e)
         (setq h e
               j (rem (+ (angle d e) r 1) r)
               L (- (max j k)(min j k))))
      ((equal p d)
         (setq h d
               j (rem (+ (angle d e) r 1) r)
               L (- (max j k)(min j k))))
      ((equal p e)
         (setq h e
               j (rem (+ (angle e d) r 1) r)
               L (- (max j k)(min j k))))
   )
   (cond
      ((< L 0.01)
         (setq i g))
      (T (setq i f))
```

Function 12-31. Cleaning up wall corner intersections (*continued*)

```
   )
   (eval (command "layer" "s" v  "" "elev" 0 z))
   (eval (command "line" h i ""))
)

(defun cnrcln3(a d)
   (setq c (inters (cadr a)(caddr a)
                   (cadr d)(caddr d) nil))
   (setq x a y d)
   (cond
      ((not (null c))
         (setq x (append x (list c))
               o (distance c b)
               y (append y (list c))
               n (1+ n))
         (cond
            ((null p)
               (setq p (list o c))
               (setq q p))
            ((> o (car p))
               (setq p (list o c)))
            ((< o (car q))
               (setq q (list o c)))
         )
      )
   )
)
```

Function 12-31. Cleaning up wall corner intersections (*continued*)

Creating Walls Parallel to Each Other

Most walls in building plan drawings are drawn at right angles to each other. All you need to do if you use Function 12-32 is type in a distance, either inside to inside or center to center. This function is unusual and may be hard to read because it does not evaluate functions. Instead, it reads lists. When the data in one list is evaluated, it in essence becomes the function. The result of this optimization is that the code takes up less memory.

```
;PARALLEL WALL DRAWING ROUTINE
;If you have a room with four walls this will draw a new wall
;parallel to it and break into the old wall perpendicular to
```

Function 12-32. Creating walls parallel to each other

```
;it.  All you need to do is type in a distance, either inside
;to inside or center to center.  This code is optimized for
;speed.  A technique is used that reads lists rather than
;evaluating functions.  Nothing is put on the atom list until
;the list is evaluated.  The only function is at the very top.
;All it does is read everything into memory.  When the data
;is evaluated it becomes a function in essence, but it takes
;up less memory.

(defun prwll ( / j k m n o p r s t aa zz
               u v x w y q aj ak
               f g h d i e ad af ac
               z L ab ae lstlay ag ah a4
               a2 a3 a5 a7 a6
               al a c ss b ai)
(setq al '(progn
        (setq a nil)
        (setq b 0)
        (setq L (sslength ss))
        (repeat l
             (setq c (ssname ss b))
             (if (= (substr (cdr (assoc 8 (entget c))) 1 5)
             "AWALL")
                    (setq a c)
             )
              (setq b (1+ b))
        )
        (setq a a)
))
(setq a4 '(progn
   (while ab
        (setq j (cdr (assoc 10 (entget aa))))
        (setq k (cdr (assoc 11 (entget aa))))
        (setq m (ssname (ssdel aa (ssget "C"
        (list (1+ (car j)) (1+
           (cadr j))) (list (1- (car j)) (1- (cadr j))))) 0))
        (setq n (ssname (ssdel aa (ssget "C"
        (list (1+ (car k)) (1+
           (cadr k))) (list (1- (car k)) (1- (cadr k))))) 0))
        (setq o (angle j k))
        (setq p (distance j k))
        (if (= ad 0) (setq ab (- ab af)))
        (setq f (cdr (assoc 10 (entget m))))
        (setq g (cdr (assoc 11 (entget m))))
        (if (> (distance j f) (distance j g))
              (progn
                (setq h g)
```

Function 12-32. Creating walls parallel to each other *(continued)*

```
                (setq g f)
                (setq f h)
             )
        )
        (setq r (polar f (angle f g) ab))
        (setq s (polar r o p))
        (setq t (inters (cdr (assoc 10 (entget n)))
        (cdr (assoc 11
          (entget n))) s r nil))
        (eval (command "line" r t ""))
        (setq u (entlast))
        (redraw aa 4)
        (setq q r aj m ak af)
        (setq v (polar r (angle f g) af))
        (setq w (polar v o p))
        (setq x (inters (cdr (assoc 10 (entget n)))
        (cdr (assoc 11
              (entget n))) w v nil))
        (eval (command "line" v x ""))
        (setq y (entlast))
        (if (= ac 1)
                        (eval (command "break" m r v
                        "break" n t x))
        )
        (setq z v)
        (setq aa y)
        (redraw aa 3)
                (setq ab (getdist z
                    "\nEnter distance to next wall: "))
    )
                        (eval a7)
))
(setq a6 '(progn
                (setq j nil k nil m nil n nil
                o nil p nil r nil s nil t nil
                u nil v nil x nil w nil y nil)
                (setq q nil aj nil ak nil
                f nil g nil h nil d nil i nil e nil)
                (setq ad nil af nil ac nil
                z nil L nil ab nil ae nil lstlay nil
                ag nil ah nil a4 nil a2 nil
                a3 nil a5 nil a7 nil)
))

(setq a7 '(progn
        (command "layer" "s" lstlay "" "elev" 0 0)
        (redraw aa 4)
        (eval a6)
        (gc)
```

Function 12-32. Creating walls parallel to each other (*continued*)

```
))
        (gc)
        (setq ac (atoi (substr (itoa (getvar "useri3")) 1 1)))
        (setq ad (atoi (substr (itoa (getvar "useri3")) 2 1)))
        (setq ae (strcat "AWALL" (substr (itoa (getvar
                                    "useri3")) 3 1)))
        (setq lstlay (getvar "clayer"))
        (setq af (getvar "tracewid"))
        (if (= ad 0) (setq ag "CENTER TO CENTER ")
                     (setq ag "INSIDE TO INSIDE "))
        (setvar "osmode" 512)
        (prompt "\nDistance between walls will be from ")
        (princ ag)
        (princ "\nEnter wall height<")
                     (setq zz (rtos (getvar "userr2") 4 2))
        (princ zz) (setq zz (getdist ">: "))
        (cond ((null zz) (setq zz (getvar "userr2"))))
        (setvar "userr2" zz)
        (setq ah (getpoint "\nPick reference wall line: "))
        (setvar "osmode" 0)
        (setq ai ah)
        (eval (setq ss (ssget "c" (list
                           (+ (car ai) 2) (+ (cadr ai) 2))
             (list (- (car ai) 2) (- (cadr ai) 2)))))
        (eval (if ss (setq aa (eval al))))
        (redraw aa 3)
        (setq ab (getdist ah
                          "\nEnter distance to next wall: "))
        (command "layer" "s" ae "" "elev" 0 (getvar "userr2"))
        (eval a4)
)
```

Function 12-32. Creating walls parallel to each other (*continued*)

Drawing Walls Using Double Lines

Function 12-33 draws walls and joins them if they come within two inches of each other. The command created is called "swall." If you transcribe this function or purchase the companion disk, you will have access to an extremely powerful and generalized program.

```
;The SWALL command draws walls using double wall lines.  This
;is an example of a generalized wall drawing command that has
;not been optimized for speed.  If you end this command within
;two or three inches of another wall it will automatically
;join the walls.
;
(defun c:swall ()
        (setq sw (getstring
          "\nOffset this wall from an intersection? (N) " ))
        (setq side (getvar "useril"))
        (setq wt (getvar "tracewid"))
        (if (= side 0) (setq dside "CENTER line "))
        (if (= side 1) (setq dside
                "RIGHT side moving clockwise "))
        (if (= side 2) (setq dside
                "LEFT side moving clockwise "))
        (prompt "\nFirst wall line will be drawn from the ")
        (princ dside)
        (if (= (strcase sw) "Y")
                (offwall)
                (drwall)
        )
)
(defun offwall ()
        (command "osnap" "int")
        (setq offint (getpoint
            "\nPick intersection to offset from: "))
        (command "osnap" "non")
        (command "osnap" "nea")
        (setq sln (car (entsel
            "\nPick wall line to start wall: ")))
        (command "osnap" "non")
        (setq offdist (getdist "\nEnter the offset distance: "))
        (prcoffset offint sln offdist)
        (setq ew (getpoint st "\nPick ending point of wall: "))
        (setq eln (findent ew))
        (setq z (+ (angle st ew) (/ pi 2)))
        (setq z2t (- (angle ew st) (/ pi 2)))
        (if (= side 0)
                (drcwall)
                (drswall)
        )
)
(defun prcoffset (stint stent stdist)
        (setq pt1 (cdr (assoc 10 (entget stent))))
        (setq pt2 (cdr (assoc 11 (entget stent))))
        (setq stdist1 stdist)
        (if (> (distance stint pt1) (distance stint pt2))
              (progn
                (setq pt3 pt2)
                (setq pt2 pt1)
```

Function 12-33. Drawing walls using double lines

```
                (setq ptl pt3)
            )
        )
        (setq slnang (angle ptl pt2))
        (if (equal ptl stdistl)
                (setq st (polar ptl slnang stdistl))
                (findoff)
        )
)

(defun findoff ()
        (print "findoff")
        (setq offadd (* (cos (- (+ pi slnang)
        (angle ptl offint)))
                (distance ptl offint)))
        (setq st (polar ptl slnang (- stdistl offadd)))
)
(defun drwall ()
        (command "osnap" "nea")
        (setq st (getpoint "\nPick starting point of wall: "))
        (command "osnap" "non")
        (setq ew (getpoint st "\nPick ending point of wall: "))
        (setq sln (findent st))
        (setq eln (findent ew))
        (setq z (+ (angle st ew) (/ pi 2)))
        (setq z2t (- (angle ew st) (/ pi 2)))
        (if (= side 0)
                (drcwall)
                (drswall)
        )
)
(defun drswall ()
        (command "line" st ew "")
        (setq wlnl (entlast))
        (if (= side 2) (setq st2 (polar st (+ z pi) wt)))
        (if (= side 1) (setq st2 (polar st z wt)))
        (if (= side 2) (setq ew2 (polar ew (+ z2t pi) wt)))
        (if (= side 1) (setq ew2 (polar ew z2t wt)))
        (eval (command "line" st2 ew2 ""))
        (setq wln2 (entlast))
        (prcwall)
)
(defun drcwall ()
        (setq w2 (/ wt 2))
        (setq stl (polar st (+ z pi) w2))
        (setq st2 (polar st z w2))
        (setq ewl (polar ew (+ z2t pi) w2))
        (setq ew2 (polar ew z2t w2))
        (eval (command "line" stl ewl ""))
        (setq wlnl (entlast))
```

Function 12-33. Drawing walls using double lines (*continued*)

```
        (eval (command "line" st2 ew2 ""))
        (setq wln2 (entlast))
        (prcwall)
)
(defun prcwall ()
        (command "change" wlnl wln2 "" "la" "awall")
        (progn
           (if sln
                (trimtees wlnl wln2 sln)
           )
           (if eln
                (trimteee wlnl wln2 eln)
           )
        )
)
(defun trimtees (wll wl2 tln)
        (print "trimstart")
        (setq intl (findinter wll tln))
        (setq int2 (findinter wl2 tln))
        (setq wll (newst wll intl))
        (setq wl2 (newst wl2 int2))
        (command "break" tln intl int2)
)
(defun trimteee (wll wl2 tln)
        (print "trimend")
        (setq intl (findinter wll tln))
        (setq int2 (findinter wl2 tln))
        (setq wll (newnd wll intl))
        (setq wl2 (newnd wl2 int2))
        (command "break" tln intl int2)
)
(defun findinter (entl ent2)
        (inters (cdr (assoc 10 (entget entl)))
             (cdr (assoc 11 (entget entl)))
             (cdr (assoc 10 (entget ent2)))
             (cdr (assoc 11 (entget ent2)))
             nil)
)
(defun newst (oldent new10)
        (setq oldente (entget oldent))
        (setq oldente (subst (append '(10) new10)
                             (assoc 10 oldente) oldente))
        (entmod oldente)
        (setq oldent oldent)
)
(defun newnd (oldent new11)
        (setq oldente (entget oldent))
        (setq oldente (subst (append '(11) new11)
                             (assoc 11 oldente) oldente))
```

Function 12-33. Drawing walls using double lines *(continued)*

```
        (entmod oldente)
        (setq oldent oldent)
)
(defun findent (pt / en)
        (print "findent")
        (setq en nil)
        (setq ss (ssget "c" (list (+ (car pt) 2)
                                  (+ (cadr pt) 2))
                            (list (- (car pt) 2)
                                  (- (cadr pt) 2))))
        (if ss
         (progn
          (setq cnt 0)
          (setq L (sslength ss))
          (repeat l
                (setq enchk (ssname ss cnt))
                (if (= (cdr (assoc 8 (entget enchk))) "AWALL")
                        (setq en enchk)
                )
               (setq cnt (1+ cnt))
          )
         )
        )
       (setq en en)
)
```

Function 12-33. Drawing walls using double lines (*continued*)

Breaking Walls

You often need to break openings in walls when you place openings for doors and windows in your building plan drawings. Of course, you can use the BREAK command to break single lines. When you break openings in walls, however, you must break two lines and close the ends of those broken lines. Function 12-34 will do this for you with a command called "wallbrk." Although this command is specifically designed for doors, it can be easily modified to work with windows. You can also use the "gang" command specified here to get the angle of a line. The command "checkent" will enable you to check an entity at a given point.

Welding Wall Breaks

After you have broken a wall, you will often want to put it back together again. The "weld" command created in Function 12-35 will accomplish this.

```
;The wallbrk command inserts a door into a wall.
;
(defun c:wallbrk ()
        (setq drwdth 36)
        (setq st (getpoint "\nPick hinge point of door"))
        (setq ss (ssget "C" (list (1+ (car st)) (1+ (cadr st)))
                            (list (1- (car st)) (1- (cadr st)))
                            ))
        (setq end (getpoint "\nPick latch side of door"))
        (setq dang (angle st end))
        (setq L (sslength ss))
        (setq cnt 0)
        (repeat 1
                (setq wall1 (ssname ss cnt))
        )
        (setq srchpt (polar st (- dang (/ pi 2)) 12))
        (command "break" wall1 st (polar st dang drwdth))
        (command "line" st srchpt "")
)
(defun c:gang ()
        (setq a (getangle "\nPick two points of angle"))
)
(defun c:chkent ()
        (setq a (getpoint "\nPick point "))
        (setq ss (ssget "C" (list
                              (1+ (car a))
                              (1+ (cadr a)))
                            (list
                              (1- (car a))
                              (1- (cadr a)))))
        (setq L (sslength ss))
        (setq cnt 0)
        (repeat 1
                (setq p (ssname ss cnt))
                (print p)
                (redraw p 3)
                (setq cnt (1+ cnt))
        )
        (entsel)
)
```

Function 12-34 Breaking walls

Cleaning Wall Crossings

After you have drawn many walls that intersect, you will want to "clean up" their intersections. When you draw double lines crossing other double lines, you will see the lines passing

```
;If you have broken a line into two segments this function
;will connect them back together again, in effect "welding"
;them back together.
;
(defun WELD ( / a b c d e f g h i)
(setq a3 '(progn
        (setq e (angle (cdr (assoc 10 (entget c)))
                       (cdr (assoc 11 (entget c)))))
        (setq f (angle (cdr (assoc 10 (entget d)))
                       (cdr (assoc 11 (entget d)))))
        (if (= (fix e) (fix f))
                (eval a1)
                (eval a2)
        )
))
(setq a1 '(progn
        (setq g (distance (cdr (assoc 10 (entget c)))
                          (cdr (assoc 11 (entget d)))))
        (setq h (distance (cdr (assoc 10 (entget d)))
                          (cdr (assoc 11 (entget c)))))
        (if (> g h)
             (progn
                (setq i (cdr (assoc 11 (entget d))))
                (entdel d)
                (setq c (entmod (subst (append '(11) i)
                (assoc 11 (entget c)) (entget c))))
            )
            (progn
                (setq i (cdr (assoc 10 (entget d))))
                (entdel d)
                (setq c (entmod (subst (append '(10) i)
                (assoc 10 (entget c)) (entget c))))
            )
        )
))
(setq a2 '(progn
        (setq g (distance (cdr (assoc 10 (entget c)))
                          (cdr (assoc 10 (entget d)))))
        (setq h (distance (cdr (assoc 11 (entget d)))
                          (cdr (assoc 11 (entget c)))))
        (if (> g h)
             (progn
                (setq i (cdr (assoc 10 (entget d))))
                (entdel d)
                (setq c (entmod (subst (append '(11) i)
                                       (assoc 11 (entget c))
                                                 (entget c))
                                                ))
```

Function 12-35. Welding wall breaks

```
            )
            (progn
                (setq i (cdr (assoc 11 (entget d))))
                (entdel d)
                (setq c (entmod (subst (append '(10) i)
                                       (assoc 10 (entget c))
                                                 (entget c))
                                                 ))
            )
        )
))
        (command "undo" "group")
        (setq a (entsel "\nSelect first line to weld: "))
        (setq a (car a))
        (redraw a 3)
        (setq b (entsel "\nSelect second line to weld: "))
        (setq b (car b))
        (redraw b 3)
        (redraw a 1)
        (redraw b 1)
        (eval (if (< a b)
             (progn
                (setq c a)
                (setq d b)
             )
        ))
        (eval (if (> a b)
             (progn
                (setq c b)
                (setq d a)
             )
        ))
        (eval a3)
        (command "undo" "end")
        (gc)
)
```

Function 12-35. Welding wall breaks (*continued*)

through each other. Instead, you want those lines to stop at the corners of walls. Function 12-36 will enable you to use "xcln" to check for wall intersections. A wall, by definition, consists of any two parallel lines that are less than a certain distance apart. All such line entities will be treated by this function.

```
;This function will clean up intersections of walls where two
;pairs of wall lines cross as an "X".
;
(defun XCLN ( / a b c d e f g h i j ss)
        (command "undo" "group")
        (prompt
   "\nPick 4 wall lines or draw crossing box around CROSS: ")
        (setq ss (ssget))
        (setq a ())
        (setq b 0)
        (setq c (sslength ss))
        (repeat c
          (setq d (ssname ss b))
          (if (not (or (equal "AWALL"
                              (substr (cdr (assoc 8 (entget d))
                               ) 1 5))
                       (equal "ARWALL" (cdr (assoc 8 (entget d)
                               )))))
                        (setq a (cons (ssname ss b) a))
                        )
                        (setq b (1+ b))
                )
        (while a
           (setq ss (ssdel (car a) ss))
           (setq a (cdr a))
        )
        (if (or (> (sslength ss) 4) (< (sslength ss) 4))
            (if (> (sslength ss) 4)
              (prompt
                "\nMore than 4 valid Wall lines were found ")
              (prompt
                "\nLess than 4 valid Wall lines were found ")
            )
                (progn
                  (print "findlineinter")
                  (setq e ())
                  (setq f 0)
                  (repeat 4
                     (setq g (ssname ss f))
                     (setq h 0)
                     (repeat 4
                        (setq i (ssname ss h))
                        (if (inters (cdr (assoc 10 (entget g)))
                                    (cdr (assoc 11 (entget g)))
                                    (cdr (assoc 10 (entget i)))
                                    (cdr (assoc 11 (entget i)))
                                    nil)
                            (progn
                               (setq j
```

Function 12-36. Cleaning wall crossings

```
                              (inters (cdr (assoc 10
                              (entget g)))
                              (cdr (assoc 11 (entget g)))
                              (cdr (assoc 10
                              (entget i))) (cdr (assoc 11
                              (entget
                              i))) nil))
                              (setq e (cons j e))
                          )
                      )
                      (setq h (1+ h))
              )
              (setq f (1+ f))
              (eval (command "break" g (car e) (last e)))
              (setq e ())
         )

     )
   )
      (command "undo" "end")
      (gc)
)
```

Function 12-36. Cleaning wall crossings (*continued*)

Drawing Simplification

When you plot a drawing that is very complex at a very small scale, you will find that the pen will often draw for too long in one small area of the drawing. When this happens, you usually see a little pool of ink on your drawing and, as a result, the plot will be worthless. In addition to this kind of disaster, the tiny drawing will take almost as long as if it were done on a much larger scale. Function 12-37 is designed to simplify a drawing by erasing anything that is smaller than a size you specify. When you run this function on a drawing, make sure you have a backup because the process is very destructive.

```
;This function takes a drawing of a floor plan of a building
;and removes any walls that are less than one foot long,
;simplifying the drawing so it can be shown at reduced scale.
;It also removes the second line of parallel wall lines, as
;well as all blocks that are not named in KEEPBLK list.

;variable names
;e      current entity
;lname  current entity layer name
;enttyp current entity type
;blknm  block name if current entity is insert
;wlen   length of line if current entity is a line
;wang   angle of line if current entity is a line (combine?)
;cent   center point of line if current entity is a
;       line (combine?)
;sp1    one corner of crossing box
;sp2    opposite corner of crossing box
;ss1    selection set in crossing box
;sscnt  counter for ssname
;ssent  entity name for current ssname
;keeplay  list of layers to keep
;keepblk  list of blocks to keep
(defun c:simp ()
    (setq cnt 0)
    (setq notss nil)
    (setq keeplay '("HOLD" "ARWALL" "AWALL1"
                    "CENTERL" "ARSPACE" "ARDOOR"))
    (setq keepblk '("DOOR" "DDOOR" "B1" "B2"
                    "SPACEID" "ID1" "GRIDNO"
                    "AID" "AID2" "AUD01D1S" "AUD02D1S"
                    "AUD03D1S" "AUD04D1S" "AUD05D1S"
                    "AUD06D1S"))
    (setq attribblk '("SPACEID" "ID1" "ID2"))
    (setq e (entnext))
    (while e
        (print cnt)
        (setq enttyp (cdr (assoc 0 (entget e))))
        (setq lname (cdr (assoc 8 (entget e))))
        (if (equal enttyp "INSERT")
            (setq blknm (cdr (assoc 2 (entget e))))
            (setq blknm nil)
        )
        (cond
            ((AND (equal enttyp "INSERT")
                  (not (member blknm keepblk)))
                       (entdel e)
                       (print "block deleted")
            )
            ((and (not (equal enttyp "INSERT"))
                  (not (member lname keeplay)))
                       (entdel e)
                       (print "line deleted")
            )
```

Function 12-37. Simplifying a drawing

```
          ((and (or (equal (substr lname 1 5) "AWALL")
                    (equal lname "ARWALL"))
                    (equal enttyp "LINE"))
               (setq wlen (distance
                             (cdr (assoc 10 (entget e)))
                             (cdr (assoc 11 (entget e)))))
               (print (cdr (assoc 0 (entget e))))
               (princ (cdr (assoc 8 (entget e))))
               (cond
                   ((<= wlen 10)
                       (entdel e)
                       (print "short wall deleted")
                   )
                   ((> wlen 10)
                       (setq wang (angle
                                   (cdr (assoc 10 (entget e)))
                                   (cdr (assoc 11 (entget e)))))
                       (setq cent (polar
                                   (cdr (assoc 10 (entget e)))
                                    wang (/ wlen 2)))
;the following two lines determine
;how far from each side of a wall line
;to search.  The number is set for 12
;inches to either side of the wall,
;but that distance can be changed.
                       (setq sp1
                         (polar cent (+ wang
                         (/ pi 2)) 12))
                       (setq sp2
                         (polar cent (- wang
                         (/ pi 2)) 12))
                       (setq ss1 nil)
                       (gc)
                       (setq ss1 (ssget "C" sp1 sp2))
                     (if ss1
                       (progn (print ss1)
                       (princ (sslength ss1))
                       (princ " ")
                       (princ (cdr (assoc 8 (entget
                       (ssname ss1 0)))))
                       (if (ssmemb e ss1)
                           (setq ss1 (ssdel e ss1))
                       )
                       (setq sscnt 0)
                       (princ (sslength ss1))
                       (repeat (sslength ss1)
                           (princ "repeating")
                           (setq ssent (ssname ss1 sscnt))
                           (cond
                               ((and
                                 (or
                                 (equal
```

Function 12-37. Simplifying a drawing (*continued*)

```
                                (substr (cdr
                                        (assoc 8 (entget ssent)
                                         )) 1 5) "AWALL")
                                        (equal
                                        (cdr
                                        (assoc 8 (entget ssent)
                                        )) "ARWALL"))
                                        (equal
                                        (cdr
                                        (assoc 0 (entget ssent)
                                        )) "LINE")
                                     (null (inters (cdr
                                       (assoc 10 (entget e)))
                                        (cdr
                                       (assoc 11 (entget e)))
                                        (cdr
                                       (assoc 10 (entget ssent)
                                       ))
                                       (cdr (assoc 11
                                            (entget ssent)))
                                            nil)))
                                           (if (<= (distance
                                           (cdr (assoc 10
                                                 (entget
                                                 ssent)))
                                           (cdr (assoc 11
                                                 (entget
                                                 ssent))))
                                                 wlen)
                                               (entdel ssent)
                                               (entdel e)
                                           )
                                       (print
                                       "wall line deleted")
                             )
                         )
                         (setq sscnt (1+ sscnt))
                     )
                     (setq notss nil)) (setq notss 1))
                 )
             )
         )
         ((member blknm attribblk)
             (setq ip (cdr (assoc 10 (entget e))))
             (setq blkno e)
             (setq e (entnext e))
             (while (not (equal (cdr (assoc 0 (entget e)))
             "SEQEND"))
                 (cond
```

Function 12-37. Simplifying a drawing (*continued*)

```
                    ((equal (cdr (assoc 2 (entget e)))
                    "AID")
                        (setq aid (cdr (assoc 1
                        (entget e))))
                    )
                )
                (setq e (entnext e))
            )
            (entdel blkno)
            (if (equal blknm "SPACEID")
              (progn
                (command "insert" "aid" ip 1 1 0 aid)
                (command "change" "l" "" "la" "ARSPACE")
              )
              (progn
                (command "insert" "aid2" ip 1 1 0 aid)
                (command "change" "l" "" "la" "ARWSPACE")
              )
            )
        )
        ((equal blknm "GRIDNO")
            (setq ip (cdr (assoc 10 (entget e))))
            (command "scale" e "" ip 2)
        )
    );end of first cond
    (setq e (entnext e))
    (setq cnt (1+ cnt))
  )
)
```

Function 12-37. Simplifying a drawing (*continued*)

As long as you carefully preserve your original drawing by making a copy of it, this function will tear through your work like termites through a sugar shack. After the drawing has been simplified, you will be able to plot a small-scale version of it without taking nearly as long or bleeding your pens. The following is a list of the objects that are deleted, and how the deletion is accomplished in each case:

- The "simp" function will delete every wall line that is less than ten inches long. It will look for every wall line pair and delete the shortest one.

Every block that is not on the list called "keepblk" will be deleted. All of the "spaceid" blocks will be changed into numbers that can be read when the drawing is reduced in scale. The "simp" function will enlarge grid line bubbles 2.5 times. Any entity that is not a block and is not on one of the layers listed in the list "keeplay" will be deleted. You can add or delete names from the lists "keeplay," "keepblk," and "attribblk" to control what is deleted and retained in your drawing.

It is important to note that on some buildings, particularly those of "tilt-up" construction, the exterior walls may have been constructed with blocks. These block names should be added to the "keepblk" list before you run "simp" on those drawings.

When the "simp" function finds a wall line, it looks for a wall line that is no more than 12 inches away from and parallel to the first line. This takes time if the drawing is large. Here is a method to reduce that time. First, turn off all of the layers with the following command:

Command: **layer off ***

Then, turn on only the layer named ARWALL. Write the entire visible drawing (wall lines only) to your hard disk using the coordinates 0,0 as the base. Turn the layers *on* and save your original drawing. Then load the drawing that you wrote as a block. Run the "simp" function on that drawing by entering the following:

Command: **load "simp"**

After the function has loaded, run it by entering "simp" on the command line. After "simp" has finished, save the drawing.

Next, load the original drawing (the one that you wrote the "arwall" layer to) and *as soon as the drawing has been loaded,* enter the following:

Command: **purge**

The PURGE command will only work if it is the first command used. Load and run the "simp" function on this drawing file. After the "simp" function has finished, you can insert the simplified wall layer back into the drawing by using the INSERT command and 0,0 coordinates for the insertion point.

Drawing Generation

You can use AutoLISP to create very elaborate functions. You can even create functions that draw entire drawings following rules, thus saving you the work. It is not easy to generalize about entire drawings, but there are some instances where the rules are simple enough to permit you to do a lot of work with very little input.

You should be careful about over-generalization in the creation of automatic drawing systems. Remember, computers cannot "think" in the complex ways that you can. Perhaps hundreds of years from now they will, but the current crop of computers—even the fastest, most expensive ones—are not very "intelligent." If you keep in mind that the computer is a tool, not a human being, you will be on the right track.

Several good examples of what you can do to generate automatic drawings are shown here. You can create complex geometry like stars, and you can create grids to use as the bases for building floor plans and elevation drawings. You can even go beyond these simple tasks, but there are limits. Beware of any system that, like an "intelligent" being, takes over very complex tasks. At least, if you will automate to that extent, be very, very careful to check the results each time you work with the system.

Creating Stars

Function 12-38, which creates the command "star," can be used to create stars rather than polygons. A star has all points on its perimeter connected to all other points except adjacent points. A polygon has all points connected only to adjacent points around the perimeter.

```
;This function draws a star given the number of parts.  Star
;calls starl, which will produce stars of N points, given the
;length of one side.  Stell will produce stellated polygons
;given the center point, inner radius and outer radius.

(defun c:star ()
    (setq vrtlst ())
    (setvar "BLIPMODE" 0)
    (setq pts (getint "\nEnter number of points for star: "))
    (starl pts)
)
(defun c:stell ( / vrtlst pts cen radl circl rad2 circ2
                                                inang outang)
    (setq vrtlst ())
    (setvar "BLIPMODE" 0)
    (setq pts (getint "\nEnter number of points for star: "))
    (setq cen (getpoint "\nPick center point of star: "))
    (setq radl (getdist cen "\nInner radius of star: "))
    (command "CIRCLE" cen radl)
    (setq circl (entlast))
    (setq rad2 (getdist cen "\nOuter radius of star: "))
    (command "CIRCLE" cen rad2)
    (setq circ2 (entlast))
    (setq outang 0)
    (setq vrtlst (cons (polar cen 0 rad2) vrtlst))
    (setq inang (+ outang (/ (* pi 2) (* 2 pts))))
    (repeat (1- pts)
        (setq vrtlst (cons (polar cen inang radl) vrtlst))
        (setq outang (+ outang (/ (* pi 2) pts)))
        (setq vrtlst (cons (polar cen outang rad2) vrtlst))
        (setq inang (+ inang (/ (* pi 2) pts)))
    )
    (setq vrtlst (cons (polar cen inang radl) vrtlst))
    (entdel circl)
    (entdel circ2)
    (dpoly vrtlst t)
)


(defun starl (pts / len vrt sang nxtang vrtlst)
    (setq len (getreal "\nEnter length of side: "))
    (setq vrt (getpoint "\nPick starting point; "))
    (setq sang (/ (* pi 2) pts))
    (setq nxtang sang)
    (setq vrtlst (cons vrt vrtlst))
    (repeat  (1- pts)
        (setq vrt (polar vrt nxtang len))
        (setq vrtlst (cons vrt vrtlst))
        (setq nxtang (- nxtang sang))
        (setq vrt (polar vrt nxtang len))
```

Function 12-38. Creating stars

```
            (setq vrtlst (cons vrt vrtlst))
            (setq nxtang (+ nxtang (* sang 2)))
        )
        (setq vrt (polar vrt nxtang len))
        (setq vrtlst (cons vrt vrtlst))
        (dpoly vrtlst t)
)
(defun dpoly (vrtlst cflag / vrt)
        (setvar "CMDECHO" 0)
        (if cflag
            (setq vrtlst (cons "C" vrtlst))
            (setq vrtlst (cons "" vrtlst))
        )
        (setq vrtlst (cons "PLINE" (reverse vrtlst)))
        (foreach vrt vrtlst (command vrt))
)
```

Function 12-38. Creating stars (*continued*)

A variation of "star," called "stell," produces stellated polygons that have internal and external radii. The "stell" command shows how you can generate very complex geometry with AutoLISP.

Creating Structural Grids

Function 12-39 shows a command called "strcgrid." This command will quickly generate a structural grid for laying out column centers on a structural plan drawing. The function is useful for engineering and architectural applications. You have a choice of numbered or lettered bubbles. In structural drawings, you will often see numbered bubbles along the north side of a building and numbered bubbles along the west side. Thus, you can refer to a column location as "E4," for example.

"strcgrid" is an example of a command that actually generates a major part of a drawing. You can probably come up with many such helpful generators yourself. Just think about the things in your drawings that you do perfunctorily and see if some of the boredom of doing them can be assigned to the computer.

```
;This command will do a structural grid, complete with
;numbered bubbles, for a building floor plan.  It will draw
;the grid, then automatically number north, south, east, and
;west bubbles.  You have the choice of numerical or lettered
;bubbles.
;
(defun c:strcgrid ()
        (setq inscol "N")
        (command "undo" "group")
        (setq strt (getpoint
          "\nIndicate lower left corner of building: "))
        (setq nobayhg (getint "\nNumber of Bays High: "))
        (setq nobaywd (getint "\nNumber of Bays Wide: "))
        (setq bayht (getdist strt "\nHeight of bay: "))
        (setq baywd (getdist strt "\nWidth of bay: "))
        (setq xtrln (getdist strt
      "\nDistance between grid bubbles and exterior walls: "))
        (calcgrid)
        (setq ds "N")
        (setq ds (strcase (getstring
          "\nReset drawing size?<N> ")))
        (if (= ds "Y")
                (allzoom)
        )
        (setq inbub "Y")
        (setq lpfl t)
        (while (not (= (strcase inbub) "N"))
          (setq inbub (strcase (getstring
            "\nInsert Gridline Bubbles?<Y> ")))
          (if (not (= (strcase inbub) "N"))
              (progn
                (insrtbub)
                  (setq inbub "Y")
                )
                  (setq lpfl nil)
                )
        )
        (command "undo" "end")
        (strcnil)
        (gc)
)
(defun calcgrid ()
        (setq xgln (+ (* nobayhg bayht) (* xtrln 2)))
        (setq ygln (+ (* nobaywd baywd) (* xtrln 2)))
```

Function 12-39. Creating structural grids

```
        (setq xglst (list (car strt) (- (cadr strt) xtrln)))
        (setq yglst (list (- (car strt) xtrln) (cadr strt)))
        (setq lstlay (getvar "CLAYER"))
        (command "layer" "s" "cntrline" "")
        (command "line" yglst
          (list (+ (car yglst) ygln) (cadr yglst)) "")
        (command "array" "l" ""  "r" (1+ nobayhg) "" bayht)
        (setq ylast (entlast))
        (command "line" xglst
          (list (car xglst) (+ (cadr xglst) xgln)) "")
        (command "array" "l" "" "r" "" (1+ nobaywd) baywd)
        (setq xlast (entlast))
        (command "layer" "s" lstlay "")
)
(defun insrtbub ()
        (command "osnap" "endpoint")
        (setq stbub (getpoint
          "\nPick end of first gridline in run: "))
        (command "osnap" "none")
        (setq ssgr (ssget "c"
          (list (1+ (car stbub)) (1+ (cadr stbub)))
          (list (1- (car stbub)) (1- (cadr stbub)))))
        (setq stline (entget (ssname ssgr 0)))
        (if (> (distance (cdr (assoc 10 stline)) strt)
          (+ xtrln 12))
          (setq ardir 0)
          (setq ardir 1)
        )
        (setq sc (getvar "userr5"));change this later
        (setq orang (angle
          (cdr (assoc 10 stline)) (cdr (assoc 11 stline))))
        (if (= (fix orang) 3) (setq xyflag 1))
        (if (= (fix orang) 0) (setq xyflag 1))
        (if (= (fix orang) 1) (setq xyflag 0))
        (if (= (fix orang) 4) (setq xyflag 0))
        (if (< (distance stbub (cdr (assoc 10 stline)))
          (distance stbub (cdr (assoc 11 stline))))
          (setq offbub (- (* sc 12)))
          (setq offbub (* sc 12))
        )
        (setq numtyp "N")
        (setq letterstring '("A" "B" "C" "D" "E"
            "F" "G" "H" "I" "J" "K"
            "L" "M" "N" "O" "P" "Q"
            "R" "S" "T" "U" "V" "W" "X" "Y" "Z"
            "AA" "BB" "CC" "DD" "EE" "FF" "GG"
            "HH" "II" "JJ" "KK" "LL"
            "MM" "NN" "OO" "PP" "QQ" "RR" "SS"
            "TT" "UU" "VV" "WW" "XX"
            "YY" "ZZ"))
```

Function 12-39. Creating structural grids (*continued*)

```
          (setq numtyp (getstring
    "\nEnter type of grid number <L>etter or <N>umber <N>: "))
         (if (= (strcase numtyp) "L")
                 (if (= xyflag 1)
                    (ltrbubbley nobayhg bayht)
                    (ltrbubblex nobaywd baywd)
                 )
                 (if (= xyflag 1)
                    (numberbubbley nobayhg bayht)
                    (numberbubblex nobaywd baywd)
                 )
         )
)
(defun numberbubbley (nb db)
        (setq strtnumb (getint
          "\nEnter starting grid number <0-99>: "))
        (setq cnt strtnumb)
        (setq insbub (list (+ offbub (car stbub)) (cadr stbub)))
        (repeat (1+ nb)
                (command "insert" "gridno" insbub sc sc 0 cnt)
                (if (= ardir 1)
                   (setq insbub (list
                     (car insbub) (+ (cadr insbub) db)))
                   (setq insbub (list
                     (car insbub) (- (cadr insbub) db)))
                )
                (setq cnt (1+ cnt))
        )
)
(defun numberbubblex (nb db)
        (setq strtnumb (getint
          "\nEnter starting grid number <0-99>: "))
        (setq cnt strtnumb)
        (setq insbub (list (car stbub) (+ offbub (cadr stbub))))
        (repeat (1+ nb)
                (command "insert" "gridno" insbub sc sc 0 cnt)
                (if (= ardir 1)
                   (setq insbub
                     (list (+ (car insbub) db) (cadr insbub)))
                   (setq insbub
                     (list (- (car insbub) db) (cadr insbub)))
                )
                (setq cnt (1+ cnt))
        )
)
(defun ltrbubbley (nb db)
        (setq strtnumb "A")
        (setq strtnumb (strcase (getstring
               "\nEnter starting grid letter <A-ZZ>: ")))
        (setq letterstring (cdr (member strtnumb letterstring)))
        (setq cnt strtnumb)
```

Function 12-39. Creating structural grids (*continued*)

```
        (setq insbub (list (+ offbub (car stbub)) (cadr stbub)))
        (repeat (1+ nb)
                (command "insert" "gridno" insbub sc sc 0 cnt)
                (if (= ardir 1)
                   (setq insbub (list
                     (car insub) (+ (cadr insbub) db)))
                   (setq insbub (list
                     (car insub) (- (cadr insbub) db)))
                )
                (setq cnt (car letterstring))
                (setq letterstring (cdr letterstring))
        )
)
(defun ltrbubblex (nb db)
        (setq strtnumb "A")
        (setq strtnumb (strcase (getstring
               "\nEnter starting grid letter <A-ZZ>: ")))
        (setq letterstring (cdr (member strtnumb letterstring)))
        (setq cnt strtnumb)
        (setq insbub (list (car stbub) (+ offbub (cadr stbub))))
        (repeat (1+ nb)
                (command "insert" "gridndo" insbub sc sc 0 cnt)
                (if (= ardir 1)
                   (setq insbub (list
                     (+ (car insbub) db) (cadr insbub)))
                   (setq insbub (list
                     (- (car insbub) db) (cadr insbub)))
                )
                (setq cnt (car letterstring)))
                (setq letterstring (cdr letterstring))
        )
)
(defun allzoom ()
        (setq maxex (getvar "extmax"))
        (setq minex (getvar "extmin"))
        (setvar "limmax" (list (+ (car maxex) 96)
        (+ (cadr maxex) 96)))
        (setvar "limmin" (list (- (car minex) 96)
        (- (cadr minex) 96)))
        (command "zoom" "a")
)
(defun strcnil ()
        (setq calcgrid nil insrtcol nil insrtbub nil
        numberbubbley nil)
```

Function 12-39. Creating structural grids (*continued*)

```
        (setq numberbubblex nil ltrbubbley nil ltrbubblex
        nil allzoom nil)
        (setq C:strcgrid nil)
)
```

Function 12-39. Creating structural grids (*continued*)

Creating Curtain Wall Grids

Like structural grids, curtain wall grids are used to locate modular building elements. Of course, in the case of a curtain wall, the elevation view of the building is shown. A curtain wall is a glazed area on a building that is, like a curtain, suspended from the building structure. The curtain wall is actually a structure in itself and must be aligned on a modular grid. Function 12-40 draws such a grid for you. The command it creates is called "strfrnt."

```
;CURTAINWALL DRAWING ROUTINE
;This command draws a curtain wall with mullions and glazing
;lines according to your start point, endpoint and number of
;lites.

(defun c:strfrnt ( / b e f g a c d h
          i j k l)
        (setq lstlay (getvar "clayer"))
        (princ "\nEnter height of window<") (setq z wht)
        (if wht (princ (rtos wht 4 2)) (princ "0"))
        (setq wht (getdist ">: "))
        (cond ((null wht) (setq wht z)))
        (setq a (getpoint
          "\nPick starting point of curtain wall: "))
        (setq b (getpoint a
          "\nPick ending point of curtainwall: "))
        (setq c (distance a b))
        (setq d (angle a b))
        (setq e (getpoint
          "\nPick exterior side of curtain wall: "))
        (princ "\nEnter width of mullion <") (setq f wmull)
        (if wmull (princ wmull) (princ "0"))
```

Function 12-40. Creating curtain-wall grids

```
      (setq wmull (getreal ">: "))
    (cond ((null wmull) (setq wmull f)))
    (princ "\nEnter depth of mullion (frame thickness) <")
      (setq g dmull)
    (if dmull (princ dmull) (princ "0"))
      (setq dmull (getreal ">: "))
    (cond ((null dmull) (setq dmull g)))
    (setq h (getint "\nEnter total number of lites: "))
    (if (and (= d 0.0) (> (angle a e) pi))
      (setq d (* pi 2)))
    (if (< (angle a e) d)
            (setq i 0)
            (setq i 1)
    )
(setq al '(progn
    (setq j (/ (- c (* wmull (1+ h))) h))
    (setq k (polar a d (/ wmull 2)))
    (if (= i 0)
      (setq L (polar
          (polar a (+ d (/ pi 2)) (/ dmull 2))
          d wmull))
    (setq L (polar
          (polar a (- d (/ pi 2)) (/ dmull 2))
          d wmull))
    )
    (command "layer" "s" "AWIND" "" "elev"
      (- (getvar "userr4") wht) wht)
    (if (equal i 0)
       (command "insert" "stffrm" a "xyz" c dmull
         wht (* d (/ 180 pi)))
       (command "insert" "stffrm" a "xyz" c
         (- dmull) wht (* d (/ 180 pi)))
    )
    (repeat h
      (if (= i 0)
       (command "insert" "cwmull" k "xyz" wmull
         dmull wht (* d (/ 180 pi)))
       (command "insert" "cwmull" k "xyz" wmull
         (- dmull) wht (* d (/ 180 pi)))
     )
     (command "line" L (polar L d j) "")
     (setq k (polar k d (+ j wmull)))
     (setq L (polar L d (+ j wmull)))
    )
      (if (= i 0)
         (command "insert" "cwmull" k wmull dmull
           (* d (/ 180 pi)))
         (command "insert" "cwmull" k wmull (- dmull)
```

Function 12-40. Creating curtain-wall grids (*continued*)

```
                (* d (/ 180 pi)))
            )
          (command "layer" "s" lstlay "" "elev" 0 0)
      ))
      (eval al)
  )
```

Function 12-40. Creating curtain-wall grids (*continued*)

Putting It All Together in 3D

Designing the Application
Creating the Symbol Library

THIRTEEN

Nothing illustrates the power and versatility of AutoCAD better than seeing how it can be used as the basis for a specific application. In previous chapters, you learned how to work with AutoCAD and how to control the program with AutoLISP. In this chapter, you will see how all of the various parts of AutoCAD's "open architecture" can be used to develop a practical AutoCAD application. You will also see how AutoCAD can be customized into a kitchen design and layout system. This system, when complete, allows the user to quickly lay out three-dimensional kitchen cabinets symbols on a floor plan, and then to change the styles of all of the cabinet fronts with a single command.

This chapter first provides you with an overview of what goes into the basic design of the system, and what parts of AutoCAD must be customized to implement this system. Next, you will be taken step-by-step through the process of developing a three-dimensional symbol library, designing and writing the AutoLISP code that manipulates those symbols, and writing the screen menus that control the system. Finally, you will learn how the AutoCAD Advanced User Interface works, how to develop your own pull-down menus and icon menus, and how to put it all together into a seamless, easy-to-use application system.

The kitchen design system described in this chapter is not meant to be a complete system, but simply an illustration of how a comprehensive application project can be designed and implemented. The basics are here, however, and it is left to you to develop this system, or one like it, to a point where it can be used in a professional environment.

Designing the Application

Before you start drawing symbols, or writing AutoLISP code, you must design your application. There are many excellent books available on software design, so this chapter will not cover a lot of theory. The most important thing to remember about a software application design is that you must have a very clear idea about what you want your software to do and a specific plan for achieving that result.

Defining the System

When you design an AutoCAD application, you must first decide exactly what you want it to be able to do. A preliminary description for the kitchen design system might be

> The system should be able to help you quickly develop a kitchen design by accurately inserting a series of different sized cabinet symbols into a three-dimensional floor plan of a kitchen. The system should be able to change the front styles of all the cabinets with a single command and be easy to use by someone who is not an AutoCAD expert. It should be able to produce presentation drawings for a client. And finally, the system should be able to produce a bill of materials for a given project.

This is a good general description, but now you must take each part of it and figure out exactly how each part should work.

Specific Design

First you need to decide how the three-dimensional symbols should look and what procedures should be used for inserting the symbols. The three-dimensional symbols should be as simple as possible, yet complete enough that they convey to the client an accurate picture of what the finished project will look like. The symbols must also be accurate so that the same presentation drawing (rotated to 2D) can be used to produce installation drawings. You will see how to actually draw these symbols later in this chapter.

The designer could insert the symbols into the drawing one at a time with the INSERT command, but there are several problems with that approach. First, it is much more difficult to accurately place symbols in a three-dimensional drawing than in a two-dimensional drawing because there are fewer visual cues in 3D (especially for a designer who is not very experienced with 3D). Second, it is preferable for the designer to develop the layout with the client, which would require a smooth routine for placing the symbols. Finally, several rules about how kitchen cabinets go together can be used to develop an AutoLISP routine to place the cabinets that would allow the designer to concentrate on the kitchen layout rather than on the mechanics of AutoCAD.

Here are some of the "rules" about how cabinets go together with which you can develop the AutoLISP routine for placing the symbols:

- Cabinets, of various widths, along with appliances, are placed in sequence along a wall.
- All base cabinets are the same depth.
- All base cabinets have countertops.
- All wall cabinets are attached to the wall and the top edges are all even with one another.
- All cabinets within a given class are identical in shape except for their width and style of front.

After you have analyzed how cabinets are laid out in a plan, you can then develop a procedure for placing the cabinets. Your outline of the procedure the designer might use to place a series of base cabinets against a wall might look like this:

1. The designer executes the base cabinet command and then is prompted to "Pick wall line for base cabinets."

2. The designer picks the desired line "Pick end of wall line to start cabinet run."

3. The designer picks a point at one end of the wall line to define the beginning of the run. Then the prompt "Pick a point inside the room." appears.

At this point, the cabinets could go on either side of the wall line. The last pick clears up that ambiguity. With these three picks, enough information has been gathered to determine the starting point of the cabinet run, and the direction and angle of the run. The designer may not want to start the cabinet run at the end of the wall line, so at this point, AutoCAD can prompt for a distance from the end of the wall line to start the cabinet run. From here on, the designer is prompted to pick a cabinet from the menu or to end the run.

There are a number of other factors to consider when laying out base cabinets, such as how to turn corners and how to place appliances, that will be left for you to develop. The AutoLISP routine for placing the base cabinets can be found at the end of this chapter.

Changing the cabinet fronts globally is simple if the design of the system is approached properly. Since the cabinets are identical except for the doors and/or drawer fronts, all you would do is make a separate symbol for the case and then a series of symbols for the various styles of fronts. You would then merely replace the cabinet front symbols with symbols of a different design. The AutoLISP routine for replacing the cabinet fronts is also found at the end of this chapter.

Now that you have seen what goes into the design of this system, you can follow along in the next few sections and develop your own version.

Creating the Symbol Library

To test and use the kitchen design system, you will need to make an assortment of base cabinet case symbols along with at least two different sets of cabinet front symbols to fit the cases. All of the symbols will be full three-dimensional symbols, and the insertion points will be at the lower left rear of the case.

Drawing the Cases

Before you draw the base cabinet symbols, you need to define four layers: BASE, CTOP, BASEDOOR, and ATTRIB.

In the AutoCAD drawing editor, with BASE set as the current layer, draw two polyline rectangles on top of one another as shown in Figure 13-1. Now place a point in the upper left corner of this figure with OSNAP ENDPoint. This point will be used as the base point of the block. Next, with the CHANGE

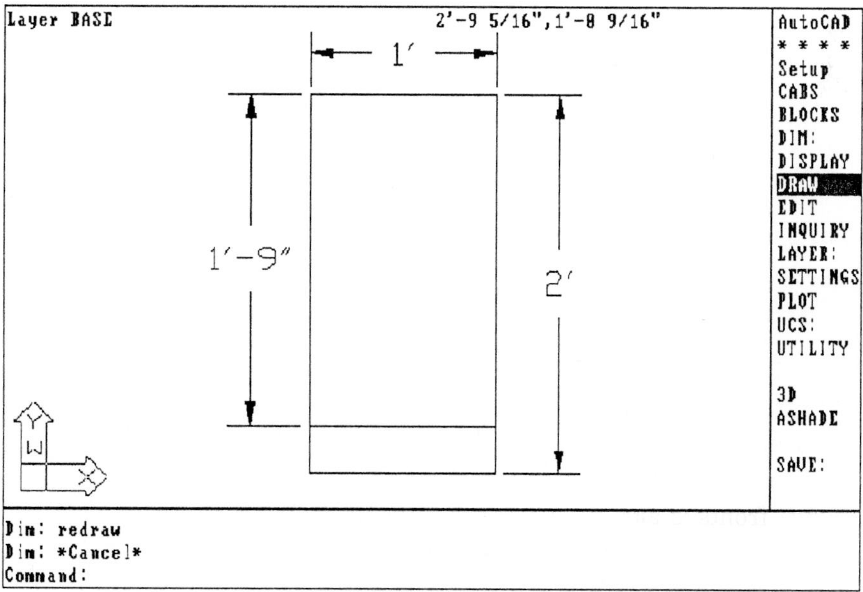

Figure 13-1. The start of the cabinet symbol

command, pick the smaller rectangle and change the thickness to 3.5 inches. Then pick the larger rectangle and change the elevation to 3.5 inches and the thickness to 31.5 inches, as shown in Figure 13-2. Use the VPOINT command to set the viewpoint to 4, −6,2. You should now have a drawing that looks like Figure 13-3.

At this point, you can save this view, so that it will be easier to return to it later, by entering

Command: **ucs**
Origin/ZAxis/3point/Entity/View/X/Y/Z/Prev/Restore/Save/Del/
?/<World>: **v**

This will make the User Coordinate System the same as this current view. Notice the UCS Icon in Figure 13-4 and compare it to the UCS Icon in Figure 13-3. Now you can save this current UCS by typing

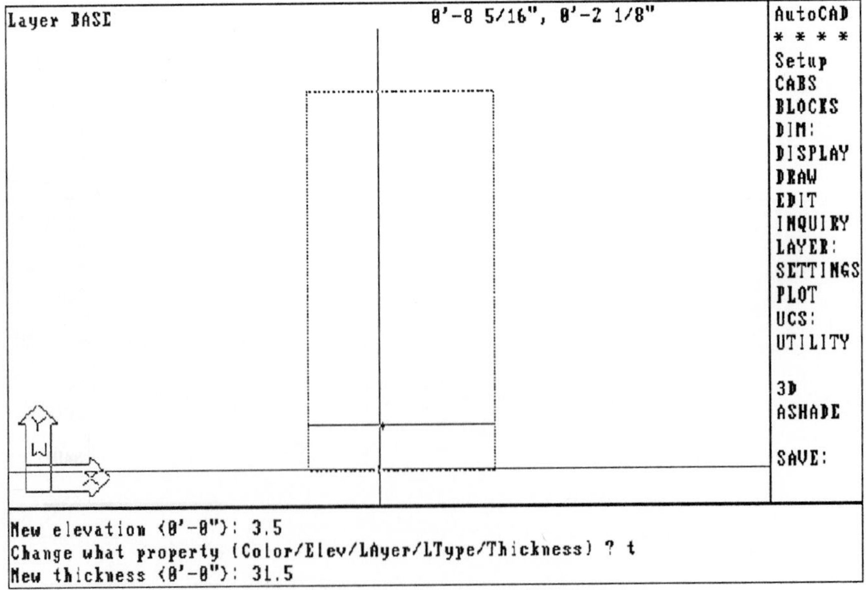

Figure 13-2. The symbol after changing thickness

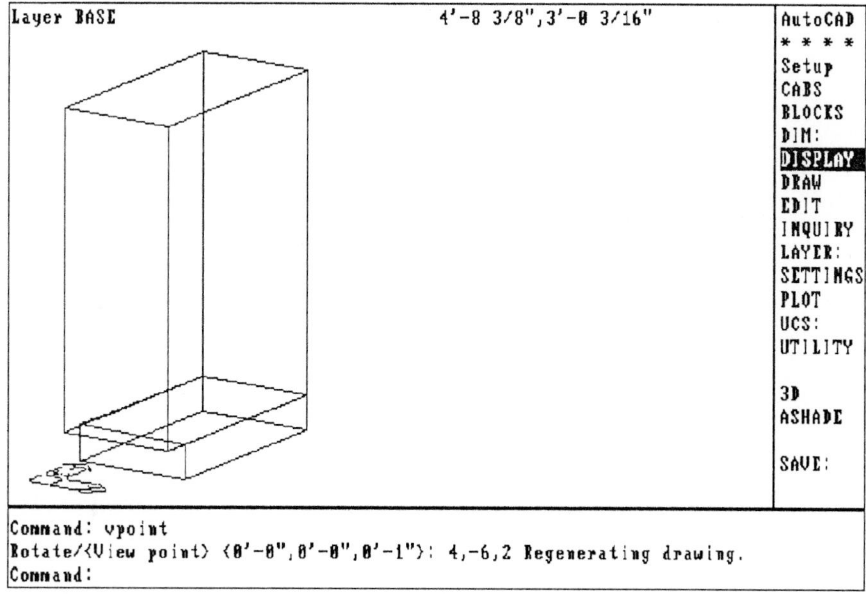

Figure 13-3. The symbol after setting the viewpoint

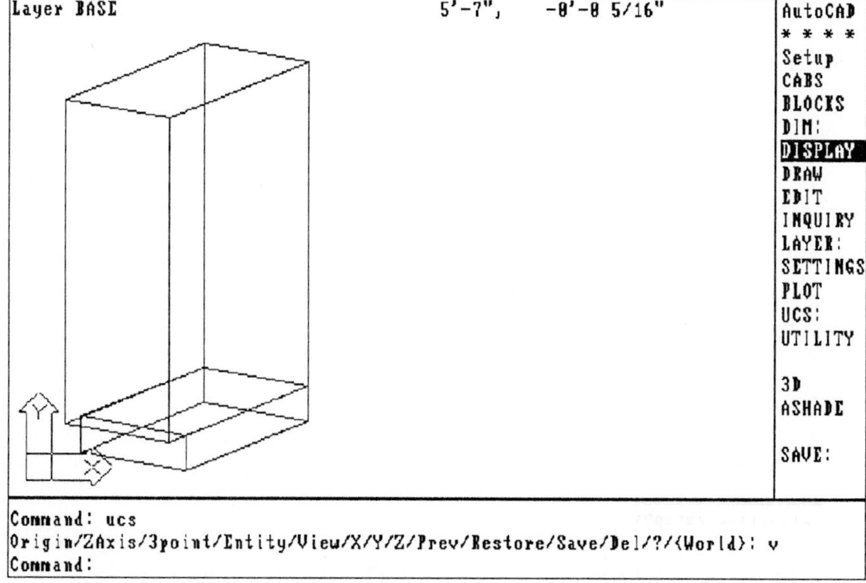

Figure 13-4. The UCS is now the same as the current view

```
Command: ucs
Origin/ZAxis/3point/Entity/View/X/Y/Z/Prev/Restore/Save/Del/
?/<World>: s
```

This will bring up the prompt

```
?/Name of UCS name: 3d
```

Enter a name for the view, such as "3D." This view can now be recalled at any time.

Now you will change the UCS so you can draw the cabinet door.

```
Command: ucs
Origin/ZAxis/3point/Entity/View/X/Y/Z/Prev/Restore/Save/Del/
?/<World>: 3
```

Enter **3** to the prompt to pick three points to determine the new UCS. Now, with OSNAP ENDPoint, pick the three points, in order, of the case drawing as shown in Figure 13-5, and the UCS will be aligned with the front face of the case. Notice that the UCS Icon in Figure 13-5 is now parallel to the front of the drawing. Save this UCS with the UCS SAVE command under the name "FRONT."

Drawing the Cabinet Fronts

Next, you can draw the slab face cabinet front by drawing two polyline rectangles on layer BASEDOOR as shown in Figure 13-6. Remember to change the thickness on these polylines to one inch. For the final touch, cover the face of these two rectangles with three-dimensional faces. Use the HIDE command to check your work. It should look like Figure 13-7. You have now drawn one base cabinet that will be the basis for all of the other base cabinet symbols.

With the COPY command, make a copy of your cabinet drawing and erase the bottom POLYLINE and 3DFACE entities on the copy. Your drawing should now look like Figure 13-8.

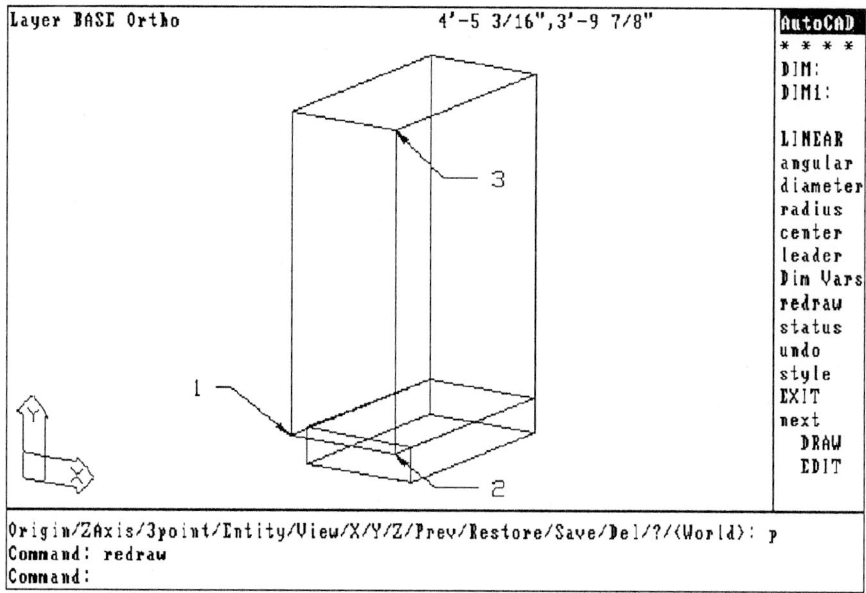

Figure 13-5. Pick these three points to align UCS

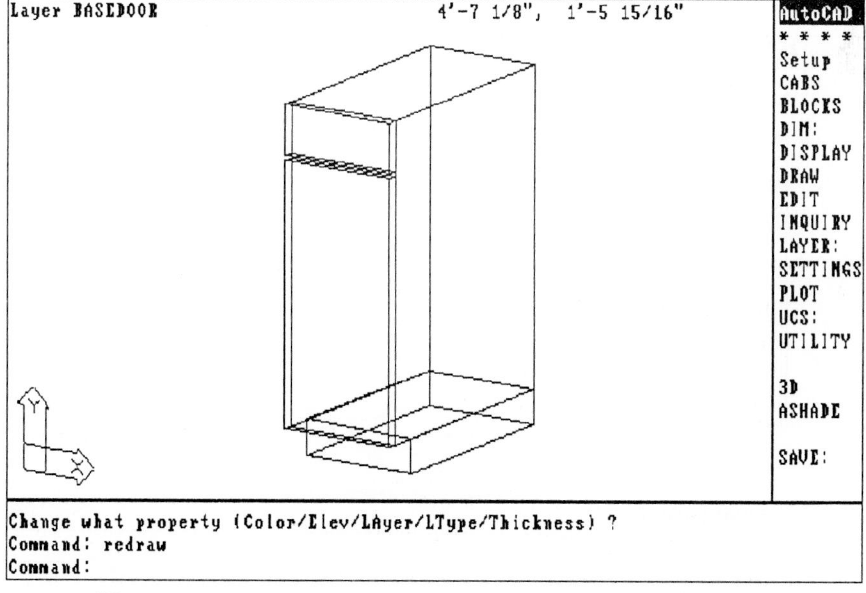

Figure 13-6. Drawing the slab face cabinet

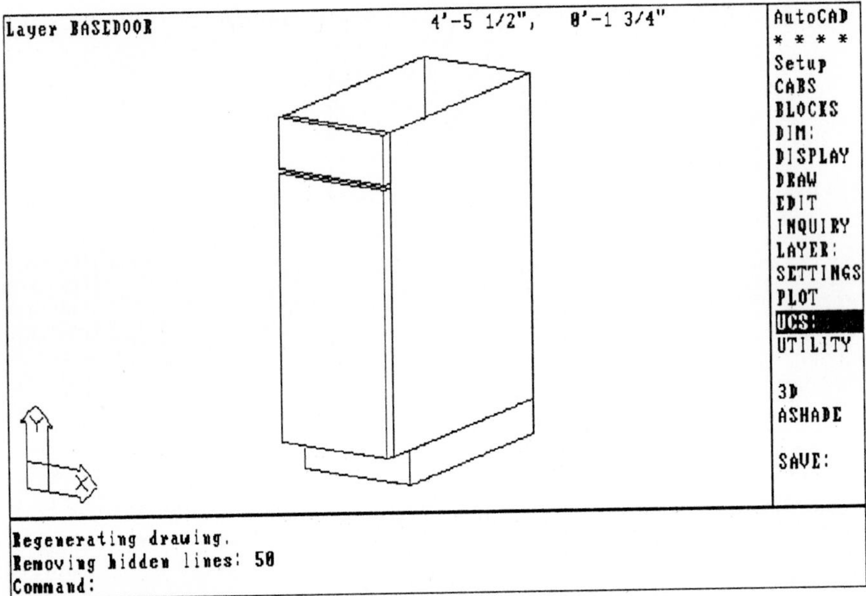

Figure 13-7. The cabinet after hidden lines were removed

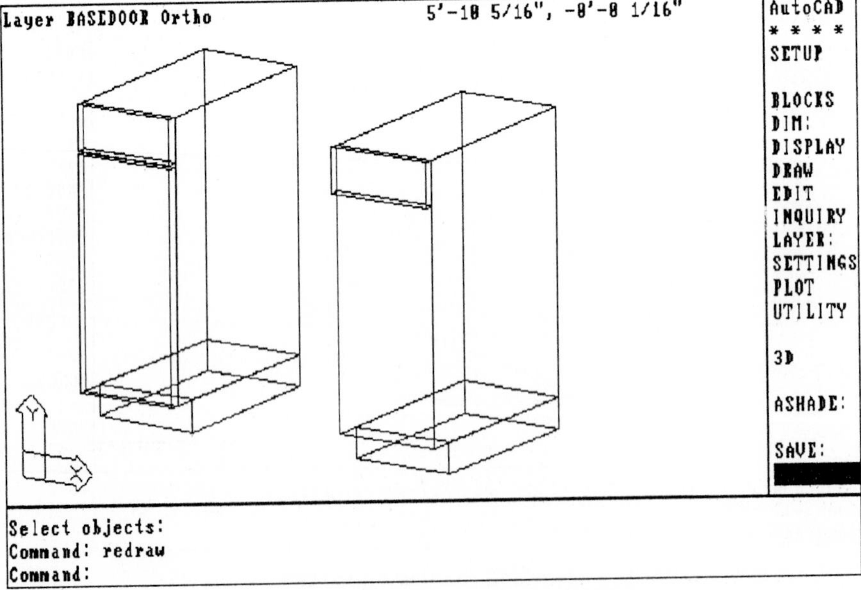

Figure 13-8. After copying the cabinet drawing

You can now draw the rail and doorfront stiles on the copied case drawing. The stiles (vertical members) are 2.5 inches wide by 26 inches high, and the rails are 2.5 inches high by 7 inches long. Draw the first rail and stile with polyline rectangles, use the CHANGE command to change the thickness to 1 inch, and add three-dimensional faces to the tops of these two rectangles. Your drawing will look like Figure 13-9. Copy the rail and stile as shown and add a 3DFACE entity in the center. Your drawing should now look like Figure 13-10.

Return the UCS and the viewpoint to the two-dimensional plan view by entering the UCS command, the letter "W," the PLAN command, and the letter "W" again.

Copy only the case part of the first cabinet (the two rectangles and point) to a point directly below the first cabinet, and move the second cabinet to a point directly above the first cabinet. Erase the two rectangles from each of the top two cabinet drawings (but not the points), and your drawing will look something like Figure 13-11.

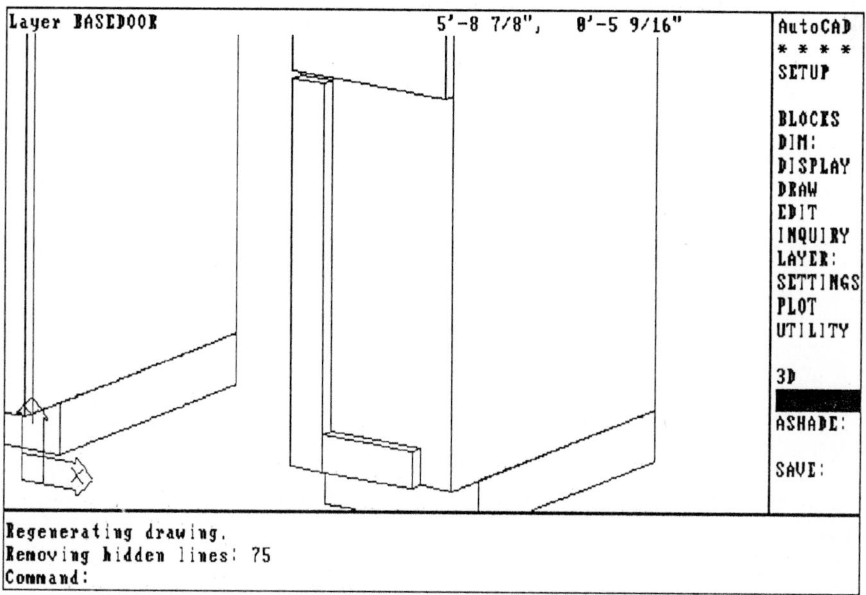

Figure 13-9. After drawing the rails and stiles

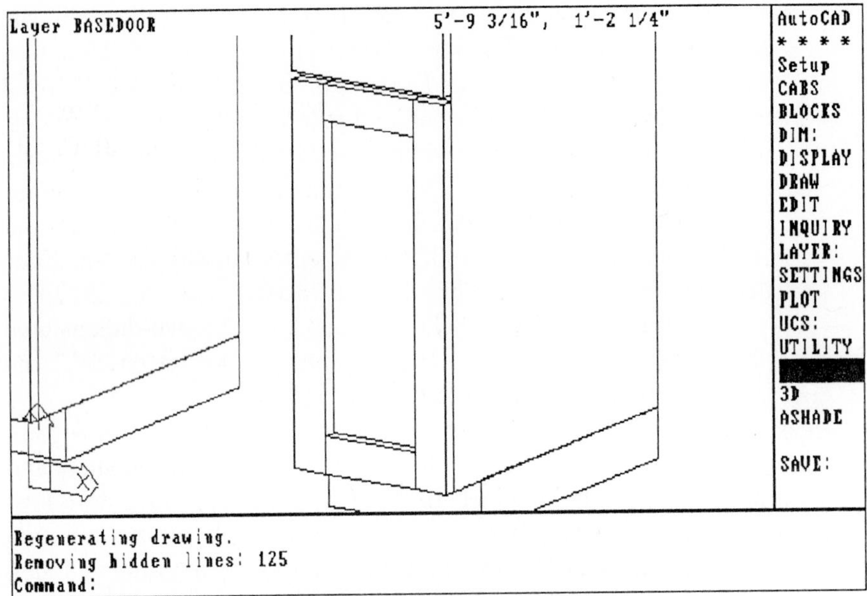

Figure 13-10. After adding a 3DFACE entity at the center

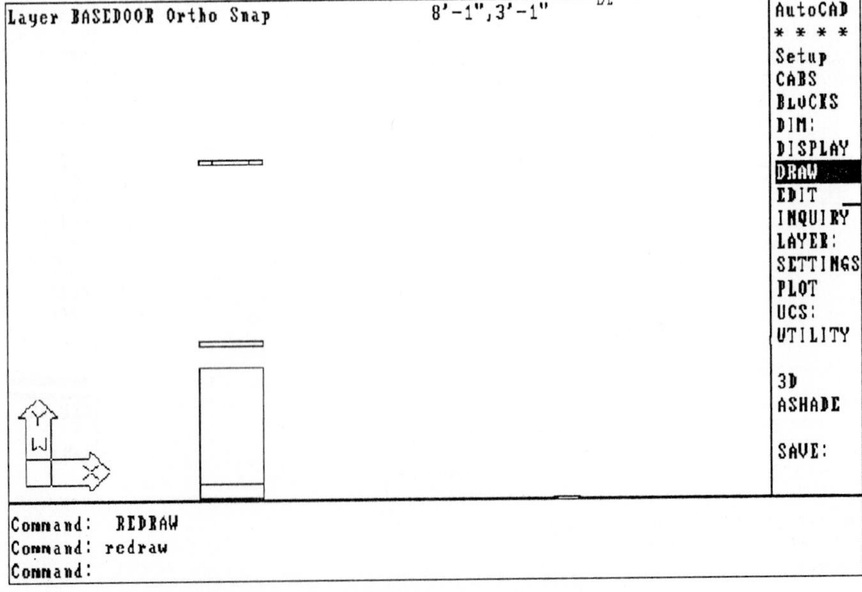

Figure 13-11. Separating the case part from the cabinet

Drawing the Countertop

Zoom in on the bottom figure (the case drawing) and set the current layer to CTOP to draw the countertop. The countertop, with backsplash and front lip, will consist of four 3DFACE entities with the edges that represent the sides of the countertop defined as invisible, so that when one cabinet block is placed against another, they will appear to be spanned by a one-piece countertop. With Figure 13-12 as a guide, draw a 3DFACE entity by using OSNAP ENDPoint and the "I" option where it is called for in the illustration. The procedure goes like this:

Command: **3dface**
First point: **end**
Second point: **i end**
Third point: **end**
Fourth point: **i end**
Third point:

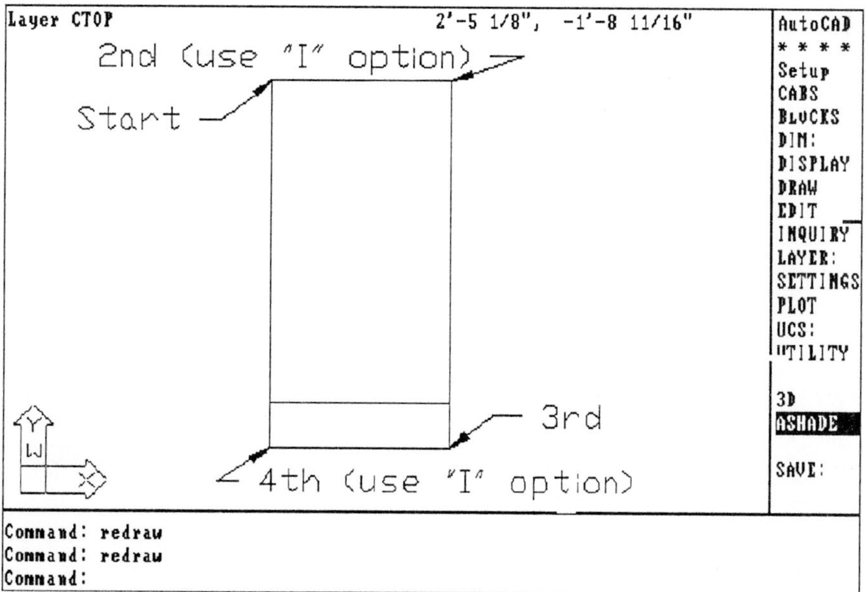

Figure 13-12. Drawing the countertop

Remember, the ENTER key is implied at the end of each of the preceding command entries. You use the "I" (invisible) option when you want the edge after the selected corner to be invisible. You just drew the 3DFACE entity on the floor. Now move it into position with the MOVE command:

Command: **move**
Select objects: **L**
Base point of displacement: **@0,0,0**
Second point of displacement: **@0,−1,36**

To place the next three 3DFACE entities accurately, you need to draw a few temporary lines. Set the current layer to 0, and draw a 1-inch by 12-inch polyline rectangle, using OSNAP ENDPoint to align it with the back of the countertop, as shown in Figure 13-13, and use the CHANGE command to change its thickness to 3.5 inches. Draw a line 12 inches long using OSNAP

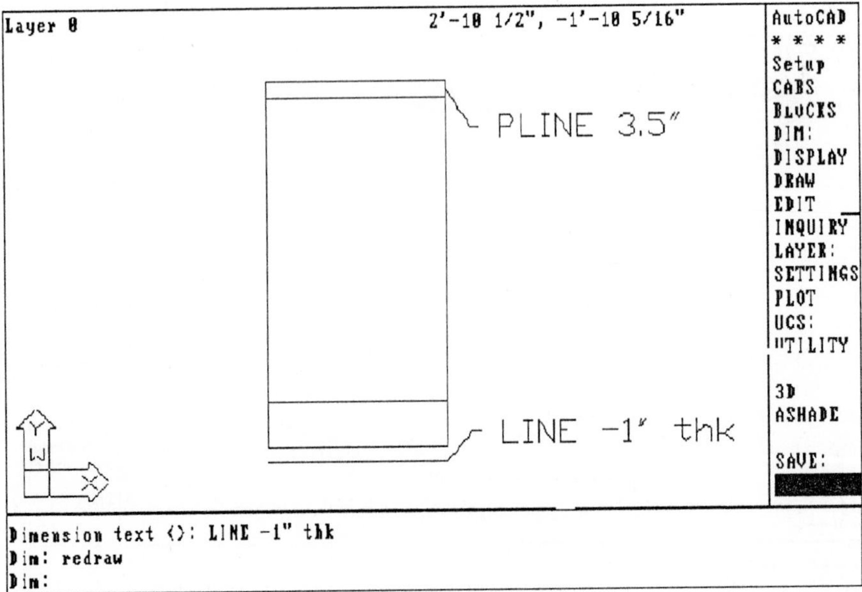

Figure 13-13. Drawing temporary lines

ENDPoint to align with the front edge of the countertop, and change the thickness of that line to −1 inch. Now restore your UCS to the one you saved as "3D," set the PLAN command for the current UCS, and zoom in on the case drawing. It should now look something like Figure 13-14 (hidden lines have been removed for clarity).

Reset the current layer to CTOP and, using the extruded polyline rectangle and the line as guides, construct three 3DFACE entities for the front edge, the backsplash face, and the backsplash top, making the side edges of these faces invisible. Turn off layer CTOP, erase the construction lines on layer 0, and then turn layer CTOP back on. Use the HIDE command to view your results—they should look like Figure 13-15.

Making Many Cabinets

Making the first cabinet was the hard part. Making six more cabinet symbols of varying widths is simple when you use the

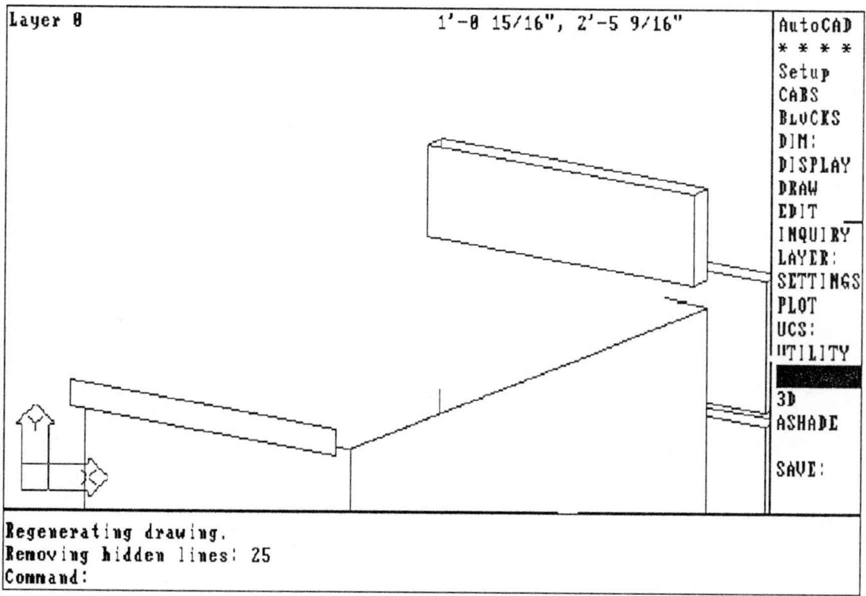

Figure 13-14. After zooming in on the case drawing

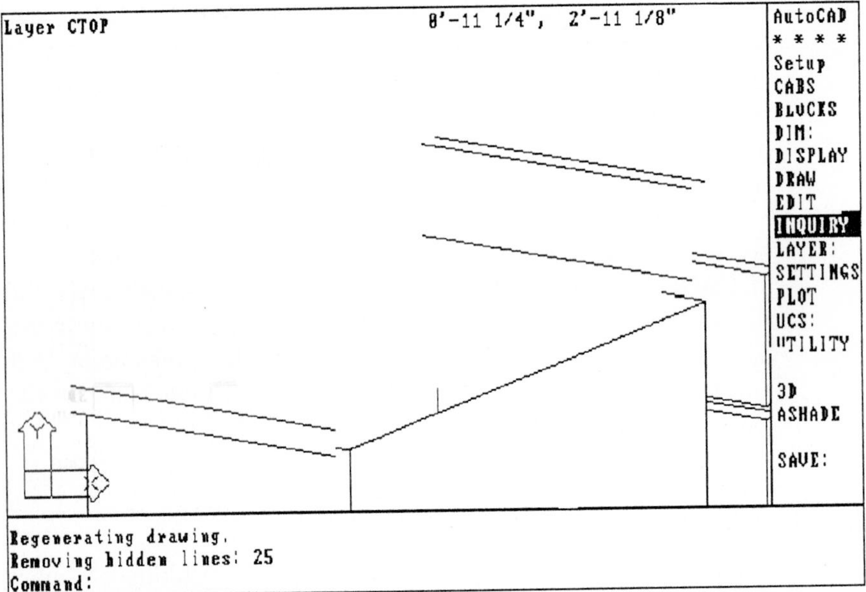

Figure 13-15. After adding the backsplash

ARRAY command to produce six more copies of the first cabinet, and then stretch each cabinet symbol with the STRETCH command to create the necessary sizes.

First, return to the World Coordinate System and the two-dimensional plan view. Next, use the ARRAY command to produce seven columns of cabinets and doors spaced 36 inches apart, as shown in Figure 13-16. Then use the STRETCH command to stretch the second through the seventh cabinets (and doors) to the right, as illustrated in Figure 13-17. Make sure that the left side of the crossing box goes through the center of the case and doors so that you will be stretching the rails and not one of the stiles in the door symbol. Each succeeding cabinet is three inches wider than the previous one. When you have stretched all of the cabinets and doors, your drawing should look like the one in Figure 13-18.

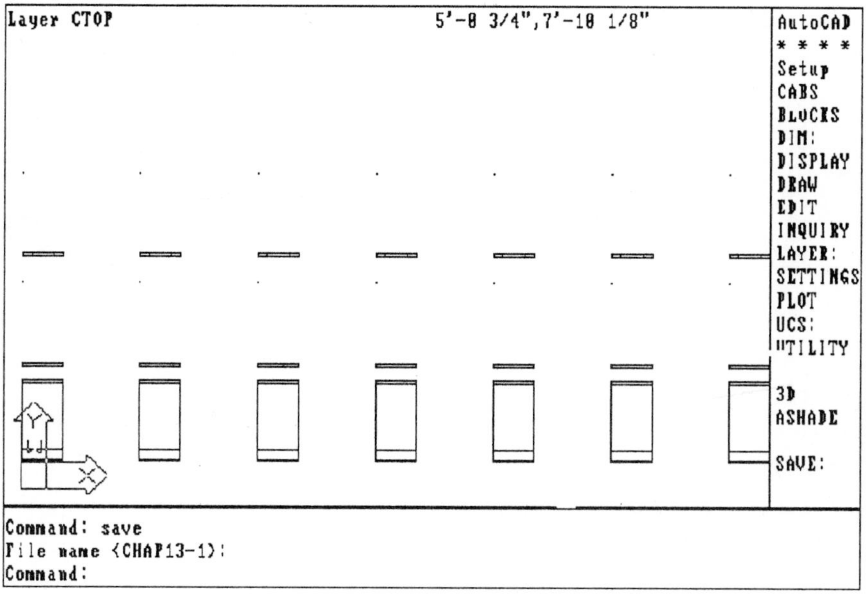

Figure 13-16. After using the ARRAY command

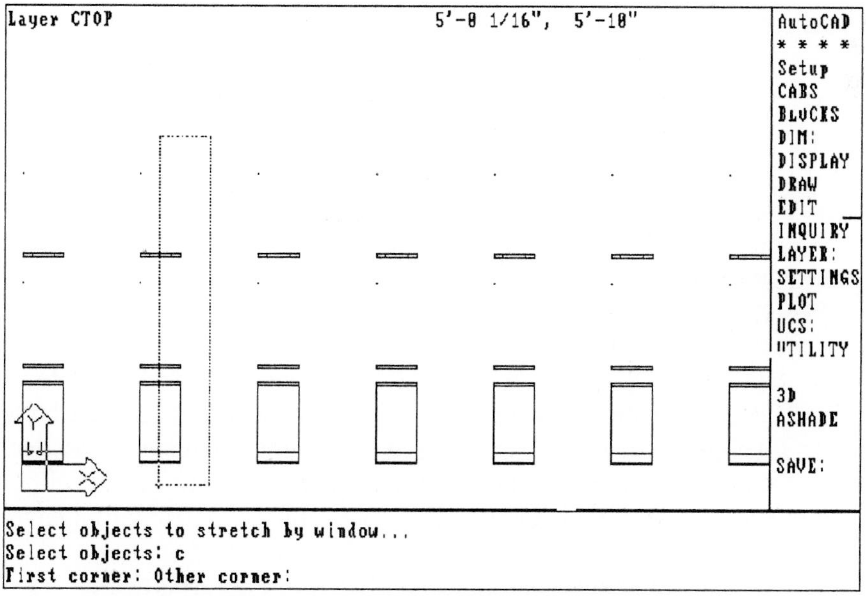

Figure 13-17. After using the STRETCH command

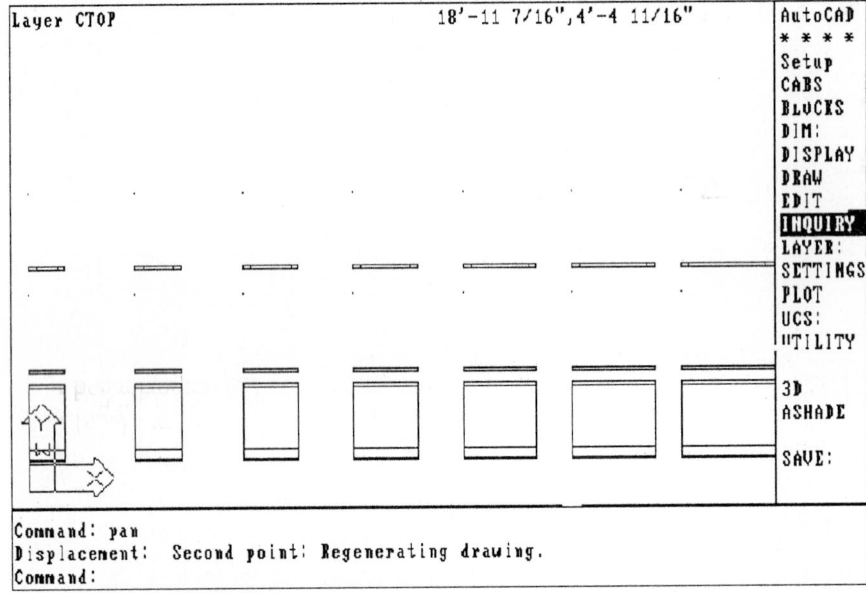

Figure 13-18. After stretching all cabinets and doors

Adding Attributes

One of the most important features of the kitchen design system is the designer's ability to quickly develop cost information for a proposed design. One of the biggest cost variables in a kitchen cabinet results from the style of the cabinet front. Using an elaborately carved hardwood door instead of a plain plastic laminate door could more than triple the project cost. Adding attributes to blocks will help you to work with such project cost variables.

Each block that is inserted into the drawing must contain data that describes what that block represents. This data is stored within the block itself in an entity called an attribute. Attributes are very flexible, and they can be defined almost any way that you want when you create the block. You can find out more about attributes by reading Chapter 9, "Attribute Management."

There should only be enough attribute information included within each block for each block insertion within a given drawing to be uniquely identified and keyed to a specific product. It is unwise, for example, to include the product pricing for each component as a symbol attribute, because you would have to update the price attribute for each block every time the prices changed. The only information that should be carried with the symbol is the product catalog number and some way to indicate the desired product finish.

Usually kitchen cabinets are ordered as a complete unit that includes the case and the front. Since this system has separate blocks for the case and the cabinet front, a method must be developed to combine the information for both the case and the cabinet front symbols into a complete product number. There are two ways to do this. The first is to extract all of the attribute data for the cases and the doors, and then combine the catalog number of the case with the catalog number of the door front to obtain a catalog number for the whole cabinet. The other way is to combine the case number attribute with the door number attribute when the door symbol is inserted, and to put the resulting number in an attribute record in the case block. This second method can be accomplished with an AutoLISP routine, as you will see later in this chapter.

The only attributes you really need are three for the case symbol and two for the door symbol. Here are the case symbol attributes:

PREFIX — This carries the base catalog number of the case.

CTLOGNO — This starts out blank, but will carry the complete catalog number, consisting of the base number, plus the front number, plus any added finish codes.

FINCODE — This will carry any desired finish code such as color and/or type of wood. This value will probably be the same for all of the cabinets in a project, so it can be added globally to all of the blocks at the end of the design session.

Next is a description of the cabinet front block attributes:

DRNO	This carries the catalog number of the door style. This number will be appended to the case PREFIX attribute in the CTLOGNO attribute.
FINCODE	This is the same as the case FINCODE except that it describes the finish of the front.

Now that you know what attributes are needed, you can add those attributes to your drawing. Figure 13-19 shows what the case and door attributes look like. All of the attributes are preset attributes, so you will not be prompted to enter attribute information when you insert the block. The attributes are all invisible except PREFIX. The attribute text for PREFIX and DRNO is three inches high, while the other attribute text is only one-half inch high. The DRNO attribute is large so that it will be easier to pick with the pick box to change the attribute value.

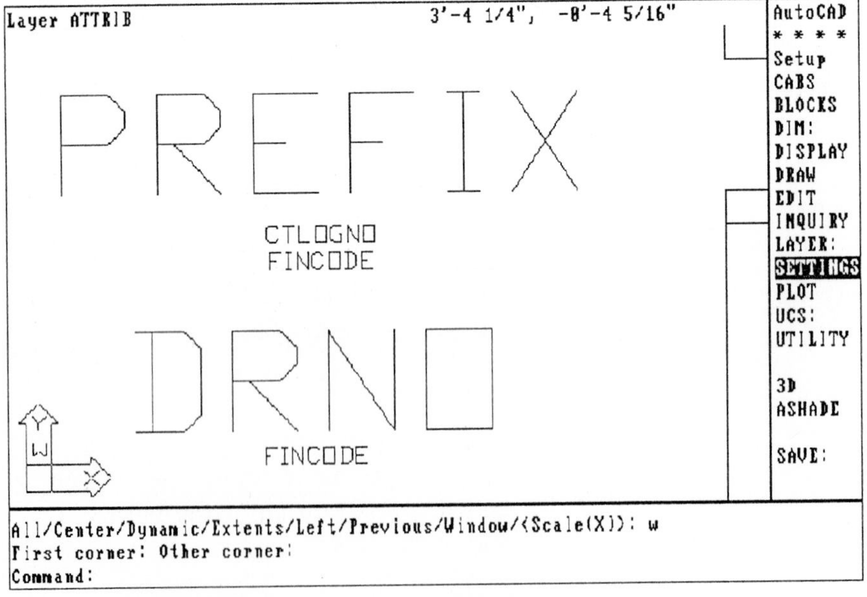

Figure 13-19. The case and door attributes

Use the ATTDEF command to define these attributes, as shown in Figure 13-19. If you have worked with 3D before, you may have noticed that if there is any text in a drawing, it will show through solid objects after the hidden lines have been removed with the HIDE command. If you give the text a little thickness, even as little as 1/100 inch, it will no longer show through any solids. So, add a little thickness to the PREFIX attribute definition with the CHANGE command.

The next step is to use the COPY command to copy these attributes to their assigned positions, as shown in Figure 13-20. Once these attribute definitions have been copied, you must use the CHANGE command to change the default attribute values of the PREFIX and DRNO attribute definitions to the proper product numbers. For the purposes of this illustrative system, product numbers B12 through B30 have been assigned for the case product numbers, the numbers RSB12 through RSB30 for the rail and stile front, and SFB12 through SFB30 for the plain cabinet fronts.

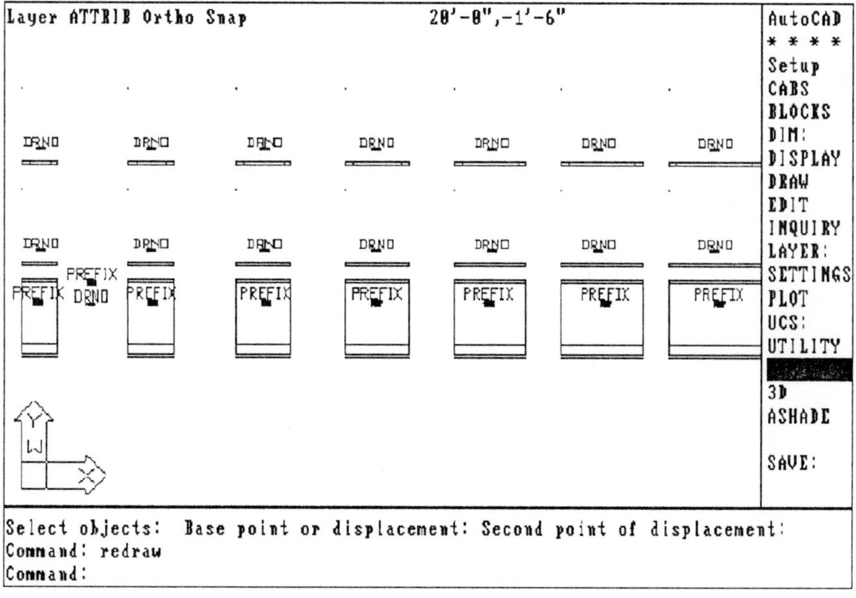

Figure 13-20. After copying attributes to their positions

Saving the Blocks

All you have left to do to create your symbol library is to save each of your case and door drawings as blocks with the BLOCK command, and then to write those blocks to your hard disk with the WBLOCK command so they can be used in other drawings.

The main consideration here is in how the blocks are named. When a block is inserted into a drawing, AutoCAD has very little information about that block except the file name. Therefore, the file names for these cabinet blocks should contain as much information about the block as possible so that when your AutoLISP program "reads" the block name, it can make a decision based on the information contained in that name.

For example, the block name for all of the base cabinet cases starts with "DBCB3" for the first five characters. The first character (or "D") might be a manufacturer's code. The next three characters ("BCB") define this block as a "Base CaBinet." The fifth character ("3") declares this to be a three-dimensional symbol. The last three characters describe the size of the block. The sixth character ("1") says that this is a standard height and depth (for a base cabinet), and the last two characters describe the width of the cabinet. Therefore, a block in this system named "DBCB3136" would be a standard size 36-inch wide, three-dimensional base cabinet symbol manufactured by a company whose code is "D."

Save each of the symbol drawings as blocks by using the OSNAP NODE to the point on the upper left corner as the block base (do not forget to include the point in the block). Use the following names:

- DBCB3112 through DBCB3130 for the cases
- DBRS3112 through DBRS3130 for the rail and stile fronts
- DBSF3112 through DBSF3130 for the plain cabinet fronts

Finally, use the WBLOCK command to write these 21 blocks to your hard disk.

Writing the AutoLISP Code

In order to implement the final system in AutoLISP, you will need to write code that is something like that shown in Functions 13-1 through 13-3. You should study these functions carefully and copy them for use with your AutoCAD system. If you do not wish to copy the code, you can purchase the companion disk for this book.

The code consists of several functions that work together to manage the kitchen cabinet design problem. The first function, shown as Function 13-1, contains the code necessary to install the base cabinets, one after the other, along a given wall. Function 13-2 shows the code needed to pick one of a number of cabinet types that appear as icons in an on-screen icon menu. The actual construction of the icon menu was already discussed. Finally, Function 13-3 shows the code necessary to replace cabinet doors, as described earlier.

The details of the code are left to you to extract. If you read the code, transcribe it, run it, and experiment by changing it, you will quickly come to understand how powerful AutoLISP can really be.

```
(defun basecab ()
    (setq start t)
    (setq off 0 wd 0)
    (setq ynlst '(0 13 32 78 89 110 121))
    (setq ylst '(0 13 32 89 121))
    (setq wln (car (entsel
         "\nPick wall line for base cabinets")))
    (setq pt1 (cdr (assoc 10 (entget wln))))
    (setq pt2 (cdr (assoc 11 (entget wln))))
    (setq tstend (getpoint
         "\n Pick end of wall line to start cabinet run: "))
    (if (< (distance pt1 tstend) (distance pt2 tstend))
        (setq stpt pt1 endpt pt2)
        (setq stpt pt2 endpt pt1)
    )
    (setq rotang (angle stpt endpt))
    (if (>= rotang (* pi 2)) (setq rotang (- rotang (* pi 2))))
    (setq runln (distance stpt endpt))
    (setq inpt (getpoint stpt
```

Function 13-1. The "basecab" function

```
          "\nPick a point inside the room"))
    (if (and (equal rotang 0.0)
             (> (angle stpt inpt) pi)
        )
        (setq rotang (* pi 2))
    )
    (if (< (angle stpt inpt) rotang)
        (setq dir 0)
        (setq dir 1 rotang (+ rotang pi))
    )
    (setq insang (* rotang (/ 180 pi)))
    (setq a nil)
    (prompt
  "\nDo you wish to offset first cabinet from the corner?<Y> ")
    (while (equal (member a ynlst) nil)
        (setq a (last (grread)))
    )
    (if (member a ylst)
        (progn
            (setq off (getreal "\nEnter offset distance: "))
            (if (equal dir 1)
                (setq stpt (polar stpt (- rotang pi) off))
                (setq stpt (polar stpt rotang off))
            )
        )
    )
    (setq runln (- runln off))
    (princ "\nPick first case from screen menu<") (princ runln)
    (setq bn (getstring ">: "))
    (setq wd (atoi (substr bn 7 2)))
    (if (equal dir 1)
        (setq stpt (polar stpt (- rotang pi) wd))
    )
    (command "insert" bn stpt 1 1 insang)
    (if (and (equal start t) (> off 0))
        (if (= dir 1)
            (command "insert" "lend" stpt 1 1 insang)
            (command "insert" "rend"
                 (polar stpt rotang wd) 1 1 insang)
        )
    )
    (if (equal dir 0)
        (setq stpt (polar stpt rotang wd))
    )
    (setq start nil)
    (setq cont t)
    (while cont
        (setq a nil)
        (prompt
             "\nDo you wish to continue this cabinet run?<Y> ")
```

Function 13-1. The "basecab" function *(continued)*

```
            (while (equal (member a ynlst) nil)
                (setq a (last (grread)))
            )
            (if (member a ylst)
                 (setq stpt (conins stpt dir))
                 (setq cont nil)
            )
        )
    )
```

Function 13-1. The "basecab" function *(continued)*

```
(defun conins (stpt dir)
    (setq runln (- runln wd))
    (princ "\nPick next case from screen menu<") (princ runln)
    (setq bn (getstring ">: "))
    (setq wd (atoi (substr bn 7 2)))
    (if (equal dir 1)
        (setq stpt (polar stpt (- rotang pi) wd))
    )
    (command "insert" bn stpt 1 1 insang)
    (if (equal dir 0)
        (setq stpt (polar stpt rotang wd))
        stpt
    )
)
```

Function 13-2. Function "conins" picks from a screen menu

```
(defun chgdoor (type)
    (setq doorlist '("RS" "SF"))
    (setq e (entnext))
    (while e
        (princ e)
        (if (equal (cdr (assoc 0 (entget e))) "INSERT")
            (progn
                (setq blnm (cdr (assoc 2 (entget e))))
                (setq bltyp (substr blnm 1 4))
                (if (equal bltyp "DBCB")
                    (progn
                        (setq ip (cdr (assoc 10 (entget e))))
                        (setq rotang (cdr (assoc 50
                             (entget e))))
                        (setq insang (* rotang (/ 180 pi)))
                        (setq wd (atoi (substr blnm 7 2)))
```

Function 13-3. Function "chgdoor" replaces a cabinet door

```
                              (setq ckss (ssget "C" (mapcar '1- ip)
                                      (mapcar '1+ ip)))
                              (setq cnt 0 delent nil)
                              (while (< cnt (sslength ckss))
                                  (setq tstent (ssname ckss cnt))
;if a door symbol exists delete it
                                  (if (equal (cdr (assoc 0
                                       (entget tstent))) "INSERT")
                                      (if (and (member (substr (cdr
                                           (assoc 2 (entget
                                               tstent))) 3 2)
                                                  doorlist)
                                          (not (equal (substr (cdr
                                               (assoc 2 (entget
                                                  tstent))) 4 1)
                                                  type)))
                                          (setq delent tstent)
                                      )
                                  )
                                  (setq cnt (1+ cnt))
                              )
                              (if delent
                                  (entdel delent)
                              )
                              (command "insert" (strcat type "31"
                                   (itoa wd))
                                  ip 1 1 insang)
                        )
                    )
                )
            )
    (setq e (entnext e))
    )
)
```

Function 13-3. Function "chgdoor" replaces a cabinet door *(continued)*

AutoCAD's Other Programming Languages

FOURTEEN

AutoLISP and custom menus are just two ways to make AutoCAD work for you. In this chapter, you will learn how to create your own text fonts, shape files, line styles, and hatch patterns. In addition, you will see how you can import other types of graphic data into AutoCAD.

Shape Files

With shape files, you can define a text font or define a library of simple symbols. Not many people involve themselves in the creation of shape files, perhaps because they think that it is too difficult a process. Actually, creating shape files is relatively simple, though developing some of the more complex and subtle shapes in certain fonts can be tedious.

Shape Files Versus Blocks

Shape files are similar to blocks in that a relatively complex figure can be inserted and moved about as one entity. There are, however, several major differences. A block is defined by using the BLOCK command, and by choosing any number of entities from a drawing to make up that block. The data vector description of that block resides within the drawing file in the BLOCK section. A shape, on the other hand, must be created outside of AutoCAD with the instructions for creating each shape written with a text editor. The description of that shape always remains in the shape file, and only a reference to that shape file exists in the drawing file.

Shapes are much more efficient to work with than blocks, because a shape's vector description is much more compact than that for a similar-looking block. Shapes are therefore significantly faster to generate within an AutoCAD drawing. Since the shape description itself is not in the AutoCAD drawing, the drawing files tend to be much smaller. For example, a block composed of 4 lines describing a square may take up as much as 320 bytes in the drawing file, but a shape definition of the same square can take up as few as 5 bytes (or as many as 13 bytes) in a shape file.

Shapes, however, have some serious limitations. Shapes cannot be exploded nor can they contain different layers. Also, shapes, unlike blocks, are not capable of carrying attribute information. Some actions that are very easy to achieve when you create a block are very difficult to do with a shape. For instance, if you want to show a hidden line in a block, you would simply define that line to have a hidden line type. With a shape, on the other hand, you would have to individually code each dashed section of that hidden line.

Use shapes to create simple symbols and text fonts. If you learn how to create your own shape (and font) files for your specific applications, you will find them to be a timesaver.

Shape File Format

Shape files are developed by using a text editor with certain codes to create an ASCII file of shape descriptions. As always with AutoCAD, you must use a straight ASCII text editor, not your word processor. A practical text editor is included on the companion disk for this book.

A shape file must have the file extension of SHP. When you have completed your shape description, you can then compile these shape descriptions (task 7 in the AutoCAD main menu) into SHX files and load them into AutoCAD for use.

You can have as many as 255 different shapes in a shape file, and each shape can consist of a maximum of 2000 bytes each. Shape files are nothing more than a description of how to move a "pen" over "paper" to draw a desired figure. For example, if you wanted to write instructions on how to draw a two-inch square on a piece of paper, it would probably go something like this:

1. Move the pen two inches to the north.
2. Move the pen two inches to the east.
3. Move the pen two inches to the south.
4. Move the pen two inches to the west.

Here is what a shape file description for the same set of instructions looks like:

```
*1,5,SQUARE
024,020,02C,028,0
```

As in this example, shape descriptions always begin with one asterisk. The two numbers that follow it are the shape number and the number of bytes in the shape description. Also on the first line, you will see the shape name, in this case "SQUARE." There will be more information about this later in the chapter. In the meantime, concentrate on the row of numbers separated by commas on the next line.

Figure 14-1 shows the square produced by the preceding shape file description. Notice how each number in the description relates to each line in the drawing.

Although this seems very cryptic at first, you will see that the coding is really very simple. There are two types of codes in shape files: vector encoded bytes and command codes. The shape description here consists entirely of vector encoded bytes.

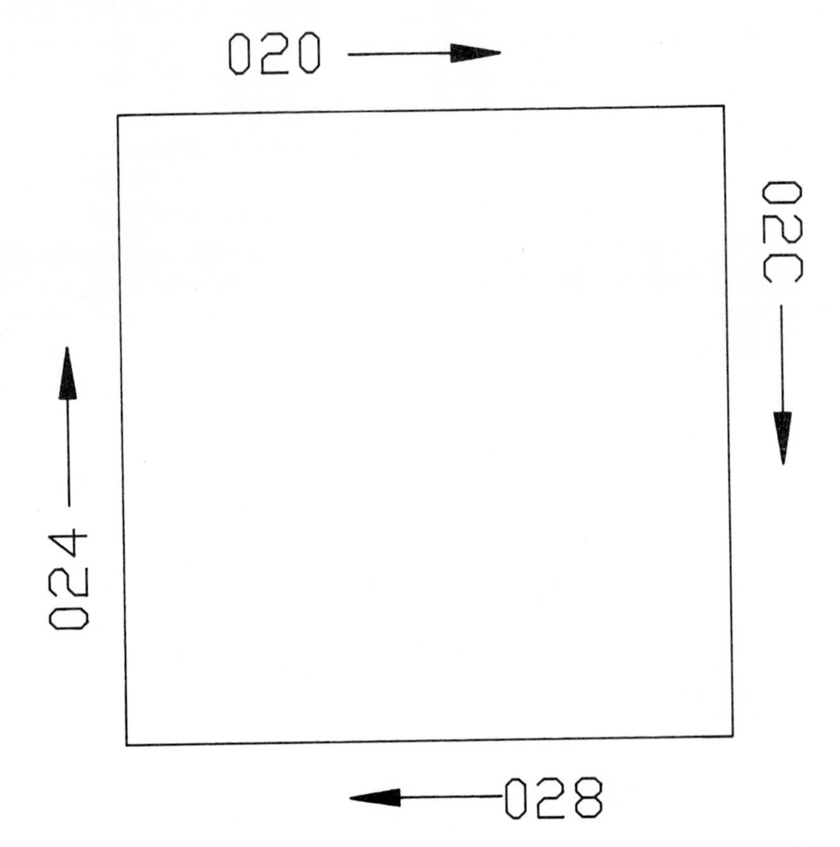

Figure 14-1. A two-unit square with shape codes

With a vector encoded byte, you can describe a line as long as 15 units in any of 16 different directions. For example, the first number of the SQUARE description describes a line 2 units long drawn in a 90-degree direction (north). If you look at the line labeled 4 in Figure 14-2, you will see that 4 is the direction for 90 degrees.

The vector encoded byte is always expressed as a hexadecimal number (base 16) from 000 to 0FF. The first digit is always 0. The second digit is the length of the line (or vector) from 0 to 15 units, and the third digit determines the direction that that vector is drawn (based on Figure 14-2).

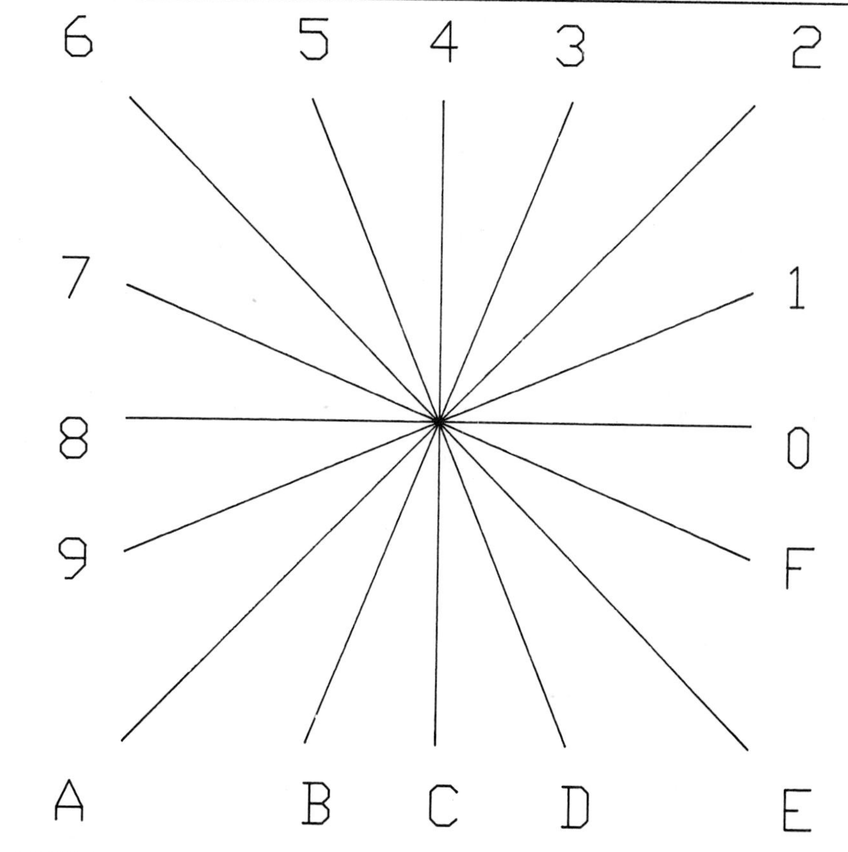

Figure 14-2. Directions and their codes

Now the SQUARE description starts to make sense. Let's take it apart and describe it byte by byte. The first line is the header line and always starts with an asterisk (*). The first number is the shape number (from 1 to 255). The second number is the total number of bytes used to describe the shape (just count the numbers in the description that follows). The last element is the name of the shape—if this is a shape file rather than a font file, the shape name must be in all uppercase characters.

The next line is the actual shape description:

024	Move 2 units in direction 4 (90 degrees)
020	Move 2 units in direction 0 (0 degrees)
02C	Move 2 units in direction C (270 degrees)
028	Move 2 units in direction 8 (180 degrees)
0	the last number in shape descriptions is always 0

For the orthogonal directions 0, 90, 180, and 270 degrees, one unit is, as expected, one unit. For the other 12 directions, the actual unit length is inscribed within a square. Each of the lines in Figure 14-1 is described as the same unit length. Look at Figure 14-3 and then look at the code that describes it. Each of the line descriptions in the shape file is two units long.

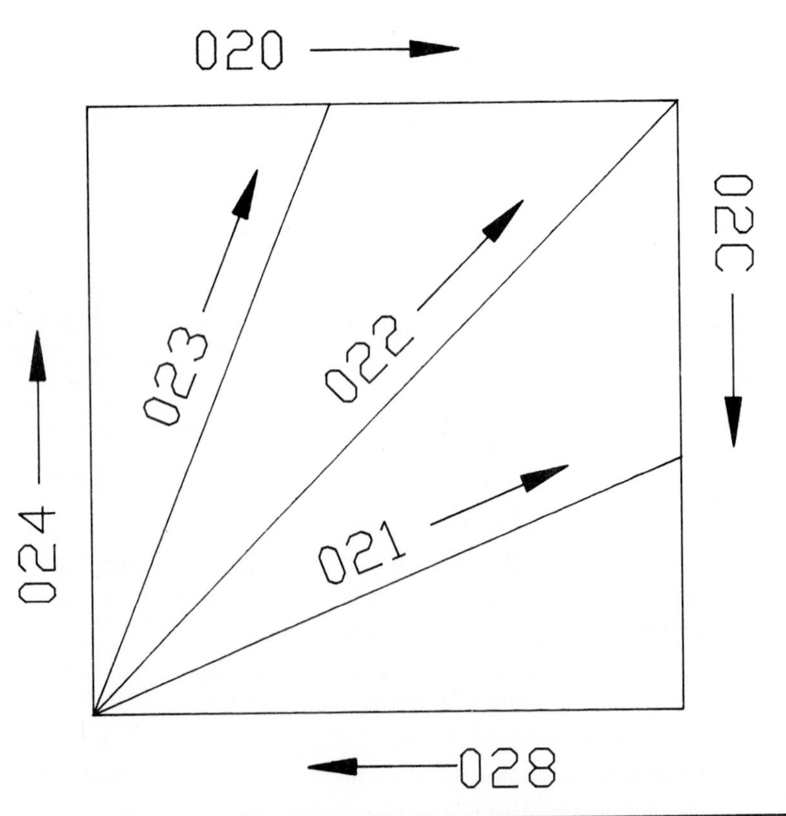

Figure 14-3. All two-unit vectors, at various angles

```
*2,14,FAN
024,020,02C,020,023,002,02B,001,022,002,02A,001,021,0
```

The numbers 001 and 002 are pen down and pen up commands, respectively. If you follow the preceding numbers, you will notice that the pen is raised or lowered depending on the last digit in each three-digit number. There are also other codes.

If you were limited to describing shapes with vector encoded bytes, you would find yourself unable to describe more complex shapes. There are 15 additional command codes that, combined with vector encoded bytes, give you the ability to describe almost any two-dimensional shape. These codes are

000	End of shape byte
001	Pen down
002	Pen up
003	Divide all vector lengths that follow by next byte
004	Multiply all vector lengths that follow by next byte
005	Push current point coordinate on stack
006	Pop a point coordinate from stack
007	Draw a subshape. The next byte is the shape number
008	The next two bytes describe an XY displacement
009	Multiple XY displacements
00A	The following two bytes describe an Octant Arc
00B	The following five bytes describe a Fractional Arc
00C	Arc defined by XY displacement and bulge (polyarc)
00D	Multiple polyarcs
00E	Used for specifying vertical text styles

All of these codes can be written in either the hexadecimal or decimal format. For example, the octant arc command can be written as either 00A or 10.

Code 000 This code indicates the end of the shape definition and must always appear as the last byte in a shape description. This code can be written as 0.

Code 001 This is the pen down code. The pen is down by default at the beginning of a shape description. This command is usually issued after a pen up (002) within a shape definition. Every command after a pen down command will result in a visible line or arc. This code can also be written as 1.

Code 002 This is the pen up code. It is used for producing a move from one point to another without anything being drawn, such as a move from the end of one text character to the beginning of the next. This code can also be written as 2.

Code 003 This is the scale down code. It will divide the lengths of all subsequent vector lengths by a scale factor indicated by the number following this command. This scale factor remains in effect until the end of the shape definition or until another scale factor is supplied in the description.

Code 004 This is the scale up code which will multiply the lengths of all subsequent vector lengths by a scale factor indicated by the next byte. This command code is the exact opposite of code 003, and these two codes are usually used together in a shape description.

If, for example, you needed a line in a shape that was 3.5 units long, you could use this code:

```
003,2,074,004,2
```

The first byte is the scale down command (003) which tells AutoCAD to divide the subsequent vector lengths by 2, the second byte. The third byte (074) says to draw a line 7 units long 90 degrees, but since the vector length has been divided by 2, the actual length is only 3.5 units long. The last two bytes (004,2) restore the vector units to their normal length by multiplying the scale factor.

These two codes have a cumulative effect. If you divide the vector length by a factor of two, and then divide it by a factor of four, the resulting vector units would only be one-eighth as long as normal. This could be particularly useful if you needed a vector length that was two-thirds of normal, for example. That could be expressed like this:

```
003,3,004,2
```

You would divide the vector length by 3 and then multiply that by 2, remembering when you have completed your two-thirds vector lengths to do the reverse as follows:

```
004,3,003,2
```

Code 005 This is the push location onto stack code. This command allows you to save a current coordinate location on a stack and, by using the POP command (006), to return to that location at a later time. This command, PUSH (005), and the next command, POP (006), can save you a lot of time and effort in writing shape descriptions, as you will see in the next command description.

Code 006 This is the pop location from stack code. This command will pop the last stored location off the stack. There are two important things to know about how this stack works. Every time PUSH (005) is used, it must be followed by a use of POP (006) somewhere within the shape description; otherwise, you will get a stack overflow or a stack underflow error when you attempt to use your shape file. The stack can only contain four locations and, because it is a stack, the last location that was stored will be the first location to be retrieved.

Here is how the example used to create Figure 14-3 can be rewritten to take advantage of the stack:

```
*3,12,FAN2
005,024,020,02C,028,021,006,005,022,006,023,0
```

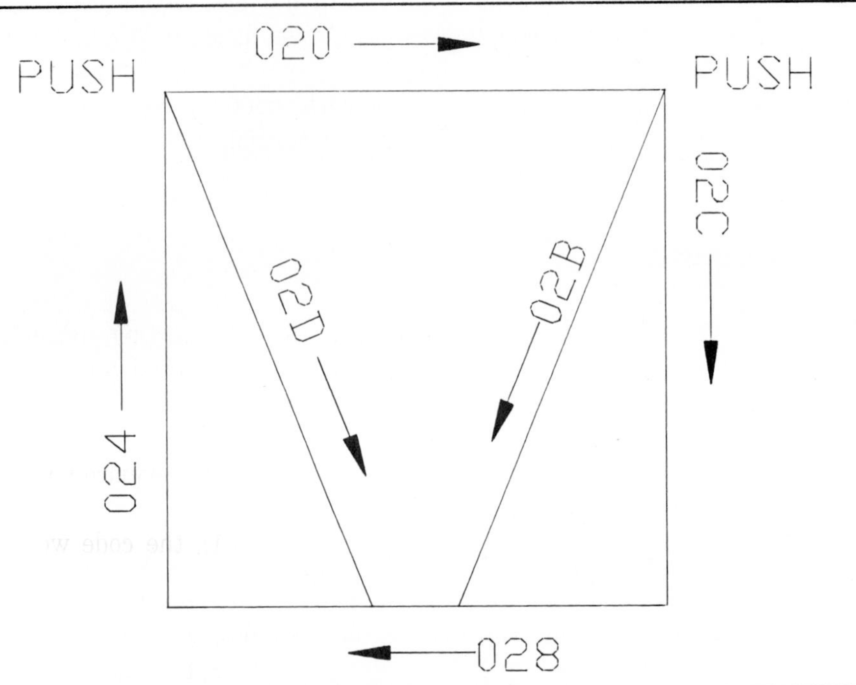

Figure 14-4. Pushing and popping

The first byte pushes the starting point on the stack, and the next four bytes describe the square. The sixth byte (021) is a 2 unit move at 22.5 degrees, and the seventh byte pops the starting point off the stack and makes it the current point. Once a location is popped off the stack, it is no longer available on the stack, so it must be pushed back on with the next command (the eighth byte). This is followed by another vector move from the starting point, a pop back to the starting point, and the final vector move.

Since the stack is four locations deep, you could push as many as four locations on the stack before you pop any back off for use. You must, however, pop the locations in the reverse order that you pushed them. Figure 14-4 is an example of a shape that uses two pushes and then two pops. Here is the code for that shape:

```
*4,11,VSQUARE
024,005,020,005,02C,028,006,02B,006,02D,0
```

Notice that the first location to be popped from the stack was the last location to be pushed onto the stack.

Code 007 This is the code to draw a subshape, the shape number being the following number. This command will include another shape description within the current shape. The starting point of this included shape will be at the pen position that is current in the shape description at the time this command is called. You can even scale this included shape with the scale commands (003 and 004).

An example would be a shape consisting of a square with a second square half the size of the first square centered within it, as in Figure 14-5. Using the BOX shape (#1), the code would look like this:

```
*10,16,2SQUARE
005,007,1,003,2,002,008,1,1,001,007,1,006,004,2,0
```

The first byte pushes the starting point onto the stack, and the second and third bytes draw the square (shape #1) at the starting point. Bytes 4 and 5 divide the vector lengths by 2 and byte 6 is a pen up. Bytes 7, 8, and 9 move the current location up 1 unit and over 1 unit (actually half units since it is scaled down). Byte 10 is a pen down command, and bytes 11 and 12 will draw shape #1—only this time at half scale. The rest of the code restores the scale and the starting point. The last part is unnecessary since this is the end of the shape description.

Code 008 This is the code for the X Y coordinate move. The two bytes immediately following this command will be X and Y coordinates respectively of a pen move. Since the numbers are all single byte numbers, the maximum X or Y distance is 255 units. Vector encoded bytes are fine for simpler shapes, but when you want a line longer than 15 units, or you need to

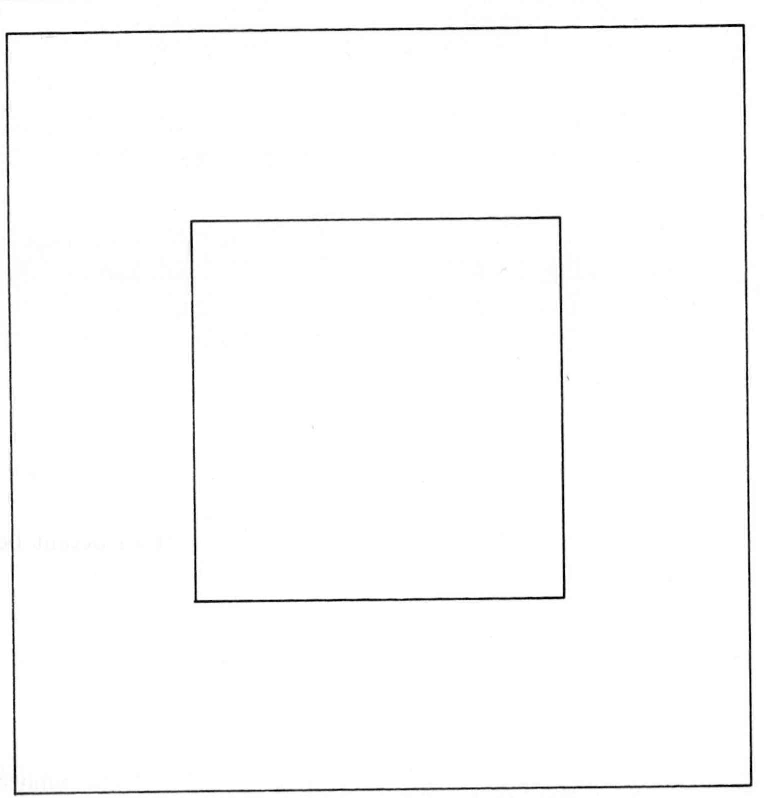

Figure 14-5. Using scale factors

describe more complex shapes, you may find that you need to use the standard XY coordinate moves that this command provides.

Here is the code for a rectangle shape that is 5 units high by 30 units wide:

```
*9,9,LONGREC
054,8,(30,0),05C,8,(-30,0),0
```

Notice that the two bytes following the 8 command are enclosed within parentheses. Although the parentheses are not necessary, it makes the shape description easier to read.

Code 009 This is the code for multiple X Y coordinate moves. This is similar to Code 8, except that this command allows you to make multiple X Y moves without using the 8 command for each move. The series of coordinate moves must always end with a 0,0 coordinate. Here is the code for a large square:

```
*8,12,LGSQUARE
9,(0,20),(20,0),(0,-20),(-20,0),(0,0),0
```

Again, the parentheses are there simply to make it easier to read the code.

Code 00A The following two bytes describe an *octant arc.* An octant arc is an arc that spans one or more 45-degree segments, or octants, and starts and ends on an octant boundary. Figure 14-6 shows a circle divided into 8 45-degree segments or octants. Each segment boundary is numbered from 0 to 7 in a counterclockwise direction. 0 is 0 degrees, 1 is 45 degrees, 2 is 90 degrees, and so on.

The first byte of the 2 bytes that describe an octant arc is the radius of the arc and it can be anything from 1 to 255 units. The second byte is an encoded hexadecimal byte, where the second digit is the starting octant boundary, and the third digit is the number of octants spanned by the arc. If the second byte is positive, the arc is drawn counterclockwise—a negative number here will generate an arc in a clockwise direction. A complete circle can be described by having the arc span eight octants.

Figure 14-6 shows six different octant arcs labeled "A" to "F." Assuming that the arcs are drawn counterclockwise, and the radius for each arc varies from between one and four units, the code that describes each arc is as follows:

Code		Radius	Start	Span
A:	00A,(1,001),	1	0	1
B:	10,(2,002),	2	0	2

Code		Radius	Start	Span
C:	10,(1,024),	1	2	4
D:	10,(3,007),	3	0	7
E:	10,(2,061),	2	6	1
F:	10,(4,008)	4	0	8 (CIRCLE)

If you wanted arc C to be generated in a clockwise direction, the code would be

10,(1, – 064)

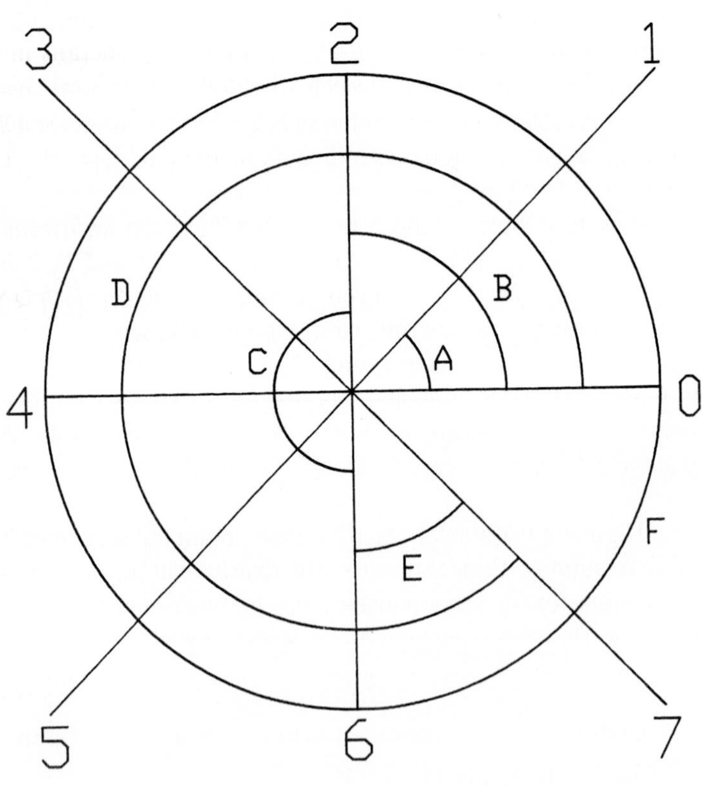

Figure 14-6. The octant measure

Figure 14-7 demonstrates how octant arcs can be used in defining a shape. Here is the shape description for that shape:

```
*21,25,NOTCH2
10,(1,043),022,10,(1,032),02e,10,(1,053),044,
10,(1,003),02a,10,(1,–072),026,10,(1,013),04C,0
```

Code 00B The following five bytes describe a fractional arc. An octant arc is fine for simpler shapes, such as that shown in Figure 14-7. However, if you need an arc where the starting or ending point does not fall on 45-degree boundaries, or where the radius must be greater than 255 units, you must use this command code for a fractional arc.

The fractional arc is similar to the octant arc in that the basic circle is divided into eight octants. Each octant in a fractional arc is further subdivided into 256 segments, with each subdivision equaling about 0.1758 degrees. Figure 14-8 shows an octant divided into 16 segments. Each segment is equal to 16

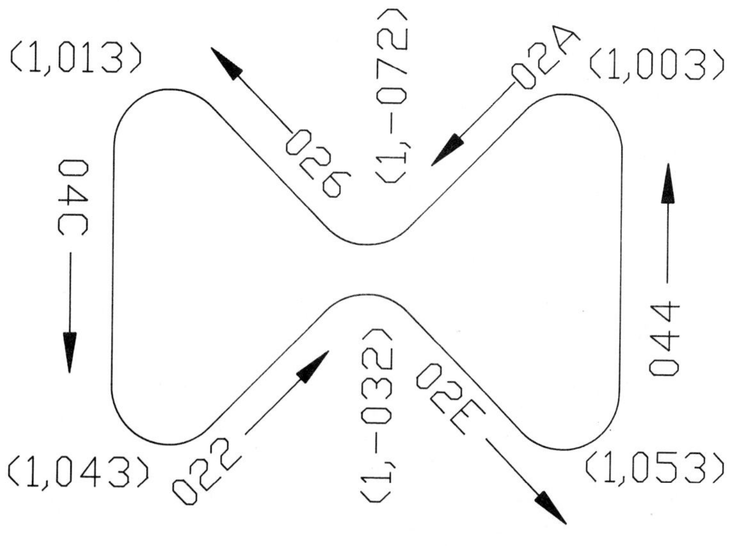

Figure 14-7. Octant arcs in use

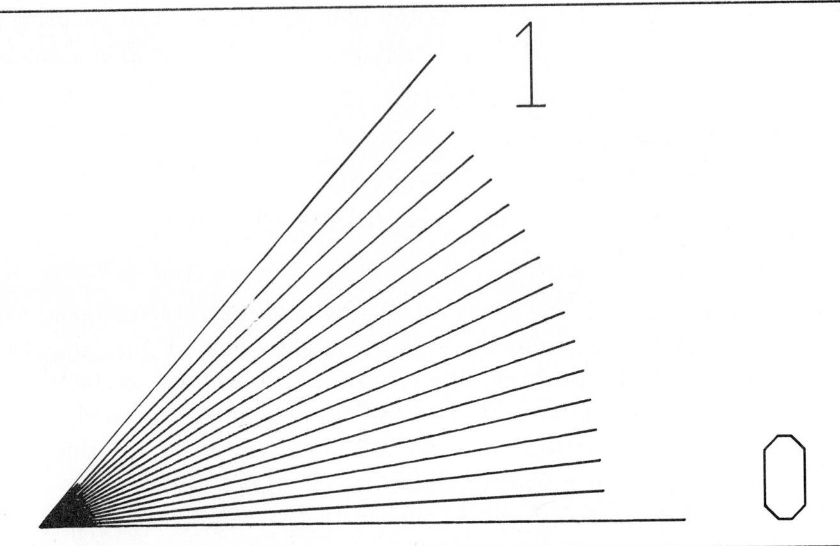

Figure 14-8. An arc divided into 16 segments

fractional arc units. Figure 14-9 shows one of the segments in Figure 14-8 divided into individual fractional arcs. While it is difficult to exactly divide a normal angle of measure into a fractional arc, the margin of error is so small that it is virtually unnoticeable.

Figure 14-9. A single segment divided 16 times

It takes five bytes to describe a fractional arc. The first two bytes are the starting and ending offsets from octant boundaries and the third and fourth bytes are the radius. If the radius is less than 255 units, the third byte is 0. The fifth byte encodes the starting boundary and the octant span the same way as in the octant arc.

The first byte in a fractional arc definition is the offset in fractional octants from the nearest octant boundary from the start of the arc. The second byte is the fractional offset from the nearest octant boundary in the direction of the arc. Visualize an arc constructed counterclockwise that starts at 5 degrees and ends at 40 degrees. The following shows how to calculate its offsets.

The angle of the starting offset is 5 degrees from the 0 octant boundary, so you multiply the starting offset angle by 256 (the number of divisions), and then divide that result by 45 (the angle of the octant). The result would be 28.44 rounded to 28—the number of fractional divisions from boundary 0 to the start of the arc. The ending offset fraction is found the same way. The angle between boundary 0 and the ending point is 40 degrees, so you multiply that by 256 and divide by 45, and the result is 227.55 rounded to 228—the ending fractional offset. If the ending angle of this arc was 50 degrees, you would calculate the ending offset from octant boundary 1, and that fraction would be 28 (that is, the arc extends 5 degrees beyond boundary 1).

Here is the code definition of these two examples, each with a radius of 8 units:

```
11,(28,228,0,8,001),        5 degrees to 40 degrees
11,(28,28,0,8,002),         5 degrees to 50 degrees
```

It is sometimes very difficult to calculate the fractional offsets of an arc, particularly if you do not know the starting and ending angles of that arc. Figure 14-10 shows a simplified version of a clear plastic overlay that has been developed for measuring the fractional parts of an arc. This overlay was drawn with AutoCAD and was plotted out at an appropiate scale onto overhead transparency material. You will see more about how this overlay can be used in the section on creating text fonts.

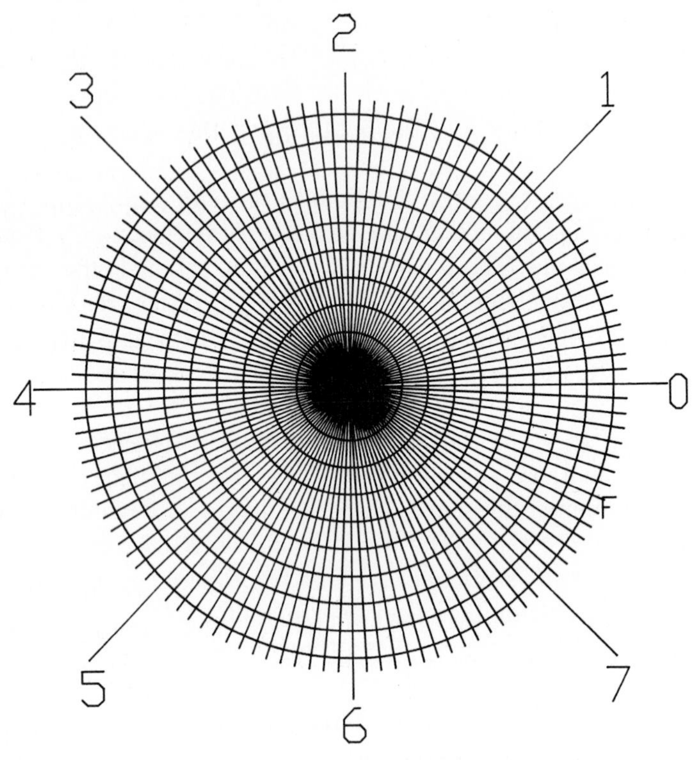

Figure 14-10. A measuring overlay

Code 00C This code creates bulge specified arcs. This code and the next code represent a different method for describing arcs that is identical to the way polyline arcs (or polyarcs) are defined in AutoCAD. The advantage of using polyarcs instead of fractional arcs in some cases is that you can specify the exact coordinate displacement of the endpoint of the arc, which is sometimes impossible to do with a fractional arc.

It takes three bytes to specify a polyarc. The first two bytes are the X and Y displacement from the starting point to the ending point of the arc. The third byte is the bulge factor that determines how much the arc is curved.

Code 00D This is the code for multiple polyarcs. This command code is similar to code 008 in that you can specify a series of polyarcs. The series must be ended with a 0,0 terminator.

Code 00E This code specifies a vertical text flag. This code is only used with text fonts that have been designed to be dual-oriented fonts. This command is used, in conjunction with other commands, to change the starting and ending points of a letter to a vertical format. If this command code is used in a font file, and if the user specifies a text style to be vertical with the STYLE command, then the next command in the shape description will be used. Otherwise, any command that follows this command will be ignored.

Font Files

Font files are simply a specialized type of shape file. They are constructed in the same way with only three minor differences. First, font files contain shape descriptions of letters and are organized so that the shape number corresponds to the ASCII character code for that letter. Second, font files contain two special shape descriptions that define the shape file as a font file and set certain scales. Finally, the shape descriptions of letter forms are scaled independently from their vector descriptions.

Let's discuss independent scale first. If you defined a 2-unit square in a shape file, and then inserted that shape into a drawing with a scale factor of 1, then that shape would be 2 units square in the drawing. If, however, you defined the letter "O" in a font file to be 50 units high, and then specified the text in a drawing to be 1 unit high, then that "O" would be 1 unit high. This scale factor is determined by the font definition shape or shape 0.

If shape 0 appears in a shape file, that shape file becomes a font file. The format for shape 0 is simple and always the same:

```
*0,4,fontname
units above,units below,mode,0
```

Figures 14-11 and 14-12 show two characters from a font overlaid with a grid with each square of the grid representing one vector unit. These samples will be used to illustrate how to create a font file. Shape 0 for this font looks like this:

```
*0,4,comp outline
50,9,0,0
```

The first byte (50) is the number of divisions from the base to the top of the uppercase character. The second byte is the number of divisions from the base to the bottom of the descender on a lowercase letter. The third byte is the mode. Zero means that this font is designed to be used in a horizontal or normal orientation only. A 2 here would mean that this font can also be used vertically. The last byte is, of course, the terminator byte.

The 50-unit height for letters is a convenient number to work with. Larger numbers tend to make the grid too fine, and fewer units tend to make the letterform too coarse.

In addition to shape 0, you need three other special shapes to make the font file function properly. These are Start of Text (1), Line Feed (10), and Carriage Return (13).

Start of Text simply pushes the starting point onto the stack:

```
*1,2,sot
5,0
```

Line Feed makes a pen up move one line down from the previous line:

```
*10,5,lf
```

Carriage Return makes a pen move all the way to the left on the current line:

```
*3,4,cr
2,8,(-75,0),0
```

The third byte (X displacement) is arrived at by adding the number of units above the base line (50) to the number of units below the baseline (9), and then adding a few extra units for clearance. You have to experiment with the clearance number.

Tips on Creating Font Files

A very effective technique for creating shape files has been developed that involves using plastic grid overlays on enlarged letters. Figure 14-11 shows a square grid overlay on a typical letterform, and Figure 14-10 illustrates a grid used to find the information about octant and fractional arcs. Here is how the technique works.

First, find a source of large letterforms about five inches high. You can either make photostat enlargements of a typeface or enlarge the letters several times on a photocopying machine. Be careful if you are planning to make your fonts commercially available, by the way, since fonts are often copyrighted.

Next, using AutoCAD, you need to create a grid of evenly spaced lines to fit your letters, similar to the grid shown in Figure 14-11. Make sure the grid lines are spaced so that the bases of the letters, the tops of the uppercase characters, the tops of the lowercase characters, and the bottoms of the lowercase descenders all fall on a grid line. Usually when the letters are enlarged, the lines in the letters become quite thick, as shown in the illustration. Make sure that the grid lines fall on the center of these lines and that your grid is wide enough to cover the wide letters such as "W" and "M." You will probably have to experiment with the scale of this grid before everything finally fits properly.

Now draw a circular grid similar to the one in Figure 14-10, making the radius of the circles the same increments as the grid spacing in the rectangular grid. Plot both of these grids onto overhead transparency material, perhaps using a different pen color to indicate base line, uppercase line, and other elements.

Tape the rectangular grid over the letterform, aligning the base line of the grid with the bottom of the letter. It should look similar to Figure 14-11. Notice how all of the lines in the letter are centered on grid lines. This is the ideal condition, but one

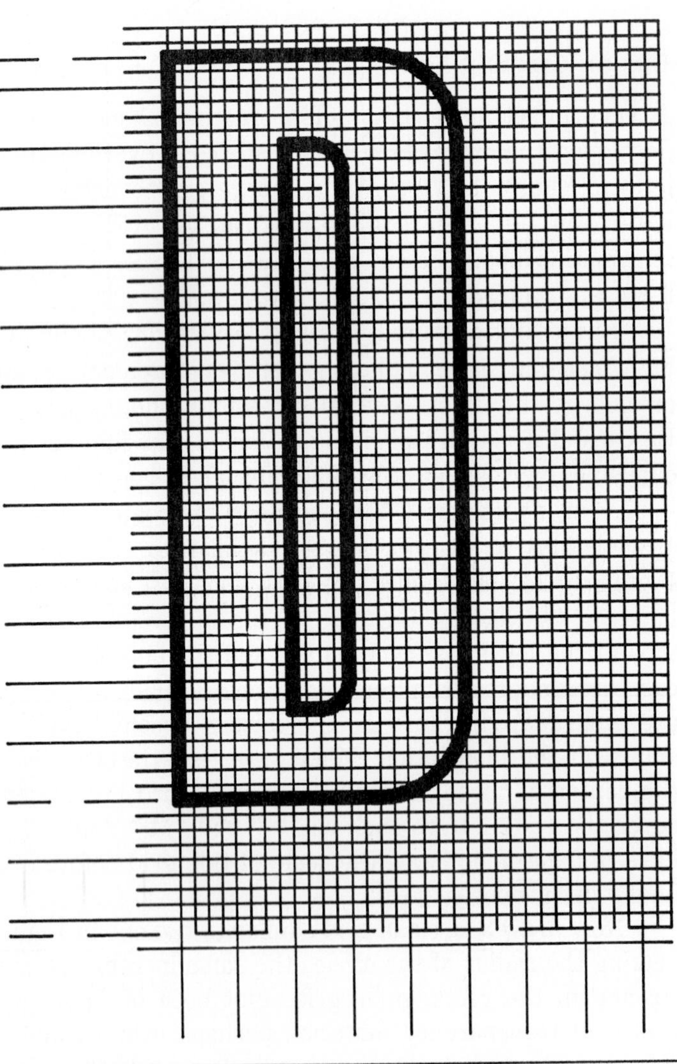

Figure 14-11. A character from a letter font

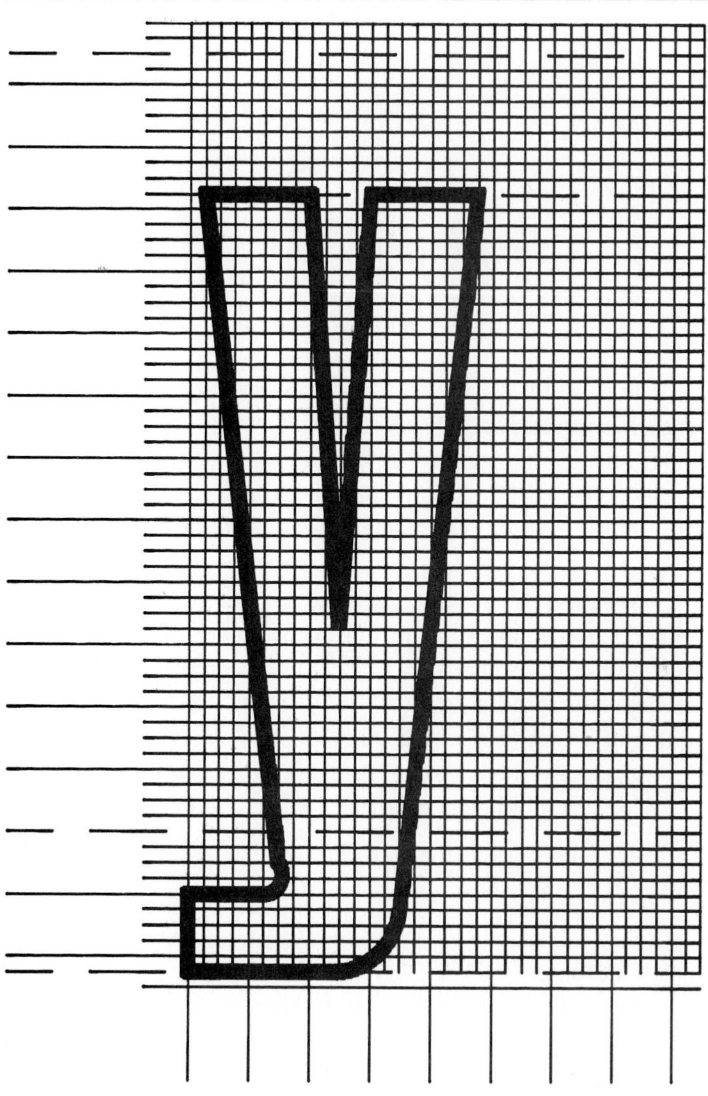

Figure 14-12. The letter "y" against a measuring grid

that you cannot always attain. Sometimes, you will need to fudge the lines just a bit.

You are now ready to start coding your shape. The letter in Figure 14-11 is relatively simple—all the lines are orthogonal and all the arcs are octant arcs. The following is the actual code used to produce this letter:

```
*68,38,ucd
8,(0,50),0E0,10,(6,-022),8,(0,-38),10,(6,-002),0E8,
2,8,(8,6),1,8,(0,38),020,10,(2,-022),8,(0,-34),10,
(2,-002),028,2,8,(16,-6),0
```

Figure 14-13 shows how the circular grid is used to find the start point, endpoint, and radius for the arcs. This grid can be used for either octant or fractional arcs. Each octant in this grid is divided into 16 parts. Usually, this is enough, but occasionally you have to estimate the offsets if they fall between division marks.

When determining compound curves, it is helpful to have two circular grids so that you can find the tangent point between two arcs. It seems that 99% of the complex curves found in letterforms can be accurately described with two arcs. The most difficult letter to do is usually an "S." Here is the code for the lowercase "y," as shown in Figure 14-12. This is a bit more difficult to code because it has two fractional arcs.

```
*121,43,lcy
2,8,(0,41),1,5,070,8,(2,-28),8,(2,28),070,8,(-5,-46),
11,(49,0,0,5,-002),098,6,5,8,(5,-43),
11,(215,0,0,2,-013),048,05C,6,2,8,(22,-41),0
```

The question still remains, why go to all this trouble when you can buy a font file, or you can at least buy a program that will convert blocks to shapes? You may need a very specific shape library or font that is not commercially available. And, as to the shape conversion software, there does not appear to be any package that does an adequate job. Usually, the shape file produced by one of these translators is five to ten times larger than one produced by hand, and it is not nearly as accurate.

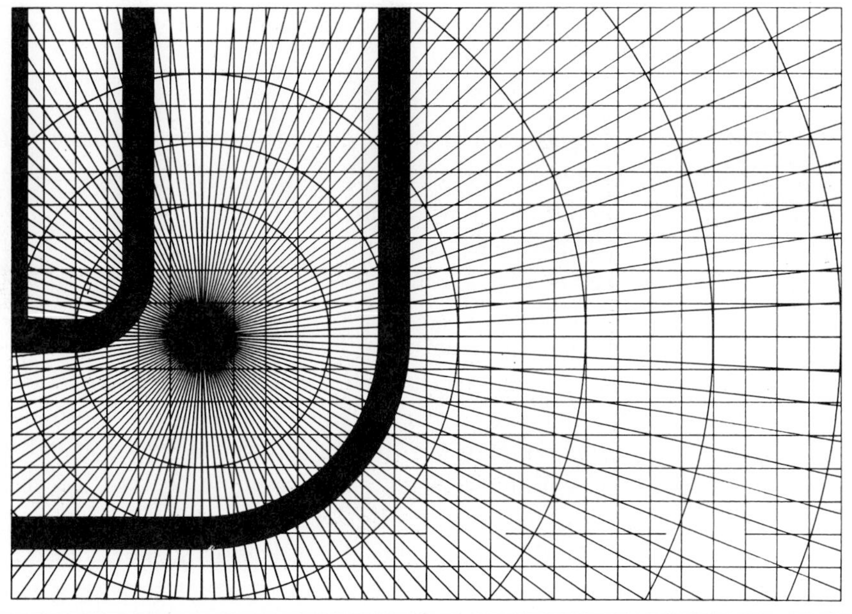

Figure 14-13. Circular grid used to code arcs

Custom Line Types

With AutoCAD, you can produce your own custom line types by varying the length of and the distance between segments of a line to produce different patterns of dots and dashes. There is not a lot that you can do with line types, but there are a few useful things that you can do with the ones you create.

The Line Type File

Line types are defined in a file called ACAD.LIN. If you look at that file with a text editor, you can see the format of these descriptions. Here are the definitions of two line types, hidden and dashdot, as they appear in that file:

```
*HIDDEN,_ _ _ _ _ _ _ _ _ _ _ _ _ _ _ _ _ _ _ _
A,.25,-.125
```

```
*DASHDOT,__ . __ . __ . __ . __ . __ .
A,.5,-.25,0,-.25
```

The first line starts with an asterisk that indicates the start of a definition followed by the name of the line type in all uppercase. The name is followed by what is called a "prose description" of the line type. This description is optional and is simply rendition of the line type in text mode that shows up on the text screen when you list the line types.

The next line starts with the letter "A," which is an alignment code that guarantees that a line created with that line type always starts and ends with a dash or a dot. The AutoCAD Reference Manual implies that this is an optional code, but a line type definition will not work unless it begins with this "A." The alignment code is followed by the actual segment description of the line type. In the hidden line type, this is a short line (.25 inch) followed by a shorter space (−.125 inch), in a pattern that is repeated for the length of the line. If the variable LTSCALE is set to 1.00000, then the length of these line segments will be as indicated. The "0" in the dashdot definition describes a dot. As you can see, the line type definition is nothing more than a list of the lengths of the segments of that line type.

Line type definitions are restricted in length to no more then 12 dimensions of segments and spaces combined, and the whole definition, including commas, must be no longer than 80 characters.

Uses of Custom Line Types

Here is one practical and one whimsical example of custom line types. When you set the LTSCALE of a drawing, it affects the scale of all of the lines in a drawing globally. You may have an occasion where you need hidden lines shown with dashes of different lengths or scales. The solution is to define several different hidden line types with different dash and space lengths. The two examples shown here and in Figure 14-14 are defined to be two and three times the scale of the original hidden line type:

```
*HIDDEN2,__ __ __ __ __ __ __ __ __
A,.5,-.25
*HIDDEN3,___ ___ ___ ___ ___ ___
A,.75,-.375
```

As you can see, the lengths in hidden2 are twice that of the hidden line type dimensions, and the lengths in hidden3 are three times its length.

The last two examples of custom line type definitions show how you can personalize your drawings with your own Morse code monogrammed line types. Samples of these line types are also shown in Figure 14-14.

```
*NJ,_ ... _
A,.5,-.25,0,-.5,0,-.25,0,-.25,.5,-.25,0,-.5
*LM,. _ .. _ _
A,0,-.25,.5,-.25,0,-.25,0,-.5,.5,-.25,.5,-.5
```

Linetype: LM

Linetype: NJ

Linetype: HIDDEN

Linetype: HIDDEN2

Linetype: HIDDEN3

Figure 14-14. Customized line types

Moving Graphic Information into AutoCAD

A whole book could be written on this subject, but this chapter will confine itself to one specific example that illustrates some of the vast potential of using other types of graphic data in AutoCAD.

Importing Map Data into AutoCAD

The U.S. Geological Survey has available, through a branch called U.S. GeoData, digital files of many of their 1:24,000 scale maps. These files are called Digital Line Graphs (DLG) and consist of all the line information derived from their accurate topographic maps. Each map is divided into several data files, and an individual file may contain hydrological, road, political boundary, or topographical data. This data is available from the USGS for a nominal cost (varying from $25 to $100 per file) and is not copyrighted. Obviously, you cannot load this map data directly into AutoCAD because the file format is incompatible. You can, however, convert the line information contained in the DLG file into a format that AutoCAD will accept with a program called DLG2DXB. The source code for DLG2DXB is shown in Function 14-1.

```
/* This program converts USGS DLG (Digital Line Graph)
** Data to AutoCAD DXB File format so that the map can be
** used as an AutoCAD drawing.  The current version will
** only convert a series of line segment coordinate points
** to a polyline.
**
** Complete information about the DLG data format can be
** obtained from the USGS as a publication called
** Digital Line Graphs from 1:24000-Scale Maps Data Users
** Guide Structure for DLG logical record number C.2.  The
** only thing used from this data in this version is the
** number of lines in the file (num_lines).  Other
** information can be used if the program is expanded.
*/
```

Function 14-1. A program to convert DLG to DXB file formats

```
#include <stdio.h>
#include <stdlib.h>
#include <math.h>

struct
{
 char category_name[20]; /* name of data category */
 char max_nodes[6];      /* max # of nodes allowable (25960) */
 char num_nodes[6];      /* actual # of nodes in file */
 char max_areas[6];      /* max # of allowable areas (25960) */
 char num_areas[6];      /* actual # of areas */
 char max_lines[6];      /* max # of lines allowed (25938)*/
 char num_lines[6];      /* maximum number of lines in file*/
 char filler[88];
} cat_info;

/* Header record for a line in the DLG file.  This record
** how many vertices make up the next line.
*/

struct
{
 char entity_type; /* either L for line N for
                      node A for area */
 char blank;       /* actually ASCII 32 */
 char line_num[6]; /* sequential from 1 to n */
 char start_node_id[6];
 char end_node_id[6];
 char left_id[6];
 char right_id[6];
 char num_pts[6]; /*number of xy coordinate pairs in line */
 char num_attrib_codes[6]; /* number of attrib codes
                              attached to this line.
                              Attribute codes are found at
                              the end of the coordinate
                              list */
 char num_attrib_chars[6]; /* not used at present */
 char filler[94];
} line_head;

/* Data structure of vertex coordinate records.  Since each
** record is 144 bytes long and the data is all ASCII,
** the data is structured as a three dimensional array
*/

struct
{
 char line_coords[12][2][6];
} line_body;

/* data structure for DXB polyline record.  This is simply written
** as-is to the input file when a new line header record is found
** in the DLG file.
*/
```

Function 14-1. A program to convert DLG to DXB file formats (*continued*)

```
struct
{
 char entity_type;      /* 19 is record ID for polyline
                           record */
 int closure_flag;      /* map lines are not usually closed */
} pline_head = {19,0};


/* Data structure for DXB Vertex record
*/
struct
{
 unsigned char entity_type;      /* 20 is record ID for
                                    vertex */
 int to_x;                       /* x coordinate of vertex */
 int to_y;                       /* y coordinate of vertex*/
} vertex = {20,0,0};


/* This is the data structure for the DXB file header
** and it is always the same.  This is the first
** thing written to the DXB file.
*/
struct
{
 char head_string[15];
 char cr;
 char lf;
 char control_z;
 char nul;
} dxb_file_head = {"AutoCAD DXB 1.0", 13, 10, 26,'\0'};

char seqend = 17; /* this byte indicates the end of a
                     polyline in a DXB file it is always
                     the last thing written after all the
                     vertex records.  */

void read_data();

char null_char = '\0';
FILE *fp;    /* pointer to input file */
FILE *fpout; /* pointer to output file */

/* global declarations */
int num_lines, line_num, num_pts;
int x_pt, y_pt;

main(argc,argv)
int argc;
char *argv[];
{
 if(argc < 3)
  {
   printf("Usage: DLG2DXB infilename outfilename.DXB \n");
   exit(1);
  }
```

Function 14-1. A program to convert DLG to DXB file formats (*continued*)

```
/* open the input file.  Although the input file is in ASCII
** format the format is of 144 byte fixed records and there
** are no carriage returns or linefeeds, so the file has
** to be treated as a binary file
*/
if ((fp=fopen(argv[1], "rb"))==NULL)
 {
  printf("cannot open file");
  exit(1);
 }

fseek(fp,1296,SEEK_SET); /* ignore first 9 records */
fread(&cat_info,sizeof(cat_info),1,fp);   /* read the 10th
                                             record */
num_lines = atoi(cat_info.num_lines);     /* to find out
                                             how many lines
                                             are in DLG
                                             file */

/* open output file */
if ((fpout = fopen(argv[2], "wb"))==NULL)
 {
  printf("cannot open output file");
  fclose(fp);
  exit(1);
 }

/* write the DXB file header first */
fwrite(&dxb_file_head,sizeof(dxb_file_head),1,fpout);

/* function calls here */
/* calls the function that reads the line data */
read_data();
fclose(fp);/*close the DLG file */
fwrite(&null_char,1,1,fpout);/* write the DXB
                                end of file mark */
fclose(fpout);/*close the DXB file*/
/*close output file*/
return 0;
} /* main */

/* This function reads all of the line data from a DLG file,
** converts the data from strings to integers and writes the
** data to the DXB file as polylines
*/
void read_data()
{
 int i, j;
 int k;
 int l;

 fread(&line_head,144,1,fp); /* read the first record */

 /* ignore area and node records */
 while(line_head.entity_type != 'L')
```

Function 14-1. A program to convert DLG to DXB file formats (*continued*)

```
      {
       fread(&line_head,144,1,fp);
      }
     /* start of line records */
     i = 0;
     while (i < num_lines)
      {
       /*writes polyline header for line*/
       fwrite(&pline_head,sizeof(pline_head),1,fpout);
       num_pts=atoi(line_head.num_pts); /* gets # of points in
                                           line */
       /*read the first record with point data*/
       fread(&line_body,144,1,fp);
       j=0;
       l=0;
       while (j<num_pts)
        {
         /* step through array of points in record and
            add coord data to DXB vertex structure */
         vertex.to_x=atoi(&line_body.line_coords[l][0][0]);
         vertex.to_y=atoi(&line_body.line_coords[l][1][0]);
         /* write vertex*/
         fwrite(&vertex,sizeof(vertex),1,fpout);
         j++;
         l++;
         k=j;
         while (k>0)
          k=k-12;
         /* if there are still points left after the whole
            record has been read */
         if (k==0 && j<num_pts)
          {
           /*read the next record */
           fread(&line_body,144,1,fp);
           l=0;
          }
        }
       i++;
       /* if there is an attribute record */
       /* read next line head */
       /* a layer could be created at this point */
       /* that would have the same */
       /* name as the attribute data */
       if (atoi(line_head.num_attrib_codes)>0)
        fread(&line_head,144,1,fp);/* skip it for this version */

       fwrite(&seqend,1,1,fpout);  /* write the SEQEND byte */
       fread(&line_head,144,1,fp); /* read the next record */
      }
    }  /* read_data */
```

Function 14-1. A program to convert DLG to DXB file formats *(continued)* so that you can study it, use it for your own purposes, or develop your own file translator application. The program was written in C language. You will need to know how to compile it with virtually any of the C compilers available on the market today. No attempt is made here to instruct you in the C language. It will be valuable for you to learn to program in C if you plan to do much of this kind of work.

This program scans through a DLG file, finds the coordinate points of the lines in the file, and then writes a DXB file using those point coordinates to create polylines. Figure 14-15 is an AutoCAD drawing based on a DLG file that was translated by the DLG2DXB program. This drawing actually consists of two separate DLG files, one consisting of hydrologic data, and the other consisting of road data. Figure 14-16 is a reproduction of the USGS topographic map of the same area.

Further Information

The DLG map data contains much more information that has been extracted with DLG2DXB. The complete file description of the DLG files is contained in a document entitled "Digital Line Graphs form 1:24000-Scale Maps Data Users Guide." This publication and the actual Digital Line Graph data is available from

National Cartographic Information Center
U. S. Geological Survey
507 National Center
Reston, VA 22092
(703) 860-6045

Several DLG files have been placed in the Autodesk Forum on CompuServe. You are free to download these files to test this program or to use in your own application. The file is called DLG.ARC.

More information about DXB files can be found in Appendix C of the AutoCAD Reference Manual or in *The AutoCAD Database Book* by Frederic H. Jones and Lloyd Martin (2d ed., Ventana Press, 1988).

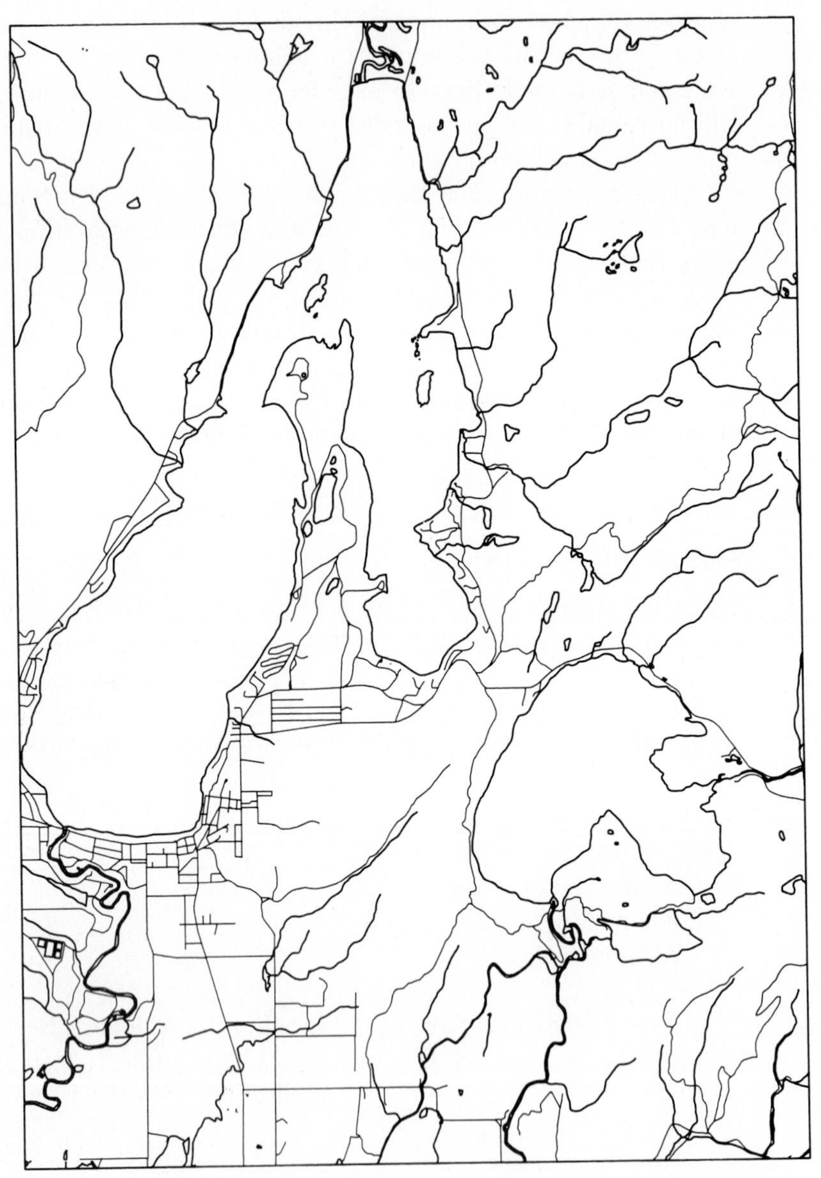

Figure 14-15. An AutoCAD drawing based on a DLG file

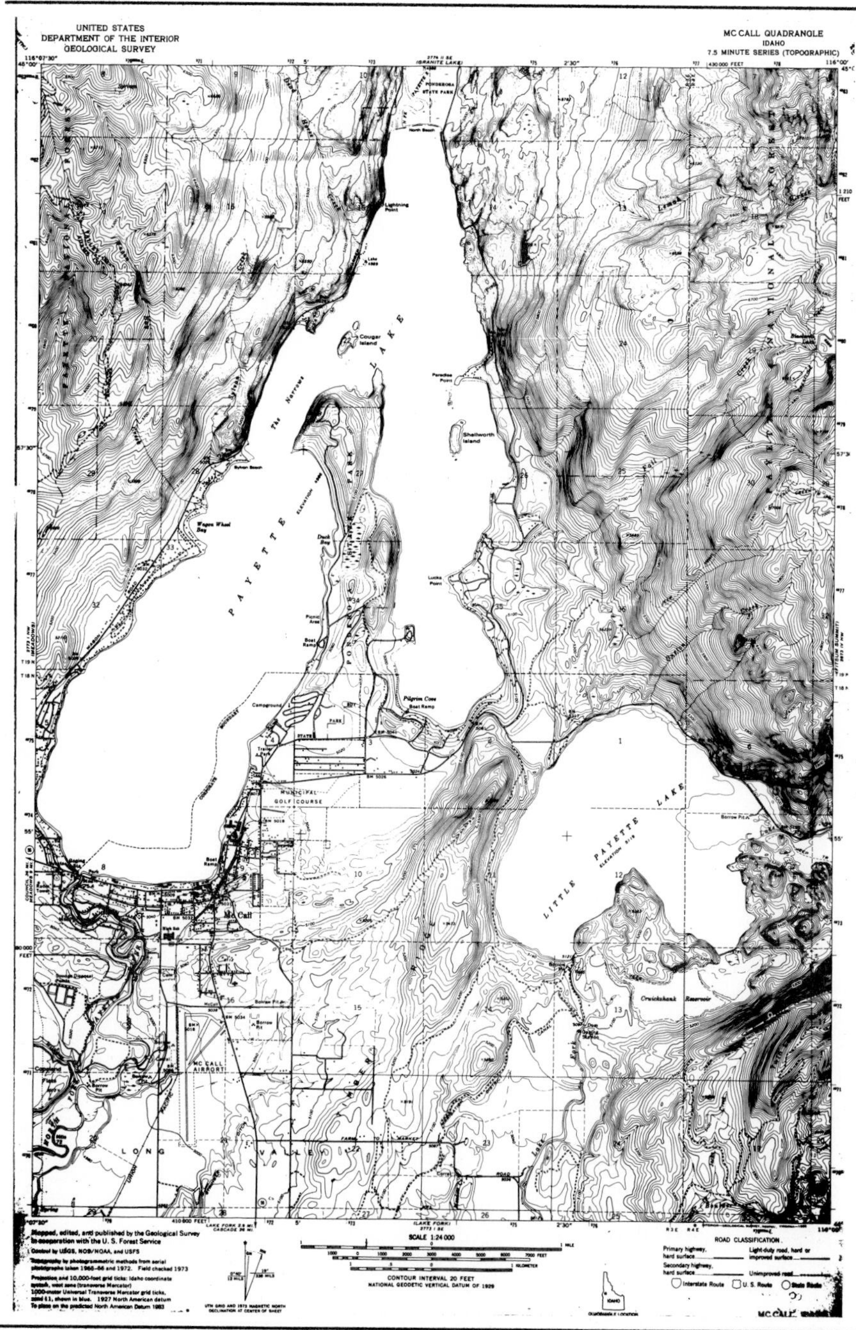

Figure 14-16. The USGS topographic map used to obtain AutoCAD drawing

Function and Command References

PART FOUR

AutoLISP Function Reference

FIFTEEN

AutoLISP Data Types

Here, for quick reference, is a list of all the data types used in AutoLISP along with the key words with which AutoLISP recognizes and describes them.

Symbols	SYM
Lists	LIST
Numbers	REAL, INT
Strings	STR

File Descriptors	FILE
Entity Names	ENAME
Selection Sets	PICKSET
Functions	LIST
Paging tables	PAGETB

These data types will be discussed in detail later in this chapter. From time to time, however, you may wish to refer to this list. You will find that there are no data types other than those listed here.

Notational Conventions

Each description of a function (or functions) in this chapter will start with the template or syntax of the function like the following:

```
(function-name <arg1> <arg2>...<argN>)
```

The template will be followed by a description of how the function works, a list of data types that can be used as arguments to the function, a list of related functions, and, finally, several examples of how the function can be used.

The Function Template

A template is a master pattern or prototype used either to create something to match the template or to make sure that something created matches the specifications of the template. In

AutoLISP, a template is used as a guide for producing correct code. An AutoLISP function must be called with the correct number of arguments, each containing data of the correct type.

The basic syntax is the same for calling all AutoLISP functions: a list enclosed by a pair of parentheses in which the first item in the list is the function name, followed by the arguments or parameters that are to be passed to that function. However, all functions do not take the same number of arguments. For example, this function for printing a blank line takes no arguments:

```
(terpri)
```

The following function takes one number and returns the square root of that number:

```
(sqrt <number>)
```

This function can take any number of arguments and add them together:

```
(+ <number1> <number2>...<numberN>)
```

So, although the preceding examples have the same basic syntax, their specific form or template will vary from function to function. The following are the rules for how the form templates are structured in this reference chapter.

The template is a list containing one or more elements. The first element in the template is the function name. Each argument prototype will begin and end with arrow brackets. The word enclosed by those brackets will describe the type(s) of data expected by that argument. This is an example of a prototype of an argument that expects a number:

```
<number>
```

If an argument is optional, it will be enclosed in square brackets. This is a prototype of an optional argument that expects a string:

```
[<string1>]
```

An ellipsis (or three dots) following an argument means that more arguments of the same type of data as the previous argument may be passed to the function. The ellipsis means that an indefinite number of arguments may be passed to the function, as in this example:

```
(list <expr1>...<exprN>)
```

This means that the function list can take one or more arguments of any valid data type.

Let's examine the templates of some different types of functions in more detail.

```
(+ <number1> <number2>...<numberN>)
```

The preceding is the template used to call a function that will add numbers. The first element of the list is, of course, the function name. The next two elements of the list represent the two arguments and the specific data type required by this function. The "number" variable refers to the type of data that is required by this particular function. The next item in this list is the ellipsis ". . .", or three dots, and means that additional arguments of the same data type as the last item may be used with this function. Here is the next template example:

```
(entnext [<entity-name>])
```

This template takes one optional argument of the data type "entity name." This is indicated by the square brackets surrounding the argument prototype.

Types of Data

"Types of data" does not have the same meaning as "data types." Some functions will accept only than one type of data, and some functions will only accept a very specific subset of one data type. For example, the function "type" will accept any data type and the function "inters" will only accept lists of drawing coordinates that are a special case of the data type LIST. What follows is a list of most of the common types of data that will be found in argument prototypes in this reference chapter:

<association-list>	Must be a valid Association List—see ASSOC
<angle>	A real number in radians
<atomN>	Can be symbol, number, or string
<entity-name>	Must be a valid entity name such as that returned by the function "entnext" or "entlast"
<exprN>	Can be any valid AutoLISP expression
<file-descriptor>	A file descriptor returned by the "open" function
<function>	Can be any valid defined function name
<argN>	Any valid data type
<list>	Any valid list
<numberN>	Can be an Integer or a Real
<promptN>	Must be a string, but not necessarily a literal
<point>	Must be a list of two or three reals that describes a coordinate

<stringN>	Must be a string
<sym>	Must be a symbol name
<selection-set>	A selection set such as that returned by the function "ssget"
<varname>	An AutoCAD drawing variable name as a string

There are several other types of data names that are each used in just a few cases. They will be described in the function descriptions where they are found.

Summary of Functions

The following is a quick summary of all of the built-in AutoLISP functions, or primitives, that are available in AutoCAD Release 10 grouped by related application.

Math Functions

Arithmetic Functions

(+) (−) (*) (/) (1+) (1−) (abs) (exp)
(expt) (fix) (float)
(gcd) (max) (min) (rem) (sqrt)

Log and Trig Functions

(atan) (cos) (log) (sin)

List Manipulation Functions

(append) (assoc) (car) (caar) (caaar) (cadar)
(caaaar) (caaadr) (caadar) (caaddr) (caadr)
(cadaar) (cadadr) (caddar) (cadddr) (caddr)
(cadr) (cdaar) (cdadr) (cdar) (cddar) (cddr)
(cdaaar) (cdaadr) (cdadar) (cdaddr) (cdr)

(cddaar) (cddadr) (cdddar) (cddddr) (cdddr)
(cons) (last) (length) (list) (member) (nth)
(reverse) (subst)

Assignment Functions
(getenv) (getvar) (quote)
(set) (setq) (setvar)

Procedural Functions
(apply) (command) (defun) (eval)
(foreach) (lambda) (mapcar)
(menucmd) (progn) (repeat)

Conditional Functions
(cond) (if) (while)

Relational Functions
(=) (/=) (<) (<=) (>) (>=) (eq) (equal)

Predicative Functions
(and) (atom) (boundp) (listp)
(minusp) (not) (null) (numberp)
(or) (type) (zerop)

String Functions
String Handling Functions
(strcase) (strcat) (strlen) (substr)
String Conversion Functions
(angtos) (ascii) (atof) (atoi) (chr)
(itoa) (read) (rtos)

Graphics Functions
Graphics Handling Functions
(angle) (distance) (inters) (osnap)
(polar) (redraw) (trans)
Screen Graphics Functions
(graphscr) (grclear) (grdraw) (grtext)

(grread) (textscr) (vports)

I/O Functions

Screen Input Functions

(getangle) (getcorner) (getdist) (getint)
(getkword) (getorient)
(getpoint) (getreal) (getstring) (initget)

Screen Output Functions

(prin1) (princ) (print) (prompt) (terpri)

File I/O Functions

(close) (findfile) (load) (open)
(read-char) (read-line)
(write-char) (write-line)

Entity Handling Functions

Selection Set Functions

(ssadd) (ssdel) (ssget) (sslength)
(ssmemb) (ssname)

Entity Name Functions

(entnext) (entlast) (entsel) (handent)

Entity Data Functions

(entdel) (entget) (entmod) (entupd)

Symbol Table Access Functions

(tblnext) (tblsearch)

Miscellaneous Functions

(_ver) (alloc) (expand) (function)
(gc) (mem) (vmon) (trace)
(untrace) (*error*) pi nil

Boolean Bit Operation Functions

(~) (boole) (logand) (logior) (lsh)

What follows is a description of each of the AutoLISP functions. The preceding conventions for specifying each function and describing variables are used, and examples for almost all functions are included. The list is current for Release 10 of AutoCAD, but may be incomplete for future releases.

Math Functions

The math functions are divided into two parts: basic arithmetic functions and log and trig functions. The math functions will always return a <number> data type. Whether the result returned is an integer or a real depends on the type of <number>s in the argument list. If all of the <number>s in the argument list are integers, the AutoLISP evaluator will perform integer arithmetic on the list and the result returned will be an integer. Integer arithmetic will throw away the remainder of the result of any arithmetic operation. Thus, the result of 47 divided by 3 in integer arithmetic will be 15 rather than 15.66667. If only one of the <number>s in the argument list is a real <number>, the evaluator will convert all of the <number>s in the list to real <number>s and will perform floating point math operations on the list. This is an important consideration when operating on integers where a fractional result may be returned, such as division.

Arithmetic Functions

AutoLISP contains a full range of arithmetic functions—from addition and subtraction to functions that will return the maximum or minimum number in a list. These functions are presented on the following pages.

(+ <number1> <number2>. . .<numberN>)

The function "+" (plus or add) adds the list of <number>s together and returns the sum. If all the <number>s in the list are integers, the result will be an integer. If even one of the <number>s in the list is a real, the result will be a real.

Examples:

```
(+ 1 2)
3
```

```
(+ 7 14 23)
44
(+ 3 5 7 9 11)
35
(+ 3 7 1.2)
11.200000
(setq a 4)
4
(setq b 7)
7
(+ a b)
11
```

(– <number1> <number2>. . .<numberN>)

The function "–" (minus or subtract) will subtract the second <number> from the first <number> and return the result. If there are more than two <number>s in the list, the third and each successive number is subtracted from the result of the previous subtraction. Another way of looking at it is that the second through the last <number>s are added together and that sum is subtracted from the first number in the list. For example, the expression

```
(- 42 7 5 3 1)
```

is the same as

```
(-(-(-(-42 7) 5) 3) 1)
```

In algebra, it would be expressed as

$$((((42-7)-5)-3)-1)$$

or

$$42-(7+5+3+1)$$

If all the <number>s in the list are integers, the result returned will be an integer. If even one of the <number>s in the list is a real, the result returned by the function will be a real.

If only one <number> is used in the argument list, the result returned will be that <number> subtracted from zero (0).

Examples:

```
(- 3 2)
1
(- 2 14)
-12
(- 47)
-47
(- 86 23 12 13 2 6)
27
(- 97 3 4 5 6 7 8 9 1.0)
54.000000
(- (+ 7 4) 9)
2
(- (+ 85 7) (- 49 6))
49
```

(* <number> <number>)

The function "*" (multiply or times) will multiply all of the <number>s together in a list and return the product of that list. If all the <number>s in the list are integers, the result returned will be an integer. If any of the <number>s in the list is a real, the result will be a real.

Examples:

```
(* 3 4)
12
(* 8 7 6)
```

```
336
(* 3 5 6 8 1.0)
720.000000
(* (+ 6 2) (* 8 9))
576
(* 0.4 4.6 7.1)
13.064000
```

Note the use of 0.4 in the previous example. A real must always begin with a whole number even if it is zero. Using .4 would be incorrect and AutoLISP would return the error message "Illegal dotted pair."

(/ <number1> <number2>. . .<numberN>)

The function "/" (divide) will divide the first <number> by the second and return the quotient as the result. If there are more than two <number>s in the argument list, the first <number> will be divided by the product of the second through the last <number>s. For example, the list

```
(/ 96 4 3 2)
```

is the same as

```
(/ 96 (* 4 3 2))
```

or in algebra

```
96 / (4*3*2)
```

If all of the <number>s in the argument list are integers, the result will be an integer. This could be a problem if the <number>s will not divide evenly and the result could be unpredictable. If you always use at least one real <number> in the argument list (even if the right side of the decimal is zero), all of the integers in the argument list will be converted to reals before the list is evaluated.

Examples:

```
(/ 72 6)
12
(/ 6 72)
0
(/ 6 72.0)
0.083333
(/ 180 9 5 2)
2
(/ 240 16 3 7)
0
(/ 240 16 3 7.0)
0.714286
```

(1+ <number>)
(1− <number>)

The two functions "1+" (one plus) and "1−" (one minus) are grouped together here because they are both primarily used as counters. "1+" will take a <number> passed to it and increment it by 1, the same as (+ <number> 1). "1−" will take a <number> and decrement it by 1, equivalent to (− <number> 1). These functions are recommended for incrementing or decrementing <number>s in a loop because they make it clear that the purpose is to count <number>s rather than to add or subtract.

Examples:

```
(1+ 2)
3
(1+ -2)
-1
(1- 1)
0
```

```
(1- -1)
-2
(1- 3.4)
2.400000
```

Here is how a counter can be used in a loop:

```
(setq count 1 count1 10)
(while (< count 10)
     (1+ count)
     (1- count1)
     (print count)
     (print count1)
)
```

(abs <number>)

The function "abs" (ABSolute) will return the absolute value of a <number>, either a real or an integer. That is, it removes the minus sign from a negative number.

The "abs" function is particularly valuable for filtering out negative angle values when comparing two angles. For example, for all practical purposes, the angle 3.14 is identical to the angle −3.14. However, suppose you were comparing the two angles for equality like this:

```
(equal 3.14 -3.14)
nil
```

AutoLISP would say that the angles were not identical. The correct form would be

```
(equal (abs 3.14) (abs -3.14))
T
```

Examples:

```
(abs 7)
7
(abs -3.987)
3.987000
```

(exp <number>)

The "exp" (e to the X Power) function will return e (the natural log base 2.718282) raised to the <number> power (natural antilog). It will return a real. The expression

```
(exp 2)
7.389056
```

is approximately the same as

```
(expt 2.718282 2)
7.389057
```

or

```
(* 2.718282 2.718282)
7.389057
```

The difference in the last digit is due to an internal rounding error since the log base is carried to 16 decimal places internally. This function is the opposite of the function "log." Thus

```
(log (exp 5))
5.000000
```

and

```
(exp (log 5))
5.000000
```

seemingly return the same value until you try this:

```
(equal (log (exp 5)) (exp (log 5)))
nil
```

This again is due to internal rounding error, and points out possible dangers in testing for equality with numbers that have had floating point operations applied to them before they are compared. You can use the "fuzz" argument in "equal" to control the tolerance within which the other arguments will be accepted as equal.

Examples:

```
(exp 1)
2.718282

(exp 5.0)
148.413200
```

(expt <base> <power>)

The function "expt" (EXPonenT) will raise the <base> argument to the specified <power> argument. If both <base> and <power> are integers, this function will return an integer. If only one of these arguments is a real, the result will be a real.

Examples:

```
(expt 9 3)
729

(expt 3 3.0)
27.000000
```

(fix <number>)

The function "fix" will return the value of <number> as an integer. It does this by truncating the <number> rather than by rounding. The <number> can either be a real or an integer.

Here is a simple function appropriately called "round," that you can use to round a <number>:

```
(defun round (a)
(fix (+0. 5a)))
```

This function adds one half to the argument and then truncates the result.

Examples:

```
(fix 47)
47

(fix 868.25)
868

(fix 99.999999)
99
```

(float <number>)

The function "float" is the opposite of "fix." "Float" takes a <number> and promotes it to a real. This function seems to be a holdover from when LISP did not have built-in functions to automatically promote the arguments to reals if one argument was a real.

Examples:

```
(float 9)
9.000000

(float 56.3)
56.300000
```

(gcd <integer1> <integer2>)

The function "gcd" (Greatest Common Denominator) will return the greatest common denominator of <integer1> and <integer2>. Both arguments must be non-negative integers that fall within the range of 0 to 32,767; otherwise, an error message will be returned.

Examples:

```
(gcd 11 33)
11

(gcd 12345 12346)
1

(gcd 24 78)
6

(gcd 36 -78)
error: improper argument
Must be a positive number.
```

(max <number1> <number2>. . .<numberN>)
(min <number1> <number2>. . .<numberN>)

The functions "max" and "min" will return the maximum or minimum value of <number>s in a list respectively. These <number>s can be reals or integers. If a real appears in the argument list, the result will be a real. The list of numbers must be part of the argument list and not appear as a nested list. You can, however, use the "apply" function to pass a list to "max" or "min."

Examples:

```
(max 27 32 3 -10)
32

(max 47 862.2 987)
987.000000

(min 43 2 -897)
```

```
-897

(min 23 2 97.0)
2.000000
```

Here is how you can apply "max" or "min" to a quoted list of numbers:

```
(setq a '(23 46 29 40.1 -4 89))

(apply 'max a)
89.000000

(apply 'min a)
-4.000000
```

(rem <number1> <number2>. . .<numberN>)

The function "rem" (REMainder) will divide the first <number> by the second <number> and will return only the fractional part of the quotient expressed as a remaining value integer. If there are more than two arguments, the second through the last <number>s will be multiplied together, and the first <number> will be divided by that product. If all of the arguments are integers, the result will be an integer. If even one argument is a real, all of the arguments will be promoted to reals before the function is executed, and the return value will be a real. "Rem" is closely related to the "divide" function, and the following examples compare that relationship.

Examples:

```
(/ 368 17.0)
21.647060

(rem 368 17)
11
```

```
(/ 16 4)
4

(rem 16 4)
0

(rem 16 4)
0

(/ 4 16.0)
0.250000

(rem 4 16.0)
16.000000
```

(sqrt <number>)

The function "sqrt" (SQuare RooT) will return the square root of a <number> as a real. Here is a function, based on the Pythagorean theorem, that will return the hypotenuse of a right triangle given the two sides as arguments:

```
(defun hypot (a b)
     (sqrt (+ (expt a 2) (expt b 2)))
)
```

This is quite a simple process. The two sides, a and b, are squared by raising their numbers by the power of two, they are added together, and the square root of that sum is found.

Examples:

```
(sqrt 16)
4.000000

(sqrt 37)
```

6.082763

(sqrt 2.0)
1.414214

Log and Trig Functions

(atan <number1> [<number2>])

If only the first argument is supplied, "atan" returns the arctangent of <number1> in radians. If both arguments are supplied, "atan" computes the arctangent of <number1>/<number2>.

(cos <angle>)

The function "cos" returns the cosine of the argument <angle>. "Cos" expects that the <angle> will be expressed in radians.

(log <number>)

"Log" returns the natural log of the argument <number> as a real.

(sin <angle>)

The "sin" function will return the sine of the argument <angle>. The argument <angle> must be expressed as a radian.

List Manipulation Functions

Many of the functions in AutoLISP, such as math and string functions, are common to most programming languages. List manipulation functions, however, are unique to LISP. The functions that follow are at the heart of AutoLISP and give you some powerful tools for manipulating symbols.

Here is some specific information on how lists are structured.

A list can be made up of symbols, numbers, strings, or other lists. A symbol is created only when it is declared as the second element of a list that starts with the AutoLISP functions "defun," "setq," or "quote." Every symbol that is created is added to the atomlist, and every time that symbol is evaluated in an expression, AutoLISP must first search the atomlist for that symbol name.

AutoLISP memory is made up of a series of nodes. Each node is 10 bytes long (12 bytes long in Extended AutoLISP) and has a specific address.

When a symbol is created and added to the atomlist, a memory address is included with that symbol name in the atomlist that points to the node containing the symbol. If the symbol is bound to a value, the node containing the symbol will contain a memory address that points to a node containing the value bound to the symbol.

If a symbol is bound to a list, the node that holds the symbol will point to the node that contains the first element of a list, and that node in turn will point to a node containing the next element in the list, and so on.

In more complex lists, such as a list that contains other lists, "'((a b) (c d))" for example, the first list will have a node that points to both the second list and the first symbol of the first list.

Understanding how AutoLISP creates and holds symbols and lists in memory is important when you want to develop an efficient method for writing AutoLISP programs. AutoLISP code that is written to take into consideration the way symbols and lists are held in memory will execute much faster than code that is written in a conventional manner. The following are some programming methods that you may find useful in developing your own code based on the way that AutoLISP is structured.

Keep all symbol names to six characters or fewer. If a symbol name is more than six characters, it will not fit in the node space, and the node will then have a pointer to another area of memory that contains the actual symbol name. This can use up a lot of extra memory. This is less of a consideration with Extended AutoLISP, but even then, keeping the symbol name in the node means that there is one less memory access.

Minimize the number of symbols that you define. Every time you define a symbol, the symbol is added to the atomlist, and each time that symbol is used in an expression, the atomlist must be searched to find that symbol. The longer the atomlist, the longer that search will take.

Bind symbols locally whenever possible within the function within which they will be used, and then reuse the same symbol names in other functions.

It is always faster to pass the return value of a function to another function directly, rather than to set a symbol to the return value of the first function, and then to use that symbol value as an argument to other functions. For example,

```
(* (/ 180 pi) rot)
```

will run faster and will take less memory than

```
(setq a (/ 180 pi))
(* a rot)
```

Avoid writing trivial functions. A function to convert radians to degrees is a good example of a trivial function. Do the conversion in the code when it is needed—this is usually faster than having to do an additional function call. For example, if you had written a function called "rtod" (to convert radians to degrees), you might use it like this:

```
(setq rotang (rtod rot))
(command "insert" blknm ip x y rotang)
```

This form is a little better since it creates one less symbol:

```
(command "insert" blknm ip x y (rtod rot))
```

The preferred way to do this, however, is to calculate your angle conversion within the function argument like this:

```
(command "insert" blknm ip x y (* (/ 180 pi) rot))
```

The built-in AutoLISP functions may execute ten times faster than any "user-defined" functions. You should always experiment, however, because there are no simple rules.

Always write your functions to be as general purpose as possible and you will find that you can use the same functions over and over again for different applications. Also, always write your functions so the only symbols operated on by that function are passed to its parameter list, and so the return value of that function is always made explicit. The following example constitutes poor practice:

```
(defun test (a)
     (setq b 2)
     (if (< a b)
     (setq c 4)
     )
)
```

Since the symbols "b" and "c" are not bound within the function, they are bound globally outside the function. Changing the values of these symbols may inadvertently change values in another part of your program. Also, what value is returned by this function if "a" is greater than "b?" Here is how this function should be written:

```
(defun test (a / b c)      ;b and c declared as locals
     (setq b 2)
     (if (< a b)
        (setq c 4)
        (setq c 2)         ;some value has to be returned
     )                     ;if a is greater than b

)
```

An even better way would be the following:

```
(defun test (a))
(if (<a 2) 4 2))
```

(append <list1>. . .<listN>)

The "append" function will append a series of lists together into a single list. This function is particularly helpful when you want to combine several lists into a single list for easier manipulation. The arguments to append must be lists.

"Append" is one of three list building functions (the other two are "cons" and "list"). Each function has a specific purpose and each will build a list differently. There is a lot of confusion about using these three functions, so several examples comparing these functions follow.

Examples:

```
(append '(a b c) '(d e f))
(a b c d e f)

(setq a (this is))
(THIS IS)
(setq b (a list))
(A LIST)
(append a b)
(THIS IS A LIST)

(append '(d e f) '((g h i) (j k l))
         '(m n o p) '(q))
(D E F (G H I) (J K L) M N O P Q)
```

The following is how to append a symbol to a list:

```
(append '(x y) (list 'a))
(X Y A)
```

(assoc <arg> <association-list>)

The association list (sometimes called an "a-list") is a list that contains sublists. The first element of each of these sublists is called the "key." The "assoc" function will search a given association list for a specific key and will return the first sublist that contains that key. Each entity record in AutoCAD is formatted as an association list. "Assoc" is so fast that it can search an association list containing several hundred sublists in less than a second. Any time you want to search through a database, you should format it into an association list.

Here are two examples of association lists:

```
(setq animal
    '(
    (cats persian siamese)
    (dogs shepherd terrier)
    (horses morgan quarter)
    )
)

(setq persian
    '(
    (fur long)
    (face flat)
    )
)
```

The first a-list is accessed by

```
(assoc 'cats animal)
(CATS PERSIAN SIAMESE)
```

The second list is accessed by

```
(assoc 'face persian)
(FACE FLAT)
```

Note that the symbol bound to the second list "persian" is also found in the first a-list under the key "cats." Once the second list is evaluated, it becomes a sublist of the first a-list. The second list can be accessed through the first list with this form:

```
(assoc 'face (eval (cadr (assoc 'cats animals))))
(FACE FLAT)
```

Both of the a-lists can be seen as structured as one list like this:

```
(setq animal
     '(
      (cats (persian
               (fur long)
               (face flat)
            )
            siamese)
     (dogs shepherd terrier)
     (horses morgan quarter)
     )
)
```

Association lists are not limited to symbols, but can also be created from strings. The advantage of strings is that they do not take up space on the atomlist to slow things down. Here is an association list made up of strings:

```
(setq phone '(("Joe" "555-3457")
              ("John" "555-4288")
              ("Jerry" "555-2030")))
```

Here is how to find Jerry's phone number simply:

```
(assoc "Jerry" phone)
("Jerry" "555-2030")
```

The only thing that will appear on the atomlist is the symbol PHONE.

Association lists are usually created with the function "cons." You will see an example of a function that will create an association list from a data file in the section on the "cons" function.

Warning: Never create an association list with more than one sublist with the same key. The second sublist with the duplicate key in the a-list will never be found.

Examples:

Here is what a line entity looks like from the AutoCAD database:

```
((−1 . <Entity name: 60000014>) (0 . "LINE") (8 . "0")
(10 1.000000 1.000000) (11 9.000000 1.000000))
```

(car <list>)
(cdr <list>)

The functions "car" and "cdr" are designed to take a list apart. "Car" will return the first element of the list passed to it as an argument and "cdr" will return the list minus the first element. If the list is empty, both of these functions will return nil. This is very simple yet powerful, as you will see in the examples.

Examples:

```
(car '(a b c))
A

(cdr '(a b c))
(B C)
```

If the list is a dotted pair list, "cdr" will return the last element in that list:

```
(cdr '(0 . "LINE"))
"LINE"
```

"Car" and "cdr" are particularly handy for taking a list apart symbol by symbol so that each symbol on the list can be operated on in turn. Here is a code fragment example of such a use:

```
(setq lklist '(a b c d e f g h i j k)) ;declare the list
(while lklist                          ;begin the loop
     (setq symbop (car lklist))  ;sets symbop to first item
     (setq lklist (cdr lklist))   ;removes first item in list
;do something here to symbop
)
;loop repeats until lklist is empty
```

"Car" and "cdr" can be combined together to return elements that are deeply nested within a list. The following is one such example:

```
(car (cdr '(a b c)))
B

(car (cdr (cdr '(a b c))))
C
```

Or you can reach into a sublist of a list like this:

```
(car (cdr '((a b c) (d e f))))
(D E F)
```

You can go even deeper, as in this example:

```
(car (cdr (car (cdr '((a b c) (d e f))))))
E

(car (cdr (car (cdr '(((a b) (c d)) ((e f) (g h)))))))
G
```

As you can see, using "car" and "cdr" to extract elements buried deeply in a list can get quite complicated. There is a slightly easier way to do this. There are 28 functions that are the equivalent of using various combinations of "car" and "cdr" to extract elements of a list. These functions are known as the concatenations of "car" and "cdr" and will be covered in great detail in the next section.

The Concatenations of "car" and "cdr" The 28 different functions that represent the different combinations of "car" and "cdr" are listed here:

```
(caar ) (caaar ) (cadar ) (caaaar ) (caaadr )
(caadar ) (caaddr ) (caadr ) (cadaar ) (cadadr )
(caddar ) (cadddr ) (caddr ) (cadr ) (cdaar )
(cdadr ) (cdar ) (cddar ) (cddr ) (cdaaar )
(cdaadr ) (cdadar ) (cdaddr ) (cddaar ) (cddadr )
(cdddar ) (cddddr ) (cdddr )
```

You will probably never need to use more than two of these: "cadr" and "caddr":

```
(cadr <list>)
(caddr <list>)
```

The function "cadr" will return the second element of a list, while "caddr" will return the third element of a list. These two functions are used, along with "car," to extract the X, Y, and Z coordinates from a coordinate list.

Examples:

The expression

```
(cadr <list>)
```

is the same as

```
(car (cdr <list>))
```

```
(cadr '(a b c))
B
```

```
(car (cdr '(a b c)))
B
```

The expression

```
(caddr <list>)
```

is the same as

```
(car (cdr (cdr <list>)))
(caddr '(a b c))
C

(car (cdr (cdr '(a b c))))
C
```

The 28 concatenations of "car" and "cdr" can be divided into 4 groups, with the division based on how deeply they can extract elements from a nested list.

The first group will only extract elements from the top level of a list. Given the following list

```
(setq tl '(a b c d e))
```

then

Function	Returns	Equivalent
(car tl)	A	(car tl)
(cadr tl)	B	(car (cdr tl))
(caddr tl)	C	(car (cdr (cdr tl)))
(cadddr tl)	D	(car (cdr (cdr (cdr tl))))
(cdr tl)	(B C D E)	(cdr tl)
(cddr tl)	(C D E)	(cdr (cdr tl))
(cdddr tl)	(D E)	(cdr (cdr (cdr tl)))
(cddddr tl)	(E)	(cdr (cdr (cdr (cdr tl))))

The second group of functions will extract elements from the second level of nesting in a list. With the following list as an example

```
(setq sl '((a b c d) (e f g h) (i j k l)))
```

then

Function	Returns	Equivalent
(caar sl)	A	(car (car sl))
(cadar sl)	B	(car (cdr (car sl)))
(caddar sl)	C	(car (cdr (cdr (car sl))))
(caadr sl)	E	(car (car (cdr sl)))
(cadadr sl)	F	(car (cdr (car (cdr sl))))
(caaddr sl)	I	(car (car (cdr (cdr sl))))
(cdar sl)	(B C D)	(cdr (car sl))
(cddar sl)	(C D)	(cdr (cdr (car sl)))
(cdddar sl)	(D)	(cdr (cdr (cdr (car sl))))
(cdadr sl)	(F G H)	(cdr (car (cdr sl)))
(cddadr sl)	(G H)	(cdr (cdr (car (cdr sl))))
(cdaddr sl)	(J K L)	(cdr (car (cdr (cdr sl))))

The third group of functions will extract elements nested three levels deep in a list. With the following list

```
(setq tl '(((a b c) (d e f)) ((g h i) (j k l))))
```

then

Function	Returns	Equivalent
(caaar tl)	A	(car (car (car tl)))
(cadaar tl)	B	(car (cdr (car (car tl))))
(caadar tl)	D	(car (car (cdr (car tl))))
(caaadr tl)	G	(car (car (car (cdr tl))))
(cddaar tl)	(C)	(cdr (cdr (car (car tl))))
(cdaar tl)	(B C)	(cdr (car (car tl)))
(cdadar tl)	(E F)	(cdr (car (cdr (car tl))))
(cdaadr tl)	(H I)	(cdr (car (car (cdr tl))))

Finally, the two functions in the fourth group will extract elements buried four levels deep in a list. Given this list,

```
(setq fl '((((a b c)))))
```

then

Function	Returns	Equivalent
(caaaar fl)	A	(car (car (car (car fl))))
(cdaaar fl)	(B C)	(cdr (car (car (car fl))))

You can, of course, combine these functions to go even deeper into a list like this:

```
(cadr (cdaaar fl))
```

If you examine these function names, you will see how the names are structured.

If the first two characters in the name are "ca," that function starts with a "car."

If the first two characters in the name are "cd," that function starts with a "cdr."

If the last two characters in the name are "ar," that function ends with a "car."

If the last two characters in the name are "dr," that function ends with a "cdr."

An "a" character between the first two and last two characters represents a "car" function in that position.

A "d" character between the first two and last two characters represents a "cdr" function in that position.

Following these rules, you could even write your own list extraction function. For example, a function to extract the "I" element from list "tl" would look like this:

```
(defun caddaadr (tl)
     (cadr (cdaadr tl))
)
```

This is the same as the following:

```
(car (cdr (cdr (car (car (cdr tl))))))
I
```

(cons <new-first-element> <list>)

The function "cons" (or CONStruct) is one of the three functions designed to build a list. "Cons" will take a new first element as the first argument, either an atom or list, and a list as the second argument, and return that list with the new first element added to the front of that list.

"Cons" will also take an atom as the second argument and return what is known as a dotted pair list of those two arguments. A dotted pair list is a three item list where the second item is a dot (or a period) and the third element is always an atom. A dotted pair list takes up less memory than a two element list. The last element can be extracted with "cdr." The only way that a dotted pair list can be constructed is with "cons." "Cons" can create lists of strings.

Examples:

```
(cons 'a '(b c))
(A B C)

(cons "these" '("are" "strings"))
("these" "are" "strings")

(cons '(a b) '(c d))
```

```
((A B) C D)

(cons '(a b) '( ))
((A B))

(cons 'a '( ))
(A)
```

Here are examples of dotted pair lists:

```
(setq a (cons 'b 'c))
(B . C)
```

And here is how the elements are extracted:

```
(car a)
B

(cdr a)
C

(cons '("another" "string") 'c)
(("another" "string") . C)
```

The following is a function to demonstrate how an association list can be created with "cons" from a simple data file. This function will create an association list that will contain sublists with two strings, the first string being the key for that sublist. Assume that the data file is structured with each element on a separate line like this:

```
"John"
"555-2345"
"Joe"
"555-4242"
"Jim"
"555-6742"
```

and so on . . .

```
(defun bldlist ( / sublist fname l a)
;creates two empty lists to put the data in
     (setq association-list ( ) sublist ( ))
;prompts for a file name
     (setq fname (getstring "File name to read: "))
;opens the file
     (setq l (open (strcat fname ) "r"))
;reads the first line in the file to A
     (setq a (read-line l))
;as long as there are lines in the file do the loop
     (while a
;read two lines for each list
     (repeat 2
;put the current line in sublist with cons
          (setq sublist (cons a sublist))
;read the next line of the file
          (setq a (read-line l))
     )
;when two lines are read reverse the order of sublist to
;put the key at the beginning of the list
        (setq sublist (reverse sublist))
;add the sublist to the association-list with cons
        (setq association-list (cons sublist
                                  association-list))
;clear out the sublist
        (setq sublist ( ))
     );end of the while loop
     (close l);close the data file
(setq association-list (reverse association list))
)
```

After this function has read the example data file, the association list that it has created will look like this:

```
(("John" "555-2345")
("Joe" "555-4242")
("Jim" "555-6742"))
```

Here is a function that will save an association list to a data file in the same format as the last example:

```
(defun svlist ( / slist sublist fname l)
;prompt for name of a-list to save
     (setq slist (getstring "A-List to save: "))
;converts string to symbol
     (setq slist (read slist))
;gets list pointed to by symbols list
     (setq slist (eval slist))
;prompts for a file name
     (setq fname (getstring "File name to write: "))
;opens the file
     (setq l (open (strcat fname "w")))
;as long as there is anything in SLIST do the loop
     (while slist
;sets sublist to the first sub-list in the a-list
        (setq sublist (car slist))
;return all but the first element in the list
        (setq slist (cdr slist))
;while there is anything in the sublist
        (while sublist
;write the first element of the sublist
           (write-line (car sublist) l)
;return all but the first element in the list
           (setq sublist (cdr sublist))
        )
     )
     (close l);close the data file
)
```

(last <list>)

The function "last" will return the last element of a list. Be cautious with this one when manipulating point lists. Many times, the last element of a list is not what you think it is.

Examples:

```
(last '(a b c))
C

(last '((a b c) (d (e f))))
(D (E F))
```

(length <list>)

The function "length" will return an integer reporting the number of elements in a list.

Examples:

```
(length '(a b c))
3

(length '((a b) (c d (e f))))
2

(length (cadr '((a b) (c d (e f)))))
3

(length '( ))
0
```

(list <expr1>. . .<exprN>)

The function "list" will take any number of valid LISP expressions (including strings) and concatenate them together into a list. "List" is one of three AutoLISP functions that will create lists.

Examples:

```
(list 'a 'b 'c)
(A B C)
```

```
(list '(x y z) '(o x p))
((X Y Z) (O X P))

(list '33.1 '47.9)
(33.100000 47.00000)
```

"List" is very useful for creating lists to manipulate two- and three-dimensional coordinates. Suppose you had a coordinate point and you wished to generate a box measuring two-by-two units beginning with the lower left corner. Here is that code:

```
(defun dbox (ip)            ;ip must be a list of two reals
  (command "line"
   ip                                     ;starting point
   (list (+ 2 (car ip)) (cadr ip))        ;lower right pt
   (list (+ 2 (car ip)) (+ 2 (cdr ip)))   ;upper right pt
   (list (car ip) (+ 2 (cadr ip)))        ;upper left pt
   "c"                                    ;close to start
  )
)
```

See the "polar" function for another version of this function.

(member <expr> <list>)

"Member" will search <list> for the first instance of <expr> in that <list> and will return the balance of the <list> from <expr> to the end. If <expr> is not found, "member" returns nil.

"Member" can be used either to return something of value from a <list> or to simply test whether <expr> is in <list>.

Examples:

```
(member 'l '(j k l m n o))
(L M N O)

(member "these" '("are" "these" "strings"))
```

```
("these" "strings")

(member "THESE" '("are" "these" "strings"))
nil
```

When you search for strings in lists with "member" and "assoc," you must be aware of the case of the strings. While AutoLISP is not case sensitive with symbols, it is with strings.

Here is an example of some AutoLISP code that uses "member" to test for the presence of <expr> in a <list>. This code will read the keyboard directly within a loop and will only drop out of that loop if either the Y or the N key is pressed.

```
    (setq a nil)
;list of ASCII codes for Y, y, N, n, return and space
;anything desired for a valid key stroke can be added here
    (setq ynlst '(0 13 32 78 89 110 121))
;if A isn't in the list continue to loop
    (while (not (member a ynlst))
;read the keyboard and set A to ASCII value of pressed key
        (setq a (last (grread)))
    )
;do something here depending on the key pressed
```

(nth <posit-num> <list>)

"Nth" will return the "nth" (or <posit-num>) element of <list>. The positions in a list are always numbered from right to left starting from zero, that is, the first element in a list is numbered zero. <posit-num> must always be a positive integer. If <posit-num> is greater than the number of elements in a list minus one, nil is returned.

Examples:

```
(nth 3 '(f g h i j k))
I
```

```
(nth 0 '(f g h i j k))
F

(nth 2 '((f g h) (i j k) (l m n)))
(L M N)
```

(reverse <list>)

"Reverse" returns the argument <list> with all of its elements in reverse order.

Since lists are normally created by adding elements to the front of the list, "reverse" is often used to place the applied list in the correct order. See the function in the example for building an association list for an illustration of this use.

Examples:

```
(reverse '(d e f))
(F E D)

(reverse '(g h (i j)))
((I J) H G)
```

"Reverse" only operates on the top level of the list.

(subst <new-arg> <old-arg> <list>)

The function "subst" (SUBSTitute) will search <list> for any instances of <old-arg> and then return a copy of that <list> with every case of <old-arg> replaced by <new-arg>. If <old-arg> is not found in <list>, <list> is returned without being modified. "Subst" is one of the most unique functions in LISP. With "subst," you can change anything in the drawing database and you can even alter the AutoLISP code itself.

The use of "subst" to modify the drawing database will be discussed in more detail in the "Entity Data Functions" section later in this chapter. This section only concerns itself with more general applications of "subst."

Examples:

"Subst" is frequently used to update data in association lists. The first few examples deal with association lists:

```
(setq phone '(("John" "555-2345")
              ("Joe" "555-4242")
              ("Jim" "555-6742")
              ("Jerry" 555-4234")))
```

Suppose Joe has a new phone number and you want to update your phone list. First, get Joe's number and put it in a symbol like this:

```
(setq old (assoc "Joe" phone))
("Joe" "555-4242")
```

Now the symbol OLD is bound to the sublist with Joe's name and number. This gives you <old-arg>. Now you can use "subst" to substitute the new phone number for the old one:

```
(setq phone (subst '("Joe" "555-9696") old phone))
```

This returns

```
(("John" "555-2345")
("Joe" "555-9696")
("Jim" "555-6742")
("Jerry" 555-4234"))
```

In this example, <new-arg> was just placed in the expression, but it would not be too difficult to write code to create the <new-arg> from user input.

Remember, "subst" does not actually modify the original list, but only returns a modified copy of that list. To make the substitution permanent, you must use "setq" to bind the modified copy of the list to the original symbol.

So far you have seen how "subst" can replace a sublist within the top level of a list. With a little symbol manipulation, you can dig as deeply as necessary into a complex list and use "subst" to change individual symbols within that list. Consider this simple association list:

```
(setq tlist '((a b) (c d)))
```

Suppose you want to change the "b" in the first sublist to a "z." Here is the code to do that:

```
(subst (subst 'z (cadr (assoc 'a tlist))
                 (assoc 'a tlist))
   (assoc 'a tlist) tlist)
   ((A Z) (C D))
```

This looks complex, so let's break it down into several individual steps. Retrieve the first sublist with "assoc:"

```
(setq ol (assoc 'a tlist))
(A B)
```

Now use "subst" to change "b" to "z" and bind that list to a new symbol:

```
(setq nl (subst 'z (cadr ol) ol))
```

Finally, replace the old sublist in the association list with "subst" like this:

```
(setq tlist (subst nl ol tlist))
((A Z) (C D))
```

This three-step process is identical to the more complex expression that was presented earlier. It is better to use the more complex expression, because it does not add symbols to the atomlist and is therefore faster and uses less memory.

Assignment Functions

The next group of functions are functions that assign or read values within AutoCAD and AutoLISP.

(getenv <var-name>)

Your operating system has an environment storage array that contains environment variable names. The most common example of an environment variable is the DOS PATH variable. You can read more about PATH and the environment in your DOS manual. AutoCAD uses certain environment variables itself. You can use the "getenv" function to return the contents of these variables.

Examples:

```
(getenv "PATH")
"c/acad"
(getenv "ACAD")
"/acad"
```

(getvar <var-name>)

The function "getvar" returns the current value of an AutoCAD system variable. The argument <var-name> must be a valid system variable and <var-name> must be enclosed in quotes (since it is a string). If <var-name> is not a valid system variable, "getvar" will return nil.

Information about all of the AutoCAD system variables can be found in Chapter 16, "AutoCAD Command Reference," or by typing **SETVAR <return> ? <return>** on the AutoCAD command line.

As a common practice, <var-name> is usually typed in uppercase to distinguish it from AutoLISP symbols.

Examples:

```
(getvar "MENUNAME")
ACAD

(getvar "ORTHOMODE")
0
```

(quote <expr>)

The "quote" function will return an expression without evaluation. Putting an apostrophe in front of an expression is the shorthand version of "quote."

Examples:

```
(quote a)
A

(quote (+ 9 7.1))
(+ 9 7.1)
```

is the same as

```
'(+ 9 7.1)
(+ 9 7.1)
```

(set <sym> <expr>)

The function "set" will set the value of <sym>, if <sym> is a quoted symbol, to the value of <expr>, and returns that value. The expression

```
(set (quote a) 6)
6
```

or

```
(set 'a 6)
6
```

is identical to

```
(setq a 6)
6
```

If you just want to bind the value of an expression to a symbol, it is more straightforward to use the "setq" function. "Set" does, however, have the unique ability to reassign a value of a symbol indirectly, as you will see in the following examples.

Examples:

```
(set 'x 4.0)
4.000000

(set (quote y) '(g h l))
(G H L)

(set 'z 'x)
X
```

In this case, "set" provides a link between <sym> "z" and <sym> "x." Now, if you assign a value to Z (without the quote)

```
(set z 980)
980
```

You will find that <sym> "x" will also be bound to the value of 980.

(setq <sym> <expr> [<sym> <expr1>. . .<exprN>])

The function "setq" (SET Quote) will assign (or bind) the value of <expr> to <sym>. "Setq" can assign an indefinite number of expressions to a like number of symbols.

"Setq" (along with "defun") is the main assignment function in AutoLISP. Most versions of LISP have a function called "defvar" that must be used to declare a symbol before the symbol can be used. AutoLISP, on the other hand, allows the programmer to both declare and define symbols at any point in the program.

"Setq," "set," and "defun" are the only functions that will add symbols to the atomlist. For that reason, you should use these functions sparingly when you write AutoLISP code since execution speed is somewhat dependent on the length of the atomlist.

If a symbol does not exist, it will be created by "setq." "Setq" and "set" can be used to define a symbol locally if the symbol name appears in the argument list of a function definition. For example, examine the following function:

```
(setq x 98.6)
(setq d 45)
(defun test (a b / c d)
     (setq c 47)          ;Binds a value locally
     (print c)            ;Prints the local value of c
     (setq x 62)          ;Binds a new value globally
     (print x)            ;Prints x
     (setq d "D")         ;Binds a local value
     (print d)            ;Prints the local value of d
)
(print d)                 ;Prints the global value of d
(print a)                 ;Prints value of a (nil)
```

In the preceding function, the symbol "d" is declared to be both global (defined outside the function) and local (defined within the function). The value of the symbol "d" can change while the function is executing and return to its original global value once the function has ended. This is a very important feature, since it means that the same symbols can be used over and over again, thus keeping the atomlist short to maximize execution speed.

Be very careful when you choose names for your symbols because "setq" can also redefine the built-in AutoLISP functions. If the name of a built-in function is used as a variable, the original function becomes inaccessible.

Examples:

```
(setq a 47)
47

(setq b 63.1)
63.1

(setq a 23 b 45.1 c 29.2)
29.2
```

Remember, a function only returns the result of the last expression that it evaluated. In this case, it returns the value bound to the symbol C. Just to check, you could find the values bound to symbols A and B like this:

```
!a
23
!b
45.1

(setq x 36)
36
(setq c x)
```

```
36

(setq d 'x)
X
```

Since the symbol X is quoted in the last example, X is not evaluated.

(setvar <var-name> <value>)

"Setvar" (SET VARiable) is used to set the <value> of an AutoCAD system variable <var-name> and returns <value>. The <var-name> must be a string (enclosed in quotes) and must be a valid AutoCAD system variable name.

The <value> must be of a data type that is within the valid value range for the particular system variable being set. For example, the system variable INSBASE expects a list containing two or three reals, SNAPANG expects a real and CMDECHO requires an integer between the range of zero and one.

The function "setvar" is identical in use to the AutoCAD command SETVAR. See Chapter 16, "AutoCAD Command Reference," for a complete list of all of the AutoCAD system variables along with a description of what each one controls.

Examples:

```
(setvar "INSBASE" '(3.0 2.1 0.0))
(3.0 2.1 0.0)

(setvar "TEXTSIZE" 1.25)
1.25

(setvar "MENUECHO" 2)
2
```

The following two functions are practical examples of the functions "setvar" and "getvar" and how they can be used to store numerous user variables in an AutoCAD drawing.

This first function will separately set the value of each individual digit of one of the user variables (USERI1 to USERI5). This enables you to have as many as 25 user variables set in a drawing instead of 5.

The first digit of the USERI variable can be set from 1 to 2, and the other four digits can be set from 0 to 9. This function is usually called from another function, and the arguments passed to it are as follows:

intvar	The integer user variable string—from USERI1 to USERI5
varpos	The digit to which you wish to set a value—1 to 5
subvar	The new value to which you wish to set the digit

```
(defun codevar (intvar varpos subvar / newstr vartocd fststr
                                       lststr newvar)
    (setq newstr (itoa subvar))
    (setq vartocd (itoa (getvar intvar)))
    (if (> varpos 1)
        (setq fststr (substr vartocd 1 (1- varpos)))
    )
    (if (< varpos 5)
        (setq lststr (substr vartocd (1+ varpos)))
    )
    (if (> varpos 1)
        (if (< varpos 5)
          (setq newvar (atoi (strcat fststr newstr lststr)))
          (setq newvar (atoi (strcat fststr newstr)))
        )
        (setq newvar (atoi (strcat newstr lststr)))
    )
    (setvar intvar newvar)
)
```

The "lkupvar" function reads the "sub-variable" that was set in the preceding function "codevar." "Intvar" is the name of the integer variable that contains the desired "sub-variable" and "varpos" is the digit position of the "sub-variable." This function returns the value that is contained in the "sub-variable."

```
(defun lkupvar (intvar varpos / vartocd)
    (setq vartocd (itoa (getvar intvar)))
    (atoi (substr vartocd varpos 1))
)
```

Procedural Functions

Procedural functions are used to describe a series of step-by-step instructions for the computer to execute. Procedural functions or procedures are common to all computer languages.

(apply <function> <list>)

"Apply" will take the specified <function> pass <list> to it as that function's arguments and return the result of executing that <function>. <Function> can be a built-in function, a user-defined function, or an anonymous function created with lambda.

The <list> must contain the same arguments that would be used in the <function> argument list.

"Apply" is particularly useful when you want to operate on lists of data that would not normally be evaluated. For example, consider the following quoted list:

```
(setq a '(1 2 3 4 5 6 7 8))
(1 2 3 4 5 6 7 8)
```

If you wanted to find the maximum value contained in this list, you might try the following form:

```
(max a)
```

But since the list is quoted, this function will fail because AutoLISP will try to evaluate the symbol itself rather than the list bound to the symbol. "Apply," however, will work in this situation since it already expects a list as an argument:

```
(apply 'max a)
8
```

The only other way to find the maximum value in "a" is this:

```
(eval (cons max a))
8
```

"Apply" is a little tricky to use, because when "apply" actually passes <list> to the <function>, it essentially adds the function name to the beginning of the list and evaluates the resulting single list as in the previous example. If you do not understand this fact, the following might seem to be a reasonable way to return the first element in the list "a:"

```
(apply 'car a)
```

But this will fail, because once the <list> is passed to the <function> "car," it is no longer a list and "apply" would be trying to evaluate something that looks like this:

```
(car 1 2 3 4 5 6 7 8)
```

The correct form for this expression would be to make sure that the list "a" is passed as a list to "car" like the following:

```
(apply 'car (list a))
1
```

The way to prove that "apply" does not really pass <list> intact is to test it like this:

```
(apply 'type a)
INT
```

The function "type" only looks at the first element passed to it by "apply."

Examples:

```
(apply '1- '4)
3

(setq a '(1 2 3 4 5 6 7 8))
(apply '- a)
-34
```

(command <command> <command-args1>. . . <command-argsN>)

The function "command" calls the AutoCAD command processor, passes <command> to the command line, and then passes <command-args> to the AutoCAD command that was called. The data contained in the argument list of "command" is treated as if it had been typed from the keyboard at the command prompt. "Command" always returns nil.

"Command" is the only AutoLISP function that will add entity records to the drawing database. Most other functions will only alter existing records to a limited degree. If you want to add a line to a drawing with AutoLISP, you would use the "command" function to call the LINE command.

"Command" will call any valid AutoCAD command, including a user-defined command created with the C option of "defun."

Here is a simple example of how the "command" function is used to draw a polyline square with "mapcar:"

```
(defun c:square ()
    (setq a (getpoint "\nPick lower left corner: "))
    (setq b (getreal "\nLength of side: "))
    (command "PLINE"
                a              ;start point
                (mapcar '+ a (list b 0));second point
```

```
                (mapcar '+ a (list b b));third point
                (mapcar '+ a (list 0 b));fourth point
                "C")                    ;close polyline
)
```

The following is a more complex example of a function that draws a polyline using a list of points passed to the function as an argument:

```
(defun newpoly (vrtlst / n)
;Adds the string "C" to the list to close polyline at end.
     (setq vrtlst (reverse (cons "C" (reverse vrtlst)))
;Invokes the PLINE command.
     (command "PLINE")
;Passes each point in turn through the command function
     (foreach n vrtlst (command n)))
)
```

Notice that "command" is called a number of times, once for PLINE and once for each point in the list. As long as the command called by the "command" function is not terminated, you can call the "command" function as many times as you want to complete the data set required by the specific command being called. The preceding example can be simplified even more by placing the string "PLINE" in the list with "cons" and by using the "foreach" function to make all of the "command" function calls like this:

```
(defun newpoly (vrtlst / n)
     (setq vrtlst (cons "C" (reverse vrtlst)))
     (setq vrtlst (reverse vrtlst))
;Add the string "PLINE" to the beginning of the list.
     (setq vrtlst (cons "PLINE" vrtlst))
;Pass everything in the list through command with foreach.
     (foreach n vrtlst (command n))
)
```

Obviously, the "command" function is very powerful and useful. There are, however, a few things that you have to be very careful about when you use this function.

None of the user input functions (such as "getpoint," "getstring," "getint," and so on) will work as an AutoLISP expression inside the "command" function. AutoCAD will return an error message and cancel the entire function (usually causing a failure of your whole AutoLISP program). If you need user input for the "command" function, use the user input functions before the "command" function is called.

If you want to pause the execution of a "command" function for user input, you can use the predefined symbol PAUSE in the appropriate location. Just make sure that the AutoCAD system variable TEXTEVAL is set to 1; otherwise, AutoLISP will interpret the PAUSE symbol as the string "PAUSE" and try to force that string into the command (usually crashing the program).

Always double-check the number of <command-args> being used with a specific <command>. Many times commands such as COPY and ERASE require an extra carriage return to terminate the selection process.

Make sure that the correct command options are being specified, such as the "XYZ" option in INSERT if you want to specify a Z coordinate for an insertion.

Check out the command by typing it on the command line and noting all of the necessary inputs and options before you put it in your AutoLISP code.

If you are using another AutoLISP expression as part of the argument list of "command," make certain that the expression will return the value that is expected for that argument. Generally, loops do not work inside the "command" function because they usually only return the value of the last iteration.

Example:

```
(setq ssa (ssget "X" (list (cons 0 "CIRCLE"))))
<selection-set 1>
(command "ERASE" ssa "")
nil
```

This example will erase all circles in a drawing. Selection sets can be passed to any command that will take LAST as a selection option.

The following example illustrates how the symbol PAUSE is used in the "command" function to pause execution for user input. This example will invoke the MOVE command, pause to allow the user to pick the object to move (the "Select Object" prompt is issued), and then cause the object to be moved four units to the right. The system variable TEXTEVAL is first set to 1 so that the PAUSE symbol will not be interpreted as a string.

```
(setvar "TEXTEVAL" 1)

(command "MOVE" pause "" '(0 0) '(4 0)) nil
```

The problem with using the PAUSE symbol is that AutoCAD will accept any input and will not check to see if it is valid before passing it to the command. Thus, if the user inadvertently hit the ENTER key or typed a word from the keyboard, this function would crash. A more crashproof way of implementing user input to a "command" function would be to request user input, and to check the validity of the input before passing the input data to the "command" function. Here is an example of how that can be implemented:

```
(defun c:mymove ( / c)
     (setq c nil)
     (while (null c)
          (setq c (car (entsel)))
     )
     (command "MOVE" c""'(0 0) '(4 0))
)
```

In this example, the "Select Object" prompt will not go away until you have picked an entity. Typing from the keyboard, pressing ENTER, or picking an empty spot on the screen will have no effect.

This final example not only checks for a valid entity selection, but also checks to see if the proper type of entity has been selected. This function will convert any circle to a 32-sided polygon inscribed within the area bound by the circle. It would be simple to add a user input prompt to request the number of sides for the polygon.

```
(defun c:c2pgon ( )
     (setq circ (car (entsel
               "\nPick circle for conversion:" )))
     (if (equal (cdr (assoc 0 (entget circ))) "CIRCLE")
          (progn
               (setq rad (cdr (assoc 40 (entget circ))))
               (setq cen (cdr (assoc 10 (entget circ))))
               (entdel circ)
               (command "POLYGON" 32 cen "I" rad)
          )
          (princ "\nEntity picked is not a circle ")
     )
     (princ)
)
```

(defun <func-name> <argument-list> <expr1>. . .<exprN>)

"Defun" (DEfine FUNction) defines a function named <func-name>. <Argument-list> contains a list of arguments (if any) passed to the definition and may, optionally, contain a list of locally declared symbols followed by <expr> which contains the function definition itself. "Defun" returns the <func-name> if it has been successfully loaded by AutoLISP.

"Defun" is the function that you will use when you want to create your own AutoLISP functions. In fact, you cannot do anything with AutoLISP unless you first define what it is you want to do with a function.

A function is the smallest complete unit of a LISP program, and a single function can be a complete LISP program. A function may be called by another LISP function and executed, or it can be invoked and executed directly from the AutoCAD command line.

A function is simply a set of step-by-step instructions telling AutoLISP exactly what you want it to do. Functions are similar to programs, functions, procedures, or subroutines in other programming languages. Some books on LISP divide functions into two types—functions and procedures, depending on what each one is designed to accomplish. In LISP, all procedures are functions, but not all functions are procedures. The distinction is minor and since the AutoLISP Programmer's Reference does not mention procedures, this book will not confuse the issue.

The first item in the function definition list is the word "defun," which tells AutoLISP that what follows is a function definition, binds that definition to the symbol that follows <func-name>, and places <func-name> on the atomlist so it can be accessed by other functions. This is why it seems to take a long time to load a LISP file.

The name of the function <func-name> is followed by <argument-list>, sometimes called the parameter list. An argument is an independent variable, or in this case a symbol, that takes the value given it when the function is called, and uses that value within the function. Some functions have no arguments while other functions may have many.

The <argument-list> can also contain symbols that have been declared locally within the given function. The arguments and the locally declared symbols must be separated by a slash and a space " / " within <argument-list>. Here are some examples of how <argument-list> is used:

```
(defun tst ( ) <expr>)          ;no arguments or local
                                ;symbols
(defun tst (x) <expr>)          ;one argument, no local
                                ;symbols
(defun tst (x y) <expr>)        ;two arguments, no local
                                ;symbols
(defun tst (x y / z) <expr>)    ;two arguments, one local
                                ;symbol
(defun tst (/ x y) <expr>)      ;no arguments, two local
                                ;symbols
```

```
(defun c:tst (/ x) <expr>)          ;defined as command, one
                                    ;local symbol
```

The rest of the list contains the function definition <expr>. Here is an example of a simple function:

```
(defun tst (x) (* x 2))
```

(eval <expr>)

The function "eval" (EVALuate) forces an evaluation of <expr> and returns the result of evaluating that expression.

"Eval" is a useful function for two reasons. Adding "eval" to a function can sometimes speed up execution of that function and, more important, "eval" can evaluate a quoted expression.

In LISP, there is essentailly no difference between data and programs—they are both lists. It has been said that in LISP a procedure is only a piece of data until it has been evaluated. This means that there can be AutoLISP programs that can be read in as data and evaluated as a procedure until they are needed. The following example illustrates this:

```
(setq a '(1 2 3 4 5 6 7 8))
(1 2 3 4 5 6 7 8)

(setq b (cons '+ a))
(+ 1 2 3 4 5 6 7 8)
```

Notice that the last expression returned a list with "+" as the first symbol unevaluated.

```
(eval b)
36
```

And finally the expression is evaluated only when it is needed. This is a very simple example, but very complex and subtle programs can be created with this technique. For instance, the data list does not have to be kept in the same .LSP file with the rest of the program, but can be read in from a separate data file or can even be an attribute value contained in a block.

Examples:

```
(eval (command "break" ent "F" pt1 pt2))

(setq a 0 b "LINE")
"LINE"

(setq c '(cons a b))
(cons a b)

(eval c)
(0 . "LINE")
```

(foreach <name> <list> <expr1>. . .<exprN>)

For each element in the <list>, the element is assigned to <name>. For each <name> so assigned, each <expr> is evaluated. The value of the last <expr> evaluated with the last member of the list is returned.

Example:

```
(foreach bolt '(plate arm base) (print bolt))
```

(lambda <arguments> <expr1>. . .<exprN>)

If you want to avoid the overhead of defining a new function, you can use "lambda." The entire function is presented where it is used, rather than by being defined somewhere else. As usual, the return value is the value of the last <expr>.

Example:

```
(apply '(lambda (a b c) (- a (+ b c))) '(3 6 9))
12
```

(mapcar <function> <list> [<list1>. . .<listN>])

"Mapcar" will execute a function using lists, element by element. Each list will be read starting from the list that is the farthest to the left. Each element in each list will be passed to the function in turn.

Example:

```
(setq q 10 r 5 s 20 t 4)
(mapcar '/ (list q s)(list r t))
(2 5)
```

(menucmd <string>)

An AutoCAD menu contains submenus. With "menucmd," you can switch between them. In this way, you can use AutoLISP to control a menu file. You must supply a <string> in the form "section=submenu". The section must be one of the valid section names such as "S, I, B, P1 - P10, A1 or T1 - T4," as discussed in Chapter 10, "Customizing Menus."

Example:

```
(menucmd "S=LINE")
```

(progn <expr1>. . .<exprN>)

The function "progn" evaluates a list of expressions. Each <expr> in the expression list is evaluated, one by one, returning only the value of the last expression. You can force an evaluation of more than one expression by a function that only expects one expression.

Example:

```
(if (/= x y) (progn (setq x (* y 3)) (setq y (* x 4))))
```

(repeat <number> <expr1>. . .<exprN>)

If you wish to repeat an expression a finite number of times, you can use the "repeat" function. The <expr> will simply be repeated <number> of times. The value returned will be that of the last expression.

Example:

```
(setq a 1)
1
(repeat 10 (setq x (1+ x)))
11
```

Conditional Functions

Conditional functions are those which test the results of expressions and perform specified operations depending on the results of the tests. For example, the expression "If you want a burrito, go to the store" is a conditional expression because it tests the results of the expression "you want a burrito." Depending on whether you want a burrito or not, the test will be true or false.

In AutoLISP, you can perform three basic types of conditional tests, "cond," "if," and "while." Each type of test has its own unique properties.

(cond (<test-expr1> <result-expr1>. . . <result-exprN>). . .)

The "cond" function evaluates lists where the first member of the list is a test expression. You can supply any number of lists, each containing expressions to evaluate if the test expression is not nil. The "cond" function will evaluate each list's first item until it reaches one that has a value that is not nil. When it reaches such a list, it evaluates all the following expressions for that list, returning the value of the last expression evaluated.

Example:

```
(setq a 12)
12
(cond ((= a 12) 1) ((= a 13) 0))
1
```

(if <test-expr> <then-expr> [<else-expr>])

The conditional function "if" takes a test expression, evaluates it, and branches to one of two following expressions depending on the result. If not nil, the first following expression <then-expr> is evaluated. If <test-expr> is not nil, however, the <else-expr> is evaluated.

Example:

```
(setq shoes "purple")
PURPLE
(if (= shoes "purple") "Weird shoes." "Normal shoes.")
"Weird shoes."
```

(while <test-expr> <expr1>. . .<exprN>)

The "while" conditional function continues to evaluate <test-expr> until it returns nil. As long as the result of <test-expr> is not nil, the expressions following are evaluated.

Example:

```
(setq a 12)
12
```

```
(setq b 1)
1
(while (1– a) (1+ b))
12
```

Relational Functions

Relational functions return the results of a test of the relationship between several atoms. Atoms may be equal to each other, not equal to each other, less than each other, and may have many other relationships. AutoLISP enables you to test these relationships with the following functions.

(= <atom1> <atom2>. . .<atomN>)

If all of the atoms in the series of atoms are equal to each other, the "=" function returns T. Remember, atoms may be of any type, including numbers and strings. In AutoLISP, integer numbers (without decimal parts) are the same as decimal numbers with zero following the decimal point. Identical strings will return T.

Example:

```
(setq a 1)
1
(setq b 1)
1
(setq c 1)
1
(= a b c)
T
```

(/= <atom1> <atom2>)

The "/=" function returns T only if the two atoms are not equal. If they are equal, the function returns nil. Unlike the "=" function, only two atoms are allowed.

Example:

```
(setq a 1)
1
(setq b 2)
2
(/= a b)
T
```

(< <atom1> <atom2>. . .<atomN>)

The "<" relational function returns T if each atom in the list of atoms is less than the one following it. In other words, the list must increase in value from left to right.

Example:

```
(setq a 1)
1
(setq b 2)
2
(setq c 3)
3
(< a b c)
T
```

(<= <atom1> <atom2>. . .<atomN>)

The "<=" relational function, like the preceding "<" function, compares atoms from left to right. The function will return T if the atoms ascend in value from left to right, even if atoms that share the same value appear next to each other in the list.

Example:

```
(<= 1 2 3 3.0 3 4 5 5 5 5)
T
```

(> <atom1> <atom2>. . .<atomN>)

Like the "<" function, the ">" function tests the relationship of several atoms. If all the atoms in the series are greater than each other, from left to right, the function returns T.

Examples:

```
(> 3 2 1)
T
(> 3 2 2 1)
nil
```

(>= <atom1> <atom2>. . .<atomN>)

Like the "<=" function, the ">=" function tests to determine the relationship that exists between several atoms. This time, the test is to determine if the values decrease from left to right, allowing any contiguous group of atoms to be considered as one atom of the same value. Atoms may be equal as long as they are next to each other.

Examples:

```
(>= 3 2 2 1)
T
(>= 3 2 3 1)
nil
```

(eq <expr> <expr>)

Do not confuse this function with the "=" or the "equal" function. The "eq" function tests not only the equality of value of the two expressions, but it tests whether or not they share the same object by being bound to it. Note that with the "=" function, atoms are compared, not expressions.

Examples:

```
(setq a '(c d e f))
(c d e f)
(setq b '(c d e f))
```

```
(c d e f)
(setq g b)
(c d e f)

(eq g b)
T
(eq a g)
nil
```

(equal <expr> <expr> [<variation>])

You can test two expressions for equality without testing whether they are bound to the same object. To perform this test, you use the "equal" function. If you wish to specify a <variation> for the values, the test will be T if the expressions evaluate within the range of the variation from each other.

Examples:

```
(setq x 3.14159)
3.14159
(setq y 3.141593)
3.141593

(equal x y 0.00001)
T
(equal x y)
nil
```

Predicative Functions

Predicative functions are those which produce an effect based on a test of one or more expressions. The subject is the expression to be tested and the predicate is the result of the test.

(and <expr1>. . .<exprN>)

The various expressions will be logically combined with the "and" function. The return will be the logical AND of all the expressions. If any of the expressions evaluates to nil, the evaluation is stopped.

Examples:

```
(setq x 1)
1
(setq y 2)
2
(setq z (equal 1 2))
nil
(setq r "abc")
"abc"
(and 2 x y r)
T
(and x y z r)
nil
```

(atom <arg>)

You use the "atom" function to find out if an argument is an atom or not. If the <arg> is not an atom, the "atom" function returns nil; otherwise, it returns T.

Examples:

```
(setq x 'a)
'a
(setq y '(a b c))
(a b c)
(atom 'x)
T
(atom x)
T
(atom 'y)
```

```
T
(atom y)
nil
```

(boundp <atom1>)

If you want to determine whether or not an atom is bound to an argument, you use the "boundp" function. If the atom has something bound to it, the "boundp" function returns T; otherwise, it returns nil.

Examples:

```
(setq x nil)
nil
(boundp 'x)
nil
(setq x 1)
1
(boundp 'x)
T
```

(listp <arg>)

The "listp" function returns T if the argument is a list and nil if the argument is anything else.

Examples:

```
(setq a 1)
1
(listp a)
nil
(setq a '(x y z))
```

```
(x y z)
(listp a)
T
```

(minusp <arg>)

If you want to test to see if an argument is integer or real and negative, you use the "minusp" function.

Examples:

```
(minusp 10)
nil
(minusp -3.14159)
T
(setq a "my string")
"my string"
(minusp a)
nil
```

(not <arg>)

The "not" function will return the reverse of the value of an argument. If the argument evaluates to T, the "not" function will return nil. If the argument evaluates to nil, the "not" function will return T.

Examples:

```
(setq x 1)
1
(not x)
nil
(setq x nil)
```

```
nil
(not x)
T
```

(null <arg>)

You may want to test whether an argument is bound to nil. If you use the "null" function, the return value will be T if the argument is bound to nil and nil if it is not.

Examples:

```
(setq x nil)
nil
(null x)
T
(setq x 1)
1
(null x)
nil
```

(numberp <arg>)

If you use the "numberp" function with an argument, it will return T if the argument is an integer or real value; otherwise, it will return nil.

Examples:

```
(numberp 1)
T
(numberp 3.14159)
T
```

```
(setq x "my string")
"my string"
(numberp x)
nil
```

(or <expr1>. . .<exprN>)

As with the "and" function, the "or" function will relate all expressions in the list using the logical OR operator. If any of the expressions is not nil, the evaluation halts at that expression and the return value is T.

Examples:

```
(setq a nil)
nil
(setq b nil)
nil
(or a b)
nil
(setq c 1)
1
(or a b c)
T
```

(type <arg>)

If you want to know the type of an argument, the "type" function will return it to you.

Examples:

```
(setq x 3.14159)
3.14159
(type x)
REAL
```

(type 'x)
SYM
(type "my string")
STR

(zerop <arg>)

You can use the "zerop" function to determine whether or not an argument is an integer or a real number and evaluates to zero. The function returns T if the argument is an integer or real and is zero; otherwise, it returns nil.

Examples:

(zerop 1)
nil
(zerop "my string")
nil
(zerop 0)
T
(zerop (– 1 1))
T

String Functions

You can manipulate strings of characters with AutoLISP. The string manipulation functions enable you to display strings, test them, compare them, and otherwise modify their characteristics.

String Handling Functions

(strcase <string1> [<upper-lower>])

The "strcase" function will take a string and convert all the characters in it to upper- or lowercase depending on the value of the <upper-lower> argument. If <upper-lower> is present and not nil, all characters will be converted to lowercase. If <upper-lower> is not present, or it evaluates to nil, the string will be converted to uppercase.

Examples:

```
(setq s "my string")
(strcase s nil)
"MY STRING"
(strcase s 1)
"my string"
(strcase s)
"MY STRING"
```

(strcat <string1> <string2>. . .<stringN>)

You can concatenate strings with the "strcat" function. Concatenation means that the strings will be combined to make one string consisting of all the strings in the list placed end to end. The concatenation will be in the order in which the strings appear in the list.

Example:

```
(strcat "I" " like" " AutoLISP.")
"I like AutoLISP."
```

(strlen <string1>)

If you wish to find the length of a string, you can use the "strlen" function. It returns the length as an integer.

Example:

```
(setq s "AutoLISP")
"AutoLISP"
```

```
(strlen s)
8
```

(substr <string1> <first-character> [<characters>])

You can use the "substr" function to extract a substring from a string. Starting at the <first-character>, the substring, consisting of the number of <characters> that follow, will be returned to you. If <characters> is omitted, the rest of the string starting at <first-character> will be returned.

Examples:

```
(substr "I like AutoLISP", 8)
"AutoLISP"
(substr "I like AutoLISP", 3, 4)
"like"
```

String Conversion Functions

(angtos <angle1> [<method> [<precision>]])

The "angtos" function will convert an angle to a string. The <angle1> argument must be a real number expressed in radians. The method is based on the DINZIN system variable. If DINZIN is 0, the string will be expressed with degrees symbols. If 1, the format will be "degrees/minutes/seconds." If 2, the method will be to express the string in grads. If 3, the string will be shown in radian measure. Finally, if <method> is 4, the string will be in surveyor's units.

If present, <precision> must be an integer that expresses the number of decimal places of precision you want. The <method> and <precision> arguments perform the same functions as the AUNITS and AUPREC system variables. The <method> and <precision> arguments are optional. The current values of the system variables will be used.

Examples:

(angtos (/ pi 2) 0 2)
"90.00"
(angtos (/ pi 2) 3 3)
"1.571r"

(ascii <string1>)

The ASCII code for a character is a number that conforms to a standard in the computer industry. The ASCII codes for the printable characters are from 32 to 127.

Examples:

(ascii "Try AutoLISP")
84
(ascii "T")
84
(ascii "U")
85
(ascii "u")
117

(atof <string1>)

Perhaps you have a string that contains a number expression. The "atof" function will convert that string to a real number.

Examples:

(atof "3.14259")
3.14159
(atof "number 13")
0,0

(atoi <string1>)

If you need to convert a string containing a number expression into an integer, you can pass the string as an argument to the "atoi" function.

Examples:

(atoi "3.14159")
3
(atoi "72")
72
(atoi "number 72")
0

(chr <number1>)

You can convert an ASCII character code into an ASCII character with the "chr" function. See the "ascii" function for the inverse process.

Examples:

(chr 83)
"S"
(chr 115)
"s"

(itoa <integer>)

Conversion from an integer to an ASCII string is done with the "itoa" function.

Examples:

(itoa −25)
"−25"
(itoa 1988)
"1988"

(read <string1>)

The "read" function returns the first atom or list from a string. There must be no blanks in the string.

Example:

```
(setq a "AutoCAD")
(read a)
AUTOCAD
```

(rtos <number1> [<method> [<precision>]])

You can use "rtos" to return a string, like "itoa," but the number can be formatted as it is read into the string. If you supply a <method>, it must be one of the following. Method 1 creates a string in scientific notation. Method 2 creates a decimal string. Method 3 creates engineering notation (feet and decimal inches). Method 4 creates architectural notation (feet and fractions of inches). Method 5 creates simple fractions. The <method> corresponds to the LUNITS variable. The <precision> argument corresponds to the number of decimal places as contained in the LUPREC system variable.

Examples:

```
(rtos pi 5 8)
"3 1/8"
(rtos pi 1 4)
"3.1416E+00"
```

Graphics Functions

Graphics functions in AUTOLISP are broken into two main classes. You can add graphics entities to your database with one class of functions, or you can manipulate graphics on the computer screen using the other class of functions.

Graphics Handling Functions

You can use AutoLISP to manipulate graphics in very powerful ways. Almost anything you can do with AutoCAD's commands can be done with AutoLISP. In addition, because AutoLISP is a real programming language, your ability to enhance and modify the AutoCAD vocabulary of commands is almost limitless. This is one of the benefits obtained from true "open architecture" system design.

(angle <point1> <point2>)

The "angle" function returns the angle of a line in the User Coordinate System. You pass the endpoint coordinates as two lists to the "angle" function and the angle is returned in radians.

Example:

```
(angle '(2.0 2.0) '(5.0 5.0))
0.3927
```

(distance <point1> <point2>)

The distance between two points is returned by the "distance" function. The points may be in three-dimensional space, but the Z axis value will be ignored.

Example:

```
(distance '(2.0 2.0) '(5.0 5.0))
4.242641
```

(inters <point1> <point2> <point3> <point4> [<infinite>])

You can find the intersection point of two lines with the "inters" function. The function returns nil if the lines do not intersect. If the <infinite> argument is not present, the lines will be considered to be finite in length, terminated by their endpoints. If the <infinite> argument is present and nil, the lines will be considered to be infinite in length. If <infinite> is present but not nil, the effect will be the same as if it were not present.

Example:

```
(setq L1s '(0 0) L1e '(1 1))
(1 1)
(setq L2s '(0 1) L2e '(1 0))
(1 0)
(inters L1s L1e L2s L2e)
(0.5 0.5)
```

(osnap <point1> <method>)

Object snap is accomplished by using the "osnap" function. The snap point achieved will be returned, if any. If no snap is achieved, nil is returned. The method used to snap is "midpoint," "center," "endp," corresponding to the snap modes of AutoCAD.

Example:

```
(osnap '(1.0 1.0) "midp")
(0.75 1.0)
```

(polar <point> <angle> <distance>)

You can obtain the point at an <angle> from the X axis at a <distance> from a starting <point> with the "polar" function.

Example:

```
(polar '(0 0) 45.0 1)
(0.7071 0.7071)
```

(redraw [<entity-name> [<method>]])

The "redraw" function redraws everything in the current viewport if no arguments are given. If an <entity-name> is given, only that entity in the current viewport will be redrawn. If the

<method> code is given, one of four methods will be used to redraw. If <method> is 1, the entity will be redrawn on the screen. If <method> is 2, the entity will be undrawn. If <method> is 3, the entity will be highlighted if the display is capable of being highlighted. Finally, if <method> is 4, the entity will be unhighlighted if it is highlighted and the screen is capable of being highlighted.

(trans <point> <start> <end> [<displacement>])

You can translate a point from one coordinate system to another with the "trans" function. The <point> may be in three-dimensional space. The <start> and <end> codes are required and refer to the coordinate systems to be used as the starting and ending systems. If <start> or <end> are 0, the coordinate system is the World Coordinate System. If 1, the system is the User Coordinate System. If 2, the system is the Display Coordinate System. You can also give an entity name as either the <start> or the <end> and the Entity Coordinate System of that entity will be used. For information about coordinate systems, refer to Chapter 1, "Quick Start," Chapter 2, "Drawing," and Chapter 4, "Working with Blocks." See Chapter 2, "Drawing," for examples of User Coordinate Systems.

Screen Graphics Functions

AutoLISP contains functions that control the status of the graphics display. The following functions will enable you to clear, draw, read, and do many other tasks involving the display.

(graphscr)

There are two modes in AutoCAD, graphics and text. You use the function "graphscr" to switch to graphics modes.

(grclear)

The "grclear" function clears the graphics viewport that is in effect when the function is called. All other parts of the display are unaffected.

(grdraw <start> <end> <color> [<highlight>])

A line is drawn between two points, <start> and <end>, when you call "grdraw." You can use any of AutoCAD's allowable colors. If you use a −1 for the <color>, the line will be XORed onto the screen, complementing any colors it passes over and neutralizing itself if redrawn over itself. If your system supports highlighting, the <highlight> argument, if present and non-zero, will cause the line to be highlighted.

(grtext [<box> <text> [<highlight>]])

You can write text to non-graphic portions of the AutoCAD screen with the "grtext" function. The text you supply will be written into the numbered box (from 0 to the highest menu type number available less 1). As with the "grdraw" function, you can use highlighting if your system allows it.

(grread [<coordinates>])

The "grread" function reads the AutoCAD pointing device and returns a list. The first element of this list is a number that specifies which type of device sent the information that follows. The following is a list of the codes and the devices they represent:

2	(keyboard-character ascii-code)
3	(point-selected coordinate-list)
4	(screen-menu-cell box-number)
5	(drag-mode coordinates)
6	(buttons-menu-item button-number)
7	(tablet1-menu-item box-number)
8	(tablet2-menu-item box-number)
9	(tablet3-menu-item box-number)
10	(tablet4-menu-item box-number)

11	(aux1-menu-item box-number)
12	(pointer-button-coordinates pointer-button)
13	(screen-menu-item box-number)

(textscr)

There are two modes in AutoCAD, text and graphics. You can set the screen to text mode with the "textscr" function.

(vports)

Each viewport has a list of descriptors that determine the viewport's size and location. If you use the "vports" function, you will return the viewport descriptors for those viewports that are currently active.

Each viewport description consists of the viewport number followed by two pairs of real numbers. These numbers are not coordinates. Instead, they refer to the fraction of the screen occupied by a given viewport. The first pair of numbers refers to the lower left corner of the viewport, while the second pair of numbers refers to the upper right corner. If there is only one viewport, the entire screen is taken up by it, and the lower left corner's coordinates would be (0.0 0.0) and the upper right corner's coordinates would be (1.0 1.0). As the number of viewports increases, the fraction of the total screen dimension decreases. Thus, a viewport that took up half of the screen would have its lower left corner at (0.0 0.5) and its upper right corner at (1.0 1.0).

Example:

```
(viewports)
((1 (0.0 0.0) (0.5 1.0))
(2 (0.5 0.0) (1.0 1.0)))
```

I/O Functions

To communicate with AutoLISP and, through it, with AutoCAD, you must be able to get values from the user. There are many ways to communicate with AutoCAD. You can type responses from the keyboard, pick values from a digitizer, or use a mouse. AutoLISP provides a basic set of functions with which you can communicate with AutoCAD.

Screen Input Functions

(getangle [<point>] [<prompt1>])

The function "getangle" gets an angular expression from the user. You can express a point to be used as a base point for the derivation of the angle. You also have the option of displaying a prompt for the angle. The angle will be returned in radians, although the angle may be entered by the user in the prevailing units format. The user's response to the prompt may be to pick the angle with a rubber-band line.

Examples:

```
(getangle)
Input angle: 1.276
1.276
(setq a '(12.34 45.67))
(12.34 45.67)
(getangle a "Enter angle: ")
Input angle: 2.7654
2.7654
```

(getcorner <point> [<prompt1>])

You can prompt the user for the second corner of a box that the user can pick with a rubber-band rectangle. The "getcorner" function is passed the coordinates of a point as an argument and can be passed an optional prompt. After you begin the function, the rectangle will originate at the point you specify and you can then rubber band the rectangle until you choose to pick the final corner location.

Example:

```
(getcorner '(10.0 11.345) "Pick the opposite corner: ")
(20.34 25.35)
```

(getdist [<point>] [<prompt1>])

You can use the "getdist" function to get a distance from the user. The distance can be in response to a prompt that you specify. If you use a point as an argument, that point will be used as the starting point for the distance; otherwise, the user can pick a starting point.

Examples:

```
(getdist)
Input distance: 23.45
23.45
(getdist '(12.34 56.78) "Please pick a distance: ")
Input distance: 45.67
45.67
```

(getint [<prompt1>])

If you wish to get an integer number from the user, you can use the "getint" function. Optionally, you can supply a prompt as an argument that will be displayed when the "getint" function begins running.

Example:

```
(getint "Enter an integer: ")
1
```

(getkword [<prompt1>])

The function "getkword" allows you to prompt the user for a response that must be one of a list of possible responses. To create the list, you must use the "initget" function described later in this chapter. If the word entered by the user is not in the list of possible words, AutoCAD will prompt the user to repeat the entry.

Example:

```
(initget 3 "Angle Base")
(getkword "Enter Angle or Base: ")
"Angle"
```

(getorient [<point>] [<prompt1>])

You can get angles in two ways. The usual angle in AutoLISP is relative to the positive X axis as zero degrees with positive angles increasing in the counterclockwise direction. It is possible, of course, to set a different base and direction orientation with the ANGBASE and ANGDIR system variables. The user can also use the UNITS command to change the base angle and direction of rotation. The "getorient" function returns angular measure in terms of the current settings of the base angle and direction of increasing angle.

Example:

```
(getangle)
Input angle: 0.7854
0.7854
; The base angle is 45 degrees and direction is
; clockwise. For such an environment:
(getorient)
Input orientation: 2.7489
2.7489
```

(getpoint [<point>] [<prompt1>])

You can get a point from the user with the "getpoint" function. You can use an optional base point and an optional prompt. The base point, if present, will stimulate the use of a rubber-band line from that point to the moving crosshairs location.

Example:

```
(getpoint '(3.45 12.34) "Please enter a point: ")
(12.35 23.45)
```

(getreal [<prompt1>])

As with the "getint" function, you can get a number with the "getreal" function, except that the number will be interpreted as a real number rather than as an integer.

Example:

```
(getreal "Please enter real number (decimal allowed): ")
3.14159
```

(getstring [<carriage-return>] [<prompt1>])

You can get a string from the user by using the "getstring" function. If the optional <carriage-return> argument is present and not nil, the string may contain spaces; otherwise, any space characters input by the user will terminate the function. As with most of the "get" functions, you can supply a prompt string if you wish.

Example:

```
(getstring 1 "Please enter the name of this object: ")
"Computer monitor."
```

(initget [<bitfield>] [<string1>])

The "initget" function initializes the entire family of "get" functions. There are many possible ways a user can provide responses to prompts. You will probably want to screen out invalid or inappropriate responses, which is partly the purpose of the "initget" function.

To use this function, you must understand the concept of binary ANDing. The number 1 in binary is, for example, 000001 (if six bits are used). The number 2 is 000010. The number 4 is 000100, and so on.

Notice that you can add these numbers together. Try adding 1, 2, and 4 together in binary. You get 00111. The process is simple. Here it is added in a column for you:

Decimal	Binary
1	000001
2	000010
4	000100
8	001000
16	010000
32	100000
Total 63	111111

How can this phenomenon be used? You can add the numbers together in various ways and get any combination of bits on or off depending upon which numbers you choose. Thus, 1 plus 4 will create a pattern of bits like this: 000101. If you have six different possible states, any or all of which can be true at any time, you can use this numbering technique to convey information about which states are true.

To choose the states you want to use in conjunction with the "initget" function, you can add the numbers together. The numbers each have meanings as follows:

1	"Does not allow null input."
2	"Does not allow values of zero."
4	"Does not allow negative values."
8	"Does not check limits—whether LIMCHECK is on or not."
16	"Three-dimensional points instead of two-dimensional points to be returned.

32 "Express rubber-band boxes and lines with dashes."

Screen Output Functions

Just as you can get input from the user, you can send output from AutoLISP to the screen. You saw the use of one form of screen text output in the prompts associated with the "get" family of functions. Now you will see how AutoLISP sends text to the screen without waiting for a user response.

(prin1 <expr1> [<file-descriptor>])

The function "prin1" takes as arguments an expression and an optional file descriptor. The expression may be any expression that is of a type allowed by AutoLISP. You can print strings, integers, and reals among the many types supported. If a file descriptor is present, it is assumed that a file has been opened and the descriptor is valid.

Examples:

```
(setq x 34.56)
34.56
(prin1 x)
34.56
(prin1 'x)
X
(setq x "AutoLISP is fun.")
(prin1 x)
"AutoLISP is fun."
(setq y (open "funfile" "w"))
<File #001>
(prin1 x y)
"AutoLISP is fun."
```

(princ <expr1> [<file-descriptor>])

The function "princ" is almost identical to "prin1." The only difference is that control characters that appear in the expression are not expanded. The "princ" function is appropriate for use with the "read-line" function. You should use "prin1" with "load."

Example:

```
(setq x "\nTry this on for size.")
"\nTry this on for size."
(princ x)
"\nTry this on for size."
; This is literally what is printed on the screen.
; If you had used "prin1" the newline (\n) would
; have added a new line before printing.
```

(print <expr1> [<file-descriptor>])

The "print" function does essentially the same thing as "prin1". The only difference is that a new line is added before printing the string, and a space is provided at the end. Thus, a string such as "This is my string." is printed as though it were "\nThis is my string.\n".

Example:

```
(print "This is a line of text.")
"This is a line of text."
; This is what appears on screen:
This is a line of text.
```

(prompt <message>)

If you want to print a prompt and have the cursor wait at the end of the prompt, you can use the "prompt" function. The advantage that this function has over the "prin" family of functions is that the message will appear on both screens of a two screen system.

Example:

```
(prompt "Do you wish to continue? ")
nil
```

(terpri)

The "terpri" function performs the simple task of printing a single new line on the screen.

Example:

```
(terpri)
nil
; A new line is printed on the screen.
```

File I/O Functions

AutoLISP is capable of writing, appending, and reading files. To do this, AutoLISP gives you access to the usual operating system function calls through its own mechanism. If you are familiar with the C language, you will find that the AutoLISP mechanism does not differ greatly from the file access methods you already know.

(close <file-descriptor>)

If you open a file, you must close it again with the "close" function to avoid accumulating too many open files and to make sure all data has been written to the file on output. It is poor programming practice to leave files open. To close a file, you supply the file descriptor of the file you opened. If the file is already closed, an error will result.

Example:

```
(close filehand)
nil
```

(findfile <filename>)

If you wish to find a file and determine if it exists, or in which directory it exists, you can use the "findfile" function. You specify the file name and a search is made in the usual manner supported by your operating system. If you are using DOS, for example, the search will be made starting at the current directory, and then along any path that may be set in the environment. You should consult your DOS manual for detailed information about the path and environment.

Examples:

```
(findfile "command.com")
"/COMMAND.COM"
(findfile "/acad/acad.exe")
"/acad/acad.exe"
; Your path is set to /myfiles for the following.
(setq a (findfile "rosebud"))
"/myfiles/rosebud"
(open a "r")
<File #001>
```

(load <filename> [<when-fails>])

You can load AutoLISP expressions and immediately evaluate them with the "load" function. You supply the file name in the same way as for the "open" function discussed in the next section. If the optional <when-fails> argument is supplied, the value supplied will be returned if the "load" function fails for any reason.

Example:

```
(load "myfunc" -1)
-1
; The load failed.
```

(open <filename> <method>)

To read or write to a file, you must open the file. The "open" function takes as arguments the file name and method of access. The file name can be any name that is allowed by your operating system, including a path. The method must be one of three lowercase letters. If "w," the file is to be opened for writing. If the file exists, it will be overwritten. If "r," the file must exist and you will only be able to read from it. If "a," the file will be created if it does not exist (like "w"). If it exists, it will be opened and anything written to it will be appended to the information already there.

Examples:

```
(setq filehand (open "notafile" "r"));"not a file" does not
                                      ;exist
nil
(setq filehand (open "/myfiles/sled" "w"))
<File #001>
(setq filehand (open "notafile" "a"))
<File #002>
```

(read-char [<file-descriptor>])

If you want to read a single character from a file, you can use the "read-char" function. If you pass a valid file descriptor, the file that has been opened for reading as that descriptor will be used. If you do not supply a file descriptor, the keyboard will be read. If no character is waiting in the keyboard buffer, the function will *wait* until the user presses a key.

Examples:

```
(read-char)
; If no key has been pressed this will wait.
97
; Aha! The user has pressed the letter "a".
(read-char)
104
(read-char)
97
```

(read-line [<file-descriptor>])

You can read a line from a file up to the next linefeed character with the "read-line" function. The line of text typed from the keyboard (if there is no file descriptor) or from the file will be returned. If you reach the end of a file, nil will be returned.

Examples:

```
(read-line)
; The user now types a line and enters it.
"Aha! I've typed this from the keyboard."
(read-line filehand)
"This is the first line in the file."
(read-line filehand)
"This is the last line."
(read-line filehand)
nil
```

(write-char <number> [<file-descriptor>])

You can write a single character to the screen if you omit the file descriptor argument from the "write-char" function. If you supply a valid file descriptor, the character will be written to a file.

The number is the ASCII code for the character to be written.

Examples:

```
(write-char (ascii "N"))
"N"
(write-char (74) filehand)
"J"
```

(write-line <string1> [<file-descriptor>])

If you want to write a string to a file, you can use the "write-line" function. As in the "write" and "read" family of functions in general, you can omit the file descriptor to cause a write to the screen.

Examples:

```
(write-line "AutoLISP is like C in some ways.")
AutoLISP is like C in some ways.
(write-line "The best of both worlds." filehand)
The best of both worlds.
; When written to a file the string is not quoted
; in the file.
```

Entity Handling Functions

With AutoCAD, you can create many types of entities. AutoLISP has a family of functions that help you manipulate those entities.

Selection Set Functions

(ssadd [<entity-name> [<selection-set>]])

The function "ssadd" adds a selection set, creating a new one if no arguments are supplied. If you call "ssadd" with just an entity name, the function creates a new selection set and adds that entity name to it. If an entity name and a selection set are given as arguments to the function, the entity name is added to the designated selection set.

Example:

```
(setq newset (ssadd))
(ssadd entity2 newset)
```

(ssdel <entity-name> <selection-set>)

If you want to delete an entity name from a selection set, you use the "ssdel" function. You must supply an entity name and the name of a selection set from which that entity name is to be removed.

Example:

```
(ssdel "MYBLOCK" set)
```

(ssget "X" <filters>)

The "ssget" function filters the entities in a drawing using various filter criteria. The <filters> used consist of an association list. You could return a selection set of all the green lines on a certain layer in your drawing, for example. The filter list must contain pairs of group codes followed by names. The group codes that identify the names used in the association list are as follows:

0	Type of entity
2	Name of block
6	Name of line type
7	Name of text style
8	Name of layer
39	Thickness (real)

62	Number of color
66	Attributes
210	3 reals define extrusion direction

The association list uses the group codes to identify the type of name that follows each code.

Example:

```
(setq set (ssget "X" (list (cons 2 "MYBLOCK"))))
; This would return any blocks named MYBLOCK.
```

(sslength <selection-set>)

If you use "ssget," you can find the length of the selection set returned by the function. To do this, you give the name of the set as an argument to the "sslength" function.

Example:

```
(setq set (ssget "X" (list (cons 2 "MYBLOCK"))))
; This would return any blocks named MYBLOCK.
(sslength set)
25
; There were 25 insertions of MYBLOCK found in the
;drawing.
```

(ssmemb <entity-name> <selection-set>)

If you have a selection set and you want to discover whether or not a given entity name is in it, you can use the "ssmemb" function.

Examples:

```
(ssmemb "BENT" set)
nil
```

```
(ssadd entity2 newset)
(ssmemb entity2 newset)
ENTITY2
```

(ssname <selection-set> <index>)

If you have used "ssget" to get a selection set of entities used in a drawing, you can use the "ssname" function to retrieve the name of any of the entities in the set by an index number. If you know how many entities are in the selection set (perhaps you used "sslength" to find out), you can examine the set by index. The index starts numbering at zero.

Example:

```
(setq set (ssget "X" (list (cons 2 "MYBLOCK"))))
; This would return any blocks named MYBLOCK.
(sslength set)
25
; There were 25 entities found in the drawing.
(ssname set 24) ; This gets name of last entity.
```

Entity Name Functions

You can find out about entity names by using the functions in AutoLISP that manipulate them. These functions operate on the entire AutoCAD database. You can, for example, find out about the next entity, the last entity, or prompt the user to select an object.

(entnext [<entity-name>])

If you want to know the name of the first entity in the database, just use the return value from "entnext," called with no arguments. If you want to know the name of the next entity after a named entity, just pass the entity name to "entnext" and the next entity name after the named entity will be returned. You can use the "entnext" function to traverse the drawing database, using the next entity name as the argument to "entnext." If any entities have been deleted, their names will not be returned. If no entities follow the named entity, the function will return nil.

Example:

```
(setq entity1 (entnext))
(setq entity2 (entnext entity1))
```

(entlast)

If you call the "entlast" function, the name of the last entity in the drawing will be returned to you. As in "entnext," if any entities have been deleted, they will not be returned.

Example:

```
(setq entity1 (entlast))
```

(entsel [<prompt1>])

If you want the user to select an entity, you must use the "entsel" function. You can supply an optional prompt. The return is a list with the first element the entity name, and the second element the coordinate pair that identifies the pick point used to select the entity.

Example:

```
(setq entity1 (entsel "Select an object: "))
; The user selects an object and the entity name is
; returned.
```

(handent <entity-handle>)

If you know an entity's handle and wish to obtain the current name for that entity, you can use the "handent" function. Entity handles are eternal, whereas an entity is renamed when the drawing is loaded.

Example:

```
(handent "1B75D")
<Entity name: 60000023>
```

Entity Data Functions

You can delete entities, get entity information, modify entities, and update them. The entity data functions are AutoLISP's way of changing the information contained within entities.

(entdel <entity-name>)

You can delete an entity by name with the "entdel" function. This function is a toggle, which means that if the entity has been deleted, it will be "un-deleted."

Example:

```
(entdel (entlast))
; The last entity has now been deleted.
```

(entget <entity-name>)

The "entget" function returns a list of entity definition data regarding the named entity. The list is in the same form as the filter lists in the "ssget" function, consisting of a group code followed by a name. All the possible group codes are allowed.

Example:

```
(setq elist1 (entget (entnext)))
((−1 . <Entity name: 60000023>)
```

```
(0 . "LINE")
(8 . "MYLYR")
(10 3.4 10.9 3.0)
(11 12.0 12.1 3.0))
```

(entmod <entity-list>)

To do the reverse of the "entget" function, you must use the "entmod" function. While the "entget" function returns a list of the data that makes up the named entity, the "entmod" function takes an entity list and replaces the named entity's data with it.

Example:

```
; Assume the above "elist1" list contains the data:
(setq elist1
      (subst (cons 10 0.0 0.0 0.0)
             (assoc 10 elist1)
             elist1))
(entmod elist1)
```

(entupd <entity-name>)

When you use the "entmod" function in conjunction with complex objects such as PLINES, you will not see the entity on the screen change. To view the changed entity after the change has been made, you can call the "entupd" function with the name of the entity you changed.

Example:

```
; Changes have been made as above.
(entupd ename)
```

Symbol Table Access Functions

AutoCAD uses tables to store information about a drawing and about how the drawing is being viewed. You can also find out about layers, line types, and other information by reading the symbol tables.

(tblnext <table-name> [<reset>])

You can examine the LAYER, LTYPE, STYLE, UCS, BLOCK, and VPORT tables. Each time you use "tblnext," the next value in the named table will be returned. If the <reset> argument is there and is not nil, the "tblnext" function is reset to the beginning of the table. At the end of the table, the function will return nil. The return for each element in the table is a list in the form shown for the "entget" function.

Example:

```
(tblnext "layer")
```

(tblsearch <table-name> <entry-name> [<next>])

While the "tblnext" function reads table information step by step, the "tblsearch" function will search for an entry in a table. If the <next> argument is present and is not nil, the next element in the table after the named entry will be returned.

Example:

```
(tblsearch "layer" "mylayer")
```

Miscellaneous Functions

Several AutoLISP functions are hard to categorize but are valuable nevertheless. The following functions include one that returns the current AutoLISP version number, one that allocates more string space, and one that expands node space. You will probably find a use for many of these functions in your AutoLISP programs. Just because they do not fall into clearly defined categories does not mean they are not helpful.

(_ver)

The "_ver" function returns the number of the current version of AutoLISP. You can use it in your programs to make sure features are supported by the version that is running. You can screen out unsupported features or provide work-arounds for them.

Example:

```
(_ver)
"AutoLISP Release 10.0"
```

(alloc <number1>)

The "alloc" function sets the size of the memory allocation request when the "expand" function is used or more nodes are requested by the evaluation. You supply the number of 512 node allocations you want AutoLISP to make for future allocation requests.

Example:

```
(alloc 600)
512
```

(expand <number1>)

You can ask for more segments within AutoCAD to run AutoLISP before they are needed. You use the "expand" function to expand the space according to a number that will be multiplied by the setting of ALLOC in the environment.

Example:

(expand 5)
10240; returns number of segments allocated to nodespace

(gc)

Garbage collection is the process AutoLISP carries out when it is required to retrieve nodes that are no longer in use. You can force garbage collection at any time with the "gc" function.

(mem)

You can find out how much memory you have left if you use the "mem" function. The amount of memory for nodes, free nodes, segments, allocation, and collection will be displayed. The return value is nil.

(vmon)

The "vmon" function enables the AutoLISP *virtual function page.* If enabled, virtual function paging will allow your total program space to grow beyond the limits of available node space. You must execute "vmon" before you use any "defun" functions for the functions to be pageable. The paging process greatly increases the capacity of your system because pages of code are swapped onto and off the drive or extended memory as required.

(trace <function1>. . .<functionN>)

You can monitor the functioning of any functions you name in the list following the "trace" command with the "trace" function.

As each function in the list is evaluated, you will see the beginning and ending of the function.

Example:

```
(trace bolts holes)
HOLES
```

(untrace <function1>. . .<functionN>)

You can turn off the "trace" command for any functions that have been set to be traced if you pass those function names as arguments to the "untrace" function.

(*error* <string1>)

The "*error*" function enables you to control the error exit process. You must declare it as a function.

Example:

```
(defun *error* (message)
     (princ "Error: ")
     (princ message)
     (terpri))
```

pi

The value of pi is 3.141592654. . . . Used in AutoLISP, the symbol "pi" is a constant that will evaluate to that number.

nil

The value of nil is very special. It does not mean zero. Instead, it means "nothing has been defined or bound."

Boolean Bit Operation Functions

A Boolean bit operation is one in which an integer is tested against a logical operator. The available logical expressions are "logand", "logior", "~", and "boole".

(~ <number1>)

You may wish to test a number to find its bitwise NOT. In such a test all bits are inverted. The return value of the "~" function will be a number that has all of the 1 bits of the argument set to 0 and all of the 0 bits set to 1.

Examples:

```
; Number 9 in binary: 1001
(~ 9)
-10          ; return is 0110
(~ 3)
-4           ; two's complement of one's complement
```

(boole <operator> <integer1> <integer2>)

You can use the "boole" function to return the result of applying a specified operator to a pair of integers. The operator is a 4-bit number from 0 to 15. There are 16 possible functions that can be performed with the two variables, Integer1 and Integer2. Several useful values for the operator are 6 (XOR), 7 (OR), and 8 (NOT). If the operator is 7, for example, the function will work like this:

```
(boole 7 4 2)
6
```

(logand <number1> <number2>. . .<numberN>)

If the "boole" function is too confusing, use the "logand" function to return the logical bitwise AND of a list of numbers.

Example:

```
; This is the same AND performed above under "boole".
(logand 10 5)
0
```

(logior <number1> <number2>. . .<numberN>)

While the "logand" function logically bitwise ANDs a list of integers, the "logior" function logically bitwise ORs a list of integers.

Example:

```
; This is the same OR performed above under "boole".
(logior 10 4)
14
```

(lsh <number1> <bits>)

You can shift bits of integers with the "lsh" function. If the <bits> argument is positive, the bits will be shifted left. If negative, the bits will be shifted right. Bit shifting discards bits that go beyond the size of the word. (On IBM AT computers, the word is 16 bits. On larger systems, the word may be 32 bits.) If a word is shifted right, the rightmost bits are lost. They "fall off" the right of the word. If a 1 bit is shifted into the leftmost position of a word, the sign is changed to negative. If a 0 bit is shifted into the leftmost position of a word, the sign is changed to positive.

Examples:

```
; The number 10 decimal (00001010 binary)
; will be shifted left 1 bit.
(lsh 10 +1)
```

```
20                    ; 20 decimal (00010100 binary)
; Now the number will be shifted right 3 places.
(lsh 20 -3)
2                     ; 2 decimal (00000010 binary)
```

The entire collection of AutoLISP functions could be the subject of a complete book, not just a chapter. Nevertheless, this chapter has tried to provide you with helpful information about all the functions you will use regularly in your AutoLISP programming work.

AutoCAD Command Reference

You will find the AutoCAD command set presented here in alphabetical order, for easy reference. The commands shown here are also used in many other places in this book. As you read the rest of this book, you should often return to this chapter to read about the range of options that are available with each command.

The AutoCAD commands are presented in alphabetical order as though they were entered at the command prompt. You will see each command in the way it will probably appear when you use it. For example, the following is the invocation for the "three-point" ARC command. The angle brackets (<>) indicate the default response for each prompt:

Command: **arc**
Center/<Start point>:
Center/End/<Second point>:
Endpoint:

In this case, the start point, second point, and endpoint have each been picked with the pointing device; hence, you see no coordinates. When you do not see an entry following the colon (:), it must be assumed that you picked or entered something. As usual, you can enter a coordinate pair or letter at many of the prompts. The command sequences will usually appear exactly as you would see them after you had entered them.

When a command has several options, the command expression shown will be the default sequence for the command. This method of presentation quickly explains by example so you will not need to spend a lot of time figuring out what to do. For most commands, you can literally copy the command expression found in this reference.

Certain commands can be used while other commands are being executed. If you are at a prompt in most AutoCAD command sequences, and the command is designated as "transparent" by the use of an apostrophe (') before the command name, you can run the command at the prompt by putting an apostrophe before it. For example, the DDEMODES command can be run during the execution of the ARC command as follows:

Command: **arc**
Center/<Start point>: **'ddemodes**
Center/<Start point>:
Center/End/<Second point>:
Endpoint:

This command sequence will display a Current Properties Dialog Box, wait for you to change properties, and then return to the command sequence when you are finished. See the DDEMODES command for more information.

APERTURE

Command: **aperture**
Object snap target height (1-50 pixels) <20>:

The **target box** used when object snap is in effect is a small square that is centered on the crosshairs. Anything that appears within the target box when you pick will be a candidate for object snap. The APERTURE command permits you to change the size of this box. The units are in pixels. You do not need to use the APERTURE command to change the size of the target box, but you can also use the SETVAR command to change the APERTURE system variable.

ARC

Command: **arc**
Center/<Start point>:

An arc is an incomplete circle. There are many methods you can use to draw arcs with AutoCAD. The method already shown is the command sequence for the three-point arc. Depending upon which method you choose, you will see different prompt sequences.

Options:

A	Angle (included)
C	Center point
D	Direction (starting)
E	Endpoint
ENTER OR BLANK	(as reply to Start point) sets start point and direction as end of last Line or Arc
L	chord Length
R	Radius

Three-Point Arcs

Command: **arc**
Center/<Start point>:
Center/End/<Second point>:
Endpoint:

With this method, you select three points and the arc rubber bands into position. The three points must each be different; otherwise, the arc will be indeterminate.

Start-Center-End Arcs

```
Command: arc
Center/End/<Second point>: c
Center:
Angle/Length of chord/<Endpoint>:
```

Note that the line that extends from the center of the arc defines the endpoint. You can move this line around until it reveals the arc you desire.

Start-Center-Angle Arcs

```
Command: arc
Center/<Start point>:
Center/End/<Second point>: c
Center:
Angle/Length of chord/<Endpoint>: a
Included angle:
```

With this method, you specify the starting point, the center point, and then the included angle. Note that the angle is defined by the orientation from the X axis to the drag line taken in the counterclockwise direction.

Start-Center-Length Arcs

```
Command: arc
Center/<Start point>:
```

Center/End/<Second point>: **c**
Center:
Angle/Length of chord/<Endpoint>: **l**
Length of chord:

With this arc's construction, you know in advance that you need an arc distance of some value. This command gives you the ability to lay out curves that have known lengths. You first specify a start point, then a center point, and finally the known length of a chord.

Start-End-Angle Arcs

Command: **arc**
Center/<Start point>:
Center/End/<Second point>: **e**
Endpoint:
Angle/Direction/Radius/<Center point>: **a**
Included angle:

This arc is defined without reference to the center. All that is required is that you specify the required angle and AutoCAD will determine where the center lies.

Start-End-Radius Arcs

Command: **arc**
Center/<Start point>:
Center/End/<Second point: **e**
Endpoint:
Angle/Direction/Radius/<Center point>: **r**
Radius:

If you define the radius as less than half the distance between the start point and the endpoint, the arc cannot be drawn, but there is no danger if you use the pointing device. The proposed arc will rubber band to the correct location.

Start-End-Direction Arcs

Command: **arc**
Center/<Start point>:
Center/End/<Second point>: **e**
Endpoint:
Angle/Direction/Radius/<Center point>: **d**
Direction from start point:

You can create an arc by specifying the start point, endpoint, and the direction from the start point that the arc is to be drawn. This method projects the arc starting at the first point you specify, connecting to the endpoint, and with a tangent relationship defined between a rubber-band line and the arc to be drawn. As usual, the line is rubber banded to the point of tangency. The arc is drawn repeatedly as you move the pointing device. If you hold the pointing device still long enough, the complete arc will be drawn.

Center-Start-End Arcs

Command: **arc**
Center/<Start point>: **c**
Center:
Start point:
Angle/Length of chord/<Endpoint>:

You can draw an arc by specifying the center, then the starting point, and finally the ending point. This is the method for drawing arcs with which you may be the most familiar. When you draw an arc manually, you usually start by knowing the center and at least one point. Matching the arc to two points would require you to construct a perpendicular bisector between the starting and ending points. You would also need to measure the radius from either the start or the end to find the center before the arc could be drawn. Of course, with AutoCAD you can experiment with many combinations for every arc you draw. It is harder to do this manually.

Center-Start-Angle Arcs

Command: **arc**
Center/<Start point>: **c**
Center:
Start point:
Angle/Length of chord/<Endpoint>: **a**
Included angle:

Remember that with angles, the angle specification line will use AutoCAD's standard angular frame of reference. Zero degrees is defined by the X axis and points to the right. Angles increase in a counterclockwise direction from the X axis. In this case, you specify the center, starting point, and the desired angle to be subtended by the arc.

Center-Start-Length Arcs

Command: **arc**
Center/<Start point>: **c**
Center:
Start point:
Angle/Length of chord/<Endpoint>: **l**
Length of chord:

Here the center was specified first, then the starting point, and finally the chord length was dragged from the start point. Merely dragging the required length in any direction will have the same effect as specifying the chord length.

Continuation of Arcs

Command: **arc**
Center/<Start point>:
Endpoint:

The last way to define arcs is one of the more powerful functions in AutoCAD. Its power comes from its sheer simplicity. You will find a great deal of use for drawing arcs in continuation. As each arc is drawn and terminated, the next arc connects with the preceding arc by a common point of tangency. This gives each arc a smooth transition. You start the continuation process with any of the preceding ten methods. To continue on to the next arc, you give the CONTIN: command, or you merely press ENTER in response to the first prompt of the ARC command.

You can see the great variety of methods for drawing arcs available to you with AutoCAD. As you work with AutoCAD, you will find that you will need to use one or another of these methods as you try to fit arcs into your drawings.

AREA

Command: **area**
<First point>/Entity/Add/Subtract:

You can compute the area of a circle, polygon, or polyline with the AREA command. The areas derived by successive exercise of the AREA command are accumulated in the AREA system variable. The area, perimeter, and total area will be reported. The total area may be cleared by using the SETVAR command to set the AREA system variable to zero.

If you set "Add" mode, you will accumulate areas in the AREA system variable. If you set subtract mode, areas will be subtracted from the AREA system variable. If you choose to compute areas with the "Entity" mode, you will be prompted to pick a circle, polyline, or polygon, after which the area(s) of such will be be accumulated. The "First point to be picked" option is useful for beginning a series of points that define a perimeter, the area of which will be computed. Finally, the "Subtract" mode will do the reverse of the "Add" mode, in that areas will be subtracted from, rather than added to, the AREA system variable.

Options:

A	Add mode is set
E	Entity select—area of circle, polyline, or polygon selected will be reported
F	First point will be picked
S	Subtract mode is set

ARRAY

Command: **array**
Select objects:

An array is an arrangement of a number of duplicates of an object. Arrays may be polar or rectangular. In a polar array, an array will consist of a number of duplicates arranged at equal distances around a central point. If rectangular, the objects will be arranged in rows and columns, much like the dates on a calendar.

Options:

P	Polar array
R	Rectangular array

Polar Arrays

Command: **array**
Select objects:

Rectangular or Polar array (R/P): **p**
Center point of array:
Number of items:
Angle to fill:
Rotate objects as they are copied? <Y>

If you choose the "Polar" option of the ARRAY command, you will be prompted for the center point of the circular array after you select the object(s) to be used in the array. After you select the center, you will be prompted for the number of times the object is to be copied. The angle to be filled by the object (equally spaced) is entered next. You can use positive numbers for the angle, in which case angles will be counterclockwise (CCW); if negative numbers are used, angles will be clockwise (CW). Finally, you choose whether the objects are to be rotated so that they are always oriented normal to rays directed from the center point or not.

Rectangular Arrays

Command: **array**
Select objects:
Rectangular or Polar array (R/P): **r**
Number of rows (---) <1>:
Number of columns (¦¦¦) <1>:
Unit cell or distance between rows (---):
Distance between columns (¦¦¦):

You can make copies of objects in a rectangular array form if you use the ARRAY command with the "R" option. In rectangular arrays, the rows are horizontally arranged while columns are vertically arranged. The selected object(s) will be propagated in any number of rows and columns. For example, to generate an array of squares consisting of five rows and four columns, you could select one square, use the "R" option (as in the preceding example), enter the desired number of rows (five) and columns (four), and proceed to enter the distances requested. If you elect to use the "Unit cell," you can pick a rectangle that represents both the horizontal and vertical distances between rows and columns. There would then be no need to enter the distance between columns. If you do not elect to use the "Unit cell," you must enter a distance between rows as well as a distance between columns. See Chapter 3, "Editing," for more information on the ARRAY command.

ATTDEF

Command: **attdef**
Attribute modes—Invisible:N Constant:N Verify:N
Preset:N
Enter (ICVP) to change, RETURN when done:
Attribute tag:
Attribute prompt:
Default Attribute value:

Attributes may be defined and used in blocks within an AutoCAD drawing. As discussed thoroughly in Chapter 9, "Attribute Management," an attribute is a text string that is identified by a name.

You can use a combination of modes by selecting "Invisible," "Constant," "Verify," or "Preset." See Chapters 5, "Dimensioning," and Chapter 9, "Attribute Management," for more information about these modes. The attribute tag is the name you want to be associated with the attribute you create. The attribute prompt is the prompt you wish to see when the attribute is used in a block. The default attribute value is the default text string you want to be used if the user does not enter anything new when using the attribute.

If "Invisible," the attribute will not be shown on the screen (unless overridden by the ATTDISP command). If "Constant," the attribute value will not be prompted for, but will always be the value you enter. In the case of "Constant" attributes, the final prompt will be "Attribute value:" rather than "Default Attribute value:." If you select "Verify" mode, the user will be forced to double check a value before it is accepted. If "Preset," the value you enter as the default may be changed, but it will not be prompted for when the attribute is used in a block.

Options:

I	Invisible attribute (or visible if not set)
C	Constant mode set (or variable if not set)
V	Verify mode set
P	Preset mode set

ATTDISP

Command: **attdisp**
Normal/On/Off <current>:

You can control the visibility of attributes for your drawing as a whole with the ATTDISP command. Normally, the attributes in your drawing will be visible only if the "Invisible" option of the ATTDEF command was set to off when the attributes were created. You may wish to see all attributes, even if many of them were set to be invisible, in order to edit them. On the other hand, you may not wish to see even those attributes that were defined to be visible.

You can select "Normal," "On," or "Off" in response to the prompt. Be sure to use the entire words "On" or "Off," or you will be prompted to resolve an ambiguous response. The letter "O" will not suffice.

Options:

N	visibility set Normally as required by each attribute
ON	All Attributes forced to be visible
OFF	All Attributes forced to be nonvisible

ATTEDIT

Command: **attedit**
Edit attributes one at a time? <y>:

After you have created attributes and used them in blocks in your drawing, you can edit them with the ATTEDIT command. This command enables you to edit attributes one at a time or globally. You can select only the attributes that you pick, or you can select all attributes in the drawing that conform to specific selection criteria.

Attributes, like other entities in AutoCAD, have properties such as value, position, height, angle, and text style. You can change any of these properties for any or all attributes during the editing session.

To edit only the attributes you want to pick from the attributes visible on your screen, you can choose the default for the following "Edit attributes one at a time?" prompt.

Command: **attedit**
Edit attributes one at a time? <Y>:
Block name specification <*>:
Attribute tag specification <*>:
Attribute value specification <*>:
Select Attributes:
Value/Position/Height/Angle/Style/Layer/Color/Next <N>:

In this case (as with all invocations of the ATTEDIT command), you will be prompted first for a "filter" to select suitable candidates for editing. Since attributes must always be used within blocks, you can specify a block name to filter out attributes that are not in a given block. Alternatively, you can use the wildcard default (symbolized by the asterisk character). As with the block name, you can specify an attribute tag name that will limit the search to only the attribute tag you specify. Finally, the filter can include a specific attribute value. If you specify anything but the wildcard character (*) for any of the three filters, you will only be able to change attributes that satisfy the filter criteria. Obviously, if you use the wildcard for all three filters, there will be no limit to the attributes you can change in the current editing session.

After setting your filter criteria, you will be prompted to select the attributes you wish to edit. You do so in the usual manner, picking attributes or windowing. After you select the attributes, you will be prompted to change the properties of the attributes, one by one, as attributes that meet the selection criteria are presented to you.

If you select the "Value" option, you will be prompted to "Change or Replace?" the string value. If you choose the default ("Replace"), you will be prompted only for a "New Attribute value:"; otherwise, you will be prompted first for the "String to change:", then for the "New string:". After you enter the new string, all instances of the string will be changed in the selection set.

Global editing of attributes is accomplished by answering **N** to the "Edit attributes one at a time?" prompt, as in the following example.

Command: **attedit**
Edit attributes one at a time? <Y>: **n**
Block name specification <*>:
Attribute tag specification <*>:
Attribute value specification <*>:
Global edit of Attribute values.
Edit only Attributes visible on screen? <Y>

You will not be prompted to select attributes in this case. Instead, all the attributes that meet the filter criteria will be presented to you, one by one, either for the drawing as a whole, or only for attributes that are visible on the screen. You can select whether or not you want to confine your edit to only those attributes that are on the screen by responding to the "Edit only Attributes visible on screen?" prompt. If you respond with a **Y**, you will limit your edit, ignoring those attributes that are not on the screen. The word "visible" in this context does not mean that only visible attributes will be edited. Even attributes that are not set to be visible will be edited if they fall within the current viewport.

After you select whether you wish to confine your editing to the screen or not, you will be prompted for the "String to change:" and then for the "New string:." After you enter appropriate values, all instances in the selection set will be changed.

ATTEXT

Command: **attext**
CDF, SDF or DXF Attribute extract (or Entities)? <C>:
Template file <default>:
Extract file name <drawing name>:

To use attribute information in the world outside your drawing, you must extract such information. AutoCAD provides the ATTEXT command for this purpose. You have the choice of three formats for extraction. You can also choose to extract all attributes from a drawing or limit your extraction to only objects you select.

If you choose the "Entities" response, you will be prompted to select the objects that contain attributes you wish to extract, and then you will be able to choose the desired extraction format.

Comma-delimited format ("CDF") gives you one record per block. Fields in the record are separated by commas, and strings are quoted. If you have used the BASIC programming language, you will be familiar with this way of storing data. You can read CDF files with BASIC or dBASE III.

Space-delimited format ("SDF") is appropriate for use with dBASE III. You can use SDF files directly in dBASE. Consult your dBASE documentation for the "SDF" option. In the SDF format, fields are not delimited and are of fixed length, padded by space characters. Strings are not enclosed by quote characters.

The Drawing eXchange Format produced by the ATTEXT command is similar to the usual AutoCAD DXF protocol. Not all drawing information is extracted, however. Only the "Attribute," "Block Reference," and "End of Sequence" entities are extracted.

The "Template file" required for the extraction is a specially formatted file you must provide. This file controls all aspects of the extraction, governing the way in which each named property of each attribute is to be reported. You must use an ASCII text editor to prepare the file. A specially designed text editor is provided as part of the companion software for this book to enable you to create text files such as this. AutoCAD cannot tolerate the use of TAB characters or other special characters that are included by word processors.

Attributes may contain many different properties, as shown in the preceding discussion. These properties are referred to as follows in the template file:

(your tag)	Cwww000
(your tag)	Nwwwppp
BL:LEVEL	Nwww000
BL:NAME	Cwww000
BL:NUMBER	Nwww000
BL:HANDLE	Cwww000
BL:LAYER	Cwww000
BL:ORIENT	Nwwwppp
BL:X	Nwwwppp
BL:Y	Nwwwppp
BL:Z	Nwwwppp
BL:XSCALE	Nwwwppp
BL:YSCALE	Nwwwppp
BL:ZSCALE	Nwwwppp
BL:XEXTRUDE	Nwwwppp
BL:YEXTRUDE	Nwwwppp
BL:ZEXTRUDE	Nwwwppp

The symbols used in the template file are as follows:

N	Numeric field
C	Character field
w	"width" as in C language's [width].[precision]
p	"precision" as in C language's [width].[precision]

The field names shown have specific meanings. You can use your own tag names, either character or numeric. Apart from these tag names, the properties of the attributes, including their position, scale, and extrusion factors, can be extracted if you include their format information. The "Cwww000" information as shown in the preceding information means "Character field, three decimals width, three zeros denoting no precision appropriate." For example, a character field 20 characters wide for a tag called SPROCKET would look like this:

SPROCKET C020000

The meaning of precision applies only to floating-point numbers, not integers. An integer is of the form "Nwww000," whereas a floating point real is of the form "Nwwwppp," in which the "ppp" refers to the number of places to the right of the decimal point.

You do not need to use all the fields shown in the preceding list in your template file. You only need to use fields that are appropriate for the extraction file you intend to produce.

Options:

C	CDF comma-delimited extraction format
D	DXF extraction format
E	Extract selected objects only
S	SDF extraction format

AXIS

Command: **axis**
Tick spacing(X) or ON/OFF/Snap/Aspect <current>:

You can show tick marks on the right and bottom borders of the graphics area of your screen with the AXIS command. Tick marks are small lines that project outward from each border line at equidistant spacing. They are helpful for quickly locating the crosshairs at a desired grid point.

You can use any of the above options to control the appearance of the tick marks displayed along horizontal and vertical axes. You can turn the axes on or off (be sure to use complete words "ON" and "OFF" as "O" will not suffice). The spacing can be set to a number. If the number is 0 the spacing will be set to the current snap grid spacing. If the number is followed by an "X," the spacing will be set to a multiple of the snap grid spacing.

Options:

S	locks the tick mark spacing to Snap interval
A	Aspect of ticks is set differently for X and Y axes
number	spacing will be set to this number (0 means "use snap spacing")
numberX	spacing is set to a multiple of the snap spacing
ON	turns the axis marks ON
OFF	turns the axis marks OFF

BASE

Command: **base**
Base point <current>:

The base insertion point is the origin that will be used for a drawing when it is inserted in another drawing. You can specify the base insertion point with the BASE command.

You can pick any point as the new base point for the drawing. When you save the drawing and start to work on a different drawing, you can insert the previous drawing in the new drawing. When you do so, the base point you selected for the first drawing will be used as the origin of the insertion. The origin of the drawing to be inserted will be at the crosshairs location.

BLIPMODE

Command: **blipmode**
ON/OFF <current>:

You can control the appearance of *blips* (markers) with the BLIPMODE command. Blips are tiny crosses that appear when you select objects. These crosses are sometimes valuable because they record the exact location of a pick. At times, however, they can be annoying and you may wish to turn them off. The BLIPMODE command enables you to do so.

BLIPMODE is also a system variable. You can turn BLIPMODE on and off with the SETVAR command as well as with the BLIPMODE command. You can also access the BLIPMODE system variable by using AutoLISP. Be sure to use the complete words "On" or "Off," or you will be prompted to be more specific.

Options:

ON	marker blips ON
OFF	marker blips OFF

BLOCK

Command: **block**
Block name (or ?):
Insertion base point:
Select objects:

You can create a new object from objects you select if you use the BLOCK command. The object you create is known as a *compound object* because it is made of a collection of other objects. Compound objects may contain entities or other compound objects limited only by the capacity of your system.

The first option of the BLOCK command is to list the blocks in your drawing. You choose this option by using the question mark (?) in response to the "Block name (or ?):" prompt. If you give a name in response to the "Block name (or ?):" prompt, that name will be used as the name for the block. If the name is already in use, you will be prompted for another one.

After giving a desired name, you must select the "Insertion base point:". This is the point you wish to be at the crosshairs location when the block is later inserted into a drawing. You select the objects you wish to include in the block with any of the AutoCAD selection methods, including picking and windowing.

After you finish the creation of a block, you can insert the block into the same drawing with the INSERT command. To use the block in a different drawing, you must use the WBLOCK command to write the block to disk.

Options:

?	names of blocks in drawing will be listed
name	desired name to be used to identify the block

BREAK

Command: **break**
Select object:
Enter second point (of F for first point):

You can erase part of an object with the BREAK command. The command works for circles, arcs, two-dimensional polylines, lines, and traces. You select the first and second points for the break, and the part of the object that lies between the two points is removed. Two new objects of the same type as the original object are created, each with a new ending and beginning point respectively.

The preceding command like all the examples in this chapter, assumes that you are picking rather than entering numbers. If you pick the object, it is assumed that the pick point is the start of the break. If you wish to reenter the start point, however, you should enter an "F" response rather than a pick. After you pick the second point, the break will be performed.

Option:

F the First point is to be respecified

CHAMFER

Command: **chamfer**
Polyline/Distances/<Select first line>:
Select second line:

In order to "square the corner" where two lines intersect, you can create a *chamfer.* Such squared corners are often used in engineering design where materials are forced to be continuous, yet contain sharp angles. Under such circumstances, stresses are concentrated at the location of the abrupt change in direction of the materials. By squaring the intersection, the stresses are more smoothly distributed, resulting in less likelihood of rupture.

AutoCAD enables engineers to easily install chamfers at corners, but the value of the chamfer is not limited to use by engineers alone. With a chamfer, intersections can be converted into squared corners for any purpose. You can use the FILLET command to do much the same thing as can be done with the CHAMFER command, except that fillets are rounded rather than squared.

You can perform several separate operations with the CHAMFER command. There are two distances involved, represented by the system variables CHAMFERA and CHAMFERB. You can use SETVAR or AutoLISP to set these variables, or you can select the "Distances" option. If you use the "Distances" option, you will be prompted for the first chamfer distance, then the second. These distances refer to the distance from the intersection of the two lines to be chamfered. The two distances will be equal unless you specifically set them to different values. Ordinarily, a chamfer will be at a 45-degree angle to the base angle.

If you choose the "Polyline" option, you will be prompted to select a polyline to chamfer. If the polyline is appropriately constructed, each intersection will be chamfered. The number of chamfers that were attempted but failed will be reported in the event that the polyline was not properly constructed.

Assuming the distances have been set and you do not wish to chamfer an entire polyline, you can select the two lines you do want to chamfer. After you select the two intersecting lines, they will be chamfered.

Options:

D	chamfer Distances are set
P	an entire Polyline is to be chamfered

CHANGE

Command: **change**
Select objects:

Properties/<Change point>: **p**
Change what property (Color/Elev/LAyer/LType/
Thickness) ?

After you have created an entity and used it in your drawing, you may wish to change its properties. In order to do this, you can use the CHANGE command. You have many options for changing properties. You will be prompted according to the entity type, and you can also change the common properties of entities.

If you choose to change properties as in the preceding command sequence, you will be able to change color, elevation, layer, line type, or thickness. Each choice ("C," "E," "LA," "LT," or "T") will display a prompt of the form "New (property) <default>:." You can then use the default value or supply a new value. For example, the color prompt might be "New color <2 (green)>:," to which you might respond with "3" or "BLUE."

You can change only the point that the entity is placed in the drawing if you use the default. If the entity is a line, you can change its length by moving the start point. You can also use an "L" response to avoid selecting "P" (for property), then selecting LA (for layer), when you wish to change the layer name. In this case, just pick a new point and the selected objects will be moved to that position. If any of the objects is a text object, however, you will be prompted as follows:

Command: **change**
Select objects:
Properties/<Change point>:
Text style: STANDARD
New style or RETURN for no change:
New height <0.20>:
New rotation angle <0>:
New text <My text>:

Options:

C	change Color
E	change Elevation
LA	change Layer
LT	change Linetype
P	Properties of objects to be changed
T	change 3D Thickness

CHPROP

Command: **chprop**
Select objects:
Change what property (Color/LAyer/LType/Thickness) ?

You can use the CHPROP command if you want to change only the common entity properties of color, layer, line type, and thickness. This command is more limited than the CHANGE command, but may be easier to use if you know that only the common properties (not text height and other specific properties) need to be changed.

For each property you elect to change, the existing value will be displayed and you will be prompted for a new value. The method of changing values is the same as for the CHANGE command.

Options:

C	change Color
L	change Layer
LT	change Linetype
T	change Thickness

CIRCLE

command: **circle**
3P/2P/TTR/<centerpoint>:

You can use several methods to draw circles with AutoCAD. The product of the CIRCLE command is always a full circle. If you want to draw parts of circles, you should use the ARC command.

There are many combinations of command options with which you can draw circles. It is sufficient to show a few possible combinations. The rest will be easy to infer from the examples.

Options:

C	enter Center point
D	enter Diameter to specify circle
2P	2 endPoints of diameter are specified
3P	3 Points on circumference are specified
R	enter Radius to specify circle
TTR	Two Tangent points and Radius are specified

"Radius"

Command: **circle**
3P/2P/TTR/<Center point>:
Diameter/<Radius>:
Radius:

To draw a circle using the radius method, you first enter the CIRCLE command by typing it on the command line or by selecting it from a menu. Then you specify the radius and the circle is drawn. This is perhaps the most common way you will draw circles.

"Diameter"

Command: **circle**
3P/2P/TTR/<Center point>:
Diameter/<Radius>: **d**
Diameter:

Just as you created a circle by using the radius, you can create a circle by using the diameter.

"Two Points"

Command: **circle**
3P/2P/TTR/<Center point>: **2p**
First point on diameter:
Second point on diameter:

A two-point circle is defined by first placing one point to be on the circumference of the circle, not on the circle's center. The second point becomes the endpoint of the circle's diameter.

"Three Points"

Command: **circle**
3P/2P/TTR/<Center point>: **2p**
First point on diameter:
Second point on diameter:

You may have encountered the formula for the three-point circle in a high school or an undergraduate analytic geometry course. Any three points determine a circle, as long as the three points do not lie on a straight line (not colinear). If you choose the 3 POINT menu item, you will be prompted for three points, and, when you place the last point, the circle will be drawn.

"Tangent Tangent Radius"

Command: **circle**
3P/2P/TTR/<Center point>: **ttr**
Enter Tangent spec:
Enter second Tangent spec:
Radius:

You can select any two entities (circles or lines) to which a circle of a given radius will be constructed, if possible. You must first draw the two lines or circles, then pick them in response to the "Tangent spec" prompts. When you supply the desired radius, the circle will be drawn. If more than one circle could be drawn matching the criteria you specify, the circle that matches the nearest points you specified when you picked the tangent entities will be constructed.

COLOR

Command: **color**
New entity color <current>:

When you draw with AutoCAD entities, the color used for drawing will be the color that has been most recently set by the COLOR command. You can change the current color setting by entering a new color number or name, or you can assign the color to the color used by the current layer or block.

You can use a number or a name to specify the color. If you use a number, it must be from 1 to 255. You can also use a standard color name. The ability of your display to support the color you specify must be taken into account when you specify colors, or you may not see what you expect. If you use the BYBLOCK key word, the objects you draw will be colored until they are included in blocks. When such entities are made part of compound objects, the block color will be used to draw them. With the BYLAYER key word, the color of the current layer will be assigned to each object drawn in that layer.

Options:

number	entity color set by number
name	entity color set to standard color name
BYBLOCK	entity color set by current block
BYLAYER	entity color set by layer

COPY

Command: **copy**
Select objects:

You can copy objects from one location to another with the COPY command. You can either copy just once for each execution of the command, or you can choose the "Multiple" option and make numerous copies without reentering the command.

Option:

M	Multiple copies desired

To make single copies, you simply pick the objects you wish to copy, then select a base point and a displacement, as in the following example:

Command: **copy**
Select objects:
<Base point or displacement>/Multiple:
Second point of displacement:

The base point is an arbitrary point that establishes the source of the copy in space. The destination is the second point you pick. After the copy, you will see new copies of the objects you selected. The new copies will be displaced from the base point you selected as the first point, and that base point will appear at the second point.

You can make multiple copies with the "Multiple" option, as in the following example:

Command: **copy**
Select objects:
<Base point or displacement>/Multiple: **m**
Base point:
Second point of displacement:
Second point of displacement:

You can go on picking second points until you cancel or press ENTER. At each second point, a fresh copy of the object(s) you selected will be placed.

DBLIST

Command: **dblist**

You can list the contents of the entire drawing database with the DBLIST command.

DDATTE

Command: **ddatte**
Select block:

You can use the DDATTE command to display a dialog box that will enable editing of attributes. You must use the Advanced User Interface to enable dialog boxes.

When you select a block that contains attributes, you will see a dialog box that allows you to edit the contents of displayed attribute fields.

DDEMODES

Command: **'ddemodes**

With the Advanced User Interface you can change current properties such as color, layer, line type, elevation, and thickness by using a dialog box.

DDLMODES

Command: **'ddlmodes**

You can use the DDLMODES command to change layer information for your current drawing. You can change the layer name. You can turn layers on or off. You can freeze layers, assign colors, and assign line types to layers. You can also add new layers. If you are using the Advanced User Interface, a dialog box will appear that enables you to change the layer information.

DDRMODES

Command: **'ddrmodes**

If you are using the Advanced User Interface, you can display a single dialog box that allows you to change the snap interval, the grid interval, the axis, ortho mode, blips, and isometric modes. You can interactively change all the variables controlled by the ISOPLANE, ORTHO, BLIPMODE, SNAP, GRID, and AXIS commands.

DDUCS

Command: **'dducs**

The DDUCS command enables users of the Advanced User Interface to control all aspects of the User Coordinate System. You can select the coordinate system that is to be made current, and you can list and delete any coordinate system you have created. You can also create a new user coordinate system, defining the name, the origin, the Z axis origin, and the rotation of the system about the X, Y, and Z axes. You can specify alignment with a view or an entity as well.

DELAY

Command: **delay**
Delay time in milliseconds:

Some AutoCAD operations happen so quickly that it may not be possible to see what is happening. You may wish to give a demonstration of an AutoCAD operation to illustrate it. The DELAY command allows you to slow down the operation enough so that people can see what is happening. You can enter a number from 1 to 32,767. This number represents the approximate number of milliseconds AutoCAD is to delay the execution of each step as it executes commands. This command is intended for use with command scripts.

DIM and DIM1

Command: **dim** (or **dim1**)
Dim:

AutoCAD has a complete command language contained within its command language. This language, which implements AutoCAD's dimensioning capabilities, consists of a set of subcommands that are invoked by the DIM command. Once you enter the DIM command, you will see a new command prompt "Dim:" that will act much like the "Command:" prompt with which you are familiar. Instead of handling the regular AutoCAD commands, however, you can enter only dimensioning subcommands with this command prompt.

The DIM1 command is like the DIM command, with one exception. While the DIM command returns you to the "Dim:" prompt after each subcommand, the DIM1 command returns you to the "Command:" prompt. You can use DIM if you know you will be staying in dimensioning mode and you wish to avoid reentering DIM1. On the other hand, you can use the DIM1 command if you want to execute only one of the dimensioning subcommands and then return to the "Command:" prompt. Refer to Chapter 5, "Dimensioning," for illustrations of many of the dimensioning techniques summarized here.

With the dimensioning subcommands, you can create dimensions with a variety of methods. You can use angular, linear, and diameter dimensioning. In addition, you can control the sizes and types of arrowheads, text strings, and much more. Each dimensioning subcommand can be executed by entering only the first three letters of the command name. You do not need, for example, to type "aligned", only "ali".

ALIGNED

Dim: **aligned**
First extension line origin or RETURN to select:

Select line, arc or circle:
Dimension line location:
Dimension text <derived>:

The ALIGNED dimensioning subcommand creates dimensions that are aligned with the objects they are dimensioning. The linear dimension of the line, arc, or circle being dimensioned is used to create the dimension text. You locate the dimension line and the dimension is automatically derived for you.

ANGULAR

Dim: **angular**
Select first line:
Second line:
Enter dimension line arc location:
Dimension text <derived>:
Enter text location:

You can create an angular dimension line between two lines by using the ANGULAR subcommand. The angular relationship between the two lines will be used to derive the dimension text. You can substitute your own text if you wish. In addition, the text can be located inside or outside the dimension line arc.

BASELINE

Dim: **baseline**

The BASELINE subcommand will repeat the last entered HORIZONTAL, VERTICAL, ROTATED, or ALIGNED subcommand using the same starting callout. Thus, all such dimensions will originate at the same place.

CENTER

Dim: **center**
Select arc or circle:

You can automatically dimension to a center mark for circles and arcs if you use the CENTER subcommand. A dimension will automatically be drawn from a center mark to the perimeter of the circle or arc at the location you pick.

CONTINUE

Dim: **continue**

Like the BASELINE subcommand, the CONTINUE subcommand creates a series of repetitions of a HORIZONTAL, VERTICAL, ROTATED, or ALIGNED subcommand. The dimensions will be placed end to end in a continuous manner.

DIAMETER

Dim: **diameter**
Select arc or circle:
Dimension text <derived>:

While the CENTER subcommand dimensions from a center point, the DIAMETER subcommand dimensions the diameter of a circle or arc. You select the circle or arc and the dimension is drawn across the diameter at the point you picked.

EXIT

Dim: **exit**

To return to the "Command:" prompt from the "Dim:" prompt, you should use the EXIT subcommand. You can also cancel at the "Dim:" prompt and achieve the same effect.

HOMETEXT

Dim: **hometext**
Select objects:

The HOMETEXT subcommand will place the text strings associated with selected dimension entities at their default locations if they have been moved to non-default locations.

HORIZONTAL

Dim: **horizontal**
First extension line origin or RETURN to select:
Second extension line origin:
Dimension line location:
Dimension text <derived>:

You can generate horizontal dimensions with the HORIZONTAL subcommand. You will first be prompted for the extension line origin. If you press ENTER in response to this prompt, you will be prompted to select an object. The horizontal dimension of the selected line, circle, or arc entity will then be used to automatically derive the dimension.

If you do not press ENTER in response to the "First extension line" prompt, you can pick a point that will be used as the origin of the dimension. You pick the origin of the second extension line and then the dimension line location. Finally, you have the option of using the derived dimension text or of entering your own text. After going through the command sequence, the horizontal dimension will be drawn.

LEADER

Dim: **leader**
Leader start point:
To point:
Dimension text <derived from last dimension>:

The leader will have an arrowhead at the start point and as many segments as you pick in response to the "To point:" prompt(s). The dimension text can either be the default or any text you wish to enter. You are limited to only one line of text per leader, although you could create an AutoLISP routine to add more than one line of text.

NEWTEXT

Dim: **newtext**
Enter new dimension text:
Select objects:

The new dimension text will be substituted for any dimension objects you select. If you use a pair of angle brackets (<>), the measured dimension will be substituted for the angle brackets in the dimension string.

RADIUS

Dim: **radius**
Select arc or circle:
Dimension text <derived>:

You can use the RADIUS subcommand to draw a radius dimension from the center of a circle or arc to the point you select on the perimeter. You can use the default text or enter your own text.

REDRAW

Dim: **redraw**

Just as in normal command mode, you can generate a redraw with the dimensioning subcommand REDRAW.

ROTATED

Dim: **rotated**
Dimension line angle <0>:
First extension line origin or RETURN to select:
Second extension line origin:
Dimension line location:
Dimension text <derived>:

Like the HORIZONTAL, VERTICAL, and ALIGNED subcommands, the ROTATED subcommand draws dimensions that can be based on picked origins or on entity properties. With the ROTATED subcommand, however, the dimension line can be rotated to a different angle from the horizontal, vertical, or entity alignment. The dimension line angle can be expressed explicitly or dragged with a rubber-band line.

STATUS

Dim: **status**

The STATUS subcommand displays the current status of all the dimensioning variables. Do not confuse the dimensioning STATUS subcommand with the STATUS command you enter at the command prompt. In the following list, a variable is either on or off unless otherwise specified. If on or off, the on state is the one shown. The list of variables with their meanings is as follows:

DIMALT	Dimension Alternate Units enabled
DIMALTD	Dimension Alternate Units Decimal Places integer
DIMALTF	Dimension Alternate Units Factor real number
DIMAPOST	Dimension Alternate Postfix String
DIMASO	Associative Dimensioning used
DIMASZ	Dimension Arrow Size in units
DIMBLK	Dimension Block for use instead of arrow
DIMBLK1	Dimension Block for first end of extension line for DIMSAH on
DIMBLK2	Dimension Block for second end of extension line for DIMSAH on
DIMCEN	Dimension Center Mark Size in units
DIMDLE	Dimension Line Extension beyond dimension line in units
DIMDLI	Dimension Line Increment in units
DIMEXE	Dimension Extension Line Extension in units
DIMEXO	Dimension Extension Line Offset in units
DIMLFAC	Dimension Length Factor real number
DIMLIM	Dimension Limits shown
DIMPOST	Dimension Postfix String
DIMRND	Dimension Rounding Value in units
DIMSAH	Dimension Separate Arrow Heads
DIMSCALE	Dimension Scale Factor real number
DIMSE1	Suppress Extension line 1
DIMSE2	Suppress Extension line 2
DIMSHO	Show New Dimension recomputes associative dimensions
DIMSOXD	Suppress Outside Extension Line Dimension Lines
DIMTAD	Dimension Text Above Dimension Line

DIMTIH	Dimension Text Inside Horizontal
DIMTIX	Text Forced Between Extension Lines
DIMTM	Dimension Tolerance Minus in units
DIMTOFL	Text Outside, Force Line forces dimension line between extension lines
DIMTOH	Dimension Text Outside Horizontal
DIMTOL	Dimension Tolerance shown
DIMTP	Dimension Tolerance Plus in units
DIMTSZ	Dimension Tick Size in units (non-zero forces tick marks)
DIMTVP	Dimension Text Vertical Position in units
DIMTXT	Dimension Text Size height in units
DIMZIN	Dimension Zero Suppression integer
	if 1 means suppress zero feet and zero inches
	if 2 means allow zero feet and zero inches
	if 3 means allow zero feet and suppress zero inches
	if 4 means suppress zero feet and allow zero inches

STYLE

Dim: **style**
New text style <default style>:

You can change the current text style during the dimensioning session by using the STYLE subcommand. After you do so, the new style will be used for all future dimensioning text.

UNDO

Dim: **undo**

Like the normal AutoCAD UNDO command, the UNDO subcommand will undo dimensioning commands you have entered. You can only undo back to the beginning of the DIM command. The dimensioning version of the U command does the same thing as the dimensioning UNDO subcommand.

UPDATE

Dim: **update**
Select objects:

You can update any dimension entities you select in response to the UPDATE subcommand. The dimensions will be made to reflect the current settings of all system variables and any other changes you may have made since the last update.

VERTICAL

Dim: **vertical**
First extension line origin or RETURN to select:
Second extension line origin:
Dimension line location:
Dimension text <derived>:

You can generate vertical dimensions if you use the VERTICAL subcommand. You will first be prompted for the extension line origin. If you press ENTER in response to this prompt, you will be prompted to select an object, and then the vertical dimension of the selected line, circle, or arc entity will be used to automatically derive the dimension.

If you do not press ENTER in response to the "First extension line" prompt, you can pick a point that will be used as the origin of the dimension. You pick the origin of the second extension line and then the dimension line location. Finally, you have the option of using the derived dimension text or of entering your own text. After going through the command sequence, the vertical dimension will be drawn.

DIST

Command: **dist**
First point:
Second point:
Distance = <derived>
Angle in X−Y plane = <derived>
Angle from X−Y plane = <derived>
Delta X = <derived> Delta Y = <derived> Delta Z = <derived>

The DIST command derives the current distance between two points in space. You can access the DISTANCE system variable with the SETVAR command to discover the distance at any time after the DIST command has been used.

DIVIDE

Command: **divide**
Select object to divide:
<Number of segments>/Block:
Block name to insert:
Align block with object? <Y>
Number of segments:

The DIVIDE command can be used to place node points along an object, dividing it into any number of equal parts. If you set the PD MODE system variable to 3, you will be able to see the node points. You can optionally identify a block name to insert and choose to align the inserted blocks with the object at each point they are inserted. The block you name must, of course, be in the drawing database. You can choose the number of segments and the object will be divided for you. Markers will be used at each division point. You can snap to those markers if object snap is enabled.

DOUGHNUT, DONUT

Command: **doughnut** (or **donut**)
Inside diameter <default>:
Outside diameter <default>:

Doughnut shapes are, as the name implies, circular, and usually have holes in their centers. The DOUGHNUT (or DONUT) command creates doughnut objects by drawing two concentric circles, one smaller than the other, and by filling the area between the circles' circumferences. Doughnuts can be created quickly and used, for example, as insertion holes in printed circuit boards.

You have the option of setting an inside diameter, which is the diameter of the "hole." The inside diameter can be zero, in which case the doughnut becomes a filled circle.

After you specify the inside diameter, you can specify the outside diameter of the doughnut. One invocation of the DOUGHNUT command will permit you to create multiple copies of the doughnut, until you press ENTER in response to the "Outside diameter" prompt.

DRAGMODE

Command: **dragmode**
ON/OFF/Auto <default>:

You can use the DRAGMODE command or the DRAGMODE system variable to control whether rubber-band lines and boxes are allowed to be dragged into position as responses to prompts. If DRAGMODE is on, dragging is enabled for all prompts that allow dragging. You must use the DRAG keyword, however, to start the drag. If DRAGMODE is set to "Auto," you do not need to use the DRAG keyword—it will automatically be enabled. If DRAGMODE is off, dragging will not be possible even if you use the DRAG key word. You can use the system variables DRAGP1 and DRAGP2 to control the frequency with which AutoCAD starts the drawing of the image of the object being dragged.

Options:

A	Automatic drag, whenever possible
ON	allow drag when drag key word used
OFF	disable drag

DTEXT

Command: **dtext**
Text:

Dynamic text allows you to use AutoCAD like a text editor. Instead of entering one line of text at a time (as with the TEXT command), you can start a new line by simply pressing ENTER at the end of the current line. You can use the BACKSPACE key to backspace over text, even back to the line above the one you are editing. You will see an outline text cursor that shows the size of the characters you will be using. Other aspects of the DTEXT command are the same as for the TEXT command.

DVIEW

Command: **dview**
Select objects:
CAmera/TArget/Distance/POints/PAn/Zoom/TWist/CLip/
Hide/Off/Undo/<eXit>:

Dynamic views can be set up with the DVIEW command. When you select the objects you wish to view, you will see a series of options as in the preceding command prompt. Each option uses slider bars that enable you to position the objects, the artificial camera, and the other aspects of the view you are creating.

Slider bars are icons that appear at various places on the screen. A typical slider bar will have a small box or cross (the slider) that moves along the bar icon, dynamically setting an aspect of the view as it moves. You will see the view be regenerated for each change in the slider position.

Options:

CA	the CAmera angle is selected
CL	back and front CLipping planes are set
D	perspective is turned on and Distance to object set
H	Hidden lines are removed for selected objects
OFF	perspective is turned OFF
PA	drawing is PAnned across the screen
PO	camera and target POints are selected
TA	the TArget point is rotated about the camera
TW	the view is TWisted around the line of sight
U	a dview subcommand is Undone
X	the dview command is eXited
Z	camera lens is Zoomed in and out

DXBIN

Command: **dxbin**
DXB file:

If you have prepared a file with AutoSHADE, you can insert the file into your AutoCAD drawing by using the DXBIN command. The DXB file format is a binary form of drawing exchange file. Do not use the ".dxb" extension in the file name you supply, since AutoCAD will add it for you.

DXFIN

Command: **dxfin**
File name:

You can insert DXF files into your drawing with the DXFIN command. DXF files are created by software other than AutoCAD and represent a de facto industry standard for the exchange of computer-aided design drawing files. AutoCAD can create a DXF file for you if you use the DXFOUT command. As always, do not include the ".dxf" extension in the file name.

DXFOUT

Command: **dxfout**
File name <current>:
Enter decimal places of accuracy (0 to 16)/Entities/Binary <4>: **e**
Select objects:
Enter decimal places of accuracy (0 to 16)/Binary <4>:

You can create an industry standard DXF file by converting your AutoCAD drawing. You simply supply a file name and select the objects you wish to convert and/or enter a numeric precision for the conversion. Do not use the ".dxf" extension in your file name.

Option:

E select objects to convert

EDGESURF

Command: **edgesurf**
Select edge 1:

```
Select edge 2:
Select edge 3:
Select edge 4:
```

You can create a bicubic surface interpolated between four adjoining edges by using the EDGESURF command. The surface is also referred to as a "Coons Patch." The surface is divided into parts along the direction of the edge first picked, according to a number stored in the SURFTAB1 system variable. Likewise, the surface is divided into parts along the direction that is at right angles to the first direction that is using a number stored in the SURFTAB2 system variable. The edges may be arcs, lines, or non-closed polylines in two- or three-dimensional space. The four edges *must* meet at their endpoints.

ELEV

```
Command: elev
New current elevation <default>:
New current thickness <default>:
```

Entities may be drawn at an elevation along the Z axis that is other than zero. You can set the current elevation with the ELEV command and you can also set the extrusion thickness for two-dimensional entities. The thickness of a two-dimensional entity is the distance along the Z axis, starting at the elevation the entity was drawn, that the entity will be extruded when it is viewed. You can also use SETVAR to set the system variables ELEVATION and THICKNESS.

ELLIPSE

```
Command: ellipse
<Axis endpoint 1>/Center/Isocircle:
Axis endpoint 2:
<Other axis distance>/Rotation:
```

With the ELLIPSE command, you can draw ellipses using several different methods. If you respond to the first prompt of the command by picking a point, you can determine the angle of the ellipse by picking a second point. You will then be prompted to pick the "Other axis distance." Picking this point will determine the size of the axis of the ellipse that is perpendicular to the first axis, whether larger or smaller.

You can also specify an ellipse by specifying two points and then a rotation angle that will determine the size of the second axis. Yet another way to draw the ellipse is to choose the center of the ellipse. If you use this method, you will be prompted for the "Center of ellipse:" and then the "Other axis distance/Rotation:." If the SNAP command has enabled "Isometric" snap mode, the ellipse will automatically be made to conform to the isometric drawing plane if you choose the "Isocircle" option.

Options:

C	Center point instead of first axis endpoint specified
R	Rotation instead of second axis used to specify eccentricity
I	Isometric circle drawn as ellipse in current ISOPLANE

END

Command: **end**

The END command updates the drawing, saves it, and returns you to the Main Menu. There is not a prompt to verify that you wish to continue. The command is a quick way to safely end a session.

ERASE

Command: **erase**
Select objects:

If you wish to erase any number of objects from your drawing, you use the ERASE command. Any of the methods of selection, including picking and windowing, may be used. You can respond to the "Select objects:" prompt with an "L" to erase the last object drawn.

EXPLODE

Command: **explode**
Select block reference, polyline, dimension or mesh:

Objects such as blocks and polylines are stored as indivisible objects. If you want to erase part of a polyline, for example, you will find that the entire polyline is erased instead. You can use the EXPLODE command to break up such objects into separate line and arc segments. The appearance of most objects remains the same, but each individual exploded part may then be modified separately.

EXTEND

Command: **extend**
Select boundary edge(s). . .
Select objects:
Select object to extend:

The EXTEND command increases the lengths of objects until they meet other objects selected as boundaries. Once you define the boundaries by selecting boundary objects, you can select any number of other objects that will then be extended until they meet the boundaries. All objects used as boundaries must be parallel to the Z axis of the User Coordinate System in effect. The extrusion must be parallel to the User Coordinate System. Only lines, polylines, and arcs may be extended.

FILES

Command: **files**

The FILES command displays the AutoCAD File Utility Menu. You can list drawing files, list specified files, delete files, rename files, and copy files from this menu.

FILL

Command: **fill**
ON/OFF <default>:

If you use the FILL command to turn on AutoCAD's automatic fill capabilities, solids, wide polylines, and traces will be filled when they are generated on the screen. If the FILLMODE system variable (as set by the FILL command, the SETVAR command, or AutoLISP) is not set to on, fills will not be performed during a plotting session. Turning FILLMODE off during test plots greatly decreases plotting time.

Options:

ON	automatically fill solids, wide polylines, and traces
OFF	outline solids, wide polylines, and traces

FILLET

Command: **fillet**
Polyline/Radius/<Select two objects>:

You can generate fillet curves between two lines, circles, or arcs with the FILLET command. The FILLET "Radius" option enables you to set the radius of the arc that will be used as the fillet. If you select the "Polyline" option, an entire polyline will automatically be filleted; in other words, its corners will be rounded. Depending on which two objects you select for the fillet, the command will behave differently. Under certain circumstances, the fillet will not be possible. For example, two circles may be too far apart to permit the fillet radius to create an arc that joins them. If your fillet is not drawn, you should suspect that the objects did not come close enough together to permit the fillet to connect with them. Lines that extend beyond a fillet will automatically be trimmed at their intersection points on the fillet curve.

Options:

P	entire Polyline will be filleted
R	fillet Radius will be set

FILMROLL

Command: **filmroll**
Enter the filmroll file name <current>:

AutoSHADE enables you to render AutoCAD drawings. To prepare the drawing for use with AutoSHADE, you must convert it into a shade file with the FILMROLL command.

GRAPHSCR

Command: **'graphscr**

If your display is in text mode, you can switch to graphics mode by using the GRAPHSCR command. If you are at a prompt in any other AutoCAD command, you can use the GRAPHSCR command transparently by preceding it with a single apostrophe character as in the preceding example. You can also use the F1 key to switch between graphics and text screens.

GRID

Command: **grid**
Grid spacing<X> or ON/OFF/Snap/Aspect <default>:

You can display a grid composed of dots spaced at specified intervals with the GRID command. You can turn grids on or off, set the grid intervals to be the same as the snap intervals, or determine an aspect ratio between horizontal and vertical grid points. The grid is only displayed within the define drawing limits. This makes the grid a quick and convenient way to view the limits of your drawing.

Options:

A	grid Aspect set (X–Y spacings differ)
ON	grid ON
OFF	grid OFF
S	grid Spacing locked to snap resolution
number	grid spacing (0 means "use snap spacing")
numberX	spacing set to multiple of snap spacing

HANDLES

Command: **handles**
Handles are OFF. . .
ON/DESTROY:

Each entity in your drawing can be given a unique number, or entity handle numbers can be removed, with the HANDLES command. If an entity has a handle, it can be referred to by that handle in future work with that drawing. The HANDLES system variable is set to 1 if handles are on.

ON	all entities are assigned handles (system variable HANDLES set to 1)
DESTROY	DESTROYs all entity handles

HATCH

Command: **hatch**
Pattern (? or name/U,style) <current>: **u**
Angle for crosshatch lines <current>:
Spacing between lines <current>:
Double hatch area? <current>:

If you want to crosshatch an object, you can use the HATCH command. You can use the "?" option to list the pattern names available. You can then supply the name of a desired pattern or use the "U" option and supply a style name. The "U" option enables you to create a pattern without using a pattern name. The pattern is created in response to the three prompts shown in the preceding example. You supply the crosshatching angle, the spacing between the lines, and tell AutoCAD whether you want the lines to be drawn in only one direction or in a checkerboard pattern.

With the "U" option, you can only use straight lines of a specified style. The styles available are "N" (normal), "O" (outermost areas), and "I" (ignore internal features). If you choose "Normal" (or do not choose a style), the pen will be raised and lowered each time it crosses a line. If you choose "Outermost," only the outermost lines will trigger a pen-up or pen-down. The "Internal" option will simply draw the pattern over the entire figure, covering everything within the outermost lines.

You can use much more complex patterns if you choose one of the standard patterns available in the "acad.pat" file. Named crosshatching patterns require you to select a scale and an angle for the pattern, instead of the angle, spacing, and double hatch prompts.

Options:

I	internal features to be Ignored
N	hatch line turned off and on as internal lines are crossed
O	Outermost portion hatched only

HELP

Command: **'help** or **'?**

The HELP command (also entered with the question mark) will display a list of currently available commands. You can also obtain help in a context sensitive manner depending on the command you are in when you execute 'HELP as a transparent command.

HIDE

Command: **hide**

The HIDE command will automatically process your drawing to remove lines that are hidden by three-dimensional surfaces and extruded shapes. You will see a message that shows the number of lines that have been removed. The message will be continuously updated to show that the computer is working on removing hidden lines. Depending on the hardware you are using and the complexity of your drawing, the process may take a few seconds, a few minutes, or a few hours.

ID

Command: **id**
Point:
X = <coordinate> Y = <coordinate> Z = <coordinate>

You can use the ID command in two ways. You can point to a location in your drawing's space and that point's coordinates will then be displayed. Alternatively, you can enter two- or three-dimensional coordinates as numbers separated by commas, and a marker you can see will be placed at the point in AutoCAD space.

IGESIN

Command: **igesin**
File name:

Files created to conform to the Initial Graphics. Exchange Standard (IGES) can be converted to AutoCAD drawings if you use the IGESIN command.

IGESOUT

Command: **igesout**
File name:

AutoCAD will export your drawing into a file whose format conforms to IGES rules if you use the IGESOUT command.

INSERT

Command: **insert**
Block name (or ?):
Insertion point:
X scale factor <1> / Corner / XYZ:
Y scale factor (default=X):
Rotation angle <0>:

There are two ways in which you can use the INSERT command to insert previously prepared drawings into a drawing on which you are working. If you have used the BLOCK or WBLOCK commands, the blocks you created can be inserted into your drawing. When blocks are written to disk, they are the same as drawings, so you can use the INSERT command to insert either. All you need to do is provide the name of an existing block or drawing, an insertion point, a scale factor, and a rotation angle, and the insertion will be performed.

Options:

name	insert a block or file by this name
block=name	use a file under "name" and create "block"
*name	individual part entities to be retained
?	names of existing blocks to be listed

C	(X scale prompt reply) specifies scale using two Corner points
XYZ	(X scale prompt replay) predefines X, Y, and Z scales

ISOPLANE

Command: **isoplane**
Left/Top/Right/(Toggle):

The ISOPLANE command makes the plane of an isometric grid the current orthogonal plane. You can choose one of three planes, or you can toggle through the planes, one by one. Isometric grids have axes at 90, 150, and 30 degrees.

Options:

L	Left plane (90 and 150 degree pair)
R	Right plane (30 and 150 degree pair)
T	Top plane (90 and 30 degree pair)
ENTER	rotate planes in left, top, right sequence

LAYERS

Command: **layer**
?/Make/Set/New/ON/OFF/Color/Ltype/Freeze/Thaw:

The LAYER command gives you control over all aspects of the AutoCAD layering system. You can list available layers, set the current layer, create new layers, and turn layers on and off. A layer can be set to a certain color or line type. Finally, a layer can be frozen or thawed. Each of these options will be discussed separately.

Options:

?	layers listed (with color and linetype info)
C color	layers set to Color
F alayer, blayer	alayer and blayer Frozen
L linetype	layers set to Linetype
M alayer	alayer Made the current layer, creating it if necessary
N alayer, blayer	New layers alayer and blayer created
ON alayer, blayer	layers alayer and blayer turned ON
OFF alayer, blayer	layers alayer and blayer turned OFF
S alayer	current layer Set to existing layer alayer
T alayer, blayer	layers alayer and blayer Thawed

"?"

Command: **layer**
?/Make/Set/New/ON/OFF/Color/Ltype/Freeze/Thaw: ?
Layer name(s) for listing <*>:

You can obtain a list of layers with the question mark option of the LAYER command ("?"). You will see a report of the available layers, including their states, colors, line types, and the name of the current layer.

"Color"

```
Command: layer
?/Make/Set/New/ON/OFF/Color/Ltype/Freeze/Thaw: c
Color:
Layer name(s) for color n <default>:
```

You reply to the "Color:" prompt with the number or name of a color. At the "Layer name(s)" prompt, you supply a single layer name or a list of layer names separated by commas. The designated layers will be set to the specified color.

"Freeze"

```
Command: layer
?/Make/Set/New/ON/OFF/Color/Ltype/Freeze/Thaw: f
Layer name(s) to Freeze:
```

If you freeze a layer, you can increase the speed of AutoCAD's operation, particularly when zooming, panning, regenerating, or setting a viewpoint. The frozen layer does not appear to exist until it is thawed. AutoCAD does not need to figure out how to treat the layer, so the software runs faster.

"Linetype," "Ltype"

```
Command: layer
?/Make/Set/New/ON/OFF/Color/Ltype/Freeze/Thaw: l
Linetype (or ?) <CONTINUOUS>:
Layer name(s) for linetype CONTINUOUS <default>:
```

The name of the line type you supply will be associated with the layers you name, as long as the layers and line types exist. Later on in your drawing activities for the current drawing, you can use the "BYLAYER" key word to use the line types associated with various layers by default.

"Make"

Command: **layer**
?/Make/Set/New/ON/OFF/Color/Ltype/Freeze/Thaw: **m**
New current layer <default>:

If you use the "Make" option of the LAYER command, you can make the current layer any one of the existing layers. All you need to do is supply an existing layer name and that layer will be made the current layer. From then on, your drawing will be done on that layer, until you make another layer current.

"New"

Command: **layer**
?/Make/Set/New/ON/OFF/Color/Ltype/Freeze/Thaw: **n**
New layer name(s):

The "New" option of the LAYER command permits you to create new layers without making them current. You might wish to use this option instead of the "Make" option when you do not want to disturb the current layer.

"ON" and "OFF"

Command: **layer**
?/Make/Set/New/ON/OFF/Color/Ltype/Freeze/Thaw: **OFF**
Layer name(s) to turn Off:

Command: **layer**
?/Make/Set/New/ON/OFF/Color/Ltype/Freeze/Thaw: **ON**
Layer name(s) to turn On:

If a layer is turned off, the entities on that layer are not visible on the screen, nor are they plotted. If the current layer is off, you will be able to draw, but you *will not see any entities as they are drawn.* If you turn a layer on, you will see the entities on that layer. If frozen, a layer must be thawed before it will become visible, even if you turn it on.

"Set"

```
Command: layer
?/Make/Set/New/ON/OFF/Color/Ltype/Freeze/Thaw: s
New current layer <default>:
```

The "Set" option of the LAYER command will not make a new layer as does the "Make" option. The "Set" option will set the current layer to a layer you name.

"Thaw"

```
Command: layer
?/Make/Set/New/ON/OFF/Color/Ltype/Freeze/Thaw: t
Layer name(s) to Thaw:
```

If you have frozen any layers, you must thaw them before you can use them again. Thawing is accomplished with the "Thaw" option of the LAYER command. A thaw sometimes requires the use of the REGEN command to see the thawed layers.

LIMITS

```
Command: limits
ON/OFF/<Lower left corner> <default>:
Upper right corner <default>:
```

Limits of drawings are checked for most entity drawing operations as a way of informing you that you are drawing "off the paper." You will see an "Outside limits" error message if you attempt to draw outside the limits you specify (or the default limits) for the drawing. The message is only a reminder and is not cause for panic. Even if you draw outside the drawing limits, the entities you create will be as normal as if they were drawn within the limits. You can even move them into the limits later on or change the limits to include them. You can disable checks on the limits so the message does not appear.

Options:

L	Lower left/upper right drawing limits set
ON	limits checking enabled
OFF	limits checking disabled

LINE

Command: **line**
From point:
To point:

The LINE command is used to draw straight lines. You are prompted for the starting point, and then you are prompted repeatedly for ending points until you press ENTER to terminate the command. If you press ENTER in response to the "From point:" prompt, AutoCAD will use the previous ending point of a line or arc as the starting point for the next line.

There are two options for the LINE command. You can respond to a "To point:" prompt with a "C" (upper- or lowercase) to close a polygon that has been created with at least two line segments. You can also respond to a "To point:" prompt with a "U" to undo the previous line segment.

Options:

C	(as reply to "To point;") close polygon
ENTER	(as reply to "From point:") start at end of previous Line or Arc

ENTER	(as reply to "To point:") end the LINE command
U	(as reply to "To point:") undo segment

LINETYPE

Command: **linetype**
?/Create/Load/Set:

The LINETYPE command is used to define line types, load line types from libraries, and set the current line type. You can also list the line types that are available.

"?"

Command: **linetype**
?/Create/Load/Set: **?**
File to list <default>:

To see a list of line types that are available for use in your current drawing, press the question mark key (?) in response to the "?/Create/Load/Set:" prompt. It is significant to visualize the AutoCAD drawing as containing not only the drawing entities but the line types, colors, and other aspects of AutoCAD drawings that *might be used* in the drawing. For line types to be available for use in the drawing, they must be created and loaded. The line types that will be listed are in a file, the default being "acad.lin." Do not add the ".lin" extension when you refer to the file.

"Create"

Command: **linetype**
?/Create/Load/Set: **c**
Name of linetype to create:
File for storage of linetype <default>:

To create a line type, you must use special letter codes. You will first be prompted for a unique name for your line type and then you will be prompted for a file in which to store it. More than one line type may be stored in a file. The default line type file is "acad.lin." Do not include the ".lin" extension if you name your own line type file.

If the line type already exists in a file, you will see a message that shows the current definition. You will be given the option of writing over it with a new definition. See Chapter 14, "AutoCAD's Other Programming Languages," for more information on line type definitions. You can edit the ".lin" file with a straight ASCII text editor, such as the one that is available with the companion software for this book.

"Load"

Command: **linetype**
?/Create/Load/Set: **l**
Linetype(s) to load:
File to search <default>:

To use line types in your drawings, you must first load them. You can load any number of line types by name, separating the names by commas. All the line types must be contained in a single file for each execution of the LINETYPE command, although you may have line types from different files in the same drawing.

"Set"

Command: **linetype**
?/Create/Load/Set: s
New entity linetype (or ?) <default>:

To assign a line type to entities as you draw them, the line type must have been loaded and it must be made current with the "Set" option of the LINETYPE command.

Options:

?	line type library is Listed
C	line type definition is Created
L	line type definition is Loaded
S	current entity line type is Set

Suboptions for "Set" option:

name	entity line type name to set
BYBLOCK	entity line type associated with block
BYLAYER	layer's line type used for entities
?	loaded line types are listed

LIST

Command: **list**
Select objects:

The LIST command will list the information in the drawing database that pertains to selected objects. The information in the list depends on the entities listed. In all cases, however, the list includes the location of the object in space relative to the User Coordinate System, the entity's type, and the entity's layer.

LOAD

Command: **load**
Name of shape file to load (or ?):

If you wish to use the SHAPE command, you must first load a set of shapes into your drawing from a shape file. To do this, you use the LOAD command. You only need to do this once per drawing, however. After you first load your shapes, AutoCAD remembers the shape file they are in and automatically loads the shapes for you. You can list the shape files that are currently loaded if you respond with a question mark (?).

Option:

? names of loaded shape files are listed

LTSCALE

Command: **ltscale**
New scale factor <current>:

When line types are drawn, the dots and dashes in them will appear to be of a certain size. You can use a global scale factor (stored in the LTSCALE system variable) to modify the sizes of the dots and dashes in the line type. You can use SETVAR or AutoLISP to change LTSCALE, or you can use the LTSCALE command. A large value of LTSCALE will create large dashes and spaces between dots and dashes, and a small value will reduce the sizes of these elements.

MEASURE

Command: **measure**
Select object to measure:
<Segment length>/Block:

Command: **measure**
Select object to measure:
<Segment length>/Block: **b**
Block name to insert:
Align block with object? <Y>:
Segment length:

You often need to divide objects into parts when you draw. A good example of this is the division of windows into parts. A window opening might be twenty feet long, too long for one continuous pane of glass. You would want to divide that length up into five-foot parts, which you could do with the MEASURE command.

To use the MEASURE command, you must first select the object to measure. The object can be a circle, polyline, line, or arc. After picking the object, you can specify a segment length. The object will be divided into segments of the given length, starting at the point closest to the point you picked. All segments will be of the specified length, unless the object length is not an even multiple of the segment length. A point entity will be placed at each division point. You can use object snap (NODE or NOD mode) to snap to such points when working with the measured object.

You can choose the "Block" option instead of supplying a segment length. If you do so, you will be prompted for a block name to insert. The block will then be inserted at the measured segment points and you can choose to align the blocks with the object. If the block was a line segment, for example, and the object was a circle, the lines would be made tangent to the circle at the insertion points. If not aligned, each line would point in the same direction.

MENU

Command: **menu**
Menu file name or . for none <default>:

If you have prepared a special menu file as described in Chapter 10, "Working with Menus," you can load it and make it visible by using the MENU command. Do not include the ".mnu" extension when you name the menu file. You can use the dot (.) response to simply reload the default menu. The command loads screen, button, tablet, and pull-down menus, which may all be defined in a single menu file.

MINSERT

Command: **minsert**
Block name (or ?):
Insertion point:
X scale factor <1> / Corner / XYZ:
Y scale factor (default=X):
Rotation angle <0>:
Number of rows (---) <1>:
Number of columns (|||) <1>:
Unit cell or distance between rows (---):
Distance between columns (|||):

The MINSERT command is essentially the same as the INSERT command in that you use it to insert blocks or drawings into your current drawing. The difference is that you can create an array of multiple insertions with this one command rather than repeat the INSERT command at different grid locations.

Like the ARRAY command, the MINSERT command enables you to specify a number of rows and columns to fashion the array. If the array is larger than 1 in either direction, you will be prompted for either a unit cell (just as with the ARRAY command), or for a pair of distances.

Options:

name	insert a block or file by this name
block=name	use a file under "name" and create "block"

?	names of existing blocks to be listed
C	(X scale prompt reply) specifies scale using two Corner points
XYZ	(X scale prompt replay) predefines X, Y, and Z scales

MIRROR

Command: **mirror**
Select objects:
First point of mirror line:
Second point:
Delete old objects? <N>

If you wish to create a mirror image of an object, you can use the MIRROR command. The command works the same way a mirror would if you placed the mirror edgewise against a sheet of paper. The mirror line is the line where the mirror contacts the paper. You first select the objects you wish to mirror, then you pick the beginning and ending points of the mirror line. After you pick the mirror line, you may optionally delete the objects that were mirrored, leaving only the mirrored version of those objects. You can use SETVAR to set the MIRRTEXT system variable to zero, in which case text will not be mirrored. Text and attribute entities will read normally and will not be inverted.

MOVE

Command: **move**
Select objects:
Base point of displacement:
Second point of displacement:

Moving objects from one location to another is a very straightforward operation. You use the MOVE command to select the objects to move, selecting a base point for the start of the move and a second point for the destination. You can optionally drag the objects to their new locations, in which case the objects will be repeatedly drawn as you change the displacement.

MSLIDE

Command: **mslide**
Slide file <default>:

Slide files are special files that contain images in a different format from the drawing file. This format permits slide files to be displayed much more efficiently, but the files cannot be edited like drawings. You use slide files to make images visible quickly, as in a slide show. All you need to do to make the current viewport into a slide file is enter the MSLIDE command and designate a file name to store the slide. Although the extension ".sld" will be appended to the file name, do not supply the extension in response to the "Slide file" prompt.

A program called SLIDELIB is available as an AutoCAD utility. It can be used to combine slide files together into slide libraries. You can use a straight ASCII text editor (such as the one supplied on the companion disk for this book) to prepare a file that contains a list of names. The names must refer to existing slide files. You redirect the output from the file as input to the SLIDELIB program as follows:

```
C>slidelib mylib < myfiles
```

In this case, the file "myfiles" contains the list of names of slide files that are to be combined together into a library file called "mylib."

MULTIPLE

Command: **multiple** <command>

You can supply any AutoCAD command as the "<command>" that follows the MULTIPLE command as in the preceding prompt. The command you supply will be repeated until you execute a cancel (CTRL-C). You must repeat the responses to prompts for each repetition of the specified command. The MULTIPLE command saves you one press of the ENTER key for each repetition of the designated command.

OFFSET

Command: **offset**
Offset distance or Through <recent>:
Select object to offset:
Side to offset:

Command: **offset**
Offset distance or Through <recent>: **t**
Select object to offset:
Through point:

The OFFSET command enables you to create lines or curves parallel to existing lines or curves. You can either enter an offset distance or specify a point through which the offset is to pass. Note that you can only specify one object for each use of the command. If you choose to specify an offset, you will be prompted to indicate the side of the object on which the offset object is to be drawn. If you elect the "Through" option, you will be prompted for a point through which the offset will be drawn.

Options:

number	offset distance

T	prompts for specification of a point Through which the offset object is to be drawn

OOPS

Command: **oops**

If you accidentally use the ERASE command, you can get your erased entities back with the OOPS command. However, you can only restore the entities that were erased with the last execution of the ERASE command. OOPS also works for the BLOCK and WBLOCK commmands.

ORTHO

Command: **ortho**
ON/OFF:

The ORTHO command can be used to set the ORTHOMODE system variable on or off. If on, ortho mode will force all lines drawn with rubber banding to be confined to the horizontal and vertical directions of the current snap grid. You can use SETVAR or AutoLISP to set the ORTHOMODE system variable. You can use the F8 key to toggle ortho mode.

Options:

ON	lines forced to be horizontal or vertical
OFF	lines not constrained

OSNAP

Command: **osnap**
Object snap modes:

Every object you can draw with AutoCAD has certain specific locations, such as a center, an endpoint, or a midpoint, that can be identified. Object snap occurs when you respond to a "To point" type of prompt by picking near an object. Object snap makes it possible to snap not only to the object, but to a specific part of the object, or to a point that has a specific spatial relationship to an object (such as perpendicular). Although you use the OSNAP command to specify the current default snap modes, you can override the current modes with the snap options explicitly by typing them in response to points that require picking. Snap options can be specified in any combination, separated by commas, in response to the SNAP command "Object snap modes:" prompt. If there are no snap modes specified (or the "NONE" snap mode is used), object snap will be disabled. You can enter a null response by pressing the ENTER key with nothing on the line. When object snap is enabled, you will see a target box at the crosshairs intersection. The first three letters of each option name are sufficient to activate the option. The object snap options follow.

Options:

CENT	snap to CENTer of arc or circle
ENDP	snap to closest ENDPoint of arc or line
INSERT	INSERTion point of text, block, or shape
INTER	INTERsection of line, arc, or circle
MIDP	MIDPoint of arc or line
NEAR	NEARest point of arc, circle, line, or point
NODE	NODE (same as a point)
NONE	NONE (turn object snap off)
PERP	PERPendicular to arc, line, or circle
QUAD	QUADrant point of arc or circle
QUICK	QUICK mode (use first find, not nearest)
TANG	TANGent of circle or arc
OFF	turn OFF a mode

PAN

Command: **'pan**
Displacement:
Second point:

If you wish to move your drawing so that different parts of it appear in the current viewport, you can use the PAN command. The PAN command allows you to specify a distance or displacement that the viewport will be moved, as though the drawing were on a large piece of paper with the viewport sliding over it. You can specify a coordinate pair for the displacement, and just press ENTER in response to the "Second point:" prompt. In this case, the displacement will move the viewport either to the right, left, up, or down by the amount you specify. A displacement of 3,2 will move the viewport 3 units to the right and 2 units up.

If you choose a second point, the amount the viewport is moved over the drawing will be the difference obtained by subtracting the distance in the X direction given by the displacement from the distance in the X direction given by the second point. The same applies for the Y direction. If you responded to the "Displacement" prompt with 6,4 and to the "Second point:" prompt with 2,3, the viewport would pan −4 units to the left and −1 unit down.

PEDIT (Two-dimensional Polylines)

Command: **pedit**
Select polyline:
Close/Join/Width/Edit vertex/Fit curve/Spline curve/Decurve/Undo/eXit <X>:

After you have created two-dimensional polylines, you may wish to change them. You can do so with the PEDIT command. Since polylines are single entities in AutoCAD, there must be a special command to change their complex properties. Using the PEDIT command, you can fit a curve to a polyline, close an open polyline, remove curves from a polyline, and do much more.

"Close"

```
Command: pedit
Select polyline:
Close/Join/Width/Edit vertex/Fit curve/Spline
curve/Decurve/Undo/eXit <X>: c
```

As you draw a polyline, you start at a point, draw segment after segment, and end at a point. If the starting and ending points do not coincide, you can connect them together with an additional segment by using the "Close" option of the PEDIT command.

Opening Polylines

```
Command: pedit
Select polyline:
Open/Join/Width/Edit vertex/Fit curve/Spline
curve/Decurve/Undo/eXit <X>: o
```

Just as you can close a polyline that has endpoints that do not connect, you can remove the last polyline segment. Note that in the case of open or closed polylines, the command options will differ. If a polyline you select is open, you will see the "Close" option. If the polyline is closed, you will see the "Open" option. The beginning and ending points of a polyline are determined by the order in which the polyline segments are drawn.

"Join"

```
Command: pedit
Select polyline.
Close/Join/Width/Edit vertex/Fit curve/Spline
curve/Decurve/Undo/eXit <X>: j
Select objects:
```

If a polyline shares an endpoint with lines, arcs, or other polylines, you can join them together into one polyline with the "Join" option of the PEDIT command. The endpoints must exactly coincide in order to be joined. AutoCAD also tells you how many segments were joined.

"Width"

Command: **pedit**
Select polyline:
Close/Join/Width/Edit vertex/Fit curve/Spline curve/Decurve/Undo/eXit <X>: **w**
Enter new width for all segments:

You can change the width of an entire polyline (which can have varying widths) to a constant width by using the "Width" option of the PEDIT command. You will be prompted as in the preceding example for the new width that will be applied to all segments in the polyline.

"Edit vertex"

Command: **pedit**
Select polyline:
Close/Join/Width/Edit vertex/Fit curve/Spline curve/Decurve/Undo/eXit <X>: **e**
Next/Previous/Break/Insert/Move/Regen/Straighten/
Tangent/Width/eXit
<N>:

Even though you constructed a polyline with specific vertices, you can change the locations of those vertices with the "Edit vertex" option of the PEDIT command. When you select the polyline to edit and choose the "Edit vertex" option, you will see an "X" at the start point of the polyline. As you edit, you will see the "X" move from vertex to vertex if you use the "Next" or "Previous" options. The "X" identifies the start of the vertex that will be edited. If a tangent direction exists for this vertex, you will also see an arrow that shows the tangent direction. After marking the starting point and optional tangent direction, AutoCAD will display the "Edit vertex" option prompt. You can choose any of the editing options, which are described in the next sections.

"Fit Curve"

Command: **pedit**
Select polyline:
Close/Join/Width/Edit vertex/Fit curve/Spline curve/Decurve/Undo/eXit <X>: **f**

You can smooth a polyline using curves tangent to all segments with the "Fit curve" option of the PEDIT command. This method of smoothing uses arcs and forces tangency to the polyline segments. If enough segments do not exist, more are added to achieve tangency. You can remove the curve if you use the DECURVE command.

"Spline Curve"

Command: **pedit**
Select polyline:
Close/Join/Width/Edit vertex/Fit curve/Spline curve/Decurve/Undo/eXit <X>: s

While the "Fit curve" option uses arcs, the "Spline curve" option uses the B-spline method to generate quadratic or cubic curves. Althought an arc must achieve tangency at all points on the polyline, the spline curve uses special rules to "approach" the endpoints of polyline segments.

Think of the curve as being drawn by a pen that is free to wander. At specific intervals an evaluation is made of the pen's position with respect to the nearest node (segment endpoint).

Although terms like "quadratic" and "cubic" may seem intimidating, they refer to concepts that can be described simply. These terms refer to the rules that govern the movement of the pen as it approaches and moves away from nodes.

In the case of the quadratic form, the relationship of all points on the curve is based on each successive pair of adjacent points. The last point, the current point, and the next point are evaluated together as input to a quadratic equation. The equation determines the locations of points on the curve. The term "quadratic" refers to the requirement that three points be used. In the "cubic" form, four points are used to determine the curve. The end result is that quadratic curves are less smooth than cubic curves. The approximation used in the quadratic form, since it is based on only three points, results in less smoothness than the cubic form's approximation, which is based on four points. If you would like to know more about the generation of B-spline curves, you could read *Fundamentals of Interactive Computer Graphics*, by J.D. Foley and A. Van Dam, Addison-Wesley Publishing Co., 1982.

You can set the SPLFRAME system variable to 1 to see both the original polyline "frame" and the spline curve at once. The SPLINETYPE system variable can be set to 5 for the generation of quadratic B-splines, or 6 for the generation of cubic B-splines. As mentioned earlier, the spline curves are generated by evaluating an equation at specified intervals. You can set the interval by changing the SPLINESEGS system variable. If you set the SPLINESEGS value to a high number (8 is the default), the interval used will be smaller, resulting in more evaluations and a smoother curve. A smaller number for SPLINESEGS will result in less evaluations and a coarser curve. Since each approximation adds a polyline segment, the drawing file size will be larger if you use a large value for SPLINESEGS. The time required to generate the splines will increase as well.

"Decurve"

Command: **pedit**
Select polyline:

```
Close/Join/Width/Edit vertex/Fit curve/Spline
curve/Decurve/Undo/eXit <X>: d
```

You can reverse the effect of curve fitting or splining with the "Decurve" option of the PEDIT command. If you use this option on a polyline that has been splined or curve fitted, you will see the original "frame" polyline as it was before the curve fitting or splining was done.

"Undo"

```
Command: pedit
Select polyline:
Close/Join/Width/Edit vertex/Fit curve/Spline
curve/Decurve/Undo/eXit <X>: u
```

You can use the "Undo" option of the PEDIT command to undo the last PEDIT operation you performed, stepping back through the entire editing session with each execution of "Undo." Undoing curves is not the same as removing all curves (as with the DECURVE command). Undoing just reverses the effect of the precious curve.

"eXit"

```
Command: pedit
Select polyline:
Close/Join/Width/Edit vertex/Fit curve/Spline
curve/Decurve/Undo/eXit <X>:
```

To exit from the PEDIT command, you use the "eXit" option. This option is the default, so you only need to press ENTER in response to the PEDIT options prompt.

PEDIT (Three-dimensional Polylines)

Command: **pedit**
Select polyline:
Close/Edit vertex/Spline curve/Decurve/Undo/eXit <X>:

The editing options presented by AutoCAD when you use the PEDIT command are governed by the type of polyline you select. If the polyline is two-dimensional, you will see the options shown earlier in the "PEDIT" section. If three-dimensional, the polyline will be treated differently.

Three-dimensional polylines are edited in much the same way as two-dimensional polylines. You can use the options described for two-dimensional polylines to edit three-dimensional polylines with the exception of the "Join" and "Width" options. You cannot join three-dimensional polylines nor can you change their width. Three-dimensional polylines have no width.

When you choose the "Edit" option for a three-dimensional polyline, the "Tangent" and "Width" options will not be available. The tangent to a three-dimensional polyline curve is hard to specify and is not included in the three-dimensional polyline specification. Width is not available for three-dimensional polylines. Instead of width the concepts of "3D mesh" and "surface" are used in three-dimensional work. Instead of the series of prompts for the "Edit" option you saw for two-dimensional editing, you will see the following set of options for editing a three-dimensional polyline:

Next/Previous/Break/Insert/Move/Regen/Straighten/eXit
<N>:

Like its two-dimensional counterpart, the three-dimensional polyline can be fitted with spline curves. The "Fit" option is not available, however, because arcs are not appropriate for three-dimensional curve fitting. The same options apply, except that a three-dimensional algorithm is used to generate quadratic and cubic B-spline curves. The SPLINESEGS, SPLFRAME, and SPLINETYPE system variables work in the same way as for two-dimensional splines.

Options for three-dimensional polylines:

C	Close an open polyline
D	Decurve polyline
E	Edit vertex (see suboptions in following list)
U	Undo
O	Open a closed polyline

Options during three-dimensional vertex editing:

B	specify first vertex for Break
G	Go (perform break or straighten operation)
I	new vertex to be Inserted after current one
M	current vertex to be Moved
N	Next vertex to be made current
P	Previous vertex to be made current
R	Regenerate the polyline
S	set first vertex for Straighten
X	eXit vertex editing, cancel break, or straighten

PEDIT (Three-dimensional Polygon Mesh Surfaces)

Command: **pedit**
Select polyline:
Edit vertex/Smooth surface/Desmooth/Mclose
/Nclose/Undo/eXit <X>:

You can create polygon mesh surfaces by using the 3DMESH, EDGESURF, REVSURF, RULESURF, and TABSURF commands. After you create such surfaces, you can edit them with the PEDIT command. If the entity you select in response to the

"Select polyline:" prompt is a three-dimensional polygon mesh surface, you will see the options that are appropriate for that type of object. The options are somewhat different than for two- and three-dimensional polylines.

Mesh entities are like polylines that are drawn in a grid form rather than as linear segments. The polyline segment is equivalent to the polygon mesh "cell." Each cell in the grid of a polygon mesh has vertices, just as each segment in a polyline has vertices. Each vertex in a mesh, however, has segments that connect to it in two directions, known as the "M" and "N" directions. When you edit a polygon mesh, you must not only specify the vertex, but the direction of the segment that extends from the vertex.

"Edit vertex"

Command: **pedit**
Edit vertex/Smooth surface/Desmooth/Mclose/Nclose/
Undo/eXit <X>: **e**
Vertex (m, n).
Next/Previous/Left/Right/Up/Down/Move/REgen/eXit
<N>:

You can edit a polygon mesh vertex by using the same methods available with the two-dimensional polyline. You can work with next and previous vertices. In addition, you can move from vertex to vertex in the left, right, up, or down directions. Left and right are also referred to as the "N" direction and up and down are referred to as the "M" direction. You can use the "Move" option to move a vertex. You can regenerate the polygon mesh with the "REgen" option.

"Smooth Surface"

Command: **pedit**
Edit vertex/Smooth surface/Desmooth/Mclose/Nclose/
Undo/eXit <X>: **s**

Polygon meshes behave like polylines when you choose to smooth them. The process is a three-dimensional version of the B-spline smoothing applied to surfaces rather than lines. Like the B-spline for polylines, the B-spline for surfaces has a quadratic and a cubic form. In addition, you can specify a Bezier surface, although you cannot fit a Bezier surface to more than 11 vertices in either the M or N directions. You can set the SURFTYPE system variable to 5 and obtain quadratic B-spline surfaces. If you set SURFTYPE to 6, you can obtain cubic B-spline surfaces. Finally, if you set SURFTYPE to 8, you will generate Bezier surfaces.

The SURFU and SURFV system variables can be used to set the mesh density in the M and N directions, respectively. The SPLFRAME system variable, if set to zero, will display surfaces that have been fitted to polygon meshes. If set to any non-zero value, the SPLFRAME system variable will cause only the polygon mesh to be displayed.

"Desmooth"

Command: **pedit**
Edit vertex/Smooth surface/Desmooth/Mclose/Nclose
/Undo/eXit <X>: **d**

If you have smoothed a surface, you can remove the smoothness with the "Desmooth" option of the PEDIT command. The "Desmooth" option behaves like the "Decurve" option.

"Mclose," "Nclose," "Mopen," and "Nopen"

Command: **pedit**
Edit vertex/Smooth surface/Desmooth/Mclose/Nclose
/Undo/eXit <X>: **m**

Command: **pedit**
Edit vertex/Smooth surface/Desmooth/Mopen/Nopen
/Undo/eXit <X>: **m**

As with the PEDIT command's use with polylines, you can open and close polygon mesh segments. If the polygon mesh is closed, you can open it with the "Mopen" or "Nopen" options, depending on the direction (either M or N) that is closed. If the polygon mesh is open, you can close it with the "Mclose" or "Nclose" options.

Options:

D	Desmooth, restoring original mesh
E	Edit mesh vertices
M	open or close the mesh in the M direction
N	open or close the mesh in the N direction
S	Smooth surface
U	Undo a PEDIT option
X	eXit PEDIT

Options during vertex editing:

D	move Down to the previous vertex in the M direction
L	move Left to the previous vertex in the N direction
M	Marked vertex repositioned
N	move to the Next vertex
P	move to the Previous vertex
R	move Right to the next vertex in the N direction
RE	REdisplay the polygon mesh
U	move Up to the next vertex in the M direction
X	eXit to the PEDIT command for the mesh

PLAN

```
Command: plan
<Current UCS>/UCS/World:
```

The PLAN command enables you to quickly switch to the plan view (the view down the Z axis) for the current UCS, a named UCS or the WCS (World Coordinate System). You can set the UCSFOLLOW system variable to 1 (on), in which case the plan view will always be shown, no matter which viewport you choose.

Options:

C	plan view of the current UCS
U	plan view of the specified UCS
W	plan view of the World Coordinate System

PLINE

```
Command: pline
From point:
Current line-width is www
Arc/Close/Halfwidth/Length/Undo/Width/<Endpoint
of line>:
```

Simple lines drawn with the LINE command have no width. To draw lines that have width and other special properties, you use the PLINE command. After you enter the PLINE command, you specify the starting point for the polyline and you then have several options.

"Arc"

If you decide to use the "Arc" option of the PLINE command, you will see several additional options. You will be able to specify an arc according to the options for arcs as follows:

Angle/CEnter/CLose/Direction/Halfwidth/Line/
Radius/Second
pt/Undo/Width/<Endpoint of arc>:

The "Angle" option allows you to use an included angle. You will see the "Included angle:" prompt. After you specify the included angle, you will be prompted for the "Center/ Radius/<Endpoint>:." As with the ARC command, you can specify the arc by the center, radius, or endpoint.

If you choose the CEnter option, you will be prompted for a "Center point:". Then you will be prompted "Angle/ Length/<Endpoint>:." to which you respond as required to specify the rest of the arc.

You can close the polyline arc if you choose the "CLose" option. Instead of a line segment, an arc will be used to close the polyline.

You can change the direction of the arc with the "Direction" option to override the default. If you do not choose to change the direction, the arc will be drawn tangent to the last segment or arc. If you choose the "Direction" option, you will see the "Direction from starting point:" prompt.

The "Halfwidth" option enables you to specify width using the center line rather than the entire width. You will be prompted for the "Starting half-width" and the "Ending half-width."

You can switch out of arc mode with the "Line" option. If you choose this option, you will then continue with the options appropriate for straight line segments.

If you choose the "Radius" option, you will be prompted for the "Radius:" and the "Angle/<Endpoint>:." You can choose an included angle or a specific endpoint for the arc.

The "Second point:" option will prompt you for the "Second point:" and the "Endpoint:" of the arc. The options here are similar to the options for the ARC command.

You can, of course, undo any of the arcs you have created in the exercise of the PLINE command with the "Undo" option.

You can also change the width of the arc by using the "width" option, in which case you will be prompted for the "Starting width:" and the "Ending width:".

"Close"

Command: **pline**
From point:
Current line-width is www
Arc/Close/Halfwidth/Length/Undo/Width/<Endpoint
of line>: **c**

You can close a polyline if you choose the "Close" option of the PLINE command. A straight line segment will be drawn between the ending point and the starting point.

"Halfwidth"

Command: **pline**
From point:
Current line-width is www
Arc/Close/Halfwidth/Length/Undo/Width/<Endpoint
of line>: **h**
Starting half-width <default>:
Ending half-width <default>:

The "Halfwidth" option of the PLINE command can be used to specify the width of a polyline by reference to the center line of the polyline. You indicate half of the width from the center line and that "half-width" is duplicated on the other side of the center line.

"Length"

Command: **pline**
From point:
Current line-width is www
Arc/Close/Halfwidth/Length/Undo/Width/<Endpoint
of line>: **l**

If you choose the "Length" option of the PLINE command, you will be able to extend the previous segment in the same direction by a length you specify. The line will be a tangent if the last part of the polyline was an arc.

"Undo"

Command: **pline**
From point:
Current line-width is www
Arc/Close/Halfwidth/Length/Undo/Width/<Endpoint
of line>: **u**

The "Undo" option of the PLINE command works like the UNDO command. It will undo back to the beginning of the PLINE command.

"Width"

Command: **pline**
From point:
Current line-width is www
Arc/Close/Halfwidth/Length/Undo/Width/<Endpoint
of line>: **w**
Starting width <default>:
Ending width <default>:

You can specify a polyline width which can be different at each end of the polyline arc or segment. If the width for the starting point differs from the width at the ending point, the polyline will be tapered from one end to the other. The default starting width is the same as the ending width of the last arc or segment.

Options:

H	set new Halfwidth
U	Undo previous segment or arc
W	set new polyline Width
ENTER	Exit PLINE command

In line mode:

A	change to Arc mode from line segment mode
C	Close using straight segment
L	segment Length (same direction as previous segment)

In arc mode:

A	included Angle
CE	CEnter point
CL	CLose using arc segment
D	starting Direction
L	chord Length (or switch to line mode from arc mode)
R	specify arc by Radius
S	three-point arc Second point

PLOT

Command: **plot**
What to plot—Display, Extents, Limits, View, or Window <D>:

The PLOT command enables you to plot your drawing with a pen plotter. You can plot the current display, the drawing extents, the drawing limits, the current view, or the contents of a window you specify. If you do not choose an option, you will plot the contents of the display.

```
Command: plot
What to plot — Display, Extents, Limits, View, or Window
<D>:
Plot will NOT be  written to a selected file
Sizes are in Inches
Plot origin is at (x.xx,y.yy)
Plotting area is a.aa  wide by b.bb high (MAX size)
Plot is NOT rotated 90 degrees
Pen width is a.aa
Area fill will NOT be adjusted for pen width
Hidden lines will be removed
Plot will be scaled to fit available area

Do you want to change anything? <N> y
Write plot to a file? <default>
Enter file name for plot <default>:
Size units (Inches or Millimeters) <default>:
Plot origin in inches <default>:

Standard values for plotting size
Size      Width      Height
A         10.50       8.00
B         16.00      10.00
MAX       17.00      11.00
USER      11.00       8.50

Enter the Size or Width,Height (in inches)  <default>:
Rotate 2D plots 90 degrees clockwise? <N>
Pen width <default>:
Adjust area fill boundaries for pen width? <N>
Remove hidden lines? <N>
Specify scale by  entering:
Plotted inches=Drawing units or Fit or ? <default>:
```

If you respond to the "Do you want to change anything?" prompt with a "Y" (for "Yes"), you will see the available plotting area sizes for your plotter. You can change the size if you wish. After you accept or change the plotting area size, you will be prompted to change the preceding plotting parameters. See

Chapter 8, "Working with Plotters," for more detailed information on responses that may be appropriate for these prompts.

```
Entity        Pen  Line Pen        Entity      Pen  Line Pen
Color         No.  Type Speed      Color       No.  Type Speed
1 (red)       1    0    38         9           1    0    38
2 (yellow)    2    0    38         10          1    0    38
3 (green)     3    0    38         11          1    0    38
4 (cyan)      4    0    38         12          1    0    38
5 (blue)      5    0    38         13          1    0    38
6 (magenta)   6    0    38         14          1    0    38
7 (white)     7    0    38         15          1    0    38
8             8    0    38

Line types  0 = continuous line
            1 = ...............
            2 = . . . . . . . .
            3 = ---------------
            4 = - - - - - - - -

Do you want to change any of these parameters? <N> y
Enter values. blank=Next value, Cn=Color n, S=Show current
values, X=Exit

Entity     Pen  Line Pen
Color      No.  Type Speed
1 (red)    1     0    38
```

When you choose a plot option, you will see the default specifications that were entered when you configured your plotter. You can change any of them. You can also change entity color, pen number, line type, and pen speed if applicable to your plotter. You will see options as shown in the preceding example. See Chapter 8, "Working with Plotters," for a full explanation of the options available to you.

POINT

Command: **point**
Point:

To draw a single point using the current color on the current layer, you can enter the POINT command. Just move the crosshairs to the location for the point in response to the "Point:"

prompt and press the pick button. Alternatively, you can enter a pair of coordinate numbers separated by a comma.

You can use the system variables PDSIZE and PDMODE to change the points you draw. The PDSIZE system variable can contain a positive or negative real number. If positive and not 0 or 1, the number will set the absolute size for all points. If negative, the number represents a percentage of the overall size of the screen. Such points will always appear to be the same size no matter how you zoom to change the apparent size of the drawing.

If you set the PDMODE system variable to 0, you will see a single dot for each point. This is the default condition. If you use a 1 for PDMODE, no points will appear, although their locations will still be recorded in the database. If 2, the points you draw will appear as crosses. If 3, points will appear as X marks. Finally, if 4, the PDMODE variable will cause points to be expressed as small vertical lines extending upward from the point location. You can cause a figure to surround a point if you use the numbers 32, 64, or 96 for the PDMODE variable. If 32, a circle will be drawn around each point. If 64, a square will be drawn around each point. If 96, a circle *and* a square will be drawn around each point. Remember, if you use a lot of marks other than points and combine them into a block, the results can be surprising. Be sure to remove such marks before creating blocks that include them.

POLYGON

Command: **polygon**
Number of sides:
Edge/<Center of polygon>:
Inscribed in circle/Circumscribed about circle (I/C): **c**

Command: **polygon**
Number of sides:
Edge/<Center of polygon>: **e**
First endpoint of edge:
Second endpoint of edge:

You can draw polygons in two fundamentally different ways with the POLYGON command. You can specify the center of a circle that will be taken as the center of the polygon. To do this, you must specify, in addition to the number of sides, whether you wish to circumscribe or inscribe the polygon. If you circumscribe the polygon, it will be drawn outside an imaginary circle and touching it at the center points of all sides. If you choose to inscribe the polygon, it will be drawn with all vertices on the circle, and inside the imaginary circle. You must specify the circle's radius, after which the polygon will be drawn.

If you choose to draw the polygon based on the specification of a single edge, you will be prompted for the endpoints of the edge. You can select any two points (as long as they do not coincide) and the polygon will be constructed with the two endpoints as the endpoints of one of its sides. It will be drawn counterclockwise, using the edge you specify as the starting segment. All the sides of the polygon will have the same length as the edge you specified.

Options:

E	polygon specified using one Edge
C	polygon specified using Center

Suboptions for Center method:

C	polygon Circumscribed around circle
I	polygon Inscribed within circle

PRPLOT

Command: **prplot**
What to plot – Display, Extents, Limits, View, or Window <D>:

If you have a printer plotter and have configured AutoCAD to use it, you may use the PRPLOT command to plot your drawing on it. The PRPLOT is almost the same as the PLOT command.

Refer to the PLOT command in this chapter or read Chapter 8, "Working with Plotters" for more information on printer plotting and plotting in general.

PURGE

Command: **purge**
Purge unused Blocks/LAyers/LTypes/SHapes/STyles/All:

As you work on a drawing, you will often create blocks, load shapes, create layers, and other object types and properties but you may not use all of them in your drawing. Even if they have not been used, these objects, layers, and properties take up space in your drawing database. You can get rid of them by using the PURGE command. The command is very straightforward. Just select one of the options presented and you will see a list of the unused objects, prompting you to decide whether or not to remove each one. The command works at any time during the editing session. Certain objects cannot be purged, for example, layer 0, the CONTINUOUS line type, and the standard text style.

Options:

A	purge All unused objects by name
B	purge unused Blocks
LA	purge unused LAyers
LT	purge unused LTypes
SH	purge unused SHape files
ST	purge unused text STyles

QTEXT

Command: **qtext**
ON/OFF <default>:

When you regenerate or plot drawings containting a lot of text entities, you may find that the process is unacceptably slow. Especially if you do not need to see text but are working on graphics alone, you may wish to use the QTEXT command to enable Quick Text. If the QTEXTMODE system variable (set by the QTEXT command, SETVAR, or AutoLISP) is on, all text in your drawing will be shown as rectangular outline boxes only. The locations and sizes of text strings will be shown by the locations and sizes of the outlined areas, thus the process of drawing each character can be avoided.

Options:

ON	set quick text mode ON
OFF	set quick text mode OFF

QUIT

Command: **quit**
Really want to discard all changes to drawing?

If you wish to quit drawing and return to the AutoCAD Main Menu, you can execute the QUIT command. All changes you may have made will be discarded. You will be prompted to make sure you wish to discard the changes you have made before returning to the main menu.

REDEFINE

Command: **redefine**
Command name:

If you have used the UNDEFINE command to make any built-in AutoCAD command invisible, you can use the REDEFINE command to make it visible again. You may wish to undefine built-in commands to create your own commands that have the same names as AutoCAD's built-in commands. See Chapter 15, "AutoLISP Function Reference," for more information on creating your own commands with AutoLISP. The built-in commands are those listed in this chapter, no more, no less.

REDO

Command: **redo**

You may have used the UNDO command (or U) to eliminate the effects of a command you may have entered by mistake. You can use the REDO command to redo the last undo as long as you do not enter any other commands before you enter REDO. The effect will be to allow you to experiment by undoing several times, then redoing the whole set of undos. Just be sure you do not undo a few commands, enter a command other than REDO, and then try to use the REDO command. This will not work, and you will have lost the commands that were undone.

REDRAW

Command: **'redraw**

You can refresh the current viewport if you use the REDRAW command. As you draw, you will find that certain commands place markers on the screen and also leave fragments of lines on the screen for various reasons. You can get rid of such extraneous fragments and see the current status of your drawing in the current viewport quickly if you use REDRAW. The REDRAW command does not thoroughly regenerate your drawing. See also the REGEN command.

REDRAWALL

Command: **'redrawall**

To clean up all viewports, you can use the REDRAWALL command. Unlike the REDRAW command, which only redraws the current viewport, the REDRAWALL command will redraw all viewports you have defined.

REGEN

Command: **regen**

Occasionally you may wish to regenerate the entire drawing and redraw the viewport. You may need to do this to make sure all of the drawing has been made current after changing system variables, for example. The process takes considerably longer than the REDRAW command, and you should not need to use it very often.

REGENALL

Command: **regenall**

Like the REGEN command, the REGENALL command regenerates and updates the drawing, redrawing to show the current drawing in complete agreement with the drawing database and all system variables. While the REGEN command regenerates only the current viewport, however, the REGENALL command regenerates all viewports.

REGENAUTO

Command: **regenauto**
ON/OFF <default>:

The REGENAUTO command sets the REGENMODE system variable to be on or off. If on, each time AutoCAD attempts to regenerate the drawing, you will see a prompt as follows:

About to regen, proceed? <Y>

If you answer "Y," the drawing will be regenerated, but you can avoid the regeneration process by answering "N." If the REGENMODE system variable is off, you will not be prompted when regeneration takes place for commands that automatically regenerate the drawing.

Options:

ON automatic regeneration ON
OFF automatic regeneration OFF

RENAME

Command: **rename**
Block/LAyer/LType/Style/Ucs/VIew/VPort:
Old (object) name:
New (object) name:

To change the name of a named object such as a block, layer, line type, or style, you can use the RENAME command. Just choose the object type from the options available and you will be prompted for the name of the object to change. After you enter a name, you will be prompted for the new name. You can use up to 31 characters in a name. The name may contain letters of the alphabet, digits, the dollar sign ($), the hyphen (-), and the underscore character (_). You may enter the name in lowercase, but AutoCAD will convert all object names to uppercase. The CONTINUOUS line type and layer 0 cannot be renamed.

Options:

B	Block to be renamed
LA	LAyer to be renamed
LT	LineType to be renamed
S	text Style to be renamed
U	Ucs to be renamed
VI	VIew to be renamed
VP	ViewPort to be renamed

RESUME

Command: **'resume**

If you are using a script of AutoCAD commands, you can interrupt it by canceling it or by pressing the BACKSPACE key. The command script will also be interrupted if an error is encountered while the command script is running. You can resume the running of the script from the place it was interrupted by using the RESUME command. If the script was stopped in the middle of a command, the transparent form (with a leading apostrophe) can be used at a command prompt.

REVSURF

Command: **revsurf**
Select path curve:
Select axis of revolution:
Start angle <0>:
Included angle (+ = ccw, − = cw) <Full circle>:

A surface of revolution is the three-dimensional surface created by revolving a curve around an axis. The curve defines the surface by sweeping through a given angle.

You can approximate a surface of revolution using AutoCAD. If you create a two- or three-dimensional polyline, line, arc, or circle, you can use it as the generating curve for a surface of revolution. You can select such an entity as the path curve in response to the first prompt of the REVSURF command. You then draw a two- or three-dimensional line or open polyline as the axis of revolution. You can then select the axis of revolution.

Surfaces are drawn as polygon meshes. Polygon meshes always have an M direction and an N direction. The path curve is always the N direction of the mesh that constitutes the surface of revolution. The M direction of the mesh is determined by the direction of the axis of revolution.

You can start the surface at a specific angle that can be measured counterclockwise (ccw) or clockwise (cw) around the axis of revolution. If the angle is positive, the surface will be generated in the counterclockwise direction. If the angle is negative, the mesh will be generated in the clockwise direction.

You can use the SURFTAB1 and SURFTAB2 system variables to control the mesh density. The SURFTAB1 variable determines how many mesh intervals will exist in the direction of rotation of the generating curve. The SURFTAB2 variable, which only applies to circles and arcs, determines how many mesh segments will be applied to circles or arcs along the generating curve. The two variables, acting together, will determine the number of mesh faces that subdivide the surface. A large number for either variable will result in many small mesh cells, a larger drawing database, and more time for processing.

ROTATE

Command: **rotate**
Select objects:

Base point:
<Rotation angle>/Reference

You can rotate objects around a given base point with the ROTATE command. You first select the objects you wish to rotate and you then pick a base point that will be used as the center of rotation. You can then enter a rotation angle or choose the "Reference" option. If you enter an angle, the objects you selected will be rotated by that angle from their starting locations. If you choose the "Reference" option, you will first be prompted for a reference angle which may be an angle that exists in the drawing. You can pick the reference angle by pointing to the two endpoints of a line. If you have chosen the "Reference" option and have indicated a reference angle, you can then instruct AutoCAD to make that reference angle into a "New angle:". A reference angle is useful because it means you can change an existing angle rather than estimate how much to rotate objects from their current positions.

Option:

R change a Reference angle to a new angle

RSCRIPT

Command: **rscript**

To continuously rerun a given script, you can use the RSCRIPT command. The last command in the script file must be QUIT Y or END. You can run script files in two ways. You can use a DOS command line like this:

C>acad x myscript

ACAD is the name of the AutoCAD program. The letter "X" means "play the following script." The "myscript" will be displayed. Such a script as this would run continuously as long as it was terminated by a QUIT Y or an END command. If you wanted to start such a script with the SCRIPT command from within AutoCAD, however, you could quickly rerun it by entering the RSCRIPT command. If the script itself had as its last line the RSCRIPT command, it would run continuously once it was run with the SCRIPT command.

RULESURF

Command: **rulesurf**
Select first defining curve:
Select second defining curve:

If you have two objects which are two- or three-dimensional polylines, arcs, circles, points, or lines, you can generate a ruled surface between them. The ruled surface is approximated by a polygon mesh.

The vertices of the mesh are placed at equal intervals along each generating curve. The SURFTAB1 system variable determines the number of vertices that will be used. The REVSURF command is similar to the RULESURF command, but instead produces a surface of revolution.

SAVE

Command: **save**
File name <default>:

As you are working on a drawing, you may wish to save your work from time to time. So many things can happen during a drawing session. The power could fail. The cat could stick its paws in your floppy drive. The SAVE command will update the drawing file corresponding to the current drawing, or will write the contents of the current drawing to a file on the hard drive, a floppy disk, or a new file name you designate.

SCALE

Command: **scale**
Select objects:
Base point:
<Scale factor>/Reference:

The SCALE command allows you to change the size of selected objects. When you change the size of an object, it will be enlarged or reduced relative to a central base point. You select the desired objects, pick the base point, and enter a scale factor or select the "Reference" option to complete the scaling operation.

If you choose a scale factor, the distances between the base point and each point on the object(s) will be multiplied by the factor you specify. If you choose the "Reference" option, you will be able to specify the length of an existing object and the new length. This method gives you a "frame of reference" by enabling you to explicitly change an existing object's size to a new size.

Option:

R   change scale from Reference size to a new size

SCRIPT

Command: **script**
Script file <default>:

If you create a file with the extension ".scr" which contains a list of commands and responses to prompts (just as you would enter them from the keyboard), you can run this "script" file with the SCRIPT command. The commands in the file will then be run just as though they are being entered from your keyboard. You should also look at the DELAY, RESUME, and RSCRIPT commands in connection with the SCRIPT command.

SELECT

Command: **select**
Select objects:

Many AutoCAD commands require you to select objects. You can select objects before you execute such commands if you use the SELECT command. When you use a command that gives you a "Select objects:" prompt, you can use the objects you selected with the SELECT command if you refer to "previously selected" objects. You do this by entering the letter "P" in response to a "Select objects:" prompt.

Entity Selection Options

Whenever you see a "Select objects:" prompt as the result of an AutoCAD command, you will also see a small target box appear at the crosshairs intersection. You have many options when this prompt appears. You can select a point, or you can use the "Crossing," "Multiple" objects, "Window," or "BOX" options. You can also use the "Last," "Previous," "AUtomatic," "Undo," "Add," or "SIngle" options. You terminate selection sets by using a null response (ENTER). You discard the selection set with the cancel response (CTRL-C).

When you use the selection options you will be able to set three prevailing modes, "Add," "Remove," and "SIngle." If "Add" mode is active you will add objects to the growing selection set. If "Remove" mode is active, you will remove objects from the selection set. Finally, the "SIngle" mode will make a successful selection terminate a "Select objects:" prompt. Unless "SIngle" mode is activated, you will see the "Select objects:" prompt repeatedly until you enter a null response or cancel the command.

Pointing

The simplest response to the "Select objects:" prompt is to pick a single point. A point on a desired object, if it falls within the target box, will be selected when you press the pick button. You can also enter coordinates numerically. Be sure to pick the lines that define the entity to be selected, not filled areas. With a filled polyline, for example, you would pick the object by placing the target box over one of the edges, not in the filled area.

"Multiple"

When you pick an object that overlaps another object, you will pick only the first object encountered in the database unless you use the "Multiple" selection option. When you see the "Select objects:" prompt, just enter the letter "M" and you will be prompted for each object encountered, with the options to "Select/Remove objects:." You can add objects to the selection set in this way and you can accumulate all overlapping objects rather than only the first one encountered.

"Window"

If you wish to select all objects that fall within a window area, you can use the "Window" option of the "Select objects:" prompt. You just enter the letter "W" and you will be prompted for the "First corner:," then the "Second corner:" of a window that encloses the desired objects. You will see a rubber-band box that will change size as you move the cursor. Only visible objects will be selected with this method.

"Crossing"

When you use the "Window" option, you must enclose all objects to be selected. If any part of an object falls outside the window, it will not be included in the selection set. If you wish to include such objects, use the "Crossing" option of the "Select objects:" prompt. In this case, all objects within the crossing window and all objects crossed by the window boundary will be selected. When you enter the letter "C" in response to the "Select objects:" prompt, you will be prompted for the "First corner:" and then the "Second corner:."

"BOX"

The "BOX" option combines the "Window" and "Crossing" options. You must enter the entire word "BOX" in response to the "Select objects:" prompt. After you enter "BOX," you will be prompted for the "First corner:" and the "Second corner:." If the first corner lies to the left of the second corner, the selection will be made using the rules for window selection; otherwise, the selection will be made using the rules of crossing selection.

"AUtomatic"

If you request the "AUtomatic" selection option of the "Select objects:" prompt, you will be able to use point selection by pointing at an object. If the object falls within the target box, it will be selected as the selection set. If, however, the target box lies entirely outside of any objects when the pick is made, the "BOX" selection mode will be activated and you will be able to select a second corner. As with the "BOX" selection option, you will be able to use the "Crossing" option method if the second corner lies to the left of the first corner. Otherwise, you will be able to use the "Window" option method.

"Last"

You can select the last object created (if it is visible) by using the "Last" option of the "Select objects:" prompt. You do this by entering the letter "L."

"Previous"

If you have built a selection set with the SELECT command, or you wish to reuse the last selection set (not the last object created), you can specify the "Previous" option at the "Select objects:" prompt. You do this by entering the letter "P" at the prompt. If the last command you used was an ERASE command, the previous selection set will be empty.

"Undo"

You can use the "Undo" option of the "Select objects:" prompt if you enter the letter "U" at the prompt. This option will undo the last object you may have entered into your selection set. It will not undo the command(s) that created the object and it will only remove the object from the selection set, not from the drawing.

"Add" and "Remove"

When you select objects in response to the "Select objects:" prompt, you will add them to the selection set if you use the "Add" mode. You can specify the "Add" mode of the "Select objects:" prompt by entering the letter "A" at the prompt. The "Add" mode is the default mode. You can change the mode to remove specified objects from the selection set by using the "Remove" option. To do this, you enter the letter "R" in response to the "Select objects:" prompt.

"SIngle"

If you use the "SIngle" option of the "Select objects:" prompt by entering the letters "SI" at the prompt, you will disable the normal command dialog and select the first object (or object set) that results from the next selection option. When the command is executed successfully, the command is finished and you will not be prompted for another object selection. If the command is not successful, you will be prompted for another object.

SETVAR

Command: '**setvar**
Variable name or ?:
New value for [variable name] <default>:

System variables are storage locations known to AutoCAD and made available to you by name. You can read the values of these variables and change most of them with the SETVAR command. When you enter the SETVAR command, you will be prompted for the variable name. You can enter an optional question mark (?) response to list the variable names available. After an existing variable name has been entered, you will be prompted for the new value, or, if the variable is read-only, you will see a message showing the value and informing you that the value cannot be changed with the SETVAR command.

System variables are mentioned throughout this book in the context of commands as they are described. In addition to references in association with commands shown in various chapters, a list of the system variables follows.

AutoCAD's System Variables

The AutoCAD system variables are used to store current information for use with many AutoCAD commands. Where a default value is shown for a given command, it is usually to be found in a system variable as well, and can usually be changed with the SETVAR command or through AutoLISP.

The following is a list of all current AutoCAD system variables. Depending on the release of your particular software, however, there may be more than those listed here, or some may have been removed or changed. You can use the SETVAR command with the "?" option to view the list of currently available system variables.

ACADPREFIX
Type: string

This read-only variable contains the directory name from the environment, set under the ACAD environment variable.

ACADVER
Type: string

This read-only variable contains the AutoCAD version number.

AFLAGS
Type: integer

This number contains the sum of the attribute flags for the ATTDEF command.

	0	1	2	3	4	5	6	7	8	9	10	11	12	13	14	15
1 Invisible	N	Y	N	Y	N	Y	N	Y	N	Y	N	Y	N	Y	N	Y
2 Constant	N	N	Y	Y	N	N	Y	Y	N	N	Y	Y	N	N	Y	Y
3 Verify	N	N	N	N	Y	Y	Y	Y	N	N	N	N	Y	Y	Y	Y
4 Preset	N	N	N	N	N	N	N	N	Y	Y	Y	Y	Y	Y	Y	Y

ANGBASE
Type: real

This variable contains the direction of angle 0 (relative to current UCS).

ANGDIR
Type: integer

The ANGDIR system variable stores the angle drawing direction relative to current UCS.

0	Means counterclockwise angles (or negative values)
1	Means clockwise angles (or positive values)

APERTURE
Type: integer

This is the object snap target height in pixels.

AREA
Type: real

The AREA, DBLIST, or LIST command produces this area.

ATTDIA
Type: integer

This variable determines whether a dialog box will be used for attribute entry.

0	Enter attributes by prompts
1	Enter attributes by dialog box

ATTMODE
Type: integer

The attribute display mode is controlled by this variable.

0	Off
1	Normal
2	On

ATTREQ
Type: integer

This variable determines whether or not attribute values will be requested when a block containing attributes is inserted in a drawing.

0	Default values of attributes will be used
1	User will be prompted for attribute values

AUNITS
Type: integer

Angular units mode is determined by this variable.

0	Decimal degrees
1	Degrees/minutes/seconds
2	Grads
3	Radians
4	Surveyors' units

AUPREC
Type: integer

This variable expresses the number of decimal places for angular units.

AXISMODE
Type: integer

The AXISMODE variable determines whether the axis ruler line is on or off. The axis mode is determined by the AXISMODE variable.

0	Off
1	On

AXISUNIT
Type: 2D point

This variable determines the axis spacing, different in the X and Y directions. It is therefore a coordinate value.

BACKZ
Type: real

If the "Back clipping" bit of VIEWMODE is on, this variable sets the back clipping plane offset, in drawing units, for the current viewport. Subtract BACKZ from the camera-to-target distance to get the distance of the back clipping plane to the camera.

BLIPMODE
Type: integer

This variable determines whether marker blips are on or off.

0	Marker blips are off
1	Marker blips are on

CDATE
Type: real

This read-only variable delivers the current date and time. The number contains the date as follows:

yyyymmdd.hhmmssxxx
yyyy is the year
mm is the month (01-12)
dd is the day (01-31)
hh is the hour (00-23)
mm is the minute (00-59)
ss is the second (00-59)
xxx is the number of milliseconds (000-999)

CECOLOR
Type: string

The CECOLOR variable contains the current entity color. The default value is BYLAYER. Color can be set by layer and by block.

CELTYPE
Type: string

The current entity line type is contained in the CELTYPE variable. The default value is BYLAYER. You can only alter the CELTYPE variable with the LINETYPE command.

CHAMFERA
Type: real

This is the first chamfer distance. See the CHAMFER command.

CHAMFERB
Type: real

This is the second chamfer distance. See the CHAMFER command.

CLAYER
Type: string

The current layer name is contained in this string variable.

CMDECHO
Type: integer

This variable is used to control whether AutoLISP will echo commands used with the "command" function.

0	Input and prompts will *not* be echoed
1	Input and prompts will be echoed

COORDS
Type: integer

The COORDS system variable determines when the coordinate display is updated:

0	Coordinate display will be updated only for point picks
1	Coordinate display will be continuously updated
2	Last point's angle and distance will be displayed on request of angle or distance

CVPORT
Type: integer

The current viewport's identification number will be returned.

DATE
Type: real

The DATE variable returns the current Julian date and time as a real number. The format is in [days].[fraction] so you can add and subtract times accurately.

DIMxxx
Type: (see DIM command)

There are a number of system variables that begin with the letters "DIM." These variables are shown under the DIM command because they relate to the dimensioning subcommands of AutoCAD.

DISTANCE
Type: real

This variable returns the distance computed by the last use of the DIST command.

DRAGMODE
Type: integer

The DRAGMODE system variable governs commands that enable dragging.

0	No drag
1	Drag by request
2	Automatic drag

DRAGP1
Type: integer

The DRAGP1 variable returns the regen-drag sampling rate. The sampling rate, in simple terms, is how often an object's image is redrawn as it is being dragged across the screen.

DRAGP2
Type: integer

The fast-drag input sampling rate is determined by the DRAGP2 variable. Like the DRAGP1 variable, the DRAGP2 variable controls how often an object's image is redrawn as it is dragged. The fast-drag, rather than the regen-drag, is affected.

DWGNAME
Type: string

The DWGNAME variable contains the name of the current drawing as entered by the user. The name includes any drive or subdirectory information if it was specified by the user. You can use "!s" on the command line to quickly view the drawing name. You can also use the SAVE command to do this.

DWGPREFIX
Type: string

The drive and directory prefix for the current drawing are contained in the DWGPREFIX system variable. The drawing prefix, like the drawing name, can be viewed with the SAVE command or the "!s" function.

ELEVATION
Type: real

The current elevation relative to the current UCS is contained in the ELEVATION variable.

EXPERT
Type: integer

You can control the appearance of "Are you sure?" prompts if you change the EXPERT system variable.

0	All prompts are to be normal
1	Suppress all "About to regen, proceed?" and "Really want to turn the current layer off?" prompts
2	Suppress "Block already defined. Redefine it?" and "A drawing with this name already exists. Overwrite it?" in addition to preceding
3	LINETYPE prompts for already loaded line type or creation of new line type in file where already defined, in addition to all preceding prompts
4	Suppress all "VPORTS Save" and "UCS Save" prompts if name supplied already exists, in addition to all preceding prompts

EXTMAX
Type: 3D point

This is the World Coordinate value of the upper right corner of the "drawing uses" extents. As new objects are added, this corner expands outward. You can shrink it with "ZOOM all" or "ZOOM Extents." See also EXTMIN.

EXTMIN
Type: 3D point

This is the World Coordinate value of the lower left corner of the "drawing uses" extents. See also EXTMAX.

FILLETRAD
Type: real

The FILLETRAD system variable contains the current fillet radius.

FILLMODE
Type: integer

The FILLMODE variable determines whether fills will be shown or not. You will not see the effects of FILLMODE until you regenerate the drawing. The FILLMODE variable controls whether fill mode is on or off.

0	Fill mode is off
1	Fill mode is on

FLATLAND
Type: integer

The FLATLAND variable is intended to help the user become familiar with Release 10. If it is set to 1, certain features of Release 10 behave as they did in earlier releases.

0	All of Release 10's new capabilities are implemented (default)
1	DXF, object snap, and AutoLISP work the same way as they did prior to Release 10

FRONTZ
Type: real

If the “Front clipping bit” of VIEWMODE is on and “Front clip not at eye” bit is on, the front clipping plane of the current viewport is set by this variable (in drawing units). You can subtract FRONTZ from the camera-to-target distance to get the distance of the front clipping plane from the camera.

GRIDMODE
Type: integer

The GRIDMODE system variable determines whether grids are on or off for the current viewport.

0	The grid is off
1	The grid is on

GRIDUNIT
Type: 2D point

The grid spacing in X and Y is determined by the GRIDUNIT system variable. The point coordinates contain the spacing values.

HANDLES
Type: integer

You can determine whether or not entity handles are enabled by reading the HANDLES system variable.

0	Entity handles are disabled
1	Entity handles are enabled

HIGHLIGHT
Type: integer

Selected objects will be highlighted, depending on the setting of this system variable.

0	Object selection highlighting will be off
1	Object selection highlighting will be on

INBASE
Type: 3D point

When you use the BASE command, this system variable is set to the current base insertion point. The point is in UCS units.

LASTANGLE
Type: real

The LASTANGLE system variable contains the end angle of the last arc you entered, relative to the XY plane of the current UCS.

LASTPOINT
Type: 3D point

The LASTPOINT system variable contains the coordinates of the last point you entered. You can use the @ character to refer to this point from the keyboard when responding to command prompts.

LASTPT3D
Type: 3D point

This variable is the same as LASTPOINT. You should use LASTPOINT instead of this variable since it will be dropped in future releases.

LENSLENGTH
Type: real

The length of the lens used to view in perspective is contained in this read-only variable. The value will be different for each viewport.

LIMCHECK
Type: integer

Limits checking is enabled or disabled by the LIMCHECK system variable.

0	Limits checking is to be disabled
1	Limits checking is to be enabled

LIMMAX
Type: 2D point

The coordinates of the upper right corner of the drawing limits are expressed relative to the World Coordinate System by the LIMMAX system variable.

LIMMIN
Type: 2D point

The coordinates of the lower left corner of the drawing limits are expressed relative to the World Coordinate System by the LIMMIN system variable.

LTSCALE
Type: real

The global line type scaling factor is contained in the LTSCALE system variable.

LUNITS
Type: integer

The linear units mode is contained in the LUNITS system variable.

1	Scientific
2	Decimal
3	Engineering
4	Architectural
5	Fractional

LUPREC
Type: integer

You can view or change the number of decimal places for linear units by using the LUPREC system variable.

MENUECHO
Type: integer

Menu echoing and prompting are controlled by the sum of the following numbers:

1	Echo of menu items is to be suppressed
2	Printing of system prompts is to be suppressed during menu use
3	Both command line echoing and printer echoing are suppressed. However, a CTRL-P still allows command line echoing
4	^P menu echo toggling is to be disabled

MENUNAME
Type: string

The MENUNAME system variable contains the name of the menu file that is currently loaded.

MIRRTEXT
Type: integer

The MIRROR command will either reflect text or not depending on the setting of the MIRRTEXT system variable.

0	Not to mirror text
1	Text is to be reflected

ORTHOMODE
Type: integer

You can control ortho mode with the ORTHO command or by setting this system variable:

0	Ortho mode is off
1	Ortho mode is on

OSMODE
Type: integer

You can control a wide range of object snap modes by adding the following numbers in various combinations:

1	Endpoint snap enabled
2	Midpoint snap enabled
4	Center snap enabled
8	Snap to Nodes enabled
16	Quadrant snap enabled
32	Intersection snap enabled
64	Insertion snap mode enabled
128	Snap to Perpendicular enabled
256	Snap to Tangent enabled
512	Snap to Nearest enabled
1024	Quick snap enabled

PDMODE
Type: integer

About 20 point descriptions are available in AutoCAD. You can change the point entity display mode with the PDMODE system variable.

0	A dot is to be drawn at the point
1	No point is to be drawn
2	A cross is to be drawn
3	An X is to be drawn at the point
4	A small line is to be drawn upward from the point

PDSIZE
Type: real

You can change the size of point entities by using the PDSIZE system variable.

32	A circle is to be drawn around each point
64	A square is to be drawn around each point
96	Both a square and a circle are to be drawn

PERIMETER
Type: real

The read-only system variable PERIMETER contains the perimeter computed by the LIST, DBLIST, or AREA command.

PICKBOX
Type: integer

The PICKBOX system variable contains the height of the object selection target box in pixels.

POPUPS
Type: integer

The capabilities of the current display are reported in the read-only POPUPS system variable.

0	Advanced User Interface feature not available
1	The current display driver supports dialog boxes, pull-down menus, the menu bar, and icon menus

QTEXTMODE
Type: integer

The QTEXTMODE system variable controls quicktext mode. See also the QTEXT command.

0	Quicktext mode is to be off
1	Quicktext mode is to be on

REGENMODE
Type: integer

Eight AutoCAD commands require REGEN to complete their processing or initiation. Automatic regeneration is controlled by the REGENMODE system variable.

0	REGENAUTO is off
1	REGENAUTO is on

SCREENSIZE
Type: 2D point

The size of the current viewport in pixels is reported by a coordinate pair in the SCREENSIZE system variable. This is a read-only variable.

SKETCHINC
Type: real

The sketch record increment is contained in the SKETCHINC system variable.

SKPOLY
Type: integer

The SKPOLY system variable determines whether the SKETCH command will draw lines or polylines.

0	Lines will be drawn
1	Polylines will be drawn

SNAPANG
Type: real

The snap grid rotation angle for the current UCS is determined by the SNAPANG system variable.

SNAPBASE
Type: 2D point

The origin of the current snap grid in the current viewport in UCS coordinates is determined by the SNAPBASE system variable.

SNAPISOPAIR
Type: integer

The current isometric plane is governed by the SNAPISOPAIR system variable.

0	Left plane
1	Top plane
2	Right plane

SNAPMODE
Type: integer

The current snap mode is contained in the SNAPMODE system variable.

0	Snap is off
1	Snap is on

SNAPSTYL
Type: integer

The snap style for the current viewport is contained in the SNAPSTYL system variable.

0	Standard
1	Isometric

SNAPUNIT
Type: 2D point

The snap spacing for the current viewport is contained in the SNAPUNIT system variable as the coordinates of a two-dimensional point. You can have different X and Y axis spacings.

SPLFRAME
Type: integer

The SPLFRAME system variable determines the behavior of the display of polygon frames and splines.

0	Polygons, polygon meshes, and invisible edges of 3D faces will not be displayed
1	Polygons, polygon meshes, and invisible edges of 3D faces will be displayed in addition to spline curves and surfaces based on these objects

SPLINESEGS
Type: integer

The SPLINESEGS system variable determines the number of line segments that will be generated for a given spline patch. If you use a negative value for SPLINESEGS, the absolute value is used for the number of segments. A curve is then fitted by using arcs rather than line segments. The resulting curve is smoother.

SPLINETYPE
Type: integer

The "PEDIT Spline" command option generates spline curves of two types. The type that will be generated by the next use of PEDIT will be contained in the SPLINETYPE system variable.

5	Quadratic B-spline will be generated
6	Cubic B-spline will be generated

SURFTAB1
Type: integer

The SURFTAB1 system variable determines the number of tabulations that will be generated for the TABSURF and RULESURF commands. The variable also determines the density of the mesh in the M direction produced by the EDGESURF and REVSURF commands.

SURFTAB2
Type: integer

The SURFTAB2 system variable determines the density of the mesh generated in the N direction by the EDGESURF and REVSURF commands.

SURFTYPE
Type: integer

The "PEDIT Smooth" command option produces surface fits with three methods. The method to be used is determined by the SURFTYPE command.

5	Generate quadratic B-spline surface
6	Generate cubic B-spline surface
7	Generate Bezier surface

SURFU
Type: integer

The SURFU system variable determines the surface density in the M direction.

SURFV
Type: integer

The SURFV system variable determines the surface density in the N direction.

TARGET
Type: 3D point

The target point of the current viewport is determined by the TARGET system variable. The target point is the point at which the viewer is looking, in UCS coordinates.

TDCREATE
Type: real

The time and date of the current drawing is shown by the TDCREATE read-only system variable. The form is the same as for the DATE system variable.

TDINDWG
Type: real

The TDINDWG system variable returns the amount of time you have spent in the current drawing session. The variable is read-only and is in the same form as the DATE system variable.

TDUPDATE
Type: real

The TDUPDATE system variable contains the date and time of the last database update in the same form as the DATE system variable.

TDUSRTIMER
Type: real

The TDUSRTIMER contains the current elapsed time based on a time that is set by the user.

TEMPPREFIX
Type: string

The TEMPPREFIX system variable contains the directory name to be used for temporary files. A path separator is appended as required.

TEXTEVAL
Type: integer

Text can be evaluated as an AutoLISP expression if desired. You can set the TEXTEVAL system variable so that text is treated literally or as an AutoLISP expression. To be treated as an expression by AutoLISP, the text string must begin with an exclamation point (!) or a left parenthesis character. If TEXTEVAL is 0, text responses to prompts will be taken literally. If 1, text responses will be evaluated as AutoLISP expressions if the first character is an exclamation point or a left parenthesis character.

TEXTSIZE
Type: real

The TEXTSIZE system variable contains the default height for text entities drawn in a style that permits variable height.

TEXTSTYLE
Type: string

The read-only system variable TEXTSTYLE contains the current text style.

THICKNESS
Type: real

The THICKNESS system variable contains the current three-dimensional thickness. Changing this variable will affect future thickness, but objects created using the previous thickness will not be changed.

TRACEWID
Type: real

The current trace width is contained in the TRACEWID system variable.

UCSFOLLOW
Type: integer

To see the plan view automatically each time you change the User Coordinate System, you can set the UCSFOLLOW system variable.

0	Changing UCS does not change the view
1	Changing UCS always automatically changes to plan view for the current viewport

UCSICON
Type: integer

The appearance and location of the User Coordinate System icon is controlled by the UCSICON system variable.

1	The icon display is enabled and the icon appears at the lower left corner of the screen
2	The icon is at the origin of the UCS whenever viewable on the screen, and otherwise at the lower left corner of the screen, *but* the icon is not visible
3	The icon is at the origin of the UCS and is visible

UCSNAME
Type: string

The name of the current User Coordinate System is contained in the UCSNAME read-only system variable.

UCSORG
Type: 3D point

The read-only UCSORG system variable contains the origin of the current User Coordinate System in World Coordinates.

UCSXDIR
Type: 3D point

The X direction of the current User Coordinate System is contained in the UCSXDIR read-only system variable.

UCSYDIR
Type: 3D point

The Y direction of the current User Coordinate System is contained in the UCSYDIR read-only system variable.

USERI1–5
Type: integer

If you are writing AutoLISP Software, you can use one of five integer variables that have been reserved. See more about this in Chapter 12, "Programs in AutoLISP."

USERR1–5
Type: real

If you are writing AutoLISP software, you can use one of five real variables that have been reserved. You can read more about this in Chapter 12, "Programs in AutoLISP."

VIEWCTR
Type: 3D point

The center point for the view in the current viewport, in UCS coordinates, is contained in the VIEWCTR read-only system variable.

VIEWDIR
Type: 3D point

An imaginary line drawn between the point contained in the VIEWDIR read-only system variable and the point contained in the TARGET variable, determines the viewing direction of the current viewport. The artificial camera is placed at the VIEW-DIR point and points at the TARGET point.

VIEWMODE
Type: integer

Viewing within a viewport is governed by five flags which may be on or off. The VIEWMODE system variable can be set to a number that is the sum of any of the five possible flags.

1	Perspective view is active
2	The front clipping plane is on
4	The back clipping plane is on
8	The UCS follow mode is on (see UCSFOLLOW variable)

16	The system variable FRONTZ determines the distance of the front clipping plane from the camera; otherwise, the front clipping plane passes through the VIEWDIR point

VIEWSIZE
Type: real

The VIEWSIZE read-only system variable contains the current viewport's view height.

VIEWTWIST
Type: real

The VIEWTWIST read-only system variable reports the twist angle of the view in the current viewport.

VPOINTX
Type: real

The VPOINTX read-only system variable contains the X component of the VIEWDIR point.

VPOINTY
Type: real

The VPOINTY read-only system variable contains the Y component of the VIEWDIR point.

VPOINTZ
Type: real

The VPOINTZ read-only system variable contains the Z component of the VIEWDIR point.

VSMAX
Type: 3D point

The VSMAX read-only system variable contains the UCS coordinates of the upper right corner of the virtual screen of the current viewport.

VSMIN
Type: 3D point

The VSMIN read-only system variable contains the UCS coordinates of the lower left corner of the virtual screen of the current viewport.

WORLDUCS
Type: integer

The WORLDUCS system variable determines whether or not the current User Coordinate System is the same as the World Coordinate System.

0	The UCS is *not* the same as the WCS
1	The UCS is the same as the WCS

WORLDVIEW
Type: integer

Ordinarily, the VPOINT and DVIEW commands expect input in the form of UCS coordinates. The WORLDVIEW system variable determines whether these commands will expect their input in terms of the current User Coordinate System or the World Coordinate System.

0	The input for the VPOINT and DVIEW commands will be expected in UCS units
1	The input for the VPOINT and DVIEW commands will be expected in WCS units

SH

Command: **sh**
DOS command:

If you use the SHELL command (described later in the chapter), you may find that your system does not have enough memory. In that case, you can use the SH command to run the DOS internal commands, but not external commands. See your DOS manual for a description of the difference between internal and external DOS commands.

SHAPE

Command: **shape**
Shape name (or ?) <default>:
Starting point:
Height <1.0>:
Rotation angle <0.0>:

To draw shapes that have been previously defined, you use the SHAPE command. When the shape is drawn, you have control over its location in your drawing by specifying a starting point. You can change the height of the shape as well as the shape's rotation angle. Shapes behave like blocks, but they are not nearly as easy to create. Shapes are even more similar to text characters. In fact, text is created with a special form of shape table.

Option:

? available shape names will be listed

SHELL

Command: **shell**
DOS command:

"Shell" is one of those words in computer jargon that often intimidates the uninitiated. If you think of a shell as a kind of enclosure, like a clam shell, you are on the right track. Think of a shell as a program that can be executed from within a program. In this sense, the program that is executed is like a shell that wraps around the program that executed it. This image is really inaccurate, however, because it is not what really happens.

In reality, the program that executes the "shell" program just stops running, saving its place until the shell program is finished. Then the program just starts up again from where it left off. Your operating system is capable of running programs from within programs until it runs out of memory. AutoCAD makes use of this characteristic of the operating system to enable you to run programs as though from your operating system's command line. It does this through the SHELL command.

If you use the SHELL command, be careful not to disrupt devices and files that AutoCAD may be using. For example, you should not change the serial port parameters if a digitizer or plotter is attached to a serial port. Likewise, you should not use CHKDSK with the "/F" option because this will attempt to fix your disk when AutoCAD is in the middle of working with open files. In general, do not use the SHELL command unless you know exactly what the DOS commands you intend to use will do to AutoCAD while it is running.

SKETCH

Command: **sketch**
Record increment <default>:

Sometimes you may wish to trace a drawing with a digitizer. It is much too tedious to construct free form drawings one straight line at a time. You can use the SKETCH command to activate a special free form drawing editor that draws a continuous flow of lines as long as the pen is down. The SKPOLY system variable controls whether lines or polylines will be used.

To set the resolution of the sketch, you modify the "Record increment" by responding to the prompt with a number. If the number is small, you will not need to move the pen much to generate a new line segment. Each time the pen moves beyond the increment distance, a new line is drawn.

As you are sketching, lines will appear in green until you record the lines or exit the command. You have a series of options that enable a limited amount of editing while you are sketching. You can use the period key to draw a straight line from the endpoint of the last line you sketched to the current pen position when the pen is up. You can use the E key to delete the last line segment. The C key can be used to continue with the sketch even if you have raised the pen. You can record the sketch in the drawing using the current drawing color if you press the R key. An X, space character, or ENTER will record the sketched lines and exit the command. A Q or CTRL-C will cancel the entire sketch.

Options:

C	Connect sketch at last point (button 6)
E	last sketched line will be Erased (button 5)
P	sketching Pen raised or lowered (pick button)
Q	sketched lines discarded, command exited (button 4)
R	sketched lines Recorded
X	sketched lines recorded, command eXited (button 3)

SNAP

Command: **snap**
Snap spacing or ON/OFF/Aspect/Rotate/Style <default>:

Snapping refers to the movement of the crosshairs when snap mode is enabled. You can define a snap grid with the SNAP command. This grid will determine where the crosshairs may be located when snap mode is on. When snap mode is off, the crosshairs will move smoothly under the control of your pointing device. Otherwise, the snap grid will determine where the crosshairs may be located and the crosshairs will appear to jump from grid point to grid point. The SNAP command options enable you to set snap spacing, turn snap mode on or off, set a snap grid aspect ratio, set grid rotation angle, and snap style. Six system variables relate to the SNAP command. You can use CTRL-B to turn snap mode on or off.

"Snap spacing"

Command: **snap**
Snap spacing or ON/OFF/Aspect/Rotate/Style <default>: **1**

You can quickly set the snap grid spacing by entering a number in response to the SNAP command prompt. The number you enter will be used as the grid interval for the new snap grid. The grid will have the same spacing in both the X and Y directions.

"ON," "OFF"

Command: **snap**
Snap spacing or ON/OFF/Aspect/Rotate/Style<default>: **ON**

You can enable or disable the snap grid by using the "ON" and "OFF" options of the SNAP command. When you turn the snap grid on, you will be able to snap to the grid intervals. Note that the whole words "ON" and "OFF" must be used or AutoCAD will prompt you for an unambiguous response.

"Aspect"

Command: **snap**
Snap spacing or ON/OFF/Aspect/Rotate/Style <default>: **a**
Horizontal spacing <1.0>:
Vertical spacing <0.5>:

The same snap grid may have different intervals in the X and Y directions. You can set the horizontal (X) and the vertical (Y) intervals to be different with the "Aspect" option of the SNAP command.

"Rotate"

Command: **snap**
Snap spacing or ON/OFF/Aspect/Rotate/Style <default>: **r**
Base point <0,0>:
Rotation angle <0>:

The snap grid can be rotated. The "+" direction is counterclockwise; the "−" direction is clockwise. If you choose the "Rotate" option of the SNAP command, you will be prompted for a base point and a rotation angle. When you respond with these, the new grid will be aligned with the base point and will be oriented to the rotation angle you specify. You can use object snap (see the OSNAP command) to pick the base point and rotation angle.

"Standard," "Isometric"

Command: **snap**
Snap spacing or ON/OFF/Aspect/Rotate/Style <default>: **s**
Standard/Isometric <default>: **i**
Vertical spacing <1.2>:

An isometric grid enables you to draft isometric drawings, which are based on a grid that contains angles that are multiples of 60 degrees. You can set the vertical distance between isometric grid points with the "Isometric" option of the SNAP command. You can return to a normal 90-degree grid by using the "Standard" option.

Options:

number	set snap grid spacing
ON	crosshairs will snap to grid intervals
OFF	crosshairs will move smoothly
A	Aspect ratio for different X and Y spacings
R	snap grid Rotated
S	select standard or isometric Style

SOLID

Command: **solid**
First point:
Second point:
Third point:
Fourth point:

If you need to draw solid-filled figures that are composed of quadrilateral (four-sided) and triangular (three-sided) polygons, you can use the SOLID command. You select up to four points for each figure, but if you enter a null response at the fourth point, you will generate a triangular solid. Points must be entered diagonally or in a triangular sequence. Entering two null responses in a row will terminate the command. If fill mode is off, the figures will be drawn without filling. If fill mode is on, the figures will be filled, even if they were drawn unfilled when fill mode was off. You must use the REGEN command to fill solid polygons after turning fill mode on. You can turn fill mode on or off with the FILL command.

STATUS

Command: **status**

The STATUS command reports the current status of the drawing, including information on the number of entities, the drawing limits, the drawing area, and the display area. The insertion base point, snap resolution, and grid spacing will be reported. You will also see the current layer, color, line type, and elevation. The on or off status of the axis, fill, grid, ortho, qtext, snap, and tablet will be reported. You will see a list of the current snap modes. Finally, for IBM PCs and compatibles, you will see the amount of free RAM, free disk space, I/O page space, and extended I/O page space.

STRETCH

Command: **stretch**
Select objects to stretch by window. . .
Select objects:
Base point:
New point:

You may want to stretch an object if you have drawn it and later need it to be longer or shorter. Lines, traces, arcs, polylines, and solids may all be stretched.

To stretch a group of entities, you select them by window. Any objects that are completely contained in the selection window will be left as they are, but moved by the new deflection amount. Any entities that are crossed by the window will be stretched so the endpoints that lie within the window are moved, but so the endpoints that lie outside the window remain where they were. Use the "Crossing" option to select objects to stretch.

STYLE

Command: **style**
Text style name (or ?) <default>:
Font file <default>:
Height <default>:
Width factor <default>:
Obliquing angle <default>:
Backwards? <Y/N>
Upside-down? <Y/N>
Vertical? <Y/N>
(style name) is now the current text style.

You can draw text with various fonts, and you can modify each font by using a style. The style changes the height, width, and obliquing angle of the font's characters. You can also determine whether the text will be drawn backwards, upside-down, or vertically (one character above the other). You can save styles and recall them for use by name. The STYLE command is discussed thoroughly in Chapter 7, "Text and Fonts."

Option:

? currently defined text styles listed

TABLET

Command: **tablet**
Option (ON/OFF/CAL/CFG):

The digitizer tablet can be used to trace drawings or as a menu device. The TABLET command enables you to align drawings on your tablet so that AutoCAD knows the dimensional frame of reference. You can then transfer accurate coordinates from the tablet into the drawing space. You can also set up the tablet for use with a tablet menu.

"CAL"

Command: **tablet**
Option (ON/OFF/CAL/CFG): **cal**
Calibrate tablet for use. . .
Digitize first known point:
Enter coordinates for first point:
Digitize second known point:
Enter coordinates for second point:

To trace drawings with a digitizing tablet accurately, you must calibrate the tablet with the TABLET command's "CAL" option. Calibration involves selecting X,Y coordinates on the drawing you wish to trace. For each point, you will be prompted for the coordinates AutoCAD is to use for that point. By comparing the information from the digitizer and the coordinates for each point, AutoCAD is able to map all points on the digitizer drawing surface to all coordinates for those points in AutoCAD's drawing space. After you select the two points and indicate what coordinates they represent, you will be able to trace your drawing accurately.

"CFG"

Command: **tablet**
Option (ON/OFF/CAL/CFG): **cfg**
Enter number of tablet menus desired (0-4) <default>:
Do you want to realign tablet menu areas? <N>
Digitize upper left corner of menu area (n):
Digitize lower left corner of menu area (n):
Digitize lower right corner of menu area (n):
Enter the number of columns for menu area (n):
Enter the number of rows for menu area (n):
Do you want to respecify the screen pointing area? <N>
Digitize lower left corner of screen pointing area:
Digitize upper right corner of screen pointing area:

You may use up to four menu areas on your digitizer tablet. For each menu area, you must have a corresponding ".mnx" file loaded to use the tablet menu for that menu number. In addition, you must respond to the preceding series of prompts for each menu area. You must indicate three points that identify the corners of each menu area "n," as well as the number of columns and rows in each menu area. After you configure all desired menus, you will be prompted to determine if you want to use a screen pointing area. Such an area enables you to use a designated part of the tablet to point in the graphics area. You can use the area to position the crosshairs and draw.

Options:

ON	turn calibrated mode ON
OFF	turn calibrated mode OFF
CAL	CALibrate tablet
CFG	ConFiGure tablet menus and pointing area

"ON," "OFF"

Command: **tablet**
Option (ON/OFF/CAL/CFG): **off**

Command: **tablet**
Option (ON/OFF/CAL/CFG): **on**

You can enable or disable calibrated mode if you use the TABLET command with the "ON" or "OFF" option. You must enter the entire words "ON" and "OFF" or AutoCAD will display a message explaining that you have entered an ambiguous response. When the tablet is on, you will be able to use it to move the crosshairs to trace drawings according to settings made under the "CAL" option. If you have used the "CAL" option, the tablet will be set to a mode wherein the tablet will be mapped to the AutoCAD drawing area. The tablet will be on. If you turn it off, you will be able to use the tablet to point normally, which will include selecting from the onscreen menu areas.

TABSURF

Command: **tabsurf**
Select path curve:
Select direction vector:

A tabulated surface is created by using a path curve and projecting the curve in the direction and to the distance represented by the direction vector. A soup can, for example, illustrates a cylindrical tabulated surface. The path curve of the soup can is a circle. The direction vector is at right angles to the plane of the circle, and extends to the depth of the soup can.

Tabulated surfaces in AutoCAD are created with polygon meshes. The mesh density is controlled by the SURFTAB1 system variable. SURFTAB1 determines how many tabulations will be used in the N direction (the direction along the path curve).

TEXT

Command: **text**
Start point or Align/Center/Fit/Middle/Right/Style:

You can enter text into your drawings with the TEXT command. With this command, you have several options. You can pick a start point, align the text between two points, center the text on a point, and fit text of a specified height between two points. You can center both horizontally and vertically (The "Middle" options), right justify text, and select a text style. Text is set by the STYLE command. Read Chapter 7, "Text and Fonts," to find out more about the use of text and fonts in your drawings. See also the DTEXT command for onscreen editing.

Options:

A	text will be Aligned between two points, a width factor being used to adjust the character height proportionally
C	text will be Centered horizontally
F	text will be Fit between two points, but the height will be maintained while the width is adjusted to fit
M	text will be centered horizontally and vertically, in the Middle
R	text will be Right justified
S	select text Style

TEXTSCR

Command: '**textscr**

If you are using a single screen system, you can use the F1 key to flip from graphics to text mode and back again. If you are using menus or command scripts, however, you can use the TEXTSCR command to accomplish the same thing.

3DFACE

Command: **3dface**
First point:
Second point:
Third point:
Fourth point:

A 3D face is similar to a solid created with the SOLID command. The difference is that a 3D face can be specified with three-dimensional points, rather than the two-dimensional points that pertain to a solid. The commands work in a similar fashion. You can specify up to four points per face. If you press ENTER at the prompt for the fourth point, the face will be triangular. If you press ENTER two times in a row in response to a prompt for the 3DFACE command, you will exit the command.

You can use objects created using 3D faces with AutoSHADE by using the FILMROLL command. A 3D face will be considered to be opaque by the HIDE command if the edges are on the same plane. You must enter 3D faces in a consistently counterclockwise or clockwise way. You can make an edge of a 3D face invisible by entering the letter "I," then the first point of the edge you wish to be invisible. Unlike with the SOLID command, 3D faces are not filled.

3DLINE

Command: **3dline**
From point:
To point:

The normal AutoCAD LINE command draws lines in 2D as well as in 3D. You can also use the 2DLINE command to do the same thing. The 3DLINE command will probably be removed from future releases. It remains only to provide compatibility with earlier versions of the software.

3DMESH

Command: **3dmesh**
Mesh M size:

Mesh N size:
Vertex(m,n):

Polygon meshes are composed of vertices that are connected by lines. You can specify a polygon mesh quite easily with the 3DMESH command. You specify the number of vertices in the M and N directions of the mesh and then specify the coordinates of each vertex, one by one.

3DPOLY

Command: **3dpoly**
From point:
Close/Undo/<Endpoint of line>:

The two-dimensional polyline created with the PLINE command has a three-dimensional counterpart through the use of the 3DPOLY command. With the 3DPOLY command, you can create polylines that have their segments oriented in space, rather than being confined to the X-Y plane. You can close three-dimensional polylines in much the same way as you can close two-dimensional polylines. You can undo previous segments. As with the two-dimensional polyline, you can continue to specify three-dimensional endpoints until you enter a null response to exit the command.

Options:

C	polyline Closed to the first point
U	the last segment entered is Undone
ENTER	3DPOLY command is Exited

TIME

Command: **time**
(current time information displayed)
Display/ON/OFF/Reset:

The TIME command will display the current time, the time the drawing was created, the time the last drawing update took place, the time in the current drawing editor session, and the elapsed time for a user timer. You will also see a message that indicates whether or not the timer is on. After the TIME command displays the time information, you will see a prompt that enables you to select one of four options. If you select the "Display" option, you will see the same time information displayed at the start of the TIME command. You can reset the timer, turn the timer on, and turn the timer off. If you enter the null response to the "Display/ON/OFF/Reset:" prompt, you will exit the TIME command.

Options:

D	current times Displayed
ON	elapsed timer ON
OFF	elapsed timer OFF
R	elapsed timer Reset

TRACE

Command: **trace**
Trace width <default>:
From point:
To point:

Lines drawn with the LINE command have no width. Lines and arcs drawn with the PLINE command can have a width that is different at each end, resulting in a "tapered" effect. The TRACE command enables you to draw lines that have a constant width. Drawing each segment or line is delayed until either the next segment is specified or you press ENTER to end the trace. You are first prompted for the desired width, then for the first point, and a series of points in a way that is identical to that used with the LINE command. When you have drawn your last line, you enter a null response to the "To point:" prompt to exit the TRACE command. The system variable TRACEWID contains the current default trace width.

TRIM

Command: **trim**
Select cutting edge(s). . .
Select objects:
Select object to trim:

Trimming erases the parts of entities that extend beyond cutting edges. You first select the cutting edges in response to the usual "Select objects:" prompt, and then you select the object you wish to trim. After selection, the part of the object that you pointed to will be erased up to the cutting edge or edges.

U

Command: **u**

You can undo the previous command by entering the U command. The U command will only undo one command. If you wish to undo more than one command at once or undo everything, you should use the UNDO command. Also, the U command does not work with all commands.

UCS

Command: **ucs**
Origin/ZAxis/3point/Entity/View/X/Y/Z/Prev/
Restore/Save/Del/?/<World>:

AutoCAD uses three basic coordinate systems to help the user establish a frame of reference for drawing; the World Coordinate System (WCS), the User Coordinate System (UCS), and the Entity Coordinate System (ECS). To use the features of AutoCAD after Release 10, you should understand the fundamental concept of the coordinate system. You can read about the practical use of coordinate systems in Chapter 2, "Drawing," Chapter 3, "Editing," and Chapter 4, "Working with Blocks."

A three-dimensional coordinate system consists of three direction *vectors* that are at right angles to each other. A vector is nothing more than a direction and a distance. For example, if you hold a ruler out in front of you, it establishes a vector in whatever direction you point it. The ruler has a direction and a scale of distances.

To understand how AutoCAD uses coordinate systems, you should visualize a system of three vectors. These vectors are each given names. The first two vectors are called "X" and "Y." When you start AutoCAD for a new drawing, the X vector is at the left edge of the drawing area and the Y vector is at the bottom edge of the drawing area. These vectors are also called axes. The X vector is the X axis and the Y vector is the Y axis. In addition to these two vectors, a third, the Z axis, is at the lower left corner of the drawing area and points out toward you at right angles to the drawing area surface. The three axes define a coordinate system.

When you start AutoCAD to make a new drawing, the World Coordinate System and the User Coordinate System are the same. They have the same origin or meeting place. The origin is at the lower left corner of the drawing area, with the coordinates of 0,0,0. The origin is the place where X, Y, and Z are all zero.

The World Coordinate System always stays the same. Although you may change your viewport to show the origin in a different location, the origin of the World Coordinate System will never change. It is an absolute frame of reference within which you can define User Coordinate Systems that have different origins and orientations.

When you want to define a new User Coordinate System, you must use the UCS command. The coordinate system you define may have a different origin and orientation from that of the World Coordinate System. The orientation of a coordinate system is the direction it points in space. In other words, if you rotate one coordinate system with respect to another, the two coordinate systems will have different orientations. A baseball thrown by a pitcher may be seen to be changing the origin and orientation of its coordinate system dynamically through time. The World Coordinate System could be said to be the baseball playing field, while the User Coordinate System at any given time could be said to be the baseball. The center of the baseball would be the origin of the User Coordinate System for the baseball.

When you begin to draw, you will create entities such as lines, polylines, and arcs. When you create an entity, it carries its own coordinate system with it, in an abbreviated form. The origin of the Entity Coordinate System is the same as the origin of the World Coordinate System, but its actual location in space is calculated with a special algorithm. The Z axis value is used to locate the elevation of the entity in the World Coordinate System. The two-dimensional points that define the entity in the UCS are transformed into WCS points and stored as the entity definition. Thus, the entity has an absolute set of two-dimensional points and a single Z coordinate value, rather than a set of three-dimensional points that would take longer to read and manipulate. The ECS enables AutoCAD to store and use three-dimensional objects in a very efficient way.

Even if the UCS is the same as the WCS, you will create your objects in terms of the UCS. You are always drawing in a UCS, even if you do not define a UCS, name it, or store it. If you press ENTER in response to the UCS command prompt, you will assign the World Coordinate System to a new UCS. Your work will be greatly enhanced, however, if you master the creation of User Coordinate Systems. User Coordinate Systems make it possible to place the two-dimensional surface of your pointing device anywhere in space, at any orientation. It is like having a drawing board that can be placed on any surface of a polyhedron and being able to draw there. This new capability of Release 10 makes drawing possible in new and exciting ways. You can now draw in space.

"Origin"

```
Command: ucs
Origin/ZAxis/3point/Entity/View/X/Y/Z/Prev/
Restore/Save/Del/?/<World>: o
Origin point <0,0,0>:
```

You can specify the origin of a UCS by selecting the "Origin" option of the UCS command. The origin is the point in space where X, Y, and Z are all zero. The origin is expressed in terms of the current UCS.

"ZAxis"

```
Command: ucs
Origin/ZAxis/3point/Entity/View/X/Y/Z/Prev/
Restore/Save/Del/?/<World>: za
Origin point <0,0,0>:
Point on positive portion of the Z axis <default>:
```

The orientation of the UCS can be thought of as the "direction its axes point." Of course, for each axis, the direction will be different. The Z axis, otherwise called the "extrusion direction," can be used to determine the orientation. To do this, you specify an origin point as in the preceding example, and then you pick a point that you want to be on the positive portion of the Z axis. After you pick the point, a new UCS will be defined that has the positive portion of the Z axis beginning at the origin and passing through the point you picked.

"3point"

```
Command: ucs
Origin/ZAxis/3point/Entity/View/X/Y/Z/Prev/
Restore/Save/Del/?/<World>: 3
```

Origin point <0,0,0>:
Point on positive portion of the X axis <default>:
Point on positive-Y portion of the UCS X-Y plane <default>:

You can specify the UCS using any three points in space with the "3point" option of the UCS command. When you do so, you will be prompted for an origin point, then for a point on the positive portion of the X axis, and finally for a point on the positive Y portion of the UCS X-Y plane. Although this seems complicated, what it means is that the origin point and two other points in space will define a plane that becomes the new UCS. You can use object snap to pick the three desired points, so you can use this option of the UCS command to orient a new UCS to nodes on an object.

"Entity"

Command: **ucs**
Origin/ZAxis/3point/Entity/View/X/Y/Z/Prev/
Restore/Save/Del/?/<World>: **e**

Use the "Entity" option to create a coordinate identification or Entity Coordinate System. This ECS, as it is abbreviated, can be used to set the UCS. Just pick an object in response to the UCS command prompt and the UCS will be made to conform to the ECS.

"View"

Command: **ucs**
Origin/ZAxis/3point/Entity/View/X/Y/Z/Prev/
Restore/Save/Del/?/<World>: **v**

If you choose the "View" option of the UCS command, you can set the UCS to conform to the screen. After executing the option, a new UCS will be created so that the X-Y plane is parallel to the screen. This does not change the UCS origin, however.

"X," "Y," "Z"

```
Command: ucs
Origin/ZAxis/3point/Entity/View/X/Y/Z/Prev/
Restore/Save/Del/?/<World>: x
Rotation angle about X axis <0.0>:
```

You can rotate the UCS around X, Y, or Z axis with the "X," "Y," or "Z" option of the UCS command. You supply the desired rotation amount for each of the axes desired. Positive angles are expressed as counterclockwise when viewed from the positive direction of the axis around which you are rotating. (This is also called the "right hand rule.") If you are rotating around the X axis, for example, and you look down the X axis from the positive direction, positive rotation angles will be counterclockwise from your point of view.

"Prev"

```
Command: ucs
Origin/ZAxis/3point/Entity/View/X/Y/Z/Prev/
Restore/Save/Del/?/<World>: p
```

If you use the "Prev" option of the UCS command, you will see the previous UCS that was defined. You can step back through User Coordinate Systems you have created until you reach the first one for the editing session.

"Restore"

Command: **ucs**
Origin/ZAxis/3point/Entity/View/X/Y/Z/Prev/
Restore/Save/Del/?/<World>: **r**
?/Name of UCS to restore:

You can restore a named UCS with the "Restore" option of the UCS command. Just supply the name of a previously defined UCS and it will be made the current UCS if it exists. You can also list the currently available User Coordinate Systems if you use the question mark ("?") option.

"Save"

Command: **ucs**
Origin/ZAxis/3point/Entity/View/X/Y/Z/Prev/
Restore/Save/Del/?/<World>: **s**
?/Name of UCS:

You can save the current UCS under any name you wish, using up to 31 characters. The characters that you can use are "$-_" and all the letters and digits.

"Del"

Command: **ucs**
Origin/ZAxis/3point/Entity/View/X/Y/Z/Prev/
Restore/Save/Del/?/<World>: **d**
Name of UCS to delete:

You can delete a UCS you have saved if you use the "Del" option of the UCS command. If you use wildcard operators, you can delete User Coordinate Systems globally. A question mark (?) may be used in place of any character, in which case all characters in the position of the question mark will be acceptable for a match. For example, the name "MY????" will work for

"MYUCS" as well as "MYNAME." If you use an asterisk (*), it will match all characters in a name, or all characters following any characters. In this case, the UCS name "MY*" will be the same as "MY???."

"?"

Command: **ucs**
Origin/ZAxis/3point/Entity/View/X/Y/Z/Prev/
Restore/Save/Del/?/<World>: ?

If you respond to the UCS command prompt with a question mark (?), you will see a list of saved User Coordinate Systems. You will also see the name of the current UCS. All listed coordinates are relative to the current UCS.

Options:

D	one or more saved coordinate systems may be Deleted
E	specify UCS with the same Extrusion direction as that of the selected entity
O	shift the Origin of the current coordinate system
P	Previous UCS is restored
R	previously saved UCS is Restored
S	the current UCS is Saved
V	establish a new UCS whose Z axis is parallel to the current Viewing direction
W	the current UCS is set equal to the World coordinate system
X	the current UCS is rotated around the X axis
Y	the current UCS is rotated around the Y axis
Z	the current UCS is rotated around the Z axis

ZA	UCS is defined using an origin point and a point on the positive portion of the Z Axis
?	saved coordinate systems are listed
3	UCS is defined using an origin point, a point on the positive portion of the X axis, and a point on the positive-Y portion of the X-Y plane

UCSICON

Command: **ucsicon**
ON/OFF/All/Noorigin/ORigin <default ON/OFF state>:

You can control the placement and visibility of the UCS icon. The UCS icon shows the origin and orientation of the current UCS for the current viewport.

"ON," "OFF"

Command: **ucsicon**
ON/OFF/All/Noorigin/ORigin <default ON/OFF state>: **on**

You can turn the UCS icon on and off with the "ON" and "OFF" options of the UCSICON command. Be sure to use the whole words "ON" and "OFF" or you will see a message asking you to reenter the command.

"All"

Command: **ucsicon**
ON/OFF/All/Noorigin/ORigin <default ON/OFF state>: **a**

If you want to change the location or visibility of the UCS icon in all viewports, not just the current one, you must select the "All" option of the UCSICON command. After you specify "All" for the current use of the command, you will be again prompted for the UCSICON command prompts. You may then change other settings and they will be effective for all viewports.

"Noorigin"

Command: **ucsicon**
ON/OFF/All/Noorigin/ORigin <default ON/OFF state>: **n**

When you execute the "Noorigin" option of the UCSICON command, you will force the UCS icon to be in the lower left corner of the viewport. For a new drawing session, the icon is situated in this location.

"ORigin"

Command: **ucsicon**
ON/OFF/All/Noorigin/ORigin <default ON/OFF state>: **or**

If you choose the "ORigin" option of the UCSICON command, you will set the UCS icon at the origin of the current UCS. You will see the icon at the lower left corner of the screen if the origin is out of the viewport.

Options:

A	settings will be changed in All active viewports
N	No origin; icon displayed at lower left corner of the viewport
OR	icon displayed at ORigin of current UCS if possible
OFF	disable the coordinate system icon
ON	enable the coordinate system icon

UNDEFINE

Command: **undefine**
Command name:

If you use AutoLISP's "defun" function to define a function with the same name as a built-in AutoCAD command, the built-in command will be used instead. In other words, you will not be able to use your new command. Fortunately, you can use the UNDEFINE command to undefine a built-in AutoCAD command so it will not be executed in place of the command you created with AutoLISP. See the REDEFINE command to find out what to do to get the built-in AutoCAD command back again.

UNDO

Command: **undo**
Auto/Back/Control/End/Group/Mark/<number>:

You can undo the effects of the previous command, or you can undo a number of previous commands with the UNDO command. You can also place markers at certain points so you can return to them later. If you enter a number in response to the UNDO command prompt, you will undo that number of previous commands.

"Auto"

Command: **undo**
Auto/Back/Control/End/Group/Mark/<number>: **a**
ON/OFF <default>:

If you turn automatic undo on, you will be able to undo any set of commands that have been entered from a single menu item.

When automatic mode is enabled, you will automatically perform an UNDO "Group" at the beginning of the group of commands in the menu, and an UNDO "End" at the end of the command group. One use of the U command can then undo the entire group of commands.

"Back"

Command: **undo**
Auto/Back/Control/End/Group/Mark/<number>: **b**
This will undo everything. OK? <Y>

If you choose the "Back" option of the UNDO command, you will undo everything in your drawing. If you have set a mark (or marks) with the "Mark" option of the UNDO command (described later), you will undo back to the last mark rather than to the beginning of the drawing. Marks will be removed as they are found with the "Back" option.

"Control"

Command: **undo**
Auto/Back/Control/End/Group/Mark/<number>: **c**
All/None/One <All>:

When you execute commands, AutoCAD stores them in a special list so they can be undone. You can control how much storage space is allowed for undoing if you use the "Control" option of the UNDO command. If you choose the "All" option of the "Control" option, you will enable all commands to be undone. The "None" option will disable the effects of the U and UNDO <number> commands. If you choose the "One" option, you will be able to undo only the last command. If you run out of disk space, for example, you can regain some of it with the UNDO "Control One" or UNDO "Control None" command options.

"End"

Command: **undo**
Auto/Back/Control/End/Group/Mark/<number>: **e**

You will usually use the "End" option of the UNDO command after the UNDO "Group" command option has been used. The two options, "Group" and "End," can be used to identify the beginning and ending of a group of commands. You will usually use these commands in a menu, not from the keyboard. After marking the group with the "Group" and "End" options, a single U command will undo the entire group of commands so marked.

"Group"

Command: **undo**
Auto/Back/Control/End/Group/Mark/<number>: **g**

If you use the "Group" option of the UNDO command, you will mark the beginning of a group of commands. You must then use the "End" option to mark the end of the command group. After you have done this, you will be able to undo the entire group of commands with a single U command. You normally use the "End" option in a menu rather than from the keyboard. When you group commands in menus, you can undo an entire command group under a single menu item.

"Mark"

Command: **undo**
Auto/Back/Control/End/Group/Mark/<number>: **m**

You can use the "Mark" option of the UNDO command to set a mark at the current place in the command sequence. After you set the mark, you can go back to it with the "Back" option of the UNDO command. In this way, you can undo back to a known place in the sequence. The UNDO command is useful when you wish to undo several commands at once. The UNDO feature is cleared when you do a PLOT or a PRPLOT.

Options:

number	undoes the specified number of the most recent commands
A	Automatically enables undo for groups from menus
B	undoes Back to beginning or previous mark
C	Controls (enables/disables) the undo stack
E	Ends a group of commands
G	begins a Group of commands to be treated as one command
M	Marks a place in the command sequence that you can go back to

UNITS

Command: **units**

Systems of units:	(Examples)
1. Scientific	1.55E+01
2. Decimal	15.50
3. Engineering	1′−3.50″
4. Architectural	1′−3 1/2″
5. Fractional	15 1/2

Enter choice, 1 to 5 <default>:

You can choose one of five different number formats for coordinates and distances. The UNITS command will display the five possible formats as shown. You can select any of them by number, after which you will be prompted for other information, depending on the option you select. If you choose option 1, 2, or

3, you will be prompted for the number of digits to the right of the decimal point. You may choose any number of decimal places from 0 to 8. If you choose number 4, you will be prompted for the denominator of the smallest fraction to display. You may choose 1, 2, 4, 8, 16, 32, or 64. After you select coordinate and distance units, you will be shown a list of angular units formats like the following:

Systems of angle measure:	(Examples)
1. Decimal degrees	45.0000
2. Degrees/minutes/seconds	45d0'0"
3. Grads	50.0000g
4. Radians	0.7854r
5. Surveyor's units	N 45d0'0" E Enter choice, 1 to 5 <default>:

You can choose one of five angular formats as shown. See more about the selection of angular options and expression of angular measure in Chapter 2, "Drawing."

Variables, see SETVAR

VIEW

Command: **'view**
?/Delete/Restore/Save/Window:
View name:

You can save the current viewport under a name you choose with the VIEW command. The question mark ("?") option will list the view you have already saved. To delete a view, you can use the "Delete" option. The "Restore" option will change the current viewport to the view you specify by name, assuming you have saved a view under that name. You can use the "Save" option to save the current view in the drawing file. With the "Window" option, you can select a window area in the drawing and it will be saved as the current view. A name can also be renamed using the RENAME command.

Options:

D	named view will be Deleted
R	named view will be Restored
S	current view Saved as named view
W	specified Window will be saved as named view
?	named views to be listed

VIEWPORTS, VPORTS

Command: **viewports** (or **vports**)
Save/Restore/Delete/Join/Single/?/2/<3>/4:

You can divide the display into viewports in various combinations and save them with the VIEWPORTS command. The VIEWPORTS commands can also be entered as the VPORTS command.

"Save"

The current viewport will be saved under a name you give it. The name you give in response to this option will be used to store the entire current viewport configuration. This means that all currently defined viewports will be saved, not just the viewport in which you are working.

The viewport name can be from 1 to 31 characters in length and it may contain the following characters from the ASCII character set:

abcdefghijklmnopqrstuvwxyz
ABCDEFGHIJKLMNOPQRSTUVWXYZ
0123456789 $-_

The named viewport configuration is stored with the drawing.

"Restore"

If you saved a viewport under a file name, you can restore it by choosing the "Restore" option.

"Delete"

You can delete a saved viewport if you choose the "Delete" option.

"Join"

Two viewports can be combined together into one with the "Join" option. You must select the dominant viewport which is the one whose view you wish the new viewport to inherit. You will first see the prompt "Select dominant viewport <current>:". You can either enter the desired viewport's name or pick a viewport with the crosshairs. You will see the prompt "Select viewport to merge:". You should then pick the viewport or specify a viewport identifier.

"Off"

If you choose this option, you will turn off multiple viewports and make the current viewport the dominant one.

"?"

The question mark option lists the identification numbers or names of the current configuration of viewports. AutoCAD gives each viewport a reference number which can be used as a shorthand way of referring to the viewport.

"2"

If you choose the "2" option, AutoCAD will split the current viewport in half. You will be asked whether you want to divide the viewport horizontally or vertically. The default is to divide the viewport vertically.

Refer to Figure 2-1 for a viewport that has been divided into two small viewports. The "Vertical" option was used for this division. The AutoCAD viewport can be divided into many small viewports.

If you were to use the "?" option with the viewport configuration shown in Figure 2-1, you would see the following report:

```
Current configuration:
id# 15
  corners: 0.5000,0.0000 1.0000,1.0000
id# 14
  corners: 0.0000,0.0000 0.5000,1.0000

Configuration *LAST:
  0.0000,0.0000 1.0000,1.0000
```

"3"

Like the "2" option, the "3" option divides the viewport. It is divided into three parts, however. You will see the prompt "Horizontal/Vertical/Above/Below/Left/<Right>:". If you choose "H," the viewport will be split into thirds horizontally. If you choose "V," the viewport will be split into thirds vertically.

The options that follow "Vertical" refer to the orientation of the split. Note that the viewport, when split, turns into one large and two small viewports when divided into three parts. The "A" option will place the larger of two viewports above the smaller. The "B" option will place the larger of two viewports below the smaller. Likewise, the viewport will be divided with the larger to the left or to the right of the smaller. Refer to Figure 2-2 for a viewport that has been divided into three viewports with the "Right" option.

If you were to use the "?" option with the viewport configuration shown in Figure 2-2, you would see the following report:

```
Current configuration:
id# 9
  corners: 0.5000,0.0000 1.0000,1.0000
id# 7
  corners: 0.0000,0.5000 0.5000,1.0000
id# 8
  corners: 0.0000,0.0000 0.5000,0.5000

Configuration *LAST:
  0.0000,0.0000 1.0000,1.0000
```

"4"

The current viewport will be divided into four viewports of equal size with the "4" option. Refer to Figure 2-3 for a viewport that has been divided into four viewports.

If you were to use the "?" option with the viewport configuration shown in Figure 2-3, you would see the following report:

```
Current configuration:
id# 19
  corners: 0.5000,0.0000 1.0000,0.5000
id# 16
  corners: 0.5000,0.5000 1.0000,1.0000
id# 17
  corners: 0.0000,0.5000 0.5000,1.0000
```

```
id# 18
  corners: 0.0000,0.0000 0.5000,0.5000

Configuration *LAST:
  0.0000,0.0000 1.0000,1.0000
```

Options:

D	saved viewport configuration to be Deleted
J	two viewports to be Joined (merged)
O	multiple viewports turned Off
R	saved viewport configuration to be Restored
S	current viewport configuration to be Saved
2	current viewport divided into 2 viewports
3	current viewport divided into 3 viewports
4	current viewport divided into 4 viewports
?	current and saved viewport configurations listed

VIEWRES

Command: **viewres**
Do you want fast zooms? <Y>
Enter circle zoom percent (1-20000) <100>:

Use the VIEWRES command to control the speed of zooming as well as the display resolution for circles. Fast zooms use REDRAW whenever possible for PAN, ZOOM, and VIEW restore. If you do not elect fast zooms, all such commands will regenerate the display. You can also enter the zoom percent for controlling the smoothness of circles. The default, 100 percent, will draw the number of line segments for circles as computed by a special algorithm. Five hundred percent is a preferred zoom setting. If you wish to zoom in on a circle, however, you will see the line segments that make up the circle. If you use a larger zoom percent, the circle's line segments will be greater in number and the circle will look smoother. Of course, the circle will take longer to draw because the number of line segments will be increased.

VPOINT

Command: **vpoint**
Rotate/<View point> <default>: **r**
Enter angle in X-Y plane from X axis <default>:
Enter angle from X-Y plane <default>:

The viewpoint is the direction in which you are viewing a three-dimensional object. Each viewport can have its own viewpoint. You can specify the viewpoint by entering the coordinates of a point, in which case the view direction will be directly at the point specified. You can also specify a rotation for the view direction by responding to the two additional prompts in the preceding example. Finally, the viewpoint can be specified dynamically if you press ENTER in response to the VPOINT command prompt.

Options:

R	Rotation angles used to select view direction
ENTER	compass and axes tripod used to dynamically select view direction
X,Y,Z	view point specified by coordinate entry

VSLIDE

Command: **vslide**
Slide file <default>:

If you have prepared slide files with the MSLIDE command, you may display them with the VSLIDE command. You will be prompted for the name of a slide file. You can respond with the name of a single slide contained in a ".sld" file, or you can specify the name of a slide in a library. To pre-load a slide to be viewed by the next VSLIDE command, you can precede the slide name with a single asterisk. In this way, you can use a script file to load the file before viewing it, use the DELAY command to pause, then quickly display the pre-loaded slide with a VSLIDE command without a slide file name. You can clear the slide from the screen by using REDRAW. To use a slide that is in a library, you must first specify the library name, then enclose the slide name in parentheses. For example, the name "mylib(myslide)" would refer to a slide called "myslide" in a library called "mylib."

Options:

filename	name of slide file
libname (filename)	slide filename in library libname
*filename	pre-load slide to be quickly viewed by next VSLIDE command

WBLOCK

Command: **wblock**
File name:
Block name:

If you use the BLOCK command to create a block of entities or blocks in your drawing you can write the block to a disk file under its own name or any other name you choose. You are first prompted for a file name, which can be any name permitted by your operating system. After you enter the desired file name, you are prompted for the block name you want to store under the file name you specified. You have four options for responding to this prompt. You can enter the name of a block that exists in the drawing. You can enter a single equal sign (=), which means that the drawing name is also the block name. If you enter a single asterisk (*), you will write the entire drawing to the file you have named. Finally, if you press ENTER in response to the "Block name:" prompt, you will be prompted to select objects and an insertion base point, essentially duplicating the requirements of the BLOCK command. You can use the INSERT command to insert blocks into your drawing.

Options:

filename	write block to this file
=	name of block same as name of file
*	entire drawing to be written to file
ENTER	selected objects to be written as block

ZOOM

Command: '**zoom**
All/Center/Dynamic/Extents/Left/Previous/Window/
<Scale(X)>:

You can use the ZOOM command to enlarge or reduce the size of the drawing as it appears on the display. If you use the "All" option, all of the drawing will be forced to fit within the display area. If you use the "Center" option, you can select a center point for the zoom, then a magnification factor. The "Dynamic" option enables you to use a view box to select the zoom area. The "Extents" option will enable you to display the entire drawing extents in the display area. Like the ZOOM "Center" command option, you can zoom using the left corner of an area to zoom, along with a magnification factor. You can select the previous zoom. You can use a window to select the area to zoom. Finally, you can enter a scale factor that will be used to enlarge or reduce the drawing within the display area. You can find out more about zooming in Chapter 2, "Drawing."

Options:

number	factor to be applied to original scale
numberX	factor to be applied to current scale
A	zoom All of drawing
C	zoom around Center point
D	pan and zoom Dynamically
E	zoom to Extents of drawing
L	use lower Left corner for zoom
P	use Previous zoom
W	zoom using Window

Command Summary

The following is a complete summary of all the AutoCAD commands with their options. For detailed information regarding any command, see Chapter 16, "AutoCAD Command Reference." This summary is designed to be a handy and quick reference for you to use when running AutoCAD.

APERTURE sets the size of the target box for object snap.

0	Object snap target height

ARC draws arcs (parts of circles) using several methods.

A	Angle (included)
C	Center point
D	Direction (starting)
E	Endpoint
ENTER	(as reply to Start point) sets start point and direction as end of last line or arc
L	chord Length
R	Radius

AREA determines the area contained by an object.

A	Add mode is set
E	Entity select—area of circle, polyline, or polygon selected will be reported
F	First point will be picked
S	Subtract mode is set

ARRAY places objects on nodes of a grid.

P	Polar array pattern
R	Rectangular array pattern

ATTDEF determines how attributes will be entered and viewed.

I	Invisible attribute (or visible if not set)
C	Constant mode set (or variable if not set)
V	Verify mode set
P	Preset mode set

ATTDISP determines how attributes will be displayed.

N	visibility set Normally as required by each attribute
ON	all attributes forced to be visible
OFF	all attributes forced to be nonvisible

ATTEDIT edits attributes. **ATTEXT** extracts attributes from a drawing.

C	CDF comma-delimited extraction format
D	DXF extraction format
E	Extract selected objects only
S	SDF extraction format

AXIS displays tick marks along the X and Y axes.

S	locks the tick mark spacing to Snap interval
A	Aspect of ticks is set differently for X and Y axes
number	spacing will be set to this number (0 means "usesnap spacing")
numberX	spacing is set to a multiple of the snap spacing
ON	turns the axis marks ON
OFF	turns the axis marks OFF

BASE sets the base point for the drawing.

BLIPMODE permits you to set blip markers on or off.

ON	marker blips ON
OFF	marker blips OFF

BLOCK lists or creates compound objects.

?	names of blocks in drawing will be listed
name	desired name to be used to identify the block

BREAK breaks an entity, dividing it into separate entities.

F	the First point is to be respecified

CHAMFER places a chamfer line at an intersection and trims.

D	chamfer Distances are set
P	an entire Polyline is to be chamfered

CHANGE permits you to change certain properties.

C	change Color
E	change Elevation
LA	change LAyer
LT	change Line Type
P	Properties of objects to be changed
T	change three-dimensional Thickness

CHPROP enables you to change certain properties.

C	change Color
LA	change LAyer
LT	change Line Type
T	change Thickness

CIRCLE draws circles by several methods.

C	enter Center point
D	enter Diameter to specify circle
2P	2 endPoints of diameter are specified
3P	3 Points on circumference are specified
R	enter Radius to specify circle
TTR	Two Tangent points and Radius are specified

COLOR sets the current color.

number	entity color set by number
name	entity color set to standard color name
BYBLOCK	entity color set BY current BLOCK
BYLAYER	entity color set BY LAYER

COPY copies objects from one place to another.

M	Multiple copies desired

DBLIST lists every entity in the drawing.

DDATTE enables attribute editing by dialog.

'DDEMODES displays current properties dialog box. Layer, color, line type, elevation, and thickness can be set.

'DDLMODES displays layer control dialog box.

'DDRMODES displays drawing aids dialog box.

DDUCS executes the UCS command by dialog box.

DELAY enables you to pause for a specified time in a script.

DIM (or **DIM1**) enables the dimensioning subcommands.

ALIGNED creates dimensions aligned with entity.
ANGULAR creates angular dimensions.
BASELINE begins dimensions at same base line.
CENTER dimensions to a center mark.
CONTINUE continues dimension from last end.
DIAMETER dimensions a diameter.
EXIT exits from the dimension subcommands.
HOMETEXT returns dimension text to home position.
HORIZONTAL creates horizontal dimensions.

LEADER draws a leader with an arrowhead.
NEWTEXT changes existing dimension text.
RADIUS dimensions a radius.
REDRAW redraws from subcommand level.
ROTATED creates rotated dimensions.
STATUS lists all dimensioning variables.
STYLE changes the text style for dimensions.
U (same as UNDO)
UNDO undoes the last dimensioning subcommand.
UPDATE updates dimensions using current variables.
VERTICAL creates vertical dimensions.

DIST measures angle and distance between two points.

DIVIDE divides an entity into a number of equal parts.

B	use specified Block as marker

DOUGHNUT (or **DONUT**) creates doughnut shapes.

DRAGMODE sets the drag mode, enabling or disabling drag.

A	Automatic drag, whenever possible
ON	allow drag when drag key word used
OFF	disable drag

DTEXT creates dynamic text (like a word processor for drawings).

DVIEW dynamically views objects to help you create models.

CA	the CAmera angle is selected
CL	back and front CLipping planes are set
D	perspective is turned on and Distance to object set
H	Hidden lines are removed for selected objects
OFF	perspective is turned OFF
PA	drawing is PAnned across the screen
PO	camera and target POints are selected
TA	the TArget point is rotated about the camera
TW	the view is TWisted around the line of sight
U	a DVIEW subcommand is Undone
X	the DVIEW command is eXited
Z	camera lens is Zoomed in and out

DXBIN reads binary drawing exchange files.

DXFIN reads drawing exchange files.

DXFOUT creates non-binary drawing exchange files.

B	write Binary DXF file
E	select objects to convert

EDGESURF creates edge-defined surfaces.

ELEV sets the current elevation.

ELLIPSE creates ellipse entities.

C	Center point instead of first axis endpoint specified
R	Rotation instead of second axis used to specify eccentricity
I	Isometric circle drawn as ellipse in current isoplane

END ends the drawing session, automatically saving the drawing.

ERASE erases selected entities from the drawing.

EXPLODE separates the component entities from a block.

EXTEND increases the length of an entity until it meets another.

FILES enables you to manipulate files on your disk.

FILL enables or disables automatic filling of entities.

ON	automatically fill solids, wide polylines, and traces
OFF	outline solids, wide polylines, and traces

FILLET creates a curved fillet at line intersections, trimming the excess lines.

P	entire Polyline will be filleted
R	fillet Radius will be set

FILMROLL creates a file that can be used with AutoSHADE.

'GRAPHSCR flips to the graphics screen.

GRID displays a dot grid at a given aspect ratio and spacing.

A	grid Aspect set (X-Y spacings differ)
ON	grid ON
OFF	grid OFF
S	grid Spacing locked to snap resolution
number	grid spacing (zero means "use snap spacing")
numberX	spacing set to multiple of snap spacing

HANDLES assigns unique identifiers to all entities.

HATCH crosshatches an object.

I	internal features to be Ignored
N	hatch line turned off and on as internal lines are crossed
O	Outermost portion hatched only
U	use simple User-defined hatch pattern

'HELP or '? displays the help menu.

HIDE processes the drawing to remove hidden lines.

ID shows coordinates of selected point or shows point from coordinates.

IGESIN reads an IGES file.

IGESOUT creates an IGES file.

INSERT inserts a block into the drawing.

name	insert a block or file by this name
block=name	use a file under "name" and create "block"
*name	individual part entities to be retained

?	names of existing blocks to be listed
C	(X scale prompt reply) specifies scale using two Corner points
XYZ	(X scale prompt replay) predefines X, Y, and Z scales

ISOPLANE determines the current isometric plane.

L	Left plane (90 and 150 degree pair)
R	Right plane (30 and 150 degree pair)
T	Top plane (90 and 30 degree pair)
ENTER	rotate planes in left, top, right sequence

LAYER manipulates layers within your drawing.

?	layers listed (with color and line type information)
C color	layers set to Color
F alayer, blayer, ...	alayer and blayer Frozen
L linetype	layers set to Line type
M alayer	alayer Made the current layer, creating it if necessary
N alayer, blayer, ...	New layers alayer and blayer created
ON alayer, blayer, ...	layers alayer and blayer turned ON
OFF alayer, blayer, ...	layers alayer and blayer turned OFF
S alayer	current layer Set to existing layer alayer
T alayer, blayer, ...	layers alayer and blayer Thawed

LIMITS defines limits, enables, and disables limit checking.

2 points	Lower left/upper right drawing limits set
ON	limits checking enabled
OFF	limits checking disabled

LINE draws a line from point to point.

C	(as reply to "To point:") Close polygon
ENTER	(as reply to "From point:") start at end of previous line or arc
ENTER	(as reply to "To point:") end the LINE command
U	(as reply to "To point:") Undo segment

LINETYPE lists, creates, loads, and otherwise manipulates line types.

?	line type library is Listed
C	line type definition is Created
L	line type definition is Loaded
S	current entity line type is Set

Suboptions for "Set" option:

name	entity line type name is set
BYBLOCK	entity line type associated with block
BYLAYER	layer's line type used for entities
?	loaded line types are listed

LIST lists entity data for selected objects.

LOAD loads shape files into your drawing.

?	names of loaded shape files are listed

LTSCALE enables you to set the scale factor for line types.

MEASURE divides an entity into equal parts.

B	use specified Block as marker

MENU loads a new menu from disk.

MINSERT is like INSERT, except multiple insertions are done.

name	insert a block or file by this name
block=name	use a file under "name" and create "block"
?	names of existing blocks to be listed
C	(X scale prompt reply) specifies scale using two Corner points
XYZ	(X scale prompt replay) predefines X, Y, and Z scales

MIRROR creates a mirror image of selected objects.

MOVE moves selected objects from one location to another.

MSLIDE makes a slide file from the current display.

MULTIPLE <command> enables you to execute commands without returning to the command line.

OFFSET creates an object at an offset distance from another object.

number	offset distance
T	prompts for specification of a point Through which the offset object is to be drawn

OOPS lets you get erased objects back again.

ORTHO constrains drawing to horizontal or vertical lines.

ON	lines forced to be horizontal or vertical
OFF	lines not constrained

OSNAP sets object snap mode according to the following:

CENT	snap to CENTer of arc or circle
ENDP	snap to closest ENDPoint of arc or line
INSERT	INSERTion point of text, block, or shape
INTER	INTERsection of line, arc, or circle
MIDP	MIDPoint of arc or line
NEAR	NEARest point of arc, circle, line, or point
NODE	NODE (same as a point)
NONE	NONE (turn object snap off)
PERP	PERPendicular to arc, line, or circle
QUAD	QUADrant point of arc or circle
QUICK	QUICK mode (use first find, not nearest)
TANG	TANGent of circle or arc

'PAN moves the viewport over the drawing a given displacement.

PEDIT enables you to edit polygon meshes.

D	Desmooth, restoring original mesh
E	Edit mesh vertices
M	Open or close the mesh in the M direction
N	Open or close the mesh in the N direction
S	Smooth surface
U	Undo a PEDIT option
X	eXit PEDIT

During vertex editing:

D	move Down to the previous vertex in the M direction
L	move Left to the previous vertex in the N direction
M	Marked vertex repositioned
N	move to the Next vertex
P	move to the Previous vertex
R	move Right to the next vertex in the N direction
RE	REdisplay the polygon mesh
U	move Up to the next vertex in the M direction
X	eXit to the PEDIT command for the mesh

PLAN forces plan view of the current or specified UCS.

C	plan view of the current UCS
U	plan view of the specified UCS
W	plan view of the World Coordinate System

PLINE draws polylines.

H	set new Halfwidth
U	Undo previous segment or arc
W	set new polyline Width
ENTER	Exit PLINE command

In line mode:

A	change to Arc mode from line segment mode
C	Close using straight segment

L	segment Length (same direction as previous segment)

In arc mode:

A	included Angle
CE	CEnter point
CL	CLose using arc segment
D	starting Direction
L	chord Length (or switch to line mode from arc mode)
R	specify arc by Radius
S	three-point arc Second point

PLOT plots a drawing using a pen plotter.

POINT draws points (otherwise known as nodes).

POLYGON draws polygons.

E	polygon specified using one Edge
C	polygon specified using Center

Suboptions for Center method:

C	polygon Circumscribed around circle
I	polygon Inscribed within circle

PRPLOT plots a drawing on the printer-plotter.

PURGE purges unused objects from the drawing.

A	purge All unused objects by name
B	purge unused Blocks
LA	purge unused LAyers

LT	purge unused Line Types
SH	purge unused SHape files
ST	purge unused text STyles

QTEXT enables or disables quick text mode.

ON	set quick text mode ON
OFF	set quick text mode OFF

QUIT enables you to quit without saving.

REDEFINE enables you to redefine built-in commands.

REDO will redo the last thing that UNDO undid.

'REDRAW will redraw the current viewport.

'REDRAWALL will redraw all viewports.

REGEN regenerates the current drawing viewport.

REGENALL regenerates all viewports.

REGENAUTO enables or disables automatic regeneration.

ON	automatic regeneration ON
OFF	automatic regeneration OFF

RENAME enables you to change names for blocks, layers, and other objects.

B	Block to be renamed
LA	LAyer to be renamed
LT	Line Type to be renamed
S	text Style to be renamed

U	User Coordinate System to be renamed
VI	VIew to be renamed
VP	ViewPort to be renamed

'RESUME enables you to resume a command script.

REVSURF creates surfaces of revolution.

ROTATE enables you to rotate an object.

R	change a Reference angle to a new angle

RSCRIPT enables you to restart a command script.

RULESURF creates ruled surfaces.

SAVE enables you to save drawings.

SCALE changes the sizes of objects.

R	change scale from Reference size to a new size

SCRIPT runs a script file.

SELECT enables you to create a selection set.

'SETVAR sets system variables (see Chapter 16, "AutoCAD Command References").

SH gives you the ability to execute DOS commands.

SHAPE draws shapes you have created.

?	available shape names will be listed

SHELL enables you to run programs while still in AutoCAD.

SKETCH allows you to sketch in freehand form.

.	draw line to current point
C	Connect sketch at last point (button 6)
E	last sketched line will be Erased (button 5)
P	sketching Pen raised or lowered (pick button)
Q	sketched lines discarded, command exited (button 4)
R	sketched lines Recorded (button 2)
X	sketched lines recorded, command exited (button 3), position (button 1)

SNAP creates and enables snap grids.

number	set snap grid spacing
ON	crosshairs will snap to grid intervals
OFF	crosshairs will move smoothly
A	Aspect ratio for different X and Y spacings
R	snap grid Rotated
S	select standard or isometric Style

SOLID creates polygons that are filled.

STATUS shows current drawing modes and status.

STRETCH lets you change the size of an object directionally.

STYLE sets the current text style or creates a new one.

?	currently defined text styles listed

TABLET enables, disables, calibrates, and configures the tablet.

ON	turn calibrated mode ON
OFF	turn calibrated mode OFF
CAL	CALibrate tablet
CFG	ConFiGure tablet menus and pointing area

TABSURF creates a tabulated surface.

TEXT creates text according to several rules.

A	text will be Aligned between two points, a width factor being used to adjust the character height proportionally
C	text will be Centered horizontally
F	text will be Fit between two points, but the height will be maintained while the width is adjusted to fit
M	text will be centered horizontally and vertically, in the Middle
R	text will be Right justified
S	select text Style

'TEXTSCR switches to text mode.

3DFACE draws three-dimensional faces with three or four sides.

3DLINE is the same as LINE (except for compatibility with earlier releases).

3DMESH draws a three-dimensional mesh with specified vertices.

3DPOLY draws a three-dimensional polyline.

C	polyline Closed to the first point

U	the last segment entered is Undone
ENTER	3DPOLY command is exited

TIME enables you to display time and use a timer.

D	current times Displayed
ON	elapsed timer ON
OFF	elapsed timer OFF
R	elapsed timer Reset

TRACE draws lines with constant width.

TRIM enables you to trim objects beyond a selected point.

U enables you to undo the last command.

UCS creates and manipulates User Coordinate Systems.

D	one or more saved coordinate systems may be Deleted
E	specify UCS with the same Extrusion direction as that of the selected entity
N	New User Coordinate System to be defined
O	shift the Origin of the current coordinate system
P	Previous UCS is restored
R	previously-saved UCS is Restored
S	the current UCS is Saved
V	establish a new UCS whose Z axis is parallel to the current Viewing direction
W	the current UCS is set equal to the World Coordinate System
X	the current UCS is rotated around the X axis

Y	the current UCS is rotated around the Y axis
Z	the current UCS is rotated around the Z axis
ZA	UCS is defined using an origin point and a point on the positive portion of the Z axis
?	saved coordinate systems are listed
3	UCS is defined using an origin point, a point on the positive portion of the X axis, and a point on the positive Y portion of the X-Y plane

UCSICON controls the UCS icon.

A	settings will be changed in All active viewports
OR	icon displayed at ORigin of current UCS if possible
OFF	Disable the coordinate system icon
ON	Enable the coordinate system icon

UNDEFINE disables AutoCAD built-in commands.

UNDO enables you to undo commands according to certain rules.

number	undoes the number of most recent commands
A	Automatically enables undo for groups from menus
B	undoes Back to beginning or previous mark
C	Controls (enables/disables) the undo stack
E	Ends a group of commands
G	begins a Group of commands to be treated as one command
M	Marks place in command sequence you can go back to

UNITS changes prevailing system units.

'VIEW enables you to manipulate and save named views.

D	named view will be Deleted
R	named view will be Restored
S	current view Saved as named view
W	specified Window will be saved as named view
?	named views to be listed

VIEWPORTS (or **VPORTS**) shows specified viewports.

D	saved viewport configuration to be Deleted
J	two viewports to be Joined (merged)
O	multiple viewports turned Off
R	saved viewport configuration to be Restored
S	current viewport configuration to be Saved
SI	display a SIngle viewpoint filling entire graphics area
2	current viewport divided into 2 viewports
3	current viewport divided into 3 viewports
4	current viewport divided into 4 viewports
?	current and saved viewport configurations listed

VIEWRES controls resolution for drawing circles and arcs.

VPOINT defines the viewpoint of the user as observer.

R	Rotation angles used to select view direction

ENTER	compass and axes tripod used to dynamically select view direction
x,y,z	view point specified by coordinate entry

VSLIDE views slides contained in slide files.

filename	name of slide file
libname(filename)	slide file name in library libname
*filename	preload slide to be quickly viewed by next VSLIDE command

WBLOCK writes a block to a file.

filename	write block to this file
=	name of block same as name of file
*	entire drawing to be written to file
ENTER	selected objects to be written as block

'ZOOM enables you to see your drawing at different sizes.

number	factor to be applied to original scale
numberX	factor to be applied to current scale
A	zoom All of drawing
C	zoom around Center point
D	pan and zoom Dynamically
E	zoom to Extents of drawing
L	use lower Left corner for zoom
P	use Previous zoom
W	zoom using Window

Using Drawing Exchange Files

APPENDIX B

You can exchange drawings with computer-aided design systems other than AutoCAD with AutoCAD's Drawing Exchange Files (DXF files). You can create a Drawing Exchange File by using AutoCAD's DXFOUT command. When you do so, the file you create will be of a special kind. It will contain ASCII characters and can be read by an ASCII text editor such as the one on the companion disk for this book.

You can also prepare DXF files that AutoCAD can read. To do this, you will need special software, although you could use an ASCII text editor to prepare such files directly. Most modern personal CAD software can import and export AutoCAD standard DXF files. AutoCAD can import a DXF file with the DXFIN command.

The DXF File Format

To create a DXF file, you must use a file name that has a ".dxf" extension. Otherwise, the DXFIN command will not recognize the file as a legitimate DXF file. If you use a text editor to create a DXF file, you must not use any white space characters other than the carriage return, linefeed or space characters. The

ASCII codes for all characters must be between 32 and 126 inclusive (hex 20 through hex 7E).

You can use BASIC, PASCAL, or C language to write your DXF file. If you do so, use the "text" mode for writing files. In C, for example, you could use the "fputs( )" function to put strings to the file. In BASIC, you might use the "PRINT #" function to put a string to the file. In either case, you should be sure to put strings that are terminated by a carriage return and linefeed character (in that order).

The DXF file format consists of four general sections. You must supply a header section, a tables section, a blocks section, and an entities section. At the beginning of each section, you must supply a SECTION marker. At the end of each section, you must supply an ENDSEC marker. In addition, you must supply an end-of-file statement.

Group Codes

Group codes are used to identify the meaning of a part of the file. You must start the file with a group code and follow each group code with a name that indicates the specific meaning of the group. For example, group code 0 indicates the start of a file separator, entity, or table entry. Used as a file separator, for example, the group code would look like this:

```
0
SECTION
```

This would indicate that the group is the start of a new section in the DXF file. The allowable group codes follow.

0	Table entry, start of entity, file separator
1	Primary entity text value
2	Name of block, attribute tag, etc.
3-4	Other names or text values
5	Hexadecimal string entity handle
6	Name of a line type (fixed)

7	Name of text style (fixed)
8	Name of layer (fixed)
9	Identifier of variable name (used only in header)
10	Start point of an entity (primary X coordinate)
11-18	Other X coordinates
20	Start point of an entity (primary Y coordinate) 2n must follow 1n immediately in the file
21-28	Other Y coordinates
30	Start point of an entity (primary Z coordinate) 3n must follow 2n and 1n immediately in the file
31-37	Other Z coordinates
38	Entity's elevation (output if FLATLAND system variable is set to 1)
39	Entity's thickness if non-zero (fixed)
40-48	These groups are reserved for floating-point values for use as scale factors, heights, and others
49	Repeat the previous value (when used to specify tables, a 7x group must appear before the first 49 group to indicate the table length
50-58	These groups specify angles
62	A color number is specified (fixed)
66	This group indicates entities follow (fixed flag)
70-78	These groups contain integer values for use as flags, counts, and for other purposes
210	X component of extrusion direction
220	Y component of extrusion direction
230	Z component of extrusion direction
999	The following is a comment

Group codes fall into five categories. Codes from 0 to 9 are all string values. Codes from 10 to 59 are all floating-point values.

Codes from 60 to 79 are all integer values. Codes 210 to 239 are all floating-point values. Finally, the code 999 indicates a comment and is ignored when you use DXFIN to load the DXF file.

An actual DXF file will be used to illustrate the DXF file format. The file was prepared from the standard AutoCAD drawing CUBE.DWG and is called CUBE.DXF. You should make your own sample DXF file to see how all of the parts go together. Just edit the cube drawing and use the DXFOUT command. You can learn a great deal about the construction of DXF files by preparing drawings and then using DXFOUT to see how AutoCAD interprets the drawing into the DXF format.

DXF File Header

The header section contains general drawing information in the form of variable names and values. The following is a typical DXF file header:

```
  0
SECTION
  2
HEADER
999
This is a typical comment.
999
This is a list of system variables and their values:
  9
$ACADVER
  1
AC1006
  9
$INSBASE
 10
0.0
 20
0.0
 30
0.0
  9
```

```
999
etcetera, etcetera. . .
999
You can use the variable names from Chapter 16 for the most
999
part, but there are exceptions.
  0
ENDSEC
```

The Tables Section

The tables section stores the settings for viewports. This table will determine how many viewports will be in the drawing and which one(s) will be visible. You can also have tables of line types, layers, views, styles, and user coordinate systems.

```
  0
SECTION
  2
TABLES
  0
TABLE
  2
VPORT
  70
  1
  0
VPORT
  2
999
Active viewport, line types, etc. . .
  0
ENDTAB
  0
ENDSEC
```

Block Definitions Section

Any blocks that have been defined in the drawing will be shown here. That does not mean that you must end each section with an ENDSEC.

```
    0
SECTION
    2
BLOCKS
    0
ENDSEC
```

Drawing Entities Section

After defining the drawing environment as described earlier, you must supply the entity definitions for the drawing. You use the entities section for this purpose.

```
    0
SECTION
    2
ENTITIES
999
The following defines a solid polygon.
999
The entire cube is defined here:
    0
SOLID
    8
0
    39
1.0
    10
0.0
    20
0.0
    11
1.0
```

```
     21
0.0
     12
0.0
     22
1.0
     13
1.0
     23
1.0
     0
ENDSEC
```

End of File

You must always provide an EOF at the end of a DXF file. Note that the EOF is identified by a group 0.

```
     0
EOF
```

Working with DXF Files

You will seldom try to construct DXF files with a text editor. Instead, you will usually use AutoCAD's DXFOUT command to prepare DXF files for use with other CAD software. Sometimes you will use the DXFIN command to import DXF files that have been prepared with other software. You may even write your own programs to prepare and read DXF files, although it is easier to read than to write DXF files.

You can use your own programs to read DXF files for many different purposes. For example, you can count entities or extract entities from DXF files. If you prepared a drawing that had attributes, for example, you might want to list those attributes in the form of a report.

A DXF Extraction Program in C Language

If you are using ANSI standard C language, you can probably directly use the following source code. It constitutes a program that will read a DXF file and extract certain information from it, displaying the information on your screen. The program is only an example of what can be done. Use your Turbo C, QuickC, or other compiler to compile the code. Because C language is so well standardized and the functions used are typical, you should find it easy to compile, link, and modify for your own purposes.

```
/**************************************************************
EXTRACT.C extracts data from a DXF file.
Prepared using Turbo C, Version 1.5 by Borland International
Inline parameter list declarations are not used, to maintain
compatibility with "classic" compilers.
Usage: extract filename
You specify the filename (with or without the .dxf extension)
and the program reads the DXF file.  The file must have a .dxf
extension in order to be valid.
You can redirect output from screen to a file as follows:
  C:>extract filename > outfile
**************************************************************/

#include <stdio.h>
#include <string.h>
#include <ctype.h>
#include <math.h>

typedef int boolean;

#define TRUE -1
#define FALSE 0
#define ENTITIES 1
#define TABLES 2
#define VPORT 3
#define LTYPE 4
#define LAYER 5
#define STYLE 6
#define VIEW 7
#define UCS 8
#define DWGMGR 9
#define BLOCKS 10

double x_start, y_start, z_start;
double x_end, y_end, z_end;
```

```
/************************************************************
main() is main loop for program.
Parameters: argc - number of arguments including command
            argv - array of pointers to strings
Returns: int - exit value
************************************************************/
main(argc, argv)
int argc;
char *argv[];
{
 char *dot;
 char path[70];
 FILE *stream;
 char filestr[256];
 int group;
 char layer[33];
 int marker = 0;

 if (argc > 1 && argc < 3)
  {
   dot = strrchr(argv[1], '.');
   if (dot != NULL && dot > strrchr(argv[1], '\\'))
    {
     /* if extension is not ".dxf", exit with message */
     if (strcmp(strupr(dot), ".DXF"))
      {
       printf("File extension not .DXF");
       exit(1);
      }
     strcpy(path, strupr(argv[1]));
    }
   else
    {
     strcpy(path, strupr(argv[1]));
     strcat(path, ".DXF");
    }
   /* open file, if file name not acceptable, */
   /* exit with message */
   if ((stream = fopen(path, "rt")) == NULL)
    {
     printf("Can't open %s.", path);
     exit(2);
    }
   /* extract entities as required */
   /* contents of DXF files must be assumed to alternate */
   /* between group codes and values, hence two levels */
   /* of extraction are necessary, one for group codes, */
   /* and one for group definitions */
   while (fgets(filestr, 256, stream) != NULL)
    {
     filestr[strlen(filestr)-1] = '\0';
     group = atoi(filestr);
     /* you can remove these diagnostics later if you wish */
     printf("Group code %d.\n", group);
     /* group code 0 denotes start or end of something */
     if (group == 0)
```

```
{
 while (fgets(filestr, 256, stream) != NULL)
  {
   filestr[strlen(filestr)-1] = '\0';
   printf("Group 0 marker = %s.\n", filestr);
   /* end of file marker */
   if (!strcmp(filestr, "EOF"))
    {
     printf("EOF marker encountered, normal termination.");
     exit(0);
    }
   /* section marker */
   else if (!strcmp(filestr, "SECTION"))
    break;
   /* end of section marker */
   else if (!strcmp(filestr, "ENDSEC"))
    break;
   /* end of table marker */
   else if (!strcmp(filestr, "ENDTAB"))
    break;
   /* line marker */
   else if (!strcmp(filestr, "LINE")
            && marker == ENTITIES)
    {
     while (fgets(filestr, 256, stream) != NULL)
      {
       filestr[strlen(filestr)-1] = '\0';
       group = atoi(filestr);
       if (group == 0)   /* report the line and go on */
        {
         printf("LINE on layer %s from (%f,%f,%f)\n",
                layer,x_start,y_start,z_start);
         printf("     to (%f,%f,%f).\n",
                x_end,y_end,z_end);
         break;
        }
       printf("Line group %d.\n", group);
       if (fgets(filestr, 256, stream) != NULL)
        filestr[strlen(filestr)-1] = '\0';
       printf("Value for group = %s.\n", filestr);
       switch (group)
        {
         case 8: /* layer name */
          strcpy(layer, filestr);
          break;
         case 10: /* start x */
          x_start = atof(filestr);
          break;
         case 20: /* start y */
          y_start = atof(filestr);
          break;
         case 30: /* start z */
          z_start = atof(filestr);
          break;
         case 11: /* end x */
          x_end = atof(filestr);
```

```
            break;
           case 21: /* end y */
            y_end = atof(filestr);
            break;
           case 31: /* end z */
            z_end = atof(filestr);
            break;
           default:
            printf("Unexpected group code.\n");
            break;
          }
        }
      }
     /* you could use a series of "else if's" here */
     /* to extract other entities */
     else break;
    }
  } /* if (group == 0) */
else if (group == 2)
  {
   while (fgets(filestr, 256, stream) != NULL)
    {
     filestr[strlen(filestr)-1] = '\0';
     printf("Group 2 marker = %s.\n", filestr);
     if (!strcmp(filestr, "ENTITIES"))
      marker = ENTITIES;
     else if (!strcmp(filestr, "TABLES"))
      marker = TABLES;
     else if (!strcmp(filestr, "VPORT"))
      marker = VPORT;
     else if (!strcmp(filestr, "LTYPE"))
      marker = LTYPE;
     else if (!strcmp(filestr, "LAYER"))
      marker = LAYER;
     else if (!strcmp(filestr, "STYLE"))
      marker = STYLE;
     else if (!strcmp(filestr, "VIEW"))
      marker = VIEW;
     else if (!strcmp(filestr, "UCS"))
      marker = UCS;
     else if (!strcmp(filestr, "DWGMGR"))
      marker = DWGMGR;
     else if (!strcmp(filestr, "BLOCKS"))
      marker = BLOCKS;
     else marker = 0;
     break;
    }
  } /* if (group == 2) */
else
  {
   if (fgets(filestr, 256, stream) != NULL)
    {
     filestr[strlen(filestr)-1] = '\0';
     printf("Group %d marker = %s.\n", group, filestr);
    }
  }
```

```
    }
   fclose(stream);
  }
 else
  {
   printf("Usage: extract filename\n");
   printf("File must have DXF extension,\n");
   printf("but you don't need to include it\n");
   printf("on the command line.");
  }
 /* end of file is abnormal because it should have */
 /* exited with an EOF marker (see above) */
 printf("Abnormal end of file.\n");
 return(0);
} /* main */
```

TRADEMARKS

AutoCAD, Autodesk, and AutoLISP are registered in the U.S. Patent and Trademark Office by Autodesk, Inc.

ACAD, ADI, Advanced User Interface, ATC, AUI, Autodesk Device Interface, AutoShade, and DXF are trademarks of Autodesk, Inc.

CAMM-GL1 and CAMM-3 are registered trademarks of Roland DG.

dBASE III is a registered trademark of Ashton-Tate.

DraftMaster and Hewlett-Packard are registered trademarks of Hewlett-Packard Company.

IBM is a registered trademark of International Business Machines Corporation.

MS-DOS and QuickC are registered trademarks of Microsoft Corporation.

Turbo C is a registered trademark of Borland International, Inc.

UNIX is a registered trademark of AT&T.

INDEX

The manuscript for this book was prepared and submitted to Osborne/McGraw-Hill in electronic form. The acquisitions editor for this project was Elizabeth Fisher, the technical reviewers were Robert Callori and William Kramer, and the project editor was Fran Haselsteiner. Lloyd Martin contributed much of the text and AutoLISP code in Chapters 11–15.

Cover art by Bay Graphics Design Associates. Color separation and cover supplier, Phoenix Color Corporation. Screens produced with InSet, from InSet Systems, Inc. Book printed and bound by R.R. Donnelley & Sons Company, Crawfordsville, Indiana.